A READER IN PUBLIC

PEOPLE in
Public Service

PERSONNEL ADMINISTRATION

EDITED BY

Robert T. Golembiewski <small>UNIVERSITY OF GEORGIA</small>
  AND
Michael Cohen <small>UNIVERSITY OF GEORGIA</small>

ITASCA, ILLINOIS
F. E. PEACOCK PUBLISHERS, INC.

Preface

THIS VOLUME completes a quartet of teaching aids in Public Administration, and shares with the other trio of volumes a basic underlying belief. That belief concerns a renaissance in teaching and research in Public Administration, a renaissance that has been implied by many obvious signs in the sixties but which we believe is still some years away from its flood tide. The opportunity to extend education and training in Public Administration—much on the model of business administration—has become available as never before, if only proponents can rise to the occasion. Directly, the quartet of volumes which this effort completes is intended as a small contribution to taking advantage of that opportunity.

The passage of time provides a solid rationale for this volume. We can only sample the evidence. The contemporary flood of significant research about Public Administration shows that our belief about disciplinary renaissance is well founded; the recent appearance of new programs for teaching and training public administrators reflects the same dynamic pattern; and the heartening reception of the three already published volumes of teaching aids in this series also suggests that our efforts are helping to meet a real need. Hopefully, this fourth volume will have similar good fortune. Whether it does or not, however, the renaissance in teaching and research in Public Administration will require the support of many similar efforts, in addition to many more volumes that go far beyond the modest aims of this project.

People in Public Service could not have been developed except as a combination of the talents of many. Patently, the authors of the selections below provided invaluable inputs. We trust we have respected, if not augmented, their contributions by the ways we have used them; and we thank the authors and their publishers for their kindness in granting permission to reprint the contributions here. A number of others contributed in more immediate ways to this volume. We note with thanks the efforts of Jackie Hall, Susan Sewell, and Sigrid Sanders, as well as the contributions of Gary Gummersall and John Durden.

September, 1968   Robert T. Golembiewski
Athens, Georgia   Michael Cohen

Contents

INTRODUCTION
    Table 1. Basic Organization of *People in Public Service*   xii

I. BROAD CONDITIONING ENVIRONMENTS: MAJOR INFLUENCES ON THE DEVELOPMENT OF PUBLIC PERSONNEL ADMINISTRATION   1
    A. The Political Environment: Weather Vanes in Crosswinds
        Table 2. Topics and Selections Relevant to "The Political Environment"   2
    B. The Social Environment: A Revolution of Rising Expectations and Changing Values
        Table 3. Topics and Selections Relevant to "The Social Environment"   10
    C. The Technological Environment: Cornucopias of Plenty and of Problems
        Table 4. Topics and Selections Relevant to "The Technological Environment"   18

II. MAJOR MANAGERIAL CHALLENGES: THE PRACTICE OF PUBLIC PERSONNEL ADMINISTRATION   27
    A. Developing the Personnel Function: Seeking Missions and Roles
        Table 5. Topics and Selections Relevant to "Developing the Personnel Function"   28
    B. Recruiting Human Resources: Attracting and Retaining Excellence
        Table 6. Topics and Selections Relevant to "Recruiting Human Resources"   36

C. Maintaining the Organization: Combining People and
    Structure
    Table 7. Topics and Selections Relevant to "Maintaining
             the Organization"   44
D. Training and Developing People: Guiding People up the
    Ladder
    Table 8. Topics and Selections Relevant to "Training and
             Developing People"   52
E. Planning and Developing the Organization: Anticipating
    Tommorow and the Day After
    Table 9. Topics and Selections Relevant to "Planning and
             Developing the Organization"   60

III. CONTROLS: MAJOR MONITORS OF THE PERFORMANCE OF PUBLIC
     PERSONNEL ADMINISTRATION   67
A. Internal Controls: Vigilance and Tension from Within
    Table 10. Topics and Selections Relevant to "Internal
              Controls"   68
B. External Controls: Oversight by Others
    Table 11. Topics and Selections Relevant to "External
              Controls"   74

IV. READINGS   83
1. Albouze, "The Departmental Personnel Officer's Contribution
    to Management"   85
2. Association of the Bar of the City of New York, "Conflict
    of Interest, Technological Change, and Effects on Public
    Recruitment"   93
3. Baum, "Getting Caught in the Middle on Classification
    Decisions: Parts A and B"   103
4. Cohen, "Responsibility in the Public Service"   112
5. Cohen, "The Personnel Policy-Making System"   123
6. Commission on Organization of the Executive Branch of the
    Government, "Alternative Organizations and Policy Implica-
    tions: Perspectives on the U.S. Civil Service Commission"   137
7. CED, "Selecting Specialists and Middle Managers in the
    Public Service"   140
8. CED, "Those Who Serve at the Top"   145
9. Corson and Paul, "Personnel Near the Top: Responsibility
    and Accountability"   148
10. Davis, "The Effects of Automation on Job Design"   155
11. Dolmatch, "Programmed Instruction: Two Perspectives"   173

12. Everett and Williams, "Line Management's Participation in Classification Decisions" 183
13. Foulke, "Fighting the Spoilsmen: The State of Civil Employ in the House of Representatives of 1901" 192
14. Goldwater, "The Perils of Power" 194
15. Golembiewski, "Organizational Patterns of the Future: What They Mean to Personnel Administration" 198
16. Golembiewski, "The 'Laboratory Approach' to Organization Change: Schema of a Method" 217
17. Gomersall and Myers, "Breakthrough in On-the-Job Training" 232
18. Grandpré, McQuie, and Brogan, "Three Things Wrong with the Civil Service" 249
19. Halloran, "Why Position Classification?" 256
20. Halset, "The Paradoxes of Public Administration" 261
21. Heisel and Gladstone, "Off-the-Job Conduct as a Disciplinary Problem" 267
22. Huse, "Putting in a Management Development Program That Works" 276
23. Jensen, "Cultural Bias in Selection" 286
24. Johnson, Executive Order 11397, "Authorizing Transitional Appointments of Veterans Who Have Served during the Vietnam Era" 295
25. Johnson, Executive Order 11222, "Executive Order on Ethics of Federal Employees" 297
26. Jones, "Developments in Government Manpower: A Federal Perspective" 304
27. Jones, "The Merit System, Politics, and Political Maturity" 316
28. Kaufman, "Building Identification with the Forest Service" 325
29. Kaufman, "The Rise of a 'New Politics'" 335
30. Knudson, "Enter the Personnel Generalist" 346
31. Leich, "Rank in Man or Job? Both!" 355
32. Maier, "Appraisal on the Job: Three Types of Appraisal Interviews" 366
33. McGregor, "Theory X and Theory Y" 380
34. Morse, "Shall We Bargain away the Merit System?" 381
35. Mosél, "How to Feed Back Performance Results to Trainees" 388
36. Mosher, "Features and Problems of the Federal Service: The Management of Merit" 397
37. Murphy, "Judicial Review and the Removal of Federal Employees" 409
38. Mustafa, "Aptitude Testing for Machine Operators" 415

39. Report of the National Advisory Commission on Civil Disorders, "The Police and the Community: The Problem of Grievance Mechanisms"   421
40. Nigro, "Department-Commission Relations: Some Swings of the Pendulum"   425
41. Pigors and Myers, "In Short: Personnel Administration for Line Managers"   434
42. Rose, "A Critical Look at the Hatch Act"   452
43. Sayre, "The Triumph of Techniques over Purpose"   460
44. Scott, "Appeal Activities in the Federal Government"   465
45. Uhrbrock, "The Personnel Interview"   470
46. USCSC, "Department-Commission Relations: The President's Formal Position"   493
47. USCSC, "Determining the Classification of a Position: Analyzing Positions"   496
48. USCSC, "How Federal Jobs Are Filled: Commission-Agency Roles"   501
49. USCSC, "Salaries by General Schedule (GS) Levels, with within-Grade Step Increases"   507
50. USCSC, "Structure of the Federal Position Classification Plan"   508
51. USCSC, "The Extent of the Protected/Competitive Service: Some Distinctions and Data"   515
52. Van Riper, "Spoils as Dysfunctional and Functional"   519
53. Van Riper, "The Taproots of American Public Personnel Administration   532
54. Van Riper, "Veterans' Preference: Policies at Potential Cross-Purposes"   537
55. Walker, "State and Local Manpower: A Challenge to Creative Federalism"   541

*TABLE 1. Basic Organization of
People in Public Service.*

I.   Broad Conditioning Environments: Major Influences on the Development of
                                          Public Personnel Administration
     A. The Political Environment: Weather Vanes in Crosswinds
     B. The Social Environment: A Revolution of Rising Expectations and
                                      Changing Values
     C. The Technological Environment: Cornucopias of Plenty and of Problems

II. Major Managerial Challenges: The Practice of Public Personnel Administration
     A. Developing the Personnel Function: Seeking Missions and Roles
     B. Recruiting Human Resources: Attracting and Retaining Excellence
     C. Maintaining the Organization: Combining People and Structure
     D. Training and Developing People: Guiding People up the Ladder
     E. Planning and Developing the Organization: Anticipating Tomorrow and
                                                        the Day After

III. Controls: Major Monitors of the Performance of Public Personnel
                    Administration
     A. Internal Controls: Vigilance and Tension from Within
     B. External Controls: Oversight by Others

IV. Readings

Introduction

THIS BOOK OF READINGS on public personnel administration is the fourth and last volume in a set of teaching aids designed for graduate and advanced undergraduate work in Public Administration. Earlier volumes dealt with, in historical order: selected readings suitable for survey courses in Public Administration;[1] readings intended to enrich courses in public budgeting and finance;[2] and a book of cases with learning designs suitable for emphasizing the applicability to public management of a variety of behavioral approaches and concepts.[3] *People in Public Service* completes the quartet of teaching aids, and in important senses puts the most significant title last in line. For in the final analysis, the people in the management equation play a crucial role in determining the quality of the product of the total mix of resources.

Without doubt, this last volume has posed the most difficult choices in selecting and organizing materials. This difficulty in large part inheres in the subject matter itself, for public personnel administration constitutes a mammoth challenge to both the student and the practitioner. These inherent difficulties also were compounded by our own complex goals for this volume. For our purpose here was not merely to provide a set of readings; rather our basic aim was to establish a style of approach to, and analysis of, major issues in public personnel administration.

The complex goals of this volume are usefully sketched. Even the orthodox basic framework of the volume implied significant problems for selecting and organizing materials to be reprinted, to begin with the least complicated of the

---

[1] Robert T. Golembiewski, Frank Gibson, and Geoffrey Y. Cornog (eds.), *Public Administration: Readings in Institutions, Processes and Behavior* (Chicago: Rand McNally & Co., 1966).
[2] Robert T. Golembiewski (ed.), *Public Budgeting and Finance: Readings in Theory and Practice* (Itasca, Ill.: F. E. Peacock Publishers, Inc., 1968).
[3] Robert T. Golembiewski (ed.), *Perspectives on Public Management: Cases and Learning Designs* (Itasca, Ill.: F. E. Peacock Publishers, Inc., 1968).

issues. As Table 1 reflects, our primary goal was to view Public Personnel Administration as an interacting product of:

    I.   Broad Conditioning Environments;
    II. Major Managerial Challenges; and
    III. Controls.

This is an orthodox approach, even though we are more concerned than most contributors with the social, political, and technological environments out of which public personnel evolved and within which it must function in the future.

Even this orthodox approach raised major questions for the selection and organization of materials. Primarily, we were in the wheels-within-wheels business. Each of the three major organizing foci—while distinct—was conceived as interacting with, and shaping, the others in complex ways. The sense

FIGURE 1

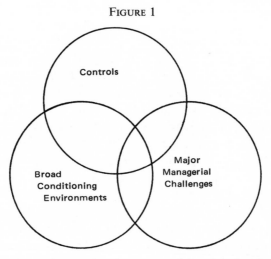

of this distinctness-cum-interaction is suggested by the sketch above. At the same time, complex linkages were conceived as existing within each of the three organizing foci, as well as between them. The sense of this dual interaction may be suggested, if only crudely. For example, three varieties of "broad conditioning environments" were distinguished—political, social, and technological. Each of these, in turn, acting individually and together, had dual effects. Thus the political, social, and technological environments helped to determine what came to be seen as major managerial challenges. Moreover, these three conditioning environments helped determine how these perceived challenges were responded to.

This static picture is complex enough, but it must be enriched substantially so as to be true to reality. That is, developments in public personnel administration have made quantum jumps. For example, early efforts in public personnel administration were preoccupied with "getting personnel out of politics," and the major managerial challenges involved the development of approaches appropriate to that end. New eras bring new problems, and the managerial challenges of today are more subtle than calls for a "wall-to-wall protected service." But the old ideas die hard, often surviving to complicate efforts at new solutions to new problems.

The complex point above may be summarized by an analogy. Assume that this book is a camera. We intend to use that camera for three purposes. That is, most simply, we will take individual snapshots of 10 major areas in Public Personnel Administration. Moreover, we also propose to establish the inter-actions of these 10 areas, as by taking multiple exposures on the same film plate. Finally, we wish to convey the sense of changes over time, both for individual areas and for the areas in interaction. The analogy suggests the complexity of the multiple exposure of Public Personnel Administration we intend to take with the camera of this volume.

Basically, then, our problem was dual. We had to choose selections that reflect complex dynamics without slighting the necessary description of the individual interacting elements. And we had to organize the selections in such a way as to reflect basic changes over time, as well as to sketch the likely demands still hidden by the future. And we had to do both without slighting that which exists.

Such complications were increased even more by our hope of simultaneously achieving diverse subgoals. Specifically, we elaborated our outline, and attempted to organize our choices of readings, in order to meet eight subgoals. These subgoals reflect the ambitions of this volume to provide:

1. A clear picture of the major *institutional features* necessary to begin coping with the complexity of public personnel administration;
2. A good sense of *historical perspective* that describes what exists today, that links the present to the past, and that outlines what the future may bring;
3. A *solid feel* for anticipating and being prepared to react to tomorrow's challenges, given our estimate that extraordinary demands will be made upon today's personnel policies, procedures, and practices;
4. A sensitization to the *value issues* in public personnel administration, value issues of today and of yesterday, and value issues that are relevant to the foundations as well as to the operating problems of public personnel administration;
5. An introduction to *new developments* relevant to public personnel administration, be they new ways of learning, or innovative policies, or new technologies for inducing change;
6. A grounding in *behavioral concepts* that will serve to acquaint students with relevant advances in useful ways of viewing people at work;
7. A familiarity with *research orientations* that have proved useful for bringing some degree of rigor and order to the study of personnel administration; and
8. An awareness of some of the interpersonal and technical *skills* that are relevant to public personnel administration.

No good models exist in Public Administration for working toward these diverse subgoals. Directly, available teaching aids in public personnel administration concentrate on Subgoals 1 and 2 above, although they certainly do not neglect Subgoals 3 through 8. In contrast, we put a heavy emphasis on the last six subgoals, especially Subgoal 3. Subgoals 4–8, in effect, detail specific ways in which we attempt to help equip and sensitize the reader for making the massive adjustments in personnel administration that are increasingly required by changes in the political, social, and technological environments.

Selecting and organizing readings to meet these diverse goals was complicated by conflicting goals, in sum. Like everyone else in a similar situation, we had to be content with what the system theorist calls suboptimizing. We developed some simple heuristics to guide our suboptimizations. These rules of thumb and organizing conventions may be listed briefly. First, the volume is divided into 10 major parts, one for each of the subheadings listed in Table 1.

Second, each major part of this volume is similarly organized. Thus a table in each part introduces the reader to its topics and subtopics. For example, as listed in Table 1 this volume will be concerned with the heading: The Technological Environment: Cornucopias of Plenty and of Problems. And that heading, in turn (Table 4) will be approached in terms of two topics:

1. Familiar Themes: Functions/Dysfunctions of Seeking Stable Ways and Means
2. Emerging Dissonances: Managing the Consequences of Rapid Change

As appropriate, subtopics also will be listed.

Third, each table in the 10 major parts of this volume will list specific readings. The same selection may be listed in more than one table. Indeed, we sought selections that could do multiple duty, such as pieces that integrate two or more topics.

Fourth, each of the 10 tables is accompanied by an introductory essay that attempts to provide some perspective on the individual selections that are reprinted below. These essays are intended to be suggestive as opposed to exhaustive, so they are typically brief. Moreover, the purpose of the essays is to provide a broad context for the several selections. The emphasis is not on abstracting or interpreting the individual selections.

Fifth, because many of the selections below are useful in more than one of the 10 major sections of this volume, the individual selections are reprinted together toward the back of the volume. The individual selections are listed under the names of their authors in alphabetical order. Each selection also is numbered, to facilitate the search process and to permit easier cross-referencing.

This arrangement provides an important option for users of this volume. Thus we have provided a framework for use of the selections, whose logic and orientation we consider useful. Users of this volume may choose to operate within that framework. Alternatively, the alphabetical listing of the various selections permits the user a wide variety of options in modifying our framework or in adopting a framework more congenial to individual interests and training.

PART I

Broad Conditioning Environments: Major Influences on the Development of Public Personnel Administration

Part I - Section A

TABLE 2. *Topics and Selections Relevant to*
"The Political Environment."

1. Familiar Themes: Seeking Protection from "Spoils Politics" and Proferring
    Neutrality
    13—Foulke, "Fighting the Spoilsmen: The State of Civil Employ in the House
    of Representatives of 1901"
    52—Van Riper, "Spoils as Dysfunctional and Functional"
    51—USCSC, "The Extent of the Protected/Competitive Service: Some Distinc-
    tions and Some Data"
    27—Jones, "The Merit System, Politics, and Political Maturity"

2. Emerging Dissonances: The Development of a "New Politics"
    a. Some Concerns about the Demise of "Spoils Politics"
        42—Rose, "A Critical Look at the Hatch Act"
    b. Some Concerns about "Administrative Politics"
        29—Kaufman, "The Rise of a 'New Politics' "
        5—Cohen, "The Personnel Policy-Making System"
    c. Public Personnel Administration and "Welfare State Politics"
        55—Walker, "State and Local Manpower: A Challenge to Creative Feder-
        alism"

The Political Environment:
Weather Vanes in Crosswinds

T HE GENERAL FORMAT in the first three sections dealing with "Broad Conditioning Environments" is a simple one. That format attempts to highlight the interplay of "familiar themes" and "emerging dissonances," using one as counterpoint to the other. Thus common opinions or interpretations about public personnel administration constitute "familiar themes," while "emerging dissonances" reflect new problems, ideas, or research findings.

A common approach underlies all three initial sections. Broadly, the conditioning environments that influenced the early development of public personnel administration can be characterized in terms of a limited number of themes, if not dogma. Sharp changes in these conditioning environments are occurring, however. Consequently, the contemporary development of public personnel administration is jostled from the pillar of the past to the post of the future. Change is tense and uncertain, at best. For policies and procedures have been evolved to meet the demands of the broad conditioning environments of the past, sometimes the long-ago past. But these policies and procedures take on a momentum borne of habit, they may be nurtured by an early history of relative usefulness, and they often seem attractive indeed compared to the difficulty of bringing off any change in any large organization. Moreover, the future does not make change an easy matter, as a general rule. If nothing else, the future is a jealous mistress of her secrets. That is, it is not always clear what developments have to be anticipated by change. The counterpoint between familiar themes and emerging dissonances is intended to illustrate the dynamic tension between the concrete adaptations to the past and the significant but mercurial demands of the future.

3

FAMILIAR THEMES:
SEEKING PROTECTION FROM "SPOILS POLITICS"
AND PROFERRING NEUTRALITY

For "The Political Environment," as Table 2 details, the contrast of familiar themes and emerging dissonances is an elemental one. Neutrality and a protected service constitute the familiar themes, and their common goal was to free the management of public affairs from the ravages of "spoils politics." The emerging dissonances are more complex, but center around the "New Politics" that has developed when administrative officials were variously insulated from "spoils politics."

The grand and familiar political themes of the early civil service movements were uncomplicated, to begin. The public official was to be protected from arbitrary replacement as different parties or factions succeeded one another; and the merit system was to be out of the reach of "spoils politics." Politics was to be kept out of public personnel administration, to put the underlying intention in its most simplistic form. There was a *quid pro quo*. In return, again simplistically, public personnel were to keep out of politics. The civil servant was idealized as a useful technician, in short, competent but politically neutral and intent only in his strivings to achieve the ends determined for him by political policy makers.

The political ferment that essentially traded protection for neutrality, the personnel reform movement following the Civil War, gained considerable momentum through the first two or three decades of the 20th century. Some of the fervor of those days is projected by a selection from Foulke, "Fighting the Spoilsmen." Foulke writes from the perspective of decades of experience with the civil service notion, and he projects utter contempt that Congress was still fouling its own personnel nest so long after the Pendleton Act of 1883. His vehemence toward Congress seems especially intense, given that the civil service concept had already made significant inroads into state and local administration, those especial dens of spoils iniquity. Foulke's brief statement is a cameolike representation of the entire personnel reform literature. That literature delights in examples of pay-for-no-work, featherbedding, nonexistent job descriptions, and the awful wastes of time and talent associated with spoils politics. And that literature roundly (even vehemently) condemns such perceived evils in personnel practices.

Despite the wide acceptance of the protection/neutrality dogma, "spoils politics" did play a variously useful role in American politics. To be sure, substandard buildings and tainted meats and wasted funds in ample volumes can be attributed to the venal and/or incompetent and/or intimidated public officials fearful of losing their jobs that were one of the major products of the spoils system. But, as Paul P. Van Riper sketches in his "Spoils as Dysfunctional and Functional," the true picture is not a monolith. Patronage or spoils helped support the development of our political parties, for example, in addition to having nurtured the delicate flower of an ethos of unprecedently wide American popular representation in politics. These are very considerable accomplishments. Moreover, spoils played a valuable role in many other useful developments, great and small. For example, Van Riper concludes about the Civil War that "there is good reason for maintaining that the war could not have been won by the North without a highly partisan exploitation of the patronage." The devil of the personnel reformers, that is, had his good days too.

The spoils system thus must be judged in terms of the ends to which it contributed, as well as a means, but there is no doubt that it has had its day. Two selections suggest the nature of a full proof of the point. Thus "The Extent of the Protected/Competitive Service," drawn from U.S. Civil Service Commission sources, presents conclusive data about the practical acceptance of the civil service idea. The 85 percent modern coverage of federal employees does not reach the wall-to-wall ideal of early reformers; but neither does it fall very short. The coverage was so extensive after two decades of Democratic presidents, for example, that Mr. Eisenhower had great difficulty in carving out even some 1,500 top jobs from the protected service to provide his administration with the leverage considered necessary to attempt to provide new direction to the federal bureaucracy. "Schedule C" jobs were distinguished to permit such leverage, as is described in "The Extent of the Protected/Competitive Service."

Moreover, the demise of spoils is reflected not only in numbers, but in significantly changed attitudes as well. Roger W. Jones analyzes such attitudinal changes in "The Merit System, Politics, and Political Maturity." Basically, he argues that politics and the merit system have evolved into "adult partners in carrying on governmental functions," from an infancy often characterized by very noisy squabbles. As a partisan of the merit system, Jones perhaps idealizes that "new maturity." But there seems no question of the existence of a great and growing mutual accommodation of the kind about which he writes. As one sign of the times, for example, one seldom reads the diatribes against public officialdom that were such good sport over the years. It has been, after all, a good many years since anyone has really put his heart into a plea that we "go back to the spoils system." In part, this good press has been earned by competent and dedicated work. In part, also, the protected service has grown so extensive and formidable that—like the lion who learned to talk—the strong tendency is to listen even when it speaks very softly.

EMERGING DISSONANCES:
THE DEVELOPMENT OF A "NEW POLITICS"

The concept of protection of a neutral and competent public service is a major social invention but, not surprisingly, a "new politics" and new political problems have tended to supplant the "old politics" and its attendant political problems. Roughly, the public official is now not likely to be an open advocate of a party. But he often is deeply involved in "administrative politics" as a partisan for his agency or his program or his own interests. In short, nature seems to abhor a vacuum in politics just as in the rest of life.

These emerging dissonances concerning the development of a New Politics will be illustrated in three ways. First, the demise of spoils has raised new political problems while solving the old. Consider Henry Rose's "A Critical Look at the Hatch Act." Basically, he stresses that public officials can be so insulated from politics as to pose a problem for their civil rights. This seems to have been the fate of an unfortunate mail carrier cited by Rose. That public servant was prominent in the activities of a pacifist religious organization, and hence was seen as having crossed over "into politics" because of the prevailing official policy sanctioning war. He not only was protected from politics, but from freedom of speech as well. His case has not become a guiding one, but it illustrates the relatively fine distinctions involved.

That one can have too much of even a good thing also is suggested by Dean E. Mann's detailed study, "The Selection of Federal Political Executives." [1] Using sampling methods, Mann was concerned with an analysis of the patterns of recruiting political appointees, officials who were unquestionably "in politics." The details of this study deserve careful reading, and although it is not reprinted here, we note one of its many two-edged findings. Thus Mann stresses the apparent importance of experience and reputation for competence in explaining the political appointments he studied, and that presumptively bodes well for public administration. But Mann also stresses the small role in such appointments of service to a political party; and he notes the short tenure of political appointees. These findings imply several significant questions relevant to the development of a New Politics. Consider only two such questions: How will our political parties adapt to such lessened patronage at top levels, at the same time that the masses of lower level jobs also are at least officially out of reach? And does the short tenure of appointees imply problems for top-level political control over the legions of public officials who have the advantage of protected tenure and of long experience at their job in their organization?

Such questions patently pose new and significant political questions. Moreover, any reasonable answers to such questions imply an enormously enhanced leverage for public officials. Some have seen the political parties fatally threatened by the merit system, indeed, although we have not recently had such a major clamor "to go back to the spoils system" as arose after World War II.

Second, many observers feel they can discern major specifics of the form of

---

[1] Dean E. Mann, "The Selection of Federal Political Executives," *American Political Science Review*, Vol. 58 (March, 1964), pp. 81–99.

leverage increasingly in the hands of public officialdom. Some of what they see is disquieting; and all of it requires careful attention in any approach to public personnel administration. Herbert Kaufman's "The Rise of a 'New Politics'" provides both broad historical sweep and detailed counterpoint concerning the ways in which "protected" and "neutral" are inadequate descriptions of our public service. In sum, Kaufman plays variously on this basic theme:

Originally, civil servants engaged in political activity to further the cause of a particular candidate or group of candidates. After the installation of the merit system and the growth of agency consciousness and professionalization, the end of political collaboration was the defense of the agency and its program, and was practiced by both parties. This was politics of a different kind.

The ironies involved in this "politics of a different kind" often are delicious. Thus, in large part, the merit system was intended to provide line administrators with capable help. But extensions of the protected service sometimes, as Kaufman notes, drove those very administrators to "pray for deliverance from their guardians." Thus upper level administrators felt limited because personnel administration was less firmly in their hands, especially hiring and firing. And not a few administrators had to contend with large numbers of employees, hired in a different time for less-demanding technologies, who still enjoyed the comfortable support of the protective/competitive service and who can provide real obstacles to necessary change. Although aggressive administrative action can still permit a public manager to staff his unit more or less to his own tastes, in sum, a new managerial broom often only raises more personnel dust. The situation is similar in much of business, and certainly at the unionized levels. So the phenomenon is not distinctly governmental. But this does not make it any less of a problem.

The irony has other facets. In his characteristic way, Norton Long highlights the crucial nature of the New Politics in discussing public administrators as "managerial mercenaries." The sense of his argument is conveyed in these words:[2]

Public administrators are a sizeable and increasing part of the governing class of this republic; they are our appointed politicians. . . . We can no longer confront the formation of their values with the fiction that they are neutral instruments to be exclusively directed by elected politicians.

Thus Long directs critical questions to both aspects of protection/neutrality.

Michael Cohen's "The Personnel Policy-Making System" provides support on both counts, surveying as he does the ways in which the Civil Service Commission

---

[2] Norton Long, "Politicians for Hire," *Public Administration Review*, Vol. 25 (June, 1965), p. 118.

does act and must act so as to assure that its interests receive due consideration. Savor the delicious irony. The U.S. Civil Service was established to safeguard the dogma of protection/neutrality. In order to perform that role, however, the Commission has had to engage in the New Politics to which Kaufman and Long direct our attention. In real senses, that is, political involvement was necessary to gain and safeguard a protected service. Happiness is all a paradox, as Peanuts might say.

Third, now more than ever before, political ends must be achieved with administrative means that are out of the direct control of those formulating the goals of public policy. This is the case, for example, with many of the grant-in-aid programs to states or localities which the federal government largely or wholly funds, but which federal officials oversee but do not directly administer. Such cases have many aspects of damned if you do and damned if you do not, in personnel matters.

That the complex and uncertain linkages of control over personnel and initiation of public policy are critical in the New Politics is demonstrated at length by David B. Walker in "State and Local Manpower: A Challenge to Creative Federalism." The programs under creative federalism envisioned by President Johnson, to illustrate the argument, rest heavily upon state and local manpower for their implementation. Such reliance is economically, politically, and managerially unavoidable. But the problems of local/federal interaction are significant, no matter what the rationale. If nothing else, state and local manpower must come to accept the general spirit of cooperative federalism and the specifics of particular programs. Relatedly, the manpower must possess the required program skills.

As Walker indicates, these "musts" are difficult to achieve. Moreover, even successful efforts to achieve one "must" may undercut the other. For example, Walker writes of legislation that authorizes the President to extend merit system requirements to more grant-in-aid programs. The intention, apparently, is to build a body of public officials of requisite competence. But the approach has important side effects, which in part work at cross-purposes to the need for enhanced flexibility in adapting to new programs. As the merit system is extended, that is, state and local public officials may be less responsive to still newer programs. Moreover, to the degree that the merit system is extended by covering incumbents—which is generally the case—it may also be more difficult to build new required skills into the work force and to remove deadwood. As the man said, it is often damned if you do, and damned if you do not.

Part I - Section B

TABLE 3. *Topics and Selections Relevant to*
"The Social Environment."

1. Familiar Themes: Seeking Merit and Loyalty
   a. Matrix Values of Civil Service: Reinforced by Government As a Model
      Employer and by Employment Uncertainty
      53—Van Riper, "The Taproots of American Public Personnel Administration"
      36—Mosher, "Features and Problems of the Federal Service: The Management of Merit"
   b. Old-fashioned Loyalty in an Economy of Scarcity: Paucity, Procedural
      Care, and Protectionism
      14—Goldwater, "The Perils of Power"
      43—Sayre, "The Triumph of Techniques over Purpose"

2. Emerging Dissonances: The Ferment in Expectations and Values
   a. Expanding the "Merit" Concept
      23—Jensen, "Cultural Bias in Selection"
      54—Van Riper, "Veterans' Preference: Policies at Potential Cross-Purposes"
      24—Executive Order 11397, "Authorizing Transitional Appointments of
         Veterans Who Have Served during the Vietnam Era"
   b. Competing and Conflicting Loyalties in a Full Employment Economy
      20—Halset, "The Paradoxes of Public Administration"
      34—Morse, "Shall We Bargain away the Merit System?"
   c. Emergence of Administrative Complexity and Abundance: "To Do What
      Has to Be Done"
      3—Baum, "Getting Caught in the Middle on Classification Decisions:
         Parts A and B"
      4—Cohen, "Responsibility in the Public Service"

The Social Environment:
A Revolution of Rising Expectations
and Changing Values

T HE SOCIAL ENVIRONMENT underlying public personnel administration also can be characterized usefully in terms of familiar themes and emerging dissonances. Even sharp distinctions can be useful for analysis, although reality tends to be of one piece. In this sense, and this sense only, we distinguish the "social environment" in this chapter from the "political environment" in the preceding chapter. This social environment will also be characterized in terms of familiar themes that over time increasingly have had to share center stage with major emerging dissonances. Table 3 develops the point in some detail. Some perspective on the thrust of this second of the broad conditioning environments will be provided by brief introductory comments concerning the selections listed in Table 3.

FAMILIAR THEMES:
SEEKING MERIT AND LOYALTY

If the early political environment of public personnel administration emphasized neutrality and protection, merit and loyalty are the dominant dual themes of the early social environment within which public personnel practices and policies were developed. Paul P. Van Riper definitively establishes the bias toward merit in "The Taproots of American Public Personnel Administration." For example, Van Riper cites the place of competitive examinations in the American experience. Their focus was on isolating a "meritocracy," period. That is, the idea of competitive examinations was not novel to America. What was novel was the "openness and availability to all" of these examinations, an obvious concern for merit alone. The examinations thus were "nation-wide in coverage, open to all on a truly competitive basis, limited to no particular universities, no social class, and no special political point of view." The contemporary British system, in contrast, had "age, degree, university, and perhaps even class limits."

Frederick Mosher validates and extends the sketch above of the matrix values of our civil service movements. His "Features and Problems of the Federal Service" massively documents the stress on merit in American public personnel administration. In addition, Mosher provides a valuable perspective on loyalty as a prime value. Thus Mosher details many specifics by which loyalty to a government service was encouraged, under the overall but not universal concept that "the government continues to operate, in many ways, as *one* employer. . . . The ground rules are very nearly universal in application and in some fields . . . they are very specific (some would say distressingly so)."

This concept of loyalty to *a* public service was massively reinforced by two characteristics of the early history of the development of our civil service. First, the federal government was a model employer in terms of wages, benefits, and personnel policies, in an era when business was at least less concerned about employee needs. In some cases, of course, business practices were frankly brutal, with arbitrary layoffs and firings being only the major external signs of that elemental spirit. This early contrast gave government work a decided advantage in the eyes of many potential employees. Second, government service implied job security in an economy characterized by more or less regular and violent fluctuations in employment. In combination with government's reputation as a model employer, the derivative consciousness about job security powerfully reinforced the concept of loyalty to a public service.

Merit and loyalty are attractive social concepts, of course, but the early development of our public personnel systems at federal and local levels often curiously shaped and misshaped attempts to achieve these concepts in action. Old-fashioned merit and loyalty in the context of an economy of relative scarcity often were affected, and sometimes changed into near opposites, by paucity, procedural care, and protectionism. This may sound precious, but we mean it in a profound way. Consider Barry Goldwater's "The Perils of Power" in which he sketches the "principle of limited government" that significantly influenced how merit and loyalty were approached in actual practice. We cannot do justice to developing the implications of limited government in any detail, but consider only two of its effects on practical approaches to merit and loyalty. Given limited funds for public purposes, and given sharp restrictions of law and custom on public officials, one could predict a general up-tightness in government personnel. Paucity, in short, would be likely to lead to an ex- aggerated demand for procedural care as well as to a correspondingly exaggerated need for protectionism of public officials. And that at least is what tended to happen, if we are willing to accept a first-order characterization of the history of our early civil service movement.

Wallace Sayre's brief and sparkling piece, "The Triumph of Techniques over

Purpose," provides evidence that the first-order characterization above is useful. Many other and longer sources could illustrate the present point, but none do so pointedly and indeed so poignantly. Consider, for example, how the laudable goal of equal treatment for all applicants for public employ and for all public employees often got transmuted into something less fine. The main practical expression of "equal treatment" in public personnel administration in the years around World War II, in the words of Gordon Clapp, was to move it "into the cold objective atmosphere of tests, scores, weighted indices and split-digit ranking" so completely that "these technical trappings have become the symbols of the merit system." Sayre sketches the triumph of technique over purpose in other revealing ways. Each approach shows how paucity, procedural care, and protectionism unevenly affected the social concepts of merit/loyalty in the early environment of public personnel administration.

EMERGING DISSONANCES:
THE FERMENT IN EXPECTATIONS AND VALUES

Time has not stood still for the social concepts of merit/loyalty. The worldwide ferment in expectations and values, and especially since World War II, has affected public personnel administration as it has all of life. A number of selections illustrate some relevant emerging dissonances that have recently begun to further complicate the difficulty of practical approaches to merit/loyalty. These readings are organized, roughly, under three headings.

First, the concept "merit" has been expanded in many and varied ways. Merit was not always better served in the process, especially if one looks only at short-run effects. On the other hand, neither was merit on balance the clear loser in even the most exuberant expansions of the concept, and especially when one takes the longer view. Ollie A. Jensen's "Cultural Bias in Selection" takes one approach to expanding the merit concept. His careful analysis reflects the real concern with "fairness" common in public personnel administration.

"Fairness" sounds hard to fault, but some varieties of concern about it do imply significant issues. Assume, for example, that a concerted drive is begun to recruit more women, or more Negroes, or more whatever for public employ. This may meet a high social purpose. The practical problems are legion, however. Encouraging such accelerated recruitment may generate a conflict, illustratively, between incompatible goals. For example, recruiting large additional numbers of individuals who have been educationally or culturally or economically deprived would require individualized remedial education to help some of them achieve the required skills or competencies. Such massive recruitment might also require that people be hired in anticipation of what they may be able to do in the future rather than because of present skills. This is a departure from the historical, and safer, emphasis on hiring for a job, and also raises serious administrative questions. Large numbers of individuals may not enter such programs unless they are given assurances about permanent employment, for example. But giving such individuals a protected status, or even a strong hope of such status, today might only mean a less-skilled but immovable work force for tomorrow. And so it goes.

Only the politically naïve person can neglect the implications of expanding the merit concept, in addition, which fact must deflate even the most fervent case made for any particular variety of "fairness." That is, broad social purposes might be achieved while political support was gained for (let us say) the U.S. Civil Service Commission. This is an attractive combination, but it has its tacky features. Paul P. Van Riper implies both features in his "Veterans' Preference." Thus an advantage to veterans in examinations for employment might be a laudable social purpose; but it also could gut the notion of merit. Similarly, the support of veterans' associations may be comforting when friends are needed to get desired legislation through Congress; but one's friends of this kind may also apply considerable pressure to see that their good offices are remembered in ways that may undercut the best of Commission intentions. In any case, the consequences of any such preference will be long with us. In December, 1965, to suggest the point, 51 percent of the total federal work force entered public service with veterans' preference. And nearly one in five of these individuals received additional consideration as a disabled veteran or as a relative of a disabled veteran.

The issue of expanding the "merit" concept is much with us, as is reflected in Executive Order 11397, "Authorizing Transitional Appointments of Veterans Who Have Served during the Vietnam Era." The Executive Order offers a *quid pro quo*: "transitional appointment" in public employ while employees gain "education or training adequate to prepare them for the future job demands." The long-run effects on merit/loyalty are not clear, even though the opportunity to upgrade the skills of veterans is an attractive one. The problems of administering such a program seem legion, however.

Second, a major emerging dissonance in public personnel administration centers around competing and conflicting loyalties in a full-employment economy. At one level, the major historical advantages of public employ have been weakened or destroyed. For example, government today has many competitors as a model employer. Moreover, at least through the 1950's, government employ was becoming less and less financially attractive at all levels than work for business. Since then, public salaries at lower levels have been raised significantly. Finally, job security has not been the pressing concern for those now in their thirties and forties that it had been for those with more vivid recollections of the Great Depression.

At the broadest level, indeed, it seems probable that our very concept of "loyalty" is changing radically. Harry Levinson makes the argument with a flourish, catching the spirit that has influenced both public and business sectors. He traces "good old-fashioned loyalty" to these roots: [1]

Loyalty is an ancient concept which goes hand in hand with honor. In feudal times a man gave his king or lord his fealty in return for the lord's beneficence or protection. To be loyal was to have a place in a formal social structure and to live according to a code of fixed relationships and mutual obligations. In return for loyalty, the more powerful took care of the less powerful. To question the lord or to act against his wishes was to be disloyal.

Levinson notes that much of this tradition still affects management thought. Crudely, this managerial approach to loyalty takes such a form: "if the employee is paid reasonably, the work place is adequately comfortable, and the boss is 'nice', the employee should do as told, and do it cheerfully. Above all, the employee should stand behind and for the man who provides his bread and butter. If he does not do so, if he does not appreciate what he is getting, he is not a loyal employee." [2]

Changing times have made such a concept of loyalty increasingly obsolete, Levinson argues. Consider only one factor. Not very long ago, loyalty was a reasonable way of assessing the value of an organization member. That is—given reasonable technical and social skills, courage, and drive—many individuals could rise to the tops of their organizations. Loyalty, traditionally defined, was as good a criterion as any to aid in the selection of those actually chosen for managerial leadership. Given the relative simplicity of most work in organization, plus the slow pace of change, it was not a serious matter if the process of selection moved leisurely, as by heavily weighting seniority.

Today, the focus must increasingly be on the early selection of individuals who can provide effective leadership to a wondrous array of professionals, engineers, and scientists. "Old-fashioned loyalty" to the organization is no particular sign of such effective leadership. Indeed, insistence on that kind of loyalty is likely to hinder the greater independence and initiative that is likely to encourage professionals, engineers, and scientists to work at their best. The conclusion is clear to Levinson. [3]

All this does not mean that loyalty is gone or will go. It means, rather, that paternalism, however disguised, is going, and the kind of loyalty which was characteristic of paternalism must necessarily go with it. The old ways of achieving loyalty—preaching it, inducing guilt, reinforcing it by tight controls and severe penalties, buying it by keeping people dependent and grateful—no longer work.

---

[1] Harry Levinson, "Whatever Happened to Loyalty?" *Public Management*, Vol. 47 (June, 1966), p. 160.

[2] *Ibid.*, p. 161.

[3] *Ibid.*, p. 163.

This broad picture can be enriched easily. For example, Walter G. Halset argues in "The Paradoxes of Public Administration" that professionalization is a growing challenge to "old-fashioned loyalty." Thus a scientist or an engineer is usually a practicing professional first and foremost, and a government employee only secondarily. If the value systems of his profession and his public employ conflict, the employee is likely to seek a more congenial organizational home. Such leave-taking may be quite casual, especially in the context of the uniquely favorable job market that has characterized the last two decades.

The growing tendency to unionize public employees also implies new and potentially severe challenges to a simple loyalty, especially concerning strikes by union members who are public officials. Muriel M. Morse's "Shall We Bargain away the Merit System?" surveys a broad range of approaches to the multiple loyalties generated by public unionization. Not all commentators see the issue in terms of merit system versus collective bargaining, as does Morse. But it is clear that Morse is correctly reacting to unionization of public employees as a source of competing loyalties that must be increasingly reckoned with in the public personnel administration of tomorrow.

Unionization and old-fashioned loyalty do not mix well. Such challenges to a simple loyalty can be generalized in terms of changes in the concept "authority." Authority was once rooted deeply in law and formal rank, and its major expression was in domination of subordinate by superior. Increasingly, authority has tended to slip such clear social moorings. Commentators increasingly place authority in the job performed, or in expertise, or even in the situation that requires remedying. Loyalty is hard to localize, as a consequence. Moreover, formal authorities are more likely to use the panoply of techniques ranging from subtle manipulation to full participation. As opposed to domination of superior to subordinate, such techniques at once show respect for existing multiple loyalties while they also help heighten them. No doubt, the superior still has powerful sanctions. But it seems very probable that his opportunities to use them with impunity have been sharply curtailed by the processes of social and technological change going on around us.

Third, the emergence of administrative complexity and abundance also implies a greater incidence of conflicting and competing loyalties in public work. In this sense, Goldwater's plea in "The Perils of Power" for limited government is at once profoundly appealing and impossibly anachronistic. Our attention must be focused on managing multiple loyalties in complex and extensive public programs. Our attention cannot be diverted by such notions as how much more simple management would be were limited government possible or desirable.

Similar effects of multiple loyalties at various levels of organization are described and analyzed in Bernard H. Baum, "Getting Caught in the Middle on Classification Decisions," especially Part B. When the federal government was smaller, to summarize his basic point, much of personnel work could be done centrally in the Washington office of the U.S. Civil Service Commission. This made life relatively easy, for a while, since competing loyalties were minimized. That day is long gone, and now many personnel actions must be taken in smallish subunits of departments and agencies. The Commission can and does oversee many of these actions, but the opportunities for competing and conflicting loyalties are many. Thus agency and Commission people can easily work into "us vs. them" postures with departmental representatives, because the plain fact is that their interests *are* different in many relevant particulars. Similarly, Washington employees of the Commission can get into a similar situation with members of their own field units, as their loyalties and interests differ. At the same time, each "us" and "them" also has other loyalties, some of them intensely shared, some of them distinct if not antagonistic. Of such stuff is administrative man made.

At a still different level, administrative complexity and abundance intensify both the need and the difficulty of keeping public servants responsible. This theme is a major burden of Michael Cohen's "Responsibility in the Public Service." Thus responsibility once could have been framed in terms of this question: For what are public employees responsible? But professionalization and unionization have given added relevance to another question: To whom are public employees responsible? The answer today is not clearly: To the public. In fact, that answer never was an adequate one. The public interest is often relied on to dignify our own needs and desires, as opposed to the lamentable special needs and desires of the other guy, whomever he may be.

A brief summary is possible but hardly adequate for this look at the familiar themes and emerging dissonances of the social environment of public personnel administration. Merit and loyalty are elusive ideals, and the approaches to them are increasingly complicated by the ongoing social ferment in expectations and values. Moreover, matters are only likely to get more complex. There is no easy way out.

Part I - Section C

TABLE 4. Topics and Selections Relevant to
"The Technological Environment."

1. Familiar Themes: Functions/Dysfunctions of Seeking Stable Ways and Means
    a. Fixation on Means and Resistance to Change
        43—Sayre, "Triumph of Techniques over Purpose"

2. Emerging Dissonances: Managing the Consequences of Rapid Change
    a. Technological Change and Personnel Policies
        36—Mosher, "Features and Problems of the Federal Service: The Management of Merit"
        2—Association of the Bar of the City of New York, "Conflict of Interest, Technological Change, and Effects on Public Recruitment"
    b. Technological Change and Personnel Procedures
        18—Grandpré, McQuie, and Brogan, "Three Things Wrong with the Civil Service"
        10—Davis, "The Effects of Automation on Job Design"
    c. Technological Change and Managing Personnel
        4—Cohen, "Responsibility in the Public Service"
        20—Halset, "The Paradoxes of Public Administration"

The Technological Environment: Cornucopias of Plenty and of Problems

T WO TRUISMS underlay the interplay of familiar themes and emerging dissonances concerning technology. Thus the early civil service movements in this country came only after the War between the States, and then current concepts of technology understandably and significantly influenced the development of early public personnel administration. Technological change has gone on at an ever accelerating pace, however, and especially since World War II. Moreover, the technology has changed in some ways that profoundly differ from the mechanistic, mass-production technology that until quite recently was held out as the ideal.[1] Consequently, public personnel administration in perhaps its most essential sense must be viewed in terms of a dynamic tension: as reaching toward innovations appropriate to changing and sometimes radically new technological requirements; and as being restrained by policies, procedures, and habits whose development came in response to an older technology.

FAMILIAR THEMES:
FUNCTIONS/DYSFUNCTIONS OF
SEEKING STABLE WAYS AND MEANS

Table 4 attempts to illustrate a dual approach to public personnel administration as reaching and as being restrained. Consider the familiar themes introduced

---

[1] Scientific Management had an enormous vogue in public administration for decades, for example, and its basic underlying technology was a simple mass-production model. See Robert T. Golembiewski, *Behavior and Organization* (Chicago: Rand McNally & Co., 1962), esp. pp. 9–26.

by that table. Any large organization must take on aspects of bureaucracy, and this necessity cuts several ways. In the orderly state, that is, many things must be done under more or less specified conditions, to meet certain standards, by individuals in specific positions, having appropriate skills relevant to the area of their delegated authority. This is a rough sketch of "bureaucracy," and it can go too far as well as not far enough. At one extreme, bureaucracy can flower into a passion for procedural care and regularity about getting something done on time without due attention to the substance of what is being done. This is just as if Lincoln took great care to cross every "t" in his Gettysburg Address, but gave little attention to its spirit and meaning. At the other extreme, pre-bureaucratic administration can be characterized by a chaos of bits and pieces, performed with a dazzling array of levels of skill, by solo performers doing what they will, how they will, when they will.

Judging from the evidence, American public personnel administration has seen some of both extremes. Wallace Sayre's "The Triumph of Techniques over Purpose" skillfully portrays the fixation on means that characterized early personnel administration. Too much of one extreme of the bureaucratic spirit got into public personnel practice, that is, and not a little of it has remained over the years. The U.S. Civil Service Commission, particularly, has made vigorous attempts of late to emphasize substance versus procedure, as in providing training, guidance, and oversight rather than in being preoccupied with the technical trappings. But old habits die hard, and hardest of all in complex organizations.

Paradoxically, then, there is evidence that bureaucratization is in important senses its own worst enemy. Consider one of the major offsprings of a passion for procedure, specifically, resistance to change. Some bureaucratic procedures can gain a momentum of their own, as individuals and groups develop a vested interest in them, and as these procedures serve to inhibit further rationalization of public officialdom. For example, the Senior Civil Service notion proposed some basic modifications in the policies and customs of the U.S. Civil Service Commission, and this threat aroused the protective instincts of those who had come to some kind of an understanding with the Commission. "Having now—after a long struggle—a centralized personnel agency to their liking," Van Riper noted of the unions of government employees, "they are loath to fragment its powers in any way. The veterans' organizations and Congress, too, often think along similar lines." [2]

---

[2] Paul P. Van Riper, "The Senior Civil Service and the Career System," *Public Administration Review*, Vol. 28 (Summer, 1958), pp. 189–200.

EMERGING DISSONANCES:
MANAGING THE CONSEQUENCES OF RAPID CHANGE

History has played cruelly with bureaucracy, exaggerating its worst features. That is, resistance to change is a common consequence of bureaucratization, but recent history has placed a major premium on planned and rapid technological change. This leaves the bureaucratic model playing from one of its major weaknesses. The predictable results are uneven responses to the massive demands imposed by technological innovation.

Three major emerging dissonances resulting from the need for rapid technological change will receive attention. In turn, the emphasis will be on personnel policies, on procedures, and on the management of men. In summary, technological change has had significant impacts on all three emphases, but timely adaptations are the exception rather than the rule.

First, technological change has had major influences on public personnel policies. To paint with a broad brush first, consider Frederick Mosher's "Features and Problems of the Federal Service." Mosher analyzes a number of features of our federal merit system that complicated adapting to technological change. A simple illustration must suffice here. Andrew Jackson's dictum that the work of the public employee could be performed by any citizen has a number of appeals, for example, and for some time that ringing populist pronouncement had a real element of truth in it. And even when time had sucked much of the marrow of truth out of that notion, it still retained manifold sources of support. Thus personnel procedures and policies developed with the Jacksonian notion in mind carried its influence well beyond its time. Moreover, the Jacksonian notion was a comforting one, in that it fitted nicely with other values of our merit system, such as it being a system open to all classes and groups. Reality had its eventual revenge, however. Technology changed more rapidly than did this convenient notion about the routine nature of public work, with the serious consequences for recruitment detailed by Mosher.

The lag in adapting personnel policies to technological change is specifically reflected in the New York City Bar Association's "Conflict of Interest, Technological Change, and Effects on Public Recruitment." Given the social value of a simple loyalty to government service built into early merit concepts, as the paper shows, determined efforts were made to separate "public" and "private" spheres of employment and to detail the cases in which a "conflict of interest" might exist between a person's private interests and his trust as a public official. Patently, such conflicts could exist and should be identified. But a useful idea can be extended ludicrously. In general, the tendency was to draw the line so sharply as to complicate recruiting for public jobs. There were some exceptions, as in the case of so-called WOC (Without Compensation) businessmen who held public offices during World War II while still attached to their private firms or organizations. But they were exceptions only. As technological demands increased, and as the line between "public" and "private" became less distinct, consequently, conflict of interest policies presented major barriers to bringing the required expertise to bear on governmental problem solving. This was particularly true in the case of the scientist, as the report of the Bar Association makes plain.

The adaptations of public personnel policies to changing conditions have come but slowly, with great effort, and often only by creating alternatives to the civil service. Thus, the major adaptation—"contracting out"—essentially by-passes civil service systems. Increasingly, that is, private businesses or curious hybrids like the RAND Corporation have been established to get important public work done while avoiding such restrictions as the ceilings on salary built into our civil service laws.[3] The point must not be exaggerated, but the changes of opinion in intellectual circles over the last decade or so have been amazing. Not long ago, informed opinion held that all public programs be handled by our civil service systems, and especially the federal service. Business was suspect, and local government perhaps even more so. Experience apparently has been a fast teacher, as Robert A. Levine reflects in explaining the troubled history of the "war on poverty" and other programs of the Great Society. Levine allows that the only way out may be to turn over to private organizations and local communities a "substantial portion of the *operation* of the Great Society programs" while retaining policy guidance for the federal government. The implications for the protected/competitive services are profound.[4]

Second, technological change also implied major emerging dissonances that affect personnel procedures. "Three Things Wrong with the Civil Service" provides specific perspective on the point. In that piece, three experienced public officials sketch areas in which they feel technological changes demand the most significant modifications of existing features of our merit system. Thus "position classification"—of which more will be said later—seems to one of the contributors to be inappropriate under modern conditions, especially in the higher reaches of public officials under the merit system. The basic American position classification at the federal levels provides for 18 grades of jobs, both high and low, and generates serious rigidities that hinder adaptations to techno-logical change. For example, roughly, position levels are defined in terms of number of people supervised and/or size of budget involved. Thus, until recently, an extraordinarily productive scientist could reach lower middle job levels only

---

[3] Bruce L. R. Smith, *The RAND Corporation* (Cambridge, Mass.: Harvard University Press, 1966); and Victor K. Heyman, "Government by Contract: Boon or Boner," *Public Administration Review*, Vol. 21 (Spring, 1961), pp. 59–64.
[4] Robert A. Levine, "Rethinking Our Social Strategies," *The Public Interest*, No. 10 (Winter, 1968), p. 86.

by leaving his scientific work. The structure of positions had serious implications for management, that is, in part because of the desire to preserve a single system and hence procedural (versus substantive) fairness for all employees. For details on position classification, see Part II, Section C, Maintaining the Organization: Combining People and Structure.

The overall view of the impact of technological change on personnel procedures tells basically the same story. Louis E. Davis provides a careful overview in "The Effects of Automation on Job Design," beginning with the propositions that the effects are still obscure. Thus Davis sketches several popular theories that profess to detail such effects, but only by contradicting one another at critical points. He provides counterpoint to this general argument by reviewing the available evidence about the specific effects of specific types of automation on the design of specific jobs. The conclusions that Davis arrives at are mixed, and he urges caution all the while. Thus he sees the upgrading of some job skills, and the downgrading of others. He is definite, however, that jobs will be up-graded, on balance. And he is certain of the need for massive changes in jobs, in training people to perform them, and in compensating employees for work.

Some major implications of automation for the public service may be hazarded, then, using Ida R. Hoos's argument as a guide.[5] Generally, the skills of the present work force must be updated and upgraded. And President Jackson's insistence on the clerklike nature of government work, consequently, ill suits the demands of the computer. Hoos also stresses the derivative need for massive doses of in-career training to use today's employees to make the adaptations necessary to provide the skills required by the technology of tomorrow and the next day. In contrast, our basic civil service policies and traditions have been oriented toward hiring for a specific job. This is anachronistic, since it is less and less clear what jobs will be required in what numbers even so short a time ahead as 10 or 15 years. And if the merit system is to continue to provide substantial employment security, the skills to perform those jobs of the future must basically come from the present public work force.

Third, and finally, technological change induces major dissonances with traditional approaches to the managing of men. Thus one observer concludes: "In short, the line supervisor of today may be faced with problems much different from those which beset his counterpart a generation ago."[6] Facing such problems is complicated by a civil service tradition liberally laced with a strong concern for procedural regularity and individual loyalty and accountability. Thus supervisors might share leadership with their technical personnel in response

---

[5] Ida R. Hoos, "The Personnel Administrator and Technological Change," *Public Personnel Review*, Vol. 24 (July, 1963), pp. 52–57.
[6] William E. Griffiths, "Supervising Technical-Specialist Personnel," *Public Personnel Review*, Vol. 26 (April, 1965), pp. 169–71.

to the new conditions, but this goes against the grain of attitudes and traditions in public service. These attitudes and traditions are rooted deeply in a history of limited government, of restricted activities and budgets, both of which are reinforced by a concern for procedure that is generally more marked than in business.

We do not wish to caricature the point, but we make it strongly nonetheless. No doubt, that is, government is and should be different than business in the elemental sense of seeking more strenuously to ensure broad public accountability. But there often has been too much of a good thing.[7] Moreover, the existing cultural lag in public adaptations to wildly different conditions is understandable on other grounds. For example, we are less than four decades away from the really small government of predepression days. Moreover, we have only a decade or so of experience with the really big public budgets of the Great Society. That the lag is understandable in the light of our limited experience, however, does not lessen the challenge.

Technological change complicates the managing of men in another major sense. Michael Cohen's "Responsibility in the Public Service" thus suggests some major difficulties of working toward the representativeness, responsibility, and responsiveness of public officials in a technologically sophisticated society. Given the Jacksonian notion of the clerklike nature of government work, and given a public service open to all ages and classes, for example, representativeness posed no great problem in theory. That problem is great today. The professionalization that is a concomitant of technological change, for example, clearly complicates the issue of who is responsible for what to whom. The employee, in effect, has multiple loyalties to his profession, to his agency, and to however he defines that awesome construct, "the public interest." These loyalties may be variously congruent; they may be played off one against another; but they complicate the matter of accountability in either case.[8]

Competition or conflict between multiple loyalties is not new in principle, of course, but it does seem more common and intense in technologically advanced societies and in large organizations. Some of the specifics of such multiple and incongruent loyalties are discussed by Walter G. Halset in "The Paradoxes of Public Administration." His focus is on the scientist, and on the kind of divergent sets of expectations he may feel in his public employment. More or

---

[7] Frank H. Weitzel, "Comptrollership Trends in the Federal Government," *The Federal Accountant*, Vol. 13 (June, 1964), pp. 4–23.

[8] Consider the case of a school psychologist who practiced an unusual kind of shock therapy on certain pupils he felt needed help: he homosexually molested them. Parents did not think much of the therapy; nor did the state courts. But the psychologist made a convincing case to school administrators that any strong action against him by them might only encourage "non-professionals" to seek greater control in areas where the professional felt his expertise should prevail. The psychologist was treated gently, indeed generously, by local school officials. Even individuals who did not esteem his practice responded to his principle.

less, his argument applies to employees having a wide range of skills in all large public organizations.

The "technological environment" escapes easy characterization, then. But it does seem fair to note that early personnel administration recognized the need to provide for stability and change, but with the emphasis on stability. The same need for a balance exists today, but the emphasis must shift more definitely toward change. Relatedly, early public personnel administration recognized the existence of multiple loyalties, but often acted on the assumption of a simple and direct loyalty. Today, that assumption is increasingly and dangerously untenable.

To be sure, we are better equipped to handle the resulting challenges of change and of multiple loyalties today than yesterday, but the question remains of whether we are only running fast enough to stand still. For there seems no question that the conflict of multiple loyalties is likely to intensify.

PART II

Major Managerial Challenges: The Practice of Public Personnel Administration

Part II - Section A

TABLE 5. Topics and Selections Relevant to
"Developing the Personnel Function."

1. Role and Development
    41—Pigors and Myers, "In Short: Personnel Administration for Line Managers"

2. Some Institutional Arrangements
    a. Commission-Congressional Relations
        5—Cohen, "The Personnel Policy-Making System"
        54—Van Riper, "Veterans' Preference: Policies at Potential Cross-Purposes"
    b. The U.S. Civil Service Commission as an Institution
        52—Van Riper, "Spoils as Dysfunctional and Functional"
        53—Van Riper, "The Taproots of American Public Personnel Administration"
        6—Commission on Organization of the Executive Branch of the Government, "Alternative Organizations and Policy Implications: Perspectives on the U.S. Civil Service Commission"
    c. Commission-Department Relations
        46—USCSC, "Department-Commission Relations: The President's Formal Position"
        40—Nigro, "Department-Commission Relations: Some Swings of the Pendulum"
        3—Baum, "Getting Caught in the Middle on Classification Decisions: Parts A and B"
    d. The Role of the Department Personnel Officer
        1—Albouze, "The Departmental Personnel Officer's Contribution to Management"

Developing the Personnel Function:
Seeking Missions and Roles

T HE PERSONNEL FUNCTION has had to struggle for its place in the organizational sun. If this is less true in some senses in government than in business, in most particulars the generalization holds more rather than less for all organizations. Moreover, although the personnel function received earlier attention in public agencies, it is fair to note that business practitioners have in general more than overcome the lead of their governmental cousins. Just as the federal government is no longer *the* model employer, so also are federal personnel programs no longer a model for policies, procedures, or programs.

How personnel missions and rules developed in public agencies, and especially at the federal level, is sketched in Table 5. Basically, the organization of this chapter is dual. A first part sketches one ideal concept of the role and development of the personnel function, and the other part sketches institutional arrangements for public personnel administration at the federal level as they diversely compare with that ideal. The ideal concept is to be used for comparative purposes only, rather than as a statement of some absolutely best condition.

ROLE AND DEVELOPMENT

In presenting an idealized picture of the role and development of the personnel function in organizations, business practice sets the standard. Paul Pigors and Charles A. Myers develop a useful amalgam of enlightened business practice in their piece, "In Short: Personnel Administration for Line Managers." Basically, personnel administration is seen as "staff." Staff provides aid or recommends or suggests to the "line," which is in the chain of command and issues orders. Pigors and Myers remain faithful to this basic concept and, consequently, their guiding principle is that "personnel administration is what

29

members of line management make it." The personnel administrator consequently is enjoined to play this role with respect to his chief executive: "At best, a personnel administrator can help a chief executive to formulate a comprehensive system of personnel policies, to explain such policies to all management representatives, and to keep track of how useful such policies are when actually applied in specific instances."

Within this role as executive helper, the ideal personnel man has much with which to concern himself. Pigors and Myers detail many specific concerns appropriate to the staff personnel function, while they also sketch the kinds of broad impacts that can be made by the personnel administrator. For example, as an "idea man," he is advised to give attention to "developing, applying, and imparting a realistic, flexible, and methodical way to think about the company situation as a whole." Moreover, the personnel man is encouraged to play a prominent role in developing and utilizing human resources, which covers much of what is most relevant in today's organizations. Given his lack of authority, that is, this image of the industrial personnel administrator is an ambitious one. Fittingly, then, the concluding section of the piece by Pigors and Myers is entitled "The Challenge of Modern Management."

SOME INSTITUTIONAL ARRANGEMENTS

Despite the fact that the U.S. Civil Service Commission as the central personnel office at the federal level early symbolized the great importance of the personnel function, the development of public personnel administration has been channeled in somewhat different ways than the ideal which Pigors and Myers prescribe. The effect has complex features and causes. Four sets of institutional arrangements that have conditioned and directed the development of public personnel administration carry the burden of demonstrating this complexity. These four sets of institutional arrangements, in order, help to

— Characterize the relations between Congress and the U.S. Civil
    Service Commission;
— Describe the Commission as an institution;
— Characterize the relations between the various levels of the
    Commission and various levels of federal agencies; and
— Sketch the role of the Departmental Personnel Officer within
    the agencies.

The relations between the Commission and Congress are multifaceted, first, and little is known about them in a systematic way. Michael Cohen samples what is known in his piece, "The Personnel Policy-Making System." Basically, the Commission seems in a three-way game. Thus it enjoys Presidential support for many of its activities, and often seeks that support actively. However, Congress and the unions provide a counterweight that balances this executive identification. The result is a somewhere-in-betweenness. Van Riper's "Veterans' Preference" implies the difficulties inherent in such a necessary Commission role, that of protecting the virtue of the merit system while preserving enough political power to have its voice heard on a wide range of matters. Such complex relations with Congress, the President, and special interest groups make the role of the central public personnel office infinitely more complicated than in the Pigors-Myers business model.

Even the brief characterization above suggests important forces-in-tension in the Commission's history. Thus the early and massive preoccupation of the Commission was with diminishing the use of public jobs as rewards for service to political parties. Relatedly, the Commission was in the business of seeking equal treatment for all applicants and employees. And yet the political devil had to be dealt with by the Commission, whether in the form of a patronage-hungry Congress, or a power-seeking President, or the Commission's own unique interests as an institution. These opposed dualities (and others) as they operated at the federal level are nicely reflected in two articles by Van Riper, his "Spoils as Dysfunctional and Functional" and "The Taproots of American Public Administration." More or less, other public personnel systems followed the lead of the federal experience.

While safeguarding its interests vigilantly in the political arena, the Commission has labored to preserve a sense of objective fairness, even when that meant drawing the line so broadly as to jeopardize other values. Basically, that is, the Commission was historically involved with protection and procedures, as opposed to a managerial concern with the effective use of human resources. Roughly, a concern for managerial effectiveness would have generated somewhat more concern for managerial flexibility and less concern for protection of the employee's job rights. But the bias was definitely the other way: the emphasis was on protection even when flexibility, timeliness, and the setting of demanding standards for the performance of employees had to be sacrificed. No doubt it was first things first, but safeguarding the status of the public employee was a preoccupation for a very long time. This bias was hardly an all-or-nothing matter, but it was a strong tendency that is only now being significantly challenged, as by determined efforts to measure performance.

The comments above lay the groundwork for describing the U.S. Civil Service Commission as an institution, second. Perhaps the basic difference between public personnel practice and the model of Pigors and Myers, is the varying but still real insulation of the U.S. Civil Service Commission from the President, the Chief Executive. For good or ill, that insulation has a simple basis. The President is "political," although he is the chief administrative officer; and the merit system is to be neutral. Roughly, that says it all. Given ebbs and flows, the Commission and the President have been kept at a substantial distance. A Congress suspicious of Presidential motives supports the pattern, as do employee unions. And the Commission itself has often resisted the Executive embrace, although it has not been above stealing a Presidential kiss now and then. Many other forces also contribute to this basic pattern of diffused power at the federal level. Thus the President appoints the Commissioners, but with the advice and consent of the Senate. In addition, the President's power is limited in other ways. Thus the Commissioners are identified as Republicans or Democrats, with the present trio including two Democrats and one Republican to give an edge to the party in power. The intent of this arrangement is to inhibit one political party from monopolizing the Commission. Although an alert President will have no difficulty in finding a member of the opposite party who is more or less congenial to the President's wishes, the arrangement does provide a potential counterweight against executive influence.

Indeed, the very organization of the Commission provides a major counterweight against Executive influence. The picture is not a simple one, but its basic implication is clear enough: the President and the Commission are to be maintained at a substantial administrative distance. Consider the piece "Alternative Organizations and Policy Implications" which summarizes four possible ways of organizing the relations of the President and the U.S. Civil Service Commission:

1. Commission with Executive Director Model;
2. Personnel Administrator and Chairman Model;
3. Coequal Administrator and Commission Model; and
4. Administrator and Advisory Board Model.

Roughly, in order, the four models give increasing power to the Administrator. Roughly, and also in order, the four models imply increasingly greater opportunities for the President to provide managerial direction to those public employees monitored by the Commission. For example, in Model 4, the Administrator would no doubt be more powerful than the present Commission chairman, while he would also probably be related more closely to the presidency as the single appointee for personnel matters. Indeed, there have been a number of proposals to approach Model 4, in each of which the Administrator was more or less clearly the President's personnel man. Generally, the fear that just such an arrangement would evolve has been the death of Model 4.

The four models also provide insight into public personnel administration in other ways. For example, roughly again in order, the four patterns imply less concern with procedures and protection and more concern with the managerial aspects of personnel. For good or ill, the present arrangement does not quite reach Model 2. The historical choice, that is, has been basically to stress the prevention of "political influence and favoritism in Federal appointments and personnel," as contrasted with a more aggressive concern with what has been called "positive personnel management." Model 4, no doubt, would significantly shift that emphasis.

It is useful to specify the institutional arrangements governing public personnel administration at various levels in the federal government, third. The following sketch charts our ballpark. The Commission is not in the usual administrative-

FIGURE 2

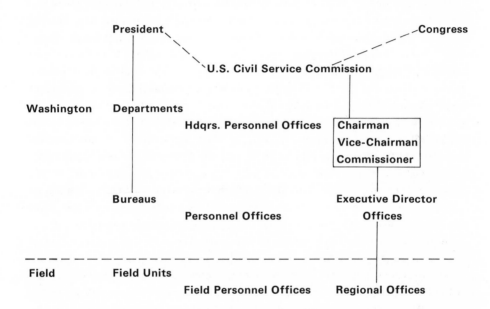

reporting relation to the President; it both helps create and responds to variously strong forces encouraging its independence from the Executive. Hence the broken line in Figure 2 between the President and the Commission. These fragmenting forces inhere in legislation passed by Congress. They also derive from tradition, from such clientele groups as labor unions and veterans' associations, and from the fear by the Commission and Congress that the protected service might be ravaged by a strong President for his own partisan purposes. Like all government agencies, the Commission also has significant relations with Congress and its committees. But nothing like a direct administrative chain of command operates in these relations. Hence the dotted line in Figure 2.

This very broad institutional picture requires substantial detail. The excerpt "Department-Commission Relations: The President's Formal Position" briefly does the job of describing the Commission's basic formal functions and roles in relation to federal departments and agencies. Note the contemporary emphasis on the Commission as "providing leadership and assistance to agencies," who do much of the actual personnel work subject to later review and inspection. The relations between the President and the Commission, to read between the lines, are clearly not like those prescribed by Pigors and Myers. The Commission is not isolated from the Executive, and particularly not of late under Chairman John Macy of the Commission. However, the description of the Commission's role implies that it keeps its own counsel to a substantial degree as protector of the merit system.

The picture of the relations between the Commission and the agencies of the federal government is not a static one, in addition. Felix Nigro provides valuable detail on broad historical trends in his piece "Department-Commission Relations: Some Swings of the Pendulum." Basically, the pattern is one of greater "decentralization" to the operating units at the departmental level or below. The movement by the Commission toward a managerial view of personnel administration also has been substantial, if tardy in relation to the 1883 establishment of the Commission as a guardian against the political disposition of jobs. Thus the title "personnel officer" in even the Washington offices of some agencies had little status at least as late as 1936, and the Commission held a tight rein over agencies and their field units as well. Increasingly, however, much of the work has been decentralized to the individual departments and to their constituent subunits. In part, necessity demanded such action. The Commission was overwhelmed with work, simply. Moreover, decentralization also signals the willingness of the Commission to risk some danger to the merit system in seeking managerial flexibility. The risk has more than paid off, in general.

Decentralization does not set straight all the relations between the Commission and federal agencies, finally. Indeed, decentralization can worsen old problems while creating some new problems as well. Baum's "Getting Caught in the Middle on Classification Decisions" documents that point from several perspectives. Differences in attitudes, work experience, job pressures, and history serve to variously set levels of the Commission against one another, as well as against the field units of the various agencies with which they interact. For example, agency personnel may look at the Commission as a partner in personnel matters or, alternatively, as a manipulator trying to get the agencies to do the work while the Commission retains the authority. In its control activities, particularly, the Commission often can generate sparks with agency officials. The Commission may be "staff," in short, but much of its "help" in effect constitutes controls over the "line." This violates the Pigors/Myers ideal, but that is the way the organizational world is.

The Departmental Personnel Officer (DPO) plays a crucial role in public personnel administration, fourth, and particularly in the context of determined efforts to change the U.S. Civil Service Commission from an action agency to one with a dominant monitoring/helping character. The consequent promise and the problems in the role of the DPO are both reflected in "The Departmental Personnel Officer's Contribution to Management," by Achille R. Albouze. One major point illustrates the character of his argument. At one time the role of the DPO was highly limited, that is, picking an employee to do a specific job that was relatively fixed, and seeing that he was paid for the difficulty of the work he did. Now, the DPO has a longer range and broader mission. Thus Albouze stresses that change is characteristic of contemporary organizations, and that the DPO has corresponding responsibility to participate in developing new jobs, in hiring new skills, and particularly in training new technical tricks to old organizational hands. In a very real sense, then, Albouze provides a statement of the modern role of personnel administration in the public service like that of Pigors and Myers.

Part II - Section B

*TABLE 6. Topics and Selections Relevant to
"Recruiting Human Resources."*

1. **Planning for Manpower Needs**
   26—Jones, "Developments in Government Manpower: A Federal Perspective"

2. **Recruiting and Selecting Executives: Political and Career Appointees**
   a. The Variety of Those at the Top
       8—CED, "Those Who Serve at the Top"
   b. Some Problems with Recruiting and Selecting Political Executives
       2—Association of the Bar of the City of New York, "Conflict of Interest, Technological Change, and Effects on Public Recruitment"

3. **Recruiting and Selecting Career Employees: The Protected Service**
   a. Recruiting Those with Competence/Potential
       48—USCSC, "How Federal Jobs Are Filled: Commission-Agency Roles"
       7—CED, "Selecting Specialists and Middle Managers in the Public Service"
   b. Testing and Selecting for Competence/Potential
       45—Uhrbrock, "The Personnel Interview"
       38—Mustafa, "Aptitude Testing for Machine Operators"

4. **Orienting the New Employee: Varieties of a Critical Activity**
   28—Kaufman, "Building Identification with the Forest Service"
   17—Gomersall and Myers, "Breakthrough in On-the-Job Training"

Recruiting Human Resources:
Attracting and Retaining Excellence

T HIS SECTION surveys an important time segment of the personnel function—that period of time extending from planning for manpower needs, through recruitment of both political executives and career employees, and including the orientation of the new employee. This is a critical time period in the employment cycle, if only that major attitudes toward public employment are often determined or reinforced by what happens to the employee in the interval. Hence the extended treatment given the topic in the editorial comments below; and hence also the variety and number of articles relevant to this section reprinted below.

PLANNING FOR MANPOWER NEEDS

At the level of concept, planning for manpower needs is straightforward; implementation is another matter. Even casual students and practitioners can detail the steps required in manpower planning, with a little help. Typically, that is, these steps are included as the major ones in manpower planning:[1]

1. Estimate the total volume of goods and services that will be required;

2. Determine which mixes of goods and services will be produced by which units of organization;

3. Anticipate the numbers and types of positions that will be required to produce the needed goods and services at the desired locations;

---

[1] Walter S. Wikstrom, "Factors in Manpower Planning," *Management Record*, Vol. 22 (September, 1960), pp. 2–5.

4. Determine how many personnel required are already employed, accounting for those who will leave in the interim;

5. Plan for the hiring required; and

6. Set up the appropriate training programs.

Beyond this superficial simplicity, however, manpower planning is all a horrendous complexity. Table 6 outlines some major dimensions of that complexity, and the following editorial comments add body to that outline. We begin by introducing Roger W. Jones, who outlines some of the complexities of manpower planning in federal personnel administration in his "Developments in Government Manpower." Jones's point of departure is the Government Employees Training Act of 1958, which he sees as playing a major role in setting the tone of contemporary and future public personnel administration. Jones ranges widely from his observation that the federal government no longer enjoys a competitive edge in the labor markets, and must therefore innovate new recruiting approaches as well as develop speedier ways of determining eligibility for appointment. The traditional approach sought procedural care at the expense of speed or even timeliness, and this legacy has proved hard to live down.

Jones also includes a vast range of other developments, even touching the question of a career service which this volume considers in greater detail in Part II, Section D. Traditionally, the merit system was concerned with hiring for a specific job, with assuring equal and fair treatment for all jobholders, as well as with keeping the system open to all comers of all ages. These biases were not career-oriented. Jones sketches the ways in which today's public service is attempting to mold these old biases with some hard realities concerning the need for career-oriented developments. Consider the elemental reality that early in a man's career it may be necessary to make some tough decisions about the likelihood of his having potential for top-management jobs, if only to provide him with appropriate training and experience. The conflict with traditional thoughtways should be obvious. The elemental reality above, that is, forces attention toward hiring for potential performance, as opposed to hiring for a specific job; it raises subtle and significant questions about fair and equal treatment, as in the rapid up-or-out promotion of hopefully gifted "jet-setters"; it may have implications for the openness of the system to lateral entry of job applicants; and it may imply promotion ceilings for individuals who were not considered early candidates for top-managerial spots and hence did not receive the benefits of accelerated training and experience. And even these brief comments, gentle reader, imply plenty of potential for conflict with traditional procedures and policies.

RECRUITING AND SELECTING EXECUTIVES:
POLITICAL AND CAREER EXECUTIVES

A good bit of the complexity in the federal manpower planning inheres in the sweep and coverage of public agencies, with resulting major problems in recruiting and retaining top-level executives. As an initial complication, there are many public personnel systems, even at the federal level: General Schedule appointments; the Post Office; Foreign Service Officers; the military; and so on. In addition, some top-level positions are political appointments, while others of them are covered by the merit system. To substantial degrees, different rules of the game apply to the two kinds of recruiting, which differences raise issues not encountered in business recruiting or management.

Some sense of the panorama of public work is suggested by an extract from the Committee for Economic Development, "Those Who Serve at the Top." The 8,600 key people described in that excerpt—both political appointees and career civil servants— are charged with helping to control a huge federal work force. They are a crucial collection of people, all the more so because of today's significant problems in developing and retaining them. For example, convincing research details numerous problems in the recruitment of political appointees, who tend to remain in office only briefly in the bargain. Both characteristics imply significant management problems.[2] As an additional complication, a very large number of top-level civil servants will be eligible for retirement in the next five years, something like one out of every two top managers will acknowledge the inevitability of time. A federal work force that grew explosively in the late thirties and forties, and which attracted young and aggressive talent that quickly rose to top levels, is now reflecting what 25–30 years of service will bring in the absence of sharp growth.

RECRUITING AND SELECTING CAREER EMPLOYEES:
THE PROTECTED SERVICE

The recruitment of career employees presents some of the same problems as the recruitment of political executives, but the basic difference is that the respective universes are hundreds of thousands versus hundreds. Our focus here is on the similarities in these problems. We concentrate on four areas only:

1. Recruiting individuals with demonstrated competence or potential;
2. Testing and selecting those with competence or potential;

---

[2] Dean E. Mann, "The Selection of Federal Political Executives," *American Political Science Review*, Vol. 58 (March, 1964), pp. 81–99.

3. Certifying and employing those recruited, tested, and selected; and

4. Orienting the new employee to his agency.

First, recruiting individuals with demonstrated competence is difficult enough to describe even broadly, let alone to accomplish. Some material published by the U.S. Civil Service Commission, "How Federal Jobs Are Filled," provides useful detail on how that recruiting job is handled. Note particularly how the Commission tries to define for itself a role that permits agencies to do much of the work of recruiting while the Commission retains control at crucial stages or provides support and help. A complex pattern of collaboration often exists between the Commission and agencies, consequently, as in the boards of civil service examiners who administer examinations for various federal positions. The members of the boards come from the agencies. But the Commission trains board members, whose work it also directs, supervises, and inspects.

There is certainly plenty of work in public personnel administration for all hands, no question about that. Excerpts from a Committee for Economic Development (CED) report, "Selecting Specialists and Middle Managers in the Public Service," conclusively demonstrate that point. For example, the article establishes both the desirability and the difficulty of attracting the entry of mid-career personnel into government service. The desirability of lateral entry has long been recognized. Thus the Herter Committee recommended that as many as 25 percent of any year's career appointments in the Foreign Service should go to "lateral entrants," that is, individuals who have not been promoted from within the U.S. Department of State. "New blood" thus can be brought into the public service, whether new in point of view or in technical skills, or both.

Bringing new perspectives and skills into the public service are laudable ends, but the CED report also develops the detailed difficulties of achieving this purpose. For example, businessmen may run a real risk to their careers by lateral entry into government service, should they elect to return to business later. The CED report also sees mid-career recruitment problems beginning as early as selection at entry grades. For example, the government is seen as getting less than its share of the topnotch graduates of our best schools. Two particular reasons are cited. First, opinion polls show that only a small percentage of college seniors and graduate students have a high regard for government employ, and this implies worlds about the difficulty of public recruiting problems. Second, compared to the most aggressive business firms, government agencies are poorly equipped for the pursuit of high-potential recruits at the entry levels. For example, expenses for recruiting visits to public agencies often have to be paid by the applicant. Many business firms have greater flexibility, and almost all of the bigger firms gladly pay for such visits to the home organization.

Second, testing and selecting those individuals with demonstrated competence or potential covers many complicated subjects. Previous selections describe in general terms the testing approach of the U.S. Civil Service Commission. Here we draw attention to only two valuable adjuncts in testing and selecting, the personnel interview and one approach to aptitude testing. Richard Uhrbrock's "The Personnel Interview" provides kaleidoscopic summary of much of what has come to be accepted as good practice in interviewing. Here we will only stress that the interview is one of the most commonly used means now available for evaluating human abilities, and particularly for managerial positions. The interview's promise and its pitfalls, then, deserve close attention.

Husain Mustafa provides another valuable perspective on the problem of testing and selecting in his "Aptitude Testing for Machine Operators." Mustafa considers the problem of selecting individuals with psychological and physical aptitudes appropriate for a difficult job, letter sorting. Mustafa sketches the problems of developing valid and reliable tests that really measure the relevant aptitudes for the task. The results cited by Mustafa also suggest the value of such testing, where it is appropriate.

Fourth, those recruited, tested or interviewed, and selected must be certified for public employment. Essentially, certification is the formal sign that an individual has passed appropriate tests or possesses qualifications that make him hireable by a public agency. Typically, lists of eligibles are prepared and circulated among agencies who have indicated specific job openings. Agencies make their choices from these lists, often after interviewing those certified so as to gather additional data about the probable success of a specific candidate. Certification may seem a small point, but it has been the source of considerable mischief. More than one eager candidate for work in a public agency has had his ardor diminished by long waits for certification and appointment, and no doubt exists but that some of the poor reputation of public employment derives from the inadequacies and delays that have become associated with certification processes.

The rationale underlying the certification process is clear enough. Basically, the examination system normally does not give much attention to "intangible factors"—personality, appearance, motivation, and the like—that may be critical in job performance. So some room for choice must be given the appointing officer from the agency in which the job candidate will actually work, but not so much as to jeopardize "fair and equal" treatment. The typical solution is to present appointing officers with a short list of eligibles, ranked in order of their performance on appropriate examinations and/or interviews, which gives the officer some (but not much) opportunity for choice between individuals based upon differences in intangible factors. As Stahl explains:[3]

In a few services, for example, the personnel agency is required by the rules in force to certify for appointment only the highest-ranking name on the list. The most common

---

[3] O. Glenn Stahl, *Public Personnel Administration* (New York: Harper and Row, 1962), p. 101.

procedure is to certify the names of the highest three on the eligible register, while in a few jurisdictions five or more names are certified when a vacancy occurs. In case of two or more vacancies it is usual to certify, according to standing on the list, a number of names sufficient to give the appointing officer a choice of two more than the number of positions to be filled. In case all names certified to the appointing officer are rejected on the basis of interviews or other information, he is ordinarily called upon to present his grounds for such rejection to the personnel agency. If these are approved, further names will be submitted.

If the rationale underlying certification processes is clear, their outcomes can be very troublesome. The experience of New York City illustrates the possible problems.[4] The city government had kaleidoscopic personnel difficulties, including an image that did not attract qualified applicants. Problems with certification made the worst out of a bad situation. Thus we are told that some jobs took as long as a year to fill. The snail's pace had various causes. Thus the local civil service agency had infrequent examinations for some positions; or it responded slowly to agency requests for specific kinds of help; or applications and examinations were processed with more than due deliberation. Not only were the recruiting/certifying processes slow, moreover, but the certification policies were such as to severely limit management choice between eligibles.

New York City also hampered management discretion in another important way. To explain, state law in New York required "rule-of-three" certification, which means that the merit office forwards to an agency a list of three people certified as eligible for a given position. The purpose is transparent: to lessen the possibility of favoritism. But the rule-of-three also has some unattractive features. Rejecting all three candidates might leave an agency in a bad light with the central personnel office, and the agency might not get as good service when attempting to fill another vacancy. This could present an agency with a dilemma, if none of the three people seemed to fit the bill. One way out is for an agency to delay action until other agencies snap up the three people on their list, whereupon they might innocently request another list of certified names. The central personnel office could counterattack by submitting any name to only a single agency at a time. If many people play either game, obviously, things can drag on and on. The rule-of-one operated in New York City, which precluded such game playing, but only at the expense of denying all choice to management about whom it wished to employ.

Much is being done at all levels to improve certification processes, fortunately. Thus examinations for many positions are held regularly and frequently, and same day certification is becoming a goal for some public personnel administrators for certain kinds of positions. The problem is still there, however.

Fifth, all public employees must be somehow oriented toward their new work,

---

[4] David T. Stanley, "Higher Skills for the City of New York," *Public Personnel Review*, Vol. 24 (July, 1963), pp. 147–51.

and how this is done can be a critical matter. Often, however, the orientation is casual and perfunctory. Two noncasual illustrations of orientation will be introduced here, both to reflect the importance of the processes as well as to illustrate two possible approaches. Herbert Kaufman outlines a traditional and effective approach in "Building Identification with the Forest Service." Kaufman draws a picture of an agency with an extended orientation program, an orientation that effectively begins during the student days of most eventual employees and follows them throughout their careers in the Forest Service. So thorough is the orientation, and so congenial are various environmental forces, that Kaufman stresses the "almost automatic tendency" for foresters to conform to the decisions of the agency leadership. Kaufman traces the various ways in which foresters "internalize" a set of perceptions, values, and premises for action that are stressed in the Forest Service. That is, the foresters identify with these agency perceptions, values, and premises so much so that—for all practical purposes—they become the perceptions, values, and premises of individual forest rangers. The result, Kaufman concludes, is "voluntary conformity."

Not all agencies can or should attempt to take the Forest Service route in orienting their employees, but neither is their way the only approach to orientation. Earl R. Gomersall and M. Scott Myers describe a promising second approach in their article "Breakthrough in On-the-Job Training." Their approach was simple. They attempted to induce a favorable atmosphere at work and, more specifically, to orient new employees so as to reduce or eliminate various causes of anxiety that were thought to contribute to low production and low satisfaction. The rationale of the investigators is worth quoting: "Anxiety on the job is characteristically assumed to be the dependent variable, gradually dropping as competence is acquired. Might not the reverse be true? Might not competence increase as a result of anxiety being decreased?" With such questions in mind, an orientation program to reduce the level of anxiety of new employees was begun. Experiments have proved very encouraging, as in drastically shortening the time required for training and in reducing absenteeism and tardiness. Such consequences patently encourage a close reading of the Gomersall and Myers article.

Part II - Section C

TABLE 7. *Topics and Selections Relevant to "Maintaining the Organization."*

1. Some Mechanics of Public Personnel Administration
    a. Position Analysis, Classification, and Salary Levels
        47—USCSC, "Determining the Classification of a Position: Analyzing Positions"
        50—USCSC, "Structure of the Federal Position Classification Plan"
        49—USCSC, "Salaries by General Schedule (GS) Levels, with Within-Grade 'Step' Increases"

2. Some Structural Basics of Public Personnel Administration
    a. Personnel as "Staff": Common Prescriptions
        1—Albouze, "The Departmental Personnel Officer's Contribution to Management"
        41—Pigors and Myers, "In Short: Personnel Administration for Line Managers"
    b. Personnel as "Staff": Typical Problems
        3—Baum, "Getting Caught in the Middle on Classification Decisions: Parts A and B"
    c. Personnel as "Staff": Some Uncommon Orientations
        12—Everett and Williams, "Line Management's Participation in Classification Decisions"
        30—Knudson, "Enter the Personnel Generalist"

3. Some Human Dynamics in Public Personnel Administration
    a. Motivation, Attitudes, and Morale: Some Empirical and Value Issues
        33—McGregor, "Theory X and Theory Y"

Maintaining the Organization:
Combining People and Structure

W<small>E DO NOT</small> generally think of our work organizations as places where creativity is allowed or fostered. We think of them, instead, as places which demand conformity to their rules, to established ways of doing things, and to the predetermined requirements of their positions. As the noted psychologist Carl Rogers makes us aware, however, organizations are badly in need of creative behavior.[1] For organizations face the challenge of solving the problems posed by rapid change in their environments. Creativity is needed to find good solutions. Without creativity, organizations drift. They respond to their changing surroundings in a mindless fashion, and repeat maladaptive responses.

Summarizing Rogers' argument of how creativity is fostered provides us with standards for judging the mechanics in the public service that are used to combine people and structure. Rogers defines creativity as the capacity to perceive and formulate new relationships, growing out of the individual's uniqueness in interaction with his circumstances. He theorizes that everyone possesses and can fulfill this capacity, if he lives in a facilitating environment. Everyone has the desire to actualize his potentialities, something which motivates creativity. Most people act defensively, however, and this aborts creativity. They are defensive either because their environments contain real threats or because real but earlier threats have been turned into a generalized defensiveness against all perceived threats, real or imaginary. To foster the creativity they need, organizations must attempt to create nonthreatening environments, allowing their employees to respond to their experiences openly. This means moving toward the condition of psychological safety and freedom.

Three basic conditions seem required for psychological safety. First, the

---

[1] Carl R. Rogers, "Toward a Theory of Creativity," in Sidney J. Parnes and Harold F. Harding, *A Source Book for Creative Thinking* (New York: Charles Scribner's Sons, 1962), pp. 63–72.

individual must feel that he is of unconditional worth. This is achieved when the facilitating person—a teacher, a supervisor, or whoever—"senses the potentialities of the individual and thus is able to have an unconditional faith in him, no matter what his present state."[2] The individual then experiences a climate of safety, gradually learning to drop his defenses and to react spontaneously and openly to his experiences. Second, the individual must be in a climate where external evaluation is absent. This is greatly freeing to the individual, who can begin to experiment with new behaviors and solutions without fear of negative evaluation. At the same time he learns to be his own judge, thus freeing himself of dependence upon others for approval and disapproval. Third, the individual must be in a climate where he is understood empathically, that is, understood from his own viewpoint. When this happens, and the individual is still accepted, then he experiences the psychological safety needed to express himself openly, a requirement for creativity.

Psychological freedom is needed along with safety. This freedom permits symbolic expression. With this freedom the individual can experiment with ideas and relationships until he creates novel solutions.

How much of a contribution does public personnel administration make to fostering creativity? We suspect it is not great, although we can only present fragments of supporting evidence in these editorial comments and in the readings reprinted below. One position needs no qualification, however. One of public personnel administration's major challenges lies in combining people and structure, and the way that is done helps determine the amount of creativity organizations will possess. Table 7 summarizes the readings reprinted below which analyze how people and structures are combined, and which also suggest how such combinations can foster or inhibit creativity. It is all too easy for technique to triumph over purpose in the areas we consider below. Hence our dual emphasis on personnel tools and on their creative conception and application.

SOME MECHANICS OF
PUBLIC PERSONNEL ADMINISTRATION

"[The] process of matching the man and the job is the heart of good personnel management." So states the U.S. Civil Service Commission in the article, "Structure of the Federal Position Classification Plan." The statement expresses well the theme of this section, which is maintaining the organization through the process of combining people and structure. How does the personnel function try to accomplish the matching of man and job? Among the most important

---

[2] *Op. cit.*, p. 69.

elements are position analysis and classification, and adequate salary schedules.

Position analysis and classification provide the groundwork for combining people and structure, so let us consider them first. Position classification, or "duties classification" as it was then called, was virtually invented in Chicago about 1910, Fred Telford informs us.[3] The necessity mothering this invention was the chaos of job titles in the Chicago public service at the time. Duties classification originally aimed at standardizing job titles to gain assurance that all those with the same title would be doing roughly the same work, and all those doing roughly the same work would have the same title. Hard as it seems to believe now, that simple assurance was largely absent until then.

"Duties classification" rapidly caught on in this country, Telford reports, evolving into present-day position analysis and classification. Only 14 years after its origin, all large jurisdictions with a centralized employment system used "duties classifications" for all or most of their public employees.[4] The popularity of "duties classification" rested on the foundation it provided for other personnel activities, such as recruiting, compensating, supervising, promoting, training, and dismissing employees. Once jobs are classified and standardized, that is, it is possible to start outlining the qualifications needed to perform them, and then to seek people with those qualifications. It also becomes possible to evaluate employees by comparing their job performances, to compensate them equitably, and so on. In short, many current efforts to combine people and structure are easily seen as rooted in position analysis and classification.

The USCSC's guidelines for analyzing and classifying positions are set forth both in "Structure of the Federal Position Classification Plan" and in "Determining the Classification of a Position: Analyzing Positions," both reprinted here. Position analysis is the process of breaking down jobs into their identifiable elements, so as to make some kind of judgment about the relative importance of the diversity of jobs in public service. On this basis, jobs are grouped together according to function, level of skill, level of responsibility, or some other principle. These groups of positions then are subdivided by grades within classes. These grades, in turn, may be related to standardized compensation plans, as shown by the chart, "Salaries by General Schedule (GS) Levels, with Within-Grade 'Step' Increases." Roughly, these are the mechanics of tying together the rank and salary structures.

Position analysis and classification are more complex than the foregoing description suggests, however. This complexity stems from the dynamic and changing character of administration. That is, for example, the performance

---

[3] Fred Telford, "The Classification and Salary Standardization Movement in the Public Service," *American Academy Annals*, Vol. 63 (May, 1924), pp. 111–20.

[4] *Op. cit.*, p. 113.

of a job normally reflects two features: elements essential to it; and elements that are transitory or that may be idiosyncratic to a particular employee. The USCSC offers guidelines to distinguish between the essential and transitory or idio-syncratic, but recognizes also that the transitory may become established and that the idiosyncracies of a particular incumbent may become expectations for his successor. Thus, these and other changes point to a continuing need for reanalysis and reclassification of positions. These changes also point out to us that maintaining the organization is an ongoing process, a series of adjustments as people enter and leave positions, as organizational needs change, as new ways of performing work are found, and so on.

How do these basic tools of personnel administration affect creativity? No simple answer is possible, but possible sources of mischief are numerous. For example, position classification is consistent with the core-value of public personnel administrations: equal pay for equal work. That is, position classi-fication provides confidence that *similar jobs* will be similarly compensated. But it may also mean that *widely different performances* on similar jobs will be similarly compensated. Emphasizing the job as opposed to the impact of the man on the job, then, sets a minimum on acceptable performance. But it does little to induce and reinforce exceptional performance.

SOME STRUCTURAL BASICS OF
PUBLIC PERSONNEL ADMINISTRATION

Maintaining the organization cannot be accomplished only by mechanical position analysis and classification, however creatively carried out. The personnel man himself helps or hinders the processes of organizational maintenance by the way he conceives his job, by the way he resolves conflicting pressures, or by the way he may redesign his job.

Let us look first at the influence the concept of the personnel job has on maintaining the organization. Paul Pigors and Charles A. Myers, in their article, "In Short: Personnel Administration for Line Managers," remind us that personnel is a function performed by management throughout the organization, not just by someone called a personnel manager or by a department of personnel. Therefore, if the personnel man relies only upon the techniques he can implement alone, he will be doing a narrow job. If, instead, he broadens his job concept to include persuading others to implement the philosophy of the personnel department, the personnel man extends himself throughout the organization, functioning indirectly to improve it.

Achille R. Albouze in "The Departmental Personnel Officer's Contribution to Management" also counsels the personnel man to take a broad view of his job. He conceives the personnel officer's primary role to be "providing personnel leadership for his agency as a catalyst, and leaving primary responsibility for personnel management in the hands of top administrators and line supervisors." Thus, the personnel officer should be concerned with keeping his own knowledge up-to-date and seeing that it gets implemented. He has the responsibility to see that top management understands the importance of committed employees and also knows how to facilitate their commitment. Again, the personnel man cannot maintain the organization alone, but he can greatly facilitate this process.

The article by Bernard H. Baum, entitled "Getting Caught in the Middle on Classification Decisions," makes us aware that how the personnel man resolves the conflicts generated by position analysis and classification can also help or hinder creative organization maintenance. Position classifications may displease those directly affected, or those who have a stake in raising their own level. Thus, the position classifier—who as a "staff" man lacks formal author-ity—may be trapped into overclassifying positions and losing uniformity between departments. The primary purpose of position classification may be undercut in this way if the personal interests of those involved are allowed to intervene.

Finally, in the last two articles in this section, the way is pointed toward reorienting the personnel function so as to increase its usefulness to the organiza-tion. R. Permin Everett and Wade J. Williams in "Line Management's Partic-ipation in Classification Decisions" report on innovation in California state government which decentralizes the function of position classification to operat-ing agencies, and which will eventually decentralize it to supervisors. The goal is to use position classification flexibly and creatively in the service of organization effectiveness, as opposed to using it woodenly.

The personnel man can also be brought closer to his immediate client group, as Harry R. Knudson, Jr., argues in "Enter the Personnel Generalist." He suggests bringing the personnel man and his techniques into a closer working relationship with people in low-level units of organization. In Knudson's plan, personnel skills are available as needed, where they are needed. The "personnel generalist" is on tap to guide the development and the commitment of employees in a small unit with which he identifies. In short, he will combine people and structure by applying and interpreting broad personnel policies for people close to him.

SOME HUMAN DYNAMICS IN PUBLIC PERSONNEL ADMINISTRATION

So far we have discussed the role and tools of the personnel function in main-taining the organization. A high degree of integration and commitment in organizations will not spring from these means alone, however. Commitment and integration derive from human dynamics in organizations, from employees' motivations, attitudes, and morale. Unless the organization satisfies needs that employees consider important, both the employee and the organization are losers. For if the employee remains dissatisfied by his world of work, the organization rarely gains the kind of commitment it needs for superior performance.

Given the possible mischief that the mechanics of Public Personnel Administration imply for creative performance, human dynamics deserve special attention. Here we can only suggest the nature of the challenge of giving effective attention to the human aspects of Public Personnel Administration. A broad view of man in organizations provides focus for the effort.

Overall, contemporary research seems to tell us that men derive their greatest satisfactions while at work from feelings of accomplishment related directly to the work they do.[5] Their greatest dissatisfactions arise from feelings of being deprived of their fair amount of factors extrinsic to the work itself, such as pay, agreeable social relations, and so on. The lesson is more complex, but we are not far wrong in such a summary: an organization which emphasizes motivations extrinsic to the work itself may keep the worst from occurring, but this does little to create an environment in which commitment thrives. To do the latter, it must satisfy employees' needs to feel a sense of accomplishment over their work. Organizations can be maintained in various ways, in short, ranging from pedestrian to creative.

The late Douglas McGregor would, if anything, sharpen the point that managers can and do choose alternative styles, and with the most significant of consequences. In "Theory X and Theory Y," McGregor urges that management philosophies and behaviors derive from basic belief systems about the nature of man and human motivation. Thus autocratic management rests on the view, called Theory X, that man finds work distasteful, needs close supervision as a prod, and can be motivated only by individualistic "bread-and-butter" threats and punishments. Theory Y supports a democratic philosophy. It assumes that man enjoys work, prefers to be self-controlling, is capable of creativity, and is often motivated within the context of social needs. McGregor's analysis permits optimism about the potential for change in management practice, and that optimism rests on substantial and growing research.

Given that techniques of supervision play their part in raising morale, and thereby in achieving greater commitment, the debate over the "best" way to supervise to accomplish this goal is far from over. Consider Robert N. McMurry's "The Case for Benevolent Autocracy," [6] which is not reprinted here.

---

[5] Frederick Herzberg, *Work and the Nature of Man* (Cleveland: The World Publishing Co., 1966).
[6] Robert N. McMurry, "The Case for Benevolent Autocracy," *Harvard Business Review*, Vol. 36 (January–February, 1958), esp. pp. 82–90.

McMurry looks critically at the long line of observers and researchers who have concluded that democratic or participative management generally increases quantity and quality of work, as well as commitment by employees. This school holds that the answer to creatively maintaining the organization lies in acting considerately, and in permitting participation. McMurry contends that most managers and supervisors are simply not capable of behaving this way, however. Ordinarily, managers and supervisors behave in an autocratic fashion, and like the character in Molière who was surprised to learn he was speaking prose, they would no doubt be surprised to learn they were autocratic. But McMurry argues that major forces prevent any significant change; and he also argues that it is foolish (or worse) to pretend otherwise.

Are the chances for gaining employee commitment lessened, then, since autocracy is likely to be the norm? Not at all, answers McMurry. Most employees are capable of contending with autocracy and, perhaps, many prefer it to any unnatural attempts by their bosses to be considerate. McMurry is basically pessimistic about the potential for change in management philosophy and practice, that is. Whatever the results of managerial behavior, in short, those results are all but inevitable and subject to only minor improvement.

Part II - Section D

TABLE 8. *Topics and Selections Relevant to "Training and Developing People."*

1. Training as a Major Function
   a. Perspectives on Defining the Problems
      22—Huse, "Putting in a Management Development Program That Works"
   b. Progress on Reducing the Problems
      26—Jones, "Developments in Government Manpower: A Federal Perspective"

2. Appraising Performance
   32—Maier, "Appraisal on the Job: Three Types of Appraisal Interviews"

3. Providing for Career Development
   31—Leich, "Rank in Man or Job? Both!"

4. Approaching Organizational and Personal Learning
   17—Gomersall and Myers, "Breakthrough in On-the-Job Training"
   35—Mosel, "How to Feed Back Performance Results to Trainees"
   11—Dolmatch, "Programmed Instruction: Two Perspectives"
   16—Golembiewski, "The 'Laboratory Approach' to Organization Change: Schema of a Method"

Training and Developing People: Guiding People up the Ladder

O RGANIZATIONS are ongoing systems, internally adjusting and adapting as external conditions and circumstances change. Given this turbulence, no wonder that the development and change of the people who work in organizations often goes on episodically. When organizations and their personnel change and develop in unplanned ways, or when they fight change, the results are seldom advantageous either to organizations or their personnel. The change and development of organizations and their personnel should be guided by responsiveness to both the needs of the person and the organization, then, which leads us to ask whether organizational ends and means are in line with each other and with changing definitions of social needs. That is, are organizations and their personnel making responses which are realistic and appropriate for what they wish to accomplish, given conditions in their environments?

In the context of dual responsiveness to personal/organizational needs, training and developing people means aiding their growth. Growth means that the individual develops a battery of responses that he can flexibly call into use as needs change. Growth also means that the individual fulfills his drive to achieve competence which is intrinsic to all humans.[1] With these as the goals of the training process, proper means to achieve them must be found.

Table 8 summarizes the readings reprinted below that help in both clarifying ends and suggesting means for guiding people up the organization ladder.

---

[1] Jerome S. Bruner, *Toward a Theory of Instruction* (New York: W. W. Norton & Co., Inc., 1966), pp. 117–24.

53

TRAINING AS A MAJOR FUNCTION

People do not grow in hostile, disciplinarian, judgmental situations. What may be called the pure theory of training is explicit on this point. Rather, growth is fostered when people are free to experiment and to accept and learn from their inevitable mistakes. This means that growth situations must be open, accepting, free of hostility, and nonjudgmental. The learner should not be blamed for making errors normal to all beginners. Edgar F. Huse, in "Putting in a Management Development Program That Works," gives life to these summary statements. He contrasts the "judgmental" and "helper" types of training programs. The helper program, called Work Planning and Review, was developed from management's objectives, namely, to assist employees to increase their competence. This led to involving employees with the trainer in review sessions where the employee discovered and enunciated his own growth needs and, with the help of the trainer, set objectives for himself. Work Planning and Review sessions took training out of the doldrums of criticism and defensiveness where it so often languishes, and placed it in an environment conducive to growth instead.

What we know in principle often has been difficult to put into practice, especially in the public service. Getting *any* kind of training has often been the more pressing problem. Overall, for example, the federal government has not provided civil servants with regular training opportunities. For many years the U.S. Civil Service Commission pressured Congress for legislation and appropriations to allow them to wholeheartedly engage in training. They were not successful until 1958, when Congress passed the Government Employees Training Act. In "Developments in Government Manpower: A Federal Perspective," Roger W. Jones discusses the value of the act in helping achieve a growth-oriented civil service. His overall theme reflects pride in the real progress that has been made, and concern about the additional advances that must be made.

APPRAISING PERFORMANCE

Growth can occur in many kinds of situations, and hence "training" should be conceived in broad terms. Formal training situations, after all, are only one group of situations in which we learn. Ideally, we can learn during most of our activities.

The appraisal of employees' performance at work provides a potentially valuable opportunity to foster individual growth in organizations. *Potentially* should be underscored. For appraisal can be used to assist growth, or it can be but another routine, *pro forma* process in which no helpful information is transmitted in either direction. Fortunately, some useful guidelines exist for making the best of an appraisal situation. Norman R. F. Maier presents a number of those guidelines in his "Appraisal on the Job: Three Types of Appraisal Interviews." For example, Maier stresses the reciprocal nature of the useful appraisal in dramatic terms: "Telling a child that he is gawky and uncoordinated does not help him to become graceful and skilled." Maier tells us that appraisals that contribute most to growth have a problem-solving quality. Problem-solving appraisal implies that people are working together for a mutual end. In this case, supervisor and subordinate are searching for improved functioning on *both of their parts* that will lead to improved performance. The other appraisal methods, "tell and sell" and "tell and listen," provide sharp contrasts. They elevate the supervisor into a judge of his subordinate, and judgmental atmospheres do not encourage problem solving. Effective problem-solving follows from open exploration of alternatives. Inhibitions and defenses by both the supervisor and the subordinate, induced by feelings of threat, inhibit the open exploration of alternatives. Therefore, the supervisor or trainer often defeats his own purpose when he acts judgmentally. Maier tells us further that the supervisor should allow the subordinate to decide how he will change; the supervisor must forego that right, while not simply letting the employee sink or swim.

Again, we preach more about making appraisals meaningful than we practice. Here we can only allude to the chronic problems experienced in the government service with performance-rating plans.[2] Successive revisions of rating forms have been adopted and abandoned; and both centralized and decentralized rating plans have been devised, but to little avail. Perhaps the reason for their failure is simple. Efficiency-rating schemes, per se, contribute little to the learning from which growth can only come. Instead, these schemes provide only judgment. They do not provide the discussion, the problem solving, the feedback which are essential to growth. And because rating plans are feared, they become political instruments, not educational ones. The following selections will provide perspectives on how to help make performance appraisal a positive learning experience rather than a punishing one. Maier's "Appraisal on the Job" has begun that task by introducing various appraisal skills and values.

PROVIDING FOR CAREER DEVELOPMENT

It is one thing to devise training and appraisal systems to aid the self-development of personnel, but training and appraising will be contraceptive experiences unless

---

[2] Mary S. Schinagl, *History of Efficiency Ratings in the Federal Government* (New York: Bookman Associates, 1966).

they are oriented toward and integrated with an employee's career development. And such career development, in turn, depends upon an agency's planning of future programs and services. The chain is very long and fragile. This section deals with career development by reviewing some of the dilemmas that have arisen on the road to this particular Elysian field, and the efforts that have been made to solve them.

Let us look briefly at some of these dilemmas and efforts at solutions. With some exceptions, provisions for career development and for satisfying personnel needs have traditionally been more *ad hoc* than planned. The distinction between *ad hoc* and planned corresponds to the distinction Harold H. Leich makes in "Rank in Man or Job? Both!" Leich distinguishes between position-oriented (or rank-in-the-job) promotion systems, and person-oriented (or rank-in-the-man) promotion systems. The distinction between the two is more a matter of degree than it is absolute. The position-oriented system tends to be *ad hoc* in the sense that it does little to plan its recruitment sources in advance, but tends to search for people to fill specific positions when the positions are open. Person-oriented systems, on the other hand, tend to be planned, in the sense that they search for and prepare individuals for openings long before they occur. This is an exaggeration, as Leich points out, since there is no necessary reason why the two approaches cannot coincide sufficiently well to avoid difficulties in filling positions as needed. In fact, this occurs in practice often enough. "Lateral recruitment" from outside the government service also can fill upper level jobs for which trained resources are not available inside the service. Still, there is always the danger that the man and job will not be simultaneously available. And beggaring your neighbor is a shortsighted strategy, especially since government agencies often cannot compete on equal terms with business organizations for the talent that is available.

Planning the career development of personnel is no panacea, for there are serious problems associated with some approaches. To take an example, several career systems already exist within subunits of the U.S. federal service, as Leich points out. They include the foreign service, the forest service, the military, and others. All of these person-oriented systems, however, have been criticized for becoming exclusive closed shops, perpetuating themselves in the same mold regardless of changes that might be required. There is some question about the truth of these allegations, but they do point to an underlying fear that closed career systems are undemocratic and foster the existence of aristocratic elites. Person-oriented career systems smack too much of a governing class, something which many Americans—including congressmen—regard with at least mixed feelings if not outright suspicion.

Developing a true career system for the entire public service covered by the General Schedule would reduce or eliminate such charges of parochialism and inbreeding in such mini-career systems as the foreign service, but such a development will not come easily. For example, the most pressing need in the General Schedule area has been to increase the supply of upper level civil servants with administrative skills. This means that the greatest pressure for developing still another person-oriented career system has been directed at creating a purely administrative career system, which would provide the proverbial "generalist administrators." Such a system would create a senior civil service, a group of experienced administrators schooled in all phases of administration in various functional areas, who could be called upon to serve where needed. But congressmen and others have scotched all such proposals. While the federal service has successfully developed a "generalist administrator" entry classification and career system, it has been unable to gain approval for developing a senior civil service class as in the theoretical rank-in-the-man model. A number of factors have prevented such an executive system from being realized. For one, many observers were concerned that such a system would allow the President greater control over the senior civil servants, to the detriment of other interests.[3] In addition, some positive values inhere in open, and *ad hoc* administrative career systems.

A recent innovation promises some progress toward flexible utilization of administrative skills, short of a senior civil service. The "career executive inventory," still in its early stages, will aid agencies in filling top-level posts. At the same time, the inventory will allow executives to have governmentwide, rather than agency-based, careers.[4] Until recently, it was not even clear how many top-level career and political officials there were, let alone who they were and what skills and training they had acquired. The computer-based career executive inventory will conveniently provide information that was unavailable in any form just a few years ago.

APPROACHING ORGANIZATIONAL AND PERSONAL LEARNING

Success in training and developing people will partly depend upon the kind of teaching and learning that occurs or, in Jerome Bruner's phrase, upon the "theory of instruction" employed.[5] Bruner makes clear that we as yet can construct only a very primitive theory of instruction to guide teaching and learning. Still, even a primitive theory of instruction is better than none, and

---

[3] Paul P. Van Riper, "The Senior Civil Service and the Career System," *Public Administration Review*, Vol. 28 (Summer, 1958), pp. 189–200.

[4] Mel H. Bolster, "The Strategic Deployment of Exceptional Talent: An Account of the Career Executive Roster's Short History," *Public Administration Review*, Vol. 27, No. 5 (December, 1967), pp. 446–51.

[5] Bruner, *op. cit.*

a few generalizations have withstood testing and use. The chances of successful training and development will certainly increase if it is based on these principles.

One element in a useful theory of instruction, for example, concerns the management of anxiety. The anxiety which learners often bring with them to the training situation is a signal of fear and defensiveness, factors which inhibit learning. In fact, in many so-called educational experiences, little if any learning occurs because of the defensive barriers erected by the learner to cope with his fears.

Earl R. Gomersall and M. Scott Myers in "Breakthrough in On-the-Job Training" report an experiment designed to reduce the anxiety felt by new employees undergoing on-the-job training. They learned that anxiety among new employees was a response to their fears of incompetence, but that anxiety decreased as feelings of competence increased. This acclimatization to the new job and environment took considerable time. Until the employees had increased their sense of competence enough to dispel their anxiety, training for complex operations was all but wasted. But after that time, they could learn rapidly. So Gomersall and Myers attempted to reduce anxiety directly, rather than to wait for competence to develop. They were successful. For example, anxiety was reduced by isolating new employees from the environmental factors which increased their feelings of incompetence and attendant anxiety.

James N. Mosel looks at the learning situation itself in "How to Feed Back Performance Results to Trainees." We learn partly by comparing successive performances with their results, Mosel reports, each time changing or improving until our new "response" or learned behavior is correct. But we can only do this if we have accurate, frequent, and rapid feedback of the results of our performances to give us a base for our new efforts. Unless we have proper feedback, trial and error becomes burdensome, and we lose interest in persisting. But not all knowledge of results is helpful, Mosel points out, and some ways of giving it are more helpful than others. He discusses what information should be given in feedback and how to give it.

Not all trainers must be people, however. Indeed, there are times when competent human trainers are not available or are wasteful. Thus mechanical training devices can be useful adjuncts or substitutions to human training situations. Theodore B. Dolmatch in "Programmed Instruction: Two Perspectives," describes programmed instruction and discusses its principles. Programmed instruction is likely to play an increasingly important role in future training and development.

Not all learning in organizations involves the learning of tasks, of course. Robert T. Golembiewski's "The 'Laboratory Approach' to Organization Change: Schema of a Method" takes us beyond training for task performance to discuss training for interpersonal performance. We ordinarily give little thought to the learning of interpersonal performance. We either take for granted that we "know how to do it" or, when our interpersonal performances turn out badly, we blame it on something vaguely called "personality clashes." We rarely recognize that *all* of our behavior, including interpersonal performance, is learned behavior and thus may be changed. A phrase like "personality clashes" is a way of denying the possibility of change, while a phrase like "interpersonal performance" recognizes that possibility.

The learning or improving of interpersonal skills proceeds in some ways like task learning. As in task learning, feedback of our performance is important in interpersonal learning. Similarly, the setting conducive to the proper transmission of feedback is important. In addition, it is important to have a non-threatening setting in which new interpersonal behavior can be tried. The T-group described by Golembiewski is designed to provide this setting. As participants learn "how they come across" to each other in T-groups, they are provided with a basis for insight into their own behavior and into the impact that their behavior has on others. With those insights, they have some of the wherewithal to judge the appropriateness of their behavior for achieving their own goals. If a person's behavior does not help him achieve his goals, further, he might decide to modify his behavior. With sufficient penetration, T-group participants can deepen their understanding of how interpersonal problems arise to be able to handle them in the future before the problems do much damage to organizational life. T-group experiences also can go a long way toward increasing interpersonal trust and confidence.

There are obvious costs to the widespread use of T-groups, however. One is the time and expense involved. Another is the amount of openness which can realistically be expected from an individual when disclosure might damage his career prospects. These problems can be avoided or at least reduced, as by a modified version of laboratory training called confrontation designs. Confrontation designs encourage "owning and openness concerning organizational issues" in order to increase trust and decrease the risks of owning and openness. Thus, as individual learning proceeds, organizational learning develops as well. Norms are built which are in line with the organization's goals. Like all useful organization training, in the final analysis, the confrontation design emphasizes the interaction of the individual and the organization.

Part II - Section E

TABLE 9. *Topics and Selections Relevant to*
"Planning and Developing the Organization"

1. Challenges to Traditional Personnel Approaches
    a. The Challenge of New Tools
        10—Davis, "The Effects of Automation on Job Design"
    b. Second Thoughts about Position Classification
        19—Halloran, "Why Position Classification?"
        31—Leich, "Rank in Man or Job? Both!"
    c. Work Relations and Organization Structure
        30—Knudson, "Enter the Personnel Generalist"

2. Specific Challenges to Innovate New Personnel Approaches
    15—Golembiewski, "Organizational Patterns of the Future: What They Mean to Personnel Administration"
    16—Golembiewski, "The 'Laboratory Approach' to Organization Change: Schema of a Method"

Planning and Developing the Organization: Anticipating Tomorrow and the Day After

P UBLIC PERSONNEL ADMINISTRATION evolved to help cope with the first-generation effects of large public organizations, with the Civil War serving as a convenient date of origin. The philosophy and techniques it developed fit the organizational forms and cultural values predominant in its youth. The organizational forms were mainly bureaucracies, often with specialized and mechanized tasks. As bureaucracies, they were erected on the "position-as-building-block" principle. This apparently provided a clear basic for assigning responsibility and ensuring discipline at work. In the ideal, responsibility and discipline could be ensured once everyone's task was clearly spelled out. The process of controlling organizational outputs was greatly facilitated by this system. Furthermore, it eventually allowed nonarbitrary treatment of employees once positions were standardized and made comparable.

Traditionally, then, public personnel administration worked within accepted organization structure. It did not change structures nor aid their development. Thus, boundaries developed between it and organizational planning and developing. But organizations, as we have argued elsewhere, are complex social systems, not easily divisible into personnel and organizational planning components. Recognition of this fact makes the distinction between personnel administration and organizational planning artificial. Thus, integrating these two foci into a unified approach is an evolving challenge to traditional personnel work. Slower than business administration to reflect this unified approach, public management has taken only tentative steps in this direction. How it will develop is not clear at this stage. But it is the leading edge of public management thinking, and we think it should be emphasized. Hence, the relevance of this section. Table 9 summarizes the readings reprinted below which examine questions of planning and developing organizations to keep them current with their culture.

CHALLENGES TO TRADITIONAL
PERSONNEL APPROACHES

A long line of social critics have deplored the restrictiveness and rigidity of traditional bureaucracies. They point out that these faults are neither inevitable nor desirable in today's world, if they ever were. In a provocative article, Warren Bennis amplifies this theme, maintaining that cultural changes are presaging organizational changes as well. These cultural changes have resulted in major human problems facing organizations. Creative solutions to these problems will prod organizations out of their bureaucratic molds, allowing more freedom and creative opportunities for their members.[1] Public personnel administration needs a sure understanding of these problems in order to assist organizational adaptation to the changed values and power balances of the contemporary world.

The human problems Bennis identifies are five: integration, social influence, collaboration, adaptation, and "revitalization." Figure 3 outlines the problems, their bureaucratic solutions, and the new conditions requiring new solutions. The chart may be summarized briefly. First, the problem of integration revolves around bringing individual needs and management goals together. Although workers once may have been considered merely passive instruments to be manipulated by rewards and punishments, that day is past. Today, it is generally recognized that management's goals can better be realized if they are consonant with workers' goals. If for no other reason, new knowledge about human behavior reveals major weaknesses in the older techniques of motivation. Thus, the problem of integration is more complex than was earlier thought. The problem of social influence arises anew in modern organizations because employees no longer accept unreservedly management's traditional unilateral use of power. Employees now have power of their own which comes with education and unionization. The problem of collaboration asks how conflicts will be managed and resolved. The present no longer admits of one-man rule when conflict breaks out as was once the case. Organizations are too complex and interdependent for that. The problem of adaptation arises because organizations are faced with increasingly turbulent environments. Technological change is more rapid now; all change is less predictable than it once was. Finally, the problem of "revitalization" means that organizations cannot avoid, as they once could, providing for their own renewal in the face of decay.

Bennis labels the future organization "organic-adaptive." It will be a place mobilizing resources quickly to tackle unforeseen problems. Now impenetrable boundaries between jobs and people will vanish, casualties of changing skills

---

[1] Warren G. Bennis, "Changing Organizations," *The Journal of Applied Behavioral Science*, Vol. 2, No. 3 (July–August–September, 1966), pp. 247–63.

FIGURE 3. HUMAN PROBLEMS CONFRONTING CONTEMPORARY ORGANIZATIONS

	Problem	Bureaucratic Solutions	New 20th-Century Conditions
Integration	The problem of how to integrate individual needs and management goals	No solution because of no problem. Individual vastly oversimplified, regarded as passive instrument or disregarded.	Emergence of human sciences and understanding of man's complexity. Rising aspirations. Humanistic-democratic ethos.
Social Influence	The problem of the distribution of power and sources of power and authority	An explicit reliance on legal-rational power but an implicit usage of coercive power. In any case, a confused, ambiguous, shifting complex of competence, coercion, and legal code.	Separation of management from ownership. Rise of trade unions and general education. Negative and unintended effects of authoritarian rule.
Collaboration	The problem of managing and resolving conflicts	The "rule of hierarchy" to resolve conflicts between ranks and the "rule of coordination" to resolve conflict between horizontal groups. "Loyalty."	Specialization and professionalization and increased need for interdependence. Leadership too complex for one-man rule or omniscience
Adaptation	The problem of responding appropriately to changes induced by the environment of the firm	Environment stable, simple, and predictable; tasks routine. Adapting to change occurs in haphazard and adventitious ways. Unanticipated consequences abound.	External environment of firm more "turbulent," less predictable. Unprecedented rate of technological change.
"Revitalization"	The problem of growth and decay	?	Rapid changes in technologies, tasks, manpower, norms and values of society, and goals of enterprise and society all make constant attention to the processes of the firm and revision imperative.

SOURCE: Warren G. Bennis, "Changing Organizations," *The Journal of Applied Behavioral Science*, Vol. 2, No. 3 (July–August–September, 1966), pp. 247–63.

and immediate needs. Enduring work groups will make way for short-term but intense associations, as peoples' skills become more mobile.

The new structure will exact a heavy psychological toll from those members whose safety and security needs are met by unchanging, tradition-laden environments. Psychological stress will diminish when members learn to know new associates quickly and to replace them with others easily. Stability will come from inner strengths, drives, and motives. Intrinsic work satisfaction will be more valuable then ever.

All of this suggests that some traditional personnel techniques might not be useful in "adaptive-organic" organizations. Where do job description and classification fit, for example, in an organization attuned to rapid mobilization for attacking problems? Does it make sense to parcel out tasks in advance and make people hew to them when the problem to be attacked is only dimly understood and subject to change? These questions become more pointed in the light of massive technological developments now occurring, which should accelerate the cultural changes Bennis sees.

The impact of these massive technological developments can be illustrated simply in terms of how automation requires changed personnel techniques.[2] With the introduction of automation, personnel men face training older workers for new tasks which they often do not understand and fear. The ordinary problems of training are magnified in such a setting. Older workers less easily define themselves as learners, to begin with, and they may not see themselves as capable of learning anything new. These barriers must be removed, along with the more usual ones, if training is to be adequate in these new situations.

In "The Effects of Automation on Job Design," Louis E. Davis takes us deeper into the world of the new organization to show us just what the new jobs in automated organizations probably will look like. Since the field itself is in flux, what Davis tells us must be tentative. On the general level, Davis points out that the jobs of narrowest scope and lowest skill are the ones being replaced by automation. In their place come the machine-front operators and the machine-back maintenance men, both of them requiring higher skills and skills of a different kind than their predecessors. Davis identified many new skills which are needed under automation, and others which are transferable from present jobs. He reminds us of Bennis' prediction that tomorrow's organizations must adapt to new skills and work forms.

The controversy between rank-in-position and rank-in-man career systems has a new dimension in the light of tomorrow's organization. This is Daniel F. Halloran's conclusion in "Why Position Classification?" He asserts that under automation a technician may easily make decisions that have wider ramifications

---

[2] Ida R. Hoos, "The Personnel Administrator and Technological Change," *Public Personnel Review*, Vol. 24 (July, 1963), pp. 152–57.

than those made by top administrators. Therefore, Halloran suggests that a rank-in-man system may be more in keeping with reality than a rank-in-position system. It would allow more equitable pay arrangements and recognize where the true power lies.

There is still other merit to the rank-in-man system over the rank-in-position system. Technological and cultural change argue for more loosely defined positions that have broader job scope and confer wider responsibility. Therefore, a classification system permitting flexibility is even more important today than it was in the past. The rank-in-man systems offer that flexibility. Harold H. Leich's "Rank in Man or Job? Both!" may also usefully be reviewed at this point for insights into differences between the two systems.

How can the personnel man himself help to bring about tomorrow's organization, and the one for the day after? We have already spoken of the changes he can make in job design, in position classification, and in training. Harry R. Knudson's "Enter the Personnel Generalist" provides valuable insight on how the personnel man can deploy himself so as to bring his tools into most flexible use. Knudson suggests the personnel man literally decentralize himself from his department to join units or teams of the organization. He attaches himself as an adjunct to these units. Thus, he becomes a specialist in each unit's specific personnel problems with ready answers for them. He can help design and implement new personnel plans as needed while on the spot. Time is saved; commitment, specialization, and flexibility are gained.

SPECIFIC CHALLENGES TO INNOVATE NEW PERSONNEL APPROACHES

Insights like Knudson's are valuable, for all evidence suggests that organization planning and development for the future will be held back by major elements in the history of public personnel administration. Robert T. Golembiewski, in "Organizational Patterns of the Future: What They Mean to Personnel Administration," points out some of the major problems inherent in the public service which must be overcome before the personnel man can deploy himself more flexibly. These problems are built into the very foundation goals of the civil service, having been legislated into being. They are the products of the use of early scientific management techniques, of the search for equal treatment, and the desire for a public career service. They have spawned techniques, structures, and behaviors that are no longer suitable, but that persist nonetheless.

Crystal gazing is always a dangerous venture, but some reasonable guesses can be made about the specific kinds of new personnel concepts and approaches that need to be innovated. "Organizational Patterns of the Future" attempts to cover much ground, treating as it does some of the basic tools of the personnel trade as well as the basic organization structure within which personnel services will be provided. From tools through broad structural environment, the story is the same. Fundamental changes are necessary in personnel concepts and approaches.

Simply innovating personnel concepts or approaches or techniques is relatively easy, however. More important, they must be adapted to the style and requirements of specific organizations. More important still, these concepts or approaches or techniques must be accepted by organization members. The personnel man meets his sternest test in these two challenges. In a rough but telling sense, the personnel man must conceive, bear, midwife, and rear new personnel approaches.

Fortunately, techniques are available to help the personnel man in anticipating tomorrow and the day after, as well as in inducing the kind of commitment by members that is increasingly necessary in today's organizations. Robert T. Golembiewski's "The 'Laboratory Approach' to Organization Change: Schema of a Method" describes one significant approach to facilitating change and development. Basically, the "laboratory approach" seeks to develop attitudes and skills in individuals that will permit greater openness in communication which should permit more effective decision making. Specific uses of the lab approach can be diverse. Thus it can be used to help overcome employee resistance to learning a new technology. Through the use of T-groups, as another example, a collection of employees can become a flexibly interacting group that is more concerned with total results than with precise boundaries between tasks.

The laboratory approach is no cure-all, but it does illustrate the kinds of new approaches that need to be added to the personnel man's stock-in-trade. Today's ongoing organizational revolution demands corresponding innovation in the ways in which personnel administration is approached.

PART III

Major Monitors
of the Performance
of Public Personnel
Administration

Part III - Section A

TABLE 10. Topics and Selections Relevant to
"Internal Controls."

1. Inside the Employee's Skin
    a.   Attitudes about Rectitude, Responsibility, Responsiveness, Representativeness
            4—Cohen, "Responsibility in the Public Service"
            21—Heisel and Gladstone, "Off-the-Job Conduct as a Disciplinary Problem"
    b.   Reconciling Perceived Cross-Pressures
            9—Corson and Paul, "Personnel Near the Top: Responsibility and Accountability"
            20—Halset, "The Paradoxes of Public Administration"

2. Inside the Employee's Agency
    a.   Appeals Systems and Redress of Specific Grievances
            44—Scott, "Appeal Activities in the Federal Government"
            21—Heisel and Gladstone, "Off-the-Job Conduct as a Disciplinary Problem"
    b.   Collective Bargaining and Control of the Broad Work Environment
            34—Morse, "Shall We Bargain away the Merit System?"

Internal Controls:
Vigilance and Tension from Within

THE QUESTION of controlling the public service is full of knotty issues. Much fear exists that bureaucrats will not follow public or legislative wishes unless their work is minutely prescribed and monitored. Yet, such prescription and monitoring often seem to go to unnecessary lengths. Many public servants are experts in complex fields, and experts expect some freedom in carrying out their jobs. This makes close oversight unwise in many cases, and may make informed oversight impossible except for well-placed experts.

Methods of achieving control are two-pronged, consisting of internal and external facets. It is not always easy to distinguish between these two facets clearly, because they are interwoven, and they are sometimes one and the same in reality. We shall try to separate them here, however. We concentrate on internal facets in this section of the reader, and on external facets in the concluding section of the volume.

But before making the separation, let us briefly look at the total subject. Michael Cohen, in "Responsibility in the Public Service," suggests using a unifying concept which makes clear how diverse and interwoven control is. The unifying concept is the sociologist Amitai Etzioni's idea of "organizational control structure." Etzioni defines this idea as "the distribution of means used by an organization to get the performance it needs and to check whether the quantities and qualities are in accord with specifications." It is apparent from this definition that our civil service control structures are vast networks of internal and external means, exhibiting little overall planning. It is important to keep this fact in mind as we proceed. Table 10 summarizes the readings which examine other facets of internal control.

INSIDE THE EMPLOYEE'S SKIN

Political theorists have long been concerned with the place of administrative organizations in political systems. The most common view of their place in democratic systems is that administrative organizations are subservient to the institutions of popular election. The bureaucracy is considered the implementer of these decisions. Popular institutions are considered the makers of policy. Indeed, in the most naïve theory, they are simply thought to translate the "public will" into policy. However, simple implementation cannot be taken for granted. For example, many misunderstandings can intervene between policymaking and policy-implementing. Therefore, special means are required to raise the probability that administrative organizations will remain responsive and responsible to political institutions. Theories of responsibility grow out of the attempt to discover these means.

Basically, all means of administrative control should tend to induce responsiveness and responsibility. Cohen's "Responsibility in the Public Service" specifies the reasons why control cannot depend on external vigilance and devices alone. These reasons are varied and complex. But no matter how anxious the political institutions are to impose only external control devices, and no matter how willing civil servants are to accept them, much public work still escapes external vigilance. Consequently, civil servants have varying amounts of discretion in deciding what they can do and how they can do it. It is commonly thought that control in these cases must come from within rather than from outside. In other words, control comes from the inner moral commitment of civil servants, from their commitment to professional values and ways of doing things. Or, as was said of Lord Normanbrook, late retired head of the British Civil Service, at the time of his death, ". . . his thinking was dominated by the need for good order in public affairs." Cohen goes more fully into the times such responsibility is most needed and the forms it may take. He also evaluates those forms.

Besides attention paid to public employees' moral conduct in carrying out their jobs, considerable attention is also directed toward their moral conduct off the job. W. D. Heisel and Richard M. Gladstone, in "Off-the-Job Conduct as a Disciplinary Problem," report a study of how public employers view their employees' off-the-job conduct. Heisel and Gladstone conducted a survey asking public managers what kind of disciplinary action they would take in a number of hypothetical situations. Briefly, they found that public employees, especially police officers and executives, are expected to exhibit more puritanical public conduct than employees in private industry. Public employees are expected to set standards for the rest of the population.

Achieving control over the public service is particularly complex and delicate, given the conflicting expectations which are often held of public employees.

In a provocative essay, not reprinted here, the psychiatrist Daniel J. Levinson clarifies some aspects of this problem.[1] From the job description point of view, responsibility is simple, since this view holds that every job is a group of unified expectations held by and about its incumbent. Levinson suggests that this view is largely a myth. He argues that while job descriptions *try* to create a set of unified expectations for each jobholder, they rarely succeed. Far from having unified expectations from a single source, he says, most employees most of the time suffer expectations from several sources. More often than not, besides, these expectations are contradictory or in conflict with each other. Thus, says Levinson, role conflicts (or cross-pressures) are very common in organizations, contrary to official beliefs. While we do not know just *how* common role conflict is, it is certainly true that a personnel theory which fails to recognize the existence of considerable role conflict (even after a thorough job survey has been done) is unrealistic.

John J. Corson and R. Shale Paul's "Personnel Near the Top: Responsibility and Accountability" documents the many sources of expectations centering on top-level civil servants who are program managers. Not all individuals and groups who may pressure the program manager expect him to do the same things. Thus he has responsibilities to his superior, subordinates, peers, public constituencies, and Congress, among others. All of them have some claim to being heard, meaning that program managers must often make an amalgam of the pressures they feel.

Cross-pressures must be accommodated to or resolved in order to avoid prolonged indecision or disruption, but many cases do not permit easy solutions. Consider the dilemmas faced by military men. We may take the cross-pressures felt by the military as extreme examples of what many civil servants feel. The military's special problems derive from the extraordinarily strong emphasis placed on their obedience. Yet, they may be issued orders they feel to be unwise or incorrect from a military or professional standpoint. Disobeying such orders has possible consequences few are willing to take. As one result, many good ideas are lost when men cannot speak their minds freely, while many poor ones are implemented because disobedience may have serious consequences.[2]

Similar dilemmas are felt by businessmen entering the government service, as pointed out by Walter G. Halset in "The Paradoxes of Public Administration." Businessmen, coming from a world of relatively free action, often grow frustrated by the greater restrictions which hem in the public administrator. The restrictions are the result of numerous regulations, which may curb administrators' powers but are also ways of weakening the power of special interest groups.

[1] Daniel J. Levinson, "Role, Personality, and Social Structure in the Organizational Setting," *Journal of Abnormal and Social Psychology*, Vol. 58 (1959), pp. 170–80.
[2] Samuel Huntington, *The Soldier and the State: The Theory and Politics of Civil Military Relations* (New York: Random House, 1964), pp. 74–79.

But businessmen rarely understand this. They tend to perceive the restrictions as "red tape," or consider themselves placed in unnecessarily conflictful situations.

Businessmen are especially dismayed by conflicts in the sets of values which underlie civil service philosophy. Thus, for example, they are enjoined to make their operations efficient, but only as this protects the public. Performing the latter may well mean costs which make realizing the former difficult. Halset maintains that the government service loses much talent because businessmen leave in frustration after short tours of duty. He proposes orientation programs, designed to make understandable the need for so many restrictions and to bring clarity to the underlying complex values, in order to retain businessmen's services.

INSIDE THE EMPLOYEE'S AGENCY

Government employees, then, are faced with a plethora of requirements and expectations, many of them conflicting. Their off-the-job conduct is also scrutinized, as we learn from Heisel and Gladstone's "Off-the-Job Conduct as a Disciplinary Problem." Many employees are likely to be disciplined under these circumstances. They may be warned, dismissed, suspended, demoted, or reduced in rank. Appeals procedures are provided by most government jurisdictions for those employees who feel wrongly accused. As well as offering protection to employees, these procedures act as controls on public managers in their dealings with subordinates. Several such grievance procedure systems are described by William G. Scott in "Appeal Activities in the Federal Government."

Faced with the possibility and reality of arbitrary control over them by their employers, workers turn to unions for protection. As time goes on, public employees are less willing to submit to controls imposed on them. Instead, they ask for limits on management's controls and for the chance to participate in setting their own limits. Unions are one means through which public employees can control their environments. As government employees' unions gain legitimacy, and their relations with public management become more formalized, their membership increases. They become, therefore, an increasingly formidable force vying with management for control over the work environment. Unionization in the public sector contains paradoxes, however, as we learn from Muriel M. Morse's "Shall We Bargain away the Merit System?" These paradoxes arise because union aims often conflict with the values of the merit system. For example, wage theory as legislated by Congress under merit principles may directly conflict with union wage theory which stresses the negotiation of wages by collective bargaining instead. Thus, Morse asks whether full-scale collective bargaining is compatible with principles of the merit system. At least one thing is clear: unions there will be. So Morse's question is a very acute one.

Part III - Section B

TABLE 11. Topics and Selections Relevant to
"External Controls."

1. Legislative Controls
   5—Cohen, "The Personnel Policy-Making System"
   2—Association of the Bar of the City of New York, "Conflict of Interest, Technological Change, and Effects on Public Recruitment"
   42—Rose, "A Critical Look at the Hatch Act"
   54—Van Riper, "Veterans' Preference: Policies at Potential Cross-Purposes"

2. Executive Controls
   6—Commission on Organization of the Executive Branch of the Government, "Alternative Organizations and Policy Implications: Perspectives on the U.S. Civil Service Commission"
   25—Executive Order 11222, "Executive Order on Ethics of Federal Employees"

3. Judicial Controls
   37—Murphy, "Judicial Review and the Removal of Federal Employees"

4. Controls through Arrangements for Power Sharing
   39—Report of the National Advisory Commission on Civil Disorders, "The Police and the Community: The Problem of Grievance Mechanisms"
   4—Cohen, "Responsibility in the Public Service"

External Controls:
Oversight by Others

I N THIS CONCLUDING SECTION of the reader, we move again to that part of the environment of public personnel administration which lies beyond the immediate organization, to look at external controls. Most of these controls are well established in traditional organs of government, but some are still being developed and debated. The former are exercised by legislative, executive, and judicial institutions. The latter are controls we call "arrangements for power sharing." They consist of techniques like the *ombudsman* and police review boards. Neither of these has yet been tried widely in the United States; both are still highly controversial. Their intent, at least at this stage of development, is to give the general public more immediate and proximate recourse against public actions than traditional institutions allow. In this sense, "arrangements for power sharing" are meant to increase representation in the control process as a whole, as shall be shown. For now, Table 11 summarizes the readings which examine external control techniques.

Our format is direct. The established institutions and technique for external control get first attention, with the major foci being on the legislative, executive, and judicial branches of government as external controls over Public Personnel Administration.

LEGISLATIVE CONTROLS

Congress exercises control over federal personnel administration in direct ways, and much of the pattern applies at state and local levels of government. Through its legislative power, Congress determines the overall framework of personnel management. For example, pay scales are legislated by Congress. The philosophy, values, or goals reflected in the application of these policies, furthermore, are set or at least influenced by Congress. For example, personnel promotion systems can be of the rank-in-job or rank-in-man type, or some combination of the two. Each system reflects a different philosophy and set of values. Congress directly influences which philosophy and values will be implemented. Congress operates episodically, however, in response to issues which confront it. This means that legislation in a substantive area is often jumpy and disconnected. The government's personnel management policies and practices, therefore, often seem jumbled and inconsistent.

The patchy quality of public personnel policies and practices is made clear in "The Personnel Policy-Making System" by Michael Cohen. He discusses the relation between major participants in the personnel policy-making system, especially the relations between Congress and the U.S. Civil Service Commission. Briefly, the participants in personnel policy-making tend to adopt different and sometimes incompatible positions. This means that, if any policy is to be processed, the participants must establish ways of accommodating their interests. Therefore, participants strive to develop ways of dealing with each other that tie them together politically. The alternative to getting part of a loaf is squabbling that may leave all policy claimants at odds.

Cohen identifies some of these accommodating relations between members of the personnel policy-making system. For example, staff members of the Civil Service Commission and the Bureau of the Budget work cooperatively in writing legislation with staff members of the House Post Office and Civil Service Committee in order to iron out differences between them. The piece of legislation they write represents a bargain which is struck among them at the time. Provisions of the bill are written in such a way as to head off important opposition, and to allow the interests of the participants to be expressed. This results in a series of gains and losses for all participants.

Congress and legislatures generally exercise other controls over personnel besides setting policy for personnel management. One area of great activity is in conflict-of-interest regulations. The overall goal is to prevent government employees from using government positions for private gain. Because of the episodic and uncoordinated nature of its policy-making machinery, however, Congress' activities in this area are inconsistent. This is clearly seen in the article by the Association of the Bar of the City of New York, titled "Conflict of Interest, Technological Change, and Effects on Public Recruitment."

The Bar Association reports, for example, that Senate Committees apply different standards as to stocks that can be held by governmental appointees. The Senate Armed Services Committee, which must confirm appointees to the Department of Defense, applies stock divestment rules which are much more stringent than other committees. This tradition works to the decided disadvantage of the Defense Department, complicating the recruitment of able personnel. The Defense Department, especially, tries to appoint middle-level business managers to its own posts, but these are the very men who suffer most by the Armed Services Committee's policy. During the period covered by the New York Bar Association's survey, two appointees asked to have their names withdrawn from the committee, while quite a few men declined in advance even to be considered. The price for the privilege of government employ was too high to pay: to dispose of stocks and of interests in family businesses, and to risk harm to their business careers.

Such costs of government service are not uniform for all professions. For example, lawyers often can take on government work without harming their later careers. Scientists, on the other hand, may be especially hurt by Congress' policies toward conflict of interest, as the Bar Association shows. Today's technically skilled personnel and scientists are increasingly businessmen as well, or at least men with business interests. An uncompromising and uncomplicated concept of conflict of interest is thus obsolete in today's world.

That conditions favor uncompromising and uncomplicated personnel concepts in legislation also is clear on a broader level. In "A Critical Look at the Hatch Act," for example, Henry Rose analyzes the still controversial issues in federal personnel policy concerning employee participation in partisan politics. The merit system itself grew out of earlier intentions to introduce neutrality into the civil service. It was meant to protect the civil service from the depredations of party politics, as well as to protect civil servants themselves from partisan raids on public jobs. The Civil Service Commission built up a large body of decisions over the years, and the limits of partisan activity which were in accord with merit system principles were set on a case-by-case basis. Rose recounts the clumsy attempt of the Hatch Act to give unity and coherence to that body of decisions, as well as to enunciate a general policy for partisan activity.

Hatch Act provisions are at issue on two counts. The first is the unbelievable inconsistency and inadequacy of handling these provisions by the Civil Service Commission, as Rose describes the matter. He points out, for example, that the law is ambiguous as to whether the Hatch Act gives legal standing to previous Civil Service Commission decisions and, if so, whether they are the precedents for future rulings. This point has not been cleared up, but the Commission and other interested parties tend to behave as though it has. Previous decisions tend to be the base for present actions. Even worse, the Commission has never systematically codified its earlier decisions, but is acting on the basis of a summary of a small number of cases. Thus, it may well be using standards containing unknown biases.

The second point at issue is whether it is any longer realistic to restrict the political activity of government employees. It can be argued that the merit principle has become well enough established and protected by other devices, and that political parties are far less corrupt than they once were, so that public employees should now have much more freedom in this area than in the past. Furthermore, surveys show that government jurisdictions apply such a variety of different political restrictions on employees as to make the entire process arbitrary and some of the restrictions discriminatory.[1] In other words, what a government employee can or cannot do in the realm of politics often depends upon which government employs him or where he lives, rather than upon the fact that he works for a government.

The best that can be said for this confused area of policy is that the federal government's Hatch Act, at least, is currently being reviewed, and is likely to be amended to bring more order into the political activities field.

Legislative policies, of course, reflect a variety of pressures which play upon Congress. Some policies may not be much more than the translation of a special interest into a public right. Veterans' preference legislation is of this kind. Paul P. Van Riper discusses this policy in "Veterans' Preference: Policies at Potential Cross-Purposes." Through veterans' preference legislation Congress is controlling the composition of the federal work force and raising a potential threat to merit principles.

EXECUTIVE CONTROLS

While the Executive Branch has the responsibility for applying controls authorized and legislated by Congress, it may itself influence and control personnel policy directly. For example, such influence inheres in the organization of the Civil Service Commission itself and its relations with the President. This is illustrated in Commission on Organization of the Executive Branch of the Government, "Alternative Organizations and Policy Implications: Perspectives on the U.S. Civil Service Commission." The Executive Branch also retains discretion in promulgating rules of ethical conduct of employees. The most recent statement on ethical conduct is contained in Lyndon B. Johnson's Executive Order 11222, "Executive Order on Ethics of Federal Employees."

Executive convenience and legislative intent may be at significant odds, moreover, for what is legitimate control for the one may seem to the other an unconscionable rape of the merit idea. For example, the notion of a "senior civil service" tied more closely to the presidency turned into a battle between the Executive and legislative branches for control over employees. Congress has generally opposed such a top-administrative class from coming into being. The Executive Branch has long done battle with Congress to gain one, however.[2]

---

[1] See, for example, Pamela Ford, *Political Activities and the Public Service* (Berkeley, Calif.: Institute of Governmental Studies, University of California, 1963).

[2] Paul P. Van Riper, "The Senior Civil Service and the Career System," *Public Administration Review*, Vol. 28 (Summer, 1958), pp. 189–200.

JUDICIAL CONTROLS

The battle lines are less precisely drawn in the case of the third branch of our government. It is conceded that the courts have jurisdiction to hear appeals from government employees who have been discharged, but there is an issue over *which* courts should hear those appeals. The possibility of gaining justice partly hinges on these grounds, as Cornelius J. Murphy argues in "Judicial Review and the Removal of Federal Employees."

Traditionally, the District Court for the District of Columbia and the United States Court of Claims have heard appeals from federal government employees who were discharged. The former has the authority to order a reinstatement, while the latter can grant relief in the form of a money judgment. This jurisdiction posed less of a problem when there were relatively few federal employees, many of whom lived in the metropolitan Washington, D.C., area. Growth of public employ and scattered federal operations put a considerable hardship on discharged employees outside Washington who wish to appeal. The prevailing practice deters them. Murphy makes a strong case for shifting jurisdiction to the regular federal District Court system. He shows that this would require a change in judicial thinking about accepting such appeals and granting relief, but such a shift in philosophy is reasonable and would improve justice considerably.

CONTROLS THROUGH
ARRANGEMENTS FOR POWER SHARING

Lastly, we come to a discussion of citizen control over personnel. The most important issue is over complaints by citizens about improper treatment by public employees. Although the United States has an extensive court system, it is rarely employed to process complaints about ill treatment at the hands of public employees. Partly, this is because the courts are poorly equipped to handle these cases quickly and knowledgeably. Perhaps even more, the people most likely to bring complaints—the poor and disadvantaged—fear and distrust the court system. These people are more likely to find a "power broker" who can intercede for them, if they make any attempt to right real or alleged wrongs.

Innovation is necessary to permit the satisfactory handling of many citizen complaints. The courts are ineffective, as are "internal" review or audit boards which agencies establish for self-policing. The courts are overloaded, as it is. And internal review or audit boards can easily become arms of defense and self-protection for the agencies they monitor. Hence the value of an "external critic" whose job it is to see that public grievances are brought forcefully to the appropriate administrator's attention.

Support for these generalizations may be found in a Report of the National Advisory Commission on Civil Disorders, "The Police and the Community: The Problem of Grievance Mechanisms." Because of the patent danger that the institution can become self-protective, the Commission concluded that "an internal review board—in which the police department itself receives and acts on complaints—regardless of its efficiency and fairness, can rarely generate the necessary community confidence, or protect the police against unfounded charges." The Commission spoke after a review of numerous civil disorders in which it learned that many police departments pay no attention to con.plaints they receive, and that residents in communities with internal police review boards think they are unfair.

The Commission also cited an urgent need for boards external to police departments to review citizens' complaints in order to improve administration and restore public confidence. They felt that most other government agencies also probably need such external review agencies. The Commission's rationale is direct and compelling. As Michael Cohen notes in "Responsibility in the Public Service," many complaints against public servants result from the inevitable differences in opinions and values between agencies and the people they deal with. An internal review board is not likely to dispel the omnipresent residual dissatisfaction and suspicion, or perhaps even to recognize them in time. A major element in a counterrationale is that such external critics would meddle in matters beyond their competence or comprehension.

The external institution most frequently mentioned for minimizing citizen concern over administration is the *ombudsman*. The *ombudsman*, as it is known in Scandinavia, is a senior official of high integrity appointed by the legislature, but not answerable to it. Citizens bring all complaints to him and he is charged with investigating all of them without discrimination. It has proven to be a very popular and effective institution in the Scandinavian countries and several other places which either have an *ombudsman* or, like Japan, its equivalent.

In recent years, critics of American administration have increasingly suggested installing an *ombudsman* here. Gellhorn questions whether the institution can be successfully transplanted to American soil, but on the whole he remains optimistic. Consider the objection that the United States is far too big for the intimate *ombudsman* to operate properly. Gellhorn notes that the *ombudsman* need not be a single man, as in Sweden, but could be a bureau. The essential thing is that the office be impartial, whether large or small. Another pessimistic objection laments the supply of men of sufficient public confidence to take such jobs. We will never know the answer to that one until we try, says Gellhorn. Finally, there is the question whether the *ombudsman's*—or for that matter any external critic's—judgment is better than that of the administrator's he is criticizing. Gellhorn believes there is a good chance it will be since the critic is likely to take both a longer time in coming to a conclusion and a longer view of the matter than the administrator. Like any new institution, therefore, the *ombudsman* should be tried with caution. As Gellhorn concludes, "The wrecks of earnest reforms lie all about us. They remind that accomplishment may not soar as high as hope." [3]

[3] Walter Gellhorn, *When Americans Complain* (Boston: Harvard University Press, 1966), esp. pp. 212–32.

PART IV

Readings

1.

THE DEPARTMENTAL PERSONNEL OFFICER'S CONTRIBUTION TO MANAGEMENT

Achille R. Albouze

In far too many public agencies, the role of the departmental personnel officer (DPO) is little understood by top management, line supervisors, and employees. There are many reasons for this lack of understanding among which may be listed: comparative newness of DPO jobs in operating agencies, relatively few detailed studies concerning functions of the DPO, and the agency administrators' lack of conviction of how important a sound personnel management program is in helping the operating agency achieve its mission and goals.

Studies made on the duties and responsibilities of the DPO show quite conclusively that he performs a great variety of assignments. Virgil L. Couch has listed over 100 different covering duties and responsibilities of the Federal DPO.[1] Recently the California State Personnel Officers' Council participated in a five-year study of the personnel management functions of its agencies. The unpublished report listed 70 pages of personnel functions for which the DPO, line supervisors, the central personnel agency, and other agencies are responsible. Canada and New York studies confirm the fact that the DPO is responsible for a multiplicity of assignments.

Two recent reports of a PPA committee develop the subject in further detail.[2]

Personnel management's objectives in the public service are no different than those of private industry. The better programs set as their goals: (1) recruitment of a well-qualified and competent work force, (2) assignment of staff so that they may work with maximum efficiency and stability and minimum size and

Reprinted from *Public Personnel Review*, Vol. 24, No. 4 (October, 1963), pp. 233–38.
[1] Virgil L. Couch, "Scope of Personnel Activities in the Federal Service," *Personnel Administration*, January 1948, pp. 1–14.
[2] "Functions of the Departmental Personnel Office," *Personnel Brief No. 23;* and "Criteria for Establishing a Departmental Personnel Office," *Personnel Brief No. 24*, Public Personnel Association, Chicago, Illinois.

(3) work shall be carried on under the best possible conditions—satisfactory to both management and employees. Few will disagree today with the concept that personnel management is a basic responsibility of line management because it is inseparable from the other components of management—money and materials. Skillful management of an enterprise is seriously impeded unless an effective personnel management program is woven into every important component of the organization.

PRIMARY FUNCTION OF DPO

What then is the primary role of the DPO in assisting his agency to achieve a good personnel management program? At the risk of some oversimplification, I would say his role is essentially one of providing personnel leadership for his agency as a catalyst, and leaving the primary responsibility for personnel management in the hands of top administrators and line supervisors. Unfortunately however, the importance of the contribution made by a good personnel program to management is too often taken for granted or considerably underestimated. The fact that public personnel administration (as we understand it today) only dates back to the early 30's may account for the fairly widespread belief that far too many heads of public agencies do not have the proper regard for what should be a forceful, dynamic, and effective personnel management program for their agency.

Too often their personnel program is considered primarily an extension of the control functions of the central personnel agency. In making this statement I am fully aware that personnel management has made great strides in many public agencies and at various levels of government.

Let us concede that significant advances have been made in many areas of personnel techniques, knowledges, and procedures; however, many important and vexing personnel problems remain to be solved. The speed and effectiveness with which these problems will be solved will depend upon our ability as personnel men to meet the four following challenges:

1. To secure more active and interested support of top management towards the personnel management program of their agency;
2. To encourage the development of a more favorable "budgetary climate" which will permit and encourage the use of present knowledge concerning human behavior in working organizations; thereby improving personnel management programs;
3. To broaden our training and experience as departmental personnel officers to become more "management-oriented" and more capable of explaining the rationale of why we do what we do, coupled with an untiring zeal to search for improved methods; and

4. To develop what has been called "wide-angle vision" towards what is happening outside of the personnel field.[3]

MANAGEMENT'S IMAGE OF DPO'S JOB

What does management expect from the departmental personnel officer? Before preparing this paper, I asked several administrators for their views on this question. One said he expected his personnel man to be his extra pair of "hands, eyes, and ears" on personnel matters. He also included the nose to "smell" out things that needed changing or disposal. Additional points which were made are summarized as follows:

1. The personnel man should be the "right hand man" of the administrator to help the latter carry out his responsibility in personnel management.
2. He should be the expert adviser to top management on all personnel matters.
3. He should know the most about the organization when areas of personnel management are at issue.
4. If any personnel trouble spots develop, he should be the first to know about it, and he should tell management what to do about it.
5. He should initiate new personnel ideas or actions which he thinks are right and "sell" these to top management.
6. He should educate and "sell" top management on good personnel management practices and then, upon acceptance, he should follow through to see that this philosophy permeates the whole organization. (How the personnel man will do this may depend a lot on his personality, not to speak of his skill and knowledge.)
7. He should try to help an administrator or supervisor solve a personnel problem.
8. If the line of personnel communication is not good within the agency, management expects its personnel man to help solve (or at least "lubricate the joints") through training devices.
9. The personnel officer should be aggressive, not passive, in promoting ideas which will mean a better personnel management program for his agency.
10. Admittedly, management is often too preoccupied with its overall management responsibilities, and there are times when the administrator does not have the time to think about personnel matters. In situations like these, the personnel officer must find a way, somehow, to have the importance of the personnel problem recognized by management and proper consideration given to the proposed solution.

---

[3] Editorial—"Needed—A Public Personnel Rationale," *Public Personnel Review*, October 1961, pp. 206.

FURTHER AREAS OF RESPONSIBILITY

11. There may be times when management does not know what the duties of the personnel officer should be. In that case, it is up to the personnel officer to develop a draft of duties, responsibilities, and areas of authority pertaining to his job for management to review, modify as needed, and to promulgate.

12. It is the responsibility of the personnel officer to find out what the philosophy of management is toward its personnel management program. If it is wrong, it is up to the personnel man to convince management where it is wrong, and to offer an acceptable substitute philosophy.

13. The personnel office should implement and maintain effective and good working relationships with all of the agency's staff including employee organizations and unions.

14. Admittedly there may be sharp and conflicting interests as between management and employees. Here is where the personnel man walks the tightrope. There can be no doubt that his loyalty belongs solely to management. If management wants to follow an unwise course on a personnel policy, the personnel man should warn of the possible consequences of ill-advised action, and substitute a better idea.

15. It is essential that the personnel officer be identified as part of the management team. Some observers have commented that personnel officers have overemphasized personnel techniques and procedures to such an extent that the personnel man often finds himself "on the bench" and definitely not a playing member of the team.

16. Let us not overemphasize the "slick management" aspects of any of the many staff functions, whether these be training, personnel, management analysis, budget control, etc. After all, these staff functions are not ends in themselves. They are only the catalysts to help the agency fulfill its program mission whether it be building highways, collecting taxes, running a mental hospital, or any of the other many governmental services.

17. Occupying a personnel officer's job does not in itself confer a title of "expert" on a man. Expert as he may be in personnel techniques and procedures, he must acquire knowledge and skill in the management of people.

18. An absolute "must" for the personnel officer—to have a working knowledge of the agency's programs.

IDENTIFY WITH MANAGEMENT

Thus, management expects its personnel officer to function as an advisor, interpreter, expert, and initiator. Management also expects its personnel staff to have mature judgment, specialized knowledge and skills, and above all, to provide effective leadership for the agency's personnel management program.

From what has been discussed thus far, we should have a good indication as to how the administrator expects the personnel program to operate. It is clear that the departmental personnel officer must be identified more closely with management if he is to be an effective member of the management team. There is a growing belief among scholars in the field of personnel management which holds that the various functions for which the DPO is now responsible may become increasingly less important or may change radically in the future. The changing needs and shifts in emphasis of programs and goals of management or the work force itself are important forces which may bring about these changes.

PRESENT AND FUTURE OBJECTIVES

The point-of-view presented here is based on the following premises:

1. The many tools, techniques, and methods used by the departmental personnel officer in such fields as recruitment, examining, position classification, and pay are fairly well advanced and generally accepted by management, central personnel agencies, employee groups, and other interested persons. (In making this statement I do not wish to imply that all agencies are performing these functions at the highest possible level.)

2. Within the limits of his work responsibilities, the relative importance of any individual function, or group of functions, for which the departmental personnel officer is responsible, will vary in accordance with his agency's needs. For example, in some organizations a stable classification and pay plan with provisions for adequate maintenance may be a primary goal; in a growing agency, the need for new positions, new concepts to meet program needs may be foremost; and in still others, the emphasis may be on employee development. Thus, what may be a major activity today, may be a minor one tomorrow. Changes in the work programs of the total agency generally produce concomitant changes in the emphasis or concentration of the work of the departmental personnel office.

3. The areas in which the departmental personnel officer of the future will be more greatly identified will be in assisting management to develop better and well defined programs for implementing and improving:
   (a) employee morale;
   (b) employee motivation;
   (c) communications between management and employees; and
   (d) selection of leaders.

Whatever the departmental personnel officer may have contributed to management in the past, the greatest challenge which the future presents to him is within the four last mentioned activities. If we, as personnel officers, can make worthwhile contributions to management within these areas, we will have made our greatest contribution. In so doing we shall dispel the frequently-mouthed criticisms that as personnel people we have been preoccupied with personnel gadgetry, gimmicks, techniques, and procedures at the expense of meeting the more important personnel needs of management.

In making this statement, I do not wish to make a blanket criticism of the present day performance of all departmental personnel offices. There are some agencies which have done, and will continue to do, exemplary and progressive jobs in the field of personnel management. However, we must admit there are others in which we would find less creditable records of performance within their departmental personnel offices.

To the person who has made any diligent study of the new dimensions of personnel administration—in private industry as well as in the public service—the direction of the future is quite clear. The future emphasis of management will be to develop and utilize manpower in a manner best suited to achieve maximum benefits for the whole organization. This objective is not new, but the emphasis that will be placed on the personnel component of management is new—judged from a review of public personnel management over the past 30 years.

EMPLOYEE MORALE AND MOTIVATION

Few persons would disagree with the importance to management of employee morale and motivation. Cecil E. Goode[4] has observed that in these areas, our knowledge comes almost entirely from the research of social scientists in private industry and business even though some of the research has been supported by public funds with a view toward its general public value.

O. Glenn Stahl[5] has observed that employee "morale is being recognized as the most important single aspect of administration and production. It is more important than mechanical techniques, than procedures, than time and motion studies. Further, it is influenced more by the attention and recognition received by the individual worker than it is by physical working conditions, by direct appeals for increased production, or even by pay. . . . The core of the problem is in devising those working arrangements and relationships which contribute

---

[4] Cecil E. Goode, "Personnel Research Frontiers," *Public Personnel Association*, Chicago, Illinois, 1958.

[5] O. Glenn Stahl, *Public Personnel Administration*, 4th edition (New York, 1956), p. 272.

most to the employee's sense of security, achievement, and belongingness—the elements of job satisfaction."

If employee morale and motivation are such important elements of a good personnel program, you may ask why are they so often neglected, even among the better programs? The reason for this may be because of the difficulty involved in utilization and application of available research findings. Further, there are still questions in the minds of many knowledgeable persons in this field as to the length of time it will take management in the public service to recognize, utilize, and adapt the results of this research to a governmental setting. In the light of this, the departmental personnel officer must not only extend his knowledge in this field, but he must also study results obtained by the experimentation of those public agencies which operate in a climate where a pioneering boldness in manpower management is encouraged.

Employee attitude surveys, employee counseling, effective grievance procedures, employee suggestion systems, and supervisory training programs are devices now frequently used by agencies which are aware of the importance of employee morale. The progressive departmental personnel officer will recognize the increasing importance of the "human relations" side of the organization and he will help shape the agency's personnel program around this need.

The concept that man works only to satisfy purely economic needs has been largely discarded following the research findings of Roethlisberger and his group at the Hawthorne plant of the Western Electric Co. Challenging work, recognition for a job well done, a better work environment, and opportunities for creativity and growth are among the incentives to maximum effort by the work group.

COMMUNICATIONS

We all appreciate the importance of an effective two-way communications system—oral and written—by which management keeps employees informed on what is going on in the organization and vice versa, listens to what employees have to say on problems and aims of the organization.

In recent discussions with other departmental personnel officers, I was repeatedly reminded that to maintain an effective communications system between management and employees on personnel information required continuing and laborious efforts. In the public service, there is the additional line of communication with the central personnel agency to add to the complexity and burden of the departmental personnel officer.

My brief reference to this facet of personnel work is not intended to minimize its importance. May I leave the thought with you that communications—like safety—is a continuing and difficult job which cannot be neglected and permitted to deteriorate if an organization is concerned about the working effectiveness of its employees.

SELECTION OF LEADERS

How are abilities for top management leadership to be identified, recruited, and trained? J. D. Millett[6] has observed that "entrance into the public service in the United States is largely upon a professional basis, that is, upon the basis of an individual's experience or knowledge in performing specific kinds of substantive work. Because of these recruitment patterns, the public service must provide adequate training for the identification and development of those persons within the service who display administrative capacities and to prepare them by study and varied experience for management duties."

Progress has been made in identifying the personal qualifications which are essential for leaders in administrative enterprises through research conducted by the Kellogg Foundation, Carroll Shartle at Ohio State University, and others. However, a crying need has often been expressed for more basic research to improve our present methods of recruiting and training personnel for administrative positions in the public service.

Cecil E. Goode[7] points out that several studies "are showing that the managers in American industry who achieve the highest performance and best results are deviating substantially from what prevailing practices specify as 'correct'." Mr. Goode points out the "need for basic modifications in existing management theory and practices. Argyris, Haire, Likert, and McGregor are some of those who feel that management and organizational theory and practice will undergo a major change during the next decade. The impact of these changes on the selection, training, and development of administrators—public and private—will be substantial. To achieve these new insights will require continued and intensified research attention and—equally important—an inquiring attitude and genuine desire for improvement on the part of organizational leaders."

DPO MUST GROW WITH MANAGEMENT

The departmental personnel officer now, and in the future, faces an ever-increasing responsibility of bringing his knowledge up to date and to sharpen his skills by assisting management in the recruitment, identification and training of its manpower selected for leadership.

---

[6] John D. Millett, *Management in the Public Service* (New York, McGraw-Hill, 1954), p. 53.
[7] Cecil E. Goode, *op. cit.*

In this presentation I hope that my views have not appeared to minimize the importance of the departmental personnel officer's day-to-day work assignment as a member of the management team. Wherever a tone of criticism was evident in my preceding remarks, it was prompted by a sincere desire to spark a more critical evaluation of what we do, how we do it, and most importantly, why we do it.

I have the greatest respect for the "hard-rock" day-to-day tasks of the personnel man. But to meet the challenges of the future for even greater contributions to management, the departmental personnel officer will need to emphasize those activities which will permit him to grow with management; to help solve the vexing and newer problems of manpower in the years ahead; to substitute better for good leadership in the personnel management programs of tomorrow; and, to pump new ideas and imagination into the bloodstream of personnel management to keep it from developing—as Wallace Sayre has expressed it—into a "triumph of technique over purpose."

2.

CONFLICT OF INTEREST, TECHNOLOGICAL CHANGE, AND EFFECTS ON PUBLIC RECRUITMENT

ASSOCIATION OF THE BAR OF THE CITY
OF NEW YORK

To what extent do existing conflict of interest restraints deter recruitment of government personnel? The issue has never been adequately explored or debated. Except to a minor extent in the case of Section 1914, Congress gave no consideration to the recruitment problem in any recorded legislative history of the conflict of interest statutes. Mid-nineteenth century political debate could not be expected to concern itself seriously with the problem. Not until World War I, and not again until World War II, did Congress face up to the emergency shortage of executives by authorizing the use of WOCs and relaxing certain of the conflict of interest restrictions. The statutes and the episodic concern of senatorial confirming committees with the conflict of interest problem are

---

Reprinted from Association of the Bar of the City of New York, *Conflict of Interest and the Federal Service* (Cambridge, Mass.: Harvard University Press, 1960), pp. 152–64.

properly seen as a disconnected string of events, not as part of any over-all program balancing the need for ethical protection against the need for qualified government personnel. The effects the present system has on recruitment are largely accidental.

CIVIL SERVICE PERSONNEL

Conflict of interest restrictions bear upon civil service employees in a variety of ways. If the civil service employee is a lawyer or accountant or other specialist, he may occasionally find himself affected by the statutory bars on assisting outsiders in claims against the government. Once in a while, he may be required to disqualify himself under Section 434 because of conflicting interests. He may, though it is less likely in the case of a permanent employee, have to forego certain outside compensation because of Section 1914. And when he leaves government service, he may be substantially restricted in his relations with the government—and consequently in his job choice—by the post-employment restrictions of his agency's regulations and by Sections 99 and 284.

But the problems most often encountered by the civil service worker involve either outside employment related to his agency or the acceptance of small gratuities, neither of which is covered by the statutes. A relatively short work week makes it possible for thousands of government employees to carry an outside job to supplement their income. The employee with a special skill or experience that he uses in his government work may want to make use of it in outside work as well. But an employee of the Federal Housing Administration who conducts an outside real estate business, for example, may seriously embarrass the agency, and regulations commonly prohibit such related activity.[1] These regulations mainly affect career personnel rather than the executive employees in Washington on temporary appointment. The other most frequent conflict of interest problem of the civil servant is the small gratuity—the dinner out, the Christmas ham, or the bottle of whiskey at New Year's, paid for by a company or individual dealing with the employee's agency. This annoying problem, calling for constant line-drawing and tact in dealing with others, is nearly always a subject of agency regulations.[2]

The recurrent problem to the agency, if not to the individual employee, is the flow of civil service employees into private companies and organizations doing business with the agency. . . . It is enough to note here that during negotiations for such transfers, the employee will often be disqualified by regulation from dealing for the agency with his prospective employer.[3]

---

[1] Federal Housing Administration, *Your Job in FHA, a Handbook for Employees* (1955) 48–50.
[2] See discussion, Chap. IV *supra*, under "Gratuities." [Chap. IV not reprinted here.]
[3] S.E.C. 17 C.F.R. § 203.5 (Supp. 1959) (negotiation for private employment).

Conflict of interest restraints thus touch upon the civil service in many ways. Nothing in the available evidence suggests, however, that the present pattern of restraints in any way deters the recruitment of civil service employees.

POLITICAL EXECUTIVES

In the federal government today approximately 1,100 executive positions are filled on a full-time but temporary basis by political appointment of the President or the heads of agencies.[4] Less than half of these require senatorial confirmation. These 1,100 jobs are the top policy-making jobs in the executive establishment. They have become increasingly difficult to fill.

... The prospective appointee learns in one way or another that he may have to make some adjustments in his personal economic interests while he is in Washington and for a period after he leaves Washington, and that these adjustments may entail substantial personal sacrifice. Out of the welter of influences pressing upon him, the political appointee himself often cannot after the event assess to what extent his decision to decline was attributable to the burdens of the conflict of interest restraints, or to what extent his decision to accept was delayed, or made conditional, or otherwise limited by them. Available evidence supports the conclusion, however, that the conflict of interest restrictions have substantially contributed to the government's difficulties in recruiting executives.

Appointment Subject to Senate Confirmation

The positions most affected have been Defense Department posts subject to confirmation by the Senate. The rigid attitude of the Senate Armed Services Committee on stock divestment has been the source of the difficulty. In at least two cases since 1953, presidential appointees who had already appeared before the Committee withdrew their names when the Committee insisted upon its stock sale requirement.[5] The evidence is that many prospective appointees to Department of Defense positions have declined in advance to be considered, in large

---

[4] See Bernstein, *The Job of the Federal Executive* (1958) 10–11.

[5] Robert Sprague was nominated as Assistant Secretary of the Air Force in January 1953. The Senate Armed Services Committee opposed his confirmation because he refused to sell his shares in his family firm, The Sprague Electric Company. His nomination was thereupon withdrawn, on February 11, 1953. In 1957 Willard F. Rockwell served as Acting Chairman of the Army-Navy Munitions Board after being nominated as Assistant Secretary of Defense for Logistics and Supply. He served several months before the Senate Committee refused to confirm his nomination because he declined to sell stocks in two family concerns, the Rockwell Manufacturing Company and the Rockwell Standard Corporation. On August 4, 1953, he requested the President to withdraw his nomination, and he resigned his government post on September 24, 1953.

part because of the Committee's practice of forced divestment. The Secretary of Defense is reported to have written to Senator Russell on April 5, 1956, that it had been factually demonstrated in the Department's efforts to recruit outstanding people for top posts that the policy of the Senate Armed Service Committee had made it extremely difficult—even impossible—to secure the best qualified persons for particular positions.

In discussing obstacles to executive recruitment in the Department of Defense, a leading official in 1957 went even further:

> The conflict of interest statutes cause us more trouble in recruiting than any other single thing, including inadequate salary. Some time ago, several executives in the department divided up a list of 57 names to fill an important executive post. We felt that any one on the list would be all right. We were not successful. In about half of the cases, conflict of interest under the statutes kept us from getting men who otherwise would have been willing to come to Washington for two or four years. We have to find a better solution to this problem to enable the department to get its fair share of executive talent.
>
> We recently had a difficult job in research development to fill. Person after person declined the job because of conflict of interest. One fellow we wanted badly had several thousand shares of stock in a company he had worked in for 35 years. He is good for at least a few more years of executive work. He would love to come to Washington, but will not sell his stock in order to do so.[6]

Interviews with Defense Department officials and former officials, and with persons declining executive appointments to the Department, provide further support for the conclusion that confirmation policies of the Senate Armed Services Committee and the existing conflict of interest restraints have hampered recruitment of departmental personnel.[7]

Although top executives of large publicly held companies are among those deterred from government service by the stock divestment requirement, it appears that the persons hardest hit by the Committee's rule are not of this group. The man most affected is the executive who owns and operates a family business. For such a man, sale of his company's stock is more than the sale of an investment or the sale of shares in an employing company; it is the disposition of the family company itself to outsiders, and the relinquishment of a future career for himself and for his children.[8]

The evidence of hindrance to recruitment arising out of the Committee's rule on stock divestment relates mainly to business executives. This is in part because stock ownership is common among this group and in part because business executives are those most apt to be appointed to the Defense Depart-

---

[6] Quoted in Bernstein, *The Job of the Federal Executive* (1958) 158–59.

[7] For example, interviews indicate that in a recent year thirty-five persons refused to take research and development posts in Defense, and that some critical research and development posts had remained vacant for as long as six months.

[8] Both Messrs. Sprague and Rockwell were in this category.

ment. The Committee's rule, however, applies to all occupations and has an equal effect on any appointee holding stock. For example, lawyers appointed as General Counsel of the Defense Department have been required to dispose of small and incidental stock investments in companies with which they had no other business affiliation.[9]

As discussed earlier, no Senate Committee other than the Armed Services Committee has shown in its confirmation proceedings a sustained concern with the conflict of interest issue. Correspondingly, no evidence available suggests obstacles to executive recruitment arising from the conduct of these Committees. And no evidence has been seen that any appointee who was willing to accept the standards imposed by a Senate confirming committee boggled at the requirements of the conflict of interest statutes or regulations.

Other Full-Time Appointments

Less clear are the deterrent effects of the conflict of interest restraints on recruitment for posts not requiring Senate confirmation.

It will be recalled that there is nothing in the statutes themselves that requires divestment of stockholdings. As a 1958 study stated, instances of forced stock divestment "undoubtedly received tremendous publicity all out of proportion to their significance in terms of numbers of jobs affected since only 5% of the responding present or former B[usiness] M[en in] G[overnment] stated that they were required to relinquish their investments. This problem appears to be limited to a very small number of businessmen who serve, probably those in the most important positions. On the other hand, it could mean that a considerable number of businessmen declined government jobs because they refused to dispose of their investments." [10]

Except in the case of lawyers, discussed below, the most troublesome statute is Section 1914, prohibiting outside compensation. Its deterrent effect is undeniable. Inadequate salary scales are among the major stumbling blocks to government recruitment efforts. Many employers are willing to grant a leave of absence to an employee while he is on a temporary government assignment, and to continue his former salary, or supplement his government salary. Section 1914 prevents this, though the employer has no business relations of any kind with the employee's agency or with the government generally. Many people who would otherwise be willing to accept government appointment are prevented by this section from doing so.

The deterrent effect of Section 1914 does not primarily fall on the highest

[9] *Hearings Before the Senate Committee on Armed Services on Nominations of Robert Dechert [and others]*, 85th Cong., 1st Sess. (1957).

[10] Harvard Business School Club of Washington, D.C., *Businessmen in Government, An Appraisal of Experience* 26 (1958).

ranking executives of the largest companies, or upon the senior men at the peak
of their business careers; for these men salary is often of secondary consequence.
The group most affected by Section 1914 is the middle rank of executives.
These younger men usually have heavy continuing financial commitments in
the form of house mortgages and school bills. To them immediate and regular
cash salary payments at a steady or rising level are essential. A voluntary slash
in salary, at this critical stage of their careers, especially when coupled with the
increased expense of a move to Washington, is out of the question.

The full effect of Section 1914 is blurred by its uncertain meaning. As noted
earlier, opinions vary widely on the extent to which it prevents government
employees from continuing their participation in retirement, insurance, and
other such security plans common today in all institutions. If a strict construction of Section 1914 is followed, a prospective appointee faces an abandonment
of his long-range retirement and insurance plans. Even if the plan permits
the employee to go on leave of absence and the employer stops making payments
under the plan, it is arguable that the section does not permit the employee to
continue even his status as a qualified member of the plan. In any case, the
amount of the payments required to be made into the plans is normally beyond
the reach of the middle-ranking executive, especially if he is simultaneously
facing a salary cut and increased living expenses in accepting government
appointment. Altogether, Section 1914 is a serious obstacle to recruitment of
men for government office at an age when they are apt to be most vigorous
and productive.

Probably this effect of Section 1914 is most marked in the business community.
Logically Section 1914 would be thought to have the same effects on men recruited for government service from the universities, especially if one recalls
the origin of the section as a bar to prevent nonprofit institutions from supple-
menting the salaries of men in the Bureau of Education. But the Attorney
General has expressed the opinion that a university professor might work for
the government on a leave of absence, even while continuing compensation
from his university, since the university was not paying him "in connection with"
his government work.[11]   And it is quite unlikely that a teacher's continued
participation in a university insurance or retirement plan would be held to violate
the section. The situations of the university employee and the business company
employee are different in some degree, and a distinction in result under Section
1914 might be justified in most circumstances. There are situations, however,
such as allocation of research grants, in which the university man and the
businessman in government can raise exactly the same problems of conflicting
interests, and here a disparity in the law applicable to them is hard to explain.
Since Section 1914 is an over-all prohibition against outside compensation, it

---

[11] See 39 *Ops. Att'y Gen.* 501 (1940).

leaves no room for refined rules adapted to the employee's particular government assignment or to the particular source of his outside compensation.

Section 434, requiring disqualification of the government employee, appears to have only incidental effect on the recruitment of personnel. Occasionally an individual spot job may absolutely require the holder to deal with a particular company. An aluminum resources administrator could hardly avoid dealing with Alcoa, and an appointee with an interest in that company would have to disqualify himself so often that he could not perform his government job; he would in effect be faced with declining the appointment or disposing of the interest. Instances of this kind can occur, and have occurred, but are rare.

Section 216, forbidding payments to government employees for aid in securing government contracts, is almost a bribery statute and has no observable effect on recruitment of personnel.

The position of lawyers under the conflict of interest statutes is unique. The point was made earlier that the four statutes dealing with prosecution of "claims" mainly affect lawyers since they limit exactly the kind of representational services normally performed by their profession. In addition it happens that a combination of three extrinsic circumstances spectacularly steps up the voltage of these statutes for lawyers.

For centuries the law has said that a partner is responsible for the acts of his partners and that the acts and knowledge of one partner will be "imputed" to the others. This is an assertion of a legal policy, useful in many contexts; it is a proposition often uttered and accepted, however, as though it were a description of a fact, a proposition springing in some mysterious way from the word "partnership," but not from other words of organizational form such as "corporation." Second, the law, mainly for historical reasons, forbids lawyers to practice in the organizational form we call the corporation and requires all joint practice to be cast in the form of partnerships. Finally, the growth of the federal government, the development of a mixed public-private economy, and the increase in tax levels have brought every enterprise into abrasive contact with the government. As a result, a significant part of almost every lawyer's practice is the representation of his clients in matters in which the federal government is or may be an adverse party.

The combination of these three factors—the doctrine of imputation of partners' acts, the compulsory use by lawyers of partnerships, and the growth of private contacts with the government—dramatically increase the effect of the conflict of interest statutes on lawyers. If a lawyer becomes a government employee, not only is he forbidden to undertake representations that fall within the statutes, but by the doctrine of imputation he may be in violation if his partners undertake such representation. Conversely, rigorous application of the imputation doctrine imputes to his partners knowledge of facts the employee may have learned in his government service, whether or not his partners are in fact aware of them.[12] As a consequence the lawyer who enters government service is usually forced to resign from his law partnership or impose on the firm the severe handicap of staying out of legal matters involving the government. Further, under Sections 99 and 284 he must usually, as a practical matter, not rejoin the firm for a period of two years after he leaves employment.

With the main fire of the conflict of interest statutes trained squarely on the lawyer and his practice, it would be thought that the government would encounter particular difficulty from this source in its efforts to recruit lawyers into full-time governmental service. But in spite of the restrictive conflict of interest restraints, and in spite of the fact that lawyers recruited for a particular post will often decline it because of the conflict of interest statutes, the government has consistently been able to find others willing to accept a full-time government appointment likely to last two or three years. The profession's tradition of government service accounts for much of this. Possibly law firms are more sympathetic than most employers to the lawyer's desire to serve a stint in government, and are more ready to permit him to go without losing ground in the firm. There are important practical considerations as well. Unlike the corporate executive, the lawyer finds his loss measured primarily by the reduction, if any, in his current income, since most deferred compensation plans and stock options, deductible pension plans and other fringe group-benefits, are, under the tax laws, limited as a practical matter to business in corporate form, and are not therefore characteristic of the lawyers' partnership. Moreover, the lawyer has more incentive to enter government service: his work there will usually be more directly applicable to and related to his professional work, and his experience and contacts gained there more directly usable in his practice after leaving government. Unlike the businessman, he is apt to add to his professional stature as a result of his government service. It is true that when, after some two or three years, he leaves government employment and returns to private practice, he is subject to the postemployment restrictions of Sections 284 and 99, and these can be troublesome. Nevertheless, for whatever reasons, the conflict of interest restrictions do not appear seriously to embarrass the government's efforts to recruit lawyers for full-time government appointment. As will be seen, recruitment of lawyers for intermittent government service is quite another matter.

INTERMITTENT EMPLOYEES

Present conflict of interest restraints affect intermittent personnel differently from regular full-time personnel. In some respects their deterrent effect on recruit-

---

[12] See *United States* v. *Standard Oil Co.*, 136 F. Supp. 345 (S.D.N.Y. 1955).

ment of intermittent personnel is even greater.

Intermittent employees have seldom if ever come before the Senate for confirmation. The compulsory stock divestment practices of Senate committees therefore are not a factor in their recruitment.

The businessman who may be deterred by the conflict of interest restrictions from accepting full-time appointment is relatively free to serve in an advisory capacity. Asked to be a consultant one day a month, the businessman generally accepts unhesitatingly insofar as the conflict of interest restrictions are concerned. He seldom, if ever, considers himself a government "employee" by virtue of his advisory services, and he makes little or no adjustment in his private affairs on accepting the assignment. Section 1914 may raise problems, but they are usually ignored by intermittent employees. If properly advised, the consultant would be aware that he is subject to Section 434 and would avoid self-dealing situations when he is actually on the job in Washington. But this restraint is a comparatively easy one for a consultant to comply with, since he is seldom representing the government in a direct transaction of business with outside entities. The other statutes affect the businessman consultant almost not at all.

When one turns to advisory or other intermittent services by the lawyer, however, the teeth of the statutes cut the other way, and the situation alters abruptly. The evidence is overwhelming that conflict of interest restraints effectively block the government's efforts to secure the services of lawyers to serve on its hundreds of advisory committees.

More aware of the statutes and more professionally concerned about the legality of his position, the lawyer sees the advisory appointment to bristle with problems. He will recognize that, as a consultant, he is an "employee" of the United States and that while he is an employee, whenever that may be, he and his partners are subject to the restrictions of the statutes. Section 1914 will raise interesting, and insoluble, intellectual puzzles for him. But, far more important, as soon as he becomes a United States employee of any kind, the full weight of Sections 281, 283, 284, and Section 99 crashes down upon him and his partners. That means that his law firm can do no tax work or patent work or antitrust work involving the United States without exposing him to prosecution. And even after he formally resigns as a consultant or his appointment is terminated, he faces the statutory two-year bar. His only safe recourse is to resign from his firm. But he cannot and will not resign from his law practice and his firm in order to stand by, awaiting an occasional call to spend a few hours in consultation with the government.

The result is inevitable. Lawyers with special experience or skill—often acquired while on an earlier full-time tour of duty with the government—are regularly requested by government agencies to serve as continuing consultants to help the government. They are usually forced to refuse for no reason whatever except the conflict of interest statutes.

UNCERTAINTY AS A DETERRENT

An unmeasurable but unmistakable impetus is given to the deterrent effect of the conflict of interest statutes by their uncertainty. At many critical points they defy understanding or prediction. The lawyer asked to advise his client on the applicability of the statutes to his particular circumstances is in a difficult position. In the matter of personal conflicting interests, the political appointee occupies the most exposed position imaginable. There is no better political ammunition than the charge of conflict of interest; the party out of power will spare no efforts to smoke out the rascals; and like the foreign agent disowned by his own government if discovered, the executive appointee detected in a questionable conflict of interest position can expect little protection or defense from his own party or the administration that appointed him. Some elements of the press, radio, and television stand ever ready to raise the hue and cry. All but one of the statutes provide criminal penalties—felony penalties, comparable to those for theft or bribery—and, while prosecutions have not been frequent, no one can predict when the next prosecution will occur, perhaps not totally free of partisan overtones. Conviction, prosecution followed by acquittal, or even indictment under one of these statutes can disgrace a man for life. And so when the prospective appointee asks his lawyer for counsel on the application of the conflicts statutes to his particular situation, the careful lawyer tends to be especially cautious. The more strict the lawyer's interpretation, the more likely that the appointee will decide that the personal costs of compliance with the statutes are too great and that he had better decline the appointment.

RELATED ADVERSE EFFECTS

Existing conflict of interest restraints have other adverse effects that are related to their deterrent influence on recruitment. Many of the same forces that tend to deter people from going into government service tend to induce them to leave it. Much of the government's recruitment problem derives from its difficulties in retaining staff already on the job. In many situations it is even more important to the government to retain trained men than it is to be able to recruit untrained replacements. The conflict of interest restraints, particularly in their prohibitions on outside compensation, add to the other factors that make it difficult for the government to keep its staff.

A second consequence is that as a result of the impact of the conflict of interest restraints, government officials tend to develop informal channels for securing the assistance of men deterred from accepting formal appointment. An expert who will not come to the office as an employee once a month can frequently be reached for informal consultation in his home on the weekend. From the standpoint of the government's need for his services, this informal advice is better than nothing. Yet if there are risks in the use of outside consultants, they are surely magnified where there is no record of the consultation, no method of controlling the agenda, and no institutional arrangement for general supervision. Consultation should be as overt a matter of public record as possible, to prevent the very risks against which the conflict of interest restraints are directed. Misdirected restrictions defeat their own purposes.

Finally, the general tendency of the conflict of interest restraints is to erect a barrier around the government through which it is difficult for information to move in one direction or the other. This blockage of information flow may be the most dangerous consequence of all, judged by the demands that the twentieth century has placed upon American government. The government's programs for scientific development probably offer the best illustration of the point. . . .

3.

GETTING CAUGHT IN THE MIDDLE
ON CLASSIFICATION DECISIONS

Bernard H. Baum

PART A. CIVIL SERVICE COMMISSION AS WATCHDOG: UPWARD AND DOWNWARD CLASSIFICATION PRESSURES

One of the principal functions of the Commission in its task of implementing the merit system is position classification. Position classification is the determination of the grade and consequent salary level of a specified group of duties to provide a system whereby "equal work" receives "equal pay." The Commission publishes classification standards that are used as the guides and bases for the allocation of any given position to any particular grade (salary) level. Currently, these grades range from a low of one to a high of fifteen in the classified Civil Service. The grades sixteen through eighteen are also in use but these "supergrades" are allocated only by the Central Office of the Commission. Therefore, they are not of immediate concern.

Bernard H. Baum, *Decentralization of Authority in a Bureaucracy*, © 1961. pp. 89–129. Reprinted by permission of Prentice-Hall, Inc., Englewood Cliffs, New Jersey.

Since 1949 the authority for taking position classification actions, without prior approval from the Commission, has been decentralized and vested with the agencies.

In general terms, the objective of a duties classification is to lay the foundation for equitable treatment of employees by the accurate definition, orderly arrangement, and fair evaluation of positions. The "correct" classification of positions is clearly a difficult and hazardous task. To perform it well requires classification investigators and analysts who are both technically proficient and endowed with more than an average degree of social intelligence, since their opportunity to create enmity as well as disappointment is almost without bounds. Theoretically they must be so eminently fair that even disappointed employees and administrative officers will recognize their fairness. They must possess the impartiality and objectivity of the judge while collecting the evidence. In view of the applicability of the classification plan on a government-wide basis, theoretically they must have a government-wide, not an insular viewpoint. Presumably, their first loyalty is to the position classification plan and to the Commission's program and standards.

It should be noted at this point that in evaluating the agencies' implementation of this authority, including evaluation of "violation rates," that prior approval from the Commission is available. Thus, although the authority has been decentralized, it need not be assumed. This, incidently, is true for all authority delegated by the Commission to the agencies. But, obviously, the program would be self-defeating if this practice were widespread. Indeed, the converse holds true. There is relatively little requesting of prior approval on actions of any kind. The exceptions are those cases where pressure is being exerted by an agency head on a personnel officer. They are not the result of inability on the part of the personnel officer to make the necessary decision.

· · ·

Table 3.1 is a summary and analysis of 1,353 classification actions audited by the Inspection Division of the Regional Office under consideration.

It will be noted that, on the basis of Commission inspection, 16.0 percent of the actions taken by the agencies were changed. Whether this figure means that the agencies are not highly competent to do this work, or whether it means that standards are so difficult to apply that there is much room for differences of opinion, or whether it means that this is about as good or satisfactory a percentage of correct actions as can be expected by anyone, is difficult to determine. Such a determination is, in the last analysis, arbitrary.

We are not primarily concerned with this aspect of position classification under decentralized authority. However, a breakdown of this figure, that is into actions changed upward and actions changed downward, is quite revealing

TABLE 3.1

Summary and Analysis of a Midwestern Region, U.S. Civil Service Commission, Audits of Agency Position Classifications [a]

Agency	Actions Audited [b]	Actions Changed		Changes Up		Changes Down		Percent of Changes:	
		No.	Per-cent	No.	Per-cent	No.	Per-cent	Up	Down
Agriculture	108	20	18.5	10	9.3	10	9.3	50.0	50.0
Air Force	11	4	36.4	1	9.1	3	27.3	25.0	75.0
Army	395	84	21.3	9	2.3	75	19.0	10.7	89.3
Civil Service Commission	5	—	—	—	—	—	—	—	—
Commerce	17	4	23.5	1	5.9	3	17.6	25.0	75.0
Federal Civil Defense Administration . . .	37	16	43.2	1	2.7	15	40.5	6.3	93.8
Housing and Home Financing Agency . .	24	1	4.2	—	—	1	4.2	—	100.0
Justice	55	6	10.9	3	5.5	3	5.5	50.0	50.0
Navy	11	4	36.4	1	9.1	3	27.3	25.0	75.0
Railroad Retirement Board	81	6	7.4	—	—	6	7.4	—	100.0
Selective Service	6	5	83.3	—	—	5	83.3	—	100.0
Treasury	166	39	23.5	10	6.0	29	17.5	25.6	74.4
Veterans Administration	344	25	7.3	5	1.5	20	5.8	20.0	80.0
TOTAL	1,353	217	16.0	40	3.3	177	13.1	18.4	81.6

[a] Fiscal Year 1955; 2nd and 3rd Quarters Fiscal Year 1956. These are the only reports available. They are assumed to be representative.

[b] Actions Audited constitute approximately a 10 per cent sample of actions taken.

for our study. There are only these two alternatives available if an action is to be changed. That is, on the one hand, an action may be considered by Commission inspectors to be correct, in which case no change is called for. If, however, a change is called for, it must be either up or down; that is to say, the agency should have classified, according to Commission standards as interpreted by Commission inspectors, a position as being of a higher grade or of a lower grade.

The findings clearly indicate the existence of an upward pressure of classification within the agencies. The first source of pressure is the individual employee or incumbent of a position who views himself as not being paid what he is worth and what the job is worth. The "worth" of an incumbent is theoretically not a factor in position classification, as it is the position which is being classified and not the individual who holds the position. An incumbent may feel and, in fact, be underpaid for his knowledge, skills, and abilities, but this is a question of job placement rather than position classification. Pressure from incumbents is based on three considerations: first, by and large, each person views his own position as being particularly difficult and significant; second, the desire for greater monetary remuneration, and third, the desire for increased social status issuing from higher classification.

This pressure frequently is in line with the second major source of pressure for upward classification—the agency head. Upward classification is, after all, a form of "empire building." . . .

Such pressures as are illustrated here can, of course, wreck a classification system but they are, in part, counterbalanced by certain stabilizing pressures. Other interests are involved and may be broadly classified into five groups:

1. The investigatory and advisory functions of the Commission
2. The sense of professional responsibility of classification men
3. The ever-possible contigency of Congressional investigation of abuse
4. The influence of organized Civil Service unions, who do push for an *over-all* raise, but also push for strict classification free of bias
5. The tax-paying public's concern to hold allocation and pay within the strict limits of law.

Having presented a review of the pressures involved, it can clearly be seen that the classification system is characterized by an inherent conflict between the Commission and operating agencies. Under the former system of administration, the Commission was the body authorized to make and enforce the allocation. Consequently, it was the Commission that found itself in the midst of these conflicting pressures. Under decentralized authority, however, it is the agency personnel officer who is in the midst of these conflicting pressures. No law can be drafted so precisely and in so much detail as to exclude the necessity for informed judgment in allocating positions. The law presumably is the outer limit within which an informed discretion, acting on successive cases, gradually reduces discretion to a minimum. The process of allocation thus becomes one of comparison and relativity. . . .

PART B. REACTIONS TO BEING IN THE MIDDLE: ATTITUDINAL VARIATIONS ON A THEME

. . . The decentralization of authority program has created a sizable auditing problem, i.e., the exercise of adequate controls to maintain the merit system. The relationship between the rules, regulations, and policies of the merit system and actual operations becomes, ultimately, a quasi-legal question and reflects the disparity between law and actual human behavior. What appears from the sociological point of view an even more crucial question is the relationship between the internalization on the part of officials of merit system principles and the amount and degree of their authority to implement it. Statements by two inspectors in the Regional Office of the Commission we are studying serve to illustrate the significance and implications of this consideration.

The following statement was made by an inspector who had been a member of an agency's personnel staff prior to his coming to the Commission:

Several years ago I became involved in the following case when all employees at the installation were invited to voluntarily participate in the chest X-ray mobile unit health program.

One World War II veteran was discovered to have active tuberculosis which necessitated his immediate hospitalization in a state sanitarium. He was married, had two small children, and was the sole provider for the family. He had about eight years of service and was recognized as an above-average employee with favorable quality and quantity of work.

The agency head was familiar with the individual case and desired, in some way, to assist the family. It was decided that the best way would be to offer the wife employment during the hospitalization of her husband. As I recall, her typing ability was no of sufficient caliber to permit her to pass the typist test so a position was established for a clerk GS-2. Indefinite appointments were permitted at the time and her appointment was made without regard to the existing register.

While the action violated the principle of the merit system, the agency head and his personnel staff felt that the action taken was humane and justified. While the circumstances surrounding the situation are unusual, it does tend to point up the fact that in some instances the regulations serve to "handcuff" the agency head and do not provide him the opportunity common to private industry in exercising his judgment in effecting certain personnel actions or placement changes.

It is, of course, precisely in the last statement that we find the crucial element. It is exactly the agency head's judgment that was not only exercised but effectively implemented. The question involved is not one of right or wrong, good or bad, but one of how this squares with decentralization of authority. The material is presented neither in criticism nor praise, but rather to highlight the fact that organization is people, and rules are enforced and used by people. The Commission is staffed by people. The same inspector who made the statement above, while an agency personnel man, arranged that a cancer victim not be fired and added a job to cover for the work not being done by him.

Appreciating the frankness of the inspector, we followed up with the question: "Now that you are an inspector, what would you do?" Answer: "I would have to write it up." Question: "Would you?" Answer: "Yes."

The other inspector's statement related to the practices within the Commission Regional Office:

Let's face it. We don't do in this office what we tell agencies to do. Our ———— (name of position) man should be a 9 (GS-9); he's an 11. His Clerk-Steno is a 4. It would be busted to 3 on the spot in an agency audit. There are no evaluation interviews, no orientation.

That the basic issue involved here is a real one is attested to by the fact that when the author was initially employed by the Commission, it was after more than ten candidates for the position had been interviewed for it. This was possible, the rule of selecting from the top three eligibles on a single register not-withstanding, by (1) interviewing the top three eligibles on several Registers, and (2) sending names from the top of a Register out to agencies for consideration while interviewing those next down on the Register.

Our interviews with Commission personnel reflected a vague feeling of uneasiness regarding their role vis-à-vis the agencies. The uneasiness is based on the resolution of two conflicting pressures. As stated by a highly placed Commission official, "There is a tendency on our part, on the one hand, to exaggerate deviations to show the need for the Commission, and, on the other, to hold down the number to keep the work in the agencies."

Pursuing this question regarding the realism or accuracy of the written inspection reports and the extent to which they reflect actual findings, the interviewee stated, "We are probably more prone to minimize (in *written* reports) all except the most flagrant violations. After all, we have to stay in business."

We can conclude from this that inspectors' activities and reports are signif-icantly conditioned by their consideration of keeping the *status quo* of the system which, after all, is a vested interest. . . .

Some of the Commission staff members' statements about there being no alternative but to require strict adherence to the law are manifestly unrealistic since corrections are made only where errors are discovered. Presumably, if a three percent violation rate occurs in a sample, for every thirty-three cases beyond the sample there is an uncorrected error. The fact is, in this connection, that although the law is conceived of as 100 percent applicable, a three percent violation rate is considered as satisfactory according to the Chief of Regional Inspection and Classification. This, of course, is an unwritten guideline. Indeed, the Commission does not do a 100 percent audit except, according to the Inspection Chief, in "the most flagrant cases."

In conclusion, let it be noted that decentralized authority has never been revoked for reasons of undue violations; the only reasons it has been revoked have been minor recentralizations of authority for Commission administrative purposes. For example, the Commission set up a register for specific positions formerly filled directly by the agencies. . . .

It was, for example, not an agency official but a high-ranking Commission official who said:

Actually decentralization of authority should be called delegation of authority. We still have the final authority. Congress always figures delegation of authority will decrease our work, but it increases it. We don't really get enough money to implement the system. It's like a balloon—squeeze it here, but the air just shifts, the volume remains the same and the pressure (the work of Commission auditing) is added.

On the whole, this Commission official saw the decentralization of authority program as an ineffective effort to delegate work, but, at the same time, deplored the fact that it opens the door to agency machinations. . . .

Another Commission official's response was more in terms of decentralization of authority as a technique:

It reflects the inability of a small group of people to cope realistically, promptly, and efficiently with the many different and the numerous problems that field agencies of an organization, scattered over a wide area, have. It was centralized in stable times, and a loose labor market when speed was not a consideration and one could afford to err consistently in the direction of conservatism. This can't be applied in a fast-moving personnel situation, and the labor market is such that speed is required which can't be achieved in a highly centralized system. Any decentralization, of course, confronts the inevitable problem that authority becomes vested in a large number of people who represent a considerable variety of background, orientation, and working situations. In order to achieve speed and realism in operations, you court greater subjectivity.

In this official's response is caught what is probably the most accurate, most realistic view of decentralization of authority in operation. It highlights the technical considerations involved, specifically "speed" and "realism" while, at the same time, giving succinct recognition to the increased subjectivity of decisions which might be out of line with more rigid Commission standards.

Two other aspects of the meaning of decentralization of authority were brought out by Commission officials. One official pointed to the decentralization of authority program as a change in the role of the Commission within the total configuration:

Before decentralization of authority, when dealing with an agency, it was in terms of, "They want an announcement." Our function was to determine the agencies' need and make recommendations. We were an intermediate service agency. Now we just go ahead and do what is needed. Now we are more intense. Contacts become more goal-directed. There are more contacts initiated by the Commission now. Before World War II, we were just a buffer between the Washington D.C. Commission and the establishments.

This is a particularly interesting response in that it places emphasis on the subtle, but nevertheless true, fact that decentralization of authority is not purely a change in organizational structure per se, but the consequence of change in the Commission's role, involving a broader responsibility. The other aspect was one that receives a great deal of attention in the literature on the subject of decentralization of authority but was mentioned by only one Commission official and one agency personnel director. This is the human consideration of greater participation and development of individual potential under decentralized authority. . . .

To one agency personnel director, the decentralization of authority program is a series of emotionally charged problems. In response to the general question, he said:

I've got some real feelings on this—some critical. For the most part, we've got authority. We know that what the Commission gives is limited by Congress. What I object to is that while I believe we have to be subjected to some review, I feel the Commission hasn't kept pace with the agencies. The Commission sends out children to do men's work. The central personnel agency sends out fellows who obviously lack experience. The result is a situation where they're mouthing policy and recommend, but don't know why. They can't reason through.

I believe that what the Commission is trying to do is right but hasn't kept pace in terms of training its own staff. For example, in classification, we're faced with a terrific steno-typist recruiting problem. The test is beyond what private employers require. There's a consequent loss of people. On top of it, we face the classification system. We're supposed to hold the job to the true level. The Commission's Chief of Classification on the one hand said, "Be realistic. Give it (a GS-3 position) a GS-4." On the phone I said, "But it's a GS-3." So he said, "Why can't you write something into it?" I told him, "Because then your auditor will down grade it!" This is not an isolated instance.

Again, where, on the surface, decentralization gives us the authority we need in recruitment, I can't agree with the necessity for such complete coordination of recruitment. The Commission expects us to do the recruiting, but the Regional Office isn't staffed for full and sound coordination.

The personnel director is rated by the Commission as "excellent" as is the personnel administration in his agency. He represents the perceptive personnel director who, although he accepts what the Commission has decentralized as authority, still recognizes the problems inherent in the operation of such a program of decentralization. . . .

The typical expression of the personnel director who viewed the decentralization of authority program as a device for putting the work on the agencies was:

By doing the work ourselves, now we can operate faster but that's about all. The fact is, there is still a lack of real authority, for example, age limits. They are arbitrary, yet the Commission sets them. One way or the other, high or low, the agency should determine them or, the written examinations. They may or may not be appropriate, but the Commission should let the agency decide—as long as merit is retained.

These statements serve to illustrate patterns of thinking regarding the meaning of the decentralization of authority program. They represent the human variable as relevant to the formal, bureaucratic conception. Undoubtedly, the major observation that draws together much of the operating officials' thinking is that agency heads and personnel directors, favoring a wide area of control, are highly critical of the Commission's claims of decentralization. These agency officials tend to view such claims as an effort on the part of the Commission to disguise the fact that agency management has little freedom in decision-making for personnel administration. . . .

Agency officials, "en masse," list only advantages to the decentralization of authority program as compared to the old system. The disadvantages mentioned all relate to the shortcomings of the program as compared to decentralization of authority as it might ideally be.

The overshadowing advantage is speed, stated in various ways:

The main advantage is that it provides speedier service to all employees. In the old days when everything had to be documented, actions sometimes took months. It reduces paper work. I can't think of any disadvantages. It's all to the advantage of the agency.

Decentralization of authority is all on the advantage side except for some inefficiency of Commission personnel and their lack of training. Under the old system, and I'm familiar with it, it was an inefficient and cumbersome system. We really didn't have a personnel program. It was record-keeping—and "keep the rascals out."

The major advantages that the Commission people saw, other than speed, are typified by the following statements of Commission officials: "Decisions are made in full knowledge of local conditions and the local situation." "There is optimum flexibility in terms of special needs."

One Commission official answered the question regarding advantages in the following terms:

All lean toward the agencies' benefit. They know better than the Commission what they want. If they're honest, it's better all the way around. Generally speaking, agencies are honest. Of course, in certain cases in military agencies, the Commanding Officer says to the Personnel Officer, "Do it or get fired." The Commanding Officer can always work up charges.

Implicit in this response is the statement of a disadvantage of decentralization of authority from the point of view of the Commission man dedicated to the rigid upholding of the merit system, i.e., that there are certain cases where the decentralization of authority program makes possible circumvention. The same respondent went on to say:

It all goes back to the original Civil Service Act, that is, all appointments made on the basis of merit. We never had appointment authority but we did certify. That was the merit system! The fact is that the Commission is still charged with the responsibility of enforcing regulations. This makes us more and more like policemen. When things go wrong, the Commission is the "whipping boy." We have trouble getting funds. Actually, when we inspect, we're supposed to be helpful but, in the nature of things, we have to look for the wrong things.

Another Commission official cited as a disadvantage, "The greater necessity for careful, written standards and the still inevitable variety of application: loss of uniformity." The same official recognized a problem in this particular setting in that, "Decentralization is from a central agency concerned only with personnel and it sometimes becomes a problem to agencies where it is only a partial concern." What, in essence, this Commission official is saying is that decentralization of authority makes it possible for the agency officials to relegate personnel administration to such a role within the operation of the agency as the particular hierarchy of values held by the agency head dictates. This, from the

Commission point of view, limits cooperation and is thus seen as a disadvantage. The loss of uniformity represents no problem to the agencies, whereas to the Commission it may well foreshadow the cessation of a single system of personnel administration within the total Civil Service. . . .

4.

RESPONSIBILITY IN THE PUBLIC SERVICE

MICHAEL COHEN

THE PROBLEM OF DISCRETION

The need for responsibility in the public service arises in those areas where judgment or discretion must be exercised. Where the administrator's task is simple and clear-cut, we tend to speak of his *duty* or *obligation*, but where his task is open to discretion, we tend to speak of his *responsibility*. In both cases, the requirement that the administrator must be accountable for his actions is central. But in the former case, there are clear-cut rules by which he can be held accountable, while in the latter, guidelines are subjective or less clear-cut.[1]

The granting of discretion to public administrators has always been viewed with considerable ambivalence, because it can be put to divergent uses. Positively, discretion facilitates an administrative flexibility which is useful and even necessary. Negatively, it opens the door to administering policy inconsistently or shortsightedly, and even to misinterpreting or subverting it. How to avoid the dangers of discretion while not sacrificing its benefits are the twin requirements that must be satisfied before responsibility can be achieved.

APPROACHES TO THE PROBLEM

Several approaches to the problem of discretion have been taken, although none has proved entirely adequate so far. Some have been pessimistic. Herman Finer, for example, believing that the dangers of discretion far exceed any of its

---

This essay was prepared especially for this volume.

[1] J. Roland Pennock, "The Problem of Responsibility," in Carl J. Friedrich (ed.), *Responsibility* (New York: Liberal Arts Press, 1960), pp. 3–27.

benefits, argued strongly against granting any discretion to the bureaucracy.[2] He advocated, instead, that legislation be detailed enough to reduce discretion as much as possible. He would then use punishment or its threat to prevent administrators from overstepping their bounds. Others have taken a more optimistic view. Carl Friedrich, for example, believed that the loss of valuable judgment was too high a price to pay for depriving administrators of discretion.[3] He thought the answer lay in relying upon professionals, who have a body of knowledge and the evaluation of their fellows to guide them. Evaluation by the professional community, he felt, would insure good judgments while avoiding the dangers of discretion.

But most observers recognize that neither of these approaches to the problem of discretion is adequate in a world where legislatures continue to make broad and unclear grants of authority to bureaucracies, where professionals are often narrow technical specialists, and where, in any case, public employees cannot be constantly scrutinized. The question remains whether useful mechanisms for achieving administrative responsibility are possible. The major task of this essay is to look closely at the times when such mechanisms are most necessary, and to evaluate the ones we have. But this task requires a broad perspective. Accordingly, the concept of administrative responsibility will first be considered as it was used in earlier administrative theory, and will then be considered in the context of more recent theory, which has developed the useful concept of organizational control structures.

THE CONCEPT OF ADMINISTRATIVE
RESPONSIBILITY IN REFORM THEORY

The concept of administrative responsibility had a significant place in the political theory developed by the post-Civil War administrative reform movement. This theory tried to solve the problem of assuring that the bureaucracy would implement with fidelity only policies decided in the legislative process. It drew a sharp distinction between *policy-making* or legislating, and *policy-implementing* or administration. Via this distinction, the reform theory intended to make policy-making a purely popular political process, and administration a purely technical one. The concept of administrative responsibility legitimated the authority granted to the bureaucracy, just as the concept of political responsibility

---

[2] Herman Finer, "Administrative Responsibility in Democratic Government," in Francis E. Rourke (ed.), *Bureaucratic Power in National Politics* (Boston: Little, Brown & Co., Inc., 1965), pp. 176–87.

[3] Carl J. Friedrich, "Public Policy and the Nature of Administrative Responsibility," in Rourke, *op. cit.*, pp. 165–75; and, "The Dilemma of Administrative Responsibility," in Friedrich, *op. cit.*, pp. 189–202.

and theories of representation legitimated society's grants of authority to elected officials. Administrative responsibility was to be achieved through a variety of means, including legislative oversight and internalized ethical and professional values.

But this solution to the problem of achieving responsibility met conceptual and empirical difficulties, making it inadequate as either an explanation or a goal of the administrative process. Empirically, the reform theory could never grapple adequately with the fact that most legislation requires substantial administrative judgment in its implementing. Nor could it adequately deal with the realities of a growing jumble of ambiguities and inconsistencies in legislative policy, which are so easily open to diverse interpretations. Conceptually, the reform theory could not maintain the distinction between policy-making and policy-implementing as two entirely separate processes. In practice, they are densely interwoven, leading to the recognition that administrators are legitimately involved in the entire process. When these factors are taken into account, it becomes apparent that achieving administrative responsibility is a far more complex process than was earlier believed.

Earlier reform theory, then, could not provide a realistic framework for treating significant problems of administrative responsibility. An appropriate theory must take into account many more subtleties about the legislative and administrative processes than it did. It must take into account the fact that legislative grants of authority to the bureaucracy are often broader and more ambiguous than reform theory allowed; that policy-making cannot anticipate all the uncertainties and risks involved in implementation; that total surveillance and monitoring of the bureaucracy is neither possible nor wise; and that, due to the increasing use of technical experts, only a few can understand and evaluate much that the bureaucracy does.

In short, inevitable and growing administrative discretion necessarily exists. But discretion generates the fear that it will open the door to inconsistent, unwise, or shortsighted actions, even by devoted and conscientious public administrators. The solution presented by earlier theory is inadequate. Being insulated in various ways from the political process, public administrators may substitute their own wishes for what the public wants or needs. Or, because the legislature may speak unclearly or in several tongues, administrators may have difficulty interpreting its policy. Given these factors, a more adequate framework for viewing responsibility must be devised before the problem can be met.

ORGANIZATIONAL CONTROL STRUCTURES

We believe that this more adequate framework is provided by the concept of organizational control structure. This concept helps us see more clearly just where and how the opportunities for bureaucratic irresponsibility arise. It also brings into view some overlooked processes of social control.

Organizational control structures, according to Etzioni, are the distribution of means used by an organization to get the performance it needs and to check whether the quantities and qualities are in accord with specifications.[4] Looking at the federal bureaucracy with this definition in mind, it is apparent that a large and varied number of means are used. There are administrative review and oversight employed by Congressional committees;[5] interest in programs taken by individual Congressmen, along with the "casework" they do; Budget Bureau and GAO fiscal controls; Presidential interest and program coordination;[6] interest group influence; agency practices in authority relations, supervisory techniques, leadership behavior, and rule setting; punishment, reward, and incentive systems for employees; court review and citizens committee review methods; and so on. All of these means, along with others, constitute the general control structure of the government bureaucracy. Guides for achieving responsibility should be seen as a part, albeit an important one, of this whole.

How the broad control structure took on these characteristics is instructive. Primarily, like Topsy, it just growed. That is, the control structure has grown by adopting new techniques when pressures arose for correcting what a powerful enough group or interest considered a failure. New techniques have been piled on old, not always superseding them, but sometimes overshadowing them. New budgetary controls, for example, have been added, while the old continue to generate information no longer necessary.

The question arises whether codifying or rationalizing this broad control structure would erase the problem of administrative responsibility. We will leave aside whether codification is even possible, given the pluralistic nature of our political system and the incremental fashion in which it changes. Instead, we argue that codification probably would not help. The very complexity of the control structure means that some personal goals and interests of employees will continue to evade surveillance. Monitoring devices cannot be total except in a police state, after all, and personal freedom is equally important for an employee of government as for an employee of private industry. In addition, there exist ever-present possibilities of varying interpretations of policy. And, further, there is the frequent necessity for administrators to take action in situations where clear policy does not exist. Administrative discretion will always be with us, then, and some provision must be made for it.[7]

---

[4] Amitai Etzioni, *Modern Organizations* (Englewood Cliffs; N.J.: Prentice-Hall, Inc., 1964), pp. 58–59.

[5] Joseph P. Harris, *Congressional Control of Administration* (Garden City, N.Y.: Doubleday Anchor Books, 1965).

[6] Richard E. Neustadt, "Presidency and Legislation: Planning the President's Program," *American Political Science Review*, Vol. 49 (December, 1955), pp. 980–1021.

[7] Anthony Downs, *Inside Bureaucracy* (Boston: Little, Brown & Co., Inc., 1967), p. 136.

If, now, we think of administrative responsibility as helping to guide behavior and decisions when monitoring and control are difficult, if not impossible, our task is clear. The questions that need answering are, what kinds of irresponsibility are likely to arise, what criteria may be employed to guide administrators toward responsibility, and how good are the criteria?

THE CRITICAL PROBLEMS OF ADMINISTRATIVE IRRESPONSIBILITY

A survey of the field suggests there are four critical problems of administrative irresponsibility. These divide roughly into two categories: irresponsibility toward a program or agency, and irresponsibility to the public as individuals. In the first category are problems associated with responding to interest group pressures and with using professional expertise. The second category concerns problems of value and social biases of individual officials and of improper treatment of the public.

THE PROBLEM OF INTEREST GROUP PRESSURES

Let us look at the issue of responsiveness to interest group pressures, first. The question of responsibility arises because administrators are often faced with interest groups attempting to influence the bureaucracy directly without going through the political institutions, or perhaps after failing to gain demands through them. Administrators are often accused of irresponsibility when they yield to these influences.

Writers are divided on how responsive the bureaucracy should be in these cases. It is often felt that a fairly rigid wall should separate the bureaucracy from these influence attempts, although it is sometimes considered a sign of good health for a government agency to respond. The question is, are there times when the agency should respond, and, if it does, what criterion should it use to choose among the demands, which are sometimes conflicting? All the while, of course, our general political preferences support the desirability of administrative openness to popular needs and opinions.

The dilemma is a hard one to resolve in terms of moral or ethical principles because what occurs in this area can often be understood only in the framework of *realpolitik*. Compromise, negotiation, and yielding to interest group demands are often the only means open to an agency in its attempts to maintain administrative and program viability, or even sometimes a modicum of strength. For, as we have pointed out, many agencies are not administering a clear-cut, well-agreed-upon piece of legislation passed by an overwhelming majority of

Congress and backed by widespread popular support. Rather, much major legislation going through Congress is highly controversial (it would probably not be in Congress otherwise) and, when passed, thanks are often due to the adroit maneuverings of Presidential forces through the obstructions and pitfalls put out by the opposition. Congress is more like a battleground than a debating society. Passage of a major piece of legislation is the end result of a process of compromise, bargaining, log-rolling, negotiating, parliamentary maneuvering, calendar manipulation, skill in tactics and debate, influence in choosing personnel for key positions, and so on. And the battle often resumes as soon as an agency attempts to put the legislative intent into practice. Since legislation is often general at best, and ambiguous or muddled at worst, ample opportunities exist for aggrieved parties to find new battlegrounds.

In other words, the opposition always has to be reckoned with, and while it may have temporarily lain down, it is rarely dead. At least, not in the important issues of our time. Nor is any legislation secure at this point. There is always the danger that Congress will later emasculate it through the appropriations, amendment, or review processes. Top-level administrators know this and are constrained by this knowledge.

Administrators are often faced, then, with gaining acceptability for a program after legislation is passed.[8] Often, the guidelines are vague and administrators are left on their own. It is as though the President said to them: "We managed to get this through Congress, now see what you can do about gaining acceptance for it so that it can be made effective. I may not be able to come to your assistance very often, if at all, and in any case I don't have much time to devote to this any more, so you're on your own. See what you can do." The stage is now set for negotiations with legislative committees, interest groups, and constituencies in order to effectuate a policy or gain compliance. It is true that the administrator often will gain White House and/or Congressional clearance before making major interpretations or changes, but it may be on his information that the approval is given. This complicates the problem of assigning responsibility. In the final analysis, then, when dealing with interest group pressures the administrator's responsibility may be to keeping the program alive. If he does this, and at the same time maintains the major part of the program's integrity, even if he has to bargain with it at the margins, he may be discharging the only responsibility he has. If he is unable to do this, however, it may well be because the odds against him are too great, not because he is irresponsible. Responsiveness to pressures is not to be equated with irresponsibility, then, since circumstances determine how responsible it is.

One solution to this problem is Paul Appleby's insight that achieving program

---

[8] For a case study stressing this point, see Philip Selznick, *TVA and the Grass Roots* (Berkeley, Calif.: University of California Press, 1949).

or agency responsibility is a process, not a single act.[9] No single act, point of time, or judgment will tell us whether responsibility has been achieved. It is a collective process. Appleby suggests that with the widespread involvement and consultation over time of many interested, knowledgeable, and authoritative parties, the policy will be the most realistic and acceptable that can be achieved. Commitment to a program, to a job, or to values embodied in the policy will be the best clue as to how responsible any individual involved in the process is. In these cases, then, administrative responsibility is gained by several means: By choosing administrators whose values are compatible with the program they will administer. By choosing men who have known ability to operate in this realm. And by insuring that there are open and widespread consultations with all interests. When these guidelines are used, administrative responsibility comes close to being realized. When these conditions are not met, administrative responsibility is problematic.

THE PROBLEM OF PROFESSIONAL EXPERTISE

It is a commonplace that the public service hires a larger and larger percentage of professionals and technical experts as time goes on. Several problems of responsibility are associated with this trend. One arises when politicians are unable to evaluate professional and technical advice. Another arises because professionals can often only be supervised by their peers, placing them outside the usual bureaucratic controls. Both of these conditions place an extra burden of responsibility on professionals.

The problems are especially acute when a policy which affects the whole society must be adopted on the advice of a few, as in defense or international relations. But even in narrower areas, as in city planning, the problem is apparent.[10] For, the well-known biases that experts exhibit toward their own fields ("A way of seeing is always a way of not seeing.")[11] sometimes means that they fall short of a more-encompassing objectivity than their own discipline claims. Furthermore, commitment to professional values, such as the best kind of roadway to build, may conflict with political or social values, such as where it is most needed, or whom it is designed to assist. Gaining accountability among professionals, then, poses special problems.

The solutions traditionally suggested for overcoming these problems are themselves not free of defect. They include keeping the professional in a subordinate position, belief that systems of professional ethics provide considerable safe-

---

[9] Paul Appleby, *Morality and Administration* (Baton Rouge: Louisiana State University Press, 1952), pp. 104–05.

[10] Alan Altshuler, *The City Planning Process* (Ithaca; N.Y.: Cornell University Press, 1965).

[11] Kenneth Burke, *Permanence and Change* (New York: New Republic, Inc., 1935), p. 70.

guards, reliance upon self-supervision among professionals, and the advice that to be truly responsible a professional must make his decision on all the knowledge available in his field. Some consider these solutions adequate for solving much of the problem of administrative responsibility in general because so many public employees are professionals.

But we said that the solutions are themselves not problem-free. For one, as Victor Thompson so persuasively argues, technical knowledge is often compelling since no one can contradict it.[12] No matter how willing the expert is to stay "on tap" he ends up "on top." Secondly, recent empirical research on the professions suggests that systems of professional ethics, supposedly internalized during professional training, do not necessarily "take." [13] They are often superficial and unenforceable. Thirdly, relying upon professionals to supervise themselves may only succeed in changing the locus of the problem since someone must still supervise the supervisors. Besides, the mechanism itself is hardly foolproof. Professional standards often permit great latitude. Moreover, even when standards are clear, professionals have a difficult time observing each other's behavior adequately enough to make judgments.[14]

Finally, to consider the solution that the professional has achieved responsibility if he takes into account all knowledge available in his field. Carl Friedrich, in his well-known discussions of administrative responsibility, strongly favors this argument.[15] He reasons that the professional is capable of discounting the work of the obviously unqualified and of knowing what the "best" thinking in his field is. He also argues that since the professional belongs to a community of professionals, his methods and judgment will be scrutinized by the "fellowship of science."

While Friedrich makes a strong case for his view, it raises enough questions to make it a faulty guideline. For one thing, the injunction to take account of all knowledge available in a field is piously unrealistic, given the great amount of information available. For another, "the fellowship of science" is probably better thought of as "the fellowships of science," since there are schools among professionals, each one of which claims to be the bearer of the "best" thought. Which school's views are to be accepted? The quantity and quality of information each used in forming a judgment is not necessarily a good criterion. And, besides, the advice is utopian, since there is no way of knowing when all the

---

[12] Victor Thompson, *Modern Organization* (New York: Alfred A. Knopf, Inc., 1961).

[13] See, for example, Jerome Carlin, *Lawyers' Ethics* (New York: Russell Sage Foundation, 1966).

[14] See, for example, the study of control among physicians by Mary E. Goss, "Influence and Authority among Physicians in an Out-Patient Clinic," *American Sociological Review*, Vol. 26 (1961), pp. 39–50.

[15] Carl J. Friedrich, "Public Policy and the Nature of Administrative Responsibility," *op. cit.;* and, "The Dilemma of Administrative Responsibility." *op. cit.*

knowledge possibilities have been exhausted. It is not always even apparent what constitutes all the knowledge in a field.

Other, and stronger objections to Friedrich's argument have been raised by Herman Finer.[16] In one sense, Finer's objections apply to all the solutions to the problem of responsibility advanced so far. For Finer rejects all non-legal means of bureaucratic control. Unlike Friedrich, he does not accept the inevitability of administrative discretion, but argues that it results from a faulty legislative process which oversteps its bounds when it delegates discretion to the bureaucracy. Finer advises that we avoid the dangers of administrative discretion by improving the legislative process. He argues that otherwise administrators will substitute their own wishes for public wants. He further argues that there is no clearer nor more certain guide to public policy-making than what the public wants, and if the public is unclear or divided, then the government should wait until a consensus emerges before acting. Under no circumstances should the bureaucracy act without a very clear mandate. Any abuse of administrative authority, according to Finer, should be handled by law courts, and by punishing and discharging employees.

As we argued earlier in this essay, it is clear that much of the drift of events has gone contrary to Finer's argument. Since, in fact, our legislative process continues to grant wide latitude to the bureaucracy, standards to hold it accountable must be developed.

Turning to a defense of professionals, it should be mentioned that some of the problems associated with using their advice are not their fault, but stem from a too sanguine belief in the validity and availability of technical information to solve problems. Often, the fault of irresponsible advice giving is not the professional's, but society's (or its political representatives) who exaggerate the availability of knowledge for their own purposes, and who neglect the qualifications which often accompany it.

Some of the problems of overcoming the irresponsibility of experts can be met by accepting their advice more tentatively, by implementing it with less than total commitment, and by reviewing the results more frequently and regularly. In other words, knowledge has to be tested and "debugged" in all new situations. If our society and its political decision-makers were more cognizant of this fact, the knowledge-purveyors might not seem so irresponsible.

THE PROBLEM OF BIASED PUBLIC OFFICIALS

Now, let us turn to the category of problems associated with responsibility to the public as individuals. Perhaps the major problem is caused by the social

---

[16] Herman Finer, *op. cit.*

and value biases of public employees. Such biases lead to distorting public policy, whether consciously or not. This is the familiar problem of the white police officer who treats Negroes differently than whites, or the middle-class public welfare worker who is hostile toward lower-class clients.

The best remedy for this problem has usually been prevention, that is, screening out those whose values do not coincide with the values of the program they will need to administer. This solution is not fool-proof, however. Prospective employees are often not aware of their true feelings, or they may mask them. Examiners don't always have the observational capacity to make such judgments reliably. And occupations which have a hard time recruiting often must hire people without inquiring too deeply into their beliefs, values, and motives.

Sometimes, the "keepers" of the policy are as much to blame for distorting it as their subordinates are. Despite the official pronouncements of agencies, their administrators may sometimes hold differing views. Employees often learn in these cases that they are expected to abide, not by the official, but by the unofficial, norms, which are more likely to bring them rewards. As an example, public welfare agencies, despite their official norms of service, have unofficial and contradictory norms of keeping caseloads low. Employees know this, and learn that they will be rewarded not for how well they service clients, but for how many clients they can fend off. In this case—and no doubt in many others like it—the irresponsibility has its roots in society's irresponsibility, and it is there that the blame ultimately lies.

THE PROBLEM OF
IMPROPER TREATMENT OF THE PUBLIC

Finally, let us look at the problem of improper treatment of the public. That is, those times when public employees abuse or show favoritism toward the public. This area is hard to analyze, and complaints may always be heard. For, it is difficult to verify what happened during unobserved encounters, and the way we label much behavior depends upon our perceptions and judgment. What one person considers neutral, business-like behavior, another may consider cold and brusque. Some people are annoyed by behavior of which others may not be aware. The same person may take offense at a type of behavior one time, and not be aware of the same behavior another time. There may be no absolute solutions to these problems.

Largely, we are talking about the huge range of daily encounters where individuals with contradictory values must inevitably rub shoulders. Strangely, some of the very ways we have of making these contacts efficient may also produce friction. For, it is useful in such fleeting contacts to treat people tangentially or stereotypically, yet in so doing we overlook differences between them, perhaps unjustly. The public employee may not always be at fault. The person on either side of the relationship may be guilty of this. Public employees, furthermore, are often unenviably the object of displaced hostilities meant for a program, another public figure, or the government itself. As officials, they may become objects of generalized hostility toward authority. They may be abused as much as they abuse.

Behavior problems in this realm are not so different from those that occur ordinarily, and perhaps are no more amenable to control.[17] Norms of politeness are the most general socially developed ways we have of avoiding and treating such difficulties. Official role behavior stresses these norms, along with the related ones of neutrality and impersonality, as further ways of avoiding favoritism or abuse in direct dealings.

Official forms may not always govern, however, so institutional mechanisms have appeared to protect the public. These include various review and appeal boards, and the regular legal system. The federal government has recently begun opening centers where complaints about service may be taken, some local governments have installed *ombudsmen*, and elected officials have traditionally investigated their constituents' complaints about the bureaucracy.

CONCLUSION

This turn of the discussion to institutional and legal mechanisms ends our survey of administrative responsibility, reminding us that guidelines for the use of discretion are never a full answer to problems of control. They only play a part. Some, like Herman Finer, question whether they add anything, maintaining that responsibility is achieved only through threat of punishment and legal action. But reality instructs that we try to do more. The dilemma remains, then, although it is well to remember that the control structure of the bureaucracy is inevitably an interweaving of many strands, among which administrative responsibility, however defined, is only one.

---

[17] Walter Gellhorn, *When Americans Complain* (Cambridge, Mass.: Harvard University Press, 1966), p. 5.

5.

THE PERSONNEL POLICY-MAKING SYSTEM

MICHAEL COHEN

Federal civilian personnel policies are shaped by many influences, including the institutions through which they pass on their way to becoming established. This essay attempts to increase understanding of these policies by looking at some of these institutions and their interrelationships. First, it sketches the way government policy-making institutions are interrelated politically. Then, it applies this sketch to the case of federal personnel policies. It is important to note also some things this essay does not do. No attempt is made to assess the relative amount of influence the political process has on the final policies, compared, for example, with values, cognitions or other factors. Nor does the essay deal with all parts of the process. Rather, it offers one way of analyzing personnel policy-making in order to single out one class of important events. Furthermore, it is more concerned with analyzing the process by which policies are made than with the substance of the policies themselves. Information for the study comes from both the literature and from interviews. The essay is limited to civilian personnel policy-making in the federal government, and to those institutions about which we have most information.

Policy-making has been studied extensively before this, of course. Several conclusions are available to help as we proceed. First, the institutional networks through which policies pass can fruitfully be viewed as political processes. This means that the policies often generate divergent interests and opinions which must be adjusted in order for agreement to be reached. For two reasons other ways of proceeding are usually closed. One is that the interests and opinions are usually backed by independent sources of power, including institutions, experts, and allies. The other is that all the interests and opinions may have some claim to legitimacy. Consequently, reaching agreement depends upon mutually adjusting the differences by such means as negotiating compromises and bargains, which is the essence of the political process.[1]

Second, one cannot properly speak of policy-making in the singular, as though all policies were alike. They are not. A useful distinction is between policies which initiate new programs and those which revise existing ones. Areas

---

This essay was prepared especially for this volume.

[1] Cf., Charles E. Lindblom, *The Intelligence of Democracy* (New York: The Free Press, 1965), pp. 87–101.

in which policies and procedures have long been established may be called, in Anthony Downs' phrase, "policy dense," in contrast to areas of newly defined public concern where established policies, interests, and expectations are absent.[2] In the latter areas of public concern, policies must be initiated in the true sense. In policy-dense areas, by contrast, existing policies and procedures usually are subject to revision, amendment, and correction. That is, there is a base from which to work. Personnel, along with other policy areas, exhibits both kinds of policy-making.

This distinction also helps remove some of the conundrum-like quality from the question, where do policies come from? In policy-dense areas, they often derive from what is already there. Their revision or replacement, furthermore, is likely to be an outgrowth of activities internal to the process itself. Several of these may be specified. First, the people who daily administer policies are likely to consider and suggest revisions. Second, revisions may be proposals which were defeated earlier, only to be reintroduced at opportune times. Third, policy-dense areas include specialized roles or sub-units designed to search out, formulate, and suggest both policy revisions and innovations. Examples include planning groups or policy-coordinating committees. These specialized units are joined in a network of consultation, both among themselves and with other units in their environment.[3] In sum, in a policy-dense area, policy-making is an ongoing process where the ground was broken long ago, and where processes for searching out and proposing innovations and revisions are well developed and institutionalized.

Now, to turn attention to personnel policy-making specifically. The general framework developed for the budgetary process, as described below, offers a tool for sorting out events in the personnel policy-making system in order to give shape to them. The use of this framework is, of course, open to the criticism that events may have been chosen or modified to fit into it. Despite that possibility, it seems to me that *some* order must be brought to these events besides simple chronology in order to choose the significant political ones and treat them systematically. The framework chosen seems the most suitable. The description of the budgetary process is meant to typify that process only, and thus, of course, it neglects minor variations and exceptions.[4]

Briefly, in the budgetary process all the important units of government involved develop characteristic strategies for dealing with each other which both serve their own interests and allow accommodations to be worked out

---

[2] Anthony Downs, *Inside Bureaucracy* (Boston: Little, Brown & Co., 1967), p. 220.

[3] This is not to say that such networks are always effective, or even important, sources of new information; but they exist.

[4] The following description of the budgetary process comes from Aaron Wildavsky, "Toward a Radical Incrementalism," in Alfred de Grazia (ed.), *Congress: The First Branch of Government* (Garden City, N.Y.: Doubleday Anchor Books, 1967), pp. 111–53.

among them. Consider the agencies and departments first. Because they are under constant pressure to develop new programs and enlarge old ones, agencies characteristically escalate their budget requests each year. The Budget Bureau, which is charged with helping the President realize his goals, thus receives greater competing demands from agencies than can be met. In the interests of setting priorities and balancing requests with potentially available funds, it characteristically responds to these competing demands by cutting agency requests. The House Appropriations Subcommittees, to which the budget initially goes in Congress, reconcile their perceived dual roles as "guardians of the Treasury" and "representatives of constituency interests" by also cutting budget requests, but not so much that amounts will not be greater than the previous year's. Thus, they try to satisfy some demands, and at the same time make a record for saving money. Finally, the Senate Appropriations Subcommittees, which take up the budget after the House Subcommittees, act as appeal boards before which agencies can protest the cuts made earlier. The Senate Subcommittees restore the cuts when they feel it is justified to do so.

The above description suggests that organizations participating in a common process develop characteristic, if sometimes conflicting, stances. They become familiar with each other's stances over time and these stances become sets of expectations, or roles. Finally, once members of the involved organizations can count upon each other to behave in given ways, they each develop strategies for maximizing their interests which take these probable responses into account. This has the further consequence of reducing conflict and fostering cooperation among the participants, since they know with some probability what they can achieve. In short, a system of norms develops which governs the behavior of the participants.

In the personnel policy-making process we will analyze the characteristic roles and relationships of the organizations about which we have most information: the U.S. Civil Service Commission, the Budget Bureau, and the House and Senate Post Office and Civil Service Committees. Other organizations which may also be important participants, such as operating agencies, will not be considered here.

Let us begin with the U.S. Civil Service Commission (CSC). The CSC acts as a primary formulator, advocate, and promoter of civilian personnel policies. It takes the lead in proposing policies because it receives information, pressures and feedback which keep it primed for discharging that responsibility.[5] It has a policy review and development division which continuously evaluates extant policy. Its 80 field inspectors are on the watch for new developments or needed changes. It sponsors an elaborate committee of federal personnel officers with

---

[5] Cf., Richard E. Neustadt, "Presidency and Legislation: The Growth of Central Clearance," *American Political Science Review*, Vol. 48, No. 3 (September, 1954), pp. 641–71.

secretariat, called the Interagency Advisory Group, who meet regularly to study policies, consult with the CSC staff, and suggest changes. It receives suggestions from agencies either directly or indirectly through the Interagency Advisory Group. It maintains a consultation network with employee unions and veterans' groups. Good government and professional personnel organizations keep it abreast of thought. When the President, congressional committees, and members of Congress have policy preferences, these are made known. As a CSC employee put it: "It's hard to see how anything could escape notice now." In sum, the CSC has developed an extensive network which searches out and receives information, processing it into policy proposals and revisions. This activity thrusts it into the role of advocate of policy change and initiation.

The above discussion does not intend to suggest that the CSC is the only initiator of new policies or policy revisions in the system. Rather, this is a characteristic role for it. Some of the other sources of policy proposals include the President, congressional committees, and special task forces and studies, held at the instigation of either the President or Congress. For example, the House Post Office and Civil Service Committee initiated a full-scale study of position classification on its own when it discovered a number of problems associated with it. Both Presidents Kennedy and Johnson frequently appointed task forces to investigate matters of interest to them. The President's authority in matters of pay, retirement, and fringe benefits means that the President must take the initiative in these areas.

Returning to the CSC, it has also become the advocate for personnel policies which stress the development of employee growth and commitment, as opposed to policies which stress the regulation and protection of employees. For example, the CSC increasingly emphasizes training programs and enlarged career opportunities for federal employees. It is also increasingly interested in personnel development.[6] Thus, it advocates using the procedures for hiring, rewarding, and firing employees to promote a committed work force, not just a tenured one.

But developmental personnel policies are not always popular with other participants in the process who may still prefer the more traditional and minimal personnel programs. So the CSC has developed strategies for dealing with these opponents. Thus, for example, if personnel policies are to be useful developmental tools, they must be flexible. To achieve this goal, the CSC prefers general authorizations from Congress, hoping to prevent policies from becoming "embalmed" in legislation. It also tries to make do with existing authority or with Presidential Executive Orders wherever possible. It may consult with the Budget Bureau in these cases. Characteristically, then, the CSC searches through

---

[6] Herman M. Somers, "The President, the Congress, and the Federal Government Service," in The American Assembly, *The Federal Government Service* (2nd ed.; Englewood Cliffs, N.J.: Prentice-Hall, Inc., 1965), p. 92.

existing legislation for authority on which to base policy changes and, when no such authority is available, it seeks non-detailed legislation.

These strategies are realistic from the CSC's standpoint for several reasons. One is the legislative process itself, which is lengthy, difficult, and contains unforeseen complications. The CSC tries to avoid becoming embroiled in it.[7] For the same reason, once policies are established by legislation, the process of changing them is equally complex. In addition, the legislative process is often sympathetic to the CSC's adversaries, such as veterans' associations and unions, another reason for avoiding it. These adversaries and others frequently oppose developmental personnel administration, non-detailed legislation, or spending money.

The CSC has other strategies for heading off its opposition. CSC chairmen, in company with other top bureaucrats, are partly chosen and evaluated, in fact, for their ability to use these strategies. One strategy is good timing. For example, not pushing for a program when key individuals are known to be opposed, avoiding not only outright defeat but loss of goodwill. One CSC chairman, for example, referring to legislation he decided not to seek, said he "would not blunt [his] sword on that one." Another strategy counsels consultation with interested parties and possible opponents in advance. The CSC musters support this way, and flushes out opposition early so that hopefully it can be appeased before it does damage. In another strategy, the CSC conducts studies and conferences to provide information for backing up policy requests, the better to persuade reluctant congressmen. For example, it took the CSC ten years to persuade the House Government Operations Committee to report legislation allowing agencies to pay certain travel costs of some employees who were transferred. The persuading artillery was a study showing that employees lost money upon transfer. Another strategy of the CSC is to provide useful services to the administrations for which it receives Presidential support. As example of this, the CSC played a role in aiding the transition from Eisenhower's administration to Kennedy's. And under the Johnson administration, the CSC has taken on such jobs as responsibility for monitoring voting rights violations. Finally, especially since 1964, the CSC has provided a variety of training and development programs for federal agencies that have been well-received. This goodwill provides a source of support when the CSC needs it. These strategies show that the CSC is not entirely defenseless against opposition.

The part played by individuals and by personal relationships in establishing the CSC's stance and in affecting its strategies is difficult to assess. So far, individuals as factors in the process have been ignored. This essay does not

---

[7] Cf., Roger Hilsman, "Congressional-Executive Relations and the Foreign Policy Process," in Andrew Scott and Raymond Dawson (eds.), *Readings in the Making of American Foreign Policy* (New York: The Macmillan Co., 1965), p. 201.

imply, however, that it is irrelevant to know who occupies positions in the organizations for understanding the actions they take, at least in the short run. We have argued, to be sure, that organizations develop characteristic stances and roles because of their assigned tasks. But individuals, their roles, and their interrelationships are also significant if one wishes to understand policy-making.

We do not know much about how individuals and personal relations influence the making of personnel policy. But we can make a start. We will concentrate upon the CSC, leaving discussion of other individuals to later parts of the essay.

The chairman of the CSC is certainly the most important individual in the organization, occupying as he does a position of greater authority and discretion than anyone else. Although there are two other commissioners, the chairman's role has been strengthened to the degree that he is now *the* active commissioner who manages the organization and sets its tone. Other commissioners make recommendations as to policy changes and innovations and provide review of CSC operations.

A chairman can influence the role and success of the CSC by the vigor with which he formulates and pursues goals. In one observer's opinion, at least, increased activity in personnel policy-making in recent years is partly due to the current chairman's vigor in promoting policies. In addition, a chairman is also in the position of being able to promote policies by building alliances and developing support for his organization on a personal basis with other participants in the process.

Of late, particularly, CSC chairmen have developed close relations with the President. A chairman is a Presidential appointee, of course, so there is likely to be a basic alliance between them. But there may be opportunities to cultivate the alliance further. For example, he may be asked to take on the task of recruiting for policy-making posts, as several have.

To summarize the CSC's role in the policy-making process, it is compounded of institutional, task, and personal factors. It acts as a primary formulator of policy innovations and revisions in the process, befitting its place in the Executive Branch. It has developed a widespread apparatus for gathering and screening information to facilitate this task. Moreover, the CSC reflects a general trend away from viewing personnel policies as merely regulatory. Since these policies are increasingly seen as useful administrative tools for aiding the management and development of employees, however, this brings the CSC into conflict with those participants (notably in Congress) which adhere to the regulatory view, and those (notably employee unions) which want policies spelled out in great detail in the law to protect employees. If it is to use personnel policies to promote the development and commitment of employees, the CSC believes that it must have flexible policies. This leads it to prefer non-detailed legislation. One way of achieving its ends is to avoid the legislative process when it can. This is understandable. CSC adversaries have influence in the legislative area, and negotiating through the legislative process is difficult and its outcome is unpredictable. The CSC has several other strategies it can use to maximize its interests. These include consultation with other participants, and the informal personal alliances which CSC chairmen establish.

Next, let us turn to an analysis of the Budget Bureau's role in the process of making personnel policies. As the agency with primary responsibility for seeing that the President's interests are respected, the Budget Bureau exerts significant influence. Its tasks of coordinating the President's legislative program and of preparing his budget give it power in determining policy outcomes. It is the needle's eye through which the departments' and agencies' camels must pass to gain Presidential backing. To have these magic words, "in accord with the program of the President," granted by the Budget Bureau to an agency proposal provides an often-useful entrée into Congress.

From the CSC standpoint the Budget Bureau is well worth cultivating. Like most agencies, CSC frequently consults with the Budget Bureau to insure that any differences over policies will be worked out early enough to avoid conflict later. The Bureau is valuable for helping to muster Presidential support for CSC. Since both their jurisdictions cut across agency lines, the Bureau can be valuable for helping to spread the CSC's viewpoint, and vice versa. In all, the Bureau can be and is a useful ally of the CSC.

This alliance may be a reflection of the set of personal relationships in which the Bureau is enmeshed. A recent assistant to the Director is a former chairman of the CSC, and has been personnel coordinator for the State Department. Some Bureau employees formerly worked for the CSC. Contemporary CSC chairmen have enjoyed close relations with top Bureau personnel. Top personnel of both the Bureau and the CSC have enjoyed close relations with Congress. In short, as we have seen elsewhere, cooperativeness in the policy process is facilitated by an informal network of interpersonal relations in which the Bureau participates.

The Budget Bureau is generally allied with the CSC in the policy-making process, in sum, although it exercises its authority to curb spending. Proposals are cleared in advance with the Bureau or written with the Bureau's help to insure its approval. This cooperation is facilitated by an underlying personal network which joins the Bureau to other participants in the process.

Now, let us turn our attention to an analysis of the role Congress plays in the process of making personnel policies. While over-all policy direction tends to come from the Presidency and the bureaucracy, Congress actively influences the process.[8] It can support, modify, delay, or defeat Executive branch proposals; it can bargain with interests independently of the President. In short, Congress is a power to be reckoned with in setting personnel policies.

---

[8] Neustadt, *op. cit.*

Congressional outcomes result from complex factors. Some overarch the entire legislative process, such as the values which prevail in Congress and the moods which periodically sweep through it. Other factors are narrower, such as the relationships centered in the committees Congress has developed to provide specialization and continuity. We shall look at both kinds of factors.

First, consider the committees most closely connected with civilian personnel policy-making. The important ones are the Committees on Post Office and Civil Service, followed by those on Appropriations, and then Government Operations. The Post Office and Civil Service Committees, first, are critically important for several reasons. Most personnel legislation is referred to them for consideration, and they oversee CSC operations, "their agency," as Committee staff members refer to it. The House Committee exceeds its Senate counterpart in importance, as reflected in its heavier workload and the far larger size of the House Committee's professional staff. Several factors account for the greater importance of the House Committee. The Executive introduces most of its legislative proposals through it; the House Committee originates much legislation on its own, the most important being federal employees' pay acts; and House members, not being on other Committees as Senators are, can give more time to it.

While these Committees are important for personnel policy-making, they are not sought-after assignments among congressmen. Studies show that they suffer much higher turnover than most committees, and their openings are hard to fill except with freshmen congressmen, who are given no choice.[9] Personnel committee assignments are not sought after for several reasons. First, their work is considered relatively less important than the subject-matter areas assigned to other committees. Thus, they offer congressmen little opportunity to make their mark on the Hill, or to gain visibility among their constituents. Second, the legislation they recommend, according to House Committee staff, can make enemies without the compensation of satisfying large constituency groups. For example, federal employees' pay increases voted by the Committees are never as high as employees and their unions demand, so that even the handful of congressmen who count a large number of federal employees among their constituents are in danger of losing that support.

The Committees' unpopularity and high turnover may affect their policy-making, but there are compensating factors.[10] For one, while rank-and-file members may be inexperienced, Committee chairmen and ranking members have seniority and congressional experience. For another, at least the House Com-

[9] Data from Warren E. Miller, as cited by Donald G. Tacheron and Morris K. Udall, *The Job of the Congressman* (Indianapolis, Ind.: The Bobbs-Merrill Co., Inc., 1966), p. 153.
[10] The view that these committees have lowered competence and effectiveness is taken by Kenneth Kofmehl, *Professional Staffs of Congress* (West Lafayette, Ind.: Purdue University Press, 1962), p. 21.

mittee currently has a sub-committee for each Democratic member to head, allowing these men more responsibility and permitting them to become knowledgeable sooner than usual. Furthermore, information and expertise pour into the Committees from their own professional staffs, the research they conduct, the CSC, and other sources. Even the high transfer rate of members has its value, since it gives the Committees allies elsewhere in Congress. On balance, then, the Committees' low ranking may not mean poor performance.

Several factors influence the Committees' actions significantly. They include Congress' prevailing values about personnel administration, and the relationships established with other members of the policy-making process. Let us look at the values first.

Since the Pendleton Act established a rudimentary merit system, most of Congress' personnel legislation has emphasized control, regulation, and protection of federal employees, tempered by occasional flirtations with spoils. These values long stimulated civil service reform, but their hold has loosened. Prodded by the CSC and others, developmental personnel administration is gradually gaining ground, although many congressmen are still suspicious of it. The legislative history behind the Government Employees' Training Act of 1958 is an instructive example.[11] Federal agencies which first sought funds for training were opposed by the Comptroller-General and Congress on the ground that good recruitment pre-supposed trained people. Until World War II, agencies either neglected training altogether or could only wrest approval from the Comptroller to train an occasional employee, so strong was Congressional opposition. But with the need for trained personnel during the War, Congress relented enough in 1942 to establish a Training Division. However, the Division could only advise agencies on training programs. The still-strong opposition to any training at all was exemplified by the statement of Congressman Wigglesworth, a member of the Appropriations Committee, in 1943 that, "the real way to get at the root of the trouble [is] to appoint competent people in the first place. . . . Why should we set up another brand new agency to teach the Civil Service Commission how to teach the teachers at various agencies how to teach the employees? You can carry that idea on almost indefinitely." [12] Finally, in the late 1950's, a combination of the Executive branch's salesmanship and growing demands for scientific and technical training in agencies resulted in the first major breach, the Training Act of 1958. But even this Act stressed training for efficiency and economy, not as the CSC hoped, for development. CSC, however, has been instrumental in obtaining a great deal of congressional

---

[11] The following example is summarized from Arthur D. Kallen, "Training in the Federal Service—170 Years to Accept," *Public Administration Review*, Vol. 19, No. 4 (Winter, 1959), pp. 36–46.

[12] Quoted by Kallen, *op. cit.*, p. 42.

support for many uses of the Training Act authority which cannot be automatically measured in terms of dollar savings—the usual connotation of the words "efficiency and economy." Today, there is relatively little congressional criticism of operations under the Government Employees' Training Act.

Now, for a description of the second set of factors influencing the Committees' actions, their relations with other participants in the policy-making process. This description will relate mainly to the House Committee, which has been studied more thoroughly.

Befitting its complexity, the House Committee sustains manifold relationships with other organizations. Its relations with the CSC and the Budget Bureau have been cooperative, at least in recent years, while its relations with federal employees' unions have been somewhat cooler. Its relations with other congressional committees have been subject to both cooperation and conflict.

Consider the Committee's relations with the CSC and Budget Bureau first. Legislation which the Committee considers is frequently written by its staff in collaboration with these two agencies. In the process, differences are accommodated and conflict is reduced. Potential congressional opposition can be taken into account when drafting the bill. If the Committee is divided in any way, the bill can be made acceptable to both sides. Stalemate is often avoided since all participants make some gains. Despite such arrangements, which function to integrate the policy-making system, it may take as much as ten years for a major, new proposal to become law. Powerful sponsors can accelerate the process, however. For example, Marion Folsom, an undersecretary in HEW in the first Eisenhower administration, was shocked by the lack of group life insurance for federal employees. He pushed the program through Congress in six months. But such examples are rare. The process of persuading congressmen that change is needed is usually long and tedious. So is the process of persuading them to vote money for new programs. Cooperation in drafting bills integrates legislative and executive; it does not guarantee fast results.[13]

Not all is cooperation between the Committees and the CSC, of course, and not all differences are resolved to everyone's satisfaction. One notable example is the continuing contention over supergrade allocations. The supergrades are the top scientific, technical, and administrative posts short of cabinet level. They can only be created in agencies by acts of Congress, although the Committees have granted many exceptions to this rule over the years. The Committees wish to continue their control over the remaining positions to use them as bargaining counters with agencies, and to prevent the CSC's power from increasing. The

[13] For a similar view of coordination, see Ralph K. Huitt, "Congressional Organization and Operations in the Field of Money and Credit," in William Fellner, *et al.* (eds.), *Fiscal and Debt Management Policies* (Englewood Cliffs, N.J.: Prentice-Hall, Inc., 1963), p. 405; and G. Russell Pipe, "Congressional Liaison," *Public Administration Review*, Vol. 26, No. 1 (March, 1966), p. 17.

CSC, however, would like to have flexibility to create and allocate these positions as needed. So far, the Committees have refused to give up control over about one-fourth of these positions, although the CSC keeps trying to persuade them to do so.

Relations between the Committees and federal employees' unions are subject to more coolness than those we have just described. The unions undoubtedly are the most important and strongest non-governmental organizations involved in the personnel policy-making process, participating via their relationship with Congress. Two reasons account for this closeness. First, while unions are interested in all policy proposals which affect their membership, they have traditionally been interested in none so much as pay increases, and it is Congress which grants those, at least for white collar employees. Second, one hope unions have of winning their controversies with the CSC is to get Congress to legislate their views into existence. Congress, then, is the natural object of pressure from the unions.

Let us look briefly at these two union interests, wages and facilitating legislation. Until recent years salary negotiations were begun by the unions, for example, the National Association of Letter Carriers with a large membership, which proposed increases to the Committees. Increases were generally higher than Congress and the Executive branch were willing to grant. Thus began a process of negotiation among the unions, the Committees, and the Executive to work out a compromise. During the bargaining, the unions brought pressure to bear on as many sensitive spots as they could. Thus they might send delegations of letter carriers to pressure vulnerable congressmen. According to participants, the usual solution had been to set the increase somewhere between union demands and the government's proposals.

This particular relationship has been undergoing change, however, as a result of the salary comparability principle contained in the 1962 Salary Reform Act. In that Act, Congress upon proposal by the Executive, adopted the policy that federal salaries should be comparable with salaries in private enterprise for the same levels of work, and the Act gave to the Executive the initiative in proposing the steps to reach and maintain comparability. While the unions still make their bids to the Committees, they do so only after they have been consulted by the Bureau and the CSC about annual surveys (compiled by the Bureau of Labor Statistics) of the prevailing levels of salary in private enterprise for positions comparable to those in the Federal government. Once comparability is reached, which the 1967 salary law prescribes for July 1, 1969, there will probably be far less controversy between and among the unions, the Executive Branch, and the Committees.

One traditionally complicating factor in pay negotiations has been Congress' unwillingness to let the bureaucracy's salaries rise above its own.[14] The result of this has been to depress salaries at the upper levels of the public service, which complicates recruiting for these posts.[15] One consequence has been the development of public-private organizations, such as the RAND Corporation, with which the government contracts for research. These organizations can set their own salary scales to attract people to do work for the government who otherwise would not.

Disagreements between the unions and CSC lead the unions to attempt persuading Congress to legislate their views. The unions tend to seek more liberal benefits and more closely protected working conditions than the CSC considers wise for good management practice. In a recent case, for example, the unions tried to get Congress to approve a bill making it mandatory for employees to be sent home at the first warning of a hurricane. The unions became interested because a recent experience suggested inadequacies in protection for employees during hurricanes in Florida. The CSC is opposed to such legislation, since it is seen as decreasing management flexibility during crises. So it has kept the bill bottled up in Committee by showing congressmen they were already handling the matter, and in a manner better than the bill proposes.

The Post Office and Civil Service Committees, in summary, are the congressional committees most involved in civilian personnel policy-making. They write much legislation in cooperation with the CSC and Budget Bureau, as a way of accommodating differences, if not necessarily reflecting identity of interest. For the Committees do have opinions and interests which conflict with Executive agencies. These differences reflect both outside pressures and values held by congressmen. In the former case, when the CSC's views are contrary to their own, unions attempt to protect their position and legislate their own views instead by pressuring Congress. In the latter case, the CSC sometimes finds itself at odds with the views of personnel administration held by congressmen. For a number of congressmen still reflect a policeman's view of personnel administration, while the CSC reflects the views of developmental personnel administration. In all, these organizations appear to have developed a *modus vivendi* which prevents policy-making from becoming overly disruptive. In the event, who is the winner and who the loser is hard to tell, if indeed such a clearcut distinction is possible at all.

Let us turn next to an analysis of the Appropriations Committees. The effect of their influence on personnel policies via the budget is unknown since data are lacking on how their budgets are treated. However, information is available

---

[14] *Congressional Quarterly Almanac,* 1965 (Washington, D.C.: Congressional Quarterly, Inc., 1966), p. 653.
[15] Marver Bernstein, *The Job of the Federal Executive* (Washington, D.C.: The Brookings Institution, 1958).

on a second set of influences which the Appropriations Committees exert on personnel policy.

These influences occur outside the regular process of personnel policy-making, where the participants have learned what to expect from each other and have adjusted accordingly. For these are the times when the Committees regulate government spending and staffing, arbitrarily from the CSC's viewpoint, by placing limitations on personnel, in effect making policy by doing so. Such committee action is most likely during one of Congress' periodic economy drives, or "mood sweeps." But they may also occur when congressmen take exception to certain kinds of staffing, or to the activities of a particular agency.

The Appropriations Committees have two ways of implementing their will in these cases. One is by striking or reducing items for personnel from agency budgets. Joseph Harris considers this to be Congress' most effective control of staffing.[16] The other way is more colorful, involving riders to appropriations bills which limit the numbers or kind of personnel that may be hired, or which fix the status of certain employees. Several famous examples may be cited, most of them products of Congress' post-World War II economizing efforts. One was the Jensen Rider which placed limits on filling vacancies, thus reducing staff size. Another was the Whitten Amendment which also placed limits on new appointments. A similar limitation on filling vacancies was contained in the 1968 tax bill. Under it, as a general rule, agencies may fill only three out of four vacancies in permanent, full-time positions until government employment is reduced to the level of June 30, 1966. Exceptions to this have already been enacted, as, for example, in the Post Office Department, but the principle remains.

Riders which have been used to prevent agencies or the CSC from carrying out certain functions include the Byrd Rider which curtailed the government's publicity efforts by cutting the size of publicity staffs throughout the federal service by 25 percent for two years. Similarly, an appropriations rider in 1960 prohibited the CSC from using funds to establish a Career Executive Board, something it had hoped to do. In this case, the Appropriations Committees were acting at the request of the House Post Office and Civil Service Committees, which opposed the Career Executive Board but could not prevent it, in the House.[17]

The McKellar Rider, first attached to the CSC's appropriations bill in 1944, is an example of one which limits some employees' status. It prohibits using funds to pay a Board of Legal Examiners, which means that the CSC cannot give competitive examinations to lawyers. As a result all lawyers are in the excepted service, curtailing their job transferability.

---

[16] Joseph Harris, *Congressional Control of Administration* (Garden City, N.Y.: Doubleday Anchor Books, 1965), p. 222.
[17] Harris, *op. cit.*, p. 206.

Conflicts occasionally crop up between the Post Office and Civil Service Committees and the Appropriations Committees because of their cross-cutting jurisdictions. Each may see the other as encroaching on its territory, or the Appropriations Committees may fail to grant sufficient funds for programs already enacted. But these conflicts are unusual. As Fenno reports, the two sets of committees frequently negotiate their differences informally.[18]

In summary, the Appropriations Committees become involved in personnel policy-making not to control the direction that policy is taking, but as a side effect of the appropriations process itself. For, one good way these Committees have of restricting budgets is by placing limits on funds spent for personnel. They can also on occasion hinder certain activities of the administration by prohibiting funds for staffing them. From the standpoint of other participants in the process, these Committees act in unexpected and arbitrary ways, disregarding established practices. But this is probably because their occasional involvement in personnel policy is only incidental to their primary involvement, which is the budgetary process.

Finally, let us look briefly at the Government Operations Committees. They too only occasionally participate in making personnel policy, but this is because their personnel jurisdiction is limited to questions of travel expenses for federal employees. But, as we saw earlier, this has been a policy area of concern in recent years, bringing these Committees into the process. When they do participate, they occupy much the same position vis-à-vis the CSC and Budget Bureau as the Post Office and Civil Service Committees do. That is, they are slightly at odds with the Executive branch's views of personnel policy and more withholding than the Executive branch would like them to be. They must be persuaded to approve Executive branch proposals, rather than acceding to them at the outset. Thus, they too become part of the *modus vivendi* by which differences are accommodated and conflict is muted, although again, this does not insure an outcome satisfactory to all.

Let us conclude this survey by reviewing a few major points. Personnel policy does not generate the most politically divisive issues of our time, but it has its conflicts. Some of these conflicts are sharp, although they may not involve very many interests. The few organizations which have been reviewed here have developed a *modus vivendi* of institutional and informal relationships which allows them to proceed without undue disruption. For, while their own interests and opinions are important to the participants, even more important to them is their need to work together and come to some decisions. They are under this restraint, if only because certain legislative decisions are demanded. Besides

---

[18] Richard F. Fenno, Jr., "The Internal Distribution of Influence: The House," in The American Assembly, *The Congress and America's Future* (Englewood Cliffs, N.J.: Prentice-Hall, Inc., 1965), p. 73.

they know they will survive to fight another day. The politics of the personnel process only occasionally results in clear-cut victory or defeat. Most of the time the gains any participant makes are small and hard-won; and the defeats are less than total.

6.

ALTERNATIVE ORGANIZATIONS AND POLICY IMPLICATIONS: PERSPECTIVES ON THE U.S. CIVIL SERVICE COMMISSION

COMMISSION ON ORGANIZATION OF THE EXECUTIVE BRANCH OF THE GOVERNMENT

In effect, the U.S. Civil Service Commission has a dual mandate. First, it must serve as protector of the merit system. The derivative objective, in the words of the 1949 *Task Force Report on Federal Personnel*, is "to prevent political influence and favoritism in Federal appointments and personnel relations." Second, the Commission must serve a role that has been designated "positive personnel management." The derivative objective, again relying on the *Task Force Report*, is "to attract, select, develop and retain well-qualified personnel in the Federal Service."

Given these distinct tasks, at least four basic ways of organizing the Commission may be identified as:

1. *The Commission-Executive Director Arrangement*
2. *The Administrator-Chairman Arrangement*
3. *The Coequal Commission-Administrator Arrangement*
4. *The Administrator-Advisory Board Arrangement*

These four alternative arrangements are sketched in Figure 6.1.

The choice of any one of these four patterns of organizing is an issue of great consequence, for the patterns imply that significantly different policy alternatives will receive primary attention. For example, Figure 6.2 depicts a likely

---

Commission on Organization of the Executive Branch of the Government, *Task Force Report on Federal Personnel* (Washington, D.C.: U.S. Government Printing Office, 1949), esp. pp. 80, 82.

FIGURE 6.1. FOUR POSSIBLE WAYS OF ORGANIZING THE U.S. CIVIL SERVICE COMMISSION AT THE TOP LEVEL.

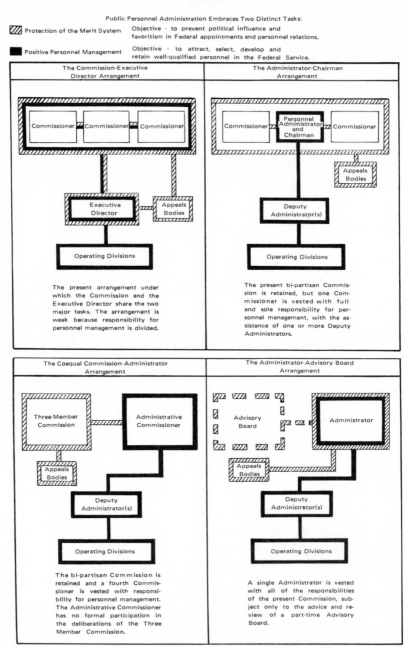

SOURCE: Commission on Organization of the Executive Branch of the Government, *Task Force Report on Federal Personnel*, (Washington, D.C.: U.S. Government Printing Office, 1949), p. 80.

FIGURE 6.2. TOP-LEVEL ORGANIZATION UNDER THE ADMINISTRATOR-
CHAIRMAN ARRANGEMENT.

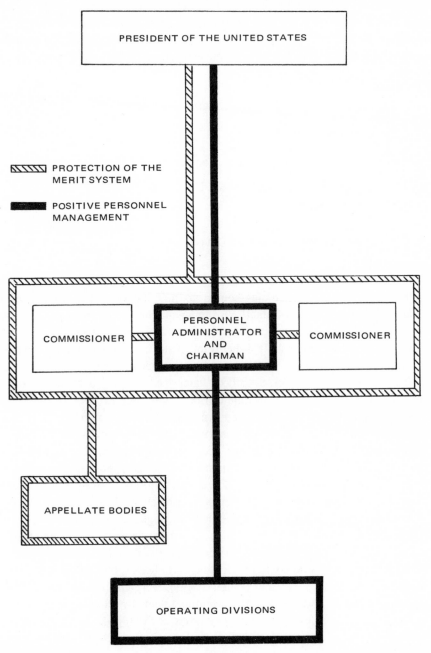

SOURCE: Commission on Organization of the Executive Branch of the Government, *Task Force Report on Federal Personnel*, (Washington, D.C.: U.S. Government Printing Office, 1949), p. 82.

pattern of relations with the President under the Administrator–Chairman Arrangement. "Positive personnel management," reasonably, probably would get especial attention under this arrangement. And such attention might even conflict with the goal of "protection of the merit system" as, for example, efforts might be made to release personnel considered to be "deadwood."

7.

SELECTING SPECIALISTS AND MIDDLE MANAGERS IN THE PUBLIC SERVICE

COMMITTEE FOR ECONOMIC DEVELOPMENT

Every recent administration has sought to find outside talent to bolster its management and technical strength. Bringing qualified people into any organization may serve any one or more of three purposes. It is a means of obtaining new scientific or technical skills; it helps to "shake up" the outfit that is coasting or fading in effectiveness; and it provides management with better yardsticks for executive performance. So-called "lateral entry" has been used both in government and industry, from time to time, to accomplish each of these ends.

The need for "new blood" in government has been emphasized by many observers. The Herter Committee, in 1963, recommended that lateral entry in the Foreign Service should be encouraged and "should normally range up to not more than 25 percent of the total number of career appointments in a given year." The foreign aid program has had special need for businessmen capable of managing large economic development projects.

Scientists and engineers have come in to manage new scientific programs in many agencies. From 1951 to 1961 the number of scientists and engineers at grades GS-13 and up in federal service more than tripled, posing a difficult recruitment problem that could not possibly have been solved solely from within. Moreover, Public Law 313 and similar statutes were enacted to enable federal agencies to attract and retain better scientific talent, by allowing these agencies to recruit skilled professionals with pay levels at the top of the career services.

Some agencies have developed close and continuing relationships with uni-

Reprinted from *Improving Executive Management in the Federal Government*, July, 1964, pp. 28–34.

versity faculties. There is a fertile field here for interchange of qualified personnel in the natural sciences, and perhaps with graduate schools of business and of public administration.

While federal agencies have had some success in bringing in specialized scientific talent and in recruiting businessmen to head up exciting new programs, they have not done so well in recruiting executives to revitalize lagging agencies or to provide the yardsticks by which agency managers can measure the performance of their top career people. Many agencies have not been touched by any significant influx of competitive talent from the outside; and some managers rely almost entirely on promotion from within to fill top posts.

Just as government could benefit from an increased infusion of highly qualified people and outstanding industrial talent, so might industry profit from the services of responsible federal executives who are knowledgeable about governmental administration. But, despite the advantages to both parties, there are significant obstacles to the achievement of a freer interchange.

As matters now stand, the upper-level business executive who contributes his services to government for a limited period of time often faces serious difficulties in returning to his company. Mid-career businessmen rightly fear even greater problems, in spite of notable instances of such men returning from tours of government service to better, more important jobs than they had held. They, as well as their companies, benefited from their experience.

Past efforts to encourage interchange have been disappointing. Some observers argue that the problem defies solution, noting that superior officials—both in government and business—are often flatly hostile to such interludes. It may be conceded that those sought and needed are the best, and the present employer is reluctant to release them. The potential long range values—for companies, government, and executives—justify determined efforts to overcome the difficulties.

Transfer conditions are somewhat easier for professionals and supporting staff managers. The lawyer who enters the Patent Office, or the Internal Revenue Service, or the Justice Department, may gain experience invaluable to himself and his firm. Similarly, the scientist or engineer who works in the space program or in the Department of Defense may provide his company with a broader understanding of the government's need for space and military items. But even in the professions, key people are hard to spare. In both managerial and professional groups retention or reinstatement privileges in retirement and insurance rights would simplify exchanges.

Despite the obvious difficulties and past failures, we believe that both government and business would benefit from an increased interchange of people, and we propose three steps.

1. We recommend re-examination of department and agency programs, to

determine the high-level technical, scientific, and managerial skills needed from outside the government; and to assess the adequacy of current agency efforts to recruit outside mid-career talent.

2. We recommend that the business community as a whole, and individual companies in particular, take positive steps to encourage freer exchange of high quality personnel between industry and government.

These steps might include: explicit recognition in industrial executive development programs of the usefulness of government service in broadening the individual executive's understanding of his working environment; provision for reinstatement in company retirement systems; and restoration of fringe benefits, within the limits of conflict of interest statutes.

3. We recommend that the federal government actively enlist industrial executives for one- to four-year periods, and that it stimulate its professional and executive personnel to reciprocate through service in the private sector.

Each agency should adjust its development programs to these objectives. Federal policy should be changed to provide suitable severance benefits for industrial employees who come into government for short periods, and to provide for continuance of fringe benefits for federal employees who devote portions of their careers to industrial service. Many federal employees have a substantial capability—through specialized knowledge and experience or managerial competence or both—that is potentially valuable to business concerns. This capability—demonstrated by retired military officers, for one example—should be made more fully available to the private sector, in reciprocity for the special talents drawn from business firms into government. Individual federal employees should be allowed to take leave of absence without penalty either in status or in promotion prospects.

Before leaving this subject we would note the constructive possibilities that may exist in interchanges at these levels between the federal services and those of state and local governments. There are a number of the latter with exemplary standards, both in personnel and in operating efficiency. It might well be rewarding to explore the possibilities for systematic interchanges with the best of these, to mutual advantage.

SELECTION AT THE ENTRY GRADES

The critical importance of recruiting at the entry grades is shown by the fact that most of the 8,600 men and women now at the top of the federal service were promoted from within. For some thirty years—beginning with the programs inaugurated under the leadership of Professor Leonard D. White as a member of the Civil Service Commission—special efforts have been made to attract exceptional talent from graduating university classes. The Junior Management Assistant and Management Intern programs have drawn from 200 to 300 able young people into the service annually. Yet, recruiting at these starting levels has been somewhat disappointing, although there appears to have been recent improvement.

The evidence is inconclusive, but those conducting the recruiting process are concerned that they may not be getting a proportionate share of the top-notch graduates from the best colleges and universities, particularly in such fields as engineering, science, business administration, and economics. Although at these levels the federal government appears to be offering salaries almost equivalent to those prevailing generally in industry, recruiters from major business concerns have greater flexibility in salary and other features of first employment. Hence, business firms can offer special inducements for exceptional talent.

The government has two specific handicaps. First, attitude surveys show that college seniors and graduate students have a rather low regard for federal employment, only 9 to 12 percent viewing it more favorably than private employment. Second, the efforts of many federal agencies to recruit capable people at entry grades are often less well adapted and less sustained than those of industry. In some agencies security checks require delays in clearances discouraging to prospective employees. Unfortunately, also, recruiting budgets are prime targets for agency cost-cutting efforts whenever long-range needs are subordinated to immediate pressures.

Foundation support has permitted initiation and encouragement of numerous university efforts to supply well trained administrative and professional personnel for governmental organizations at all levels, although grants have usually been limited in term. These efforts may have tended to obscure the obligation of the government itself to assure the steady flow of high talent into federal service, to the end that expenditure of vast sums of taxpayers' money may be well managed.

For a century the traditional view was widely held in this country that the supply of candidates for any civilian governmental post always exceeds the demand, and that—consequently—there was no need for the federal government to concern itself far in advance with the quality or quantity of its future employees. Corollary to this view was the idea that each candidate for federal employment was expected to bear sole and personal responsibility for his own career preparation. These propositions have undoubted merits—emphasizing the aspect of free competition for employment on the one hand and the concept of self-reliance on the other.

The personnel systems of modern business concerns have accepted a modification of these views, as applied to their prospective managerial and professional personnel. There is less willingness to trust to chance that our educational institutions will automatically produce an adequate supply of highly qualified future managers and professionals with the specialized kinds of training required. Concern over curricula and the flow of qualified people through graduate schools has led to closer business-university collaboration. Several of the better managed federal agencies have now adopted a comparable outlook.

There are agencies, of course, with aggressive recruiting programs yielding excellent results. Notably successful programs usually include some of the following elements, most of which are also characteristic of the best industrial recruiting systems.

1. Mounting recurrent recruiting drives in some hundreds of universities throughout the country, focused on graduate students with bachelor's degrees from smaller colleges who were in the top 25 percent of their classes, and who are identified by their department heads as promising.
2. Placing program administrators, scientists, and technicians—men of standing able to arouse interest in the agency's work—on recruiting teams.
3. Providing summer fellowship programs for promising young undergraduates and graduate students.
4. Concentrating efforts in geographic areas where student awareness of agency programs is strongest.
5. Preparing brochures highlighting the importance of the agency's programs to the nation, stressing the future contribution of the individual applicant in furthering these programs, and giving details on pay, promotional opportunities, and chances for further education and growth in the agency.
6. Authorizing recruiters to make firm commitments and to offer outstanding candidates expense-paid visits to agency operations.[1]

In addition to the higher regard for federal service which we think would follow from adoption of recommendations made elsewhere in this statement— with the improved climate of excellence in federal administration that we would expect to result—we propose four specific steps to improve the federal recruiting efforts.

1. We recommend that agency recruiting programs at the entry grades involve participation by line managers and program people, wherever this practice has not yet been adopted, and that the professional association and university ties of these key people be utilized.

2. We recommend that agency personnel officers analyze their "successes" in entry level recruiting, to identify those aspects of their efforts that are most productive.

---

[1] Present law prevents payment of these costs for recruitment to the competitive service; but pending legislation would correct this situation if enacted.

3.   We recommend that outstanding agency and industry recruiting programs be identified and described, that their useful elements be adapted to specific situations, and that recruitment offices be encouraged and not hampered in their application.

Another aspect of this problem deserves emphasis.   Many of the nation's leading universities have educational programs, both graduate and under-graduate, designed to equip students for useful careers in government service. These efforts—especially those aimed specifically at preparation for federal service—have been less well coordinated with the manpower needs of the federal government than their possibilities would justify.   Federal officials have met with university leaders in recent years to establish better communications on this and related subjects, and it is hoped that closer collaboration may develop.

4.   We recommend intensive inquiries into ways of relating university programs to long-range federal needs for upper-level manpower; and that means be found for opening channels into the federal service, at home and abroad, for the ablest university graduates choosing this career.

8.

THOSE WHO SERVE AT THE TOP

COMMITTEE FOR ECONOMIC DEVELOPMENT

The 8,600 key people are found in four categories—Presidential appointees, civilian career executives and professionals, military officers, and foreign service officers.

1. Top Presidential Appointees, about 500 of them, bear the brunt of translating the philosophy and aims of the current administration into practical programs.[1] This group includes the secretaries and assistant secretaries of cabinet depart-ments, agency heads and their deputies, heads and members of boards and commissions with fixed terms, and chiefs and directors of major bureaus, divisions, and services.   Appointments to many of these politically sensitive

---

Reprinted from Committee for Economic Development, *Improving Executive Management in the Federal Government* (New York: CED, 1964), pp. 15–18.
[1] There are other Presidential appointments to lower-echelon posts, such as U.S. Marshals and Attorneys, with a traditional patronage aspect. These are excluded from our total of 500 because they have little or no management responsibility.

positions are made on recommendation by department or agency heads, but all are presumably responsive to Presidential leadership.

One qualification for office at this level is that there be no basic disagreement with Presidential political philosophy, at least so far as administrative judgments and actions are concerned. Apart from the bi-partisan boards and commissions, these men are normally identified with the political party of the President, or are sympathetic to it, although there are exceptions.

There are four distinguishable kinds of top Presidential appointees, including:

> Those whom the President selects at the outset to establish immediate and effective control over the government (e.g.—Cabinet secretaries, agency heads, his own White House staff and Executive Office personnel).
>
> Those selected by department and agency heads in order to establish control within their respective organizations (e.g.—assistant secretaries, deputies, assistants to, and major line posts in some bureaus and divisions).
>
> High-level appointees who—though often requiring clearance through political or interest group channels, or both—must have known scientific or professional competence (e.g.—the Surgeon General, the Commissioner of Education).
>
> Those named to residual positions traditionally filled on a partisan patronage basis.

These appointees are regarded primarily as policymakers and as overseers of policy execution. In practice, however, they usually have substantial responsibilities in line management, often requiring a thorough knowledge of substantive agency programs.

2. Civilian Career Executives and Professionals, about 5,500 of them, occupy positions in the three upper grades under the Classification Act (GS-16, GS-17, and GS-18),[2] or in the postal field service (grades 18, 19, and 20), or in high posts under Public Law 313 which was enacted to facilitate recruitment of needed scientific or specialized skills. Also included are comparable positions in the Atomic Energy Commission, the Tennessee Valley Authority, the United States Public Health Service, the Veterans Administration Department of Medicine and Surgery, and other agencies outside the Classification Act.

Supergrade personnel are responsible for executing policies established by

---

[2] The "GS" Grades: GS is an abbreviation for "General Schedule." Grades GS-1 through GS-4 are low-level clerical and comparable workers; university graduates usually enter at grades GS-5 or GS-7; holders of master's degrees usually enter at GS-9; doctoral degree holders may enter at GS-11; and holders of GS-13, GS-14, and GS-15 grades usually have significant supervisory or managerial duties, or responsible professional or staff support roles.

The "supergrades," GS-16, GS-17, and GS-18, superimposed on the former structure in 1949, were designed to distinguish higher levels of responsibility and competence.

These—and their opposite numbers outside the classified civil service—are the central interest of this statement.

their superiors. They also play a significant part in formulating policies. They provide the experience, the intimate knowledge, and often the insights on which the 500 Presidential appointees rely in discharging their policymaking and managerial responsibilities.

Not all of these 5,500 have risen from the ranks of the career services. There are 500 Classification Act positions lacking standard career protection—the "Schedule C" jobs described elsewhere in this statement. Over half of these 500 positions are filled by career employees from lower civil service ranks, who can fall back to their classified service grades if called upon to do so; the other half of the 500, plus a few others among the 5,500, are regarded as political appointees without tenure.

Most career executives have achieved their present rank and status by dint of demonstrated technical competence and after a lengthy apprenticeship, as in many large and long-established private firms. In the government, about 90 percent have had ten years or more of federal service, and about half were first recruited at middle or lower grades. Only a small percentage has been brought into government from comparable outside posts.

Most top career servants, whether promoted to their positions from within or recruited from outside, have tended to "stay put." For example, two-thirds of a large sample studied recently had worked only in one or two departments or bureaus in their entire public careers although most were long-time federal employees. Hence their experience, lengthy though it may be, lacks breadth.

3. Military Flag Officers.—Nearly 1,300 generals and admirals play a major part in formulating the policies, planning the expenditures, and directing operations for 2.6 million persons on active military duty, and some one million civilians in the defense establishment. Responsible, in turn, to civilian secretariats, they execute day-to-day assignments similar in many ways to those of the so-called "supergrade" civil servants (GS-16, GS-17, and GS-18) and of persons holding positions under Public Law 313.

Ordinarily, flag officers reach their senior positions through promotion from within. Over 90 percent of flag-rank officers in the Navy, two-thirds in the Army, and one-third in the Air Force were first recruited through the service academies, and most have earned one or more university degrees. They have been trained, rotated, and selectively promoted until those judged most capable have reached general officer levels, although seniority has a major influence.

4. Foreign Service Officers.—Over 1,300, including reserve officers, serve in foreign affairs agencies (State Department, Agency for International Development, and the United States Information Agency, for example) at home or in diplomatic posts.[3] They are responsible for the detailed conduct of consular,

---

[3] Individuals in this group are those in the Foreign Service, in the Foreign Service Reserve, or in Staff categories at grades comparable to FSO (Foreign Service Officers) 1 and 2, in addition to Career Ambassadors and Career Ministers.

economic, political, and administrative operations in more than 100 foreign countries.

Recruitment sources vary from agency to agency. About 80 percent of those in the State Department attained their present positions through promotion, although a number were brought in at upper grades as a result of the lateral appointment provisions of the Foreign Service Act of 1946, and the subsequent Wriston Program of 1954. On the other hand, the Agency for International Development (AID) has relied almost exclusively on persons brought in at middle and upper grades. The pattern in the United States Information Agency (USIA) is midway between State and AID.

9.

PERSONNEL NEAR THE TOP: RESPONSIBILITY AND ACCOUNTABILITY

JOHN J. CORSON AND R. SHALE PAUL

What does examination of the day-by-day activities of upper-level career civil servants reveal as to the nature of "management" as it is practiced in the federal government? What does such an examination reveal as to the character of the responsibilities borne by those who direct federal programs?

How broad are their responsibilities? Do they encompass the carrying out of an objective precisely defined in statutes, prevailing plans, or regulations? Or do they extend to the accomplishment of less specifically stated objectives (e.g., the protection of the public against adulterated foods)?

And to whom are these upper-level career civil servants accountable? To a single superior, a boss? Or is the "program manager" accountable in some degree to a number of individuals and groups concerned with the program for which he is responsible? . . .

[There follows, in the original text, brief summaries of the responsibilities of four typical program managers, drawn from a sample of some 400. Corson and Paul draw major conclusions from their intensive study of the total sample of managers, and these conclusions are reprinted below.]

We have pictured the ways that typical program managers meet six different

Reprinted from John J. Corson and R. Shale Paul, *Men Near the Top: Filling Key Posts in the Federal Service*, (Baltimore: The Johns Hopkins Press, 1966), pp. 23, 43–51. With permission of the Committee for Economic Development, and the publisher.

kinds of responsibilities. These activities, together with the managers' own estimates and records, show somewhat more clearly how these top-level career servants actually manage. They show, for example, that 60 percent of the program managers' time is spent "managing," that is, in applying the so-called *command skills* of direction, staffing, controlling, planning, and evaluating. But, as their activities have illustrated, program managers spend a significant proportion of their time—more than 20 percent—in managing by means short of overt direction. These managers seek to persuade others (over whom they have no control) to their viewpoints, and they try to get the best for their programs; they coordinate related activities in their own and other programs. And they, as representatives of their programs and agencies, strive to put their best foot forward before Congress, private industry, and the public . . . . however, they call on their supporting staff managers for these same persuasive skills.

Still, managers are directly involved in the substance of their programs. Those in this study report an average 24.4 hours spent (during the week surveyed) in specialized or functional activities. In contrast, they reported only 4.1 hours spent on general or administrative activities. While most of these activities were accomplished with others, the program managers reportedly put in an average of thirteen hours a week *alone* (perhaps one-third of it at home after working hours) reading, writing, dictating, and reviewing correspondence.

To what do these findings add up? We believe that six generalizations can be drawn out of this cross-section of federal experience.

1. *Management in the federal service is integrally and inextricably interrelated to an understanding of, and a dedication to, the objectives of the program being managed.*

Dr. Chalmers Sherwin, Deputy Director of Defense Research and Engineering in the Department of Defense, has written of the passing of the "general purpose manager."

This type of person always has been and always will be essential to many parts of business and government [he wrote]. He is not, however, a suitable person either to operate the law courts, or to direct modern technological enterprises (although he did quite well at managing the relatively simple technical operations of the industrial revolution, particularly operations based on mechanical devices). A lawyer or a businessman can master in a few weeks the essential technical aspects of the operation of a railroad or a busline. But just let him try to rationally guide the development of an inertial guidance system, a laser communications system, or a radical new computer!

The kind of technical knowledge needed in these matters, along with the subtle skills of management which bring out the creative efforts of scientists and engineers, simply cannot be picked up after hours or as part of a job. It can only be obtained one way: by a systematic, thorough technical education plus extensive professional experience in research and engineering. Unfortunately, the lingo of science is easy to pick up. But, as any experienced technical person well knows, there is nothing so depressing as to listen to a "general-purpose" manager using all the right words without real comprehension.[1]

The evidence provided by the record of what career program managers do belies Dr. Sherwin's suggestion that the general purpose manager still is useful in the older and less changing activities of government (e.g., the collection of taxes—and there are those who would question this assertion!). Together, Dr. Sherwin's contention and the record of what career program managers do, challenge a prevailing belief that the manager is a generalist who delegates technical and administrative details and relies on others for the substance of policies and processes, and then focuses his time and energies on interpreting and executing these approved policies. The practice of program managers suggests that such an administrator is rare.

The analysis of a complex technical report presented by one's staff, discussions of troublesome problems with members of Congress and interest groups, the gathering of seasoned judgments from highly specialized staff members, and the negotiating with his peers in related fields involve the program manager in the warp and woof of the program. The capacity to represent his staff and to persuade the congressional committee or constituent group often requires not only understanding, but a dedication to the program and its objectives.

It is not surprising, therefore, that most program managers have spent the larger part of their adult careers in the fields in which they are now working. The Director of the Bureau of Restraint of Trade in the Federal Trade Commission, for example, joined the FTC in 1925, after obtaining a law degree. He has worked successively in various fields of legal investigation for 39 years, as an examiner, assistant chief examiner, associate director (Office of Legal Investigations), before becoming bureau director. Similarly, the Director of the Division of Timber Management joined the Forest Service after graduating from college with a degree in forestry in 1925. After starting as a grade GS-5, Assistant Forest Ranger, he served as a Forest Ranger, a member of a Forest Supervisor's technical staff, an Assistant Forester engaged in forest products research, an Assistant Forest Supervisor (general administration), and Assistant Regional Forester, before being promoted to his present job. Both men gained the capacities required in their present posts by dint of long experience in specialized fields.

The program managers' concern with the substance of the program is confirmed by their designation of those activities they engage in that they believe to be most significant. In four of every five instances, the activities that they designated involved substantive (as distinguished from administrative) considerations. Supervising the progress of the case handled by a staff of attorneys,

---

[1] *Saturday Review*, August 1, 1964, p. 39 (based on an article which appeared in the *Naval Research Reviews*).

evaluating a technical report on the Alaska fishing industry, or planning a regulatory commission's programs for the coming year are illustrative activities identified by these managers. Such activities require that the program manager be familiar with the technical intricacies of the program he manages.

This dedication to the program is usually associated with a deep sense of responsibility to the whole citizenry. The attitudes of many top-level civil servants are marked by a true feeling of public service, of belief that they are doing something or providing services of great value to all citizens. This attitude is less often observable in the activities of business executives of like rank.

2. *Management is, in substantial part, an entrepreneurial function; it involves the responsibility for continual innovation, i.e., for taking the lead in bringing about changes in legislation, in policy, and in processes of execution.*

Much of the program manager's time goes into activities that are undertaken to develop amendments to existing law, changes in prevailing policies or improvements in processes and procedures. The pressure for change, for growth, and for improvement comes from the day-by-day experience in administration. But simultaneously the pressure for innovation may come from political superiors who strive to fulfill political promises or to achieve political gains, and such pressure will continually come from constituent groups.

The entrepreneurial function of the career program manager[2] is that of having his staff develop the change that is in the public interest and then of engineering the consensus required—among staff, the representatives of other executive departments, the Executive Office, constituent groups, and the congressional committees, or such groupings as are required in a particular instance.

3. *Management is the task of continually interrelating forces and groups within and without the agency in the achievement of program objectives.*

The program manager is located at the hub—not the apex—of the groups and forces he must influence if he is to get things done, i.e., if he is to carry out existing law and policy, and is to initiate the continual and progressive

---

[2] The analogous entrepreneurial function of the manager in private business is aptly described by Peter F. Drucker in his book, *Managing for Results* (New York: Harper & Row, 1964), pp. 3–14.

Drucker suggests, later in his book, that this function has, as yet, not been completely realized. He notes: "Managers have become a leadership group in the last two decades largely because they have developed such a discipline for the managerial half of their job: the planning, building, and leading of the human organization of a business. But for the other, the entrepreneurial, half—the half that deals with the specific and unique economic function of business enterprise—the systematic discipline has yet to be evolved. All over the world, executives have committed themselves to management as a discipline. Now they have to commit themselves to purposeful entrepreneurship. Only when entrepreneurship is presented as a discipline and practiced as the specific task that systematically directs resources to economic performance and results, will an educated layman be able to understand what business—industrial society's economic organ—is trying to do, and to respect what it is doing. Only then can society truly accept that business is a rational pursuit and that the executive in business has an important contribution to make." (P. 227).

change required. He is involved in a never-ending process of adjusting, balancing, and interrelating the views, expectations, and pressures of:

superiors, including his immediate boss, and those "up the line," even perhaps the President;

subordinates, most of them specialists in a number of separate and sometimes little related fields, e.g., the biologist and the lawyer in the Food and Drug Administration;

peers, other career men both within and without the department of which his agency is a part, who are responsible for parallel programs and compete with him for funds and for the support of the Executive Branch, constituencies, and the Congress; concurrently, they are partners in meeting over-all objectives of the Executive Branch;

advisors and supporting specialists, outsiders who contribute economic, scientific, public relations, or other viewpoints deemed related to the agency problems and to the achievement of agency objectives;

members of Congress who represent the views of constituents and who, as members of key substantive or fiscal committees, can significantly affect the administrator's batting average in getting needed legislation through or in obtaining requisite funds;

representatives of special interest groups (e.g., labor, industry, agriculture, and veterans organizations) who seek to influence the administrator and the agency by plying their special interest wherever they can gain an audience.

And importantly, the manager must reconcile these many obligations with his own personal sense of responsibility to himself. The process of management, in terms of this reconciliation, involves discovery or development of the solution, policy, or action which will serve the public interest, maximize concurrence among the several constituent groups, and yet leave the manager with the conviction that he has acted according to his own highest sense of right.

The task is similar to the role Marya Mannes pictures for the conductor of a private orchestra. He is responsible as an artist for relating the contributions of pianists, flutists, violinists, and others, while at the same time he is occupied with harmonizing the demands of the musicians' union and his board of trustees and with stimulating the interest and approval of the press, of prospective customers in other cities, and of contributors wherever he can find them.[3] Leonard Sayles has identified thirteen similar groups or forces with which the business executive must cope.[4]

---

[3] Marya Mannes, *But Will It Sell?* (New York: J. B. Lippincott & Co., 1964), pp. 238–39.
[4] He includes among these groups those "... for whom he is doing work, ... to whom he, in turn, contracts out work, ... from whom he gets parts, materials, or services ... who control the access to equipment, space, and other resources ... to whom he will send what he has processed ... who are doing things in other parts of the organization that directly or indirectly impinge on his activities." "Executives Need This Skill," by Leonard P. Sayles, *Nation's Business*, © August, 1964, p. 49.

4. *Management is essentially a process of negotiation and persuasion; it is, at the most, only partially a process of command.*

In developing a solution, a policy, or an action that will serve the public interest and maximize concurrence,

... who has authority over whom is a moot point. The balance of power, of status and influence tends to be ambiguous. These types of interaction, therefore, require enormously more personality abilities than did jobs under simpler kinds of technologies. Much more skill and time has to be given to negotiation-like behavior patterns, to interviewing, and a whole host of skills that are the opposite of the smothered individual which critics of large corporations tend to fret about.[5]

In the federal service even more than in private enterprise, these "personality abilities" are of prime importance. For no matter how great are the career civil servant's professional attainments, no matter how long is his service or how rich his experience, and no matter how clearly his competence is recognized, he always occupies a secondary or even tertiary position in the federal service. If J. Edgar Hoover has achieved a primary role in the determination of what policies shall govern and how federal law enforcement activities shall be carried out, he constitutes the exception that proves a valid and generally prevailing rule. The career civil servant, while he may be clearly responsible for the conduct of a particular service, is the subordinate of a politically appointed superior who is expected to approve the policies that shall prevail and to oversee the manner in which they are executed.

5. *Management is primarily a group process; it is seldom the task of an all powerful individual working alone.*

The activities which consume a major portion of the program manager's time (perhaps three-fifths of all his working hours), and most (over 75 percent) of the activities which he regards as "most significant," are group activities, i.e., conferences, meetings, and group discussions. The program manager spends a minor part of his time alone. He has relatively little time to focus his talents and experience alone on the problems for which he is responsible, little time to read, to write, and to deliberate.

This characteristic of the program manager's activities derives in large part from the fact that the career civil servant is often only responsible for a part of a total governmental effort. For example, the career official in the Department of Agriculture responsible for shipping surplus agricultural commodities to the developing countries provides but a portion of the aid the United States makes available to these countries. Technical experts, machinery, equipment, and perhaps loans may be provided by AID, while military equipment and military advisors may be supplied by the Department of Defense. These activities must be carried on in consonance with objectives set by the State Department

---

[5] *Ibid.,* p. 50.

if the resources provided by each of these separate programs are to accomplish this country's foreign policy ends.

The decisions made by the program manager arise far more often out of consultation than out of his single-minded judgments. The decision usually reflects the informed and debated views of those involved in the problem. It may, at times, represent the abdication by the program manager of the responsibility for making the decision to the will of a majority.

6. *Management demands of the manager skill in communication, perhaps to a greater degree than any other skill.*

The Deputy Treasurer of the United States, who is responsible for an organization which provides general banking services and related activities for the entire federal government, wrote of his own job: "The talking, conferring, dictating, reading, and writing constitute a continuing communication with superiors, subordinates, personal staff, equals in other bureaus and departments, Congressmen and their assistants, committees of Congress, members of the general public, and the press."

In other words, the program manager's accomplishment, this official indicates, depends largely on his ability to communicate with others—in writing and orally—to gather needed facts and views; to instill subordinates with the confidence that he understands the problems they are attempting to resolve and the programs they are engaged in; to persuade these subordinates of the wisdom of following and supporting his leadership; to sell his program to peers, bosses, interest groups, Congress, and the public; and to win the support of powerful and interested groups for his agency's programs.

This requires a large capacity for putting scientific and economic jargon into terms that the boss, a Congressman, or a newspaper reporter can understand. The possession or lack of this capacity can make or break a program by itself.

Of special importance to the American form of government is the ability of the program manager to translate the program to and to educate his politically appointed boss. Indeed, it is the only way the political appointee learns about his own department—and his learning is of vital importance.

Finally, the program manager must manifest an ability to sense the reactions of each of the groups with which he deals. It is by these reactions that he measures his accomplishments; for he is usually denied the neat quantitative measures that guide the private business executive.

James A. Perkins, the able president of Cornell University, aptly described this needed communication skill in response to the question: "How do you tell whether you're doing well in your job?"

From the reactions of the public with whom I deal, [he replied]. If the various boards you deal with start asking a lot of small questions or arguing small points, you can figure you're doing something wrong.

Or if you find yourself repeatedly under attack from the faculty, or from the students

(I pay attention to the student newspaper), or if many alumni are restive—you're in trouble.

On the other hand, if these people say—or give the impression—that they're kind of pleased, then you feel you're doing all right. You have to trust your personal radar to a great extent.[6]

So it is with the federal program manager. He will often have quantitative measures he can use to claim accomplishment. But in the end, he must possess that communication skill that Perkins describes as his "personal radar" to measure his accomplishment continually.

10.

THE EFFECTS OF AUTOMATION ON JOB DESIGN

Louis E. Davis

Anyone who attempts to study the effects of automation on job design quickly discovers what amounts to a factual desert. Like all deserts it is replete with oases, which upon close examination turn out to be mirages. Only the sketchiest sorts of objective data are available on such questions as what jobs will be like under automation, the skills that will be required, the types of jobs and industries that will be most changed, and how many workers will be affected. However, the paucity of data has not inhibited in the slightest either the outpouring of testimony before governmental bodies[1] or the writing of learned treatises. In fact, we now have an Act which was passed by the United States Congress in its desire to do something about the problem.[2]

A careful examination of the present state of knowledge about automation shows a large collection of unknowns. Although information is available on certain technical aspects of automation, answers to important questions con-

---

[6] "An Informal Call on James A. Perkins Far Above Cayuga's Waters," by William McCleery, *University* (a quarterly publication of Princeton University), © March, 1965, p. 19.

Reprinted from *Industrial Relations*, Vol. 2 (October, 1962), pp. 53–71.

[1] *New Views on Automation*, Joint Economic Committee, Subcommittee on Automation and Energy Resources, 86th Cong., 2d sess. (Washington, D.C.: U.S. Government Printing Office, 1960); *Impact of Automation*, U.S. Bureau of Labor Statistics, Bull. No. 1287 (Washington, D.C.: U.S. Government Printing Office, 1960); *Governor's Conference on Automation*, State of New York (Albany, N.Y.: 1960).

[2] *Manpower Development and Training Act of 1962*, enacted March 15, 1962.

cerned with the public interest are virtually unobtainable. These questions deal with what kinds of jobs and how many will be affected by automation and what will happen to the content of jobs and to the skills required to hold them. The following pages, however, will be restricted to the areas in which there are some factual data and which incidentally happen to be the areas of competence of the author. It is difficult enough to attempt to provide some order to the data and to indicate trends with respect to changes in job designs in the next 10 to 15 years. As interesting and vital for public policy as they are, the questions of how many and what kinds of jobs will be needed, and where they will be needed, are excluded from this discussion.

The article will take the form of a review of published material in the subject area. In addition, estimates will be made regarding job content, based on projections of experimental and empirical data available today and on analyses of the evolving technology. These are influenced, of course, by the author's experience and observations of automation in industry and his own research findings in job design.

POPULAR THEORIES REGARDING AUTOMATION

From the confusion of myth, fact, fancy, and apprehension surrounding automation, a number of propositions stand out and influence most of what has been said about the subject. The first of these is a forecast made by Peter Drucker in 1955, in which he predicted "the greatest upgrading of the labor force ever seen." [3] By upgrading, Drucker meant the elimination of low-level routine jobs and an increase in the number of people in maintenance, technical, and professional occupations. His forecast has greatly influenced all subsequent discussion of automation.

A second proposition logically derives from Drucker's forecast. The upgrading will require high skills and therefore considerable additional training for workers in automated situations. These requirements will effectively constitute a technological lockout unless labor, business, and government get busy and see to it that workers' skills are raised. A third proposition, starting with a different set of premises, states that even if workers can become skillful enough to work in automated systems, job satisfaction will be diminished. This prognosis is supported by the arguments that not only will there be more machines and less men in the system but the larger size of the machines will result in greater isolation of workers, making them mute cogs in a large, machine-dominated organization. A fourth proposition which is considerably more

---

[3] Peter F. Drucker, "Integration of People and Planning," *Harvard Business Review*, XXXIII (May–June, 1955), 38.

familiar to all of us is that automation means elimination of people from production systems, since the new machines can do human tasks and therefore make the human being obsolete.

Supporting or refuting these propositions would add little to our knowledge. I propose rather to indicate the confusions, assumptions, and misconceptions underlying them and in so doing to point out the research that is needed to provide data from which solutions can be developed.

Examining Drucker's forecast now after seven years: is it a fanciful wish or will it come to pass? The answer seems to depend on whether the economy as a whole or an individual company is being considered and what is meant by work force and worker. For the economy as a whole, Drucker's forecast appears to be valid. Jobs consisting largely of repetitive routine tasks are being replaced by automated equipment. This is taking place or is impending not only on the factory floor and in the office but also in management, particularly on middle management levels. The latter change has been well characterized by Leavitt and Whisler[4] in their forecast of management in the 1980's. When the capabilities of the technology of automation are considered, it becomes obvious that repetitive and predictive jobs can be automated either in the factory or the office. What is needed for meaningful public policy making is an examination and evaluation of the decision process by which management, faced with the possibility of adopting automated equipment, will choose one production system versus another.

Within the individual company, Drucker's forecast also appears to be valid, if by "worker" we mean everyone in the company. The application of automation makes it possible to reduce the number of personnel whose present jobs are tending or feeding machines, moving material, performing routine information transmission, and similar activities. At the same time, the need for skilled managerial and technical manpower is increased.

Automation also increases the technical complexity of production, whether "production" means providing goods or services or transforming information. Close technical integration of the processing equipment and information components in a system become necessary. The very large capital investment in equipment, coupled with technical inflexibility of automated systems, impose the requirement of long-range planning and decision making on the organization. Even the apparently narrow problem of minimizing downtime has vast ramifications, calling for elegant analytic methods in the development of solutions. These needs, plus those of providing the means for instructing (programming) and designing equipment, have resulted in a large influx of scientists and engineers into business and industry. Thus there *has* been a rise in the skills within an

---

[4] H. J. Leavitt and T. L. Whisler, "Management in the 1980's," *Harvard Business Review,* XXXVI (November–December, 1958), 41–48.

organization. An examination of the simple statistics of the ratio of engineers to workers in American manufacturing industries supports this statement. In 1940 there was approximately 1 engineer for every 200 production workers, but by 1958–1960 the ratio was 1 engineer for each 60 workers.

The second proposition, that high skills will cause a technological lockout, depends in part on what is meant by work force and workers and in part on what is meant by skills. If the concern is with those presently considered to be workers, is the reference to workers at the front of the machine or those behind the machine? Almost forgotten is the fact that automation is evolving and that even those skills presently identified as necessary for automation are only transitional. Bright emphasizes this, and his contribution is very important.[5] Walker's findings do not make the same emphasis, but support Bright's conclusions and indicate that partial automation may retain repetitiveness and other negative aspects, as well as increase tensions at work.[6]

At a later point the details of skills that will be required in the future will be considered. An examination of these skills will indicate that there is little relationship between them and skills existing at present. In general, present-day skills in the factory and office are to a large extent sensorimotor and control skills, coupled with an acquired body of rules of procedure learned through apprenticeship or direct training. Jobs approaching those at the technician levels, such as toolmaking, require a body of acquired technical knowledge coupled with sensorimotor skills. For machine operators in current automation systems, the skills required are generally associated with monitoring, adjusting, controlling, and with failure procedures for stopping the equipment. Experience reported by Crossman and by others indicates that these skills are specific to their particular situation and are nontransferable.[7] Notably they are not associated with manipulating controls or speeds, but are observational and interpretative. This applies both to the factory and office situations. Bright indicates this and further shows that, as automation reaches its final development, even these skills will change, since vigilance and adjusting activities will diminish or be eliminated.

As for the third proposition, that job satisfaction will be reduced under automation, it is difficult to determine whether or not this will be the case. There is evidence given by Walker that this is not the case and that dissatisfactions appear to be features of the period of transition.[8] Examination of automated systems indicates some developments that may approach the effects predicted by Drucker, i.e., stimulating and interesting jobs. Present systems

[5] James R. Bright, "Does Automation Raise Skill Requirements?" *Harvard Business Review*, XXXVI (July–August, 1958), 85–98.

[6] Charles R. Walker, "Life in the Automatic Factory," *Harvard Business Review*, XXXVI (January–February, 1958), 111–19.

[7] E. R. F. W. Crossman, *Automation and Skill* (London: H. M. Stationery Office, 1960), pp. 15–16.

[8] Walker, *op. cit.*

tend to show: (1) the operator's work pace becomes more independent of machine or belt as automation progresses; (2) working conditions are safer and the physical environment more pleasant under automation; (3) operators have a wider range of technical information, a wider overview of a larger segment of the process, and considerably larger responsibility, as well as a broader sense of the consequences; (4) operators' jobs have minimal physical activity and long periods of inactivity as well as minimal contact with machines or processes and materials, which may have adverse effects on operator performance; (5) shift work is increased and will become the usual pattern; and (6) work locations are more isolated physically, but jobs are more closely integrated in terms of contacts and information transmission on the part of operators with technicians, maintenance personnel, engineers, and managers. Crossman indicates that these operators "seem to exercise greater influence than their formal training would merit." [9] Perhaps the pessimistic view of the effects of automation on the individual expressed by industrial sociologists can be explained by their disappointment over the failure of Drucker's prediction to materialize.

The fourth proposition, that automation means elimination of people from production organizations and the obsolescence of human beings, can either be approached with apprehension—the disaster approach—or data can be obtained which would permit planning to take place. Not well identified at present are the criteria used by management in determining replacement of the more usual types of production or processing systems. Substantive knowledge is unavailable on the changes and patterns of manpower and job distributions within automated systems. In formulating solutions, it is important to distinguish between what will be technologically possible, in terms of fully automated, workerless production systems, and what will be economically feasible. Present predictions are that where automation is installed it will probably be carried only to the state presently found in oil refineries and similar industries. This is one reason why the study of jobs and occupation profiles in these industries should be undertaken.

In approaching this problem, Simon postulates two invariants—which may or may not be as invariant as he believes—having to do with the use of human resources.[10] These are: (1) that automation will have transitional effects but that after its installation the human resources of society will be substantially fully employed; and (2) that the distribution of intelligence and ability in our society will remain the same as at present after automation is fully installed, although a much larger percentage of adults will have completed college education. Both of these lead to his prediction that the occupational distribution of

---

[9] Crossman, *op. cit.*

[10] H. A. Simon, "The Corporation: Will It Be Managed by Machine?" in M. Anshen and G. L. Bach (eds.), *Management and Corporations, 1985* (New York: McGraw-Hill Book Co., 1960), pp. 17–56.

employment may be greatly changed. This appears to be sound, for it is not quite as dependent on the prerequisite invariants as he seems to indicate. Specific changes depend on the well-known economic principle, the doctrine of comparative advantage. Whether men or machines are employed in a production system depends not simply on their relative productivity, but on their cost as well, which means on their price. Given the productivities of processes in current technology, human employment will become smaller relative to total labor force in occupations and industries in which automatic equipment has the greatest comparative cost advantage. Human employment will become relatively greater in occupations and industries in which automatic equipment has the least comparative cost advantage.

TYPES OF AUTOMATION

Economic motivations and the development of technology both contribute to the changing of production systems from the order type (job shop) and batch type (including mass production) to the process or continuous type of production system. Automation, which is characterized by both integrated, automatic movement of materials through a production system and by built-in self-control or regulation of the production units, frequently has been erroneously viewed as equivalent to continuous production. Automation, however, makes it possible to *convert* discrete production of individual units, as in the Detroit type of mass production or in batch production, into production systems similar in characteristics to the continuous type of production. Automation can also exist within other production systems.

For the sake of this review which is mainly concerned with job design, both automatic-control processes, similar to those found in the chemical industry, and continuous-flow production, by means of transfer machines and built-in self-control or regulation, can be considered to be alike; that is, they appear to require operators having similar job characteristics.

A second type of automated production system can be called the programmed-machine system and can exist within other production systems. It consists of numerically controlled production machines in which production tools are guided by instructions on magnetic tapes or punched paper tapes. Electronic computers or electronic data processing machines are the office counterparts of numerically controlled machines. Both operate by means of programs or instructions developed prior to the work done on the machines.

A third type of automation system, which may be no more than a variation on the first two indicated, utilizes the centralized remote-control center. The center is removed from the actual work done and the operations performed by the equipment are inaccessible to the controller. Such control systems are present in chemical plants, power plants, and railroad control centers.

FEATURES OF AUTOMATION
WHICH AFFECT JOB DESIGN

Automated production equipment and computers affect jobs at all levels in an organization. Our particular concern here is with jobs of production workers, although the effects on other levels will be touched on.

Automated production equipment and computers are evolving through a series of stages. In the present stage, workers monitor equipment performance, make adjustments, diagnose difficulties, and make repairs. Although relieved of physical exertion and pacing effects, workers are part of the functioning of the system, or are "in line" with the system. Both Walker and Bright indicate that where workers are in line with the system, either because of equipment limitations or flexibility requirements, their jobs may retain some of the repetitiveness of, and may create more tensions than, similar jobs in nonautomated systems.[11] Contemporary automation provides us with an opportunity to study the aspects of jobs which are likely to be retained in completely developed automated systems.

At the moment, the somewhat uneven development of computers and automated production equipment is having some rather unfortunate consequences, insofar as the jobs of production workers are concerned. The superior capabilities of computers in solving programming problems and the relative lack of information regarding job design is leading to peculiar misapplications in the balancing of assembly lines. What is being balanced is unknown. There are no criteria other than minimum delay time, and because the factors influencing job performance are not well defined, they are ignored. Computational programs are used to balance the output of work stations and lines using numbers representing performance times of workers at work stations. What we appear to have is a numbers game divorced from the reality of job performance determinants. Unfortunately, this trend is going to continue for some time, because it is easier to develop computational programs than to determine job design factors.

Present jobs under automation have greatly diminished sensorimotor and increased vigilance requirements. The jobs provide a broad sense of consequences and a wider process knowledge, as well as increased responsibility. The trend seems to be toward more self-controlled jobs having higher interactions between engineers, technicians, and managers. Compared to operators with similar education and skills in conventional production systems, operators in automated systems appear to exercise more influence because of their information roles in an integrated system.

In the ultimate development of automated systems there will be computers

---

[11] Walker, *op. cit.*

that can program computers—heuristic programs by which electronic computers can "think" and learn. Automated equipment will be available that can monitor itself for failures and breakdowns and possibly perform some repairs. Equipment designs will stress minimization of downtime and easy, routine maintenance. Repairs will consist of simply removing defective units and plugging in replacements. The consequence of these additional removals of in-line activities for the worker will be to enhance further his responsibility for larger spans of the production systems and to raise the requirements for technical understanding. He may also take on new jobs, such as set-up, inspection, and repair. In the discussion below of the results of job design studies, the value of greater operator control over the job and more comprehensive duties is indicated. These findings, coupled with increased responsibilities under more complete automation, lead to the prediction of comprehensive, self-contained, less directed jobs. For the present this raises some problems in overcoming the rigidity of existing job classifications.

When we turn to the effects of the application of automation on the organization and its structure, we can anticipate that organizations will be smaller, i.e., they will require less manpower per unit of output or unit of production equipment. There will be a strong move to recentralize planning and control functions based on information systems providing rapid feedback of performance results; coordination of manpower will become less of a problem. The distance between organizational levels will increase, both because of diminished needs for coordination and more comprehensive self-contained jobs at all levels. A shift in emphasis can be expected in management away from personal factors, i.e., away from manpower management, toward technology or analysis. The high capital investment and inflexibility of automated systems will require long-term planning and place great emphasis on analyses which determine patterns of demand and on programs to minimize downtime and control inventory, waste, scrap, product combination, etc. Scientists, engineers, and suitably trained analytic specialists are expected to be highly placed in management and probably in top management because of the policy decisions that will have to be made on investment and operation, as well as on maintenance.

The communication and coordination deficiencies prevalent today in the typical line and staff organization may cause radical modifications. The need for rapid communication between equipment monitors, maintenance personnel, and technical specialists will help bring about this modification, as will the coordination needs of engineers and other technical specialists who plan the operation of a production system and have to modify its defects. In addition, as described by Leavitt and Whisler, a withering away of the managerial family can be expected.[12] Large numbers of middle managers will disappear to be

---

[12] Leavitt and Whisler, *op. cit.*

replaced by information system programs involved in automatic decision making. Present functional specialist divisions will be modified because of the need for rapid communication and coordination. What appears likely to result are organizational units built around products or processes and consisting of specialists of various kinds. The job of foreman or supervisor may also see radical alteration; such workers may become technical experts who direct monitors, diagnosticians, repairers, etc., or they may supervise record keeping or record data checking. In any event, the foreman's job will have fewer personnel managing elements in it.

At the upper levels of the organization the accelerated growth in research and development activities will cause a continued increase in the numbers of scientists, engineers, and other analysts. Their positions, rewards, and advancement will require modification of the traditional organization. The resulting organizational structure will look something like a football sitting on top of a rather narrow pyramid. Within the football will be the top managers, operating a very centralized organization, surrounded by various subgroups of researchers, innovators, and programmers, whose organizational relationships are likely to be changeable and somewhat amorphous. Below the football will be the operating and more programmed portion of the organization. This structure will be more clearly pyramidal than at present, with relatively few middle managers at the apex.

The producing segments of the organization will be characterized by complex equipment and systems which have high capital requirements. Increased technical complexity will require much closer integration of the information process and the production equipment system. Information systems will therefore continue to develop, and computers will occupy a more central role in the operation of the organization.

The requirements of integration and high capital outlays place a great premium on long production runs and minimum downtime. These, in turn, provide incentives for continuing to automate in order to achieve minimum downtime and to adapt both the organization and jobs to permit rapid communication and action to be taken in an emergency. An interesting study by Davis and Werling in a West Coast chemical plant indicates some of the kinds of job changes likely to take place, so that minimum downtime can be achieved in a continuous process operation.[13] The jobs of maintenance workers were enlarged to include five skills; the workers were superior in two of the skills and supportive in three other skills. These changes permitted the assignment of maintenance personnel on an area basis rather than by skill or craft and thereby permitted rapid repair of processing equipment.

---

[13] L. E. Davis and R. Werling, "Job Design Factors," *Occupational Psychology*, XXXIV (April, 1960), 109.

Lastly, we shall look at the effects on job design of compensation and reward systems in automated plants. Present reward systems, built on payment by output units for individual performance, are likely to be unsuitable. If anything, payment should reflect base performance of teams of individuals responsible for equipment or processes or of the entire plant. Such reward systems, if possible, should be related to yield or utilization. Team or plantwide reward schemes, such as the Scanlon Plan, which emphasize cost reduction or yield increase on the part of all members of an organization, may be expected to increase.[14] With the de-emphasis of reward systems based on the output of individuals, there is likely to be a growth in the use of merit-rating plans.

The future and importance of job evaluation under automated systems is uncertain. Large steps will exist between the levels of operators, technicians, and engineers. In addition, flexibility in job assignments would seem to be of rather critical importance under automated systems. One of the unforeseen side effects of job evaluation programs has been the development of rigid descriptions and assignments; such restrictions tend to hamper the development of job assignments to suit new automation and information systems. In fact, one of the problems that will increasingly confront both management and labor is the need to construct new agreements which permit increased freedom of assignment. For the immediate future, job evaluation classification schemes will prove to be a source of difficulty and will require radical modifications to permit the needed changes to develop.

JOB DESIGN RESEARCH

A small research program carried on at a few universities is beginning to have widespread effects on the design of jobs. Neither the effects nor the magnitude of application can be compared with those of automation. However, because this research seeks to determine job design factors which enhance job performance, it is important to examine its findings particularly as these may be coupled with the job requirements stemming from automation.

In the last ten years, considerable progress has been made through automation and system analysis in the development of optimal man-machine assignments and the provision of decision bases for allocating tasks. Nevertheless, these bases are still serious problems for the system designer when he is faced with relating individual jobs to process, organization, over-all system, and human performance requirements. Job design research attempts to provide data which will assist in the design of effective jobs. The organization of a job to satisfy the technical and organizational requirements of the work to be accomplished

---

[14] F. G. Lesieur (ed.), *The Scanlon Plan* (New York: John Wiley & Sons, Inc., 1958).

and the personal requirements of the worker has been defined as job design.[15] It can be conceptualized in a framework having technical, organizational, and personal dimensions. The technical dimension derives from the production process which includes man-machine systems, work flow, methods, inspection, performance standards, tools, equipment, and product design. The organizational dimension derives from the structure of the organization—levels, specialization, communication, methods of coordination, practices and traditions regarding delegation of authority and responsibility, reward systems, etc. The personal dimension derives from personal values, needs, skill levels, attitudes, relationships, perceptions, aspirations, rewards, etc.

The research program has been concerned with developing criteria of performance effectiveness which will be useful in supporting job design decisions and in identifying job factors or components related to effective performance. The findings which are slowly accumulating come from field and experimental studies. Curiously, they are being accepted rather widely by business and industry and applied in many situations. The term "job enlargement" is frequently used in describing the changes. However, there is far from unanimous support by psychologists. Some strongly support the concepts with findings from their own studies.[16] Others see little objective evidence in favor of these concepts and ask for a return to the well-known approaches of selection and placement, even if these are known not to have yielded good solutions in maximizing the job holder's performance.[17]

In general, the findings of the research point in a particular direction.[18] The indications are that effectiveness of performance is related to control by job holders over methods, rate of performance, quality, and variety, as well as completion activities, and auxiliary and related tasks. Effectiveness also appears to increase as skills, job knowledge, and responsibilities of the job holder are enlarged. In addition to improved performance effectiveness as measured by objective criteria of output and quality, jobs having enlarged skill, control, and responsibility seem to produce workers who are responsive in a positive way to many problems and issues of concern to management. This responsiveness seems to be what management is striving for in its attempts to develop "job interest." [19]

---

[15] L. E. Davis and R. R. Canter, "Job Design," *Journal of Industrial Engineering*, VI (January–February, 1955), 3.

[16] C. Argyris, "The Individual and Organization: An Empirical Test," *Administrative Science Quarterly*, IV (September, 1959), 145; L. R. Sayles, "Introduction to Technology, Social Relations, and Performance," *Human Organization*, XVII (April, 1958), 2.

[17] A. C. McKinney, P. F. Wernimont, and W. O. Galitz, "Has Specialization Reduced Job Satisfaction?" *Personnel*, XXXIX (January–February, 1962), 8–17.

[18] L. E. Davis, "Toward a Theory of Job Design," *Journal of Industrial Engineering*, VIII (September–October, 1957), 305.

[19] Davis and Werling, *op. cit.*, p. 130.

Job design findings indicate that performance effectiveness is positively influenced by larger, self-contained, comprehensive jobs. At the same time, automation points to the development of enlarged jobs. The physical isolation of the equipment and the worker, his minimal sensorimotor activities, his intimate participation in the information transmission process, and his close integration with technicians, engineers, and managers all seem to support the prediction that automated jobs will, after the transition period, be comprehensive. We would expect to see the boundaries between machine-front and machine-back functions become indistinct and disappear. Under developed automation, the monitor will also be the regulator, repairer, and machine adjuster. In nonautomated situations the same prediction can be made. Only in the interim situations of shifting from nonautomated to automated systems would we expect the prediction not to hold.

JOB CONTENT AND SKILL UNDER AUTOMATION

Having reviewed both the general setting for jobs in automated systems and the influences flowing from job design research and equipment development, we are ready to examine job content and skill under automation.

Job content is discussed here as it is likely to exist under future automated systems of production, given the expected development of technology. These jobs are derived by examining present-day automated production systems and projecting the requirements of prospective jobs.

It is well to remember in an abstract discussion of job content that jobs are made up of a series of related tasks—preparation, set-up, feeding of material, removal of material, inspection and detection, and adjustment and control of the tools and/or machinery. At present, under mass production, jobs have been fractionized, resulting in the assignment of a single task as a complete job. In discussing job content it is far easier to specify or predict what people will have to do in automated systems than it is to consider skills. This is particularly so in cases where there is difficulty defining what is meant by skill. For example, at present, skills are thought of as requiring training or particular experience. To avoid perpetuating misconceptions, the term "skill" is used here as meaning any particular ability, inherent or acquired. Let us turn now to machine-front personnel or operators in different automated systems and look at the contents of their jobs.

Operators of continuous-flow production systems, during the transitional phase, perform as monitors, adjusting equipment in a continuous process to maintain quality of output and avoid breakdowns. This requires monitoring of gauges, controls, and other devices, with consequent complex decision making based on observation of the read-out devices. Sensorimotor skills, so necessary in the operation of production machines, are required to a very minimum extent. The operator has to control independent variables by observing different indicators of performance. He may be required to patrol the equipment, to detect trouble, and to prepare reports and records of performance at specific time intervals. He may also be required to perform routine maintenance, and here we come across some possible restrictions in present job evaluation plans. The skills referred to will be discussed in somewhat greater detail below.

These jobs have no definite work cycles, as presently identified in machine or assembly-line work, and little physical activity or exertion is required. There are occasional periods of rather intense effort as operators start up or shut down a piece of equipment or switch over from one to another. Although individual operators and their units may be physically isolated, there is close contact between them, the technical staff, and management, particularly because of the need for high and rapid information transmission. Shift work increases, and the swing- and night-shift workers have larger responsibility than day-shift operators because of the presence of fewer engineers and technicians. Judging by the chemical industry, we may anticipate that employment will be stable for those who have jobs, because of long-term scheduling of production units in order to maximize the return on high capital investment.

On numerically controlled production machines or computers, machine-front operators carry out scheduled assignments by providing inputs in the form of either taped instructions or card instructions and by controlling and monitoring the operations of the equipment. Providing supplies or feeding of the equipment may also be necessary, but this task is likely to be of a restricted nature. The opportunity for meeting chance demands is limited, since the scope of alternatives for the operator is very precisely defined. Recordkeeping and communication are also required in these jobs. Operators need to know the machine's language or logic and something about the machine's faults or weaknesses so that estimates can be made of the causes of failures or stoppages. Here again sensorimotor and control skills are not required. Nor are operators required to monitor gauges or other read-out equipment or to make fine adjustments to the machines. If development of programs or instructions is not included, then computers make the same demands on operators as do numerically controlled production machines. The main differences are that the production machines require skilled machinists to set up tools and holding devices and have more serious maintenance problems.

For remote-control operations, the main requirement is to interpret arrays of indicators, relating these to each other and making quick decisions. The operators require knowledge and understanding of the operation of the system. In most instances, the indicators are abstractions of the actual working system. The operator evaluates coded information and makes decisions rapidly between well-defined alternatives. The information-handling skills seem to be: (1) selective vigilance, in which the operator must be receptive to some of the incoming signals but not to others and have the ability to determine which signals he should attend to; (2) the ability to translate incoming data, i.e., relate incoming symbolic information to actual occurrences; (3) decision making, i.e., optimizing performance by using knowledge of the system rather than rule of thumb response; (4) a short-term memory for events, combined with an ability to forget them shortly after they have occurred. Unfortunately, human operators are good at long-term memory and poor at short-term memory.

All three types of automated systems call for increased vigilance on the part of the operators. This requirement, in turn, is leading to further technological developments which will eliminate the need for vigilance. The vigilance discussed here is the ability to interpret quickly information presented after a long period of inactivity. Human beings have difficulty responding effectively to such performance demands. We may therefore expect to see these demands reduced in the future by means of equipment.

Which of the skills referred to above are required of operators of automatic plant equipment at present? The identification of these skills or abilities is precisely what is needed today in preparation for entering into the period of more widespread automation. When automation equipment has been fully developed, some of these skills will be taken over by sensing devices within the equipment itself. For example: (1) regulation or stabilization, in which the operators keep processes running under prescribed conditions, making adjustments as necessary; (2) optimization, in which the operator adjusts the process according to certain criteria provided to maximize yield, quality, etc.; (3) making changeovers rapidly from one type of process or product to another; (4) observing, predicting, and assessing breakdowns or stoppages; and (5) minimizing the downtime of equipment should the latter occur. These skills or abilities are presently required of operators in chemical plants and other process plants. Experience seems to indicate that they are nontransferable. The prior skill background of operators who have been taught these skills appears to be not very different from that of semiskilled workers in mass-production plants. The practice of chemical plants has been to select semiskilled operators and train them to perform the necessary regulatory and control activities on specific processes. This program has provided chemical plants with very good operators.

The control skills which seem to be nontransferable appear to be comprised of five components. These are: (1) sensing, which requires the ability to detect by various means how the process is proceeding; (2) perceiving, which is the ability to interpret the read-outs or the information which has been sensed; (3) prediction, which is assessing the consequences of what has been perceived; (4) specific familiarity with the process in terms of which controls are to be manipulated to secure a desired effect; and (5) decision, which is the ability to select the control action which will achieve the optimal result under the circumstances. Decision making is at present the subject of a great deal of empirical and laboratory investigation. Indications are that poor operators decide on the basis of rules of thumb which they have acquired and that good operators follow a mental model of the process and appear to use intuition in the course of determining what is going on and what to do about it. Good operators appear not to use any rational or logical approach which can be identified.[20] Decision making, of course, can take place using a purely logical approach—the worker consciously reasons out the consequences of various steps and comes to a rational decision. Interestingly enough, good operators are able to secure better performance from the process intuitively than are engineers who, as designers of the system, use a purely rational method of control.

For industries that approximate continuous-flow production by means of transfer machines, such as the automotive industry, the general demands and skill requirements of the operators are very similar to those of the process operators previously described. In addition, they are skilled craftsmen engaged in finding ways to maintain quality levels, given the particular faults of the machine tools.

The skill requirements for remote-control process operators appear to be the same as for continuous-flow production operators. The skills of operators of programmed machines, including both numerically controlled production machines and computers, appear to be fewer than those required by continuous-process operators. Since adjustments are not possible, control skills and monitoring are not required. Since programs have built-in checks there is little that an operator can do other than return a program, should error or stoppage occur. If error or stoppage persists, again there is little the operator can do other than to return the program to the programmers or report the difficulty to the technical or maintenance staff.

Given these skill descriptions for machine-front personnel or operators it becomes difficult to assess whether they represent upgrading or downgrading of skills for operators. What is certain is that the work done is completely different from present work, and so are its skill requirements. One way of considering the skill question is to examine the educational and intellectual prerequisites of operators. Indications so far are that the levels required for semiskilled, mass-production jobs will be suitable for operators of automated equipment. Bright's exposition[21] appears to be an accurate forecast. What he holds is that there are 17 levels of mechanization, ranging from manual control to complete control by the equipment (automation). Skills, mental effort, and education required rise to high levels at approximately the middle

---

[20] E. R. F. W. Crossman and J. E. Cooke, "Manual Control of Slow Response Systems," *Proceedings*, Institute of Radio Engineers, International Congress on Human Factors in Electronics, Long Beach, Calif., May 3–4, 1962.
[21] Bright, *op. cit.*

of the continuum and then fall to levels approximating those necessary for purely manual work. The rise is associated with the variability of the process and the interposition of the operator in sensing, adjusting, and regulating the equipment and is not associated with the complexity of the equipment. In fact, where the equipment reaches its ultimate state of complexity, self-sensing and self-adjusting are built into the equipment. However, Bright's conclusion, concurred in here, is that responsibility will increase for operators of automated equipment. This is likely to occur because there may be a joining of machine-front and machine-back activities to make a new type of operator's job.

In industries characterized by rapidly changing technologies, stabilization of processes and ultimate refinement of equipment will not take place. In these industries the skill and education requirements of operators will have to increase as more complex equipment is introduced. It is anticipated, however, that such instances will affect relatively few individuals.

JOBS AND SKILLS OF MACHINE-BACK PERSONNEL

High capital costs, equipment-sequence rigidity, and long-term schedules place a greater premium than ever on management's ability to minimize downtime and related production losses in automated systems. Great effort and research are going into the development of solutions in this problem area. Some of the solutions are transitional, such as the development of repair methods: critical path scheduling, stock banks and spare machine programs, and diagnostic routines. Research is also progressing on long-range solutions to such problems as the matching of the lives of tools and parts (in this the Russians are considerably in advance of the United States), design for maintenance rather than just operation, development of replacement plug-in packing units, self-identification of failure by automatic equipment, and automation of garden-variety maintenance tasks.

Maintenance jobs and skills have to be discussed both in terms of the transitional stage and in terms of the ultimate development of automated equipment. During the present transitional period we find that the maintenance function and its personnel are growing, while the number of operators is decreasing. Will this trend continue? Industries that have automated have increased the ratio of maintenance personnel to operators, and the chemical industry which is at the present time the most advanced in automation shows approximately two maintenance workers for each operator.

The balance of skills within the maintenance labor force appears to remain the same under automation, aside from the introduction of large numbers of electronic technicians and instrument mechanics. Bright indicates that the skills of most of the maintenance crafts are also unaffected in terms of their present levels, if it is assumed that maintenance electricians cannot be converted to electronic technicians.[22]

Maintenance work can be divided into two general classes: routine preventive maintenance and trouble shooting and repair. In both classes, knowledge of control theory, electronic circuitry, and control devices is needed. The trouble-shooting maintenance activity places heavy emphasis on diagnostic techniques for tracking down causes of stoppages. Individual differences in diagnostic skills appear to be rather great, given the same amount of technical training and knowledge.

Some interesting developments are under way which may have a marked effect on the skills of maintenance workers in automated industries. One of these was noted in the job design research study reported on by Davis and Werling.[23] In this study the skills of maintenance workers were broadened. The result was decreased costs of maintenance (with higher wage rates), decreased downtime, increased maintenance quality, and increased quality of product. This sort of change forecasts the likely future pattern of development of maintenance skills in automated industries, particularly in the trouble-shooting and repair segments of maintenance work. A similar development has already taken place in France: the *polyvalent* craftsman. This multiskilled craftsman is trained in both electrical and mechanical practice so that he can service modern equipment in which the electrical and mechanical parts and controls are interlocked.

A third development which the technology of automation demands and which has yet to take place is the creation of the control technician. Control technicians will be trained in electronics, servo-mechanisms, and control theory and will be capable of setting up, servicing automatic controls and instruments, and diagnosing operating faults. The types of control systems present in automated equipment are: hydraulic, pneumatic, electrical, electronic, and mechanical. This is a growing area of skill need with which our educational system has not dealt very well. The technical institutes prevalent in many European countries are missing from the educational scene here. Given the failure to provide such training and skills, industry has to provide them internally or through arrangements with nearby training institutions.

INDIRECT WORK

Nothing has been said thus far about indirect work since the traditional division between direct and indirect work will change with automation and become

---

[22] *Ibid.*
[23] Davis and Werling, *op. cit.*

relatively slight. The probability is that specialized control technicians, present-day set-up operators, set-up specialists, and programmers for computers will be needed for the present. As automation progresses to its final evolution the demand for these people will be reduced, although a few will remain as specialists within the organization.

Numerically controlled machines require programmers of considerable technical education. Such programmers, few in each organization, will have university-level educations in engineering or mathematics. However, in the final development of automation machinery computers will be preparing programs. As at present, the operator of automatic equipment will be unaffected by the skills and technical competence of programmers and set-up specialists. Although it is not clear at present, the findings of job design research indicate that increased productivity and quality result from the inclusion of set-up, inspection, and control among the tasks of operators. For some automated systems, then, there is a distinct possibility that the jobs of operators, or direct workers, will be combined with those of indirect workers.

CONCLUSIONS

1.   Under automation, work and jobs at the operator level are so different from more conventional production jobs that there are no means for making direct comparisons of content or skills. Some serious questions should be raised about the feasibility of public policies directed toward raising and changing skill levels when so little knowledge is available.

2.   Skills for operator jobs appear to be nontransferable and consist largely of monitoring or information handling, adjusting, and making judgments and taking actions which will minimize downtime. These skills have been acquired by workers drawn from backgrounds equivalent to those of semiskilled operators in present mass-production industries. The fears expressed in some quarters concerning a technological lockout of workers seeking to enter automated industries appear to be unwarranted.

3.   The pessimistic views expressed by sociologists regarding the effects of jobs in automated industries may be interpreted as reflecting their disappointment over the failure of the predictions that automation would raise skill levels, remove drudgery, and generally provide a new world of jobs for workers. Automation represents a continuation of the rationalization and mechanization of the production of goods and services which began about 150 years ago. The significant differences between jobs under automation and those in mass-production systems are that automation increases the operator's responsibility, his over-view of the process, his technical information, his sense of consequences, and his informational integration with technicians and engineers.

4.   In the area of union-management agreements, new approaches will have to be developed for providing compensation above base levels and for the evaluation of jobs. Present job evaluation schemes with their built-in inflexibility will prove to be inhibiting to the application of automation.

5.   The ultimate development of operator jobs under automation will probably result in a breakdown of the boundaries between machine-front and machine-back work.   These jobs will combine monitoring, regulating, adjusting, and spot maintenance. The prediction is based upon the trends toward job enlargement stemming from job design research, the development of relative self-reliance, and the increased responsibility characteristic of automated jobs.

6.   For maintenance work there will be an increase in skills and content. For the same job-enlargement reasons, our equivalent to the *polyvalent* craftsman will probably be developed.   Control system technicians will also be developed and may well become a new type of maintenance technician.

7.   Considering industry and business as a whole, there will be an upgrading of jobs as a consequence of automation, in that the relative number of engineers, scientists, and analysts will continue to increase.

11.

PROGRAMMED INSTRUCTION: TWO PERSPECTIVES

THEODORE B. DOLMATCH

A.   PROGRAMMED INSTRUCTION: THE BASIC VOCABULARY

In any new field, a technical vocabulary develops along with the subject area itself. In programmed learning, the special vocabulary is already large, and it is still growing. Some time may be needed before there is general agreement—even among the experts—about the meaning of every term. It is certainly a mistake to rely on the usual dictionary definitions, or even on any single specialist's definitions, to provide an understanding of programmed instruction.   The

Reprinted by permission of the publisher from *Revolution in Training: Programmed Instruction in Industry*, by Theodore B. Dolmatch, Elizabeth Marting, and Robert E. Finley. © 1962 by the American Management Association, Inc.

word "programming" itself, for example, may suggest parallels between computer programming and programmed instruction that do not in fact exist. Nevertheless, a brief review of some of the key concepts and the terms most generally used to designate them will serve to make discussion easier and more consistent.

Common Words and Phrases

In programmed instruction, a *program* is a sequence of *items*, *steps*, or *frames* which presents material to the learner. Each frame contains new information and/or a recapitulation of information, combined with some material requiring a response (called the *stimulus*). This may be a question, a fill-in, or a problem to be solved. The size of each frame varies with the programming technique used and with the special requirements of the subject matter.

After each of his responses, the learner is provided with information about the correctness, quality, or appropriateness of his response (*feedback*). On the basis of this feedback, the learner determines whether or not he has grasped the material. Since the material in each frame is carefully structured and builds very precisely on preceding information, errors should be minimal. Thus the learner has the *reward* of being frequently correct. This gratification is both *reinforcement* and a stimulus to future learning.

Since the learner is continuously involved and is guided toward learning by the nature of the material itself (aided sometimes by *augmenting statements* or by *prompts*), programmed instruction is said to *control behavior* during the learning process.

Basic to every program, according to the *NEA Journal*, are controlled presentation of material, the active response of the learner, the use of *cues* (prompts) to elicit the correct responses, immediate confirmation of success or failure, and reinforcement of correct responses to encourage the individual learner to move ahead at his own pace from familiar material to some previously determined terminal point.

The Major Approaches

Just as it is easy to become confounded by the jargon, so we can too easily become partisans of one or another of the various schools of programming to the exclusion of the others. This partisanship can result in our stressing the differences among the various techniques, rather than in our using any and all methodologies that help us reach our goal: learning.

One of the major approaches to programming follows principles enunciated by Dr. B. F. Skinner, a professor of psychology at Harvard. It is distinguished by its use of two techniques, both designed to produce rapid, error-free learning:

1. A *linear* or single-track form. The program is designed to lead the student

through the material in an unbroken sequence of steps. This is differentiated from the *branching* form of programming, which provides parallel tracks onto which the student moves if he chooses an answer other than that which is considered the "best" one.

2. The *constructed response.* The student is required to compose his own response to each question (or other testing opportunity). A fill-in would be a typical constructed response. This type of response should be differentiated from that which requires the learner to choose one from a number of possible —that is, rational but not necessarily true—responses already provided in the text (*multiple-choice*).

Skinnerian programmers believe that errors inhibit or are *aversive* to learning. By making each step in the learning process small, by using prompts, and by basing each small increment of learning on previously learned material, they reduce the chance that the student will fail to grasp the information correctly. Therefore, they also reduce the chance that the student's constructed response will be incorrect. While these programs need not be completely error-free, the number of possible errors should be rigorously controlled.

Another approach to programming, that favored by Norman A. Crowder, employs the multiple-choice response and generally provides more information per frame. Learners who make the wrong choice from among those presented find themselves shunted onto another track or branch which corrects their error or further clarifies the point in question. The branching sequence may continue for a number of frames, again depending on the student's responses, before the learner finds himself back on the main track. Crowder's *intrinsic programming* focuses on determining whether the communication of information from program to learner is successful, and through branching provides a remedy in case of failure.

As programming techniques develop and other specialists enter this growing field, certain combinations of techniques are appearing that make classification more and more difficult. Thus there are now linear programs which contain multiple-choice frames, and there are basically linear programs with branching sequences. This development reinforces the belief that the major differences between Skinner and Crowder lie more in the realm of philosophy than in the kind of track or in the kind of stimulus provided. . . .

B. A MANAGERIAL PERSPECTIVE ON PROGRAMMED INSTRUCTION

The typical position description for the job of "training director" very likely includes a statement that the training director's responsibilities include "keeping informed about new methods and techniques for training."

Teaching machines and programmed learning have been very much in the news lately. Both the popular press and the business magazines have reported on these new instructional concepts. Meetings of training specialists have been held, till by now it is quite clear that the training director must look into teaching machines and programmed learning in order to meet his responsibilities and capitalize on his opportunities.

Shortly after he gets involved in the field, however, the training man may become disenchanted. The jargon, the number of new gimmicks and gadgets, and the expense of some of the paraphernalia to his mind add up to one thing: Teaching machines and programmed learning—whatever they may offer—are something he can do without for the time being. Perhaps he can be sold on them later, but not now.

There is no doubt that, like many other new areas of inquiry, programmed learning has its special terminology, its cabalistic expertise, and its marginal practitioners. The field seems to be growing so quickly that self-professed experts are having a field day, everyone wants to get into the act, and some undercapitalized and undertalented entrepreneurs see only the opportunity for a quick dollar. The idea that this field is something very complicated and arcane, requiring the help of costly advisers, is a very attractive idea—for those advisers. The phrase "teaching machine" itself calls to mind boxes full of electronic gadgetry, and the cost of some of these teaching machines is enough—despite projected savings—to make strong controllers weep.

Nevertheless, programmed instruction is a significant new tool for the training director, and it may be helpful to try to put it in its proper perspective—proper for the training director and the executive, that is. The educational psychologist and the research man have their own special requirements, but it should be helpful to avoid some of the complexity that a consideration of their needs always seems to produce.

Wrong Choice of Words

To make a start, it might be best to avoid the phrase "teaching machine" altogether. It is an attractive combination of words, calling to mind flashing lights and robots. It seems to imply an application of modern technology to that old-fashioned process called "learning." However, it is misleading, and we might be better off if it had never been invented.

If a "teaching machine" is a man-made device that instructs, then a book is a teaching machine, and so is an educational film or recording. So are the Link trainer, the mockups of company products and equipment used in many training programs, and other simulation mechanisms, some of them very elaborate. Since "teaching machine" can describe so many different instructional devices, whether or not any new concepts or principles are involved, many producers of films, tapes, and records have set themselves up as teaching-machine specialists. And it is the rare "teaching-machine exhibit" that does not include instructional devices in rapid and remedial reading, foreign-language records, and similar helpful tools. How natural it is for some producers of these instructional devices to pick up the fashionable designation, dropping the old label until the time comes to pick it up again. How natural, too, for the user of instructional aids to be confused and irritated.

The term "teaching machine" produces an unfortunate reaction in many people. Some teachers see themselves becoming obsolete because of this new-fangled machine, and some training directors wonder secretly whether they too will be casualties of automation. Their feelings are similar to those the accountant had when he was first faced with the computer. Indeed, the same training director who once gave courses to accounting personnel designed to allay the fears of technological change may now need the same sort of reassurance he provided for them.

He can have them. He and the teacher will not be replaced any more than the accountant was. As a matter of fact, there are few parallels between the effects of the data-processing machine and the teaching machine except those suggested by the unfortunate term "teaching machine" itself. The chief similarities are two: First, this kind of instruction may accelerate learning just as data processing speeded up data collection. Second, it should upgrade the job of the training man, just as EDP upgraded the financial and information-gathering functions. But these similarities are fortuitous, and they are not enhanced by the designation "teaching machine."

The term has one other major disadvantage. It gratuitously provides ammunition for the pseudo-intellectuals who persist in seeing teaching as a mystical communion between teacher (in tweeds with pipe) and student (with shining eyes). In an era of extensive mechanization, are we to automate that last citadel of the intellect—teaching? Even if the answer is a clear "no," the purist may still react viscerally to that loaded word "machine."

The Case for "Programmed Instruction"

It may be optimistic to hope that the "teaching machine" idea will lose its fascination, particularly since the Sunday supplements are addicted to such catchy concepts. In any case, a much better term is "programmed instruction," for it describes what is being done and has appropriate overtones of the organized, systematic approach to the act of instruction which is the key to this new method.

Programmed instruction, as the term is used here, means more than the simple ordering of course material. It is instruction that meets these specific criteria:

1. It is individualized; that is, one person learns at a time. The device speaks to him without the intercession of a monitor or tutor.

2. The device presents material to be learned in minimal increments. It operates on the principle that we learn better in small doses, and that we also learn better if we avoid error. By proceeding in small steps, we obviously reduce the likelihood of error.

3. That which is to be taught is rigorously ordered. Because of the desire to hold errors to an absolute or pre-ordained minimum, each step in the learning process has to follow logically, as well as closely, the one preceding it.

4. Students progress at their own pace. Instead of being restricted to a classroom situation where the norm of learning must become the pace of every student in the room, each user of a programmed instructional device learns as quickly as he is able. His rate of accomplishment is established by his performance alone.

5. The student's answer is almost instantaneously checked against the correct response, which appears before the next question is asked. In this way, the student receives the reassurance that his answer (response) is correct, and the very appearance of the correct answer reinforces his learning. If the answer is incorrect, he can easily locate the reason for his error, without, as in traditional learning, discovering that he is—all at once—at sea.

Any instructional device can be accepted or rejected on its own merits, whether or not it meets these five criteria. Calling any audiovisual or other educational tool a "teaching machine" does not make it one, and even if all these criteria are met, it is optimisitic to assume that programmed instruction, simply by virtue of its *being* programmed instruction, teaches any better or any worse than other kinds of instruction.

There are good and bad programs, just as there are good and bad teachers. The good ones do the job well, and the poorest are probably worse than nothing at all. At this time, in the infancy of programmed instruction, we are more likely to find programs that do not meet our standards, but this should not deter us from searching out the good programs and benefiting from them.

Keys to the Evaluation Problem

Determining which *are* the good programs is vital, and it is not much more difficult than determining the quality of any other brand of instruction. Evaluation, in short, requires pre-established standards. Most instruction has as its goal *changed behavior*, but it is rather discouraging to note how little this goal is analyzed or even considered when the quality of instruction is measured. The academic world can, if it chooses, evaluate teaching by counting its teachers' advanced degrees and frequency of publication, by having supervisors make annual classroom visits, or by similar criteria. Teaching in industry cannot be weighed by these factors.

Industry is, in fact, more fortunate than the college in this respect. We need not rely on examinations for data. We have many more valid measurements of performance, if we will identify and use them. The great amount of numerical data available to us, the graphs, charts, and balance sheets that are a fundamental part of industry, should be our starting point. Management cannot afford to accept intuition as a measure, and it has no need to do so.

The need for evaluation in the training department is of course not confined to its use of programmed instruction. Every kind of training, every method, every approach is amenable to proper testing and should be evaluated in this way. It is not surprising that so much industrial training is done on faith; the analogue we find in the academic world encourages us to accept it without question. But faith isn't enough. In industry, we train in order to produce more and better products, and we have production and quality control records to tell us whether we are getting them. We train to get more work done per hour, and time records tell us whether we are succeeding. We train to get better supervisors, and in addition to these production, quality control, and time data we have attendance, grievance, turnover, maintenance, safety, and many other records with which to measure our supervision. Finally, we have balance sheets and a variety of financial records—the payoff—which provide a kind of final examination for the company as a whole.

Improvement in performance, demonstrated by positive changes in these data, is the goal of training. It is the training director's job to search out the correlations between his program and performance—not to manufacture the correlations or ride along on the coattails of a recession that reduces turnover, absenteeism, or grievances. And it is also his job to provide the best possible training to produce improved performance.

The Conflict of the Theorists

In his search for effective training methods, the specialist has discovered programmed instruction. Experiments in schools and in the military indicate that it is truly an important new concept, with applications of great potential significance to business and industrial training. It is also a new concept with a great many conflicting theories and practices. Should the program be "linear," "branching," multiple-choice, or what have you? What subject matter is appropriate for programming? Who will help us construct a program?

At this time, one of the most unrewarding of practices is for the average training man to attempt to become an expert in programming itself. A few pioneer training departments are in fact developing programmers within the company, and the day may come when industry will handle its own program construction as a matter of course, but that day isn't here yet. Some directors may be interested in finding out all about the conflicting schools of programming and the complex experimentation that has influenced their thinking and is still going on; for them, the bibliography at the end of this book will give an idea of the available literature.[1] I have a feeling, however, that too much concern with theory might complicate the complicated and allow the primary job—getting improved performance—to be sidetracked, perhaps forever.

As a matter of fact, the odds are great that much of the current conflict among the theorists will be resolved as more programs are issued and evaluated. At present, many of the companies working in the field seem more interested in the "machines" than in the instruction.

A More Logical Emphasis

There may be a parallel here in the development of the safety razor. When it first appeared, it was an expensive device; the blades were very much an after-thought. It eventually became clear, however, that not only did the blade do the shaving but there was more money in blades. And there was also something to be said for blades which fitted many different razors.

In terms of marketing, it would seem logical for the companies involved in programmed learning to emphasize the program rather than the device carrying it—the blade, rather than the razor. This doesn't seem to be the case now, although some purveyors of programmed learning (shall we call them "manufac-turers," "publishers," "programmers," or what?) are beginning to pay more attention to the material itself. The time may come, of course, when the program —complete and ready for use—will be available as a unit that includes its own "machinery."

Such a unit has already been achieved by certain book publishers, who have issued "scrambled books" or programs that look like books on the outside but have text pages designed according to the principles of programmed learning. Unfortunately, these programmed books are somewhat unwieldy to use, and they do not motivate the learner as some of the machines do. Indeed, even though one would wish otherwise, the "look of the book" seems to have negative effects on many students, regardless of the look of the inside pages.

Experimentation now going on indicates the probability of new devices that will be less expensive than some that are now being sold. It also seems most likely that the form of the particular device may eventually depend on the program

---

[1] I would recommend three books in particular: (1) A. A. Lumsdaine and Robert Glaser (editors), *Teaching Machines and Programmed Learning: A Source Book*, National Education Association, Department of Audio-Visual Instruction, Washington, D.C., 1960; (2) Jerome P. Lysaught (editor), *Programmed Learning: Evolving Principles and Industrial Applications*, The Foundation for Research on Human Behavior, Ann Arbor, Michigan, 1961; (3) Eugene Galanter (editor), *Automatic Teaching: The State of the Art*, John Wiley & Sons, New York, 1959.

it carries. Thus programming an assembly operation may require a machine that includes motion pictures, special earphones, and other complex attachments —and be very much worthwhile—while programming a course in supervision may call for no more than a text which a man can carry in his pocket.

Constructors of programs, now arguing over the relative merits of branching or linear methods, may find that some subjects require one technique, some another. Or they may discover that both methods can combine to provide better instruction than either alone. Or, as they learn more about the subject, they may find that a new method, neither linear nor branching, works better yet. The test lies in the student's responses, not in the theoretician's.

In short, the validation, not the organization, of the program is the key to its use.

What Can a Company Do?

At the present time, with so many variations among programs and machines, it seems questionable whether a company should commit itself to large capital expenditures for instructional apparatus. There are, of course, certain specific situations where a particular machine program, whose efficacy in similar circumstances has already been demonstrated, may be called for. Much experimentation with programmed learning can be done by paper-and-pencil methods, however.

If the manual devices somehow do not reproduce the motivation of the electronic gadgets, that is too bad—but it also may be more realistic to face facts from the start. Every new gadget supplies, while it is new, a special motivation: people like to play with it. This motivation may speed learning now, but it is likely to wear off as the gadget becomes familiar. Even the paper devices provide some incentives based on their newness and format, but why evaluate the success of an instructional device on the basis of evanescent advantages?

It also seems likely that experimentation will reveal that certain subjects can be best taught by one kind of program, that other subjects call for another kind, and that still other subjects call for combinations of programming methods that now seem to be imcompatible.

It would seem appropriate for the training specialist to try different kinds of programs—for skill training, for supervisory development, and for all the other training areas for which he is responsible. He should, for economies in time and money, select those that seem immediately applicable and are the work of well-known producers of sound programmed materials. He should search for validation, but he should try not to be too impressed by studies which prove that carefully structured programmed instruction produces better results than "traditional" instruction. The real question is *what kind* of traditional methods were used. Ideally, we should compare different methods of similar quality, but how often has this been done so far?

Arguments in Favor of Programming

Even if a good program and good traditional instruction produce the same level of performance and the same retention of knowledge, there may be very good reasons to use programmed instruction in industry whenever possible.

First, the time spent in conventional training costs a great deal of money. It is time taken away from production time. If programmed instruction speeds learning, then it is a cost-cutting (time-saving) tool of great significance.

Second, the consistency of the program—with each learner getting the same material—may solve many problems. The swing shift can expect to be taught as well as the day shift, even though the best human instructor is home with his family. Equivalent training should produce equivalent performance, which is always desirable.

Third, since programmed instruction is a solo affair, the juggling of schedules to get a class together is unnecessary. And each learner gets his training at his own pace, so that the fast students can be made productive more rapidly, without being held back by the class.

Fourth, programmed instruction by its design provides a great deal of motivation beyond that supplied by the device itself. It sets up a situation in which the student is virtually compelled to learn by the subtle pressures of the program and his desire to learn is increased by immediate reinforcement.

Finally, programmed instruction gives the training director a new role in industry. He can subordinate his role as instructor, attendance-checker, and test administrator. Relieved of these tasks, he can spend more time searching for the correlations between training and performance, refining his courses of instruction to increase their tie-in with actual company needs. He can identify the specific areas needing more instruction and help the students in the precise areas where they are having special difficulty. In short, like the finance man with EDP, he has a new tool to help him and a new competency through which he can help his company.

12.

LINE MANAGEMENT'S PARTICIPATION IN CLASSIFICATION DECISIONS

R. Permin Everett and Wade J. Williams

What role should line management play in making classification decisions? We believe personnel management in California state government has developed to the point that line management is willing and ready to accept the responsibility —and the accountability—for classification decisions without preaudit. In this article we focus attention on a program to encourage management's participation in classification decisions and the benefits to be derived from such a program.

Each agency must decide whether, and to what extent, operating departments will participate in classification decisions. This decision depends on such factors as the acceptance of the merit principle by the departments, the maturity of the organization, the political environment within which it operates, and its basic goals and objectives. If the personnel department is primarily engaged in fighting the spoils system and does not enjoy the active cooperation of line management, the central personnel department is probably making all classification decisions. The more mature merit system, which has won the acceptance and cooperation of line management, will typically have broadened its program with more emphasis on other aspects of personnel management and will have been able to delegate a large percentage of classification decisions to the operating departments.

CLASSIFICATION IS NOT A GAME

When the central personnel department makes all of the classification decisions, an interesting type of gamesmanship often develops. It challenges some line managers to push for reclassifications they might not approve if they were held accountable for the decision. There is no penalty for trying, and the line manager finds he is neither responsible nor accountable for the accuracy of the decisions.

With this attitude of gamesmanship, the line manager may not be too careful in seeing that all of the facts are presented to the central personnel department. He does not necessarily present misinformation. He is more likely to present the

Reprinted from *Public Personnel Review*, Vol. 24, No. 1 (January, 1963), pp. 30–36.

information most favorable to his case and leave it up to the personnel department to bring to light contradictory information. Where this condition exists, there will be continuing conflict between agencies and central personnel. The resulting opponent-proponent relationship has had unfortunate consequences. More than one central personnel department has had to ask itself whether "winning all of the classification battles" has sacrificed cooperative working relationships with agency management and reduced its effectiveness over other aspects of personnel administration such as employee appraisal and development, employee utilization, and employee motivation and discipline.

This opponent-proponent relationship also provides a framework which encourages the central personnel department analyst to be on the lookout for areas of difference. Interestingly, the magnitude of the differences which develop between central personnel analysts and department management often are enlarged out of proportion to the total problem. Big differences sometimes arise over small or insignificant problems. These differences then block or lengthen the solution of the main problem.

All virtue does not reside in the central personnel department, and the active participation of line management in classification decisions brings many advantages to the central personnel department. The primary advantage stems from improved relations between the personnel staff and line management. The reduction of time spent on individual position allocation disputes releases staff time to develop broad forward-looking personnel management programs. The essential problem is obtaining line management acceptance of the responsibility and accountability for accurate allocation of its positions.

MODIFIED CLASSIFICATION REVIEW

The experience of the California State Personnel Board indicates that one of the best ways to assure acceptance of responsibility by management is to have management participate in the establishment of position allocation standards. Typically, disagreements on position allocations that arise between line management and the central personnel department are not over facts but over differences in understanding and interpretation of the allocation standards. Active participation by line management in the development of the standards has the interesting result that they accept the standards as their own, rather than standards imposed upon them.

As this understanding and acceptance of classification standards has grown in the California state service, the Personnel Board has gradually adopted a program of delegation of classification decisions to department management. We have titled our program "Modified Classification Review" and it is now commonly referred to as "MCR."

The Personnel Board's Modified Classification Review Program began very inauspiciously and has grown gradually over a period of eight years. In its essentials, it consists of two lists of classes, List I and List II, which meet established criteria listed below. Appointment to positions in classes on MCR are not given a preaudit by Personnel Board analysts. Although appointments are thus processed without preaudit, the State Personnel Board is still responsible for the proper classification of positions in state service as provided by Constitutional provision. This duty is performed by appropriate post-audit programs, one of which is the Personnel Board's departmental classification survey. These surveys have not disclosed an increase in misclassified positions following inauguration of the MCR program.

MCR Policy

The policy of the State Personnel Board is that as many classes as possible should be placed on Modified Classification Review. There are, however, a small number of classes which are excluded from MCR and retained for prior review of all allocations by a Personnel Board analyst. Examples of these exemptions are:

1. One-position classes (most of which are high-level administrative and management classes), the filling of which is likely to have important organizational implications.
2. Classes for which no written allocation standards or levels descriptions have been developed and agreed upon by the operating agencies and the Personnel Board staff. As such standards or levels descriptions are agreed upon, these classes will be considered for addition to List I or II.
3. Classes for which specifications are under study for revision and sufficient questions have arisen about the allocation of positions to warrant the classes being removed from List I or II.

Criteria for MCR

Classes are included in Modified Classification Review List I if they meet one of the following criteria:

1. Classes for which the consequence of an individual position allocation error is relatively minor and the filling of a position would not have important organizational implications.
2. Classes in which the levels are clearly defined and the characteristics which distinguish the levels are clearly identified.
3. Classes which are on continuous testing.

Classes included in Modified Classification Review List II are those classes that do not fully meet the criteria listed for classes on List I but are not specifically excluded from MCR. These are classes in which initial allocation of positions by a Personnel Board analyst is required. Subsequent filling of positions in these classes will not require review by the analyst when the agency certifies that there are no substantive changes in the duties of the position.

MCR Expansion

Over the eight-year period, application of MCR criteria has resulted in 1,011 classes being included in List I and 1,286 on List II, out of a total of 2,815 classes in state service. Furthermore, most of the populous classes are included on List I with the consequence that 81 per cent of the appointments in state service are made without a prior classification review by a personnel analyst in the Personnel Board.

To further the assumption of responsibility for classification by the operating departments, several approaches have been developed. In the Department of Water Resources an experimental program is underway in which the Department management plans to place more responsibility for position allocation decisions on line supervisors. This is presented as Case 1. Another approach is discussed as Case 2 where classification responsibility was also delegated to the department head of the State Compensation Insurance Fund who has assigned it primarily to the departmental personnel office.

CASE 1. DEPARTMENT OF WATER RESOURCES

During the classification survey of the California State Department of Water Resources, the Personnel Board staff found that many supervisors, knowing that final responsibility for position classification rested elsewhere, felt no personal responsibility for the accurate classification of their positions. After discussing this fact with the top management of the Department, a program was developed to emphasize the responsibility of the line supervisor for position classification decisions.

To assist in this program, the director of the department appointed seven professional engineers at the first and second supervisory levels to serve on a committee to: (1) determine the appropriate engineering class series needed by the department, (2) review professional and nonprofessional engineering positions to identify factors which are significant in determining proper classification levels, (3) develop objective standards for classification of professional and nonprofessional positions, and (4) recommend methods of developing supervisory acceptance of these standards and of training supervisors in their administration. In addition to the professional engineers, there were representatives of the departmental personnel office and the State Personnel Board on the committee.

Staff members of the departmental personnel office and the State Personnel Board actively participated in the discussions. It was also their responsibility to schedule meetings, gather and disseminate information during and between meetings, act as a catalyst for development of ideas and see that all participants were given the opportunity to present their points of view. The Personnel Board retained final responsibility for the content of standards for classification of both professional and nonprofessional positions.

Role of Classification Workshop Committee

The Department of Water Resources Classification Workshop Committee held a series of weekly half-day meetings for a period of six months. The end product of these meetings was a committee recommendation, jointly agreed to by the Personnel Board staff, which recommended:

1. Establishment of new classes and revisions of others.
2. Departmental acceptance of accountability and responsibility for classification without preaudit by the Personnel Board.
3. In carrying out this classification responsibility, the levels descriptions developed by the Committee be used.
4. To effect this program, line supervisors be provided training in the following subjects:
   a. Use of levels descriptions.
   b. Limitations of levels descriptions.
   c. Supervisor's responsibility for correct classification by level and by class.
   d. Use of classification as a supervisory tool.
   e. Classification concepts of the classes used in the department.

Primary emphasis by the Classification Workshop Committee was on engineering classes. Levels descriptions for the Geology, Drafting, and Clerical series were also prepared jointly by the staffs of the department and the Personnel Board, and these classes were included in the MCR lists.

The Director accepted these recommendations and the Personnel Board staff developed a program to put them into effect. This program is described below. (Due to two very substantial reorganizations in the department, all of the program has not yet been effected.)

Because this proposal went further than previous uses of MCR, it was believed desirable to clarify the responsibilities of the Personnel Board and the Department of Water Resources in a letter of understanding between the Executive

Officer of the Personnel Board and the Department Director. Future programs will typically not be formalized to this extent, but will merely be outlined in a letter to the department from the Personnel Board staff. The letter of understanding covered in detail the following matters:

1. Assumption of classification responsibility by the Department.
2. The standards for adding other classes to the MCR program in the future.
3. The acceptance of the levels descriptions and their use by line supervisors in allocating individual positions.
4. Responsibility of the Department and the Personnel Board to discuss revisions in the levels descriptions in cases where the levels descriptions are not clear or a new type of work develops.
5. The training program.
6. The post-audit program and the development of periodic reports on staffing ratios, position reallocations, and new positions.

The Department then embarked on a training program to provide line supervisors with the skills necessary for the accurate allocation of positions supervised by them.

Position Allocation Training

The training sessions consisted of four hours of training for all engineering supervisors. The training sessions were divided into an hour and one half general session and then smaller conference groups of 10 to 15 supervisors for the remaining two and one half hours. At the general session, top management made a presentation covering the development of the program, the interest of the Department Director in having line supervisors assume a more active role and responsibility for position classification, and the advantages of the program to the Department. The departmental personnel office developed a supervisor's handbook explaining position classification and the supervisor's responsibilities. This handbook plus the allocation standards and a written report on the program were furnished to each supervisor and a film strip was presented covering the supervisor's handbook.

The conference groups of 10 to 15 supervisors were led by one of the professional engineers who participated in the development of the program or by a personnel analyst from the departmental personnel office. The small conferences permitted supervisors to ask questions concerning the allocation standards and their role in the program. There also was opportunity for each group to work through two or three allocation case problems to test the levels descriptions and the training the supervisors had received.

Postaudit

The Water Resources proposals call for the development of a postaudit program, which has not yet been inaugurated. The extension of the Modified Classification Review to a department is not conditioned upon a formal postaudit program. It was developed here at the request of the Department of Water Resources to provide adequate management reports which would assure the Director that they were operating the classification plan correctly.

The proposed program provides that the department will:

1. Prepare a quarterly listing which shows the ratio of various levels in their class series by division and department-wide.
2. Develop with the State Personnel Board general tolerances which will encompass normal variations in staffing ratios.
3. Maintain a register of new position allocations and reclassifications to facilitate sample postaudits of these actions.
4. Make special classification reviews in those divisions where staffing ratios exceed the tolerances to identify the reasons therefore.

The State Personnel Board will:

1. Review with the Department semiannually the staffing ratios described in paragraph 1 above. This review is for the purpose of informing the Board staff as to (a) variations in the staffing ratios, (b) staffing trends, and (c) reclassification actions.
2. Conduct desk audits of a random sample of classification decisions on new positions and reclassified positions and others as indicated by the review of staffing ratios. Where the determination of the Board staff member differs from that of the Department, the item is to be discussed with the personnel staff of the agency to determine whether this difference was due to inadequate standards or differences in the interpretation of the standards. In the former case, the Department and the Board will prepare revisions to the standards. In the latter case, if it is agreed that the supervisor was in error, the Department will call it to the attention of the supervisor concerned and an appropriate course of corrective action is to be taken.
3. After five years, conduct a complete classification audit to determine the accuracy of the Department's classification program.

At the time the Department of Water Resources was surveyed, it had 1,649 permanent civil service positions allocated to 197 different classes. Approximately 23 per cent of the Department's classes were under the Modified Classification Review program at the start of the classification survey. Following the adoption of the program listed above in April, 1961, 80 per cent of the Department's classes were under the MCR program and this included approximately 90 per cent of the Department's employees.

CASE 2.   CALIFORNIA STATE
COMPENSATION INSURANCE FUND

The California State Compensation Insurance Fund has 1,100 employees located in the headquarters office in San Francisco and 17 field offices. The State Fund's participation in an expanded Modified Classification Review Program developed as a natural outgrowth of a long history of general agreement on allocation standards between the Personnel Board and the State Fund. By reason of this close working relationship, the Personnel Board suggested the State Fund consider an expanded Modified Classification Review program to eliminate the duplicate review of position allocation documents. The State Fund personnel officer and the Personnel Board analyst developed a proposed MCR program.

The climate was right for consideration of change since top management had previously shown in other areas of operation a desire to implement new and improved management and personnel programs. In response to management's questions on the advantages of the proposed program over the existing preaudit of personnel documents by the Personnel Board, the personnel officer indicated the advantages were:

1. Clearer identification of the personnel officer's role as an advisor and consultant on personnel and organization to line staff rather than a middle man between the line staff and the Personnel Board.

2. Quicker action with less documentation.

3. The proper climate for the development of a greater feeling of responsibility for classification decisions by line division chiefs and subordinates.

Management recognized that in accepting this type of program, they were assuming classification responsibility and accountability. Decisions would be made by management rather than passing them on to the Personnel Board to be acted upon.

Extent of MCR Coverage

The proposed expanded MCR program which was accepted by State Fund added 27 technical and clerical classes covering 500 positions to the existing MCR List I. The expanded MCR program, coupled with the existing classes on MCR, resulted in all but the Assistant General Manager class being on MCR.

Levels descriptions for the delegated classes were prepared jointly by the Personnel Board and State Fund and then approved by State Fund and the Personnel Board staff.

The expanded MCR program was implemented in the agency on February 1, 1962, by a letter from the Personnel Board to the Department, outlining the program. The Department then presented the program in writing and in oral presentation to their top management officers at the division chief level and above.

Postaudit

The Compensation Insurance Fund postaudit program consists of frequent verbal discussions between the Personnel Officer and the Personnel Board analyst concerning proposed allocations which are on the fringes of the levels descriptions. The levels descriptions are then modified if necessary to cover these positions. There will also be periodic sample inspections of the records in the departmental personnel office to see how the program is working. Desk audits can be made if needed, but primary emphasis in the postaudit is placed on a review of the written record, such as position duty statements.

The department believes the most beneficial aspects of the whole program have been (1) the recognition by line staff of the need to develop better planning to present effectively requests to management for organization changes, classification changes and staffing needs, and (2) the inclusion of the personnel office in the early planning stages for consultation and advice. An unanticipated further benefit was that the line staff found it to their advantage to develop a complete package concerning their proposed request rather than thinking of personnel as one aspect to be dealt with separately from other considerations. Still another benefit is that classification decisions are clearly identified as having been made by the department. If line staff is not happy with a particular classification decision at least they know they failed to sell top management rather than rationalize that a third party, the Personnel Board, didn't understand their problem.

SUMMARY

The State Personnel Board has followed a program of gradual delegation of responsibility for position classification decisions to operating agencies. One of the long-range goals is the ultimate assumption of this responsibility by line supervisors. However, this is not a condition of delegation and the extent of this further delegation has been left to the operating department's discretion. As the staff has worked with the departments in developing programs of further delegation, realized and potential advantages have become apparent.

1. It makes possible the transfer of analyst time from individual classification decision to the development of allocation standards.
2. Focuses attention on the responsibility of the agencies for proper classifica-

tion and results in more attention by agency management to position classification.

3. The de-emphasis of the Personnel Board's "policeman" role, and resulting better relationship between the Personnel Board technical staff and the operating departments facilitates more effective personnel service to the departments.

4. The joint development of allocation standards with line management contributes to the willing acceptance of these standards.

5. Creates a better climate for joint discussion of the broader aspects of personnel management.

6. Supervisors learn to use classification as a tool of supervision and an integral part of the normal process of establishing positions, assigning duties and classifying the resulting job.

7. Assumption of this responsibility has resulted in supervisors doing a better job of management planning.

8. Places the departmental personnel officer in the role of advisor to management rather than intermediary between line management and the Personnel Board.

We have been pleased with the operation of the Modified Classification Review program. There will be other specific programs developed, tailor-made to meet each particular department's needs.

13.

FIGHTING THE SPOILSMEN: THE STATE OF CIVIL EMPLOY IN THE HOUSE OF REPRESENTATIVES OF 1901

WILLIAM DUDLEY FOULKE

... Persons appointed to perform certain work were assigned to occupations entirely different. Thus the House telegrapher worked in the stationery room, while the man who actually performed the work of telegrapher was paid from an appropriation of $900 for the "hire of horses and wagons and cartage for

Reprinted from William Dudley Foulke, *Fighting the Spoilsmen* (New York: G. P. Putnam's Sons, 1919), pp. 137–39.

use of clerk's office." Meanwhile the man who received $1200 as telegrapher spent his time in the library compiling biographies of the members of Congress, a "leisurely place" where "you didn't have to perspire a great deal," though $400 additional appropriation was recommended by the clerk in evident appreciation of the statesmanship recorded in these biographies. One of the pages "who could not read and write" was put to driving a team and the man employed as driver cleaned the floors and scrubbed the spittoons. The locksmith served as a messenger and though he was absent from April until after the Christmas holidays, he received $1440 a year.

The librarian and his subordinates were also absent for long periods and the library, consisting of some 300,000 volumes was scattered from dome to basement with piles of books in unused rooms until the librarian himself testified that it would be all right for a barnyard but for books it was terrible.

One Smith, who was pretty fond of "old barleycorn" got an appropriation of $600 for "loafing about." He had a good run of the books which were in the rubbish pile and knew to what part of the pile to go for certain volumes. The business of keeping this rubbish pile was farmed out by other employees to this man.

The folders were absent a great deal and others were employed and paid to do their work.

The door-keeper testified, "I do not like to criticize members, but that is the situation. They go and say, 'I have got to have my man home' and he must go home."

The door-keeper was further asked: "Have there been any other cases of absenteeism except among the folders?" To which he replied, "No, except those who naturally go." Of this our committee observed: "It would appear that these two classes, those who naturally go and those who go through the artificial assistance of Congressmen form a pretty large aggregate."

There were dozens who were paid when they were not there at all. One of the employees in the cloakroom was there on and off for only three or four months during a period of three years and he was spared from going to Washington even to receive his salary. The vouchers were sent to him and he filed receipts in the disbursing clerk's office "just as all the other gentlemen who go home do."

The disbursing officer testified: "It is no question for me to find out whether they are there or not."

The office which kept such admirable check upon expenditures itself cost about $14,000 a year.

14.

THE PERILS OF POWER

The New Deal, Dean Acheson wrote approvingly in a book called *A Democrat Looks At His Party*, "conceived of the federal government as the whole people organized to do what had to be done." A year later Mr. Larson wrote *A Republican Looks At His Party*, and made much the same claim in his book for Modern Republicans. The "underlying philosophy" of the New Republicanism, said Mr. Larson, is that "if a job has to be done to meet the needs of the people, and no one else can do it, then it is the proper function of the federal government."

Here we have, by prominent spokesmen of both political parties, an unqualified repudiation of the principle of limited government. There is no reference by either of them to the Constitution, or any attempt to define the legitimate functions of government. The government can do whatever *needs* to be done; note, too, the implicit but necessary assumption that it is the government itself that determines *what* needs to be done. We must not, I think underrate the importance of these statements. They reflect the view of a majority of the leaders of one of our parties, and of a strong minority among the leaders of the other, and they propound the first principle of totalitarianism: that the State is competent to do all things and is limited in what it actually does only by the will of those who control the State.

It is clear that this view is in direct conflict with the Constitution which is an instrument, above all, for *limiting* the functions of government, and which is as binding today as when it was written. But we are advised to go a step further and ask why the Constitution's framers restricted the scope of government. Conservatives are often charged, and in a sense rightly so, with having an overly mechanistic view of the Constitution: "It is America's enabling document; we are American citizens; therefore," the Conservatives' theme runs, "we are morally and legally obliged to comply with the document." All true. But the Constitution has a broader claim on our loyalty than that. The founding fathers had a *reason* for endorsing the principle of limited government; and this reason recommends defense of the constitutional scheme even to those who take their citizenship obligations lightly. The reason is simple, and it lies at the heart of the Conservative philosophy.

Reprinted from Barry Goldwater, *The Conscience of a Conservative* (New York: MacFadden Books, 1964), pp. 15–24. Copyright © 1960 by Victor Publishing Company.

Throughout history, government has proved to be the chief instrument for thwarting man's liberty. Government represents power in the hands of some men to control and regulate the lives of other men. And power, as Lord Acton said, *corrupts* men. "Absolute power," he added, "corrupts absolutely."

State power, considered in the abstract, need not restrict freedom: but absolute state power always does. The *legitimate* functions of government are actually conducive to freedom. Maintaining internal order, keeping foreign foes at bay, administering justice, removing obstacles to the free interchange of goods—the exercise of these powers makes it possible for men to follow their chosen pursuits with maximum freedom. But note that the very instrument by which these desirable ends are achieved *can* be the instrument for achieving undesirable ends—that government can, instead of extending freedom, restrict freedom. And note, secondly, that the "can" quickly becomes "will" the moment the holders of government power are left to their own devices. This is because of the corrupting influence of power, the natural tendency of men who possess *some* power to take unto themselves *more* power. The tendency leads eventually to the acquisition of *all* power—whether in the hands of one or many makes little difference to the freedom of those left on the outside.

Such, then, is history's lesson, which Messrs. Acheson and Larson evidently did not read: release the holders of state power from any restraints other than those they wish to impose upon themselves, and you are swinging down the well-travelled road to absolutism.

The framers of the Constitution had learned the lesson. They were not only students of history, but victims of it: they knew from vivid, personal experience that freedom depends on effective restraints against the accumulation of power in a single authority. And that is what the Constitution is: a *system of restraints against the natural tendency of government to expand in the direction of absolutism.* We all know the main components of the system. The first is the limitation of the federal government's authority to specific, delegated powers. The second, a corollary of the first, is the reservation to the States and the people of all power not delegated to the federal government. The third is a careful division of the federal government's power among three separate branches. The fourth is a prohibition against impetuous alteration of the system—namely, Article V's tortuous, but wise, amendment procedures.

Was it then a *Democracy* the framers created? Hardly. The system of restraints, on the face of it, was directed not only against individual tyrants, but also against a tyranny of the masses. The framers were well aware of the danger posed by self-seeking demagogues—that they might persuade a majority of the people to confer on government vast powers in return for deceptive promises of economic gain. And so they forbade such a transfer of power—first by declaring, in effect, that certain activities are outside the natural and legitimate scope of the public authority, and secondly by dispersing public authority among several levels and branches of government in the hope that each seat of authority, jealous of its own prerogatives, would have a natural incentive to resist aggression by the others.

But the framers were not visionaries. They knew that rules of government, however brilliantly calculated to cope with the imperfect nature of man, however carefully designed to avoid the pitfalls of power, would be no match for men who were determined to disregard them. In the last analysis their system of government would prosper only if the governed were sufficiently determined that it should. "What have you given us?" a woman asked Ben Franklin toward the close of the Constitutional Convention. "A Republic," he said, "*if you can keep it. . . .*"

We have not kept it. The Achesons and Larsons have had their way. The system of restraints has fallen into disrepair. The federal government has moved into every field in which it believes its services are needed. The state governments are either excluded from their rightful functions by federal preemption, or they are allowed to act at the sufferance of the federal government. Inside the federal government both the executive and judicial branches have roamed far outside their constitutional boundary lines. And all of these things have come to pass without regard to the amendment procedures prescribed by Article V. The result is a Leviathan, a vast national authority out of touch with the people, and out of their control. This monolith of power is bounded only by the will of those who sit in high places.

There are a number of ways in which the power of government can be measured.

One is the size of its financial operations. Federal spending is now approaching a hundred billion dollars a year (compared with three and one-half billion less than three decades ago.)

Another is the scope of its activities. A study recently conducted by the *Chicago Tribune* showed that the federal government is now the "biggest land owner, property manager, renter, mover and hauler, medical clinician, lender, insurer, mortgage broker, employer, debtor, taxer and spender in all history."

Still another is the portion of the people's earnings government appropriates for its own use: nearly a third of earnings are taken every year in the form of taxes.

A fourth is the extent of government interference in the daily lives of individuals. The farmer is told how much wheat he can grow. The wage earner is at the mercy of national union leaders whose great power is a direct consequence of federal labor legislation. The businessman is hampered by a maze of government regulations, and often by direct government competition. The government takes six per cent of most payrolls in Social Security Taxes and thus compels millions of individuals to postpone until later years the enjoyment of wealth they might otherwise enjoy today. Increasingly, the federal government sets standards of education, health and safety.

How did it happen? How did our national government grow from a servant with sharply limited powers into a master with virtually unlimited power?

In part, we were swindled. There are occasions when we have elevated men and political parties to power that promised to restore limited government and then proceeded, after their election, to expand the activities of government. But let us be honest with ourselves. Broken promises are not the major causes of our trouble. *Kept* promises are. All too often we have put men in office who have suggested spending a little more on this, a little more on that, who have proposed a new welfare program, who have thought of another variety of "security." We have taken the bait, preferring to put off to another day the recapture of freedom and the restoration of our constitutional system. We have gone the way of many a democratic society that has lost its freedom by persuading itself that if "the people" rule, all is well.

The Frenchman, Alexis de Tocqueville, probably the most clairvoyant political observer of modern times, saw the danger when he visited this country in the 1830's. Even then he foresaw decay for a society that tended to put more emphasis on its democracy than on its republicanism. He predicted that America would produce, not tyrants but "guardians." And that the American people would "console themselves for being in tutelage by the reflection that they have chosen their own guardians. Every man allows himself to be put in lead-strings, because he sees that it is not a person nor a class of persons, but the people at large that hold the end of his chain."

Our tendency to concentrate power in the hands of a few men deeply concerns me. We can be conquered by bombs or by subversion; but we can also be conquered by neglect—by ignoring the Constitution and disregarding the principles of limited government. Our defenses against the accumulation of unlimited power in Washington are in poorer shape, I fear, than our defenses against the aggressive designs of Moscow. Like so many other nations before us, we may succumb through internal weakness rather than fall before a foreign foe.

I am convinced that most Americans now want to reverse the trend. I think that concern for our vanishing freedoms is genuine. I think that the people's uneasiness in the stifling omnipresence of government has turned into something approaching alarm. But bemoaning the evil will not drive it back, and accusing fingers will not shrink government.

The turn will come when we entrust the conduct of our affairs to men who understand that their first duty as public officials is to divest themselves of the power they have been given. It will come when Americans, in hundreds of communities throughout the nation, decide to put the man in office who is pledged to enforce the Constitution and restore the Republic. Who will proclaim in a campaign speech: "I have little interest in streamlining government or in making it more efficient, for I mean to reduce its size. I do not undertake to promote welfare, for I propose to extend freedom. My aim is not to pass laws, but to repeal them. It is not to inaugurate new programs, but to cancel old ones that do violence to the Constitution, or that have failed in their purpose, or that impose on the people an unwarranted financial burden. I will not attempt to discover whether legislation is 'needed' before I have first determined whether it is constitutionally permissible. And if I should later be attacked for neglecting my constituents' 'interests,' I shall reply that I was informed their main interest is liberty and that in that cause I am doing the very best I can."

15.

ORGANIZATIONAL PATTERNS OF THE FUTURE: WHAT THEY MEAN TO PERSONNEL ADMINISTRATION

ROBERT T. GOLEMBIEWSKI

Profound debate rages concerning the ways in which people view organizations, and this debate has major implications for personnel administration. This paper sketches two such managerial views, and gives special attention to organizational arrangements congenial to one of these managerial views. The focus throughout is on the challenges to personnel administration and to personnel administrators implied by these organizational arrangements.

TWO MANAGERIAL WORLD-VIEWS

Two major contenders receive support in the debate over managerial world-views, or major ideas about what the administrative world is and how it should be. The first and dominant view amounts to a kind of managerial *push-theory*. In it, the employee scrambles and innovates and burns the midnight oil to avoid possible and perhaps inevitable harsh outcomes. In one version of this view,

---

This article will appear, in part, in *Personnel Administration*, with whose permission it is here reprinted.

men work hard because it is morally bad to do otherwise. The properties of this view are like those of McGregor's Theory X or 9,1 on the Grid.

Whyte's *The Organization Man* illustrates the managerial push-theory, and laments its demise. Gone are the old stimuli to heroic effort such as survival-of-the-fittest "training programs" that tested a man's desire and skills, or broke him. In their place, Whyte saw manifold nicely-nicelies such as longish training programs that effectively closed the school of hard-knocks. In Whyte's view, organization men were whistling their way through the dark, hand-in-hand, neglecting harsh realities for which they were less and less prepared. No harshness, given the push-theory, no progress.

In the managerial *pull-theory*, the focus is more on what you are reaching toward than on what you are seeking to avoid. In it, the employee also scrambles and innovates and burns the midnight oil. However, work is so need-satisfying that it elicits massive employee efforts. The goal is dual: doing the job better, and doing it in ways that permit unprecedented personal freedom in organizations. Indeed, this view almost says that *it is only through greater personal freedom* that a better job can be accomplished. Organization life is demanding in this view, but it does promise fulfillment at work. Warren Bennis articulates both emphases clearly:[1]

> I think that the future I describe is not necessarily a "happy" one. Coping with rapid change, living in temporary work systems, developing meaningful relations and then breaking them—all augur social strains and psychological tensions....
>
> In these new organizations of the future, participants will be called upon to use their minds more than at any other time in history. Fantasy, imagination and creativity will be legitimate in ways that today seem strange. Social structures will no longer be instruments of psychic repression but will increasingly promote play and freedom on behalf of curiosity and thought.

The managerial pull-theory seeks to accommodate personal needs and organizational demands, then.[2] Skeletally, the underlying rationale proposes that:

1. Many individuals find little satisfaction in their work, and this is a major deprivation for them personally and for their organization.
2. Many or all individuals will be more productive as they exercise greater control over their work, and as work permits satisfaction of a broadening range of needs.
3. Organizations increasingly need superior output from more and more of their employees, and technological and skill requirements are such that these contributions must be elicited more than forced. Expenditures to redesign jobs and work relations, and to change managerial styles or techniques are reasonable, consequently. Indeed, in the longer run they are probably necessary.

---

[1] Warren G. Bennis, "Beyond Bureaucracy," *Trans-Action*, Vol. 2 (July–August, 1965), p. 35.
[2] See especially Chris Argyris, *Integrating the Individual and the Organization* (New York: John Wiley & Sons, Inc., 1964).

CONSCIOUS AND DELIBERATE CONCERN
WITH MANAGERIAL WORLD-VIEWS:
GENERAL DEMANDS ON PERSONNEL ADMINISTRATION

That personnel administration will have to be consciously concerned with both managerial strategies seems clear. Thus the *pull-theory* becomes increasingly appropriate as organizations move rightward on the following dimensions, and such rightward movement seems very probable:

From Basic Emphasis upon: →	*To Growing Emphasis upon:*
regularity in operations →	creativity in concept; adaptability in execution
programmed decisions →	novel decisions
stable and simple competencies, → technologies, and markets	volatile and complex competencies, technologies, and markets
stop-and-go processing →	continuous processing
stable product lines, programs →	volatile product lines, programs
monolithic product lines, programs →	variegated product lines, programs
demands of hierarchy →	demands of task, technology, profession
departmental orientation →	system orientation
expanding volume at central site →	developing national and international field units

The reader can supply the full rationale for the relevance of the pull-theory under the conditions in the right column. To illustrate, you can order someone to obey when work or decisions are programmed. Ordering creativity is quite another matter.

Personnel administration also probably will give significant attention to structure and policies consistent with the *push-theory*. Briefly, technological requirements influence which structure and managerial techniques are likely to be successful, and not all organizations will or even can move sharply rightward on the dimensions above. Certainly, at least different technologies and markets will move rightward at different times and paces. Thus today's plastics industry reflects the characteristics in the right column, but the cardboard industry does not. As compelling new evidence suggests, opposite managerial styles are effective in these two industries.[3] Roughly, the push-theory is more appropriate to the technology and market of the cardboard carton industry than to the plastics industry. To the degree that technologies and markets like the carton industry will continue to exist, then, so also will personnel administration have to give attention to structure and policies consistent with the push-theory.

---

[3] Paul R. Lawrence and Jay W. Lorsch, *Organization and Environment* (Boston: Harvard Graduate School of Business Administration, 1967).

THE MANAGERIAL PULL-THEORY:
SOME BASIC ORGANIZATIONAL PATTERNS

Since the managerial pull-theory seems congenial to the technology of the future, our focus narrows. We live in a transitional period, and the following analysis extends what is already happening into a reasonably coherent view of what the future implies for personnel administration.

Probable changes in organizational patterns consistent with the pull-theory can be described in terms of four polarities. Different times and technologies give different emphases to each. The four polarities are:

1. Differentiation/integration;
2. Repression/wriggle room;
3. Stability/newness; and
4. Function/flow of work.

Short of anarchy, no age has a real choice of structure or no structure. The emphases placed on these four polarities, however, significantly influence the kind of structure that does develop in organizations. A wide range of alternative organizational patterns are possible.

First, any organizing pattern reflects relative emphases on differentiation/integration. Following Lawrence and Lorsch, "differentiation" can be defined in terms of the development among the several units of an organization of "different formal reporting relationships, different criteria for rewards, and different control procedures." In sum, differentiation is defined in terms of "the difference in cognitive and emotional orientation among managers in different functional departments." Integration refers to "the quality of the state of collaboration that exists among departments that are required to achieve unity of effort by the demands of the environment." [4]

Organizational patterns of the near-future will no doubt emphasize integration. Early organizational experience tended to reflect integration, as in the crafts. Over the first half of this century, however, the emphasis shifted to the differentiation of functions and skills. Thus "bureaucracy" dominated this phase of organization history, and that concept is rooted in differentiation. Bureaucracy includes, that is,

1. A well-defined chain of command that vertically channels formal interaction;
2. A system of procedures and rules for dealing with all contingencies at work, which reinforces the reporting insularity of each bureau;
3. A division of labor based upon specialization by major function or process that vertically fragments a flow of work;

---

[4] *Ibid.*, pp. 10–11.

4. Promotion and selection based on technical competence defined consistent with 1–3 above; and
5. Impersonality in relations between organization members and between them and their clients.

More lately, integration has received increasing emphasis. The "system approach" and the computer are the major contemporary technical expressions of this integrative thrust. Behaviorally, the integrative emphasis seeks to meet both human needs and technical demands at work.

Second, a basic foundation of any pattern for organizing deals with the relative emphasis on repression and "wriggle room." No technical definitions seem necessary here; and "surplus repression" is commonly seen as a major product of bureaucracy. Increasingly, an emerging integrative emphasis seeks an organizational climate having the minimal constraints consistent with quality performance. This is the essence of the contemporary stress on "management by objectives." Similarly, the popularity of sensitivity training reflects massive concern about such costs of repression as withheld effort or information.

There is no mistaking the root-cause of such de-emphasis on repression. Today's organizations reflect a growing need for an organic and evolving integration, as opposed to a mechanical structuring. Adherence to a mechanics can be enforced; but commitment to an organic integration can only be elicited and encouraged. Put another way, the integrity of a stable and simple technology may be safeguarded by culling deviants. But changing and complex technologies require the careful husbanding of selected kinds of innovation or adaptability in a widening range of employees. Hence the growing importance of wriggle room.

The change in emphasis on repression/wriggle room may be characterized broadly, and with essential accuracy. The bureaucratic spirit is oriented toward developing a system to guard against man at his worst, to preclude error or venality. Hence flows of work are differentiated as functions or positions or motions, and surplus repression is the glue used to pull them together. The integrative emphasis, oppositely, strives to create an environment in which man can approach his productive best. Hence the emphasis on wriggle room, on learning how and when individuals can more often meet their own needs while contributing more effectively to a total flow of work with which they identify.

Third, the relative emphasis on stability/newness also constitutes a major decision underlying any organizing pattern. The acceleration of newness has been described in many places, even if one cannot feel it in his bones. Hence the bare notice here that all-but-overwhelming newness is a trademark of our times, and that it is poorly served by bureaucratic properties.

Fourth, different emphases on the three polarities above imply different organization structures built around *functions* and *flows of work*, respectively. Take an easy case, to begin, the organization of three activities *A*, *B*, and *C*

FIGURE 15.1. A STRUCTURE CONSISTENT WITH THE VALUES OF BUREAUCRACY: EMPHASES ON DIFFERENTIATION, REPRESSION, STABILITY, AND FUNCTION.

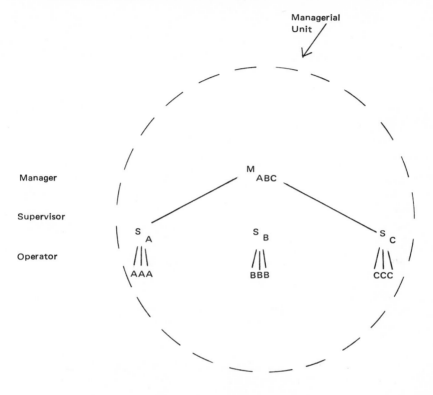

Underlying Properties

1. Authority is a vertical, or hierarchical, relation.

2. Departments are organized around the same or similar activities, called "functions" at high levels of organization and "processes" at low levels; that is, "like" activities are put together.

3. Only a relatively small number of people should report directly to any superior.

which when combined yield some product or service.[5] Figure 15.1 presents the skeletal structure consistent with these three emphases: differentiation; repression; and stability. This characterization is easy to support. For example, Figure 15.1 essentially puts the same or similar activities together in its basic

---

[5] For a comparison of these models, see Robert T. Golembiewski, *Men, Management, and Morality* (New York: McGraw-Hill Book Co., 1965).

FIGURE 15.2. AN ALTERNATIVE STRUCTURE:
EMPHASES ON INTEGRATION, WRIGGLE ROOM, NEWNESS, AND FLOW OF WORK.

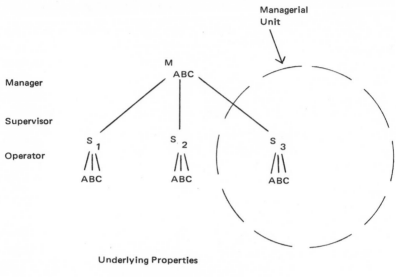

Underlying Properties

1. Authoritative relations occur up, down and
    across the organization, and all these vectors
    should be directed to similar goals by an
    effective structure.

2. Departmentation reflects the "flow of work";
    that is, related activities are put together
    whether they are "like" or "unlike."

3. A relatively large number of people may
    report to any superior, given a structure that
    facilitates measuring performance.

units of organization. That is, the model builds on departments *differentiated* by kinds of activities, usually called "functions" at high levels of organization and "processes" at lower levels. Relatedly, the narrow span of control is well designed to facilitate surplus *repression* in the details of operation. That is, the structure encourages centralization of decision-making at the level of M_{ABC}, who alone can make reasonable decisions about the flow of work $A + B + C$. Hence he alone controls a "managerial unit." Finally, the model presumes a *stable* state. The underlying model is that of a mechanical meshing of parts rather than of a dynamic flow of work.

Figure 15.2 presents an alternative structure that is consistent with prime adaptations to the on-going organizational revolution. These adaptive arrangements include: decentralization; project management; matrix overlays; independent profit centers; management by objectives; autonomous teams; and numerous other variations on a theme. In common, as the Figure 15.2 model suggests, these adaptations stress integration, wriggle room, change, and flow of work. Thus the model organizes around *integrative* departments, that is, it groups together activities that are related in a total flow of work. This integrative thrust can be extended to the operators, as through job rotation and job enlargement. In addition, the model seeks the *minimum control* that is consistent with end-item quality and quantity. The multiple opportunities for self-discipline and self-control built into the model, for example, reduce the need for external repression in tying individual needs to organizational goals. The key factors are teams which control a flow of work whose performance is easily and meaningfully comparable. Moreover, Figure 15.2 variously facilitates adapting to *change* and to *growth*. For example, Figure 15.1 structures tend to grow "tall" very quickly, with consequent increases in reaction time, in communication costs, and so on. The limited span of control is the major culprit. Figure 15.2 structures are much less growth-sensitive and can remain relatively "flat" even with manifold increases in size. Finally, Figure 15.2 structures departmentalize around *flows of work* as opposed to functions. Each *S* now controls a managerial unit.

The two structures are ideal types in that they are analytical extremes. In practice, they can be approached only in degree, often in complex mixtures. But approaches to one ideal model or the other will tend to generate significantly different consequences.

THE MANAGERIAL PULL-THEORY: SOME MAJOR IMPLICATIONS FOR PERSONNEL ADMINISTRATION

I. Differentiation/Integration.—At least three major challenges for personnel administration inhere in shifting emphasis from differentiation toward integration. In general, note that "personnel administration" below usually refers to both the staff personnel job as well as to those personnel aspects for which a line manager is responsible. Basically, the interest here is in "what" needs to be done rather than "who" will do it. "Who" questions do get some attention, however.

First, new strategies must be developed for motivating individuals and groups while facilitating interpersonal and intergroup collaboration. Inducing win-lose competition between individuals and groups has been the standby strategy, and it does have its attractions. Thus starting rivalry or conflict is easy. Keeping it within bounds often is the difficult part. Moreover, the competitive strategy can engage substantial energies. In addition, much line and staff experience has been accumulated about "cattle prod" activities useful for inducing rivalry or win-lose competition.

The disadvantages of win-lose competition loom increasingly significant,[6] and particularly in organizations with structures like that in Figure 15.1 Overall, technological demands require growing collaboration between functions or processes, but great potential for conflict and rivalry is built into a Figure 15.1 structure. For example, the work of departments in a Figure 15.1 structure is not directly comparable, which often precludes reliable and non-arbitrary measures of performance. Each department provides only a partial contribution to a variety of flows of work, which implies major problems in factoring-out departmental successes/failures. Because of this complexity, one department may "win" only as another department "loses," e.g., in a cost-accounting allocation.

Structures like that in Figure 15.2 require that S perform a managerially-integrative role, in contrast. The S takes a generalist role in fact as well as intent, in that he can make reasonable decisions about a total flow of work. These integrative features of Figure 15.2 structures have numerous advantages. Because the basic units of organization below M_{ABC} are autonomous and control an entire flow of work, for example, reliable and non-arbitrary measurement of performance is relatively simple. In addition, the basic unit of organization includes the full sequence of operations. Effort and performance are more likely to be congruent, as a consequence. Moreover, the "wins" of one department do not preclude "wins" by others. Even the competition in Figure 15.2 structures has integrative tendencies, in sum.

Since a Figure 15.2 structure may not exist, or cannot always be approached, the development of strategies for motivation that facilitate interpersonal and intergroup collaboration deserve high priority. For example, inter-departmental conflicts and rivalries encouraged by Figure 15.1 structures may be ameliorated by improving the processes of interpersonal and group interaction. Consider the chief executive of an organization patterned after Figure 15.1 who spotlighted the divisive forces induced by the traditional structure in these words:[7]

The trouble with ABC is that nobody aside from me ever gives one damn about the overall goals of this place. They're all seeing the world through the lenses of their departmental biases. What we need around here are people who wear the ABC hat, not the engineering hat or the sales hat or the production hat.

This complaint inspired the development of the *ABC* hats, a group representing several functions and hierarchical levels that filled the integrative gaps resulting from a Figure 15.1 structure. Organizational applications of sensitivity training

---

[6] To extend the argument, win-lose competition also is less useful at an inter-firm or inter-nation level. The magnitude of many projects requires exquisite coordination between "competing" firms, for example. And I have heard a major aerospace official say that, whatever the political issues between us, acute practical considerations require advanced cooperation on the SST between American firms and the French.

[7] Warren G. Bennis, "Organizations of the Future," *Personnel Administration*, Vol. 30 (September, 1967), p. 16.

seek similar integration via improved interpersonal and group relations.[8]

Improving interpersonal and intergroup relations in a Figure 15.1 structure implies an uphill struggle all the way. Whatever improvement in communication processes results from sensitivity training or from a team-building experience, that is, the structure will tend to keep on generating conflict and rivalry. Consequently, "booster shots" are necessary. Indeed, some organizations have evolved a "change-agent" role to provide just such a stimulus to effective interaction between individuals and groups. Providing change-agent services, and particularly organizing for them, will generate major problems for personnel administration.

Second, personnel administration must give massive attention to developing a viable integrative function. Consider two possible approaches: some integrative role may be grafted to the basic functional structure, in Figure 15.1; or integrative teams may become the basic units of departmentation, as in Figure 15.2. Both cases present problems. The second case is more attractive in concept, but for most organizations it would mean a major and difficult organization development effort.

Integrative roles in organizations tend to be superimposed on a Figure 15.1 structure, consequently, as via an interdepartmental coordinating committee or a "project manager." Both are integrative overlays designed to counteract the fragmenting tendencies of the traditional structure of departments organized by functions or processes. To illustrate, the project manager develops a temporary integrative team to do some specific job, making requests for personnel as necessary from the functional departments. Team members respond to two authoritative sources, then: to their more-or-less temporary project manager; and to the head of the functional department to which they will return when the project is complete. The resulting multiple lines of authority are sometimes called a "matrix overlay."

Integrative arrangements superimposed on a traditional structure can help reduce the conflict and rivalry characteristic of a Figure 15.1 structure, but they are tricky.[9] Thus questions of multiple authority may vex personnel administration. Or power may remain in the permanent functional departments, and this can make life difficult for integrative agents such as project managers or interdepartmental coordinating committees. In both cases, in addition, what is to be done with a project manager when his project is terminated? The experience in the aerospace industry does not suggest any easy ways out. Making conscious

---

[8] For an analog of sensitivity training that shows promise, see Robert T. Golembiewski and Arthur Blumberg, "Confrontation as a Training Design in Complex Organizations," *Journal of Applied Behavioral Science*, Vol. 3 (December, 1967), pp. 525–47.

[9] Richard M. Hodgetts, "Leadership Techniques in the Project Organization," *Academy of Management Journal*, Vol. 11 (June, 1968), pp. 211–20.

arrangements for an integrative role, then, implies serious problems for personnel administration.

Third, shared values that encourage organizational unity must be developed and broadly accepted. Otherwise, a significant shift of emphasis toward integration is unlikely. Prevailing organizational values—the "values of bureaucracy"—are hierarchy-serving in that they reinforce superior-subordinate relations, but they do so only at the expense of inhibiting the development of socio-emotional ties that can integrate individuals or groups performing different functions in different departments in a Figure 15.1 structure. Since today's organizations increasingly must be integrative, and since they increasingly must stress systemic knowledge-gathering because they are truth-requiring, the values of bureaucracy will increasingly generate troublesome consequences.

The alternative to the values of bureaucracy is not yet clear. However, the following "climate of beliefs" seems adaptive to the knowledge-gathering and truth-requiring demands of today's technology: [10]

1. Full and free communication, regardless of rank or power;
2. Reliance on consensual processes in dealing with conflict, as opposed to coercion or compromise;
3. Basing influence on technical competence and knowledge, as opposed to personal whim or hierarchical status;
4. An atmosphere that easily admits emotional expression as well as task-oriented behavior; and
5. Acceptance of conflict between the individual and the organization, which conflict is to be coped with openly.

Getting acceptance of such values in principle and practice should constitute a major near-future challenge for personnel administration.

II. Repression/Wriggle Room.—Two issues involved in the shift of emphasis toward wriggle room deserve special attention because they pose major problems for personnel administration. One issue involves tailoring both organization structure and interaction processes so as to meet human needs at work. The second issue deals with values and representational vehicles capable of supporting such changes in structure and interaction processes.

One major approach toward emphasizing wriggle room involves shaping organizations to fit people in the design of tasks and structure. Historically, people were fitted to the organization. Many observers have argued the merits of tailoring tasks to man,[11] as through job enlargement, so we note only two major derivative demands on personnel administration. In the federal government, "classification experts" still far outnumber "specialists in job design."

---

[10] Warren G. Bennis, *Changing Organizations* (New York: McGraw-Hill Book Co., 1966), pp. 15–16.
[11] David S. Brown, "Shaping the Organization to Fit People," *Management of Personnel Quarterly*, Vol. 5 (Summer, 1966), pp. 12–16.

A traditional personnel specialty, especially in the federal government, needs to be reoriented if more wriggle room is the goal. Moreover, job enlargement is easiest in a Figure 15.2 structure. Since a Figure 15.1 structure is what most organizations have, the implied challenge to public personnel administration is the development of a potent OD, or organization development, specialty. Experience in the federal government suggests the road will be arduous and long.

Relatedly, interaction processes can also usefully be tailored to man. Argyris has posited needs of man that are seen as typically frustrated in large organizations, and especially in organizations patterned after Figure 15.1.[12] Building satisfying interaction processes into organizations is a gargantuan task, and only scarcely begun. Thus some change-agents attempt to build sensitivity training groups directly into organizations, which raises major issues with traditional ways of organizing and managing. Others argue that building need-satisfying interaction into organizations is hopelessly utopian. Many variations exist between those anchor-positions. However matters evolve, the face of personnel administration is certain to change substantially. That much is clear from these broad values of sensitivity training that imply what is often seen as lacking in organizations: [13]

1. An attitude of inquiry, reflecting a "hypothetical spirit" and an emphasis on experimentation;
2. An expanded awareness on the part of organization members, with a corresponding sense of a broader choice of alternatives for action;
3. An undergirding system of norms that stress collaboration and a problem-solving orientation to conflict; and
4. An emphasis on the helping relationship as a major way to concretely express man's interdependence with man.

Changes in tasks and interaction processes must be supported by appropriate values and representational vehicles. As an example, greater managerial concern for due process and sharing of influence seems necessary. Either the pull-theory or the push-theory can guide how the two are approached—since due process and influence-sharing will receive major attention, for good or ill—and the choice is a matter of real consequence. That is, influence-sharing or due process can be granted with top-management support in sensitive dialog with employees whose needs and capabilities are diversely evolving; or at a polar extreme, they can be wrested away by employees after heated battle with a boulwareian management. The pull-theory recommends the former, of course.

No doubt much of the near-future resolution of issues involving due process and influence-sharing will be in familiar terms: employee unionization, more

---

[12] Chris Argyris, *Personality and Organization* (New York: Harper & Row, 1957), especially pp. 49–53.

[13] Edgar H. Schein and Warren G. Bennis (eds.), *Personal and Organizational Change Through Group Methods* (New York: John Wiley & Sons, Inc., 1965), pp. 30–35.

or less grudging management assent, and more or less successful efforts at rapprochement. Increasingly, however, the resolution will involve the breaking of new and uncertain ground. At least at managerial levels in many organizations, for example, determined efforts are underway to develop new and enhanced representational vehicles, encompassing "tell all" dinners, management councils, and God knows what. Only the brave fool would try to guess the product of this maelstrom, or even whether we can avoid a kind of organizational totalitarianism born of ineptness or unwillingness in developing appropriate values and vehicles. That personnel administration vitally depends on the outcome of the search for viable approaches to power-sharing and to organizational due-process seems undeniable.

III. Stability/Newness.—Any shift in emphasis toward newness implies at least two major issues.

First, the "change function" must be given greater priority, with such attendant challenges as better equipping people to tolerate ambiguity. We have only clues as to how to cope successfully with such an increased priority, both as to mechanics and organization.

As for mechanics, an increased priority for change implies an appropriate reward system. Existing reward systems usually are keyed to how much one produces, however, or how long one has been a producer. Neither bias facilitates change; both biases are at best irrelevant to change, if they are not inimical to it. Likely reinforcers of change imply a host of problems. I have in mind one labor agreement that rewards employees for their willingness to be continually retrained, as opposed to rewarding them for their productivity or for their seniority. Such arrangements imply very significant labor-management issues, with which we have precious little experience. One thing is clear, however. Much of the heart of traditional personnel administration—as in the classification and pay plans at the federal level—poorly suits arrangements designed to facilitate change. Nothing better could be expected of these products of our bureaucratic phase, indeed.

Organizationally, increased emphasis on change also poses real problems for personnel administration. The issues are most sharply joined in the evolving role of the "change-agent" which is devoted to facilitating change and inducing appropriate interpersonal and intergroup climates for change. Where is the change-agent to be located? Who is to be the change-agent? Working answers to such questions have tended to be unsatisfactory. Relying on "external change-agents" such as consultants has some real advantages, but this places the change-agent outside the organization's authority-and-reward structure and may compromise his effectiveness. Relying on internal change-agents ties them in to the system, but this cuts both ways. If things got rough for them, change-agents might be motivated to become a kind of non-directive and even gentle but nonetheless efficient gestapo in the pursuit of their own interests.[14] If the line manager becomes the change-agent, you avoid many ticklish authority problems but you run the risk of placing reliance for change in an individual who may be overbusy with day-to-day problems. Moreover, there is no guarantee that line officials will have the appropriate skills or training, or even the interest. Embody the change-agent role in a staff man or unit, and that implies all of the problems that have plagued line-staff relations. Managing the change-agent role, in sum, implies one grand job for personnel administration conceived in its broad sense as an amalgam of line and staff responsibilities.

Second, the shifting emphasis to newness implies a growing need to quickly develop and disband both large and small work-units. The point clearly applies to the teams formed in project management, for example. Moreover, the need to revitalize today's organizations so as to prepare them for adapting to tomorrow's markets or programs also raises questions about managing temporary social systems.

Managing temporary social systems presents a formidable task in at least two major ways. Such management requires that people develop a kind of instant but still intense commitment. This is difficult, but seemingly unavoidable. Complex systems often permit no alternative to the technical *and* social compatability of team members. In addition, organization members will need to learn how to experience the loss of one temporary social system in ways that do not inhibit their commitment to future systems.

We are gaining some experience with effective management of temporary social systems, as via "team-building." The approach uses learning analogs derived from the laboratory approach, whose purest form is the sensitivity-training group. For example, such team-building has proved useful in one multi-plant firm using periodic rotation of management teams.[15] Plant technology is based on continuous processing and delicate integration of activities, and rotation typically caused a variety of dislocations that registered as decreases in productivity and employee satisfaction. Roughly, the typical relearning dip in several plants of this firm approximated six months. Moreover, as the plant technology became more integrated, that break-in period seemed to lengthen. Now, 3- or 4-day team-building experiences are provided early in the life of each new team. The re-learning dip has been halved.

Less is known about disbanding a temporary social system in ways that do

---

[14] The temptation is great where such change-agents use sensitivity-training sessions, for example, during which much data about individuals and groups may be divulged. A similar problem faces such professionals as psychiatrists employed by organizations.

[15] "Team-building" has also been utilized on a mass scale, by such firms as Alcan and TRW. See Alexander Winn, "The Laboratory Approach to Organization Development: A Tentative Model of Planned Change." Paper read at the Annual Conference, British Psychological Conference, Oxford, September 1968.

not inhibit the commitment of its members to future systems. Work with sensitivity training suggests that such "separation anxiety" can be effectively managed. However, socio-emotional de-briefing is still uncommon.

Experience with both creating and terminating temporary social systems seems worth developing. Consider aerospace firms, which typify what many organizations are increasingly becoming. One prominent feature of aerospace experience is the socio-emotional turmoil associated with developing, and more particularly with terminating, project teams. Members of teams gear themselves up to unflinching commitment, working long and hard. When the project is concluded, depression often sets in, marital difficulties seem unusually common and severe, and so on. Both research and popular news magazines have painted an alarming picture of this new problem, which we can expect to become increasingly common.[16]

Managing temporary social systems also implies two major technical issues. One of these concerns structural arrangements that encourage quick group identification and that also permit reinforcement by reward systems keyed to meaningful measures of performance. These dual goals are within reach. That is, both identification and the measurement of performance will be facilitated as organizations move toward Figure 15.2 structures. The point is of crucial significance. At a global level, indeed, Figure 15.2 offers a way out of nagging organizational problems. Thus managing the change-agent role might be handled effectively through team effort by members of a small integrative managerial unit. A line manager and a staff personnel man could be assigned to each managerial unit, and be jointly responsible for the change-agent role. Team effort also could provide a basis for redefining line-staff relations, as is urged below. Consequently, such structural change must occupy much of the effort of personnel administrators over the near future.

Figure 15.2 structures also permit convenient changes in incentive systems and philosophy. In one Figure 15.1 structure, for example, a very complex system of different wage rates for specific jobs required an elaborate supervisory and clerical apparatus for wage administration. Under a Figure 15.2 structure, a simpler system was possible. Management negotiated a base-price tied to output with a producing team that controlled the entire flow of work, and the unit handled the internal distribution of its income.[17] That is, group incentives in a Figure 15.2 structure can help integrate a total flow of work and reinforce the allegiances encouraged by that structure. Supervision is consequently simplified. Compensation systems in Figure 15.1 structures, in contrast, tend to fragment flows of work and to complicate supervision.

---

[16] Warren G. Bennis and Philip E. Slater, *The Temporary Society* (New York: Harper & Row, 1968).

[17] P. G. Herbst, *Autonomous Group Functioning* (London: Tavistock Publications, 1962).

A second major technical issue in managing temporary social systems concerns position classification. Figure 15.2 structures, and the temporary teams within them, encourage classification plans that place rank in the man rather than the job. On this score, the federal public service can expect special problems in managing temporary social systems. Although recent policies permit some recognition of the impact of the man on the job, the federal approach to classification emphasizes rank-in-position.

IV. Function/Flow of Work.—Basic structural change that shifts emphasis from particularistic to integrative departmentation, from functions to the flow of work, will make it easier to respond effectively to the challenges facing personnel administration; but that change will be difficult. The root-need is the development of a solid core of organization development (OD) specialists who can maintain real momentum in long-run programs of change. Ideally, perhaps, every manager should be his own OD specialist. Practically, the OD function often will become a staff personnel specialty.

Redefined line-staff relations are necessary if personnel officials are to operate effectively in an OD role, it is particularly important to note. Redefinition is necessary because OD means change, change in basic attitudes and values and ways of organizing work. Hence the inappropriateness of the traditional model of staff as outside the chain of command, as advisory, and as organizationally inferior to the line. Structural arrangements for a suitable redefinition of line-staff relations also seem clear, in general. A Figure 15.2 structure, for example, could provide a common organizational home for both a line manager and a staff personnel man. Their shared responsibility for the success of a total managerial unit would encourage a team effort, rather than line vs. staff tension. The approach gets much support, both from experience[18] and from theoretical analysis.[19] In contrast, Figure 15.1 structures are organized around separate functions or processes. This encourages fragmentation of line from staff, and differentiation between line and staff.

Realistically, and especially in the public service, such a core of OD specialists can anticipate a formidable task. The difficulty is multidimensional. Unlike many business organizations, for example, OD specialists in public agencies must not only convince their top management, but they must also reach powerful legislators or standing committees as well as multiple interest groups. This gives agency sub-units—bureaus or such groups as Foreign Service Officers—an opportunity to develop a kind of iron triangle of resistance to top agency management. On this score alone, OD specialists will have their work cut out for them. In addition, the brief average tenure of political appointees adds

---

[18] Robert Blake and Jane Mouton, *Corporate Excellence Through Grid Organization Development* (Houston: Gulf Publishing Co., 1966), Appendix II.

[19] Robert T. Golembiewski, *Organizing Men and Power: Patterns of Behavior and Line-Staff Models* (Chicago: Rand McNally & Co., 1967).

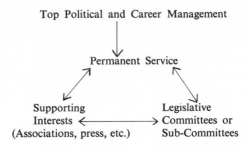

temper to that iron triangle. Finally, any protectionism induced by the civil service concept as it has evolved can serve to complicate any process of change. Perhaps the clearest reflections of the point are the complex "bumping arrangements" that apply to reductions-in-force.

Assuming the development of a core of OD specialists, three specific re-orientations in outlook also seem necessary. They will be sketched only.

First, an emphasis on flow of work as opposed to functions will require a "bottom, up" approach to organizing work *and* to locating services. The first point need not be emphasized, but the location of services has been given less attention. Given a "top, down" approach, services tend to drift upward in the typical hierarchy. For example, staff probably would report to M_{ABC} in Figure 15.1, even though many of their inputs might be made at the level of S_A or below. A "bottom, up" approach would generate a different pattern   The point may be illustrated briefly. Typically, an overhead staff unit would both design and monitor patterns of work motions. In one large electronics firm, however, "time and methods" has been handled differently. Employees are themselves instructed in the basics of motion analysis by overhead staff. These employees then design and monitor their own work-motion patterns.

Such bottom, up approaches as the example above imply multiple problems for personnel administration. Thus they may raise troublesome status questions for both M_{ABC} and the men who report to him. Moreover, suitable work environments for such approaches must have one or both of two characteristics: employee efforts must be measurable, easily and validly; or the employees must be motivated to apply the principles of motion analysis. These are major problems, but they are more soluble than the problems of enforcement/evasion likely under a top, down approach to motion analysis. For example, a Figure 15.2 structure can help significantly to reduce both mensural and motivational problems.[20]

Second, shifting emphasis to the flow of work requires a new "line-staff" concept. I have dealt with the matter at length elsewhere at the analytic level,

---

[20] *Ibid.*, pp. 90–110 and 154–73.

and fragmentary research has proved very encouraging.[21] Note here only the multiple mischief of conceiving staff as a glorified prosthetic device, as a kind of enlargement of the senses of M_{ABC} in Figure 15.1. Such a notion does encourage centralized identification and location of staff. And such identification and location always will be necessary for some staff, at least some of the time. Often too much is made of a good thing, however, with obvious costs in increased managerial complexity, heightened line-staff conflict, long communication chains, and a general rigidifying of relations at work.

Third, greater emphasis on the flow of work will require basic value reorientations in wide segments of the population. This socialization of adults will require both defusing and infusing of values, as it were. As some intriguing research demonstrates, at least "middle-class" children seem to be acquainted with the essentials of a Figure 15.1 structure as early in life as the third or fourth grade.[22] This suggests the extent of the value-defusing that will be required, and implies a major training burden that extends far beyond the workplace into the value-generating processes of the socialization of children.

There seems a solid base on which to infuse values more appropriate for Figure 15.2 structures, however. Thus many observers explain the fascination with McGregor's Theory X/Theory Y formulation in terms of a broad managerial desire to increase the congruence between their personal values and the presently-legitimate organization values. The former values tend toward Theory Y; but the latter are Theory X-ish, decidedly. In addition, some evidence shows that managers in larger and technologically sophisticated firms are more likely to reflect Theory Y attitudes.[23] This suggests that contemporary technological demands will supply push/pull forces that will help change values such as those underlying a Figure 15.1 structure.

AN IN-PROCESS SUMMARY

Our in-process summary begins with three assertions. Here the emphasis is decidedly on the challenges facing the staff personnel man.

1. To the degree that the developmental trends sketched above do in fact become reality, so will personnel administration experience profound challenges.
2. To the extent that specialists in personnel change in response to those challenges,

[21] Robert T. Golembiewski, "Personality and Organization Structure: Staff Models and Behavioral Patterns," *Journal of the Academy of Management*, Vol. 9 (September, 1966), pp. 211–30.
[22] Herbert G. Wilcox has accumulated evidence of this socialization-effect with an interesting research design. "The Culture Trait of Hierarchy in Middle-Class Children," *Public Administration Review*, Vol. 28 (May, 1968), pp. 222–35.
[23] Mason Haire, E. E. Ghiselli, and Lyman W. Porter, "Cultural Patterns in the Role of the Manager," *Industrial Relations*, Vol. 2 (February, 1963), pp. 95–118.

moreover, so will these specialists be able to ride the tiger of our on-going organizational revolution.

3. If personnel specialists do not make the required adaptations, someone else will try.

The preceding analysis also implies five major themes that will characterize successful adaptations by specialists in personnel, none of which will come easy.

First, and most broadly, reorienting the basic concept of personnel administration is in order. Crudely, the reorientation must emphasize training and organization development more than position classification or compensation or investigation. Roughly, the reorientation is away from a punitive approach and toward a participative and hopefully a rewarding approach. Such a reorientation is fortunately underway in many areas, albeit in wildly diverse degrees.

Second, specialists in personnel administration must transcend the limitations of the traditional staff role as an appendage for human needs tacked on to an immutable technical structure for work, of staff conceived of as outside the lines of command. A basic redefinition of line-staff relations is in order. Basically, a training or OD role for personnel implies broad involvement in the go-go of the organization. As was sketched above, a Figure 15.2 structure aids in developing line-staff relations necessary to permit such involvement.

Third, specialists in personnel administration must gain support for their new effort, but in an interdependent mode. That is, personnel specialists must avoid the temptation of forcing OD programs down the line, after having gained top-level backing by subtly or grossly playing the informant's role. Such things do happen,[24] and they are the death of OD programs. This more or less standard staff strategy illustrates a dependent mode of promoting an OD program, much more consistent with the push-theory than the pull-theory.

Fourth, the processes within personnel departments will have to be analogs of the processes desired in the broader organization. If integrative teams are seen as the answer to the organization's ills, for example, personnel specialists must demonstrate their willingness and ability to develop such integrative teams and participate in them. At the very least, this means that other members of such teams will have trust, backed by experience, that their openness will not return to haunt them in the form of tales carried upward in the organization.

Fifth, personnel specialists will need fine skills in managing dependence-hostility as they broaden their role. It is a mature relation, indeed, in which "help" is given and accepted, period. When the issue is the change of long-standing patterns of behavior, both dependence on the "helper" and hostility toward him will become more prevalent. Both dependence and hostility will have to be confronted willingly and openly, which only says that everyone must be more heroic and emotionally healthy.

---

[24] See Melville Dalton, *Men at Work* (New York: John Wiley & Sons, Inc., 1959), esp. pp. 18–109.

16.

THE "LABORATORY APPROACH" TO ORGANIZATION CHANGE: SCHEMA OF A METHOD

Robert T. Golembiewski

Organization change in both business and government increasingly relies on the "laboratory approach." Applications in business organizations such as Humble Oil have received massive attention in the literature and sometimes have involved thousands of employees. Public agencies have kept pace, but with far less public notice. Thus, IRS, the Peace Corps, and the New York Port Authority have utilized "lab methods" to provide opportunities for the personal growth of their employees. Other public agencies have made greater commitments. They have used the laboratory approach as a vehicle for organization change, for improving organizational procedure and policies as well as for increasing personal skills and insight. The Department of State's Project ACORD (or Action for Organization Development) is an example of the more ambitious kind.

In the following pages, the special meaning of the two key terms "organization change" and "laboratory approach" is developed. Administrative reform in public administration commonly means *formal* change, i.e., "reorganizations" or modifications in organization charts. This is in the tradition of the President's Committee on Administrative Management, the Hoover Commissions, and the municipal surveys of PAS. In contrast, "organization change" as used here has a dual meaning. It initially emphasizes *behavioral* changes in the attitudes, feelings, and beliefs of organization members, and subsequently *formal* restructuring which is facilitated and reinforced by behavioral changes. The "laboratory approach" to "organization change," as defined here, works through:

1. *The Basic T-Group*—or "sensitivity training group"—composed of individuals who do not normally work together, which focuses on expressing and unfreezing old attitudes, on developing interpersonal trust, on increasing trust and openness between group members, and on practicing new skills and behaviors; and
2. *Variant T-Groups*—variously called "core groups," "action groups," or "family groups"—composed of individuals who normally do work together,

Reprinted from *Public Administration Review*, Vol. XXVII, No. 3 (September, 1967), pp. 211–21.

which focus more on conceiving and implementing changes in the members' work.

A rough but useful contrast distinguishes the "laboratory approach" from more usual approaches to organization change. Perhaps 95 per cent of the effort in conventional organization change fixates on the *concepts* of, and deviations from, some such ideal as a "strong mayor" in city government. *Implementation* of the model gets little attention, especially in the sense of preparing organization members for the specific behavioral changes that are required. In sharp contrast, laboratory approaches to organization change give perhaps 95 per cent of the initial attention to *implementation*, to freeing and preparing organization members emotionally for full participation in "action groups" that will help conceive and implement some concept of the good administrative life.

The "laboratory approach" is multifaceted, but some sense of its complex dimensions may be conveyed through brief description of the growing agreement among *aficionados* about what the lab approach is, how it should be applied, and for what ends it should be employed in organization change. This growing agreement has five emphases touching on: (1) the boundaries of the lab approach; (2) its bias toward preparing the way for the development and implementation of action proposals; (3) the emerging normative agreement about the goals and techniques of the lab approach; (4) the broad features of life in organizations consistent with the lab approach; and (5) some of the inadequacies of the lab approach as a vehicle for organization change and development.

DIVERSE FORMS AND A COMMON PURPOSE

Basically, the lab approach to organization change variously seeks to "free-up" the individual to be a more effective participant in the molding of his own organizational life. Relevant learning therefore takes place at many levels. Three kinds of learning are considered here: (1) personal learning about the self in group situations; (2) transfer of personal learning to a worksite; and (3) restructuring the organization in ways that make it more satisfying and more rewarding to its members.

The Basic T-Group or sensitivity group deals largely with personal learning about the self in interpersonal and group situations. In roughest terms, the Basic T-Group ("T" is for "training") may be defined as a small group of a dozen or so "normals," generally strangers who meet in an "unstructured setting" for an extended period of time with a "trainer" having a strong background in the behavioral sciences. By "unstructured setting" is meant that Basic T-Groups typically have no specific task to perform, with their members concerned about learning from the interactions generated in whatever activities they engage in. Some "trainers" aggressively prod Basic T-Group members to confront the data they generate, but the stock early complaint is that trainers do not even try to help. In either case, members of Basic T-Groups typically have experiences that develop insight and behavioral skills that surprise the learners.

More specifically, Basic T-Groups have two major purposes. These purposes are to analyze the data generated by their own "here-and-now" interactions and to develop insight and behavioral skills that facilitate both analysis and action in the Basic T-Group as well as in "back-home" situations.

Unlike the "deep" analysis of psychiatry, Basic T-Groups consider mostly the "public," "here-and-now" data available to all members. The range of these target data is very wide:

1. The specific *structures* members develop in their interaction, such as the leadership rank-order;
2. The *processes* of their group life, with special attention to getting a group started, keeping it going, and then experiencing its inevitable "death";
3. Their specific *emotional reactions* to one another's behavior and to their experiences; and
4. The varying and diverse *styles* or *modes* of individual and group behavior, as in "fighting" the trainer or in "fleeing" some issue that has overwhelmed group members.

The overall goal is to increase the level of trust among group members so that each will provide to the others increasingly timely and unambiguous "feedback" concerning perceptions, feelings, or reactions. Hence the incidence of such conversational fragments: "I feel that . . . ."; "the way you come across to me . . . ."; "I believe that . . . ."; and "what I hear you saying is . . . ." Briefly, each individual is *the* expert about his own perceptions, reactions, and feelings. Being open about these gives group members data vital for acting effectively and efficiently. In contrast, failure to risk being open implies the creation of roadblocks to group and individual movements.

The typical design of a laboratory experience also provides for developing and testing insight and behavioral skills. Much of this work goes on in the Basic T-Group, but specific "exercises" which can cover an extremely broad range —from improving "listening skills" to more visceral experiences dealing with an individual's specific reactions to warm interpersonal contacts—are common. Ideally, such exercises are tailored to the specific needs of a specific Basic T-Group. Consequently, their design makes great demands on the experience and ingenuity of the trainer, for sensitivity groups can develop in an incredible diversity of ways.

Variant T-Groups have been developed to facilitate "back-home" learning, for encouraging members of organizations to experiment at the worksite with new behavioral skills or insights, and also to create more satisfying work relations. These Variant T-Groups may be called "family groups," "core groups," or "action groups." They differ from Basic T-Groups in two senses: they are composed of individuals who typically work together, and they have a relatively specific task, to develop and implement programs of organization change. The supporting rationale is that members of a Variant T-Group can rely on their "stranger" experience in a Basic T-Group to support being "open" in the company of organization peers and superiors, where greater forces would probably inhibit interaction if the individuals were not "freed up" by the earlier experience. In the great majority of cases, the intended effect is achieved to degrees beyond the expectations of most participants. Variant T-Groups tend to range widely between the "here-and-now" and the "there-and-then." That is, their members often have long and intricate common histories that do not so enrich/burden Basic T-Groups. In groups of both kinds, however, the aim is to help liberate the individual from socio-emotional impediments to his effective functioning, whether as a person or as an organization member.

Variant T-Groups can take many forms as they seek to build useful learning processes into organizations. For example, formal decision-making groups in organizations may be "instrumented" in such ways that their basic work continues pretty much as usual, except when certain indicators of the group's processes "go critical." At this point, the group stops its "organizational work" and focuses on "socio-emotional work." One decision-making group whose members often withhold important data from one another, for example, developed a list of significant dimensions of its own activity. Members individually score each meeting and mail their individual returns to a consultant. If the aggregate scores reach specified "critical points," the consultant is empowered to call an extraordinary "process conference." Much less withholding now goes on, and committee members feel they are more effective. Each member knows that if enough other members are unhappy with the committee's functioning but feel unable to voice their concern publicly, a "process conference" will be called. Consequently, everyone is motivated to be open more often and more cooperative.

The diversity of the lab approach extends far beyond these elemental distinctions, and other perspectives reflect kaleidoscopic variegation in what the lab approach is and how people respond to it. For example, much use is made of "unstructured" situations within which an incredible range of behavior may emerge. Moreover, the design of every lab experience is unique, at least nominally, and very often substantially so. Diversity is a highly probable outcome. Finally, "trainers" from the National Training Laboratories' "network" deal with "cousin," "stranger," or "interface" groups in "clusters" or "bunches" of such bewildering variety as to make it difficult even for persons with lab experiences to communicate easily what happened and why.

The underlying unity of laboratory programs of organization change is nonetheless real and marked. Although what follows is oversimplified, it illustrates that unity. The immediate analysis stresses three kinds of learning possible in both Basic T-Groups and Variant T-Groups, which variously tend toward the same end: to free individuals to be more effective while they are more themselves. The three kinds of learning are not mutually exclusive.

First, some individuals may extract learning from the lab experience that is largely cognitive and technique-oriented. Thus, some participants may emphasize after training that their committees function more smoothly because of the members' sensitization to, and increased skills in dealing with, the processes of their own functioning. Both increased sensitivity and skills in process analysis are common products of laboratory programs.[1]

Second, for many participants lab experiences highlight deep emotional needs that previously went unmet or unrecognized. Very little of this learning may properly be called "cognitive." The learning is "emotional," making the individual more aware of who he is, what he needs to function wholly, and how he can get it. Very often, the core issue is the feeling of personal repression and confinement in organizations. The consequences are multiple: the individual feels restricted, his levels of trust and comfort are low, and his performance suffers. His sense of repression and confinement is likely to grow. The lab approach can help break this cycle by allowing the individual to work on issues that are real to him but tend to be shunted aside in organizations. One highly placed executive in a federal agency expressed the point in these terms: "Many times in the last four years, I wanted to get up and walk out of a staff meeting. I asked myself what am I doing here with all these strangers. Now, after all these years, I feel a little more at home . . . more free. . . . I am starting to talk to A. . . . Staff meetings have become more open. That makes the big difference."

Third, lab approaches to organization change may primarily tap varying levels of "unfinished business." The term will not be given a rigorous definition here, but if an issue keeps intruding itself and inhibits work on other issues, that is a piece of unfinished business. Two parties may share some specific information with a third party (consultant), and each may know, or guess, that the other knows. If the issue is of mutual interest, the business remains unfinished until the two parties publicly exchange that piece of information and work on it. The issue presses on the consciousness and inhibits both as they continue to suppress it.

"Unfinished business" covers a wide range. Thus a continuing wrangle between a trainer and T-Group member about authority may come to be seen by the latter as a symbol of unresolved tensions between him and his father,

---

[1] Chris Argyris, "Interpersonal Barriers to Decision-Making," *Harvard Business Review*, Vol. 44 (March–April 1966), pp. 84–97.

for example. Or an individual may reveal (as he has perhaps long yearned to do) that his organizational aloofness hides a tormenting loneliness. One manager gave such testimony as he explained what happened to him during his only recreation, solitary sailing far out into the ocean. "I stand up in the boat and stare into the darkness, then up to the sky," he concluded. "Something surges over me. I throw my arms open wide and scream into the darkness. . . . I wait . . . listen. . . . Nobody hears me." [2]

The consequences of raising unfinished business may be diverse, but usually the consciousness of all concerned is liberated. As an example of the worst, and highly improbable, result: A serious issue is raised prematurely and with little skill by a member of a T-Group. Here, the consequences may be harmful, if time and will are short. The most effective safeguard against such an eventuality—and, in addition, against a willful mischiefmaker—is the highly cohesive character of the training group, whose members cannot be divided and conquered as easily as in the "real world" because of the participants' commitment to evaluate the processes of their own interaction. The presence of a trainer also is an important safeguard. The most salient defense, however, is one built into the dynamics of the lab approach. As mutual trust grows, so also does the capacity to state, to hear, and to work through weighty issues. This may seem a fragile defense against the inopportune raising of difficult issues, until one sees it in action.

These last-ditch defenses against deeply hurtful feedback are seldom needed, however. Very often, the public raising of unfinished business will suffice to extinguish its press on the consciousness. Or at least the group is free to work on the issue, and in a supportive way that eases the task. In the case of the lonely manager, for example, this typical deluge of emotional support from fellow group members followed his soliloquy about the sea and his loneliness: [3]

People were crying for the lonely old man. There was the look of peace on Bob's face and slowly, somehow, the loneliness was leaving.

He looked young, strong.

Softly, I said, "Do you realize you've taken us with you? You've given us the privilege of being the first on your boat."

People said, "Thank you, Bob." "You're a poet." "You've got great courage." "I could listen to you all night." "I've never known what a wonderful person you are."

Jim asked, "How old are you, Bob?"

"Forty-nine," Bob replied.

Jim exclaimed, "Is that all! You've been acting like you're an old man—like your life's over, like your career with the company was finished. You even looked old."

Jack said, "You're a young, powerful person, Bob. Look at yourself." Bob's smile

---

[2] Arthur H. Kuriloff and Stuart Atkins, "T-Group for a Work Team," *Journal of Applied Behavioral Science*, Vol. 2 (January–March 1966), p. 85.

[3] *Ibid.*

was young. He seemed overwhelmed with the adulation of the group—with the love that came by letting people in.

"Family groups" composed of individuals with close organizational ties can extend such support into the worksite, which is one basic reason for their usefulness in developing and implementing programs of organization change.

Openly raising unfinished business is no cure-all, of course. Some unfinished business cannot be settled. But raising such issues mutually and publicly at least signals the inappropriateness of overloading organizational relations with that piece of business. Some "unfinished business" may require therapy, of course. One of the trainer's important functions, indeed, is to intervene decisively when it is necessary to encourage group members to concentrate on their feelings and reactions and to avoid attempting to provide amateur psychiatric services. Group members are the experts about their own feelings and reactions and perceptions; but few are qualified for therapy.

Unfinished business is important in lab approaches to organizational change, but it is not an exclusive theme and the bulk of it is not psychologically spooky. Consider this skeletal design of a recent five-day experience for the "new management group" of a large business organization:

1. Unfinished business, largely dealing with previously unshared feelings about the "old management group" ($1^1/_2$ days).
2. Building relations among the "new management group" ($1^1/_2$ days).
3. Developing new work-related policies and procedures (2 days).

At the outset, the group felt bound up and less effective than they desired. Much suppressed old business was handled, with general pleasure at having opened up both points of agreement and disagreement. Some new relations were tentatively established in this freed-up state, and this "maintenance activity" supported some intense work on new policies and procedures. Such concentrated and monolithic attention was devoted to developing new policies and procedures, however, that some of the managers felt "pushed around" and attacked their formal head. Thus new business was generated and interpersonal relations required building or mending. And so it goes.

FACILITATING ACTION VERSUS BLUEPRINTING AN IDEAL

As the stress on freeing individuals suggests, the laboratory approach to organization change has a strong initial bias toward creating conditions which will facilitate consensual action, with far less concern about the action goals toward which that consensus should be directed. Much evidence reflects this bias toward action. For example, early experiences in a T-Group unsettle many persons. Hence the common fixation on the awkward question: "What should we talk about?" This presumes a complex consensus rather than builds toward it. Only an elemental action-oriented consensus is necessary: "Let's get something started, even if it is only talking about why we are so concerned with what we should be talking about."

In its dominant focus on action, on methods *for achieving and changing consensus*, the lab approach constitutes a truly revolutionary departure from much organizationally relevant work. For example, proponents of "scientific management" were *concept-oriented*. Realizing that their utopia could never really exist anywhere until it existed everywhere, they desired to reform "society," to create the kind of people who could live in the scientifically managed society and love it. However, they were muddled about how to achieve what that concept required, beyond the stopwatch, the micro-motion camera, and other technical appurtenances. In contrast, the lab approach concentrates on behaviorally preparing individuals to decide upon and to achieve *their* definition of the desirable organizational life. About the lab approach one may almost say that there is no such thing as a bad concept for change. Only more or less adequate behavioral commitment to a concept determines success or failure, to exaggerate the point somewhat.

Basically, a concept oriented approach encourages win-lose games, which the mixed record of conventional attempts at administrative reform suggests is awkward.[4] To be sure, win-lose games sometimes may be necessary. Perhaps President Roosevelt was tactically correct in setting up a win-lose situation by neglecting to represent Congress on the 1937 committee.[5] The costs of win-lose games tend to be substantial, and in any case, there is another way.

VALUES UNDERLYING METHODS AND USES

That the lab approach is action-oriented and emphasizes procedures *to develop and to change* consensus does not imply that its proponents prefer just any consensus. The approach is not narrowly "means-oriented." Quite the opposite is the case, in fact, as the table attempts to show. The table reflects four levels of value-related goals or methods common to laboratory programs of organizational change. Disagreements among laboratory trainers may exist about the details in the table, but not about its essence.

There is no easy way of illustrating the complexity of the table, but some of its uses may be established. Consider a "competitive" exercise in a laboratory

---

[4] Karl A. Bosworth, "The Politics of Management Improvement in the States," *American Political Science Review*, Vol. 47 (March 1953), pp. 84–99.
[5] Barry Dean Karl, *Executive Reorganization and Reform in the New Deal* (Cambridge, Mass.: Harvard University Press, 1963).

design using Basic T-Groups. Individual A, who has suffered with the muddling-through characteristic of early T-Group meetings, seizes the opportunity provided by the time pressure of the exercise to "whip his group into shape." He is well pleased with his efforts initially, but in the end his group loses badly. Moreover, he learns soon thereafter that the commitment he thought he had been instrumental in forging existed largely in his own mind. For the design of the exercise required data gathering at various stages about the involvement of group members in the competitive exercise, members' confidence in their team strategy, and so on. These data were reviewed as part of a post-exercise analysis, and they showed that most members of A's group privately reported low involvement and lack of confidence in their team.

The table provides a way of classifying the reactions of our hypothetical Individual A. His reactions will be referred to the table via a shorthand, such as reference to (A-1) to indicate that Individual A was acting in ways that reflected a critical and experimental approach to behavior.

Hypothetically, then, let us assume that (like all of us) Individual A did not enjoy losing the competitive exercise, and particularly in the presence of prestigious peers. But A is particularly disturbed that his group "held out on him" and "let him down" by failing to communicate their feelings and expectations to him. If the level of trust is high enough (C-5) and if group members generally accept the meta-values of lab work (A-1 through A-4), Individual A can begin learning from this disturbing challenge to his skill and to himself (B-4). What did he do that encouraged other group members to "lead him down the primrose path" (B-1)? What cues did he miss that he might be sensitive to in similar situations (B-2)? These are among the questions dealing with the "here-and now" (C-1) that Individual A can raise.

Only other group members can provide answers to such questions in their own reactions and feelings to the "here-and-now," however, and Individual A soon learns he will receive roughly in proportion to his giving of himself. He has revealed some openness (B-5) by confessing that he is troubled about the experience. That revelation is likely to earn him some constructive feedback (C-3) that shares with him the impact his behavior had on others (C-4). His initial openness also may save Individual A from the no-feedback that essentially rejects Individual A as well as his specific actions (C-2). Consequently, Individual A will increasingly grow to feel that he can safely level with other group members, even if leveling means that he must tell them that temporarily he has all the data he can process (C-5). For he finds that he is not rejected as a person even though others reacted strongly against his actions (C-2) during the competitive exercise. Indeed, perhaps paradoxically, A can only gain acceptance as a total person as his particularistic actions are considered significant enough to react to, whether positively or critically, and as the atmosphere permits him to be himself (C-5 and C-6).

But Individual A must go further still if he wants to learn more. For example,

LABORATORY APPROACH
Four Value-Loaded Dimensions Relevant in Laboratory Approaches to Organization Change and Development

A Meta-Values of Lab Training *	B Proximate Goals of Lab Training	C Desirable Means for Lab Training	D Organization Values Consistent with Lab Training**
1. An attitude of inquiry reflecting (among others): a. a "hypothetical spirit" b. experimentalism	1. Increased insight, self-knowledge	1. Emphasis on "here-and-now" occurrences	1. Full and free communication
2. "Expanded consciousness and sense of choice"	2. Sharpened diagnostic skills at (ideally) all levels, that is, on the levels of the a. individual b. group c. organization d. society	2. Emphasis on the individual act rather than on the "total person" acting	2. Reliance on open consensus in managing conflict, as opposed to using coercion or compromise
3. The value system of democracy, having as two core elements: a. a spirit of collaboration b. open resolution of conflict via a problem-solving orientation	3. Awareness of, and skill-practice in creating, conditions of effective functioning at (ideally) all levels	3. Emphasis on feedback that is non-evaluative in that it reports the impact on the self of other's behavior, rather than feedback that is judgmental or interpretive	3. Influence based on competence rather than on personal whim or formal power
4. An emphasis on mutual "helping relationships" as the best way to express man's interdependency with man	4. Testing self-concepts and skills in interpersonal situations	4. Emphasis on "unfreezing" behaviors the trainee feels are undesirable, on practice of replacement behaviors, and on "refreezing" new behaviors	4. Expression of emotional as well as task-oriented behavior
	5. Increased capacity to be open, to accept feelings of self and others, to risk interpersonally in rewarding ways	5. Emphasis on "trust in leveling," on psychological safety of the trainee	5. Acceptance of conflict between the individual and his organization, to be coped with willingly, openly, and rationally
		6. Emphasis on creating and maintaining an "organic community"	

* Adapted from Edgar H. Schein and Warren G. Bennis (eds.), *Personal and Organizational Change Through Group Methods* (New York: John Wiley & Sons, Inc., 1965), pp. 30–35; and Leland P. Bradford, Jack R. Gibb, and Kenneth D. Benne (eds.), *T-Group Theory and Laboratory Method* (New York: John Wiley & Sons, Inc., 1964), pp. 10, 12.
** Philip E. Slater and Warren G. Bennis, "Democracy Is Inevitable," *Harvard Business Review*, Vol. 42 (March–April 1964), pp. 51–59.

he must accept the integrity of the feelings of his colleagues (B-5), rather than defensively deny their "reasonableness." This giving and accepting of reactions, in turn, will contribute to the cohesiveness of the group (C-6). For it signals to other group members that they need not hide their reactions (C-5) for fear that they will be discounted. The results are generally happy, for the hiding of reactions not only creates "unfinished business" but also deprives everyone of data and thus inhibits everyone's learning. Moreover, as the sense of community in his training groups grows, so will Individual A feel more free to risk further exploration (B-5) of the issues related to the competitive exercise. And when Individual A acknowledges that even the "strong man" can be freer only as he acknowledges his interdependence with those about him (A-4), then has a really firm foundation been established for learning. From that base, for example, group members can collaboratively (A-3) survey the fuller range of alternatives open to Individual A (A-2), help him to work toward modifying awkward behaviors (C-4), and reinforce his efforts to experiment with other behaviors (A-1 and C-4). These notes are sketchy, and sound lifelessly stilted in the bargain, but they illustrate the dynamic linkages that underlie the static picture in the table.

VALUES GUIDING ORGANIZATION CHANGE

Individual A also might be motivated by such experiences to work actively in an "action group" to change his organizational environment. That is, Individual A may apply his "here-and-now" learnings to "there-and-then" situations, as via working to approach the five values listed in column D in the table. For the value systems of most organizations must be modified or changed to permit individual growth and productivity. For example, most organization settings discourage approaching the goal of the "expression of emotional as well as task-oriented behavior" that the table lists as a value consistent with the laboratory approach.

The Basic T-Group experience can be of varied usefulness in translating individual learning into organization change consistent with the values in column D. Consider only that:

1. The individual can be freed by his experiences in a Basic T-Group so as to remove obstacles to his interpersonal functioning and, perhaps, to his performance in organizations.
2. The Basic T-Group can provide an arena to develop and to test new skills and insights applicable to interpersonal situations that may be modified for use in "action groups" or at work.
3. The experience in the Basic T-Group can reveal the nature and importance of differences between "public" and "private" attitudes in organizations,

differences in which may be owned up to, analyzed, and perhaps reduced in ways that enhance performance in organizations.

4. The group experience can point up the limitations of existing organization norms; or

5. At least the experience in the Basic T-Group can illustrate in life that alternatives to common organizational norms are available.

6. The Basic T-Group can help generate new norms for work and help enforce them as well, as by inducing a desire in individuals to work actively in a "core group" to try to achieve at their work some of the gratification of needs they experienced in a Basic T-Group.

Value considerations are relevant at all stages of the laboratory approach, in sum, from the goals of personal learning, through techniques, and even unto the design of appropriate organizations. The lab approach is not a means to just any ends.

LABORATORY APPROACH APPLICATIONS: AGREEMENTS AND INADEQUACIES

The linkage of individual change in a Basic T-Group with organizational change was made casually above, but this does an injustice to reality. Let us remedy this injustice in two ways: by sketching three broad areas of agreement about the nature of this complex linkage and by detailing the inadequacies of existing theory to act upon these points of agreement.

Agreement I.—Organizational applications of the lab approach stress the "organic" versus the "mechanistic" nature of organizations.[6] As opposed to traditional organization theory, that is, the emphasis is on assembling the competencies necessary to do the job, on "team management," or on "problem-solving." As opposed to traditional organization theory with its emphasis on functional specialization, similarly, the lab approach stresses organizing around "flows of work," "projects," or "matrix overlays." Unfortunately, comparative testing of such alternative ways of organizing has barely begun. Line-staff relations in this regard are like the weather. For example, despite torrents of criticism, little comparative work of even a semicontrolled kind exists that will permit really doing something constructive about line-staff relations.

Agreement II.—Relatedly, points of organizational fragmentation are strategic points for applications of the lab approach. The fragmentation may set depart-

---

[6] Herbert A. Shepard, "Changing Interpersonal and Intergroup Relationships in Organizations," pp. 1115–43, in James G. March (ed.), *Handbook of Organizations* (Chicago: Rand McNally & C., 1965).

ment versus department, line versus staff, headquarters versus the field, or labor versus management. Various lab designs can help clarify the sources of tension and can set the stage for reducing them. For example, desired changes in attitudes and behaviors resulted from an effort to state and to work through some of these very complex interactions within one firm—between headquarters and a field sales force, between several departments within headquarters, and between several hierarchical levels.[7] These strategic targets for change, however, impose correspondingly great demands on the adequacy of the theory underlying applications designed to remedy matters.

Agreement III.—Applications of the lab approach stress the ideal of a change program simultaneously affecting behavior, task, and structure.[8] The ideal of simultaneous change is seldom so closely approached as at Non-Linear Systems (see footnote 2), but simultaneity comprises a major theme in many programs of organization change and development. Given the imprecision of our existing knowledge of behavior-task-structure linkages, the ideal is a lofty one.

The demands implied by these three points of agreement highlight the inadequacies of laboratory approaches to organizational change and development. The summary conclusion may be driven home in terms of three particulars. First, we lack appropriate empirical theory to guide lab approaches to organization change. Epigrammatically, the classroom reflects a complexity that more than matches the capacity of existing theory. So much more ill-equipped are applications in incredibly more complex formal organizations.

Second, and relatedly, the lack of theory is tied to the inadequate volume of research dealing with applications of the lab approach to organization change. Thus Schein and Bennis note that:[9]

Discouragingly, but not unexpectedly, the research effort seems weakest in those situations where the risks are highest and the tasks are most complex. We are referring to the uses of laboratory training in inducing change in organizations. In some organizational change programs, a great deal of attention is being paid to research, but not enough research is yet being done.

Theory and research about the application of laboratory methods to individual learning are in much better shape, in contrast. Thus much is known about who is likely to learn what in which laboratory designs. And certainly no one can doubt the considerable power of laboratory experiences to change attitudes or

---

[7] Robert T. Golembiewski and Arthur Blumberg, "Confrontation As a Training Design in Complex Organizations," *Journal of Applied Behavioral Science*, Vol. 21 (September 1967), pp. 211-20.

[8] Richard Beckhard, "An Organization Improvement Program in a Decentralized Organization," *Journal of Applied Behavioral Science*, Vol. 2 (January–March 1966), pp. 3–26.

[9] Edgar Schein and Warren G. Bennis (eds.), *Personal and Organizational Change Through Group Methods* (New York: John Wiley & Sons, Inc., 1965), p. 323.

to change behavior. More generally still, research on the personal and inter-personal aspects of laboratory training reflects all the signs of robust activity.

Third, existing research about organizational applications of the lab approach has important design limitations. Generally, much research about learning in laboratories has a strong focus on "outcomes," such as the before-after change in an individual's ability to empathize with others. Commonly, "input" or process variables receive less attention. Exceptions to this "rule" exist both early and late in the short history of sensitivity training. But the generalization still holds rather more than less.

The "outcome" bias characterizes research on laboratory approaches to organization change and development, specifically, with several interesting reservations. For example, the "outcomes" emphasized most in research about change programs in organizations tend to cover a narrow range and/or to be restricted to the feeling realm. Of course, many narrow measures of the success of laboratory approaches to organization change can be cited. For example, attitudes of both headquarters and field officials in a large organization have been changed via a modified laboratory design, as one small part of a long-run program of change.[10] As the criteria for success are broadened, however, so also does the validation of change become more elusive and problematic. Whether the attitudinal changes noted above also produced more effective work relations, for example, is just such an elusive and problematic issue. Highly placed organization members have reported that they feel their work relations are freer and more productive. Liking is an important outcome, to be sure, and for some purposes even the most important one. But other outcomes also are of scientific and practical interest.

Finally, the complexity and chancy nature of crucial events in organizations often leaves change agents exhaustedly satisfied if "things seemed to work out pretty well, on balance." This gross outcome bias I can well understand, as a participant in several major efforts in which events far beyond the change program affected it substantially.

Straightforward summary is possible concerning the third problem with the laboratory approach to organization change. With very rare exceptions,[11] lab approaches to organization change have not been validated in the broader sense of tracing their influence on such desirable states as high productivity or low employee turnover. Complexity and confounding variables make it very difficult to support rigorously the compelling circumstantial evidence of the value of laboratory programs for change. Similarly, very few change programs in large

---

[10] Golembiewski and Blumberg, *op. cit.*
[11] Louis B. Barnes and Larry E. Greiner, "Breakthrough in Organization Development," *Harvard Business Review*, Vol. 42 (November–December, 1964), pp. 139–65.

organizations have looked closely at input variables or the specific processes of the groups involved.[12] It has been, in short, "outcome" bias.

Such then is the skeleton of the laboratory approach to organization change. The startling growth of the "sensitivity training" movement suggests that the approach is likely to be increasingly relied upon. It is important to know about the real values of the approach, as well as about its disadvantages and present weaknesses.

Bibliographical Note

"Laboratory training" is a new and rapidly expanding approach to learning. The magnitudes involved are implied in one datum. Since its modest beginnings in summer 1947 under the auspices of the National Training Laboratories, some 50,000 persons have had a laboratory experience. Lab training is at once difficult to understand, new, risky, expensive, and patently much sought after.

The literature dealing with the laboratory approach is correspondingly diverse and rapidly growing. This bibliographical note introduces the reader to that literature under six heads: (1) relatively "popular" treatments of the use of sensitivity training in personal growth; (2) organizational applications of the laboratory approach; (3) comprehensive treatments of lab theory and applications in many contexts; (4) underlying theory; (5) "controlled" research; and (6) criticisms of lab training and of "applied behavioral science."

The "popular" literature is extensive. Re: sensitivity training in personal development, Alfred Marrow's *Behind the Executive Mask* (New York: American Management Association, 1964) is perhaps the most useful. For a view of the laboratory approach applied to programs of organizational change, see Chris Argyris' "T-Groups for Organizational Effectiveness," *Harvard Business Review*, Vol. 42 (March–April 1964), pp. 60–74.

Two efforts by Chris Argyris well illustrate the problems and potentials of organization applications of the lab approach in a public agency and in a business firm. See "Some Causes of Organizational Ineffectiveness Within the Department of State," *Center for International Systems Research*, Occasional Paper No. 2, January 1967; and *Interpersonal Competence and Organizational Effectiveness* (Homewood, Ill.: Dorsey Press, 1962). Herbert Shepard's "Changing Interpersonal and Intergroup Relationships in Organizations," pp. 1115–43, in James March (ed.), *Handbook of Organizations* (Chicago: Rand McNally & Co., 1965) provides generalized counterpoint to Argyris' specific cases.

Valuable comprehensive treatments of the lab approach have recently become available. Of particular interest are: Leland P. Bradford, Jack R. Gibb, and Kenneth D. Benne (eds.), *T-Group Theory and Laboratory Method* (New York: John Wiley & Sons, Inc., 1964); and Edgar H. Schein and Warren G. Bennis (eds.), *Personal and Organizational Change Through Group Methods* (New York: John Wiley & Sons, Inc., 1965). These two sources also contain extensive bibliographies.

The theory underlying the laboratory approach covers the range from personal feelings to group structure. Selectively, see W. R. Bion, *Experiences in Groups* (New York: Basic Books, Inc., Publishers, 1959); Herbert A. Thelen, *The Dynamics of Groups At Work* (Chicago: University of Chicago Press, 1954); and Robert T. Golembiewski, *The Small Group* (Chicago: University of Chicago Press, 1962).

Much "controlled" research is conveniently treated in summary articles such as Dorothy Stock's "A Survey of Research on T-Groups," in Bradford, Gibb, and Benne, *op. cit.* Major outlets for much of this research are the *Journal of Applied Behavioral Science* and various other publications of the National Training Laboratories.

Criticisms of the laboratory approach tend toward the colorful and dramatic. George

---

[12] For one exception, see Chris Argyris, *Interpersonal Competence and Organizational Effectiveness* (Homewood, Ill.: Dorsey Press, 1962).

Odiorne's "The Trouble With Sensitivity Training," *Journal of the American Society of Training Directors*, Vol. 17 (March 1963), pp. 9–20, is more or less typical. See also S. Klaw, "Two Weeks in a T-Group," *Fortune*, Vol. 64 (August 1961), pp. 114–17ff.

Social science applications in organizations, more broadly, also have received critical attention. Loren Baritz, *The Servants of Power: A History of the Use of Social Science in American Industry* (Middletown, Conn.: Wesleyan University Press, 1960) provides a comprehensive and generally measured survey of "applied behavorial science."

17.

BREAKTHROUGH IN ON-THE-JOB TRAINING

Earl R. Gomersall and
M. Scott Myers

In this article we shall describe and analyze the results of an unusual study just completed at Texas Instruments Incorporated (TI). The study dealt with the relationship between organization climate and job performance. One of the objectives was to find out what would happen in a large manufacturing department if the causes of anxiety among new employees were reduced. The following gains were accomplished:

Training time was shortened by one half.
Training costs were lowered to one third of their previous levels.
Absenteeism and tardiness dropped to one half of the previous normal.
Waste and rejects were reduced to one fifth of their previous levels.
Costs were cut as much as 15% to 30%!

We feel that similar gains can be realized in other organizations, in and out of manufacturing, if they use the approach to be described. If so, the TI study should lead to significant improvements in the efficiency of U.S. industry. Moreover, the gains are not limited to the categories just listed. In the TI manufacturing department, for instance, the results are stimulating managers to try other innovations which, in a circular fashion, are touching off chains of events leading to still more innovations and bringing about basic changes in the job and in the values of the supervisor.

JOB ENLARGEMENT

Job enlargement is a means of countering trends toward regimentation, social stratification, technological displacement, and routinized work brought about by mass production methods. Industrial engineering has traditionally applied techniques to achieve organizational goals without thoughtful regard for, and sometimes at the *expense* of, individual goals. The manager's interest in job enlargement stems not from altruism, but rather from his observation that people are motivated by meaningful work which leads to the attainment of personal as well as organizational goals.

Job enlargement efforts follow several approaches. Earliest and best known at Texas Instruments is the work simplification process which equips individuals with knowledge, skills, and attitudes to apply industrial engineering techniques to their own jobs.* Through work simplification, individuals become the willing agents rather than the defensive targets of change. Because mass production operations have gradually limited independent action, a premium is placed on group effectiveness, and job enlargement is pursued through team approaches to problem solving and goal setting.

Jobs may be enlarged horizontally and/or vertically. If an operator's job is expanded so he is now *doing* a greater variety or number of operations, it is enlarged horizontally. If the operator is involved in the *planning, organizing, and inspection*—as well as the *doing* of his work, his job is enlarged vertically. Evidence from several companies indicates that most forms of job enlargement—horizontal or vertical, individual or group—result in improved performance or, at least, less job dissatisfaction. Manufacturing processes at TI appear to improve most through vertical enlargement involving groups united by common goals or processes.

One example of successful job enlargement at TI began with 10 assemblers and their supervisor in a conference for solving problems and setting production goals for the manufacture of complex radar equipment. Through their initiative and creativity, assemblers improved manufacturing processes and gradually reduced production time by more than 50 % and exceeded labor standards (based on a previously approved method) by 100 %.

This process ultimately embraced the entire group of 700 assemblers, and it led to substantial cost reductions in the division, less absenteeism and tardiness, and fewer complaints and personnel problems. This successful group process, which granted unprecedented freedom to assemblers in managing their own work (such as rearranging their own assembly lines), also caused supervisors to begin changing their traditional authoritarian self-image to one of coordination and support.

—The Authors

* See Auren Uris, "Mogy's Work Simplification Is Working New Miracles," *Factory*, September 1965, p. 112.

SETTING OF THE STUDY

The study resulted from our cooperative efforts—one of us is a manufacturing manager and the other an industrial psychologist—in what was initially intended to be an application of motivational techniques through job enlargement (as defined, see above). Although job enlargement replicated from other TI experiments was successful, this article primarily describes innovations by line management to improve job performance through deliberate changes in the organizational climate of the manufacturing department.

The setting for the study was a rapidly growing TI department which, at the time of the experiment, included over 1,400 persons spread throughout three shifts. The department manufactured integrated circuits (microminiature circuitry units). The subjects of the study were women operators who collectively performed approximately 1,850 different operations (the most numerously replicated of these operations having only 70 operators per shift). Approximately 57% of the operators worked with microscopes, and all jobs placed a premium on visual acuity, eye-hand coordination, and mechanical aptitude. Selection standards for operators included high school education and passing scores on the General Aptitude Test Battery of the Texas Employment Commission.

The work reported here commenced with a meeting of the authors to plan the application of job-enlargement programs as practiced by other areas of the corporation. Despite the fact that all first- and second-line supervisors had attended the TI motivation seminars and knew the principles of job enlargement, the department manager felt that, in practice, these principles were not being successfully implemented. Part of the answer seemed to lie in the fact that both the supervisors and the employees were in a continuous process of adapting to rapid expansion and technological change. For this and other reasons, as will be discussed later, supervisors and employees were experiencing anxiety. This anxiety appeared to have an effect on their work.

EXHIBIT 17.1

LEARNING CURVE FOR BALL BONDERS

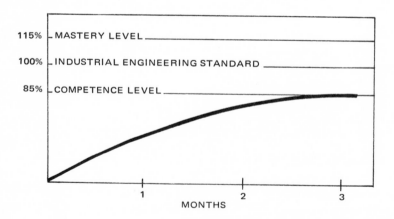

Operations were typified by a continuous training process—training new people hired for expansion and replacement purposes and retraining transferees and the technologically displaced. The consequences of this training program can be illustrated with the classical growth curve shown in Exhibit 17.1. As this curve shows:

The ball bonders required approximately three months to reach what we term the "competence" level. (The competence level is the stage at which assemblers can independently manufacture the product, but have not yet achieved the speed and accuracy ultimately expected of them to reach the labor standards set by industrial engineering. The competence level is about 85% of labor standards; a position about 115% of standard is termed the "mastery" level.)

The learning curve of ball bonders was fairly typical of production operations in the department (and, for that matter, of learning in many other companies and industries).

Competence and Creativity

A need was recognized to find out at what stage in the learning process assemblers could be meaningfully involved in the problem-solving, goal-setting process. Were they ready, for example, at one month, at which time they were halfway to the competence level? Or must they have fully reached the competence level before creative involvement in problem solving could be expected?

To answer this question, two experimental groups were selected, one comprised of individuals of one-month tenure, and the other of individuals who had been with the organization three or more months:

The one-month group, when involved in the problem-solving process, came up with maintenance-type suggestions such as:
We need more coat racks.
Standards not set right.
We don't have enough time to eat.
There aren't enough maintenance technicians around to fix machines.
Too much confusion at shift breaks.

The more seasoned group came up with over two pages of specific, technically oriented suggestions to improve the quality of operations, many not previously considered from a management standpoint. Following are examples of suggestions from the seasoned group:
Do not split manufacturing lots between operators.
Assign the same quality inspector to a given group of operators to assure continuity.
Print wiring diagrams on the backs of all lot travelers (operation sequence sheets).
Give each girl a capillary punch for capillary repair.
Technicians should always repair burnt-out electrical heaters, and girls should always change own capillaries.

This experiment corroborates earlier observations that minimal job competence is a requisite to creative problem solving. The finding seems to have quite general application. Not only do untrained employees impair the problem-solving efforts of skilled workers, but they themselves are frustrated by their inability to participate in the problem-solving activities. So there is added reason to seek ways to accelerate on-the-job learning.

EXPERIMENTS CONDUCTED

Why did the one-month group fail in the problem-solving experiment? The reason, we postulated, was not only lack of familiarity with hardware and processes, but also debilitating anxieties associated with lack of job competence during the early days of employment. These relationships were not mere conjecture. The department manager had, during the past year, followed a systematic program for interviewing individuals during the morning coffee break. The results of 135 interviews with 405 operators yielded the following facts:

Their first days on the job were anxious and disturbing ones.
"New employee initiation" practices by peers intensified anxiety.
Anxiety interfered with the training process.
Turnover of newly hired employees was caused primarily by anxiety.
The new operators were reluctant to discuss problems with their supervisors.
Their supervisors had been unsuccessful in translating motivation theory into practice.

Similar interviews conducted with the supervisors and middle managers yielded these additional conclusions:

They experienced as much anxiety as new assemblers.
They felt inadequate with seasoned, competent subordinates.
They cut off downward communication to conceal ignorance.
Supervisory defensiveness discouraged upward communication.
Motivation principles learned in the classroom were not being implemented on the assembly line.

Preliminary Analysis

Facts uncovered through these interviews underscored the importance of anxiety in inhibiting job effectiveness for both operators and supervisors. It seemed obvious that anxiety dropped as competence was achieved. The relationship between the learning curve and what was believed to be the anxiety curve of operators is illustrated in Exhibit 17.2.

To supplement information obtained through personal interviews and to gain a better understanding of the characteristics of the anxiety to be reduced, we developed a 92-item questionnaire to measure the following possible causes

EXHIBIT 17.2
RELATIONSHIP OF ANXIETY TO COMPETENCE

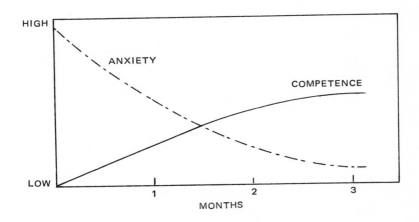

of tension or anxiety: supervision; job knowledge and skill; social acceptance; physical condition; orientation; job pressure; regimentation; vocational adjustment; personal problems; financial worries; outside social factors; and opportunities for the satisfaction of growth, achievement, responsibility, and recognition needs.

Administration of this questionnaire to short-tenure and seasoned employees identified three types of tension in the job situation—the first two harmful and the third helpful:

(1) One form of anxiety, mentioned previously, stemmed from the unpredictable and sometimes threatening new world of work and, as illustrated in Exhibit 17.2, was higher among *new* trainees.

(2) Another type of tension resulted from anxieties about non-job factors such as personal finances, domestic problems, professional status, and outside social relationships. This type existed in equal amounts in *both* groups.

(3) The third type of tension was identified as a positive, inner-directed desire for constructive self-expression. This creative tension found constructive expression best in an atmosphere of approval and self-confidence after job competence was reached.

Anxiety vs. Performance

Assuming the validity of Exhibit 17.2, we posed the following question: "Is it possible to accelerate achievement to the competence level by reducing anxiety at a faster rate?" In other words, we wanted to know if it were possible to achieve the relationships illustrated by the dotted lines in Exhibit 17.3.

EXHIBIT 17.3

Postulated Consequence of Anxiety Reduction

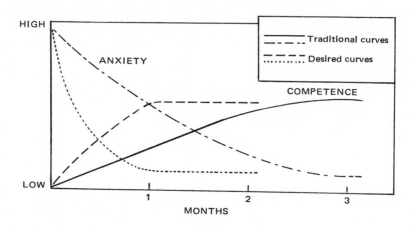

Anxiety on the job is characteristically assumed to be the dependent variable, gradually dropping as competence is acquired. Might not the reverse be true? Might not competence increase as a result of anxiety being decreased? With such questions in mind, we decided to design an orientation program to reduce the anxieties of experimental groups of new employees:

The next group of ten girls hired for bonding work on the second shift was chosen as the first experimental group. A control group was selected from the first and third shifts. Precautions were taken to avoid the "Hawthorne effect" of influencing behavior through special attention. (The "Hawthorne effect" was first reported by Elton Mayo and F. J. Roethlisberger in their experiments at Western Electric. They noticed that improvements in operators' performance often followed simply from outsiders' taking an interest in them.) The control group was oriented in the customary manner and the experimental group through a revised approach. Neither group was told of the experiment, and members of both groups had no reason to think they were being subjected to special treatment.

Conventional Indoctrination

The control group went through the usual first-day orientation, which consisted of a two-hour briefing on hours of work, insurance, parking, work rules, and employee services. This session included warnings of the consequences of failure to conform to organization expectations and, though not intended as a threat, tended to raise rather than reduce anxieties.

Following this orientation, it was customary for a bonder to be introduced to her friendly but very busy supervisor, who gave her further orientation and job instruction. Unfortunately, the supervisor's detailed familiarity with the operations had desensitized him to the technological gap between them, and the following might be typical of what the operator heard him say:

Alice, I would like you to take the sixth yellow chair on this assembly line, which is in front of bonding machine #14. On the left side of your machine you will find a wiring diagram indicating where you should bond your units. On the right-hand side of your machine you will find a carrying tray full of 14-lead packages. Pick up the headers, one at a time, using your 3-C tweezers and place them on the hot substrate below the capillary head. Grasp the cam actuator on the right-hand side of the machine and lower the hot capillary over the first bonding pad indicated by the diagram. Ball bond to the pad and, by moving the hot substrate, loop the wire to the pin indicated by the diagram. Stitch bond to this lead, raise the capillary, and check for pigtails. When you have completed all leads, put the unit back in the carrying tray.

Your training operator will be around to help you with other details. Do you have any questions?

Overwhelmed by these instructions and not wanting to offend this polite and friendly supervisor or look stupid by telling him she did not understand anything he said, the operator would go to her work station and try to learn by watching her peers on either side of her. But they, in pursuit of operating goals, had little time to assist her. Needless to say, her anxieties were increased and her learning ability was impaired. And the longer she remained unproductive, the more reluctant she was to disclose her wasted effort to her supervisor and the more difficult her job became.

Experimental Approach

The experimental group participated in a one-day program especially designed to overcome anxieties not eliminated by the usual process of job orientation. Following the two-hour orientation by Personnel, they were isolated in a conference room before they could be "initiated" by their peers. They were told there would be no work the first day, that they should relax, sit back, and have a coke or cigarette, and use this time to get acquainted with the organization and each other and to ask questions. Throughout this one-day anxiety-reduction session, questions were encouraged and answered. This orientation emphasized four points:

1. "*Your opportunity to succeed is very good.*" Company records disclosed that 99.6 % of all persons hired or transferred into this job were eventually successful in terms of their ability to learn the necessary skills. Trainees were shown learning curves illustrating the gradual buildup of competence over the learning period. They were told five or six times during the day that all members of this group could expect to be successful on the job.

2. "*Disregard 'hall talk.'*" Trainees were told of the hazing game that old em-

ployees played—scaring newcomers with exaggerated allegations about work rules, standards, disciplinary actions, and other job factors—to make the job as frightening to the newcomers as it had been for them. To prevent these distortions by peers, the trainees were given facts about both the good and the bad aspects of the job and exactly what was expected of them.

The basis for "hall talk" rumors was explained. For example, rumor stated that more than one half of the people who terminated had been fired for poor performance. The interviews mentioned earlier disclosed the fact that supervisors themselves unintentionally caused this rumor by intimating to operators that voluntary terminations (marriage, pregnancy, leaving town) were really performance terminations. Many supervisors felt this was a good negative incentive to pull up the low performers.

3. *"Take the initiative in communication."* The new operators were told of the natural reluctance of many supervisors to be talkative and that it was easier for the supervisor to do his job if they asked him questions. They were told that supervisors realized that trainees needed continuous instruction at first, that they would not understand technical terminology for a while, that they were expected to ask questions, and that supervisors would not consider them dumb for asking questions.

4. *"Get to know your supervisor."* The personality of the supervisor was described in detail. The absolute truth was the rule. A description might reveal that—

the supervisor is strict, but friendly;

his hobby is fishing and ham radio operation;

he tends to be shy sometimes, but he really likes to talk to you if you want to;

he would like you to check with him before you go on a personal break, just so he knows where you are.

Following this special day-long orientation session, members of the experimental group were introduced to their supervisor and their training operators in accordance with standard practice. Training commenced as usual, and eventually all operators went on production.

SIGNIFICANT GAINS

A difference in attitude and learning rate was apparent from the beginning in the progress of the two groups. By the end of four weeks, the experimental group was significantly outperforming the control group, as shown in Exhibit

EXHIBIT 17.4

ONE-MONTH PERFORMANCE LEVELS OF
EXPERIMENTAL AND CONTROL GROUPS

	Experimental Group	Control Group
Units per hour	93	27
Absentee rate	0.5%	2.5%
Times tardy	2	8
Training hours required	225	381

EXHIBIT 17.5

LEARNING CURVES OF EXPERIMENTAL AND CONTROL GROUPS

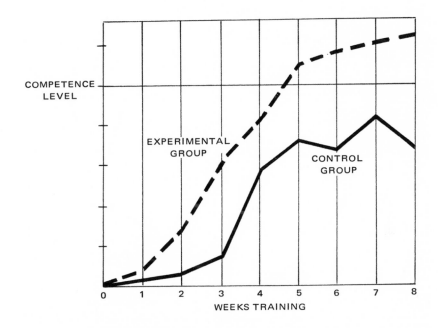

17.4. Note that the experimental group excelled in production and job attendance as well as in learning time.

Exhibit 17.5 compares the learning curves of the two groups. It is interesting to note that when anxiety is minimized, learning appears to be almost a straight-line function of time, suggesting that the area between the experimental curve and the control curve represents learning time lag caused by anxiety.

When the experimental study began showing significant results, the anxiety-reduction process was used on additional groups. Exhibit 17.6 shows performance curves reflecting similar results for more than 200 members of experimental and control groups for assembling, welding, and inspection; their absenteeism rates are also compared. It is interesting to note that the third week's methods change in the inspection department depressed the performance of the experimental group more than that of the control group, but the experimental group made a more rapid recovery.

Attaining Mastery

Now let us make a general observation: after an operator achieves an acceptable level of competence, further improvement depends on the nature of the incentive.

EXHIBIT 17.6

FURTHER COMPARISONS OF EXPERIMENTAL AND CONTROL GROUPS

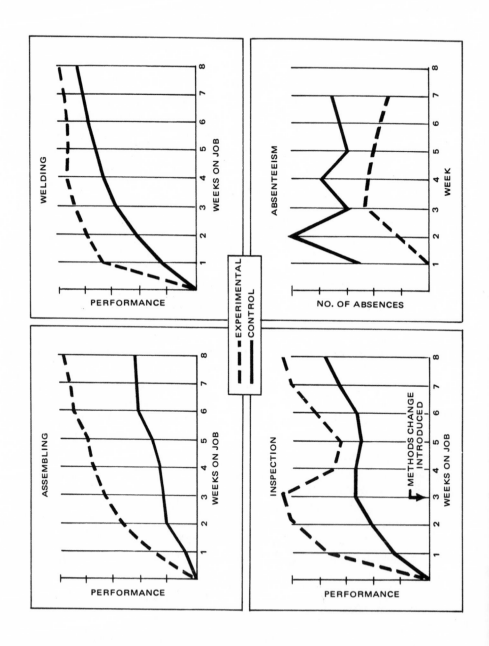

The usual practice is to set labor standards somewhat in excess of the plateau which an operator can comfortably achieve in the short run. As noted earlier, standards traditionally impose an expectation about 15 percentage points above the competence plateau. However, there is a more positive incentive for surpassing the competence plateau. This is the opportunity for self-initiated creative effort. Let us look at some aspects of the TI experiment which bear on this.

In the integrated circuits groups without methods improvement, the motivated assemblers exceeded labor standards by about 15% to achieve what we term the "mastery level." Since the mastery level is usually attained after plateauing at the competence level, members of the control group seldom reached the mastery level before the fifth month.

But in the experimental group, by contrast, the mastery level was achieved in two to three months.

EXHIBIT 17.7

MASTERY ATTAINMENT BY EXPERIMENTAL AND CONTROL GROUPS

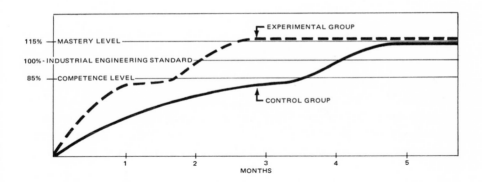

As illustrated in the smoothed curves of Exhibit 17.7, the area between control group and experimental group curves represents an improvement in performance of approximately 50%. For 100 new hires in this department at TI, that gain was equivalent to net first-year savings of at least $50,000. On the basis of reduced turnover, absenteeism, and training time, additional annual savings of $35,000 were estimated.

Spread of Confidence

As trainees with less anxiety gradually became members of the regular work force, their attitudes began influencing the performance of the work groups

EXHIBIT 17.8
COMPARATIVE PERFORMANCE OF THREE SHIFTS

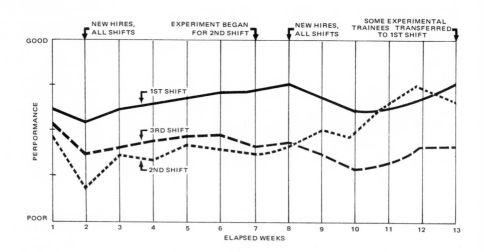

they joined. The greater confidence of the new members seemed to inspire greater confidence among their older peers; also, their higher performance established a new reference point for stimulating the natural competitiveness which existed among members of work groups. Old peers were sometimes hard pressed to maintain a superiority margin between themselves and the rapidly learning newcomers. There was evidence of improvements in quality and quantity, not only among immediate peer groups, but also among adjacent work groups who were influenced through the informal social system in the plant.

The performance of an entire shift was difficult to measure because of changing methods and standards, but Exhibit 17.8 shows the results of putting 10 operators trained under the system among 60 workers on the second shift. The second shift, which for the previous seven weeks had had the lowest productivity, became clearly the highest producer five weeks after the experiment began. Although transferring some of the 10 experimentally trained operators to the first shift in the thirteenth week dropped the performance level of the second shift, the transfusion appeared to raise the performance level of the first shift.

Quality Improvement

The new training system influenced performance in more ways than one. For example, in analyzing the causes of defects management noted that, contrary to

EXHIBIT 17.9
QUANTITY-QUALITY RELATIONSHIPS

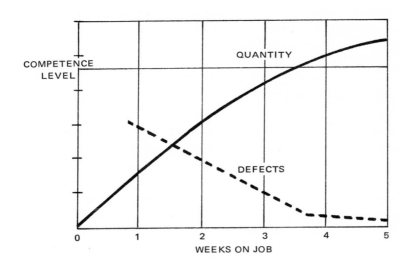

common assumptions, the faster operators (by definition, master operators) were making fewer errors. The relationship of output to defects is shown in Exhibit 17.9; note that those trainees who exceeded the competence level within four weeks were usually making products with practically no defects.

It had been the practice to subject all units to 100% inspection for nine specific reject criteria. This required one inspector for every two assembly operators. Master operators, whose defects were close to zero, were now permitted to submit completed units to quality assurance inspectors for lot inspection, thus bypassing the normal 100% inspection. The pride which these operators felt because of their accomplishment and because of being identified with the master operator group actually improved their product quality over the standards achieved through 100% inspection. The lot rejection rate dropped by a factor of five, and labor costs were lowered by 30%. Not only was pride in workmanship returned to the job, but an old manufacturers' axiom was validated: "Quality cannot be *inspected* into a product; it must be *built* into it."

BROADER IMPLICATIONS

The results of this experiments are significant to the operating manager in terms of the criteria most important to him—reduced costs, higher quality, satisfied customers, and increased profits. Without improvements in these measures, no matter how noble the other motives, experiments of this type generally have low priority.

At the same time, because this experiment has led to improvements in terms of these traditional management criteria at TI, managers have become enthusiastically involved in its implementation and, in the process, have become the agents for other changes. Now let us look at some of these effects.

New Understanding

As managers have gradually become more sensitive to the relationship between attitudes and behavior, they have begun to seek a better understanding of the causes of attitude change. Motivation theory, which they had learned as an intellectual process in a company motivation seminar, has become meaningful for them as they observe its implementation in the work situation. Job enlargement and increased motivation through the application of behavioral theory in other groups has become interesting to them; and systems for measuring attitudes, teaching problem solving, goal setting, and providing performance feedback are now seen in new perspective. These new perspectives constitute a foundation for greater managerial effectiveness at all levels and in all functions.

Improved Training

It is interesting to note that, as managers reviewed the results of anxiety reduction for production personnel, they would observe, "You know, managers have anxieties, too. . . ." And many would volunteer descriptions of their own debilitating anxieties.

Why do supervisors have anxieties about their competence as supervisors? Primarily because of mistaken concepts of the proper role of a supervisor. This error is understandable in the light of the typical man's background:

Approximately 60% of the first-line supervisory positions are filled by new college graduates. They reach industry after a life of conditioning in "superior-subordinate" relationships. After a long background of parent-child, teacher-student, officer-enlisted man experiences, it is normal for them to come to their first supervisory job with the notion that a leader is someone who "can do everything his subordinates can, only better."

Because of this traditional image of infallibility of leaders, the new supervisor understandably feels inadequate in his new role of supervising large numbers of individuals, most of whom know the operations better than he does. He does not realize that the operators recognize and accept his limitations and that it is futile and self-defeating for him to try to conceal them.

To help new supervisors gain early acceptance of their limitations and a better understanding of their supervisory role, TI developed a plan for having operators train the supervisor! Working in pairs, operators (who have received trainer training) give the new or transferred supervisor his first orientation to the assembly line, acquainting him with the pitfalls traditionally encountered by new supervisors and defining his role as it is perceived by the operators. This innovative approach serves three basic purposes:

(1) It provides a supervisor with valid information directly from the persons who have the greatest knowledge of the operations.

(2) It provides assurance to the operators that the supervisor is properly qualified and acquainted with their problems. Because they get personally involved in his training, they will seek to make him successful.

(3) Most importantly, this approach to training is significant because of its impact on the values of the supervisor. A supervisor who, in his first experience as a manager, learns to expect and seek information from subordinates, and discovers that they are creative and responsible, is conditioned or permanently "programmed" to look to, and rely on, subordinates for assistance in solving problems. And, as Douglas McGregor and many others have pointed out, people tend to rise to properly delegated expectations of supervision. Supervisors who are programmed to have high expectations of subordinates are ideally suited for pursuing job enlargement.

Fluid Communication

A significant effect of the new orientation program is the encouragement of upward communication. In the final analysis, communication depends upon the behavior of supervisors who, through the language of action, provide a climate conducive to natural and informal exchange of information. It was as a result of sensitizing supervisors to the importance of listening and maintaining fluid communication channels at all levels that the following incident took place:

An operator approached a manager during coffee break and casually struck up a conversation about the "units with little white specks on them that leaked after welding." The supervisor asked, "What little white specks?" The operator pointed out that almost all of the units that leaked after welding had little specks on them, a fact unnoted before. Verifying and investigating this fact revealed that units were placed in plastic trays while still hot from a previous process; their heat caused many of them to fuse to the plastic container. Pulling them from the container caused the units to pull away a small amount of plastic, thus insulating them during the welding process.

Once this was discovered, the problem was solved simply by delaying the placing of units in the plastic trays until they had cooled sufficiently. This single suggestion reduced rejects by a factor of four for this product—a projected cost prevention of hundreds of thousands of dollars.

The point we want to emphasize here is that casual questions and observations of the type described take place only in an atmosphere of approval, genuine respect, and interest.

CONCLUSION

As the principles of the new approach have been adopted and adapted by other departments at TI, we have been able to gain new appreciation of the respective roles of managers and behavioral scientists. The manager should look to behavioral scientists not to solve his problems, but only to provide needed information about them. To ask the scientists to do more robs the manager of his charter and violates the very principle which he is expected to implement through job enlargement.

However, the behavioral scientist is operating within his proper realm of responsibility if he serves as a change agent by assisting managers in planning the application of theories and principles and by giving visibility to their achievements. Incidentally, there should be broader recognition that, as the previous discussion indicates, behavioral science applications can be measured in traditional production indexes as well as in the more nebulous criteria of morale and attitudes.

Important Effects

The approach described in this article has had important effects on TI's manufacturing department:

(1) It has made the department more effective by reducing costs and waste and by improving quality and profitability.

(2) It has made the workplace more attractive for the employees by reducing anxiety and making work more challenging. This has resulted in less reactive behavior, better attendance, and better utilization of talent.

(3) Supervisors are becoming more effective managers. As their involvement in anxiety reduction and job enlargement results in more responsible and creative behavior on the part of operators, supervisors learn to delegate with greater confidence. This in turn frees them from details which heretofore seemed oppressively inescapable so they can spend more time on higher level developmental work.

These gains do not, of course, happen independently but, rather, in a mutually reinforcing and circular way.

The new approach can, if applied broadly, reduce the costs of personnel administration. Outside their staffing responsibilities, personnel departments traditionally devote most of their efforts to administering supplemental benefits, working on collective bargaining, settling grievances, and, in general, dealing with causes of dissatisfaction. Dissatisfaction and preoccupation with so-called "maintenance" factors (that is, parking arrangements, fringe benefits, vacation schedules, and so on) are not usually a consequence of inadequacy of these factors but a symptom of thwarted motivation needs. People in jobs which offer opportunity for growth, for achievement, responsibility, and recognition, have little incentive to get sidetracked with peripheral issues and feel no need to seek the intervention of a labor union to "police" management. In fact, on a properly designed and delegated job in a suitable organizational climate, the employee is in a real sense a manager himself. His proprietary interest in managing his job gives him a sense of company identification that causes him to see unionism as a deterrent to his effectiveness. Hence, meaningful work eliminates the wastefulness of uninspired and reactive behavior and the cost of elaborate systems for dealing with dissatisfaction.

The rate of technological displacement—and hence the need for effective training—is increasing. This fact, in combination with the current labor shortage, the entry of more young people and minority groups into industrial employment, and the deployment of new plants domestically and internationally, means that management should place more emphasis on training and other personnel management innovations than ever before. Lessened turnover and accelerated learning curves constitute a significant advantage to companies that are able to achieve them.

U.S. business has been hard pressed to match international competition. Handicapped by the pay differential, American companies have met the challenge primarily through technical innovation and superior quality. They can also meet it with management innovation. A great deal can be accomplished in this way, as our experiences with accelerated learning and job enlargement demonstrate.

18.

THREE THINGS WRONG WITH THE CIVIL SERVICE

I. CAREERS CLEAR TO THE TOP—DONN R. GRANDPRÉ

This title brought forth some reminiscences of World War II when I planned to "expose" the Army. I never did and now I notice that the things I then complained about seem to make pretty good sense.

I've had many of these changing views; sometimes representing 180 degrees turnabout. They lead me to believe, as some gentleman of note once stated,

Reprinted by permission from the July–August, 1960 issue of *Personnel Administration*, copyright 1960, Society for Personnel Administration, Suites 485–487, National Press Building, 14th and F Streets, N.W., Washington, D.C. 20004. With permission from the author, Donn R. Grandpré.

"Everything is relative." The magnitude or importance of things seems to depend on where we happen to be sitting at a given time.

At the present time, my frame of mind calls for career service personnel to fill the top slots of our bureaucracy—including the secretaries of the departments.

The findings of the second Hoover Commission don't support this, on the grounds that the party in power must retain these positions for political appointments to insure that their policies are carried out.

This may be true and is possibly a valid reason for maintaining these offices as political plums; however, it may also be true that they represent a vestige of the old "clean sweep" philosophy that prevailed during the days when the spoils belonged to the victor.

Just a brief glance back to some of our notables of the recent past, e.g., McElroy, Pace, Forrestal, Robertson, McNeil, Dulles, Marshall, gives evidence of superior ability in many political appointments. Is it fair to assume that our top drawer career people would be less able? No more than it would be to assume that soap and auto salesmen know "what's good for the country," speaking from a defense or foreign relations standpoint.

Does the business acumen and economic know-how of leading industrialists, used to figuring in terms of profit taking and beating out the competition, stand them in good stead as political appointees to one of government's top administrative positions? Possibly, but does it make up for the lack of knowledge of specific functions of their governmental organization? Or inexperience with how the government operates? You can't run the government like General Motors.

Many noncareer types who have served as assistant secretaries or secretaries admit that they were vastly confused most of the time they were in office. It seems to be the rule rather than the exception to rely almost entirely on their career staff not only for guidance but for actual policy formulation. The non-careerist spends most of his time in conference, making speeches, or in trying to unscramble some of his confusion. Some actually grasp the techniques and are well on the road to becoming effective when they leave.

Which brings up another relative factor—time. According to my wife, nine months is "never ending" when pregnant. My boys think that a like period of schooling is "forever." Two years to a drafted GI probably seems like infinity; yet, two years is the approximate average for an assistant secretary in office; hardly a spit in the ocean compared to the years required to become proficient in government administration. The record is little better for department heads. They serve an average of approximately 32 months, returning with a shout of joy, I presume, to the "outside."

What about these guys? Where, or how, did they get where they got? For the most part, they worked their way up, if not from the bottom of the ladder, at least from quite a ways down.

They got to the top by climbing; socially, over the backs of their associates, by hard work, guts, personality, dynamics, or marriage. At any rate, most of them know their business "cold" because they have been with it for 15 or 20 years.

The same applies to the career people in civil service. They climbed the same ladder, the good ones pushing ever higher, and ahead of their associates who have fallen off, become complacent in a lesser position, or branched out in other directions. The best, with exceptions, become the "supermen" of government and rise to the top career jobs open to them. Always a bridesmaid, never a bride.

This is my gripe, in short; career personnel could more effectively handle the top positions in government because of their previous experience, availability over the years, and "neutral" role in carrying out policies of the reigning dynasty.

The added incentives of "no limitations to the heights you may rise," plus the fact that they too may go down in history, just as the soap and girdle salesmen did before them, would boost the morale of career people all down the line.

II. A SHOT IN THE ARM FOR POSITION
CLASSIFICATION—Robert McQuie

During the past ten years, the voice of anguish, frustration, and reform has been raised against the Government system of salary classification. The same basic system is with us still, however, and so are its abuses. Just what fundamental changes should be made in it is highly debatable. Some desperate souls have suggested scrapping the whole system and starting over. This article suggests that only three minor changes are needed to cure the main defects of the present system, and that these changes will permit it to work fairly well until an ideal solution can be discovered.

The worst defect of the present system is that it allows the classifier to assume the supervisor's power to hand out pay increases. A second defect is the time and delay in arriving at grade level decisions.

The first defect springs from the fact that once a grade decision is made by the classifier, no effective pay incentive is left for the supervisor to hand out. The present periodic increases are automatic and are too small to be much of an incentive anyway. Ideally, the decision about pay is supposed to be split between the two people involved. The classifier, in Government or in industry, is supposed to place the job in a broad pay range (or grade) and the supervisor is supposed to decide just when and how much an employee should get, within

Reprinted by permission of the author, Robert McQuie, Kettelle Associates, Inc.

the limits of that grade. In the jargon of personnel administration, the classifier should make decisions about "position classification" and the supervisor about "pay administration."

The Government system was set up originally with this in mind, but over the years something has slipped. Allowing the periodic increases to become so small and making them automatic has taken from the supervisor any reward to hold out to or withhold from his staff. Since a grade increase then becomes the only reward he has left, the process of classification is reduced to a hassle between management and personnel in which the stronger of the two tries to get control and frustrate the intentions of the other.

A second defect is the amount of time that is consumed in handling grade level decisions. They come up too often, and the process of making each one requires too much effort and personnel. A minor readjustment in the duties of an office and the classifier must be brought in to straighten things out, an experience any supervisor would just as soon pass up. With so many different grade levels, placing a job in the right one becomes difficult and controversial, so that the classifier's decision is hard to sustain against determined opposition. This has caused the general inflation of grade levels over the past few years. The time required to arrive at each decision has caused the classification staff to grow all out of proportion to its function in the over-all personnel program. The "Federal Personnel Manual" lists eight possible functions for a personnel program, of which classification is one. The latest inventory of Government occupations lists classifiers as about one fifth of all personnel employees. In other words, there are roughly forty per cent more classifiers than the function should bear.

A look at the over-all classification pictures shows a key fact behind these two defects. The CSC publishes a Government-wide inventory of occupations by grade titled "Occupations of Federal White Collar Workers." It may be purchased at the Government Printing Office. From this inventory and some knowledge of the standards, one thing becomes immediately apparent: *non-supervisory grades in almost all occupations cluster around two or even three grade levels.* Usually, the worker is one grade level and his non-supervisory staff counterpart at higher headquarters is a grade or two higher. Sometimes the distinction is between the difficulty of work done: complicated work (whatever that is) is given one or two grades more than ordinary work. Naturally, all work is complicated. For example, most file clerks cluster around grades 2, 3, and 4. Accountants cluster around grades 9 and 11, draftsmen around 5, 6, and 7. Most mechanical engineers are in grades 11 and 12; most physicists in grades 11, 12, and 13. Most classifiers are found in grades 9 and 11, and most statisticians are in grades 11, 12, and 13.

Classification would be simplified considerably, if most non-supervisory jobs in an occupation could be placed in one grade. The fine distinctions that are now the basis of many promotions would no longer be there to take up the classifier's time and the supervisor's patience. These distinctions, moreover, are often unrealistic. The crucial genius on one small problem of a research project is often worth more money than the project director. A field classifier is often more valuable and skillful than his headquarters counterpart who writes letters. In theory different duties are the difference between different grades. In practice the classifier must evaluate performance. The better employees in an office pick up the more important work and the slower ones pick up the routine. What is important or routine differs so much from place to place that the standards cannot realistically recognize it. The complex of circumstances, politics, and talent that makes one employee ideal for problem cases and another good for only routine can be evaluated only by the supervisor. Trying to cover such intangibles by finely detailed classification standards has given classification the disreputable name it has today. The proper decisions for the classifier are much broader, and in a sense much more important.

We cannot scrap the present classification system and start over for many reasons. The most obvious one is that such a move would also scrap the classification standards. Before revised ones could be published, supervisors would have wrecked a new system in their scramble for higher pay. Retaining the present system with three simple changes will remove most of its defects.

First.—*Consolidate the number of grades to approximately half, but keep the present pay ranges.* Several ways of doing this have been suggested, but they all get about the same results. For example, GS-11 now gets from $6,400 to $8,200 and GS-12 from $7,600 to $9,500. The proposed pay range for a combined grade would run from $6,400 to $9,500.

Second.—*Eliminate the step rates and let management set an employee's pay anywhere in the broad pay range that they feel just.* This will get the classifier out of pay administration and will remove the incentive for a supervisor to force his way into classification decisions.

Third.—*Limit the percentage of total positions in each occupation that an agency can pay in each quarter of the pay range.* This will keep management from promoting everybody to the top of the grade, if budget limitations haven't done this already. For example, only 10% of the jobs might be allowed in the top quarter of the pay range and 30% in each of the other three quarters. Just how this number is distributed among various activities of an agency could remain a management decision. They could allocate the high pay where it would do the most good for the overall agency. All of the positions in the whole agency that could be paid in the top quarter of a grade might be allocated to one field activity doing particularly important work, as for example a laboratory. For some occupations, on the other hand, the top pay could be allocated to the headquarters, if there is a need to attract good field personnel into Washington. Or, the high and low pay can be divided up evenly over the total agency. With the present arrangement, higher grades are almost inevitably grouped at headquarters and the lower grades (and pay) in the field.

These three changes, by removing the easy-to-solve defects, make the classification job easier for the supervisor, for the Congress, and for the C.S.C.

To the supervisor they give back an incentive that he can use to motivate his staff without going through the intricate detail of classification. A particular employee's pay can be increased 2% or 10% as desired without pretending to assign him new duties. This transfers pressure from the classifier to the supervisor when an employee hollers, "more." It also eliminates most of the borderline decisions that cause the haggling between management and classification. With these decisions eliminated, classification can then make the remaining grade decisions quicker and with a smaller staff.

To the Congress, the proposed changes give the opportunity for a longer view when considering pay raises. They remove the need to find immediately four or five hundred million dollars every time a moderate pay raise is passed. Pay legislation could, instead, grant the raise by increasing the upper and lower levels of each grade without automatically increasing each person's next paycheck. Everyone would stay at his present rate of pay (but within the new pay ranges) until the next salary review, which could be made every six months. Because of the Congressional action, however, many would then be eligible for an increase who were at the top of their bracket under the previous pay rates. On the other hand, the total impact of the new pay rates on the budget would be spread over two or three years instead of hitting all at once. Everyone would have to work for their new raises and the anticipation of it would keep the Congressional action longer in mind than by giving it out all at once. Thus, Congress would receive recognition for authorizing the increased pay without being forced to immediately find half a billion dollars to finance it.

To the Civil Service Commission the proposed changes would give a chance to remodel the present classification system, but in a slower and more systematic fashion than by revising it all at once. The standards would still need revision in order to group as far as possible all working positions in the same large grade level. A simpler way of evaluating supervisory jobs would still be needed, perhaps similar to the one used by some wage board systems at present. The standards would still have to be clarified so that the uninitiated could understand them.

In all these areas, the CSC has shown great improvement during the past few years. If they can remove the immediate, simple defects from the system, there is every reason to expect even more improvements in the years to come. If we wait for an ideal solution, on the other hand, the Government will be caught in the classification rat race until the end of time.

III. CIVIL SERVICE ISOLATION—Raymond F. Brogan

One of the most frustrating things about the civil service, at least on the federal level, is the sense of isolation that descends upon you after a year or so. By this I mean the sense that you the individual working for Department X are bound to that department for better or worse till death, or a RIF,[1] do you part. You never get to feel that you are a part of the government. The chief reason for this feeling, as I have experienced it, is the total lack of concern by any central agency or office for the advancement and career development of individuals.

There is little or no cooperation among the various departments and agencies as far as the individual is concerned. Let me illustrate what I mean with an example. In August, 1958, I was placed on a register by the Department of Health, Education and Welfare as a GS-11 Education Specialist. After many months of waiting I called them to find out what were my expectations. The gist of their reply was that although I was on the register the department had not had an opening in so low a level in years and did not expect to have one in the foreseeable future. At the same time the Navy was looking for Education Specialists, but I was unaware of this fact. Now, I do not expect the Department of Health, Education and Welfare to hire for the Navy, but I do expect that if an examination is given for a certain position there be a reasonable hope for an appointment in the area concerned.

What can be done to relieve this situation?

The Civil Service Commission took a step in this direction a year or so ago. It ordered the various departments and agencies to set up career and promotion plans within their own jurisdictions. This was only partially successful. Some agencies put into effect well organized plans; many published token plans; few were as honest as the agency that put out a ten chapter booklet on its plans. The first ten pages detailed why the booklet was published. This was followed by nine three-page chapters. The first page gave the chapter heading and number; the second page had a one line entry: "Details to be published at a later date"; the third page was blank. This was twenty-six months after the Commission had ordered development of such plans.

The Civil Service Commission can take a leaf from the military personnel manuals. The military services have Career Management Branches, staffed by career specialists, where the individual officer's assignments are planned so as to best help him in his career. There should be a central testing and career development division of the Civil Service Commission where an employee of the government could get aid in mapping out a career and be made aware of employment opportunities. This could be done through the Commission and

---

Reprinted by permission of the author, Raymond F. Brogan.

[1] Reduction in force.

its regional offices. Actual job seeking and employment would be between the employee and the agencies concerned; but at least an eligible candidate on a register would not have to sit waiting because one agency has no openings while another agency has openings and few or no eligibles.

This would be quite an undertaking, but in this day of the Electronic Data Processing Machine it is not an unsurmountable task. With the use of an EDPM a central data processing center could be set up that would be able to keep abreast of the employment situation throughout the nation by collating information fed to it through the various regions. The central office could have facts and figures on a nation-wide basis that would be less than a week old and the regions would be only a day or two behind. A system such as this would make federal employees Government employees with something that began to approach a true career system.

19.

WHY POSITION CLASSIFICATION?

DANIEL F. HALLORAN

The two chief methods used by governments to establish hierarchical structures within the civil service are position classification and personal ranking. Position classification is essentially job-oriented and focuses attention on the organization and its immediate functions. The personal ranking system concentrates on the individual and his personal status.

The core of position classification is the concept of the "position" as an abstract entity apart from the employee. The position is viewed as a group of duties and responsibilities requiring the services of one employee. From an organizational viewpoint, a position is the smallest administrative unit of an organization. In a position classification system an individual employee is considered to "fill a position" and he achieves promotion by progressing from one "position" to a higher-level "position" within the organization's structure.

The personal ranking system, also called the "career system" or "rank classification," is oriented to the personnel of an organization rather than directly to the organizational structure. It is distinguished from position classification by establishment of a rank hierarchy which exists apart from the administrative

Reprinted from *Public Personnel Review*, Vol. 28, No. 2 (April, 1967), pp. 89–92.

structure of the organization, whereas position classification adheres rigidly to organizational lines.

The position classification method is used extensively in the United States in the federal civil service and by many state and local public jurisdictions. It is used sparingly outside of the United States by Canada, Brazil, and, to some extent, Russia. The much older personal ranking system has its roots in the class society of Western Europe and is used in the British and French civil service as well as in most other European countries. Personal ranking is not unknown in the United States with familiar applications in the academic world, military service and the foreign service.

OUTGROWTH OF SPOILS SYSTEM

Position classification, and its industrial counterpart, job evaluation, are relatively new concepts. The first application of the position classification principle was in 1909 in the Chicago Civil Service. As a coincidence, the first industrial application of job evaluation was also in Chicago in 1912. The development and application of position classification in the United States as an integral part of the civil service reform movement was in reaction to the excesses of the spoils system and the gross pay inequities that were rampant under it. Position classification served well both management and employees of the public service in the early days of reform. It gave management an orderly administrative plan for the utilization of personnel. To employees it assured equal pay for equal work in place of the erratic and meaningless salary situations which had existed. Because of its impersonal approach to salary, it had an aura of democratic fairness about it which strongly appealed to employees who had become accustomed to seeing favoritism shown in matters of pay. It is doubtful if a personal ranking system could have corrected as quickly the inequities of the spoils system in the United States.

THE BRITISH CIVIL SERVICE

The British civil service is not the product of reaction to a political "spoils system" as are its counterparts in the United States and Canada. This difference in origin has resulted in certain distinctions, not only in procedures but in underlying philosophy. In the British civil service, concern for the improvement of staff quality was of primary importance from the beginning. The American civil service movement was initially concerned primarily with stopping abuses and protecting the rights of employees. Only later did management improvement become an important objective of the civil service system in the United States. The American civil service movement resulted in the development of a body of law devoted largely to the protection of employees. In Britain, even the tenure of civil servants is based on custom rather than law.

The basic philosophy of British civil service is nowhere more evident than in the concept of the three broad Treasury classes: administrative, executive, and clerical. The structure is directly related to the educational system; recruitment is normally at an early age and directly from the appropriate educational level — university, secondary or elementary; and examinations are general in nature rather than specific, and they are designed to select candidates for a lifetime career rather than to fill particular vacant posts. Traditionally, an individual entered service at the entrance level of one of these three broad classes and planned to make his career completely within that one class.

The generalist approach to recruitment of the British service has been affected considerably by the heavy requirement by government for technical specialists. The professional, scientific, and technical classes already have more than ten times as many specialists as the generalists of the administrative class, and they are still the most rapidly growing classes. Ironically, because of the specialized qualifications required for performance of many of these jobs, some of the techniques of position classification must be adopted to analyze and define them.

THE FRENCH CIVIL SERVICE

Until 1945, the French civil service was decentralized with each ministerial department having its own personnel system, setting its own pay scale, and conducting its own examinations. In 1945, a Direction of the Public Service was founded which established a uniform classification of administrative posts into four categories: (1) civil administrators, (2) secretaries of administration, (3) administrative clerks, and (4) clerks and attendants. Independent of the administrative structure is a career structure broken down into cadres, classes, and echelons. Salary is related to the career structure rather than the administrative structure. Recruitment is largely of the generalist approach with the National School of Administration serving as the single channel of recruitment to the highest civil service level.

THE RUSSIAN SYSTEM

The Russian system, unlike the general European pattern, is basically a position classification system, possibly in reaction to the overtones of aristocratic society inherent in a personal ranking system. In 1935, a Central Committee on the Civil

Service was established. Class standards are now defined by law including duties and qualifications required.

Recruitment is not by general broad examinations but by specific examinations conducted independently by the various ministries. The educational system is highly specialized, and many of the higher educational facilities are directly related to the administrative requirements of the government. Individual students who are selected at a young age for eventual placement in high-level management positions in the government are assigned to party schools for additional training after they complete the standard curriculum.

COMPARED WITH PERSONAL RANKING

Detailed attention to the principles and practices of classification or grading in various jurisdictions is apt to lead to the conclusion that there are two completely opposite methods of grading employees which can never be reconciled. This is both an over-simplification and an inaccuracy. Actually, no position classification system exists which does not take into consideration people, nor can a personal ranking system long prevail which completely ignores the concept of position. All civil service systems are, to some extent, a combination of both methods, the distinction being one of emphasis on either positions or people in the classification process.

There are, of course, certain differences in approach and technique which readily distinguish a system as belonging to one basic type or the other. In a personal ranking system, pay is determined, to some extent, by an individual's potential rather than by actual services rendered; his pay is based on what he may reasonably be expected to do on the basis of his personal qualifications. Position classification bases pay on the duties an individual is currently performing without any regard for what he might be capable of doing.

In a civil service system patterned on the position classification principle, promotion of an individual necessarily must follow the lines of the organizational structure. Because of the natural desire to provide adequate opportunity for promotion of capable employees, a position classification system leads almost inevitably to the development of a somewhat contrived organization. Position classification and job refinement go hand-in-hand, and one of the results of the position classification-job evaluation movement in the United States was a strong tendency toward fragmentation of larger jobs, over-specialization, and over-departmentalization, and the development of organization characterized by elaborate multiple levels of technical competence and/or supervision. The objective of the position classifier often seems to be the creation of the maximum number of levels which can be accommodated within an organization rather than the minimum number of levels necessary to carry out its program.

ADMINISTRATIVE CLASS BORN

The development of a career system for the public service of a particular country does not take place without reference to the socioeconomic nature of that country including its educational structure. In Britain, the general acceptance of a horizontal stratification of society and the existence of a well developed university system made the concept of an elite administrative class in the civil service a natural and acceptable phenomenon. Even with the current movement toward greater social equality in Britain, the approach to the administrative class is to demand the easier movement of individuals into it regardless of social background, *not* to eliminate the very concept of an administrative class.

In the United States, emphasis on the democratic ideal and aversion to the concept of any sort of aristocracy have precluded so far any broad acceptance of the idea of an administrative class. Equality of opportunity had to be emphasized in the public service even at times above administrative needs.

At one time, it would have been generally unacceptable even to require a college degree for appointment to a particular level. However, the whole pattern of educational opportunity was changed after World War II with the G.I. Bill of Rights which sent through college an entire generation that might not otherwise have gone. Since then, the expansion of educational facilities and the general increase in material affluence have placed the college degree within reach of so many that it is no longer considered undemocratic to apply reasonable educational requirements to recruitment for the civil service. It is now common practice for public jurisdictions to hold annual examinations as part of broad recruitment programs for college graduates.

Although this is still far short of the establishment of an administrative class, it is a step in this direction. The Hoover Commission in its 1955 report on the federal civil service strongly urged the establishment of a Senior Civil Service which would be quite comparable to the British administrative class. One of the strongest indictments made by the Commission concerned the application of position classification technology to the upper levels of the civil service.

The civil service law and system are designed primarily for other purposes. Originating as a reaction against the spoils system, and adapted to the large-scale employment problem of 20th-century government, the present Civil Service System has not been geared to provide or develop professional administrators at the higher levels. The extension to higher posts of concepts and procedures which were designed for a large number of standardized positions at lower levels has been awkward for both non-career executives and career administrators, because such concepts disregard so completely both the personalities and the careers of individual men. New concepts, policies, and procedures are needed which are designed specifically to supply career administrators at the higher levels. We propose a program designed to meet this need.

Possibly the greatest failing of American public personnel systems is the failure to distinguish between routine clerical and technical jobs and the highest levels of administrative service. While position classification is a valuable tool in the treatment of routine jobs which exist in large numbers, its application to the uppermost areas of the civil service is of questionable value. Under the present personnel demands of government in the United States, the ideal personnel system might be one which continued to apply position classification concepts to the mass of jobs in the service, but at a particular level in the personnel structure switched to a personal ranking method in view of the unique responsibilities of most high level administrative posts and the individualistic nature of the most desirable candidates for them.

EFFECTS OF AUTOMATION

However, even before the question of how far up the administrative structure position classification can be validly applied is answered, a new problem is evolving. The rapid advance of automation is already beginning to have a disturbing impact on our traditional concept of the direct relationship between pay received and work effort exerted. The application of programming to automated processes is causing an even greater distortion of this relationship. Job evaluation and position classification, with their emphasis on complexity of duties, may find themselves as outmoded as the horse and buggy in an occupational world in which a semi-literate ADP operator can push a few buttons and outproduce a thousand highly skilled technicians. It is not unlikely that position classification will be completely unable to cope with the eventual upheaval caused by automation. A pay system based on personal ranking might have considerably less difficulty in adjusting to the effects of automation.

20.

THE PARADOXES OF PUBLIC ADMINISTRATION

WALTER G. HALSET

Frustration among public employees because of government controls, rules, regulations, and so-called "red tape" is common at almost every level of government.

Reprinted from *Public Personnel Review*, Vol. 26, No. 2 (April, 1965), pp. 66–69.

This feeling exists particularly among businessmen who accept appointments in government and among employees engaged in technical disciplines. Many businessmen leave public service within a short time because they cannot accept the governmental environment. Frustration among scientific and technical personnel is especially serious as it involves a large group of civil service personnel often charged with important, and at times, vital public projects.

A characteristic of scientists who have chosen to work in the governmental environment is that often they are not trained in political science or public administration. Many engineers, physicists, and chemists have only a smattering of the liberal arts—sometimes only the required basic civics or history courses. Interviews with senior level engineering students considering public employment revealed that liberal arts courses usually were disposed of with the least possible effort because of the heavy academic pressure of the engineering curriculum.

PROFESSIONAL LOYALTY FIRST

The engineer or scientist seldom gravitates to a government position because he wants to be a government employee. Rather, he accepts the job because it provides him an opportunity to practice his profession. He usually brings to the job a high level of professional loyalty and interest, reinforced by active professional associations. The world of government, and the art and science of public administration is a strange and unknown domain.

Many public administrators and researchers have been concerned with this problem. Its significance has become particularly important with the increased emphasis on scientific and engineering activities in government and the radical changes which have occurred in the organizational environment under which scientific and engineering development takes place. A considerable segment of scientific and engineering work now is conducted within the complex environment of government bureaucracy.

This concern has caused several studies to be conducted on the problems of scientific and engineering productivity. Much of this research has dealt with the attitudes of scientists and engineers to determine under what conditions they are most productive. Particular emphasis was placed on the attitudes of the scientific or engineering manager. The studies of Krugman and Edgerton represent an example of this type of research. However, lesser consideration has been given to the environmental situation in which the scientist or engineer finds himself when he joins a governmental bureaucracy. This is unfortunate because much of the frustration which scientists and engineers experience results from their unfamiliarity with the public environment and with the value systems which contribute to this environment.

ENTERING THE BUREAUCRATIC WORLD

Let us consider for a moment the kind of world which confronts a person who is not professionally trained in government. First, he quickly becomes aware of the many procedures, rules, regulations, and other controls which limit his activities. He soon learns that somewhere in the background is a legislature or congress which asks questions about his program, approves his budget, and limits his financial resources. He learns that a central personnel agency exercises control over his pay, his classification, and who he can hire.

Then there usually is a department budget officer who reviews his budget request, and a central budget department which exercises what seems to be almost omnipotent power over his department; and if this isn't enough, there are the public, special interest groups, political parties, the department management, the governor or president, and a host of other groups or people who seem to have their fingers in the pie—people who somehow must be satisfied. To the uninitiated, this presents a confusing and almost unintelligible picture. Is it any wonder that the businessman or the engineer becomes overwhelmed with a sense of frustration?

TRAINING HELPS UNDERSTANDING

An approach to solving this problem which has been used with some success by the author involves training aimed at assisting the employee to understand the environment within which he works. The program consists of three major elements. These are:

1. Familiarization with the forces which contribute to and constitute the governmental process.
2. Review of the value systems which underlie American government, and particularly the relationship of the seemingly opposing values which characterize American public administration.
3. Relating these forces and value systems to the responsibilities of the public administrator.

The forces which constitute the governmental process are presented in a chart. Each of the principal forces is shown as an arrow bearing upon a central circle which represents the total government process. The major forces shown on the chart are the constitution, the courts, the executive and the legislative branch. Additional forces include constitutional officers, statutes and government codes, administrative law and procedure, rules and regulations, department policies and practices, control agencies, centralized service organizations, governmental tradition, civil service, special interest groups, public opinion, and the press. The significance of each of these forces is explained and discussed, with particular emphasis on the following points:

1. There are many and varied forces which contribute to and make up the governmental environment;
2. The government process is complex;
3. Government must serve many masters.

CONFLICTING VALUES CONFUSE

The second phase of the program presents significant value systems which underlie American public administration. Analysis of these values constitutes a basic element of the program because it emphasizes that American public administration is controlled largely by these value systems, many of which are in conflict.

In other words, the public administrator lives in a world of paradoxes—a world where conflicting but equally important values are in dynamic interplay. This characteristic of public administration is emphasized because many public employees are aware of or accept only a selected few of the value systems of government, and often only those which fit their convenience or background. This inevitably results in being confronted by demands to recognize those values which were ignored or rejected and to perform in accordance with them. These demands may come from management, administrators, control agencies, legislators, or special interest groups. Much of the frustration of technical people in government results from the pressures to accept and reconcile these conflicting values. To the uninitiated, this position can be almost intolerable.

The value systems of government are presented as paradoxes to demonstrate the inherent conflicting situations which often confront the public administrator. The examples used are those which represent conflicting situations which create the greatest frustration and difficulty for the scientist or engineer. Those presented in this paper do not represent an exhaustive list of the value systems of American public administration, nor are those described below necessarily distinct or unrelated.

EFFICIENCY VS. PUBLIC PROTECTION

One of the most frustrating of the paradoxes of public administration is the paradox of *efficiency* versus *public protection*. The value of efficiency and the value of protection of the public through separation of powers, constitutional limitation, rules, regulations, audits, and so forth, are in constant conflict. The efficiency ethic is particularly strong in business executives and engineers. Often it is difficult for them to realize or accept that the people (including themselves as private citizens) value governmental safeguards to the extent that they are willing to accept a lesser efficiency in order to have them. In other words, within the environment of government, the value of efficiency must be reconciled with the value of public protection and safeguards.

Closely related to the efficiency and public protection paradox is the *action and results value* versus *legal and procedural value*. The action and results value is expressed by such statements as, "My job is to build the project, and damn the red tape." It is often exhibited by so-called crisis management—make everything an emergency—and a refusal to distinguish between a legitimate exception and a routine transaction. Persons dominated by this value are in constant conflict with the administrative officers, the legal staff, and with control agencies. They have little understanding or sympathy for the governmental environment which defines and limits their action by legal codes, rules, regulations and orderly procedures. Their tendency is toward autonomy, with a rejection of the overall values of centralized purchasing, classification, recruitment, or other government-wide services which, on the over-all basis, may provide considerable savings to the government.

UNIFIED VS. DECENTRALIZED CONTROL

Another paradox is the conflict between *unity of command* versus *decentralization of authority*. This conflict is expressed by the statement, "The control agencies exercise control but don't assume responsibility for results." It is also manifest in the conflict between the executive and the independent civil service commission. Another area of conflict is between the line organization and the staff which imposes standards, methods, and procedures upon them. The unity of command value often is accepted as being unassailable. But at the same time, the value of establishing control agencies, decentralizing executive authority in several public officials, the use of boards and commissions to formulate or review policy, or the use of staff to oversee the activities of line officers is strongly entrenched in American government, and is as realistic a value as is unity of command. The two values must live side by side in an acceptable compromise.

The paradox of the *socio-political value* versus the *technological value* is of particular significance in a scientific or engineering organization. Many scientists and engineers do not understand or have sympathy with the political process. Illustrations of this conflict are numerous, i.e., the conflict between the engineeringly proper place for a freeway versus the politically and socially acceptable location, the engineering solution to a water development problem versus the political or social views of the people affected. The technological value often is expressed by such statements as, "I'm paid to be an engineer, not a politician," while the social or political value is expressed by, "All the engineer cares about is building the freeway, and to him, the best freeway is the shortest distance between two points." The reality of the government environment is, however, that any solution to a public problem must be socially and politically acceptable. Consequently, these values must be reconciled.

MINORITY VS. MAJORITY

The conflict of the *minority value* and the *majority value* is one of the great challenges of democratic government. From a political science standpoint, this statement is an accepted and obvious principle. But from the standpoint of many public employes, it presents complex and frustrating problems. The conflict of these values has many ramifications. It can involve the conflict between the rural and urban interests, regional conflicts, the demands of special interests, or the traditional conflict between the majority and the minority political parties. The public administrator must understand the political tradition of American government that the minority interest must be recognized and reconciled. Also, he must be sensitive to the power and rights of special interests even though they may represent a comparatively small percentage of the population. The failure to recognize these realities causes serious difficulties for many public officials and employees.

An important step in developing an understanding of the environment of public administration is to discuss the basic values which constitute American public administration. This discussion should emphasize that it is essential that the public administrator understand the public environment and accept its underlying values, even though they may seem to be in conflict with one another. Certainly, the very process of accepting values presents a paradox. However, one of the basic functions and responsibilities of the public administrator is the reconciliation of these opposing values in a manner which produces the best possible results.

21.

OFF-THE-JOB CONDUCT AS A DISCIPLINARY PROBLEM

W. D. HEISEL and RICHARD M. GLADSTONE

Off-the-job conduct of public employees is an important concern of management While specific standards of conduct cannot be prescribed because of the uniqueness of each case, the public employer generally expects a higher standard of conduct from his employees than his counterpart in private industry. He expects an even higher standard of his police officers and executives.

These conclusions were reached as a result of a study of off-the-job conduct in city government conducted by the City of Cincinnati and the University of Cincinnati early in 1967. The study consisted of the analysis of a questionnaire completed by 41 city managers, mayors, and personnel administrators. The questionnaire posed 16 examples of off-the-job conduct which had possible unfavorable overtones, and asked the respondents to decide what disciplinary action, if any, they would administer in each case, assuming that the employee was otherwise competent and had no prior disciplinary record. They were also asked to explain their reasoning in arriving at their decisions. In most cases four answers were solicited: one each assuming the employee to be a laborer, a professional employee, a department head, and finally a policeman. Cases were drawn from actual experiences, although some modification was necessary to rule out extraneous considerations.

GENERAL CONCLUSIONS

In eleven of the 16 cases, there was substantial agreement among the respondents on the action to be taken. Only in five cases were the respondents widely split. (The cases themselves are presented and analyzed below.) This degree of agreement permits us to reach certain general conclusions:

(1) Administrators generally expect a higher standard of conduct of police officers than any other group. Primarily this is the "Caesar's wife" concept. Because the police enforce laws, they cannot be guilty of any shady practice, whether or not a violation of law is involved.

Reprinted from *Public Personnel Review*, Vol. 29, Number 1 (January, 1968), pp. 23–28.

(2) Administrators generally expect high standards of department heads. To some extent this expectation results from their public prominence. However, several respondents emphasized that the department official who got into trouble lost the administrator's confidence, and, therefore, became useless. Largely as a result of this viewpoint, there was a marked tendency to either fire the department head or forget the incident. As one respondent wrote, "You just don't suspend or put a reprimand on a department head's record."

(3) Generally, higher standards are expected in government than in industry. While private industry was not included in this survey, this conclusion is justified by the comparison of responses in this survey with arbitrators' decisions in parallel cases in industry. This conclusion was explained by many comments from respondents concerning the adverse effect of publicity on agency programs. Various respondents decried the fact that unfavorable publicity results from public knowledge of any improper conduct by public employees, whether on or off the job. In effect, this creates a dual standard for public and private employment which cannot be morally justified. On the other hand, from the viewpoint of the administrator trying to get his programs accomplished, there is no choice but to recognize public reaction and deal with subordinates accordingly.

(4) While precedent is important in handling disciplinary cases, each is unique. Many respondents hedged their answers when they felt they needed more specific information about the incident or the employee. This is understandable. While we predicated each case on the assumption the employee was "satisfactory," each respondent perhaps had a different standard of what constitutes satisfactory performance. Moreover, the respondents felt each case had to be decided on its own merits, and needed more information before they could be positive.

(5) Administrators were in substantial agreement that, when a law was violated, the employee should be punished. The more serious the violation—such as a felony—the more serious the punishment. Generally, misdemeanors justify only suspension; felonies dismissal. Respondents agree, however, that they should not make the decision; court action should precede disciplinary decisionmaking. In serious cases, suspension pending court adjudication is warranted; but if the employee is found not guilty, most respondents would give him back pay for time lost. Unfortunately, none of the cases posed the problem of what to do if the employee were freed by the court on a technicality, such as the failure to be notified of his constitutional rights. It appears to the authors that preponderance of evidence against the employee might lead to dismissal from public service, even though criminal guilt in the form of proof beyond a reasonable doubt were lacking.

(6) Public employees are judged by fair standards, and evidence of substance should be required before disciplinary action is taken. The polygraph, for example, was ruled out as satisfactory evidence against an employee by most respondents. Likewise, a case involving a drinking employee resulted in strong con-

sensus for a mild punishment simply because of the failure of management to promulgate a rule requiring sobriety testing. (See Case 6 below.)

(7) Outside employment is generally tolerated, provided there is no conflict of interest. An employee observed doing outside work while off duty because of alleged illness would only be suspended, not discharged, by the vast majority. However, many respondents explained that had the employee not been legitimately sick, they would recommend dismissal for fraudulent misrepresentation. (See Case 7 below.)

(8) Abuse of official position for personal gain would result in dismissal. However, most officials feel that investment in industry should not be considered a conflict of interest unless the employee's specific duties give him the opportunity to favor one business over another. Purchasing agents were cited as the one group which must be most careful about their private investments.

(9) Communists are obviously not welcome in the public service by many respondents. While opinion was divided, the majority felt that it was dangerous to have in a sensitive public post (department head or policeman) a person committed to the overthrow of the institution he served. Some also noted the dissension he might create in the work force and used this as a reason for separation.

Almost all respondents, however, would tolerate a member of another extremist organization, the John Birch Society. This organization apparently does not generate the same emotional reaction as Communism.

(10) Political activity is frowned upon by administrators, even off the job. Part of the almost unanimous action against politicking is due to the fact it is a violation of law in many cities. In addition, particularly in city manager cities, political action by subordinates of the city manager compromises his neutrality. While management seeks political neutrality, it is interesting to note that some authorities and all public employee unions are working toward a relaxation of the political restrictions that now limit public employees of many jurisdictions. A confrontation on this issue appears inevitable in the near future.

CASE ANALYSES

As indicated, the respondents were asked to judge each case solely on the basis of the facts given, and to assume satisfactory performance and a clean disciplinary record. Except where specifically noted, they were asked to give four responses for each case: L = unskilled laborer; *Pro* = professional employee; D = department head; and *Pol* = police officer. Sixteen cases were included in the survey, but two are omitted from this summary because the results obtained were not definitive.

All tables will be shown in percentages, but they may not add up to 100 per cent because a few respondents omitted certain cases. "Separation" includes requested resignation as well as dismissal. "Lesser disciplinary action" includes reprimand, suspension, demotion, and, in a few cases, transfer. "No action" obviously absolves the employee of any wrong-doing.

Case 1.—One of your employees is arrested while at work and charged with shooting and wounding a man the previous night. He asks for a jury trial and the case will not be adjudicated for several weeks.

RESPONSES

	L	Pro	D	Pol
Separation	—	—	—	—
Lesser disciplinary action	73%	76%	78%	83%
No action	17	24	22	17

The key element is that the employee has only been accused, not convicted. In many responses, the statement was made that he should be suspended pending trial, and given back pay if acquitted and dismissed if convicted. Thus the respondents believe they should be guided by judicial determination of the evidence.

Case 2.—One of your female employees is arrested and convicted of doing an obscene dance at a local night club. (She was not employed by the club.)

RESPONSES

	L	Pro	D	Pol
Separation	32%	42%	46%	39%
Lesser action.	49	46	44	49
No action	17	12	10	10

The authors had assumed that the fact this woman was not employed by the night club would lead the respondents to deduce that a psychological problem was at the root of her exhibitionism. The responses, however, showed that this was not a major consideration. A majority felt there was little or no reflection on the city and therefore recommended either no action or a minor penalty. Another significant group recommended dismissal on the basis of moral turpitude; many expressed the belief that such incidents hurt the reputation of the city. This is the first of several cases in which public reaction was to play an important role in the decisionmaking process.

Case 3.—One of your employees is arrested and convicted for molesting a ten-year-old girl while on his way home from work.

RESPONSES

	L	Pro	D	Pol
Separation	95%	95%	95%	98%
Lesser action.	5	5	5	2

Case 4.—One of your employees, on his way home from a party, strikes and

kills a pedestrian and is arrested and convicted for driving while intoxicated and involuntary manslaughter.

RESPONSES

	L	Pro	D	Pol
Separation	74%	76%	81%	86%
Lesser action.	22	20	17	12
No action	2	2	2	2

These two cases are grouped together because both involve the commission of felonies. As a general rule, it appears that the commission of a felony leads to quick removal from public employment. It is interesting to note, however, that the first case, which involves moral turpitude, produced a more extreme response than the second, in which the felony was committed without malicious intent. Molesting a child is thought of as more dastardly a crime, and is dealt with more harshly. The fact that none of the respondents gave serious attention to the possibility that either of these employees might be mentally ill surprised the authors. We can only conclude that, because of the sensational quality of both cases, the respondents were concerned over public reaction; a "soft" approach would have been politically unwise.

Case 5.—Two department heads belong to the same country club. During the course of a party at the club, after a few drinks, they get into a fight and are arrested for disorderly conduct. Both charges are dropped in court.

RESPONSES

Separation	2%
Lesser action.	83
No action	10

Although charges have been dropped in court, the key here appears to be that the department heads have shown a measure of irresponsibility and deserve light punishment. Most respondents indicated that nothing would go on their records; this was something to be handled privately by the city manager. We were surprised, however, by the absence of any consideration of whether these two men could any longer work together effectively.

Case 6.—You have a no-drinking-on-the-job rule, which states no employee can be under the influence of alcohol on duty. Your medical department uses a blood alcohol level test to determine drunkenness. An hour after starting time, one of your employees asks to go home because of an injured back; liquor is smelled on the man's breath. He admits to taking a drink *before* coming to work. The medical department tests show a blood alcohol level three times the permissible amount. However, the department nurse says he passed all the common sobriety tests. The fact that the medical department has a standard for blood alcohol *has not* been promulgated.

RESPONSES

	L	Pro	D	Pol
Separation	10%	10%	12%	15%
Lesser action.	78	80	74	78
No action	7	10	12	7

The failure to promulgate a blood-alcohol test was the principal influence on the majority thinking that this employee should be retained. Normally, appointing authorities indicate, they are tough on the alcoholic. But they also believe in fair play, and if a standard is used, it should be known by the employees. In fact, some respondents went so far as to let the employee off with no penalty simply because of the failure to publicize the procedure.

Case 7.—One of your employees has been granted permission for outside work, running a small business (servicing machines in coin operated laundries). He is away from his regular job because of illness, and has a doctor's certificate. While off, his supervisor observes him servicing his laundry machines.

RESPONSES

	L	Pro	D	Pol
Separation	12%	12%	20%	10%
Lesser action.	86	86	78	88
No action	2	2	2	2

This case illustrates the persuasiveness of the medical certificate. Was the employee really sick? If not, he was guilty of fraudulent use of sick leave, and many respondents indicated he deserved to be fired. But the doctor's certificate validated his illness, even though he engaged in an activity that should have been off limits to a sick person. Thus most respondents compromised by recommending a light punishment. The question might well be raised as to why, if he were sick, did they wish to penalize him at all?

This case also illustrates the vulnerability of the department head. When the appointing authority loses confidence in such an official, he is done. The figures indicate a much higher percentage recommending dismissal for the department head. Those respondents were saying, in effect, they did not believe the doctor's certificate, but they probably could not prove a case before a Civil Service Commission against rank-and-file employees.

Case 8.—Some material is missing from a stockroom. A supervisor, walking through the employee parking lot, sees the material in the unlocked car of an employee. This employee is not assigned to the stockroom. He denies any knowledge of how it got into his car, and there are no evidence or witnesses. He agrees to a polygraph exam. The polygraph operator concludes that he is lying when he states he has no knowledge of how the material got into his car.

RESPONSES

	L	Pro	D	Pol
Separation	22%	29%	29%	27%
Lesser action.	46	37	37	41
No action	27	29	29	27

The key to this case is the polygraph examination—the only "evidence" against the employee. A majority appeared to have sufficient confidence in this device to take some action. But only a minority had sufficient confidence to proceed with dismissal. Certainly, if there had been proof of guilt, the response in favor of dismissal would have been unanimous. Some respondents were undoubtedly influenced by the fact that in their jurisdictions, an appeal to court would be permissible, and the likelihood of judicial support of a case based solely on the polygraph would be slim.

Case 9.—Consider this next case as applying only to the professional and the department head. It has come to your attention that one of the staff of your Planning Commission has recently invested heavily in real estate of low value where the city is planning a new park. The planner was responsible for the plans for the new park.

RESPONSES

	Pro	D
Separation	76%	71%
Lesser action.	17	22
No action	5	5

Case 10.—Consider this next case as applying only to the person named. It is reported and proven to you that the wife of the head of one of your key departments owns substantial amounts of stock in the company which provided the city's stationery supplies.

RESPONSES

Separation	—
Lesser action.	12%
No action	81

These two cases were used to present extremes in conflict of interest cases. The first case indicated a rather clear-cut misuse of official information; such action would destroy public confidence in the integrity of the administration, and, therefore, justified dismissal in the opinion of a large majority. The second case, however, resulted in no recommendations for dismissal, and very few for any disciplinary action. Two principal reasons were cited: (1) the wife, not the employee, was the investor; and (2) unless the official was the Purchasing Agent, he would have little or no voice in determining the vendor. While the authors see little validity in the first reason, it is true that, in modern organizations with central purchasing departments, only the Purchasing Agent is in a decision-making position in such matters. The investments of other officials, therefore, need little control.

Case 11.—It has been reported that one of your employees is associating with known dope peddlers. The fact has not been publicized, nor is there any concrete evidence that your employee is using narcotics. The employee's explanation is that the person is an old high school friend. He is warned to discontinue the contact without threat of disciplinary action. Two weeks later the newspapers report the above situation indicating the meeting took place after your talk with the employee.

RESPONSES

	L	Pro	D	Pol
Separation	10%	12%	24%	27%
Lesser action.	51	52	42	47
No action	34	34	32	24

The divided opinion on this case apparently results from the difficulty of determining which of two conflicting factors was the more important: (1) the employee's failure to heed the warning of his supervisor; or (2) the reluctance to penalize an employee simply because of his associations. Those who opposed any disciplinary action felt that an employee should not be found guilty by association. Those voting for dismissal felt one warning was enough. The largest group, those voting for lesser disciplinary action, felt that a warning should be given officially before separation is considered. It is interesting to note that the police officer was expected to meet a higher standard for his associates than any other category.

Case 12.—One of your employees has been discovered to be a member of the Communist Party. His membership has been publicized in the local papers. Your agency has no loyalty oath.

Case 13.—The same as Case 12, only the organization is now the John Birch Society.

RESPONSES

	L	Pro	D	Pol
Case 12:				
Separation	32%	34%	46%	39%
Lesser action.	15	17	15	20
No action	51	47	37	39
Case 13:				
Separation	7	7	10	7
Lesser action.	12	15	15	15
No action	79	76	73	76

The high level of emotional involvement in the Communist issue is illustrated by Case 12. Even though the fictional agency has no loyalty oath, a substantial number of respondents would fire a Communist, particularly if he were found in the ranks of department heads or police. Yet membership in a right-wing organization would rarely be penalized. Many respondents defended their views on the basis that the Communist was sworn to overthrow the government, and, therefore, could not be trusted. This could account for the reluctance to employ a Communist as a department head or police officer, but a city laborer's job would scarcely be a strategic position from which to overthrow the government. Apparently public reaction had a heavy influence on their thinking. The public can accept right-wing membership, but simply will not tolerate Communism.

Case 14.—One of your employees has been found distributing campaign literature for a local councilman to his fellow workers on his lunch hour. He has also admitted to conversations during working hours advocating the election of this man.

RESPONSES

	L	Pro	D	Pol
Separation	37%	37%	37%	37%
Lesser action.	56	56	56	56
No action	7	7	7	7

Political activity of public employees is obviously frowned upon by administrators, according to the responses to this case. Either separation or some lesser punishment was the choice of almost all respondents. Frequently, those who voted for separation cited legislation in their jurisdictions which made political activity illegal; presumably, without such legislation they, too, would have favored milder action.

The case is important, because employee organizations are advocating greater political freedom for public employees at the same time that management is attempting to maintain a neutral posture.

IN CONCLUSION

It is apparent that decisionmakers are seriously concerned with the public acceptance of their decisions. This appeared time and again in the comments offered by respondents.

This is understandable. Serving the public requires that the public be satisfied. Administrators whose decisions are often unpopular can be replaced.

As indicated, disciplinary action is not administered in a vacuum. Each case is unique. It must be decided on the basis of all the facts. The opinions of their peers on these capsule cases, however, should assist administrators in making decisions. They may also assist in the determinations on applications for employment, in the sense that applicants should not be hired who would be fired for the same offense committed after employment.

22.

PUTTING IN A MANAGEMENT DEVELOPMENT PROGRAM THAT WORKS

Edgar F. Huse

One of the greatest challenges facing management today is to increase the skills of present and future managers. Two of the currently most popular approaches are formal management training programs and the installation of new performance appraisal systems—frequently described as management by objectives and appraisal by results. However, most of the follow-up studies on such programs have shown disappointing results; some have shown negative results.

A large, internationally famous company, an integrated organization engaged in the design, manufacturing, and marketing of complex systems for defense and civilian markets, decided to change its appraisal methods from a classic system to one best described as "management by objectives." Although the initial installation of the program did not succeed, the lessons learned allowed the company to install a subsequent program that showed gratifyingly positive and proven results at all levels of management. This corporation's experiences should be widely applicable.

Originally, the corporation considered that it had an outstanding classic performance appraisal program. Appraisals were completed annually by the immediate supervisor to provide subordinates with information and recommendations for developments and improvement and to provide bases for salary action. The appraisals were detailed, of three or four typed pages, together with a formal rating; they were reviewed by the next higher level of management and by the personnel department. After the immediate supervisor reviewed the appraisal with his subordinate, both signed the form. Completed appraisals were kept on permanent individual file. Elaborate procedures had been established and maintained to ensure that appraisals were completed properly and on time, and 98 per cent were.

A study was conducted to determine some of the effects of these performance appraisals. Performance appraisal discussions between worker and supervisor were observed *in situ*. Subordinates were interviewed before and after the appraisal discussions. In addition, a follow-up was made twelve to fourteen weeks after

Reprinted from *California Management Review*, Vol. IX, No. 2 (Winter, 1966), pp. 73–80. Copyright 1966 by the Regents of the University of California.

the discussions to determine the degree to which work had improved. The results have been described elsewhere,[1] but the conclusions will be briefly summarized here.

1. The appraisal discussion had no measurable influence on improvement of job performance as such.
2. Criticism of performance resulted in subordinate defensiveness.
3. The more the criticism, the more the defensiveness.
4. The more the defensiveness, the less the performance change noted in the subordinate.
5. Praise, in the discussion, had no measurable effect on the reaction to criticism or on later work performance.
6. Work improvement occurred only when specified goals, measurement of results, and deadlines were established and agreed upon separately from the appraisal discussion.

The findings of this study confirm the widespread criticism of performance appraisal and seemingly substantiate McGregor's comments that "the strategy of management by integration and self-control is more likely to be conducive to growth, learning and improved performance" than a performance appraisal system.[2] Company management studied these findings and decided that a new approach was necessary.

As a substitute for the performance appraisal system, it was decided to implement a modified form of Peter Drucker's "management by objectives and self-control." The program, called Work Planning and Review, can be described as a flexible process involving periodic sessions between the worker and his manager, with mutual planning of the work to be done, mutual review of progress, and mutual problem solving and assistance. The primary objective is to help the subordinate improve his work performance through a more effective working relationship with his supervisor.

Work Planning and Review (hereafter called WP&R) does not involve formal ratings. In their place, it provides an informal basis for the worker and his manager to discuss the job to be done in advance of doing it, to agree upon a plan of action and the measurement of results, and to review progress after completion of the task or project. Although there is no fixed time for such discussions, they typically take place at the beginning and end of projects, or monthly, or quarterly, depending on the job. The results of the discussions remain confidential; no copies or records go to the personnel department.

WP&R started as a pilot study. One-half of the organization continued with the classic performance appraisal, and the other half (approximately 125 man-

---

[1] E. F. Huse and E. Kay, "Improving Employee Productivity Through Work Planning," in *The Personnel Job in a Changing World*, ed. J. W. Blood (New York: American Management Association, 1964), pp. 298–315.
[2] D. McGregor, "An Uneasy Look at Performance Appraisal," *Harvard Business Review*, May–June, 1957, pp. 89–94.

agers) were "put on" WP&R. Forms were developed, and a brief booklet was prepared. The over-all principle of WP&R was explained to the managers in staff meetings. They were told that they should conduct work planning and review sessions with their subordinates rather than continuing the formal performance appraisal.

Three months later, the results were studied. The findings were largely negative. Almost universally, managers had stopped doing performance appraisals (with a great sense of relief). However, these managers had done very little of the "management by objectives" required by WP&R.

A number of factors were apparently involved in the initial failure of the program:

The managers had been given insufficient background for, and understanding of, the program.
The program was perceived as another kind of classical performance appraisal.
The timing, forms, and techniques were regarded as rigid, inflexible, and unrelated to the job.
The implementation violated some of the most important principles of the introduction of change.

At this point, I was made responsible for the implementation, acting as change agent, and the program was not abandoned, but a fresh start was made, working slowly and gradually, assisting managers in changing their behavior so that they could do a better job of assisting their subordinates in developing and improving their work performance. The focal point was shifted from the subordinate to manager, who had to change before the subordinate could.

IMPORTANT RELATIONSHIPS

Once these principles were followed, a highly successful program evolved.

The principles used to implement the successful program fall into three major dimensions.

The first is the relationship of the manager to his own supervisor, and the necessity for executive support.
The second is my relationship with the managers.
The third is the worker-manager relationship.

Manager-Supervisor Relationship.—The principle in this dimension relates to the method of using the executive hierarchy to gain support for the program. Industrial organizations are basically authoritarian, and expressed expectations of executives are more important forces for creating change than are the expectations of the subordinates.

Although change can be effective even if not started at the top, the tacit approval, if not the active support, of the top executives is extremely helpful. For this reason, the implementation of the process began at the top with heads of major departments. Individual meetings were first held with them to provide an understanding of the program and to obtain their approval, even if the support was not always wholehearted. Next, the results of the research showing the failings of the "classical" performance appraisal and the reasons for substituting WP&R were presented at the staff meetings of the department managers.

Follow-up individual coaching and counseling meetings were then held with each of the department head's immediate subordinates to obtain approval, understanding, and commitment. This combination of informational staff meetings, followed by individual coaching and counseling meetings, continued down the management hierarchy until each manager had had at least one individual meeting.

With few exceptions, changes in behavior did not occur as a result of the staff meetings. The staff meetings served to accomplish two objectives: to provide information to the staff about WP&R and to indicate to the staff that the "boss" had approved the program and expected his subordinates to implement it. The real changes in the supervisors came about as a result of the individual coaching and counseling meetings.

Relationship with managers.—Managers not only need to be involved but also need to see a "payoff" in what they are doing. As a change agent, my relationship with the managers involved three principles:

The job-centered approach.
The use of job-related material rather than abstract or theoretical material.
Increased supervisory involvement and participation.

Job-centered coaching and counseling sessions are more effective in changing behavior than are either general exhortations or off-the-job training programs.

The first attempt at implementing WP&R consisted of general explanations and "exhortations" to one-half of the managers. This was not effective.

In the second attempt, two contrasting methods were used. One was individual coaching and counseling meetings with the supervisor. The other was a fourteen-week training program which I conducted for more than thirty managers, divided into two training sections.

Very little action was taken as a result of the training program. Although the principles and rationale of WP&R were carefully explained, together with the general principles of the motivation and development of subordinates, only one or two managers began using the work planning approach. Follow-up questionnaires indicated that the managers regarded the training program as extremely helpful—but later interviews with the same managers showed that it had not resulted in implementing WP&R.

In contrast, the individual coaching and counseling sessions did result in behavior changes. The meetings centered around the manager's job, performance improvement needs of his subordinates, and ways in which he could assist his subordinates in improving their performances. I used an essentially nondirective approach in helping the manager to focus upon his job and the ways that WP&R could assist him in his work with his subordinates.

A group counseling approach was found to be successful after the managers had had an opportunity to experiment with the approach that best suited their needs and the demands of the job. These sessions were seminars conducted with small groups of supervisors who had similar jobs; they usually lasted approximately an hour and a half and were nondirective, but concentrated on the supervisors' successes and failures with work planning. The group shared experiences and picked up ideas that they could take back and try out on their jobs.

WP&R enhanced the change process by giving the supervisor meaningful and relevant material rather than "theoretical" facts.

Changes in behavior presuppose prior changes in "attitudes." Changes in attitudes presuppose modifications of perceptual process. New facts must be presented or familiar facts reorganized in different ways. To the extent that the material is meaningful, relevant, and job-centered, the change in the perceptual process is made easier.

Change in subordinates presupposes change in supervisors. The individual coaching and counseling meetings were directed toward assisting the supervisor in improving the work performance of his subordinates, and the discussion remained within job-related areas, with little abstract or "theoretical" material presented.

In addition, the supervisors were provided with more specific and relevant material through the use of questionnaires which explored the way their subordinates perceived them as supervisors. The questionnaires were given anonymously to the immediate subordinates. After I analyzed them, the results were fed back only to the immediate supervisors. Because no one superior to the supervisor ever saw the results, his defensiveness was considerably reduced and he was able to take positive corrective actions rather than defending himself to higher management.

The change process needs to be tailored to the immediate situation and to provide for the increased involvement of the supervisor.

One's own facts are much more powerful instruments of change than facts or principles generated or presented by an outside "expert." A number of approaches were used to increase supervisory involvement and participation in the change-over.

No fixed form or technique was used in WP&R. A form was developed and provided, but the manager decided whether or not the form was used. This was contrary to the classic performance appraisal which has a fixed form and a fixed date. Managers were encouraged to develop their own forms or to use other approaches that appeared best to them in the job situation.

Managers were encouraged to experiment. Although I was in charge of implementing the program, I gave little direct advice to the managers. Rather, the coaching and counseling sessions, the feedback sessions after the administration of the questionnaires, and the small group seminars—these were all directed toward problem solving, with the individual manager being encouraged to work out his own solution within his unique situation.

Managers were encouraged to approach the change-over on a mutual problem-solving basis with their subordinates. This allowed some managers to remain fairly directive in their approach, while others were much more participative. Managers were not asked to make changes in their "managerial style." Instead, they were encouraged to experiment. One manager might start with only one of his subordinates, while another might shift his entire group to WP&R.

Man-Manager Relationship.—The four principles in this area pertain to the man-manager relationship in the change-over from the classic performance appraisal system to WP&R:

Preservation of the self-concept.
Growth motives rather than deficit motives.
Development through identification.
Establishment of specific goals and criteria.

In a very real sense, it is line management and, more specifically, the immediate supervisor who has the responsibility for subordinate growth and development. Staff groups can assist but cannot assume the responsibility of the manager in this area.

Changes which enhance or, at least, do not disturb the self-concept are more easily accepted than changes which seek to modify or destroy it.

One of the most fundamental motives in human behavior is the preservation of the self-concept. Threats to the self-concept cause the individual to bring his defensive mechanisms into play. Actions which enhance or, at least, do not disturb the self-concept permit the individual to cooperate, to work with others, to avoid the win-lose dilemma so often seen in the classic performance appraisal discussions.

WP&R tends to reduce the win-lose dilemma. To the extent that the job requirements and criteria are discussed before it is done, both worker and manager have the opportunity to focus on the job rather than on the personality of the subordinate. WP&R seeks to change behavior, not to modify personality.

From the point of view of the manager, he sees as one of his duties and responsibilities that of "developing his subordinates." His self-concept is such that it is difficult for him to admit, even to himself, that he is not doing a good job in this area. At the same time, he is overburdened with more immediate and pressing tasks. He knew previously that the traditional performance appraisal method was not an effective tool for developing subordinates and resented the time it took. He conducted performance appraisal primarily because of the insistence of outside experts (the personnel department) and not because he had confidence in the method. At the same time, he felt a sense of guilt that the job pressures did not allow him to do as much as he wanted to do in the area of subordinate development. WP&R allows him to concentrate on getting the job done and, at the same time, provides a vehicle for subordinate development—a vehicle whose effectiveness he can easily see.

In addition, since work planning can be done differently by different managers, the manager's self-concept is enhanced. He is in control of the process, rather than the personnel department.

From the point of view of the subordinate, one of the most striking aspects of his self-concept is his desire to do a good job. But the subordinate's concept of "doing a good job" may not agree with his manager's. It may have mixtures of ego development and dependency needs; it may be distorted through projection, rationalization, and other defense structures. But he wants to do a good job as he sees it.

The criticism and "suggestions" received through the traditional performance appraisal procedures do not enhance or even coincide with the self-concept of the subordinate. Indeed, in many performance appraisal discussions, the manager is attempting, through such suggestions as, "Be more aggressive," to tear down defenses that the subordinate has spent years building up.

Conversely, the work planning approach, with the mutual involvement of manager and subordinate and the emphasis on doing the future job better rather than on criticism of past jobs, enhances rather than detracts from the self-concept. Such an approach builds on the desire of the subordinate to grow and develop on the job and to perform better in the service of his own need satisfaction.

Change processes which facilitate growth are more effective than deficit motivations.

The importance of the "ego" motives has been widely recognized. However, there is little research as to how these motives may be satisfied in industrial situations. Herzberg,[3] Huse,[4] and Myers,[5] among others, have pointed to the different roles played by "growth" and "hygienic" motives. In brief, the "growth" motives include feelings of achievement, recognition, and responsibility. These are conditions which must be present if productivity is to increase and work performance is to be improved. The deficit or hygienic motives, such as company policy, and administration, working conditions, and the like, are, of course, necessary pre-conditions, but "growth" motives are essential for improved work

---

[3] F. Herzberg, *et al.*, *The Motivation to Work* (New York: John Wiley & Sons, Inc., 1959).
[4] E. F. Huse, "The Motivation of Engineers and Scientists" (unpublished study, 1962).
[5] M. S. Myers, "Who Are Your Motivated Workers?" *Harvard Business Review*, January–February 1964, pp. 73–88.

performance. The direct relationship between the "ego" motives of Maslow and McGregor and the "growth" motives are fairly obvious. To the extent that our needs for achievement, recognition, and responsibility are met, "ego" motives of reputation, self-confidence, and esteem are enhanced. WP&R is one of the most effective ways to develop and satisfy these growth motives.

As discussed earlier, it is a part of the manager's self-concept that he not only needs to get his job done and satisfy his boss, but he also needs to see himself fulfilling one of his additional responsibilities, that of assisting his subordinates in getting their job done better. To the extent that these two objectives are consonant, rather than conflicting, the manager's own feelings of achievement and recognition are enhanced. In the traditional performance appraisal approach, power and responsibility were shared—with the personnel department which drew up the forms and ensured, through appropriate police action, that procedures were complied with. In WP&R, power and responsibility are still shared but with a more appropriate source—the subordinate. As Blake[6] points out, the "best balance between power and distribution and the sense of responsibility" is when both supervisor and subordinate share as equally as possible.

WP&R facilitates communication between manager and subordinate. The subordinate has a much better idea of what it is that the manager wants. Perhaps, more importantly, he has the opportunity to influence his manager in the establishment of job goals and criteria. His ego involvement in the task is thereby enhanced. In addition, the establishment of relatively short-range goals, with clearly identified criteria, makes them more understandable and attainable. The subordinate's feelings of accomplishment and recognition are built into the program, particularly since he is put into a more active role. Goals are joint, not imposed; involvement is positive, not defensive; and the relationship with his supervisor is positive and man-to-man, rather than being that of judge and defendant. Responsibility is increased through participation and involvement in planning. Achievement is increased through clear, attainable goals. Recognition is increased through work review—in a nonpunitive approach. On the other hand, the classic performance appraisal process actually reduced the opportunity for growth motivators to operate, as the research shows.

A change process which fosters the development of identification is more effective than one which impedes the identification process.

The process of identification, of incorporating into one's own personality the behavior and values of older and wiser persons, is a well-known psychological phenomenon. In addition, as Levinson has pointed out, it continues to be a mechanism for growth over a lifetime. As he puts it, "one of the significant

---

[6] R. R. Blake and J. S. Mouton, *The Managerial Grid* (Houston: Gulf Publishing Company, 1964).

differences between those who become executives and those who do not lies in the presence or absence of . . . identification models."[7]

The processes of mutually establishing job goals and criteria, mutually reviewing job progress, and mutually establishing a climate of reduced defensiveness—all these are provided in WP&R; they are also the processes that establish the best conditions for learning, growth, and development through identification.

CLIMATE FOR GROWTH

The manager has the opportunity to give the subordinate the benefit of his years of experience, and the subordinate has the opportunity to learn in an atmosphere that encourages rather than discourages the identification process. In WP&R sessions that I have observed, there appear to be four stages:

1. The subordinate takes the lead in discussing his accomplishments since the last review period—as well as his failures. (However, it is vitally important to stress that these are handled in an objective, nondefensive fashion.) The manager interjects questions and comments, but it is the subordinate who is doing the appraisal, with the assistance of his manager.
2. The next stage is subtly different. Plans for the next period are developed and here the manager takes the lead, although with the full participation of the subordinate.
3. In this stage, the interplay between manager and subordinate is almost on an equalitarian basis, as both strive to develop fair and equitable criteria for the tasks outlined in the second stage. Communication is fully open—the manager relies on his years of experience and the subordinate relies on his more intimate knowledge of the job to develop jointly acceptable criteria and priorities.
4. The final stage is, again, subtly different. In this stage, the process of identification comes to full fruition. The subordinate tends to talk about his future job plans, and the manager gives him advice and counsel.

Throughout the entire interchange, the sense of mutual problem solving and of working toward common goals stands out in a far different fashion than one finds in the traditional performance appraisal discussion. The subordinate is exposed to the thinking, ideas, and values of his manager; perhaps just as importantly, he has an opportunity, in a nonhostile climate, to freely share his ideas with his superior—with acceptance of the good ideas, rejection of unworkable ones, and the supervisor's instructive analysis of both.

The process of identification is facilitated because the supervisor is operating much more as a "coach" or "counselor" than as a judge. In the latter role, the supervisor increased the defensiveness of his subordinate.

A learning process which specifies criteria of progress and furnishes adequate

---

[7] H. Levinson, "A Psychologist Looks at Executive Development," *Harvard Business Review,* September–October, 1962, pp. 69–74.

knowledge of results is more successful in creating and maintaining change than one which does not.

Learning is an active, rather than a passive, process which does not take place in a vacuum. The work planning process is built around the basic principles that better knowledge of what was expected and the results obtained would result in changed behavior on the part of both managers and subordinates.

The classic performance appraisal system gave the manager a broad, nonspecific criterion—improve subordinate performance. The necessity, however, for sticking with a rigid format and using broad, rather than individually tailored, goals reduced the manager's effectiveness. Furthermore, the managers could not see any results from their work, and they were certainly sensitive to the fact, later borne out by research, that subordinates became defensive rather than changing their behavior.

The classic appraisal program gave the subordinate vague, nonspecific criteria such as: "Be more aggressive," but little, if any, knowledge of results. The more specific goals established in work planning, the better knowledge of what was expected, and, perhaps most important, the opportunity to discuss and understand the criteria of a job in advance—these provided an opportunity for better knowledge of results.

As communications between worker and manager increased, both could see improved results. Managers found that their job was becoming easier; subordinates found their managers easier to approach. Additional contributing factors in this context were that the work planning and review processes were held on weekly, monthly or quarterly bases, thus allowing for much more immediate feedback of results than the classic annual performance appraisal.

PROGRAM RESULTS

The effectiveness of the program was examined in three different ways:

The research conducted to determine the effectiveness of the program.
A clinical "feel" based on observations and discussions with managers and subordinates.
The results of a questionnaire completed on an anonymous basis, throughout the organization.

The research results have been reported previously in considerably greater detail,[8] but I will summarize them. Research was planned to find the actual changes in subordinates' behavior resulting from the program. The most important finding was that the work planning group, in specific actions taken to improve performance, showed a 72 per cent increase over the control group. (The control

---

[8] McGregor, *op. cit.*, pp. 89–94.

group cited specific actions to improve performance on 40 per cent of the items that they and their manager had discussed, while the work planning group had taken action on 70 per cent of the items.)

Both the work planning and performance appraisal groups completed "before" and "after" questionnaires. Both groups were equal in all respects in the "before" questionnaires but were quite different in their responses on the "after" questionnaires. The questionnaire measured five major areas:

1. Help received from manager in doing present job better.
2. Extent of mutual agreement on job goals.
3. Extent of improvement and development for the future.
4. Participation in job-related decisions.
5. Attitudes toward performance appraisal discussions.

On each of these, the performance appraisal control group showed no changes, but the work planning group showed positive and significant gains. (Significance, in this context, is at the statistical 5 per cent level or better.)

One measure of the low effectiveness of the classic performance appraisal system was that managers were forced by the personnel department to conduct appraisals on an annual basis. Unless they were continually reminded, the managers ignored the organization policy. Conversely, once managers became accustomed to the work planning process, they needed no policing. Instead, they kept it up on their own. In addition, they made a number of comments, such as: "I don't know how I managed without this," or, "This has really been a help to me," or, "At last, you people (personnel) are helping me rather than forcing me to do something I don't want to do."

Interviews with subordinates indicated that they now saw their supervisors more as helpers than as judges and that the subordinates' job goals were not only more clearly understood, but more important, far better accepted, primarily because they had greater participation in establishing the goals.

Limited experience in sitting in on work planning and review discussions indicated that there was much less defensiveness on the part of the subordinate and much greater self-measurement. Because of the research results, the decision was made to implement the program throughout the organization. Almost a year later, in late 1964, the compensation office asked all involved personnel in the organization to complete an anonymous questionnaire regarding salary practices. Because of the tightening of salary practices since 1961, all the questions regarding salary practices showed a drop from the previous questionnaire responses in 1961. One question, however, did not relate to salary practices. This question had to do with the extent to which "my manager encourages me to improve my job performance." In contrast to the rest of the questionnaire, this question showed almost 50 per cent improvement in the three years since 1961, indicating the effect of the work planning process.

SUMMARY

I have described the successful use of a management development program that works at all levels. Research on the classic performance appraisal system had demonstrated that it was not meeting its primary objective of improving work performance. As a result, it was decided to implement a modified management by objectives approach. Originally established on a pilot study basis, the program ultimately became successful (after an initial failure), when the implementation process was adapted to incorporate eight basic principles. Follow-up research indicated that there had been a 72 per cent increase over the control group in specific actions that the WP&R group had taken to improve performance. Other nonresearch data pointed to similar results.

Two major conclusions can be drawn:

A change process needs to be carefully planned and implemented.
WP&R is effective as a management development program at all levels of management in a wide variety of management positions.

23.

CULTURAL BIAS IN SELECTION

OLLIE A. JENSEN

Bias in selection can be deliberate and direct or indirect and incidental. This discussion deals with the second type of bias—the non-selection of individuals from minority ethnic groups, not because they lack potential, but because of the kind of education and experience they have had.

A conclusion which has been drawn repeatedly in the literature on ethnic group differences is that tests with high verbal skill loadings are not "fair" to all groups. This conclusion is indisputable for tests used to measure relative ability to learn (used as aptitude tests), but does not necessarily hold for tests used to measure developed abilities (used as job knowledge or achievement tests).

Reprinted from *Public Personnel Review*, Vol. 27, No. 2 (April, 1966), pp. 125–30.

WHAT'S FAIR?

Verbal skills are acquired through informal exposure and formal education. Use of a test of verbal skills to predict individual differences in ability to learn related skills is "fair" only if all test takers are approximately equally motivated and have had about the same exposure to verbal material. If there are widespread differences among the test takers in motivation or past exposure to books and good schooling, these differences, rather than differences in aptitude, will account for most of the obtained test score variance.

In contrast, the verbal skills test is "fair" to all competitors if the skills tested are required for success on a particular job and if the new employees are expected to be fully qualified after a fixed orientation or probationary period. Here, the only interest is current level of developed (immediately usable) ability.

The qualifications in the foregoing statement point up two widely differing current problems:

1. Often the level of verbal ability needed to pass a civil service test is far in excess of that required to be successful on the job. This needlessly discriminates against competitors with particular ethnic or socio-economic backgrounds.
2. While governmental agencies have routinely provided some form of orientation and skill training, they have not provided individualized remedial education. Organized minority groups are now requesting that governmental agencies do more selection on the basis of potential, and then provide whatever individualized remedial education is needed to bring achievement up to required levels.

Whether the historical position of governmental agencies is "fair," and whether governmental agencies should go into the business of remedial education, are questions the voting public will have to resolve. The point that needs to be made here is that if individualized remedial education is to be given those hired, it is inappropriate to use a job knowledge test as a ranking device. In the remedial education situation, the ranking of eligibles should be on the basis of individual differences in potential or aptitude. If there are limits on the amount or kind of remedial education authorized, the job knowledge test can be used as a pass-fail screen. It also can be used for diagnostic purposes—to indicate the kind and amount of remedial education needed to bring a particular eligible to the full working level.

MYTH OR METHOD?

Efforts to construct culture-fair aptitude tests with useful predictive validity have not been particularly fruitful. This fact has led many psychologists to assume the following peculiar (though consistently negative) position stated by Howard C. Lockwood in his paper "The Testing of Minority Applicants for Employment": ". . . there is no such animal as a culture-fair test, but if there were it would be useless in personnel selection. . . ."

There are several reasons why such pessimism is unwarranted at this time:

1. The number of studies concerned with the utility of culture-fair tests in personnel selection is relatively small.

2. Studies which use as a criterion, supervisory rating of employees' performance during their first six months or year on the job, are by definition using a biased criterion—those who come to the job with the most fully developed, immediately useable skills receive the highest ratings regardless of their long-range potential. Studies which use as criteria measures of accomplishment during five, 10, or more years following initial testing (a) are scarce, and (b) indicate that culture-fair tests have higher predictive validity than their conventional counterpart.

3. Semler and Iscoe ("Comparative and Developmental Study of Learning Abilities of Negro and White Children Under Four Conditions," *Journal of Educational Psychology*, 1963) found that learning rate scores are not related to race. Testing the ability to learn material that is equally novel to all appears to be the most direct, fair approach to predicting ability to learn on the job. The *Raven Progressive Matrices* is probably the best culture-fair, miniature-learning-situation test in general use today. This test is 30 years old; it uses only one kind of test item and one kind of test material; it certainly can be improved upon.

4. Most of the major publishers of psychological tests have reported recently that they have major culture-fair test development projects under way.

IS A CHANGE NECESSARY?

One of the features of the ongoing "social revolution of the 60's" is the increasing pressure being exerted on governmental agencies to reduce cultural bias in selection. On the other hand, a selection system which is without bias is not a merit system. The only bias-free selection system is the perfectly conceived and operated lottery. What kind of bias is desirable? What kind is undesirable?

Deliberate and direct job-related bias, selection on the basis of merit, is the stated goal of all civil service selection programs. Deliberate and direct bias that is not job related (bias for or against individuals because of politics, race, religion, sex, etc.) is undesirable and prohibited by civil service law or rule. Indirect and incidental bias is both undesirable and unregulated.

It can be assumed that the combination of law and rule, general professionalization of personnel agency staffs, and alert vested interest groups (Fair Employment Practice Commissions, organized employee groups, etc.) provide adequate curbs on deliberate and direct bias that is not job related. The same assumption cannot be made about the more insidious indirect and incidental bias. Can this pest be controlled?

Professional application of known principles of good test construction, administration, and analysis, coupled with a sincere, knowledgeable, and pervasive "equal opportunity" recruitment and hiring effort can drastically reduce indirect and incidental bias in selection. In other words, the tools are available; the job can be done—for a price.

The value of any selection program is a function of acceptance, costs, and validity. Each personnel agency implicitly or explicitly determines the relative weight to be given each of these variables on a situation-by-situation basis. In one instance, the more costly performance test (job-sample test) is used because of doubts concerning public acceptance or validity of alternate approaches; in another instance, the device with the highest validity and acceptance is rejected in favor of one with only moderate validity and acceptance but which costs substantially less to develop or administer.

Should public personnel agencies change their formulae for evaluating cost, i.e., pay the price needed to more adequately control indirect and incidental cultural bias? If some of the well-intended but technically naïve proposals of organized minority groups (e.g., elimination of the qualification appraisal interview and use of "rule of one") become law, this question will be academic.

STATUS QUO IS FOOL'S PARADISE

In any event, the *status quo* is a fool's paradise that can vanish in an instant:

Over the years, the slogan of civil service has been "equity and merit."
Over the years, the general public has come to believe that for the most part civil service personnelists are sincerely trying to do their "mediocre best" to live up to that slogan.

Over the years, the most consistent pressure on public personnel agencies has come from employees and management and has concerned classification and pay matters.

Over the years, limited budgets, increasing work loads, and the consistent pressure on classification and pay matters have forced a mechanical, superficial approach to much of the examining function.

Knowingly or unknowingly, evidence of uniformity in treatment of applicants, competitors, and eligibles has been substituted for truly equitable treatment, and face validity of selection devices and procedures has been substituted for selection on the basis of actual merit. The scattered exceptions to this rule are tributes to the effectiveness of particular local, occupational, vested interest groups.

IS THERE A DO-IT-YOURSELF KIT?

Before entering into an enumeration of specifics for reducing cultural bias in selection, there is one closely-related topic that should be touched upon. That is the importance of having a public image as an employer who is sincerely attempting to apply the principle of "equal opportunity" in day-to-day personnel practices.

A large private utility company discovered that the percentage of Negroes passing a certain written test was, with a single exception, quite low. In the exceptional case—one city in a statewide operation—the proportion of Negroes passing the test was equal to the proportion of whites passing. The only unusual feature of this case was the unstinting effort being made by the local personnel officer to convince the community that the company was an "equal opportunity" employer, and to help line supervisors put "equal opportunity" principles into practice. In this one spot, because a great many highly qualified Negroes applied for jobs, the company was able to hire a large number. As for the test, even in this exceptional situation, it probably underestimated the relative standing of those Negroes who passed; and probably an even higher percentage of Negro applicants should have received passing scores.

The point of this more-anecdotal-than-definitive study is, "Output can be no better than input, and input can be no better than the actual public image of an agency." If the input is at least an average sampling from a current labor market, what should be done to obtain an optimum output (list of eligibles)?

HOW TO REDUCE BIAS

The do's and don'ts for reducing incidental cultural bias listed below appear, for the most part, to be paraphrases or specific applications of well known principles of good test construction. This is as it should be. Technically speaking, incidental cultural bias is merely one kind of systematic error of measurement. The more professional the approach to examining, the smaller the error of measurement, regardless of source.

Rule 1.—If the purpose is to measure developed ability, explore the feasibility of using a job-sample test battery. While job-sample tests generally are somewhat troublesome to administer and to score, costs need not always be substantially greater, and carefully conceived and executed job-sample tests are well received by competitors and keep cultural bias at a minimum.

Rule 2.—If the purpose is to measure developed ability, and written tests are part of the selection battery, set up procedures for excluding verbiage, non-job-related jargon, and other terminology and phraseology which tend to favor individuals with particular educational or socio-economic backgrounds. Also, unless differences in speed of reading are important to job success, eliminate individual differences on this variable through the use of generous time limits.

Rule 3.—Whether the purpose is to measure developed ability or ability to learn, make instructions understandable to the person who barely meets the requirements for admission to the examination. Also, in the administration of each test, make certain that the instructions are understood—even at the price of an extra proctor, possible boredom of the more test-wise, and increased total test administration time.

Offer Practice Material

Closely related to "Rule 3," if not actually part of it, is "Provide adequate practice material and feedback." The instructions and practice problems included in the "Directions Page" for civil service examinations generally are adequate for promotional situations in which the competitive group consists of employees familiar with the testing process. On the other hand, when those same "Directions" are used in open competitive examinations (a standard practice) they introduce, rather than control, cultural bias. They tend to rely on the fact that most natives of the U.S. white, middle class culture have taken many tests for many purposes. This is fine for most competitors, but devastating for those with backgrounds which do not fit the mold.

The unsophisticated test taker not only needs practice with item format and with recording answers on a separate answer sheet, he also needs practice in answering subject matter questions within the item format and an opportunity to compare his answers with the key answers. Ability to pick up clues as to the level of abstraction intended, fineness or grossness of distinctions to be made, etc., is acquired through exposure. As this is a test-related (rather than job-related) ability, individual differences should be minimized. It is to be remembered that differences in test sophistication affect both power and speed.

Successive Hurdles Approach

Rule 4.—Whether the purpose is to measure developed ability or ability to learn, remember that whenever the selection process consists of a series of hurdles, the total process is no better than the worst hurdle. The input for one hurdle is the output from the previous one. If the examination publicity reaches only WASPs, only WASPs will apply. If the publicity reaches all potential competitors in the recruitment area, but one segment of the potential competitive group finds the public image of the agency unsatisfactory, then few from the unsatisfied segment will apply. This is especially true of the better qualified people in that segment.

If the group of applicants is representative, but the first test hurdle is culturally biased, then the competitive group for the next hurdle will reflect that bias. No matter how "fair" the second or succeeding tests are, the selection process will yield a culturally biased list. If more than one hurdle is culturally biased, the error is, of course, compounded. Currently, public personnel agencies all too frequently set up a series of absolute selection hurdles. An "absolute hurdle" is one which must be cleared in one try—there is no second chance; there is no provision for achieving a compensatingly high score on other hurdles.

The reasons for choosing the "successive absolute hurdles" approach usually are expediency or increased economy, not increased validity. The least expensive selection devices (which also tend to be the most culturally biased and least valid) are used as the first hurdle:

(a) Minimum qualification requirements for admission to the examination are inserted as a pretest hurdle. Often these qualifications more closely resemble "desirable qualifications" than they do minimum qualifications. In light of how difficult it has been for members of some minority groups to obtain " 'X' years of progressively responsible experience," this practice is biased in the extreme.

(b) A group written test is frequently used to reduce the number of competitors who will be evaluated further by a costly individual test or interview. Here, all too frequently, the choice of test format and item content, style, or terminology inadvertently favors one discipline over another or favors formal course study over self development.

The gist of "Rule 4" is not "abandon the successive-hurdles approach to selection"; rather, it is, "don't use the successive-hurdles approach routinely, and in each instance of use, make a separate determination on how it is to be used":

(a) Set true minimum qualifications or admit all.

(d) Selectively abandon absolute hurdles in favor of relative ones; hurdles which within situationally defined limits allow for compensating patterns of abilities.

(c) Discover and then utilize other procedures and techniques for reducing the "compounding of error on error" so characteristic of today's successive-hurdles selection programs.

Key Test to Requirements

Rule 5.—If a general aptitude test is to be used, make it appropriate in level and kind to the general aptitude requirements of the selection situation. This self-evident principle needs emphasis because it is ignored in day-to-day practice. Often the only general aptitude recognized is abstract intelligence, and the only recognition given to the differential requirements of jobs widely separated in level and kind of duties is a change in the level of abstraction, the number of questions, or the reconditeness and face validity of the vocabulary used.

The general aptitude needed for success in most low level classes is qualitatively different from abstract intelligence. It is an ability to carry out consistently a readily-learned routine with dispatch and accuracy. The key words here are "routine," "accuracy," and "consistently."

Routine.—The distinguishing feature of low level jobs is the routine nature of their duties. The routine varies widely in content and, within narrow limits, in complexity, but in all cases the required ability is being capable of following implicit or explicit sets of directions.

Accuracy.—Above a certain minimum level of speed, specific to each job, accuracy is more important than speed. The cost (time, money, manpower, public relations) for correcting one error generally offsets substantial differences in gross production.

Consistently.—On routine jobs, inconsistency is characteristic of the over-qualified as well as the under-qualified.

Shortcomings of Current Devices

The main shortcomings of most devices for measuring the ability to follow directions are

(a) They are too short. Individual differences in accuracy due to fluctuating attention are not measured.

(b) They are too highly speeded. While it is true that in a specific setting, speed and accuracy tend to be correlated, it is also true that short-burst speed is not related to sustained accuracy.

(c) They are set up to yield a single speed-accuracy scale. Depending on whether the test is to be used as a pass-fail screen or a weighted part of the examination, (1) separate speed and accuracy cutoffs should be set; or (2) a speed cutoff should be set above which ranking is in terms of relative accuracy.

Rule 6.—Don't use a low selection ratio as a substitute for careful test construction and administration. It is true that by selecting only one in 100, a test with low validity can produce an eligible list containing a high proportion of highly qualified individuals. The problem is that most of the factors contributing to the low validity of the test also contribute to its cultural bias. Consequently, the list is disproportionately loaded with white, middle-class Americans having an above average amount of formal education.

SUMMARY

The moral to be drawn from this illustrative rather than exhaustive discussion of cultural bias in selection is that expediency and tight-fisted economy in the operation of a selection program tend to produce the same result as corruption and incompetence—a downgrading of one segment of the competitive group and an upgrading of another segment for invalid reasons.

24.

AUTHORIZING TRANSITIONAL APPOINTMENTS OF VETERANS WHO HAVE SERVED DURING THE VIETNAM ERA

LYNDON B. JOHNSON

WHEREAS the Federal Government has the obligation to facilitate the transition of veterans from service in the armed forces during the Vietnam era to employment in civilian pursuits;

WHEREAS many veterans have not completed education or training adequate to prepare them for the future job demands of civilian employment;

WHEREAS the Government recognizes that the acquisition of adequate education or training is an essential element in preparing individuals for employment in our present society;

WHEREAS the Government as an employer has a continuing need for skilled employees and a corresponding duty to encourage the acquisition of adequate education or training by its employees; and

WHEREAS the acquisition of necessary education or training can be combined effectively with productive employment:

NOW, THEREFORE, by virtue of the authority vested in me by the Constitution of the United States, by sections 3301 and 3302 of title 5, United States Code, and as President of the United States, it is ordered as follows:

SECTION 1. (a) Under such regulations as the Civil Service Commission may prescribe, the head of an agency may make an excepted appointment (to be known as a "transitional appointment") to any position in the competitive

Reprinted from Executive Order 11397.

service at GS-5 or below, or the equivalent thereof, of a veteran or disabled veteran as defined in section 2108 (1), (2) of title 5, United States Code, who:

(1)   served on active duty in the armed forces of the United States during the Vietnam era;

(2)   at the time of his appointment has completed less than one year of education beyond graduation from high school, or the equivalent thereof; and

(3)   is found qualified to perform the duties of the position.

(b)   An employee given a transitional appointment under paragraph (a) of this section serves subject to:

(1)   the satisfactory performance of assigned duties; and

(2)   the satisfactory completion, within such reasonable time as is prescribed in the regulations of the Civil Service Commission, of not less than one school year of full-time approved education or training, or the equivalent thereof, except that two school years of full-time approved education or training, or the equivalent thereof, shall be required when an employee has not completed high school, or the equivalent thereof, by virtue of that education or training.

(c)   An employee who does not satisfactorily meet the conditions set forth in paragraph (b) of this section shall be removed in accordance with appropriate procedures.

(d)   An employee who satisfactorily meets the conditions set forth in paragraph (b) of this section and who has completed not less than one year of current continuous employment under a transitional appointment shall, in accordance with the regulations of the Civil Service Commission, be converted to career-conditional or career employment when he furnishes his employing agency proof of the satisfactory completion of the required education or training. An employee converted under this paragraph shall automatically acquire a competitive status.

(e)   In selecting an applicant for appointment under this section, an agency head shall not discriminate because of race, color, religion, sex, national origin, or political affiliation.

SECTION 2.   A person eligible for appointment under section 1 of this order may be appointed only within one year after his separation from the armed forces, one year following his release from hospitalization or treatment immediately following his separation from the armed forces, or one year after the effective date of this order, whichever is later. . . .

25.

EXECUTIVE ORDER ON ETHICS OF FEDERAL EMPLOYEES

LYNDON B. JOHNSON

By virtue of the authority vested in me by Section 301 of Title 3 of the United States Code, and as President of the United States, it is hereby ordered as follows:

PART I—POLICY

Section 101.—Where government is based on the consent of the governed, every citizen is entitled to have complete confidence in the integrity of his government. Each individual officer, employee, or adviser of government must help to earn and must honor that trust by his own integrity and conduct in all official actions.

PART II—STANDARDS OF CONDUCT

Section 201.—(a) Except in accordance with regulations issued pursuant to subsection (b) of this section, no employee shall solicit or accept, directly or indirectly, any gift, gratuity, favor, entertainment, loan, or any other thing of monetary value, from any person, corporation, or group which—

(1) has, or is seeking to obtain, contractual or other business or financial relationships with his agency;

(2) conducts operations or activities which are regulated by his agency; or

(3) has interests which may be substantially affected by the performance or nonperformance of his official duty.

(b) Agency heads are authorized to issue regulations, coordinated and approved by the Civil Service Commission, implementing the provisions of subsection (a) of this section and to provide for such exceptions therein as may be necessary and appropriate in view of the nature of their agency's work and the duties and responsibilities of their employees. For example, it may be

Reprint of Executive Order 11222, issued May 8, 1965. *Federal Register*, pp. 6469–6473.

appropriate to provide exceptions (1) governing obvious family or personal relationships where the circumstances make it clear that it is those relationships rather than the business of the persons concerned which are the motivating factors—the clearest illustration being the parents, children or spouses of federal employees; (2) permitting acceptance of food and refreshments available in the ordinary course of a luncheon or dinner or other meeting or on inspection tours where an employee may properly be in attendance; or (3) permitting acceptance of loans from banks or other financial institutions on customary terms to finance proper and usual activities of employees, such as home mortgage loans. This section shall be effective upon issuance of such regulations.

(c) It is the intent of this section that employees avoid any action, whether or not specifically prohibited by subsection (a), which might result in, or create the appearance of—

(1) using public office for private gain;

(2) giving preferential treatment to any organization or person;

(3) impeding government efficiency or economy;

(4) losing complete independence or impartiality of action;

(5) making a government decision outside official channels; or

(6) affecting adversely the confidence of the public in the integrity of the government.

Sec. 202.—An employee shall not engage in any outside employment, including teaching, lecturing, or writing, which might result in a conflict, or an apparent conflict, between the private interests of the employee and his official government duties and responsibilities, although such teaching, lecturing, and writing by employees are generally to be encouraged so long as the laws, the provisions of this order, and Civil Service Commission and agency regulations covering conflict of interest and outside employment are observed.

Sec. 203.—Employees may not (a) have direct or indirect financial interests that conflict substantially, or appear to conflict substantially, with their responsibilities and duties as federal employees, or (b) engage in, directly or indirectly, financial transactions as a result of, or primarily relying upon, information obtained through their employment. Aside from these restrictions, employees are free to engage in lawful financial transactions to the same extent as private citizens. Agencies may, however, further restrict such transactions in the light of the special circumstances of their individual missions.

Sec. 204.—An employee shall not use federal property of any kind for other than officially approved activities. He must protect and conserve all federal property, including equipment and supplies, entrusted or issued to him.

Sec. 205.—An employee shall not directly or indirectly make use of, or permit others to make use of, for the purpose of furthering a private interest, official information not made available to the general public.

Sec. 206.—An employee is expected to meet all just financial obligations, especially those—such as federal, state, or local taxes—which are imposed by law.

PART III—STANDARDS OF ETHICAL CONDUCT
FOR SPECIAL GOVERNMENT EMPLOYEES

Section 301.—This part applies to all "special government employees" as defined in Section 202 of Title 18 of the United States Code, who are employed in the Executive Branch.

Sec. 302.—A consultant, adviser or other special government employee must refrain from any use of his public office which is motivated by, or gives the appearance of being motivated by, the desire for private gain for himself or other persons, including particularly those with whom he has family, business, or financial ties.

Sec. 303.—A consultant, adviser, or other special government employee shall not use any inside information obtained as a result of his government service for private personal gain, either by direct action on his part or by counsel, recommendations or suggestions to others, including particularly those with whom he has family, business, or financial ties.

Sec. 304.—An adviser, consultant, or other special government employee shall not use his position in any way to coerce, or give the appearance of coercing, another person to provide any financial benefit to him or persons with whom he has family, business, or financial ties.

Sec. 305.—An adviser, consultant, or other special government employee shall not receive or solicit from persons having business with his agency anything of value as a gift, gratuity, loan or favor for himself or persons with whom he has family, business, or financial ties while employed by the government or in connection with his work with the government.

Sec. 306.—Each agency shall, at the time of employment of a consultant, adviser, or other special government employee require him to supply it with a statement of all other employment. The statement shall list the names of all the corporations, companies, firms, State or local governmental organizations, research organizations and educational or other institutions in which he is serving as employee, officer, member, owner, director, trustee, adviser, or consultant. In addition, it shall list such other financial information as the appointing department or agency shall decide is relevant in the light of the duties the appointee is to perform. The appointee may, but need not, be required to reveal precise amounts of investments. The statement shall be kept current throughout the period during which the employee is on the government rolls.

PART IV—REPORTING OF FINANCIAL INTERESTS

Section 401.—(a) Not later than ninety days after the date of this order, the head of each agency, each Presidential appointee in the Executive Office of the President who is not subordinate to the head of an agency in that Office, and each full-time member of a committee, board, or commission appointed by the President, shall submit to the Chairman of the Civil Service Commission a statement containing the following:

(1)   A list of the names of all corporations, companies, firms, or other business enterprises, partnerships, nonprofit organizations, and educational or other institutions—

(A)   with which he is connected as an employee, officer, owner, director, trustee, partner, adviser, or consultant; or

(B)   in which he has any continuing financial interests, through a pension or retirement plan, shared income, or otherwise, as a result of any current or prior employment or business or professional association; or

(C)   in which he has any financial interest through the ownership of stocks, bonds, or other securities.

(2)   A list of the names of his creditors, other than those to whom he may be indebted by reason of a mortgage on property which he occupies as a personal residence or to whom he may be indebted for current and ordinary household and living expenses.

(3)   A list of his interests in real property or rights in lands, other than property which he occupies as a personal residence.

(b)   Each person who enters upon duty after the date of this order in an office or position as to which a statement is required by this section shall submit such statement not later than thirty days after the date of his entrance on duty.

(c)   Each statement required by this section shall be kept up to date by submission of amended statements of any changes in, or additions to, the information required to be included in the original statement, on a quarterly basis.

Sec. 402.—The Civil Service Commission shall prescribe regulations, not inconsistent with this part, to require the submission of statements of financial interests by such employees, subordinate to the heads of agencies, as the Commission may designate. The Commission shall prescribe the form and content of such statements and the time or times and places for such submission.

Sec. 403.—(a) The interest of a spouse, minor child, or other members of his immediate household shall be considered to be an interest of a person required to submit a statement by or pursuant to this part.

(b)   In the event any information required to be included in a statement required by or pursuant to this part is not known to the person required to submit such statement but is known to other persons, the person concerned shall request such other persons to submit the required information on his behalf.

(c) This part shall not be construed to require the submission of any information relating to any person's connection with, or interest in, any professional society or any charitable, religious, social, fraternal, educational, recreational, public service, civic, or political organization or any similar organization not conducted as a business enterprise and which is not engaged in the ownership or conduct of a business enterprise.

Sec. 404.—The Chairman of the Civil Service Commission shall report to the President any information contained in statements required by Section 401 of this part which may indicate a conflict between the financial interests of the official concerned and the performance of his services for the government. The Commission shall report, or by regulation require reporting, to the head of the agency concerned any information contained in statements submitted pursuant to regulations issued under Section 402 of this part which may indicate a conflict between the financial interests of the officer or employee concerned and the performance of his services for the government.

Sec. 405.—The statements and amended statements required by or pursuant to this part shall be held in confidence, and no information as to the contents thereof shall be disclosed except as the Chairman of the Civil Service Commission or the head of the agency concerned may determine for good cause shown.

Sec. 406.—The statements and amended statements required by or pursuant to this part shall be in addition to, and not in substitution for, or in derogation of, any similar requirement imposed by law, regulation, or order. The submission of a statement or amended statements required by or pursuant to this part shall not be deemed to permit any person to participate in any matter in which his participation is prohibited by law, regulation, or order.

PART V—DELEGATING AUTHORITY OF THE PRESIDENT UNDER SECTIONS 205 AND 208 OF TITLE 18 OF THE UNITED STATES CODE RELATING TO CONFLICTS OF INTEREST

Section 501.—As used in this part, "department" means an executive department, "agency" means an independent agency or establishment or a government corporation, and "head of an agency" means, in the case of an agency headed by more than one person, the chairman or comparable member of such agency.

Sec. 502.—There is delegated, in accordance with and to the extent prescribed in Sections 503 and 504 of this part, the authority of the President under Sections 205 and 208(b) of Title 18, United States Code, to permit certain actions by an officer or employee of the government, including a special government employee, for appointment to whose position the President is responsible.

Sec. 503.—Insofar as the authority of the President referred to in Section 502 extends to any appointee of the President subordinate to or subject to the chairmanship of the head of a department or agency, it is delegated to such department or agency head.

Sec. 504.—Insofar as the authority of the President referred to in Section 502 extends to an appointee of the President who is within or attached to a department or agency for purposes of administration, it is delegated to the head of such department or agency.

Sec. 505.—Notwithstanding any provision of the preceding sections of this part to the contrary, this part does not include a delegation of the authority of the President referred to in Section 502 insofar as it extends to:

(a) The head of any department or agency in the Executive Branch;

(b) Presidential appointees in the Executive Office of the President who are not subordinate to the head of an agency in that Office; and

(c) Presidential appointees to committees, boards, commissions, or similar groups established by the President.

PART VI—PROVIDING FOR THE PERFORMANCE BY THE CIVIL SERVICE COMMISSION OF CERTAIN AUTHORITY VESTED IN THE PRESIDENT BY SECTION 1753 OF THE REVISED STATUTES

Section 601.—The Civil Service Commission is designated and empowered to perform, without the approval, ratification, or other action of the President, so much of the authority vested in the President by Section 1753 of the Revised Statutes of the United States (5 U.S.C. 631) as relates to establishing regulations for the conduct of persons in the civil service.

Sec. 602.—Regulations issued under the authority of Section 601 shall be consistent with the standards of ethical conduct provided elsewhere in this order.

PART VII—GENERAL PROVISIONS

Section 701.—The Civil Service Commission is authorized and directed, in addition to responsibilities assigned elsewhere in this order:

(a) To issue appropriate regulations and instructions implementing Parts II, III, and IV of this order;

(b) To review agency regulations from time to time for conformance with this order; and

(c) To recommend to the President from time to time such revisions in this order as may appear necessary to ensure the maintenance of high ethical standards within the Executive Branch.

Sec. 702.—Each agency head is hereby directed to supplement the standards provided by law, by this order, and by regulations of the Civil Service Commission with regulations of special applicability to the particular functions and activities of his agency. Each agency head is also directed to assure (1) the widest possible distribution of regulations issued pursuant to this section, and (2) the availability of counseling for those employees who request advice or interpretation.

Sec. 703.—The following are hereby revoked:

(a) Executive Order No. 10939 of May 5, 1961.

(b) Executive Order No. 11125 of October 29, 1963.

(c) Section 2(a) of Executive Order No. 10530 of May 10, 1954.

(d) White House memorandum of July 20, 1961, on "Standards of Conduct for Civilian Employees."

(e) The President's Memorandum of May 2, 1963, "Preventing Conflicts of Interest on the Part of Special Government Employees." The effective date of this revocation shall be the date of issuance by the Civil Service Commission of regulations under Section 701(a) of this order.

Sec. 704.—All actions heretofore taken by the President or by his delegates in respect of the matters affected by this order and in force at the time of the issuance of this order, including any regulations prescribed or approved by the President or by his delegates in respect of such matters, shall, except as they may be inconsistent with the provisions of this order or terminate by operation of law, remain in effect until amended, modified, or revoked pursuant to the authority conferred by this order.

Sec. 705.—As used in this order, and except as otherwise specifically provided herein, the term "agency" means any executive department, or any independent agency or any government corporation; and the term "employee" means any officer or employee of an agency.

26.

DEVELOPMENTS IN GOVERNMENT MANPOWER: A FEDERAL PERSPECTIVE

ROGER W. JONES

Any examination of what has happened in recent years to government manpower has to start with the Government Employees Training Act of 1958. Signed by the President on July 7, 1958, that Act became a benchmark of indisputable validity almost at once. In spirit and philosophy, it has provided a point of departure for significant manpower developments of several kinds, and they are not so unrelated as they may seem. Of course, everything did not fall neatly into place upon passage of the Act, but constructive movement cannot be denied.

In less than nine years, the concepts, principles, and stated purposes of the Training Act have pointed a sternly critical finger at deficiencies in: (1) manpower planning; (2) career development, with particular reference to executive training; (3) employee mobility; (4) analysis of losses and turnover; (5) pay and fringe benefits; (6) labor-management relations; (7) use of modern technology in personnel administration; (8) attitudes toward, and knowledge of, contributions which the social sciences can make to personnel administration; (9) cooperation among governments at all levels and academic institutions in defining and filling requirements for new kinds of government personnel; and (10) acceptance of Federal responsibility for trying to alleviate at least part of the crisis in intergovernmental manpower matters. A retrospective look indicates that the Federal government as a whole may have come further than many agencies realize in facing up to manpower problems—but not as far as the agencies can with the right combinations of use of existing authorities.

MANPOWER PLANNING AND CAREER DEVELOPMENT

Whatever the judgments of hindsight about timid acceptance of responsibility to make quick and full use of the 1958 Training Act, the Act and its implementing Executive Order (No. 10800, issued January 15, 1959) did have one immediate

Reprinted from *Public Administration Review*, Vol. XXVII, No. 2 (June, 1967), pp. 134-41.

consequence. Manpower planning and career development became respectable concerns—not simply of personnel officers but at the highest levels of program management and policy formulation. It was a sobering experience to many at the top to discover some of the bleaker aspects of the Federal manpower outlook, of which four deserve mention.

1. The Federal government has to compete in the marketplace to fill its manpower needs. It can no longer spend time in leisurely contemplation of ways to limit eligibility for appointment. Nor can agencies delay appointment decisions for long periods of time. Young people are not flocking to the flag of the career civil service, but they will choose government careers if: recruiting and examining are streamlined and made positive; employment offers are backed up by sensible inducements, including clear statements of duties and firm commitments that demonstrated ability will be accompanied by promotion; and mobility is not frowned upon.

2. Death, eligibility for retirement, and resignations because of attractive outsider offers—all have been taking heavy toll in the "Great Depression" generation of young competence, which entered Federal service between 1933 and 1937.

3. There is insufficient depth in replacement ranks because too little training has been done, and the effect of limited high-quality intake of college graduates during World War II (1941–45) and the Korean War (1945–54) was underestimated.

4. There has been so much pressure *to do*, for so long, that structured, planned career development and management of middle and higher-level personnel in the civilian agencies have been badly neglected.

It is no wonder, then, that the Brookings Institution's announcement in 1958 of a modest conference program for Federal executives met with wide acclaim. The program was expected to perform miracles, and it did, both in setting the stage for use of Training Act authorities and in proving the value of getting Federal executives to rub elbows and ideas in an off-the-job environment. Brookings deserves much credit for stepping up Federal awareness that executives do not just happen and that Federal program managers can profit from knowing more than how to tend their own small garden patches of activity.

The net result of the first three years of ferment about the possibilities of the Training Act was not only to make manpower planning and development respectable enterprises but, equally important, to give impetus, first, to the Civil Service Commission to shake up old ways of doing business and, second, to agency executives to get themselves into the personnel business.

The 1959, 1960, and 1961 annual reports of the Civil Service Commission, muted and low key though they were, contained flashes of small and distant lightning which showed how badly the parched fields of manpower needed the steady downpour to come.

For example, in 1959, special efforts were begun to attract scientists and engineers, to select persons with research skills needed in Federal laboratories, to train Federal employees for space programs, to recruit superior college graduates, and to put merit promotions on a firm basis. In 1960, a greatly increased effort was made in the area of management and executive development programs; in addition, the Commission established an intern program in management applications of computers. In 1961, agencies identified 11,490 positions as targets for executive development programs and forecast replacement needs. They also increased executive training available through their own agencies or at outside institutions. The Civil Service Commission began a study to determine successful career development methods and to give them continuing evaluation.

The small specifics of the years 1959–61 have been extended into developments of larger scope. Perhaps as many as twenty departments and agencies have formalized their manpower planning activities and in many cases have reinforced manpower planning with career development programs either within the agency itself or by collaboration in interagency training programs.

One of the most interesting, at least in terms of long-range potential, is the State Department's Manpower, Utilization, and Systems Technique. Although still in the experimental stage of collecting and analyzing quantitative data about requirements and resources, this program has great promise as a device for integrating manpower planning with career management.

The Budget Bureau, in cooperation with the Civil Service Commission and the National Institute of Public Affairs, is moving into the second year of an interagency program for giving university-based training to more than 100 employees a year in the techniques and uses of systematic analysis needed for installation of the planning, programming, budgeting system.

In addition to extending its series of institutes for specialized training, the Civil Service Commission now has two Executive Seminar Centers for short-course, midcareer training, one at the U.S. Merchant Marine Academy at Kings Point, New York, and the second at Berkeley, California. Demand for spaces for the forthcoming year already far outruns the capacity of the two Centers.

Almost ten years of discussion about the need for some kind of high-level civilian staff college have culminated in action. Within the last few weeks the President, acting on a recommendation of his Task Force on Career Advancement, has directed the Chairman of the Civil Service Commission "to establish a center for advanced study for executives in the upper echelons of the Civil Service." The program at the center will emphasize the major problems facing our society and the government's response to them.

Overall, interagency training has grown from opportunities for a few thousand employees in 1959 to 40,000 persons receiving some form of such training in

1964, and 65,000 in 1966. Something over 2,000 interagency courses will be available in this fiscal year of 1967.

Also worthy of note are a number of developments in training activities within specific agencies. The Internal Revenue Service's Executive Selection and Development Program has been so successful that of its 111 graduates, 2 are now regional commissioners, 11 are assistant regional commissioners, 29 are district directors, 37 are assistant district directors, and 1 is service center director.

The Federal Aviation Administration has begun a new long-term training program to develop air controllers. The program of the Foreign Service Institute has been extensively revised. The Department of Defense is in the process of establishing a Career Executive Institute for its civilian personnel. The Post Office Department has requested funds to start a Postal Management Academy. Similarly, the experience gained under the Brookings Conference Programs, the National Institute of Public Affairs Fellowships, and the Princeton Fellows Program is leading to growing use of the Training Act authorities by the agencies at a growing number of colleges and universities.

The issuance of Executive Order 11348 on April 20, 1967, changes the report of the Presidential Task Force on Career Advancement from a handbook of the desirable to an action program. (The order revokes Executive Order 10800 of January 15, 1959, referred to earlier.) The clear statements of responsibilities vested in the Civil Service Commission and in the agencies and their heads give a clear focus of action for the years ahead.

However, if the Civil Service Commission and the agencies are to avoid a start-and-stop approach to building the fully cooperative structure required by the new Executive order, four undertakings appear to be the most needed next steps:

1. Establishment of an effective and continuing system for *evaluating*: agency manpower and career development programs, agency and interagency training efforts, and the special competence of particular colleges and universities to provide curricula for specific governmental manpower training and education.

2. Early decision to define and delimit the kinds of training which can best be undertaken within the Federal government to meet its own needs and related needs of State and local governments.

3. Determination of academic capability and willingness to undertake short-term, specialized training as opposed to longer-term "horizon-broadening" education.

4. Development of a hard-core catalog of management skills needed by career executives to improve their performance.

While Federal agencies could effectively use some additional money to accelerate the progress of manpower planning and career development systems, it is just as well that they have been cautious about pressing their demands too vigorously. Development of a program and a philosophy which are not flamboyant, and do not require large infusions of new money, requires an orderly buildup. It appears that "lack of money" has been an excuse rather than a reason for the failure of some agencies to move toward more adequate manpower planning and career development programs. More money, however, clearly is needed for outside training in academic institutions. And it should be accompanied by conviction that training is a component of all personal services appropriations.

EMPLOYEE MOBILITY AND ANALYSIS OF LOSSES AND TURNOVER

The list of occupations in the Federal government has increased rapidly in the last decade as government programs have been extended into new fields. The need for most effective use both of the specialist and of the more generally trained executive or program manager also has become more pronounced. Figures supplied to the Task Force on Career Development indicate that specialists now make up 27 per cent of Federal employment, or some 761,000 persons. The report estimates that there will be need for an additional 225,000 employees in professional, administrative, and technical occupations in the decade immediately ahead, and that the gross turnover figure will be in the neighborhood of 675,000. In other words, 900,000 of a total employment estimated at 985,000 by 1975 will represent either new positions or turnover.

In some rapidly developing specialties, the percentage increase in employment will be very large. For the computer occupations, the Bureau of Labor Statistics forecasts a 74 per cent increase between 1965 and 1975; a 44 per cent increase for physicists; a 39 per cent increase for engineers; and a 36 per cent increase for chemists.

If the Federal government has to recruit 90,000 professional, administrative, and technical employees annually, it must develop more sophisticated means of analyzing turnover and sharing manpower shortages. The number of shortage occupations in American life shows no sign of decreasing, but government programs requiring shortage skills show every sign of increasing. These trends, when complicated by rapidly changing methods, technology, and content of government programs, point to needs of crisis dimensions for maximum deployment of skills where they are most needed. In other words, employee mobility (once looked upon with some disfavor) has become a requisite characteristic of Federal careers.

To meet these two needs, the Civil Service Commission has taken two important steps: creation of a Bureau of Executive Manpower and central compilation (to complement agency efforts) of an annual Federal Workforce Outlook. This publication analyzes the structure of the workforce and makes employment projections for five years ahead.

The Bureau of Executive Manpower has as its charter the development and administration of the Executive Assignment System. Due to come into full operation later this year, the System is designed to bring modern manpower management techniques to the task of finding and using the best possible talent in key executive posts in the civil service. The major components of the System will be a servicewide talent bank, reinforced by flexible recruitment of quality talent from outside the government. To meet rapidly changing technological and program needs, agencies and the Civil Service Commission will continuously relate executive manpower and organizational structure to mission requirements. A primary goal is the development of a top staff ready for assignment where needed and committed to the concept of response to overall government needs, rather than to entrenchment in a single agency or an individual program.

The new Bureau will do well, indeed, if it can devise a rational and effective system for handling a total universe of 8,750 top-level positions—so-called "supergrades" and their equivalents. Mobility, however, must begin at lower levels. The agencies, themselves, must undertake responsibility for developing the organization and procedures for sharing shortages and making best assignments of shortage skill personnel who are scattered through another 50-55 thousand positions in the next lower grades. They must also be kept fully abreast of what is happening to the incumbents of these positions in their own and related agencies. It is this level of Federal employees on whom heavy leadership responsibilities will soon fall, and they must be ready to move up. The management of this resource will require a more imaginative approach to interagency training than agencies so far have devised.

The reports of the Civil Service Commission for 1965 and 1966 and the annual catalog of interagency training courses indicate the kind of initial work which the Commission and the agencies are doing, particularly in the management sciences, supervisory techniques, and similar fields.

PAY AND FRINGE BENEFITS

The Federal Salary Reform Act of 1962, like the Government Employees Training Act of 1958, brought to fruition several years of intensive work to get badly needed manpower legislation into a satisfactory benchmark statute. Early judgment that the 1962 Salary Reform Act ranks high on the list of most important Federal personnel legislation will stand the test of time insofar as its central emphasis is concerned. The statute begins:

It is the policy of Congress that Federal pay fixing be based on the principles that—

1. there be equal pay for substantially equal work, and pay distinctions be maintained in keeping with work and performance distinctions; and
2. Federal pay rates be comparable with private enterprise pay rates for the same levels of work.

Pay levels for the several Federal statutory pay systems shall be interrelated, and pay levels shall be set and adjusted in accordance with these principles.

Although the first principle has been central to Federal policy ever since the original Classification Act was passed, the principle of comparability between Federal pay rates and private enterprise evolved slowly. In the main it reflects extensive dissatisfaction with the series of hit-or-miss pay raise bills enacted between 1945 and 1960. Although each enacted substantial average increases in civilian pay, there was no means for determining whether any one of them was soundly based or was keeping Federal pay in a competitive position.

In 1958, Congress and the Executive Branch began a series of efforts to relate Federal pay to what was happening in the economy at large. Statistical compilations and linkage studies proved that the comparability principle was sound, that its enactment into law should enable the Federal government to compete effectively in the labor market, and that it would establish a pay structure which was fair to Federal employees and to the taxpayer.

There is considerable evidence that if full comparability had been obtained in the 1962 Act, some of the difficulties encountered with pay legislation in 1964, 1965, and 1966 might have been avoided. The President, in his pay message of April 5, 1967, has proposed closing the comparability gap in three steps: a 4.5 per cent across-the-board pay increase, effective October 1, 1967, and two subsequent increases to be effective October 1, 1968, and October 1, 1969, to remove the remaining lag.

Related to this major development are two other proposals made in President Johnson's 1967 pay message. The first is for an updating adjustment of executive, legislative, and judicial salaries after receipt of the recommendations of a special Commission which reported on June 1, 1967. The second is for the establishment by law of a Joint Salary Commission, representing the three branches of the government, to examine all Federal pay systems and to report to the President or to the Congress within two years. In connection with this second recommendation, the President said:

Salary reform for the government of an increasingly complex and ever-changing society is never complete. The entire structure and interrelationships of all Federal pay systems, civilian and military, should be continually reviewed and improved. The adequacy of the basic pay system itself must be periodically re-examined.

Concurrently with efforts to establish a rational, continuing basis for setting Federal salaries, both the Congress and the Executive Branch turned their attention to the supplemental benefits structure. Over the years it had not kept up with the best practices outside the Federal structure. In September 1959, Congress enacted the Federal Employees Health Benefits Act, which went into effect in 1960. Along with the Federal Employees Group Life Insurance Act of 1954, this law provided protections which had become almost standard practice in progressive private firms.

Several basic improvements have been made in recent years, or are pending, in the civilian retirement program, including the long-sought optional retirement on unreduced annuity at age 55 after 30 years of service (enacted in 1966) and transfer of credit to the social security system for employees whose service does not earn entitlement to civil service retirement. This measure is now being considered by Congress along with a companion measure which would establish the minimum social security benefit as the minimum survivor benefit under the Civil Service retirement system.

Of significance also are three other improvements in fringe benefits. In 1964, amendment of the so-called Dual Compensation Acts established a rational basis for permitting retired personnel of the Armed Services to accept employment in civilian agencies without sacrificing all of their military retired pay benefits. In 1966, Congress completed an extensive revision and updating of the Federal Employees Compensation Act. Similarly, Congress took favorable action on recommendations of the President for greatly liberalized moving expense payments for employees transferred from one location to another and for severance pay to employees losing their jobs through no fault of their own.

LABOR-MANAGEMENT RELATIONS

The period 1961-66 ushered in a new era in employee-management cooperation in the Federal government. The report of a special Task Force designated by President Kennedy to advise him on employee-management relations in the Federal service led to the issuance, on January 16, 1962, of Executive Orders 10987 and 10988. These orders provided for:

A more uniform system of appeals within agencies and extension to nonveteran employees of rights given to veterans.

Recognition of the rights of employees to join or refrain from joining employee organizations.

Three forms of recognition for employee organizations—informal, formal, and exclusive.

Negotiations with organizations granted exclusive recognition of appropriate written agreements on matters of personnel policy and working conditions.

Adoption of advisory arbitration of grievances.

By the end of calendar year 1966, exclusive representation agreements covered 1,054,000 employees, as compared with 19,000 in 1961. There had been 598

negotiated agreements by the end of 1966, as compared with 26 in 1961. Formal
and informal recognition also was extensively used. Relationships between unions
and agency management—particularly at the local installation level—showed
marked improvement in communication with employees and in practices relating
to safety, tours of duty, health and working conditions, and the scheduling of
leave and overtime. While there have been some disputes, charges of unfair
practice, and other unsatisfactory situations, the labor-management relations
program is developing with tolerance, understanding, and resolution to make it
a success. The need for revision of Executive Order 10988 is undergoing serious study.

The program has also produced much valuable information which augurs well
for better training programs for rank and file employees and for more attention
to opportunities to advance, with proper training, from the skilled crafts into the
ranks of the technical specialists. The government's need for technicians possessing greater knowledge of professional and scientific methodology is increasing
rapidly.

The Task Force on Career Advancement has recommended that the heads of
agencies establish systems whereby:

... opportunities for upgrading to technician jobs are effectively communicated to
employees and to employee organizations; those who express interest are ranked
as to their potential for such assignments, and the best of these are trained for technical
positions.

Here again, there can be little doubt that agencies will respond affirmatively by
using Training Act authorities to unite technicians and professionals in a more
effective manpower management system.

USE OF MODERN TECHNOLOGY IN
PERSONNEL ADMINISTRATION

Modern technology, particularly the computer, points the way to dramatic developments in the personnel field. Not only will manpower planning and career
development programs depend increasingly upon automated data systems, but
these systems will also bring about a more rational differentiation among needs
for administrators, specialists, technicians, and capability in clerical and laborer
ranks. The results of the new technology on managerial effectiveness and in improved agency administration already are measurable in terms of higher productivity, lower costs, improved employee motivation, and greater flexibility to meet
the kinds of change with which government is slowly learning to live.

The implications of technology for the Executive Assignment System of the
Civil Service Commission are obvious. Less obvious, and largely because they
have not been satisfactorily explored, are the implications in development of

classroom and on-the-job training. Bold, imaginative agency executives and personnel officers are now exploring how to undertake further experimental work in this field.

THE SOCIAL SCIENCES AND
PERSONNEL ADMINISTRATION

There is little to report about increasing commitment to use the contributions of the social sciences in personnel administration. Until very recently, government administrators and personnel people have been suspicious of the behavioral sciences, which probably have seemed to many "academic" and therefore hostile to empiricism and pragmatism. For example, most Federal managers have been reluctant to make use of the findings of psychology. Some agencies are now finding that the proper use of psychological investigation will increase understanding of the way to get optimum performance. It is disappointing to note that the Civil Service Commission's "Federal Workforce Outlook for Fiscal Years 1966-69" projects no increase in employment of psychologists. Hopefully, this is an incorrect estimate. Recent meetings of personnel officers have reported interest in the appointment of psychologists, not to work in a clinical setting but as staff officers attached to personnel and management offices in Federal agencies.

Less disappointing is the Federal attitude toward development of the concept of organizations as social systems. Sociologists have found that within the social system of any large organization there exist definite and successive linkages between individual psychology, group behavior, organization functioning, and the larger body politic. They have also developed precise and highly useful definitions of the structures which exist in any social system. Improved analytical approaches to the functioning of organizations are a prerequisite to making them function more effectively.

Still another of the social sciences, economics, has added broad new vistas for managerial analysis and competence, with obvious implications on the Government manpower front. One example, referred to earlier, is systematic analysis and its application in the so-called planning, programming, and budgeting system. It is easy to joke about depersonalization of decisions reached by systematic analysis, but the fact remains that Federal managers have an obligation to collect and use systematic information on what the central government is trying to accomplish; what the best ways of accomplishing these objectives are *in the light of all available options;* and last, but not least, how Federal programs are faring when one is compared with another.

INTERGOVERNMENTAL PERSONNEL MATTERS

Without the responses made to the Training Act by the Brookings Institution, the National Institute of Public Affairs, and the graduate schools specializing in public and international affairs, it is doubtful that Federal agencies would have given much serious attention to creation of a climate for full-scale cooperation among governments at all levels and academic institutions. Joint reassessment of views about personnel required to discharge today's public functions has paid dividends—and they have been greater than the advocates of the Training Act dared to hope in 1958. The starting point may well have been early refusal of the Civil Service Commission to accept responsibility for defining agency training needs. This action spurred contacts and conversations between Federal agencies and academic institutions about training needs and the kinds of education which would improve the caliber of government manpower. Three important developments to date appear to be:

Agreement that strict reliance on usual academic disciplinary training given to teachers and researchers does not fill many government needs.

Interdisciplinary training, difficult though it may be to undertake in the present structure of most colleges and universities, presents great opportunities for solving significant public policy problems confronting our society in such broad categories as health, education, welfare, housing, transportation, crime, and urban decay.

Collaboration between academia and government is essential for what one retired Government official (now in academic life) calls "the development of means for bridging the gulf between the increasingly specialized world of the discipline-oriented academician and the problem-oriented or public policy-oriented public official."

There can be no doubt that the role of many thousands of government employees is changing. Concern with ministerial functions and attention to the needs of homogeneous, nationwide constituencies is giving way to deep involvement in applying government programs to the problems of individuals. Many tight little compartments of discrete Federal activities are disappearing. For example, cooperative financing under grant-in-aid formulas calls for new skills, different relationships with State and local governments, and broader awareness about nongovernmental activities. Bureaucratically vexing overlaps in jurisdiction have come into being and are imposing heavy responsibility upon government manpower for interagency policy and program coordination—to say nothing of interlocking, complementary efforts in program administration. The impersonal, subject-matter program authorizations affecting housing, slum clearance, and health, to give only three examples, have become much less important than the effect of program dollars on individuals and on State and local levels of government.

Perforce, the Federal government must lead the procession in finding effective and constitutional means for abandoning sporadic and less than full use of the combined powers vested in Federal, State, and local governments. Congressional grant of broad authority to deal with the large complexities of our time reflects public concern about the growing interdependence of every segment of our society. It does not mean the dissolution of State and local governments, but opportunity to advance into partnership with the Federal government in solving problems which neither they nor their people can solve for themselves. Clearly the need is for government employees who are trained to be public affairs activists.

The examination which academic institutions are making of their curricula and teaching methods and which government agencies are making of their current and future manpower requirements is as significant a development as any which has taken place in government manpower in the last decade.

Belatedly, but not reluctantly, the Federal government has recognized that it must help to alleviate the manpower crisis facing State and local governments. In response to advice and views obtained from many sources inside and outside the Federal structure, President Johnson has recommended enactment by Congress of two bills designed to assist in upgrading and training State and local governmental personnel. The emphasis of the first bill is of two kinds:

To improve the capability of administrative, professional, and technical personnel who handle over $17 billion of Federal appropriations for grant-in-aid programs and to promote merit system standards.

To bring about an effective partnership between the Federal government and State and municipal governments in recruiting, examining, and exchanging personnel between levels of government.

Separate emphasis is given in the second bill to provision of financial assistance to students who plan public service careers and to colleges and universities for improvement of all kinds of public service education.

CONCLUSION

This attempt to identify and describe some of the recent developments in the field of government manpower has presented difficult choices. Limitations of space required exclusion of many small but significant improvements. Similarly, interpretation and more than superficial discussion of reasons for most of the developments fell into discard. Abandonment of any reporting on "nondevelopments," or failures of worthy proposals, gives a bias which can be justly criticized. Much of the backdrop is indistinct and blurred. For these flaws the author assumes responsibility. It seemed better to highlight clear auguries (and a few "musts") for continued progress toward the goal of sustained competence in government manpower.

America has the right to expect high quality in the men and women who carry on the public's business. And those who choose either careers or limited tours of duty in public service have the right to expect that they will not have to make undue sacrifices for their choice—whether in pay, supplemental benefits, mobility, opportunities to improve their skills, effective use of their talents, or willingness to accept responsibility for their actions.

Although anti-intellectualism has sometimes seemed to dominate the American political scene, there appears to be solid evidence that it does not now control personnel policy. Federal manpower developments in the last nine years point to acceptance of public service as a demanding calling, and public administration as a professional way of life.

27.

THE MERIT SYSTEM, POLITICS, AND POLITICAL MATURITY

Roger W. Jones

For most of the last 80 years, it has been considered imprudent to mention politics and the merit system in the same breath, unless to attack one and extoll the other. I think the time has come to take another approach! It should be decided, in the light of several kinds of evidence, just how much political maturity the merit system has achieved, and how far politics has come toward accepting the merit system and its personnel as adult partners in carrying on governmental functions.

Passage of the Civil Service Act in 1883 effected a legislative settlement of the basic issue of merit appointments and a nonpolitical civil service. But there has been continuing argument for more than 75 years about the kind of structure which should be built on the foundations of the Pendleton Act, and the kind of people who should inhabit that structure. Much of the argument has been concerned with whether politics was still bent upon destroying merit sys-

Reprinted from *Public Personnel Review*, Vol. 25 (January, 1964), pp. 28–34.

tem concepts or, alternatively, whether a merit system extending beyond minor positions would frustrate legitimate political control of governmental actions. Actually, none of the argument settled much either way because events and history kept overtaking its premises.

The masks of good or evil assigned to politics and the merit system, depending upon one's point of view, seems to me useful only as a piece of popular folklore in which the original truth about the spoils system stands as a moral to be remembered, and the masks are but trappings belonging to an earlier stage. New needs, undeniable and important, have produced a sobering and maturing effect upon politicians and civil servants alike.

In short, I believe that politics has acquired a commendable maturity in most of its attitudes towards merit systems. Similarly, I believe that merit systems have achieved a responsible adult understanding of political forces and how to deal with them without destructive partisan involvement. When exceptions to these generalizations appear, they must be watched and worked at. Most of them are immediately recognizable as matters of conscience and proper discipline. As such, they can and should be corrected before they become issues which can be settled only by appeal to public dissatisfaction.

HOW MATURITY DEVELOPED

What has brought about this maturity and why does it augur well for further advances of merit system concepts? It seems to me that at least six interlocking developments are involved. The first three are distillates of experience in the democratic processes of seeking to govern well. The second three reflect new concepts of the role of government in America which have grown up in the twentieth century. Space limitations may cause these six developments to suffer from concentrated summarization, but I think that the main outline can be kept in focus.

1. "A public office is a public trust." Even casual reading of the papers of Presidents from George Washington to Grover Cleveland will uncover that thought expressed in many ways. Most often it is a lonely ideal which Presidents have the chief, and sometimes the sole, responsibility to pursue. After Cleveland's time, and in no small part because of his own example, the moral political man, who had been so avidly sought by the Civil Service reformers, was accepted as a prime moving force in honest and impartial government. Presidents since Cleveland have had a far easier row to hoe in insisting that public officers, as well as public laws, are servants of all the people. As this concept of personal responsibility grew, it extended outward through the ranks of political officers and downward into the ranks of the still struggling, but

rapidly growing, civil service. The use of public office primarily for the assumed good of a political party became as unpopular as it was unwise and irresponsible.

The importance of this trend was not lost upon political parties. It changed their concepts of party responsibility. First, willingness to act was accompanied, at least at the national level, by party concern for considered and positive plans of action, the results of which the party expected to be held to account. Second, administrative efficiency as a demonstrable sign of conscience and maturity in public affairs, became a concern of party leaders as well as the President, and those appointed by him as his chief lieutenants. Both factors produced a need for closer attention to strengthening working level support in a responsible and responsive bureaucracy, and greater utilization of career staff.

POLITICAL NEUTRALITY HAILED

Perhaps equally important, party leaders rallied to the cause of political neutrality in persons charged with the day-to-day administration of tasks allocated to the federal government. As early as 1887, Woodrow Wilson was loudly acclaimed even by the politicians when he said that it was a "plain business necessity" to have a "body of thoroughly trained officials serving during good behavior." This doctrine was a common sense solution, reasonably acceptable to all concerned.

This recognition of public office as a public trust began the real partnership between merit systems staffed by career people and political officers. It brought to each side a sobering realization of their respective opportunities and responsibilities. Emotional reaction to shortcomings and mistakes was replaced slowly but steadily by a more mature reaction of analysis and resolve to do better than call names and assess blame. In time, there was created a climate which made it possible to express loyalty to the government in a broad sense, and to particular programs in the narrower sense. Both conditions were necessary to the development of a mature, career, merit-system body of employees.

Furthermore, there is strong evidence that politicians, instead of civil service reformers, are playing the major part in efforts to obtain a more efficient administration of the public service through the inculcation and defense of the merit system principles. At times, the main thrust of their effort has been blurred by attempts to prove that merit with a partisan bias is to be preferred over merit for its own sake. Actually, this attitude has seldom been predominant. Instead of setting back the cause of merit systems, it has, in substantial and subtle ways, advanced the cause by creating a healthy spirit of competition between solid substantive knowledge and intuitive advocacy of party positions. It is no paradox to count among the strongest supporters of the career service a great many able and influential political officers whose initial hostility toward merit system people and ideals turned into respect, admiration, and a kind of two-fisted advocacy which has helped to bring about the present-day maturity.

LAWS ENFORCE MERIT PRINCIPLES

2. The second distillate to come from matching experience to the need to govern well is the gradual enactment of laws which clarify and nail down Congressional commitment to merit system principles. As evidence accumulated that new programs could be entrusted to civil service staffs and that improved personnel laws might advance government efficiency, Congress took action. The result had the double effect of promoting the growth of a stable career service, and relying upon it to produce politically acceptable results. Over the years it became apparent that Congress wanted the federal government to be a good employer, and also intended to provide guidelines and tools which would give the executive branch no excuse for not having an effective personnel system.

There was an initial period of antagonism to the vigor with which the Civil Service Commission, from Theodore Roosevelt's day on, enforced the Pendleton Act and other personnel legislation. Nevertheless, by the time Roosevelt became President a few years later, Congressional interest had begun to shift. Primary concern with patronage was replaced with a determined effort to play what Wallace Sayre and Fritz Mosher have called an "extensive, continuous, detailed, and intimate role" in personnel management.

Our Constitution did not give Congress authority to direct administrative agencies, but it did reserve to the legislative branch the right to create agencies, to define their personnel policies and program objectives, and to demand reports of stewardship from their officers and employees. The legislative histories of countless laws, and the record of many inquiries into executive actions, present conclusive evidence that close Congressional attention to personnel matters had a maturing effect upon the federal merit system as well as on political officers.

If career officers were inept or obviously inexpert when called before Congressional committees, not only they but their political superiors were hauled up short. The disparaging excuse, "He is only a civil servant," has almost completely disappeared.

EXPEDIENCY NO EXCUSE FOR LAXITY

One special phenomenon deserves attention. Wherever events have overtaken the limitations of the personnel laws and the merit system to produce enough good people at the right time, and fast enough to serve the Government's purpose (as happened in the 1930's and during World War II), there has been a sudden and large influx of employees with a minimum of the usual merit system kinds of screening. One might well expect that there would be pressure to extend these recruiting programs indefinitely. Presidents and the Congress, however, have seen to it that the temporary expedients have lasted only long enough to permit merit system principles to be installed.

At first, there were rather widespread "exemptions from civil service" with subsequent noncompetitive "blanketing in." An alternative to "blanketing in" was transition to independent, agency-wide merit systems comparable with the classified civil service. The personnel systems of the Tennessee Valley Authority and the Atomic Energy Commission are prime examples of this alternative. Later, administrative devices such as special types of exemptions and selective certification of eligibles having special qualifications were accepted as consistent with merit system principles. They continue to be widely used today.

It is both naïve and incorrect to assume that these departures from the standard pattern of merit system principles were designed primarily as a device for obtaining patronage in the old sense of the spoils system. Even if they had been so intended, they were no long-run success. In the first place, despite some of the more unabashed pronouncements of the early New Deal patronage czars— Postmaster General Farley and Emil Hurja—there was a final emphasis on qualifications. This was a far cry from the spoils of a half century earlier.

Political officers of the New Deal were avid partisans, but they had a high sense of responsibility—a desire to make new programs succeed and to give old programs new life. A sense of nonpartisan urgency and excitement also brought forward tens of thousands of candidates for government positions. A large proportion reflected maturity of purpose and had sound qualifications, not mere desire for jobs, badly needed though jobs were by my unemployed generation. The pattern was similar in World War II. Thousands rejected for military service brought amazing dedication and competence into civilian service, and they have stayed on for careers.

Literally hundreds of the most effective and capable senior officers and thousands in lesser positions in the career service started their Federal employment without benefit of competitive certification by the Civil Service Commission. Many certainly received some kind of political clearance before they were appointed, but they responded to the favorable climate for larger loyalties. From the start they were, and they still are, essentially nonpartisan in the discharge of their duties. Certainly both their attitudes and their actions have helped to mature the merit system. Those who have found party politics more stimulating than job challenge generally have left, but not without gaining insights and experience that have brought many of the more able back into government service as political executives. Not a few have been elected to State or national office, and still others have found rewards in service as Congressional staff. With very few exceptions, each has been, in his way, a supporter of the merit system.

CREATION OF CABINET AGENCIES

3. The third major development arising from distillation of experience in the desire to govern well began with the creation of the Department of the Interior in 1849. That Department was the first positive reorganization of governmental responsibilities which sought to bring together activities with definite constituencies and with a common interest in natural resources. Its constituency rapidly became national in scope and one which, while it transcended parties, also created vigorous interparty competition about the best philosophies and policies for the utilization, development, and conservation of natural resources. The department had to build a staff wise enough and permanent enough to keep things sorted out.

It is perhaps significant to note that every department created since 1849 has followed the same pattern of political response to the needs and interests of a national constituency. Also, each department has developed the same mature capacity to suggest for political decision alternative means to attain the statutory goals underlying its creation. Agriculture in 1862, Commerce and Labor in 1903 (reorganized into two departments in 1913), and Health, Education, and Welfare, created by Reorganization Plan in 1953, all have responsibilities to special groups. At the same time, they have both collegiate and individual responsibility to promote the general welfare of the people as a whole.

This capsule view of half of our Cabinet agencies explains, in large measure, why they found it essential to develop and maintain complementary merit system staffs. No other device could provide the personnel necessary to sort out program possibilities with institutional objectivity. And no other system could provide, to a frequently changing group of political officers, the perspective for informed reaction to complex and constant pressures from departmental constituencies.

There was, however, one unfortunate result. Most senior officers were tagged as narrow experts. It was assumed also that it was to the government's advantage, and theirs, for them to remain so. Now, thanks to the growing maturity of our personnel system, we have a broader view. We are beginning to use present-day authorities for education and training to equip able career personnel for wider use. The merit system is ready to accept the challenge of wider use. If political officers find that their mandate can be accomplished better with new faces and fresh points of view, the merit system can provide them. But in doing so, the officers and employees involved are entitled to protection of their career status. The key to ultimate success may well be found in more consistent career planning and better scheduling of long-range manpower requirements.

NEW CONCEPTS OF GOVERNMENT ROLE

The three chief developments which I have classified as reflecting 20th Century concepts of the role of the federal government are probably separable. I think, however, that in combination they produce a better focus, and perhaps, will be more understandable as evidences of growing political maturity. I define them as: (1) need for continuity in operations, (2) growth of executive agencies as a channel of communications between the people and the central government, and (3) the importance of excellence. I shall try to discuss them as parts of a whole which give depth and dimension to the first three points.

Once the people demanded that the federal government recognize the existence of national constituencies with widely differing interests and power, whether in the economy or at the ballot box, growth in the number and complexity of federal programs was certain to take place. But laws are not self-executing, and appropriations do not spend themselves. Both are given direction, force, and meaning only by continuing thought and action of people.

Thought and action, however, are not enough in themselves. They must follow or stem from logical and consistent plans. Such plans require for their execution people with varying skills and motivations—arranged in a pyramidal structure which spreads downward from the one-man apex of the presidency through statutory and administrative lines of supervision and control to the last of the two and a half million civilian employees now on our federal payroll.

Cross currents within the special interests, hopes, desires, fears, and prejudices of national constituencies automatically created rivalries and overlaps, opportunities for alliances and defections, blurred responsibilities, and incontestable needs for leadership and effective communication. Truly national policies needed to be formed, and they, perforce, had to interlock.

As the federal government increased its response to these new forces with new programs and expansion of older activities, it felt within its own structure the same kinds of cross currents. Program expertise or substantive knowledge was not enough to deal with the situation. Either could be trapped in its own burrow, if not highly sensitive to rational continuity in policy developments. Continuing attention to organization and management became essential, and the effective tools appeared to be best forged in the processes of program planning, budgeting, financial control systems, uniform personnel policies, coordination of procurement activities, clear delineation of administrative procedures, and appropriate decentralization of operations to local levels. These needs not only demanded sweeping expansion of the kinds of occupations to be found in federal employment, but they also clearly required both continuity of service and an unremitting search for excellence. It was no longer possible for political officers, no matter how capable, to do all the work or to depend upon assistants without experience.

Public Service Becomes Profession

Furthermore, the successful conduct of federal business required special skills. A new kind of supervisor extending high into staff and program management duties was needed. He must possess a capacity for patient examination of alternatives, analysis of past experience, and acceptance of shared responsibility, which is a peculiar and not unpraiseworthy manifestation of democracy in its modern aspects. But, most of all, there had to be an assured flexible maturity which only a thoroughly trained bureaucracy could provide. In short, thousands upon thousands of federal jobs increasingly demanded something more than integrity of person and purpose, common sense, and determination to work hard. Public administration became a professional way of life, as both federal need and response of our American educational system to that need have demonstrated.

Perhaps nothing had a more maturing effect upon the political sensitivity of the merit system than the communications with the people which resulted from the growth of federal activities. Throughout the 19th Century most communication between the people and the federal government focused in the legislative branch. By 1900, new channels had appeared, and they have increased and deepened rapidly ever since, particularly since 1930. Government went down to the grass roots, not because its officers wanted to sit in the living rooms of America, but because the people wanted to talk and deal at first hand with those who were administering programs affecting them. Occasional contact or correspondence with members of Congress remained available if either the bureaucracy or its political superiors tended to isolate themselves into a remote and arbitrary center of power.

Career Loyalty First

Another factor also was important. Once a federal activity was authorized, both the people and their elected representatives showed a strong disinclination to have it administered under a party label. Career loyalty to program was expected, as was accurate and dispassionate reporting about the administration of that program. In no other way could the effect of plans, policies, and procedures be adequately assessed. Partisan dispute about size, meaning, or content of program remained largely a matter for Congress and political officers to settle. If they could not, then the ballot box might decide the issue. In the meantime, however, the operators at every level were expected to carry out the orders of the day with mature goodwill and judgment. This manifestation of democratic pragmatism resulted in rapid growth of a seasoned willingness on the part of merit system employees to handle the people's business objectively, so far as substance was concerned, and with at least outward neutrality when partisan emotion or party positions came into the picture.

Presidents and their political appointees in the last 30 years have used this new channel of communication with the people as one means of providing executive leadership. By and large, the merit system has met this expression of faith in its capacity and perceptiveness by trustworthy performance. It takes political maturity for career officers to reconcile themselves to association with the kind of power possessed by their non-career superiors. The reverse is equally true. I believe that both recognize that fact, and are prepared to live with it intelligently.

Acceptance of the need for continuity, and the obvious value of good communications between executive agencies and the people, led to new efforts to bring greater excellence to the merit system. An early step in this direction was to establish common standards for qualifications and pay in many types and levels of positions. These had to be supported by better competitive examining techniques, promotion on the basis of demonstrated merit, development of a fair system under which unsatisfactory employees could be dismissed, and good employees protected against arbitrary administrative action. We have not yet achieved full effectiveness in our administration of these comcepts, but I believe we are learning how to make them work as tools, not merely as rules.

Individual Excellence vs. Equality

Perhaps the most serious remaining impediment is the confict between the need for individual excellence and the broad merit system principle of equality—equality of opportunity to compete, equality of opportunity for promotion and transfer, equality of pay for equal work, equality in sharing responsibility. I have doubts whether these concepts, good though they may be in the abstract, are necessary straight across-the-board in a mature personnel system. They can be supplemented by flexible good judgment at both political and career levels in making excellence and equality fit together more effectively.

But here both politics and the merit system tend to be conservatively doubtful of each other's maturity to pioneer in the wilderness of such matters as: New examining techniques; finding a better means of matching candidates with vacancies; flexible salary administration which recognizes other needs than competition for shortage skills; more mobility in and out of government; and the kinds of transfer of responsibility for personnel matters to the agencies that would make the Civil Service Commission more the definer of standards and policies, and less the protector and administrator of procedures and rules. I believe, however, that the history of the partnership makes it safe to predict that these problems, too, will be solved. A solution would benefit the cause of excellence in federal personnel, even though it might change the principle of equality from a position oriented base to a person oriented base.

In conclusion, I want to make a plea to merit systems at every level of government to join hands with politics in an effort to convince America that the high quality of its public servants depends as much upon intellectual attainment as it does upon skill in how to do a job. Politics and the merit system do not have to retreat from intellectual defense of program and policy into a "we do what we are told" kind of attitude of self-justification. The mark of political maturity in any person finds no higher measure than capacity to accept responsibility for his own actions. Anti-intellectualism has sometimes seemed to dominate the American political scene, but it has no place or reason for being in a mature partnership between political executives and a competent merit system.

28.

BUILDING IDENTIFICATION WITH THE FOREST SERVICE

HERBERT KAUFMAN

In addition to picking and advancing men likely to be receptive to communications from the leaders of the agency, and to "training into" these men the capacity and willingness to adhere to preformed decisions announced by the leadership, the Forest Service enjoys—largely as a result of its deliberate efforts, but partly in consequence of fortuitous circumstances—an environment conducive to an almost automatic tendency to conform to those decisions. That environment is a set of conditions promoting identification[1] of the members of the Forest Service with the well-being of the organization, linking their own positions and welfare and futures with those of the agency, fusing their perspectives with those of their colleagues and superiors. It is a set of conditions that sets them apart from all people "outside" the organization, binds them intimately with other organization members; that "injects into the very nervous systems of the organization members the criteria of decision that the organization wishes to employ," and thereby vastly increases the probability that each of them will "make decisions, by himself, as the organization would like him to decide." [2]

Reprinted from Herbert Kaufman, *The Forest Ranger* (Baltimore: The Johns Hopkins Press, 1967), pp. 175–84, 185–86, 187, 189, 190–92, 192–93, 197–99.
[1] The term "identification" is used here in the sense in which it is employed by H. A. Simon, *Administrative Behavior* (New York: The Macmillan Company, 1947, 1957), p. 205: "A person identifies himself with a group when, in making a decision, he evaluates the several alternatives of choice in terms of their consequences for the specified group."
[2] *Ibid.*, p. 103.

Without realizing it, members of the Forest Service thus "internalize" the perceptions, values, and premises of action that prevail in the bureau; unconsciously, very often, they tend to act in the agency-prescribed fashion because that is the way that has become natural to them. Much of what the Service does tends to further this process.

TRANSFER AND PROMOTION

For example, transfer of personnel is treated in the Forest Service as a device for "the development, adjustment and broadening of personnel"; consequently, men are deliberately moved a good deal, particularly during their early years in the agency. The Service does not merely wait until vacancies occur; it shifts men to replace each other in what looks like a vast game of musical chairs, but for the serious purpose of giving them a wide range of experience in preparation for advancement to positions that require a broader understanding of national forest administration than can possibly be gained in long assignments at a single duty station. If transfers can be coupled with promotions, the added incentive to move is provided; however, "horizontal transfers [i.e., in the same grade] also may be proposed as a prerequisite to possible future advancement." If an individual declines a proposed transfer, his status in his old post is not prejudiced, for transfers are recommended, not ordered formally, in most cases,[3] and the *Manual* decrees, "There will be a clear-cut determination that the transfer will not work undue hardship either on the transferee in his personal situation or on the receiving or sending unit"; nevertheless, the *Manual* also warns the Service "is forced to insist that those who wish to advance must, at times, waive personal preferences as to location, make inconvenient moves, and serve where most needed . . ." Hence, when most men are asked to move, they move; it is chiefly old hands with long years of service, no longer interested in rising any higher than they are, who furnish the few declinations. Younger men just starting their careers rarely do, for such an action might impair their futures.

The Rangers studied here have had differing experiences, but all have employment records that reflect the general statements of transfer policy. Of three with more than 20 years in the Forest Service, one was in five locations, one in four, and the third in three within a dozen years; and each moved again at least once later on. As for the younger men, one has served in four places in five years, the other in two places in seven years. Three served in one capacity or another on the staffs of forest supervisors as well as at the district level.

---

[3] One forest supervisor reported he thought he might have been brought up on charges of insubordination if he refused to move. Actually, this seems most unlikely, but this expression of concern by a high-ranking officer suggests how much importance is attached to transfer.

In ten or fifteen years, then, a man in the Forest Service is introduced to many of the problems and practices of national forest administration; he is doubtless "developed, adjusted, and broadened." But the impact of rapid transfer is more profound than training alone; it also builds identifications with the Forest Service as a whole. For during each man's early years, he never has time to sink roots in the communities in which he sojourns so briefly. He gets to know the local people who do the manual work in the woods, but not very well in the short time he spends with them. He barely becomes familiar with an area before he is moved again. Only one thing gives any continuity, any structure, to his otherwise fluid world: the Service. When he reports to a new area, his superior helps him get installed in his new living quarters, introduces him to the townsfolk who will be his neighbors, acquaints him with all the members of the local work force and fire organization, instructs him in the management of the administrative unit, supervises and evaluates and corrects his work, and prepares him to shoulder heavier responsibilities. Whenever a younger man severs his ties in a location to which he has just become adjusted and takes a new place, an experienced Forest Service officer is there to receive him, support him, guide him. To be sure, there are strains and conflicts and frictions, too. But, in general, it appears from the limited evidence of this study that the men who move rapidly are received sympathetically by those to whom they are detailed, and are taken in hand for a time as the personal as well as the official responsibilities of their immediate supervisors.[4]

Thus, the Forest Service acquires a more or less fraternal aura for its newer members. To be sure, it is the organization that uproots and shifts them in the first place, but the hardships are considerably softened by the visible team of friends and colleagues ready to help them and to make the transitions as smooth and pleasant as possible. Moreover, behind the inconveniences stands the comforting knowledge that transfer is preparation for advancement, that every assignment and detail is recorded, adding to qualifications for promotion when the opportunities arise.[5] The impersonality of the system is reduced, the sense of belonging enhanced—particularly since the frequency of transfers to different locations and administrative levels brings many of the men in each region into

---

[4] And, at times, of their subordinates. One nonprofessional employee who had served the Forest Service for almost thirty years on one district worked under a total of thirteen Rangers in that period. He took a paternal interest in the young men who supervised him, and the Ranger under whom he was serving at the time of the interviews for this study confessed his great dependence on the older man. "My chief job," the employee said, "is breaking in Rangers," a job he apparently performed proudly, gently, and with affection for those he helped.

[5] In many organizations, transfer is employed as a sanction, too. Choice assignments go to the men who fit the organization patterns, undesirable ones to those who depart from the preferred patterns, and to newcomers. (The policeman detailed to the "sticks" is a familiar case in point.) No evidence of this strategy was found in the Forest Service in the course of this study, nor did any of the men interviewed at any level seem to consider this a likely penalty. If it is used at all, it is apparently used sparingly. (However, see footnote 3.)

personal contact with each other despite the dispersion of the agency.[6] Every-where, they encounter men with similar interests, similar problems, similar objectives, similar aspirations, similar complaints. They find understanding and appreciation of their problems. Their ties with their fellow-officials are multiplied and deepened. As they become part of the organization, the organiza-tion also becomes part of them.

The opportunity for this process of organizational acculturation to have a chance to work its effects on every executive in the Forest Service (i.e., every officer at the Ranger level or higher) is maximized by two practices: One is a firm system of promotion from within for professional positions in national forest administration. The other is a policy of relatively unhurried promotion.

The Forest Service, at least as far as its professional foresters are concerned, constitutes a classic illustration of a career system. The foresters are com-paratively safe from the vicissitudes of politics and economics; the merit system has guarded them effectively since the first days of the agency, and reductions in appropriations are absorbed more by the large seasonal work force than by permanent officers. With professional staff thus stabilized, the Service has been able to recruit its new professionals to fill entering, sub-Ranger positions, and to fill virtually every job at the Ranger level and above by advancing someone from a lower grade. Says the *Manual*:

In filling a position, we should avoid or minimize the chance of bringing into the Forest Service persons about whom we know less, because of lack of service and salary records, than we do of our personnel and who might therefore be incorrectly appraised by us as being better qualified than our own personnel.

Without exception, all the Rangers interviewed, though professional foresters, served their "apprenticeships" in sub-Ranger grades; in fact, there are no Rangers now in the Service recruited directly from outside the Service. Further-more, almost all the officers higher than Ranger in national forest administration have served as Rangers at some time in their careers. To be sure, there is no single set pattern for advancement; there are many alternative ladders, many different routes upward. But they all have one thing in common: vacancies are filled by promotion and transfer, never (for all practical purposes) by lateral entry.[7] There are no "strangers" in the administrative positions in national forest administration, save for the men junior to the Rangers. There are com-pelling reasons for this practice; it is a long step indeed from forestry school to the heavy responsibilities of district management. Nevertheless, it means the ethos of the agency is subject to few jarring dissonances from within.

---

[6] Inter-regional transfers are not uncommon, but they are far less frequent than intra-regional shifts.

[7] Indeed, every Chief since Gifford Pinchot has come from inside the Service with but one exception, and even he had had extensive Forest Service experience when he was brought back under the New Deal to reorganize the bureau.

Not only are the higher positions filled by men selected from inside the Service, but men in the lower positions ordinarily occupy them long enough for the process of acculturation to take effect. In part, this is a result of circumstances beyond Forest Service control rather than planning; civil service law requires that employees remain in a grade for a year before being promoted, and, in any event, the pyramidal structure of the organization for national forest administration provides fewer openings for advancement than there are men eligible to move ahead. In part, however, it is also deliberate policy; it is estimated by the Service that it will take not less than three years to rise to the command of a Ranger district, and possibly as long as a decade. (One of the Rangers interviewed traversed this distance in less than the minimum, two took three years, one took eight years, and one was twelve in coming up.) The minimum for becoming a forest supervisor is seven or eight years, while seventeen years is a short time to ascend the ladder to regional forester; generally, most men in these positions took longer.[8]

As private industry absorbs ever larger percentages of technically trained foresters, and as intensification of forest management creates additional positions in the Forest Service, the rate of advancement tends to become more rapid. Nonetheless, forest officers are exposed for substantial periods to the environment of the agency before they are appointed to executive positions, and they remain always under the surveillance of men who have spent practically their whole adult lives in Forest Service employ. They are absorbed into the organization by a kind of gradual social osmosis, during which they, in turn, absorb many of the prevailing values, assumptions, and customary modes of operation.

Seniority does not automatically bring promotion. Periodically, the regional foresters and assistant regional foresters in each region assemble to review the records of the men under them and determine what their assignments should be. Length of service is a factor in their judgments, to be sure, but it is far outweighed by other elements—principally the evaluation of each man by his immediate superior, by the personnel management division of the regional office, and by the regional forester and his staff (most of whom will have met almost all the professional foresters in their jurisdiction in the course of visits, conferences, inspections, training meetings, and conventions of professional societies and associations, and who also have access to inspection reports, civil service performance ratings, and other appraisals of accomplishment and potential). Some men will be transferred to round out their experience; others will be left where they are to season; still others will be advanced; a number are repeatedly passed

---

[8] "The average grade 9 Forester is 41 years old and reached his present grade in 8 years. For GS-11 the same statistic is 44 years of age and 15 years of service to reach it; for GS-12, the age is 48 and elapsed time from entry to present grade is 22 years; and for GS-13, age 59, elapsed time is 23 years." W. A. Elkins, *Professional Manpower for the Forest Service* (mimeographed by the Forest Service, 1957), p. 5.

over. Some never get beyond the Ranger level, and a few serve out their years without even achieving command of their own districts; some shoot comparatively meteorically through the hierarchy, and many a veteran Ranger has been inspected by a man the Ranger himself trained a few years earlier.

It does not take most men long to learn there are attributes rewarded by the organization, and those who yearn to rise deliberately cultivate those attributes if they can. There is a striving on the part of many to demonstrate they fit into the approved pattern, and even those who profess to be indifferent to promotion cannot help picking up many of the traits of the culture in which they work. For those who fit the pattern naturally, this takes no conscious effort. For others, it takes conscious self-appraisal and adjustment; as one Ranger who failed to advance from his sub-Ranger assignments during his early years put it, "I changed my outlook and reorganized myself and my own line of thinking," and the transformation was followed by promotion. In other words, promotion is a sanction, a reward or a punishment based on excellence on the job, but excellence on the job is in practice measured by the proven predisposition to behave in the organizationally desired fashion rather than just by technical proficiency.

Promotion and transfer are thus far more than methods of staffing. As practiced in the Forest Service, they also foster in each officer identification with the agency—with its survival and welfare, with its goals, with its procedures, with its members.

THE USE OF SYMBOLS

Identification is heightened by the use of symbols. Perhaps the outstanding ones are the uniform and the badge. The whole purpose of uniforms and badges is to identify the members of organizations, to differentiate the wearers from everyone else and to link them with each other. The livery and insignia show at a glance who is "in" an agency and who is not, and establish authority and status at a glance. And they also foster a group spirit and unit, a "we" feeling, a common bond. . . .

HEADQUARTERS CONSULTATION WITH FIELD OFFICERS

Identification is further intensified by the Forest Service practice of sounding out field opinion on questions affecting field administration. Social psychologists have indicated that participation in the formulation of organization decisions tends to promote identification.[9] The Forest Service provides many opportunities and channels for such participation.

For instance, the field is sometimes polled formally. As noted earlier, the Washington office requested opinions from the field on whether uniforms should be required, and also on the style of the uniform; the attitudes of members of the Service down to the Ranger district level were obtained, and the policy eventually adopted was based in large part on their reactions. In another case, the Washington staff, anticipating legislation on overtime pay, proposed a tentative stand for the Service to present to the Secretary of Agriculture and Congress; the circular was transmitted to the field with the comment, "As usual we wish, of course, to check with you and have your advice on these—and any other related problems—before making specific recommendations to higher authority." (Reports from the regional foresters on opinion in their jurisdictions occasionally indicated that the regional foresters did not agree with the judgments of their subordinates, but they dutifully transmitted those judgments just the same. A couple of regional foresters reported comments obliquely critical of the Washington office on the overtime issue, urging headquarters to simplify and stabilize policy.) . . .

Over and above the polling techniques, the Forest Service provides many additional opportunities for field men to make their views known to their superiors. Indeed, these may be even more effective means of encouraging an upward flow of ideas and opinions from the field, for they do not restrict the comments to particular subjects. Thus, as previously noted, few men who are under inspection pass up the chance to ventilate their suggestions and criticisms —both during working hours, and even more so in the informal social hours after the close of business; this practice is not only tolerated, but encouraged, and members of the Service insist that their recommendations and complaints *do* get back to the higher levels, sometimes generate action, and do not (unless carried to an extreme) result in injury to the sources for being outspoken.

---

[9] See, for example, G. W. Allport, "The Psychology of Identification," in S. D. Hoslett (ed.), *Human Factors in Management* (1st ed., New York: Harper & Bros., 1946): "We are learning some of the conditions in which reactivity [i.e., "rebellion against authority, . . . disaffection of all sorts"] does decline. . . . Opportunities for consultation on personal problems are, somewhat surprisingly, found to be important. And as members of S.P.S.S.I. [Society for the Psychological Study of Social Issues] have shown, group decision, open discussion, and the retraining of leaders in accordance with democratic standards yield remarkable results. One of Lewin's discoveries in this connection is especially revealing. People who dislike a certain food are resistant to pressure put upon them in the form of persuasion and request; but when the individual himself as a member of a group votes, after discussion, to alter his food habits, his eagerness to reach his goal is independent of his personal like or dislike. In other words, a person ceases to be reactive and contrary in respect to a desirable course of conduct only when he himself has had a hand in declaring such a course of conduct to be desirable." (P. 259) See also M. Sherif and H. Cantril, *The Psychology of Ego-Involvements* (New York: John Wiley & Sons, Inc., 1947), pp. 369–71.

Since Rangers are inspected by supervisors' offices, regional offices, and from time to time as sample districts in their regions by the Washington office, this often permits them to air their convictions quite effectively. . . .

Conferences for budgetary, policy, or training purposes afford additional opportunities for field officers to impress their concepts on their superiors. When Rangers assemble to work out financial plans with their supervisors and the supervisors' staffs, they come with proposals of their own with regard to their programs for the fiscal period, and they bargain with each other and with their superiors to get as close to their objectives as they can. When district programs are coordinated to mesh with forest policy, forest policy is often adjusted to fit district needs as the Rangers see them. . . .

Furthermore, the Rangers are told over and over again that they are the pillars on which the Forest Service rests. According to the *Forest Service Manual* itself:

The Forest Service is dedicated to the principle that resource management begins—and belongs—on the ground. It is logical, therefore, that the ranger district constitutes the backbone of the organization.

And the Chief of the agency, in a speech to the 1958 convention of the National Woolgrowers Association (who have often been critical of Forest Service grazing policy), told the assembled sheep raisers:

The man who is responsible for making the initial decisions for the management of your individual allotments [of grazing privileges] is the district ranger. He lives in your community as a neighbor; his children go to the same schools as yours do. You can be sure that he would not propose livestock reductions that sometimes lead to bitter controversy if he were not thoroughly convinced this action is necessary . . .

We have often heard it said that the rangers and supervisors are good guys but that they are merely doing what they are told to do by some bureaucrat in Washington. It would be utterly impossible for the small staff we have in Washington to be sufficiently familiar with conditions on all of the national forests to make or even to suggest what specific decisions should be made as to the management of individual allotments. Of necessity we have had to delegate responsibility and authority to the men on the ground. We, in Washington, establish general policies and procedures. We make periodic checks and inspections to determine how well the policies and procedures are being carried out, but the responsibility for making the decisions and the authority to carry them out has been delegated to the men on the forests and ranger districts.

Lest it be thought he was trying to evade his own responsibilities, the Chief added:

In the final analysis I am responsible for the action of all the members of the Forest Service. Although we delegate responsibility and authority all the way down the line, I cannot shift the responsibility for the work of the Forest Service to anyone else's shoulders. You might say I "share" my responsibilities with the regional foresters, forest supervisors, and rangers, but in sharing it I do not escape any of the responsibility for what happens.

Skeptics might argue the speech was a smokescreen, although it is not so regarded in the Service. But even a skeptic cannot help but be impressed with the fact that the field men are so visible and respected in their communities that the Chief himself—whether engaged in a maneuver to relieve his office of pressure or sincerely depicting the realities of decision-making in his bureau—sometimes takes refuge behind them. It is persuasive evidence that they make important decisions in the Forest Service, and play significant roles in the administration of the agency. The speech was circulated to all the members of the Service on national forests in grazing regions.

Actually, the field men do not seem to need convincing on this point. If anything, it would appear difficult to *alter* their convictions about it. For their day-to-day experience has already persuaded them that all higher headquarters are heavily dependent on them—not only for executing policy pronouncements, but in formulating them as well. . . .

It does not seem likely that all the types and evidences of field participation in agency decisions were deliberately instituted or adduced to create the feeling of identification with job and organization that social psychologists say is linked with a sense of participation. Rather, the various kinds of consultation probably grew out of the nature of resource management problems. But it makes little difference for this study whether the practice was designed to enhance the sense of participation or was simply the incidental fruit of the pursuit of other objectives. The fact is, field officers *do* participate, and to a degree they seem to believe is significant. Thus, they come to identify themselves with the Forest Service and its decisions. . . .

THE INTERNALIZATION OF FOREST SERVICE
PERCEPTIONS, VALUES, AND PREMISES OF ACTION

Much that happens to a professional forester in the Forest Service thus tends to tighten the links binding him to the organization. His experiences and his environment gradually infuse into him a view of the world and a hierarchy of preferences coinciding with those of his colleagues. They tie him to his fellows, to the agency. They engender a "militant and corporate spirit," an organized "self-consciousness," dedication to the organization and its objectives, and a fierce pride in the Service. They practically merge the individual's identity with the identity of the organization; the organization is as much a part of the members as they are of it. At least some of the practices described above were probably initiated with this in mind, but a number were apparently adopted for other reasons and contributed to this result more or less accidentally. Still, whatever the purposes, one outcome of the practices is that field officers (among others) make their administrative decisions in terms of the consequences for the Forest

Service, and in terms of criteria the leaders of the Forest Service wish them to employ.

The Result: Voluntary Conformity

Forest officers are selected in a fashion that winnows out many of the men who probably lack the inherent predisposition to conform to the preformed decisions of the Forest Service, and that guarantees at least a minimum level of technical competence.   Their competence is broadened and deepened by post-entry training, both in-service and outside, and by placement, transfer, and promotion policies; the methods of improving technical skill also intensify the predisposition to conform. The predisposition is strengthened by generating identification with the agency (which at the same time adds to understanding of the announced agency objectives). As a consequence, officers of the Forest Service conform to agency decisions not simply because they have to, but because they want to. And they can because they have been equipped to do so.

"Wanting" to conform is used here not to mean an abstract desire to be obedient the way a child wants to be "good" but not to do any of the things that being good means to his parents. Rather, it is employed to mean wishing to do as a matter of personal preference the things that happen to be required. It is in *this* sense Forest Service personnel want to conform. Often, confronted by a situation in the field, there is a course of action they would "instinctively" like to follow, that seems "clearly" to be the "best" and "proper" one; a good deal of the time, this "happens" to be the action prescribed by the Service. That is, they are not consciously "conforming"; they are merely doing what is "right." Inevitably, there is little consciousness on their part of the deliberate search for the appropriate "instincts" by the leaders of the Forest Service, and of the deliberate efforts to cultivate these and weed out others.

Indeed, even when men are overruled—when their "instincts" do not move them in the same directions as their superiors—their adherence to the provisions of the higher decision comes in a sense from inside themselves. They rarely persist in opposition after judgment has been rendered, or engage in administrative sabotage, or carry appeals to higher levels. In part, of course, this obedience is based on the risks of such action.[10] In addition, however, it rests on the widely expressed sentiment that "there's no other way to run a big organization." They value the organization more than they value getting their own way; they therefore carry out directives they opposed, because doing so is "necessary" and "right"—and, though they do not seem to be aware of it, because this feeling is carefully nurtured by the organization.

---

[10] Other factors in obedience are discussed in H. A. Simon, D. W. Smithburg, and V. A. Thompson, *Public Administration* (New York: Alfred A. Knopf, Inc., 1950), pp. 188–201.

29.

THE RISE OF A "NEW POLITICS"

HERBERT KAUFMAN

The expansion of the range of its activities as well as the number of federal employees subject to its authority made the Civil Service Commission the kingpin of federal personnel administration. Formally, the personnel function was widely scattered. The basic framework was provided by legislation and by Executive Orders of the President issued under authority conferred on him both by statute and by the Constitution directly. More detailed regulations were issued by the Civil Service Commission, whose staff then either executed the provisions of the regulations or exercised surveillance over the line agencies to ensure compliance. The bulk of the personnel actions in the federal government were taken by the dozens of departments and independent agencies that make up the executive branch, operating within the laws, rules, and regulations, and under the watchful eye of the Civil Service Commission as well as with its advice, assistance, and stimulation. It was the administrators who actually appointed, assigned, promoted, transferred, trained, disciplined, and discharged government employees. After 1938, by presidential order, each major agency had a personnel office, headed by an agency personnel officer, to assist with these functions at the agency level and to serve as liaison with the Commission. In practice, however, the Commission played a key role in initiating most of the legislation and Executive Orders under which it operates, its views were invariably solicited when any other source initiated proposals, it was consulted by the heads of other agencies who did not want to run afoul of its enforcement powers, and it enjoyed strong support among civic organizations and among unions and associations of federal workers. From 1958 on, its members have had six-year, overlapping terms instead of serving at the pleasure of the President. In the partitioned world of federal personnel management, there was probably no single dominant force, but the Civil Service Commission was unquestionably the central figure.

The Rise of a "New Politics"

In but 80 years, despite great political swings, enormous governmental growth, deep depressions, and global wars, the process of neutralizing the civil service

Herbert Kaufman, "The Growth of the Federal Personnel System" in *The Federal Government Service*, Wallace S. Sayre, ed., © 1965. Reprinted by permission of Prentice-Hall Inc., Englewood Cliffs, New Jersey.

and promoting the merit system thus progressed from hesitant, uncertain be-ginnings to almost total victory in the federal government.

To be sure, it did not completely isolate the civil service from politics, a con-dition a democratic polity could not tolerate even if the condition were attainable. In point of fact, however, it is not attainable. Administrative agencies get their appropriations from Congress. Their enabling legislation comes from Congress. They are subject to investigation by Congress, and many have felt the fury of a member of the legislature embarked on a vendetta against them. They therefore do not ignore an applicant who is referred to them by someone on Capitol Hill. They do not casually send away an applicant with an introduction from a power-ful party official. This does not mean the law is violated; rather, it means that there are ways of accommodating pressures within the letter of the law, which federal administrators, in order to protect their agencies and their programs, soon learn. The vigilance of the Civil Service Commission and the increasing profes-sionalization of the federal government service tend to keep these practices at a minimum. But they are often there.

These practices are not initiated by politicians exclusively. Organization survi-val in the constantly shifting governmental environment often calls for the great-est managerial skill, expertness not only at yielding to pressure regarding per-sonnel administration but also at building systems of defensive alliances to stabilize the environment. For federal administrators, this has come to mean collabora-tion with congressional committees and with interest groups, both of which can have a profound impact on the fate of an agency, either for better or for worse. In this situation, adept use of discretion in wielding the power of appointment can be an important instrument, and it is no doubt used in this way from time to time. So it is not merely a matter of politicians assaulting the purity of the classified service; the "victim" is frequently willing, frequently the instigator. The classified service is party to a new kind of political cooperation.

It is important to distinguish between the politics played by the civil service prior to the Civil Service Act and the kind practiced after the merit system was firmly established. Originally, civil servants engaged in political activity to further the cause of a particular candidate or group of candidates. After the installation of the merit system and the growth of agency consciousness and professional-ization, the end of political collaboration was defense of the agency and its pro-gram, and was practiced by both parties. This was politics of a different kind.

So the neutralization of the civil service did not entirely stamp out all vestiges of the "old" politics, and it intensified new elements on the political scene. Nevertheless, the efforts to isolate administration from party politics through personnel management, in a span of 80 years, attained a level of completeness that its originators would doubtless regard as fulfilling their fondest hopes were they alive to see the fruit born of their labors.

NEW DILEMMAS

The Line Administrators Complain

As the merit system began to push toward its upper limits, words of criticism were heard from the very people the system was designed to assist and protect— the line administrators. Top management personnel of the line agencies, their organizations now protected against the raids of the spoilsmen, began to pray for deliverance from their guardians. They did not deny that it would be impossible to conduct effective administrative operations if their staffs were inexpert because of the influence of politics, but they contended that good administration is difficult also if personnel management is taken partly out of their hands.

No adequate explanation of this seeming paradox is possible unless two closely related facts are taken into account. One is that the federal government moved into areas calling for increasingly intensive specialization on the part of its work force described earlier. The other is that the component elements of the civil service, developing a continuity (as a result of the merit system) and a sense of the importance and difficulty of their work (as a result of specialization), began to display an awareness of themselves as identifiable bodies in society and a deep interest in expanding and perfecting the programs they administered; in a word, they gradually came to exhibit the characteristics of a series of sizable bureaucracies. Party loyalty of the patronage days gave way to program and professional loyalty.

As a result, the leaders of the line agencies grew more intolerant of incompetence than even the reformers; they developed a greater interest than the reformers in the ability of their own membership. In the first place, dedicated as they were to the welfare of their agencies and their programs, they were unwilling to see these jeopardized by lack of proficiency; they had an ideological stake to preserve. In the second place, the *esprit de corps* of the organizations and their prestige in the community engendered insistence by members of line organizations upon capable personnel; identification with, and pride in, his group constituted another stake for each civil servant. In the third place, as government workers became more and more skilled and professional, they tended to grow resentful of newcomers who received the same rewards without the same qualifications; this was another investment for them to keep safe. All in all, then, the forces at work among government employees thrust in the direction of higher attainment. To be sure, there were tendencies in the *other* direction, too, generated by the new conditions of government work. Members of tightly-knit organizations become emotionally attached to each other and to the old ways of doing things, and when it became necessary to make any changes in either or both, strong currents of resistance appeared; hardening of administrative arteries is another facet of bureaucratization. But the fact remains that federal government employment, considered over-all, had become almost a profession, and federal officials were as concerned about professional standards for their membership as anyone else.

Yet, when the officers of the line agencies tried to take personnel actions considered routine in the business world, they were on occasion prevented from doing what they wished by the interpretations placed on laws, rules, and regulations by the staff of the Civil Service Commission. Often, therefore, before even making a move, agencies checked with the Commission staff to see if the proposal would meet with disapproval. And even if they secured approval, it was sometimes slow in coming. Let them try to fill a vacancy, to transfer a man, to promote someone, to increase an employee's pay by changing the position-class to which his job is allocated, to take any of a host of such ordinary steps, and they encountered the Commission.

To a line officer, this hardly made sense. He was not less anxious than the Commission to protect the merit system. Moreover, he was apt to feel he knew the employment situation in his technical field a good deal better than anyone on the Commission. Yet he felt hemmed in from every side. The labyrinthine procedures developed to keep politics out of administration were alleged to have grown into prisons for administrators, and many administrators charged that they, like the spoilsmen, were treated by the Commission as the enemy. Their every move was suspect; the very machinery constructed to promote energetic, creative, imaginative administration, they bewailed, now obstructed it. This complaint was common in Washington, an oft-repeated story in administrative circles.

The Chief Administrator Hampered

At the same time that the professionalization of the civil service was producing dissatisfaction with the Civil Service Commission among line administrators, a kind of uneasiness sprang up among other students and practitioners of American government.

The great, sprawling complex of organizations that constitutes the executive branch was something of a patchwork, put together by bits and pieces, each added as the need for it was felt, piled on the rest without any real effort at system or order. As one outstanding administrative committee once put it, it grew like a farm—a wing added to the house now, a new barn put up later, a shed built some other time, a silo at one stage, a corn crib at another, until it was spread over the landscape in a haphazard and thoroughly confusing way. America's pragmatic genius assembled this crazy quilt because problems were attacked as they arose; it might have been done more tidily had we been functioning on a smaller scale, but we were conquering a vast and rich continent, and the rough edges of the structures we built in the process could be smoothed off whenever there was time. Besides, through the spoils system, the parties exerted substantial influence on the shape of American public administration; the parties are highly decentralized, and they therefore helped to produce a fragmented pattern of administrative organization.

Each fragment, despite its formal subordinancy to the President, became a local center of power. Congress, not out of preference but out of necessity, delegated to them authority to "sub-legislate"—that is, to issue, within the framework provided by statute, rules and regulations binding upon the people to whom they applied—and to make administrative adjudications—that is, to decide cases involving individual citizens in a quasi-judicial fashion. At first, the courts attacked this blurring of what had traditionally been considered the boundaries of the separate legislative, executive, and judicial branches, but eventually, they reluctantly admitted the inevitability of the new phenomenon in view of the needs of an industrial civilization, and administrative law took its place beside the common law, the law of equity, and statutory law. For a long time, each agency secured its own appropriations directly from Congress; there was no central review. Each agency became influential with respect to the formulation of legislation in its own sphere of expertness, and much of the legislation enacted by Congress originated with the agencies themselves. Every segment of the executive branch thus became a decision-making center, and if not every decision, considered individually, was of great significance, all of them taken in the aggregate were of tremendous importance.

Congress, too, is fragmented; the real work of Congress is done in its numerous committees, and it is in the committees that much of the real legislative power resides. With a decentralized party system, a diffused legislature, a splintered executive, and a plethora of interest groups exerting pressure at all these points, there was for a long time no place at all in the government where a coordinated policy could be worked out and a unified set of plans devised for accomplishing the ends selected. The operation of the government in each policy area devolved upon clusters of administrative agencies, congressional committees, and interest groups.

One consequence of this arrangement—or non-arrangement—with its lack of central control and direction, was the rise of familiar administrative defects in a most acute form. Agencies not only duplicated each other's work; one would sometimes unwittingly undo what others had carefully done. They not only pursued contradictory ends; they sometimes became involved in administrative wars of incredible bitterness and long duration over the shaping of policy and its execution.

A second consequence was the appearance of "self-directing bureaucracies," the agencies that began to function almost autonomously, behaving less like parts of a large team than as individual, independent establishments. With the end of the spoils system, the civil service grew steadily into a corps of specialists outlasting political officers. The politicians come and go; the civil servants remain. The transients are amateurs, laymen; the permanent body is expert. In the relations between the two groups, it was often the political officers who felt themselves at a disadvantage, psychologically, factually, technically.

If there had not been the rise of this autonomy, the defects of unplanned administrative growth might have been easier to remedy; if it were easier to control all the executive agencies, it might have been simpler to do away with the clashes and contradictions and other inefficiencies that characterize the executive branch. It is not surprising, therefore, that insulation of the civil service from political influence came under questioning. Is it possible, asked some political scientists, that insulation from political influence contributes to insulation from political control (a problem that never occurred under the spoils system)? Is it possible, inquired some administrative experts, that the way our system of personnel administration operates deprives the President, as Chief Administrator of the nation, of an important tool of management? Neither political scientists nor administrative experts advocated return to the spoils system, nor did they ascribe to one cause a complex phenomenon that was obviously the product of a large number of things. All that their questions implied is that the triumph of the merit system may have brought its own administrative difficulties.

Problems of Party and Policy Leadership

But administrative problems were not the only ones intensified by the rise of the isolated personnel system. Jobs in the government service had long been used as political currency by Presidents, enabling them to establish their authority as leader of their parties and to provide leadership in the formulation and execution of policy; a fragmented legislative body is far less able to perform these functions. Every President has found patronage a device to provide himself with the necessary currency. But once the merit system had been pushed almost to its limit, and the likelihood of the rise of new parallel bureaucracies comparable to those built under President Franklin D. Roosevelt declined, the supply of currency of this kind was almost at an end—as long as Chief Executives continued to respect the practices that have now become personnel traditions.

There is perhaps insufficient evidence to reach any hard and fast conclusions about the impact of this state of affairs on presidential-congressional relations, but there is enough to warrant some concern about the attenuation of leadership in the federal government and the tendency of the government to become paralyzed as a result of conflict among its component political (as well as administrative) units, or as a consequence of the simultaneous pursuit of mutually contradictory ends by its political (as well as administrative) constituent elements. It appears to be more than a coincidence that these symptoms were to grow most acute just at the time the patronage was reduced to a very low point. That is not to say the decline of patronage is the only cause or that restoring patronage the most advisable remedy. But the decline of patronage brought in its train many consequences besides those advertised by the reformers, and some of them were almost as vexing as the conditions the reformers sought to relieve.

NEW TRENDS AND NEW BATTLES

Anti-Isolationism

If the isolation of the civil service from politics produced these new dilemmas, then it was almost inevitable that the political scientists and administrative experts concerned with these problems should begin to wonder whether the process of neutralization had possibly gone too far. While recognizing the worst evils of the spoils system, they also concluded that the neutralization of federal employment had done its work; the quarantine had almost obliterated spoils while permitting new standards, and new forces defending those standards, to take root and flourish. If so, the time had come to return authority and discretion over personnel matters to the executive and administrative officers charged with the conduct of the government's business. The risks of revival of the spoils system seemed low; the promise of gains, in terms of solutions of the new problems, seemed great. As the new critics of "excessive" isolation saw things, the major need of government in the twentieth century was to strengthen leadership—in the departments and agencies, in the executive branch, in the processes of policy formation.

Much of the effort to strengthen leadership had little to do with the wall between politicians and the civil service. It was directed at other targets—the provision of staff assistance to Chief Executives, for example; the improvement of financial management; the rationalization of administrative structure; and delegation to executives of broader powers to reorganize the units and agencies under their command. At the presidential level, in pursuit of these goals, the movement produced the executive budget, an expanded Executive Office of the President, Reorganization Acts conferring on the President authorization (subject to congressional veto) to shift and regroup administrative agencies. At the departmental level, too, administrative management was strengthened by provision of expert staff aides, addition of undersecretaries and assistant secretaries to help top officials, and by employment of special assistants.[1] The advocates of better management achieved many notable successes in many areas.

But while they recommended sweeping changes in personnel organization, designed in large part to increase managerial discretion in this field as well, their

---

[1] See Commission on Organization of the Executive Branch of the Government, *Task Force Report on Personnel and Civil Service* (February 1955), pp. 204–209.

accomplishments were more modest. For their proposals would have reduced the isolation of the civil service from managerial direction, and this ran counter to what had become a deeply entrenched, widely accepted tradition. So when the President's Committee on Administrative Management recommended in 1937 that the Civil Service Commission be abolished, that the responsibility for personnel management be assigned to a personnel director serving in the President's immediate official family, and that the guardianship of the merit system be charged to a Civil Service Board with advisory and investigatory powers but no administrative authority, the recommendations were rejected by Congress. The intent of the proposals was to return to the Chief Executive the personnel powers that were his in form, but in substance were actually wielded by a Civil Service Commission functioning, like other specialized agencies, with remarkable independence. A single officer, close to the President and the problems of the line agencies, would be more apt to interpret his mission in terms of program accomplishments, it was contended, than in terms of technical compliance with detailed regulations regardless of the effect on program. Many reformers, the bureaucracies, and the federal employees' unions and associations resisted vigorously, and with telling effect.

Nevertheless, the pressure of the anti-isolationists continued, and the first Hoover Commission, which reported in 1949, accepted a modified version of their recommendations. The Commission advised that the administrative functions of the Civil Service Commission (examinations, position-classifications, enforcement, internal operation, etc.) be separated from its rule-making and appellate duties, the former to be assigned to the chairman alone (assisted by an executive director), the latter to be discharged by the three commissioners sitting together. President Truman offered a Reorganization Plan to put these provisions into force, and Congress did not veto the Plan; in 1949, this major change took effect.

The Hoover Commission also recommended that personnel responsibilities be decentralized to the departments and agencies. The majority, however, adopted such modest proposals in this direction that one of the commissioners, James K. Pollock, filed a minority opinion taking the majority to task, urging a full and complete decentralization, and contending that such a course of action would make it possible and reasonable to follow the advice of the Committee on Administrative Management a decade earlier regarding the dissolution of the Civil Service Commission. His presentation is still one of the most vigorous and uncompromising statements of the anti-isolationist viewpoint ever issued by a responsible and authoritative public figure, but its effect on practice at the time was negligible. It is true, however, that anti-isolationist sentiment did find its way into practice on a limited basis. The Classification Act of 1949 authorized allocation of positions to position-classes by agencies without prior reference to the Civil Service Commission (though subject to post-audit and revision by the

Commission, and even to revocation of the allocation authority). The Commission granted agencies a larger role in the examining process, and in other personnel management procedures, subject to its supervision. It also strengthened its field organization to speed service to the nine-tenths of the federal bureaucracy located outside Washington. If the strides toward anti-isolation of the government service were not momentous, they were nevertheless steps in the anti-isolationist direction. And further measures of this limited kind were taken from time to time in the years that followed.

A more dramatic stride in the same direction occurred in 1953, when President Eisenhower, having named the new chairman of the Civil Service Commission, also named him Presidential Adviser on Personnel Management, invited him to attend cabinet meetings, and relied on him as his personal lieutenant in connection with all federal personnel matters. In many respects, this came closer to the suggestions of the 1937 Committee on Administrative Management than any change in structure and relationships ever made. The tide seemed to be turning.

The Movement Stalled

But there were tides running in the opposite direction, too. The report on personnel and civil service of the Second Hoover Commission in 1955, in the long tradition of neutralization, tried to draw a precise line between political posts and permanent positions, so that "career administrators . . . should be relieved by the noncareer executives of responsibility for advocacy or defense of policies and programs and should be kept out of direct participation in political controversies." The wall of separation, originally erected to remove civil servants from the pressures and temptations of political parties, was thus to be raised another notch to keep them from the presentation or justification of their agency programs and functions. To assist department and agency heads, a large number of new political executive positions were introduced in the federal government, and the incumbents did take on many of the responsibilities urged by the Hoover Commission. While the insulation of the permanent service was something less than total, for Congress always guards jealously its access to administrative agencies, the philosophy of isolation thus continued to advance.

In the same vein was another—and, as it turned out, far more controversial—proposal of the Hoover Commission: the establishment of a Senior Civil Service. A logical product of the emphasis on separating political from career executives, it was a plan to meet the need for a reservoir of executive talent experienced in the ways of the government service, available for flexible assignment, capable of furnishing essential administrative counsel to the noncareer officials, yet easily replaceable at the discretion of agency chiefs. To this end, the plan proposed putting rank in the men (an elite corps) rather than in the jobs they would occupy, and called for them to be completely neutral politically, even to the extent "that they must avoid such emotional attachment to the policies of any administration that they cannot accept change and work in harmony with new leaders." Thus, the requirements of the government for high-level managers was to be met without blurring the line between politics and administration. The plan was never put into effect, partly because high civil servants themselves were uneasy about it, and partly because the idea of an elite group was not easy to reconcile with American governmental traditions. But the fact that it was not immediately adopted did not mean it was dead; the idea would be actively, and heatedly, discussed for many years, yet another manifestation of the deep commitment to the belief in neutralization that moved the civil service reformers for generations.

There were still other indications that the anti-isolationists would have heavy going. In 1958, as noted earlier, the Civil Service commissioners were given fixed terms instead of serving at the pleasure of the President, thus carrying the concept of civil service autonomy even further than the original reformers ever intended. In 1957, the relations between the President and the chairman of the Civil Service Commission (tightened in 1953 when President Eisenhower brought his chairman into the White House circle) were loosened again and restored to pre-1953 separatism when a new post of Special (presidential) Assistant for Personnel Management, divorced from the Commission, was created. (This was applauded by the advocates of total neutralization, who feared that the guardian functions of the Commission would be impaired by close association of the chairman and the President.) Furthermore, in 1961, the Commission's report would proclaim with pride that "for the first time in the Commission's 78-year history, all three Commissioners are career men in the executive branch of the Government," so that the self-directing tendencies of the civil service were further reinforced. And the "decentralization" announced in 1949 ended up essentially as a delegation of detail, but not of control, to the line administrators: "Decentralization," wrote Professor Van Riper, "deteriorated into a type of workload decentralization which discouraged initiative and permitted little time for any imaginative contemplation of personnel management. . . . Greater return of the personnel staff function into the main stream of line management would have to await major modification of a myriad of restrictive federal statutes." More than 15 years after the 1949 decentralization, the "rigid net of procedural controls" had not been significantly relaxed.

On balance, the efforts to return personnel management from its position of splendid isolation to a role as an instrument of administration in the hands of the government's executives must be regarded as having made little headway even after more than a quarter-century. The 1937 report of the President's Committee on Administrative Management remained the landmark of this philosophy of the personnel function in government, but the goal it set was not much closer in 1964 than it was when the report was first issued.

A New Field of Battle

It is most unlikely that the slow progress of the anti-isolationists will end in the demise of their movement. The lesson of American political history is that the proponents of any significant change win their points only if they have patience and persistence; civil service reform itself is an outstanding illustration of this principle. Moreover, the factors that produce the anti-isolation movement are likely to grow in intensity rather than to diminish; the demands for government service in a rapidly increasing population and an expanding economy will ineluctably lead to a larger federal establishment, and the pressure for executive discretion in managing this vast enterprise will rise correspondingly. The battle will not end in this century.

The outcome in the twentieth century is by no means beyond doubt. The advocates of managerial discretion in personnel matters, who correspond in background and objectives to the civil service reformers of the nineteenth century, have demonstrated that they will not let the issue drop. They are informed and articulate. The conditions they seek to correct will in all probability grow more pressing with the passage of time. And they will have the oblique support of those who support Presidents in policy matters. The resources behind critics who think neutralization of the government service has been carried to excessive lengths are thus substantial.

But the defenders of the isolation of the civil service have impressive sources of support, too. Working for them is the long history of glorification of traditional civil service reform, which has produced an atmosphere in which any who question the system on any grounds are suspect. The specter of the spoils system is a powerful ally that is easily evoked. A large coalition of groups with vested ideological, emotional, or material interests in the traditional system has developed: large numbers of federal employees, their unions, and their associations, for example, are concerned about the job rights and security built up slowly and painfully over the years under the traditional system. The Civil Service Commission and departmental experts in the intricacies of civil service procedures are unfriendly to changes that might erode the basis of their expertise. Many civil service reform organizations and civic groups find it difficult to abandon or substantially modify the time-honored premises on which they have operated, and with which they have scored so many victories. Congressmen fear loss of control over the executive agencies through the lines of access and influence established over time, and congressional committees as expert as any personnel specialists in the complexities of the old arrangements are hostile to modifications that would reduce their power. Interest groups enjoying stable relationships with the federal officials and employees who serve or regulate them are uneasy about the possibilities that greater presidential discretion over personnel might disrupt those relationships. The array of forces supporting the *status quo* is formidable.

Thus do the outlines of controversy over the federal government service shape up for the last third of the twentieth century. Some observers see in the approaching struggles a setting back of the clock of history. Others see only the correction of an imbalance brought on by excessive reforming zeal. Still others view emerging events as the swinging of the pendulum of time, the continuation of an inescapable cycle in the political affairs of men. One thing, however, is certain: the fights will be vigorous and unremitting. When values clash in the political arena, as in this case the fear of spoils conflicts with the hope for managerial effectiveness, an enduring settlement is seldom easy to find. What kind of settlement is reached in the case of the federal government service, if one is reached at all, will affect not only the service itself, but, in various ways, all the institutions of government and politics at the national level (and perhaps other levels) in the United States.

30.

ENTER THE PERSONNEL GENERALIST

HARRY R. KNUDSON, JR.

Traditionally, the hallmark of the personnel function has been specialization—a specialization which has its core in the highly trained, experienced personnel man who is equipped to handle a specific type of problem or assignment. A look at the personnel department's organization chart in almost any large company will reveal a veritable multitude of employment specialists, training specialists, wage and salary specialists, employee relations specialists, pension and benefit specialists, and so on—their number and type depending, of course, on the nature of the company's activities, its size, and the attitude of top management toward the personnel function. In most cases, each of these specialists reports to a functional manager (the employment manager or the training director) and deals with all levels and types of employees.

In many instances, this traditional arrangement has been unsuccessful, however, in accomplishing the stated objective of personnel administration: helping line management to maximize the profit potential by obtaining, main-

Reprinted by permission of the publisher from "Enter the Personnel Generalist," by H. R. Knudson, Jr., *Personnel*, March/April 1960. © 1960 by the American Management Association, Inc.

taining, developing, and utilizing an effective work force. In fact, while the traditional approach to personnel administration is meritorious in theory, it often prevents the personnel organization from operating at its optimum effectiveness. Consider, for example, the following disadvantages of specializing the personnel function:

In many instances, line management must deal with several representatives of the personnel department—a different person for each type of situation—thus preventing a high degree of rapport and empathy from developing between personnel specialists and line management.

The personnel specialist normally operates throughout the entire organization in his specialty. Thus, his contact with any particular line supervisor, or the line management of any given segment of the organization, is occasional and brief—again hindering the development of a close, continuing relationship between personnel specialists and line managers.

The abilities and experience of personnel representatives at the "working level" are often too insufficient for them to obtain the confidence and respect of line management.

Specialization limits even the best personnel representatives to operating in a narrow, sometimes artificial, area of the employer-employee relationship.

Specialization increases the tendency for a personnel representative to perform his function from his own office, rather than in the work area, thus adding another block to effective communications and understanding.

Recognizing these and other limitations to the traditional organization of personnel activities, progressive managements have been experimenting recently with a new idea—the concept of the personnel generalist. While his appearance on the business scene has revealed him to be essentially similar to his predecessor, the traditional personnel man, some noteworthy differences in his activities and in the philosophy that underlies his existence mark his debut as a significant advancement in the theory and practice of personnel administration.

The concept of the personnel generalist is deceptively simple: A qualified personnel administrator is assigned to each significant segment or group of employees within the organization. Each of these personnel generalists is supported by a small, centralized personnel unit at the company level, each one reports to the manager of his group, and each is responsible for the major personnel functions of selection, orientation, employee appraisal and development, salary administration, employee relations, policy and procedure formulation, and so on, depending upon the nature of the unit to which he is assigned. Thus, the personnel generalist performs for his unit all but two of the usual personnel functions: (1) Supervision of clerical functions, such as record keeping, reports and announcements, and paper-work processing of new employees, which is the responsibility of the central personnel unit, and (2) recruiting, which is carried out on a companywide basis by a recruiting manager and his assistants.

In effect, then, the concept gives each personnel administrator or generalist a group of employees for whom he has primary personnel responsibility. He may, of course, ask for assistance from the central personnel department (which has already assisted him appreciably by undertaking the major clerical tasks) if unusually difficult situations arise requiring highly specialized treatment. Insofar as the employees of his group are concerned, however, he *is* the personnel department.

It is important to note that this new concept does not change the basic relationship between personnel and line management. The personnel administrator acts in a staff capacity to the line supervisor of his group—he does not usurp line management's authority; he does not make line decisions. His close relationship with the group enables him, however, to provide *continuing* service, thus making line management more effective. To emphasize the significance of this point, and to illustrate how the existence of the personnel generalist eliminates many of the disadvantages of the traditional personnel arrangement, let us examine some of the reasoning upon which the new concept is based.

First of all, let us consider the prime requirement of an effective personnel program: its acceptance by the employees. This acceptance depends mainly upon the extent to which the program satisfies the actual needs of the employees concerned, the extent to which key personnel have an opportunity to participate in the program, and the effectiveness of the personnel representative in advocating or implementing it.

Since the attitudes, abilities, work needs, values, and interests of employees differ from one group to another, it is imperative to give special attention to employee groups with similar characteristics and interests (for example, engineers and their supporting personnel) if the needs of the employees are to be satisfied. But the possibility of one personnel representative having the varieties of skills, insights, tools, techniques, and personal qualities to effectively deal with all these varying employee groups is somewhat remote. The concept of the personnel generalist is, therefore, a logical alternative.

The other two ingredients of an accepted and thus a successful personnel program—the participation of key personnel and the effectiveness of the personnel representative himself — are closely tied in with each other, since the effectiveness of the personnel representative is predicated upon his ability to win personal acceptance, which, in turn, rests upon his establishing and maintaining a close and continuing relationship with the employees. The personnel generalist is better able to fulfill these requirements than the traditional personnel man mainly because located as he is within the working area itself, he is in daily contact with the operating people. This gives him a first-hand opportunity to become acquainted with and share their problems and thus to provide continuing assistance in all areas of personnel administration. This principal feature of the concept of the personnel generalist—close physical proximity to the employees he is responsible for—cannot be overstressed. Its results touch upon many of the factors inherent in good personnel management.

ADVANTAGES OF THE CONCEPT

For one thing, most personnel difficulties assume the proportions they do because of the traditional personnel man's failure to either anticipate their occurrence or to handle them properly in their early stages. The personnel generalist, however, because he works with operating personnel on a day-to-day basis, is in a good position to learn of potential problem areas and to suggest appropriate action before the problem reaches serious proportions.

Then, too, most successful management depends upon a supervisor's knowledge of the feelings, attitudes, and reactions of his subordinates. A personnel representative in daily contact with operating personnel and physically located within their domain is in a unique position to accurately interpret and advise management of the state of employee morale, and to suggest intelligent and practical approaches to keep it at a high level.

The personnel generalist also plays an important role in maintaining or increasing individual productivity. For example, effective work performance is often diminished because of problems inherent in the working environment or in the personal lives of the workers, such as friction between employees, between employees and supervisors, between one working group and another, or between a man and his wife. These problems can be minimized by understanding and intelligent counsel—but first, they must be brought out into the open. And the probability of an employee making his problem known is infinitely greater if the personnel representative is readily available, is personally known by the employee, and has the employee's respect, confidence, and acceptance.

Another main cause of employee dissatisfaction is misinformation or the lack of information. This may well result in low productivity, lack of teamwork, or excessive turnover and absenteeism. Again, a personnel representative who is in continuing contact with a particular segment of the work force is in an excellent position to advise management of the need for additional information within the segment, as well as to recommend methods by which the information could be more effectively disseminated. He is equally well placed to promote upward communications—an important aspect of employee relations that often gets little more than perfunctory attention at best.

AIDING SELF-DEVELOPMENT

Another key phase of personnel management upon which the concept of the personnel generalist leaves its mark is that of self-development. Many of the skills an executive must develop, if he does not already intuitively possess them, have to do with the management of people. Of fundamental importance here is an awareness and understanding of human behavior, to which there is probably no surer path than the endeavor to learn more about oneself. A personnel representative in daily contact with supervisory personnel is in a strong position to provide competent assistance and proper motivation and direction to line management in this crucial area of self-development.

Aside from placing the personnel administrator in the midst of the fray, so to speak, the concept of the personnel generalist has other features to recommend it. For one thing, a personnel representative, whose responsibilities encompass all the major personnel functions, is able to bring the experience and knowledge gained in one area into play in performing other duties. Thus, the concept of the personnel generalist provides an integrated personnel program in which all the important aspects in selecting, motivating, and developing employees become one continuing effort.

Also, under the generalist concept, since the personnel representatives do not purport to be specialists themselves, they are in a position to want, need, and make maximum use of the highly specialized and truly professional assistance available in the central personnel staff. This has the side effect of diminishing the friction that often occurs when one specialist attempts to assist another of lesser eminence.

Finally, under the new concept, a personnel representative is released in large measure from the overwhelming burden of paper work that seems to characterize so many personnel operations. He is thus free to devote his time and energies to the more subtle problems involving the work force that often defy quantitative treatment, yet are the essential ingredients in a successful personnel program.

These, then, are the positive features of the concept of the personnel generalist. It will be admitted that they are impressive and reflect some serious thinking about the nature of personnel administration. But any new idea is bound to have some disadvantages and before going overboard with this one, it would be as well to see what the snags are, too.

DISADVANTAGES OF THE CONCEPT

The personnel generalist system has three principal drawbacks: (1) The difficulty of maintaining a uniform and consistent personnel program; (2) expense; and (3) the difficulty of finding capable personnel.

The first disadvantage has its root in the number of personnel administrators involved in the system. Because each one handles similar personnel functions and yet is relatively dissociated from the others, continuity and uniformity of action can be a problem. This dissociation, however, is inherent in the concept of the personnel generalist—it is, in fact, the very heart of the concept. (The personnel administrator is not a member of the central personnel group—he reports only to the manager of the group he is serving.)

This disadvantage can be minimized, however, by a well-organized central personnel department with clear-cut policies and procedures and a capable personnel director who has an explicit understanding that one of his major responsibilities is to assure maximum communications between himself and each personnel administrator, as well as among the personnel administrators themselves. Without such direction, the generalist arrangement could lose much of its effectiveness, since each of its segments could conceivably be operating under significantly different policies and procedures.

The second disadvantage of the personnel generalist concept—its expense— follows from the type of person the program requires. While in actual numbers the new type of organization calls for about the same staff as is required in the traditional personnel department, the personnel generalist must be someone of considerably broader talents and experience than his traditional, specialist counterpart.

He must first be able to gain the acceptance of a whole group of employees, often of high caliber, on a continuing basis and then to take the appropriate actions to alleviate their personnel problems. In effect, therefore, the position of a personnel generalist requires someone capable of holding a position that would appear at a much higher level on a traditional personnel organization chart. This means higher salaries than would be paid to the general run of personnel specialists. But in relation to the significant investment in manpower that is becoming increasingly typical of most business concerns, the additional cost required to adequately staff a personnel organization that will yield a more effective personnel program is nominal indeed.

The third disadvantage—that of finding capable personnel to function as generalists—also arises from the high-caliber type of person required. This difficulty, while not insurmountable, should not be taken lightly, for it is crucial to the success of the program. The job of personnel generalist is not a training position for a junior personnel executive and must not be considered as such. If the system is to function effectively, it must be staffed by experienced, competent people fully capable of meeting the considerable demands of the job.

ONE COMPANY'S EXPERIENCE

So far, we have discussed the concept of the personnel generalist in theory only. But what about its practicality—does it really work? To answer this question, suppose we take a look at the personnel program based on the concept of the personnel generalist that has been in operation at the Wayland Laboratory of the Raytheon Company since the summer of 1958.

Raytheon's Wayland Laboratory, with approximately 1,500 employees, is composed of several groups of highly trained electronic and technical specialists performing classified research on a contract basis for the government. The labor force consists primarily of graduate engineers and sub-professional technical employees, with the usual complement of support and clerical personnel. In dealing with Wayland's large number of highly educated professional workers —many working on the "team" basis typical of research activities and many having a common interest in and affiliation with professional societies outside the corporate structure—the shortcomings of the traditional specialist concept of personnel administration were very pronounced. It was in an attempt to find a better method of serving this unique, high-caliber group of employees that the personnel generalist system was initiated.

A personnel administrator was assigned to the manager of each of the Laboratory's larger departments. Each administrator was given the responsibility for all personnel functions for professional and sub-professional employees within his department, with the exception of recruiting and the following central office personnel functions: central processing activities, files, reports, employee benefit administration, coordination of employee services, and all personnel activities for clerical and support employees. Special technical assistance was made available from the corporate personnel staff as needed. The program has retained this organizational structure since its inception, although some personnel changes have taken place.

The personnel administrators were selected after extremely careful screening of prospects from the entire Raytheon organization. Each one had had several years' experience with the company in important positions, either in personnel or in general administration, or both. Some of the personnel generalists had basic technical backgrounds which, it was felt, would enhance their ability to deal effectively with technical people. All of them seemed to have an intuitive understanding of people—a quality that was specifically sought out in the screening process and one that has, undoubtedly, greatly attributed to the initial success of the program.

RESULTS OF THE PROGRAM

In fact, the extensive screening process and the obvious capabilities of the personnel generalists probably accounted in large measure for their almost immediate acceptance by both the department managers and employees. The comments of the department managers, many of whom had extensive technical backgrounds, reflected an appreciation of the opportunity to have a qualified person working with them on a continuing basis to help them with problems that they themselves often felt less than expert in solving. The managers also expressed enthusiasm for having professional assistance in many areas which they felt were important, but to which they had not previously given adequate attention.

The employees, too, were uniformly enthusiastic about having someone to whom they could look for advice and assistance. Surprisingly, they showed no indications of dissatisfaction with the new arrangement. Thus, while unexpressed dissatisfaction may have existed, the employees apparently whole-heartedly welcomed the innovation. The addition to the department of a qualified person whose primary responsibility was their welfare seemed, in fact, to give them a feeling of prestige.

The high degree of enthusiasm on the part of the personnel administrators was also impressive. Although well aware that the results of the new system depended largely upon their own personal capabilities, they were, nevertheless, unanimously confident in its success. In other words, while they recognized the tremendous personal challenge in their new assignments, they also recognized the outstanding opportunity they were being afforded to contribute to the well-being of the organization.

The initial contacts of the administrators with their groups were characterized by seemingly endless demands for all kinds of specific information: "How often will my performance be evaluated?" "What effect will my extracurricular activities have on my progress with the company?" "How do I stand in the pension program?" "Will the company pay for graduate engineering courses?" These and similar questions were easily answered by the administrators. Incidentally, the extent of these questions, which was entirely unanticipated, indicated very clearly to management the shortcomings of their previous personnel operations—which, heretofore, were assumed to have been at least reasonably effective.

In addition to the demands for specific information, the administrators received a significant number of requests for general information about the company and its policies. It seemed that, in some instances, employees had received false impressions through misinterpretation of policy, rumor, or personal biases. Although this type of question was, of course, more difficult to deal with and often required more time and attention than a very specific question, the administrators were able, for the most part, to answer them satisfactorily. It was interesting to note that few employees attempted to use the new system to present obviously unfounded criticisms or unique considerations that would result only in their own personal gain. Evidently, the acceptance of the administrators was so complete that it almost precluded this type of action.

The personnel administrators did find, however, that many employees wished to discuss problems that were essentially personal in nature—problems ranging from their difficulties in finding housing to their children's poor school performance. Obviously, the administrators were not able to solve all these problems, but the employees now had a place to bring them for sympathetic understanding —and they seemed to be doing so.

Of particular significance was the tendency, on the part of many employees, to just "sorta talk things over" with the administrator, without discussing any particular problem. This was considered to be a positive indication that the administrator was becoming an integral part of his group. Not only was he accepted passively, as a non-disrupting element, but he was actually considered a member of the group. While this may have been partly attributable to the physical availability of the administrators, it seems likely that their outstanding personal qualities mainly accounted for their complete acceptance.

SOME FUTURE CONSIDERATIONS

Though these initial successes were mostly confined to the area of improved communicatons with employeees, some longer-range objectives of the program were also achieved to a rewarding degree. Each of the administrators spent considerable time with his department manager—giving advice on personnel problems, providing technical information, and generally being of assistance whenever possible. As a result of this close and continuing contact, many technically oriented managers have openly expressed a greater realization of the value of the human assets under their control. This may be only talk—but it is something of an achievement in so short a period of time, and certainly an encouraging harbinger of things to come.

It should be added that, as the program has progressed, the generalists themselves have revealed an increasing competence and confidence in handling all aspects of personnel administration rather than one specialized function. They have matured in their positions and feel that they have had a unique opportunity for their own development.

Of course, all has not been entirely smooth sailing, and there have been some problems mainly arising from situations in which there is a dual responsibility for personnel activities. For example, the individual administrators and the central personnel department share some responsibility in certain phases of employee processing, salary administration, employee counseling, and union activities. While some minor difficulties have been encountered here, viewed in the total achievements of the program to date, they are insignificant. Certainly, they can be eliminated as more experience with the generalist system is gained.

Although it is still too early to formally evaluate how far the Raytheon program is living up to expectations, all indications are that it will prove to be more effective than the traditional methods of personnel administration—at least in the Raytheon situation. Management has expressed a high degree of enthusiasm for it, and plans are currently being made to install similar programs in other Raytheon facilities.

To sum up, then, while the concept of the personnel generalist still has to meet the test of time, it is based on a well-thought-out philosophy of personnel administration and should, therefore, be of considerable interest to progressive managements dissatisfied with the traditional organization of the personnel function. Indeed, it may well turn out that the personnel generalist may prove to be *the* personnel man of the future.

31.

RANK IN MAN OR JOB? BOTH!

HAROLD H. LEICH

It is a widely held belief that there are two separate, incompatible, and even antagonistic personnel systems in the world—a personal rank system centering attention on the individual and his qualifications, title, and status opposed by a job-oriented system concentrating attention on distinctions in job levels with little regard for the persons filling the jobs. The British Civil Service, the U.S. Foreign Service, and military personnel plans often are cited as examples of the first system. The typical U.S. and Canadian civil service plans are considered to be examples of the second.

There is much evidence, however, that the differences are becoming smaller in the United States and that, in many essentials, placement systems centering on rank-in-the-man and those centering on rank-in-the-job are now similar. Our experience demonstrates, for example, that a career service (in which young people are brought into the organization to remain and advance throughout their working lives) is possible in job-oriented systems and, in fact, is thriving in many federal agencies. Under good personnel management in either system, the rank of the man matches the rank of his job.

Recent studies of public personnel practices recognize that characteristics of the two systems generally are mixed, and O. Glenn Stahl concludes: "The proper balance between the position-oriented and person-oriented approaches will continue for some time to be one of the challenging problems of public personnel administration." [1]

Reprinted from *Public Administration Review*, Vol. XX, No. 2 (Spring, 1960), pp. 92–99.
[1] O. Glenn Stahl, *Public Personnel Administration* (4th ed.; New York: Harper & Brothers, 1956), pp. 174–82. See also Norman John Powell, *Personnel Administration in Government* (Englewood Cliffs, N.J.: Prentice-Hall, Inc., 1956), pp. 345–49.

COMPARISON OF THE TWO SYSTEMS

Listed below are advantages often cited for "rank-in-the-man," not necessarily inherent but tending to emerge from it.

1. Original recruitment of persons of broad general competence for advancement in lifetime careers rather than recruitment of persons of specific competence to immediate vacancies.
2. Less emphasis on specialized experience or training for initial selection and for later advancement in the service.
3. Systematic training for higher responsibilities.
4. Ability of administrators to assign personnel to a wide variety of posts, of higher or lower status than normally required by the personal rank of the members, without change in rank or compensation.
5. Agreement by the member to accept any type of assignment in any location.
6. Careful screening for promotion (above the lower ranks) and often "selection out" for those who fail of promotion.

Military staffing, for example, displays these "personal rank" advantages. Young men of high general competence are carefully selected, given broad training for the military profession, and commissioned as ensigns or second lieutenants. Thus they achieve personal rank on the lowest step of a career ladder. They may be given a variety of assignments without changes in personal rank. After suitable experience and further systematic training, they are advanced to successively higher ranks until they reach a point in midcareer where selection for advancement becomes a matter of intense competition with their peers. Such selections are on a service-wide basis by a board of senior officers who have access to detailed service records and fitness reports. Members who fail of selection for advancement may be retained for several years, or, as they approach retirement age, they may be "selected out" on a pension.

Now, for comparison purposes, we turn to an example of the opposite approach—that part of the U.S. Federal Civil Service that operates under the Classification Act (for brevity called the Federal Civil Service from here on). The Second Hoover Commission described it as clearly rank-in-the-job: "The Civil Service System emphasizes positions, not people. Jobs are classified, ranked, rated, and their compensation determined on the bland assumption that they can always be filled like so many jugs, merely by turning the tap." [2]

But surprisingly, this prototype of the job-rank system has many of the personal-rank advantages. Let us compare current practice in the Federal Civil Service with these six advantages of personal-rank listed above.

---

[2] U.S. Commission on Organization of the Executive Branch of the Government, *Personnel and Civil Service: A Report to the Congress* (Washington, D.C.: U.S. Government Printing Office, 1955), pp. 37–38.

1. Recruitment for Lifetime Careers

In the Federal Civil Service we find two kinds of staffing patterns—"program staffing," when already trained and experienced persons are recruited for specific assignments above the entrance level without much regard to their potential for future advancement, and "career staffing," when persons of high general competence but without advanced training or experience are recruited for lifetime careers with the expectation that they will be developed for promotion by further training and rotational assignments.[3]

The Federal Civil Service has been thought of as relying largely on program staffing. But in 1956 the Civil Service Commission found from a 30-day sample survey of promotions in the competitive civil service (excluding the postal service) that there were 22 promotions per 1,000 employees compared to 19 outside appointments. In the middle ranks of the classified service, from which man-agerial-professional employees might be expected to come, there were 25 promotions per 1,000 for GS-8 through 11 employees, 21 per 1,000 for GS-12 and up. Almost surely, the outside appointments in GS-12 or higher positions were fewer than 19 per 1,000. Each employee being promoted to GS-11 or above had entered the service, on the average, more than 6 grades below the grade to which he was promoted. The Federal Civil Service, then, is operating to a considerable extent on a career staffing basis, according to this sample.

A somewhat related conclusion was reached by the personnel task force of the Second Hoover Commission after making a sample survey of the careers of top federal officials: "It appears then that several older agencies have developed their own career systems."

There are numerous examples of career services which flourish under the formal position classification plan of the Federal Civil Service—for example, the Forest Service of the Department of Agriculture, the Geological Survey and National Park Service of the Department of the Interior, the National Bureau of Standards of the Department of Commerce, and the Ammunition Inspector Group in Army Ordnance. Some of these go back many years and are almost as complete a career system as the U.S. Foreign Service or the military staff system. Furthermore, the Civil Service Commission has urged agencies without career staffing plans to consider their advantages.[4] Thus it seems that a formal position classification plan does not prevent the growth of a career staffing plan.

---

[3] This concept of program staffing vs. career staffing comes from the writings of Paul David, most recently with Ross Pollock in *Executives for Government* (Washington, D.C.: The Brookings Institution, 1957), pp. 46–66.

[4] U.S. Civil Service Commission, *Career Staffing—A Method of Manpower Planning* (Washington, D.C.: U.S. Government Printing Office, 1956).

At the same time, the point should be made that program staffing, too, has its advantages in appropriate situations: to man a new program, to provide needed specialists, or to revitalize a career leadership group.

It is true that the examples given above emphasize careers within one federal bureau—comparatively unifunctional and homogeneous—rather than across departmental lines. But apparently to an increasing extent, careers in the Federal Civil Service are being pursued across departmental lines, especially in staff activities such as personnel and budget administration. In several ways the Civil Service Commission tries to aid the process. Departmental placement officers meet every week in Washington to exchange information on vacancies and available candidates.[5] A roster maintained in the Commission's Examining Division lists the records of most federal personnel officials for referral to agencies having appropriate vacancies. A similar roster of federal scientists and engineers at GS-13 and above was established recently at the request of the President's Committee on Engineers and Scientists for Federal Government Programs. About 22,000 names are listed; some 6,000 referrals have been made.

Nevertheless, more could certainly be done to supplement the efforts of individuals to find careers on a governmentwide basis. One valiant effort of the past was the Commission's Interdepartmental Placement Service, a punch-card roster of all federal employees (except the postal service). Established in 1940, the IPS recorded the qualifications of nearly a million employees and referred names on request to federal agencies. But wartime turnover became so rapid that the job of maintaining current records bogged down, and the unit was therefore abolished.[6]

Another effort, though on a much smaller scale, was the "Federal Administrator" written test conducted during the Korean emergency to identify administrative talent in nondefense agencies for referral to defense activities. Some 4,700 employees at GS-12 and above completed the test. A number of the higher-scoring candidates were transferred to defense agencies as a result of this program.[7]

A recent small-scale study shows some hopeful results. Since January 1950 the Civil Service Commission has appointed 92 junior management assistants (now called management interns) to its own staff. By late 1959 (with exactly one decade of experience), 33 had transferred to other federal agencies, 31 still worked for the Commission, and 28 had left the federal service. As regrettable

---

[5] Clyde C. Hall, "Interdepartmental Placement," 11 *Personnel Administration* 14–17 (May, 1949).

[6] W. P. Lehman, "The Interdepartmental Placement Service," 4 *Personnel Administration* 1–7 (November, 1941).

[7] Milton M. Mandell, "Obtaining Administrative Personnel for Defense Agencies," 16 *Public Administration Review* 269–271 (Autumn, 1956).

as the loss of 33 trained and able people might be to the Commission, the net result for a government career service is healthy.[8]

In March, 1960 the Commission announced the establishment of a new Office of Career Development placed directly under the Commission's Executive Director. This was in response to memoranda from the President and his Special Assistant for Personnel Management requesting the Commission to assist in devising methods for better executive selection and development in the career service. One of the planned actions is the establishment of an inventory of career executive talent at the top levels to give placement assistance to agency heads. Here, at last, may be a workable answer to the problem of facilitating interdepartmental transfer of federal executives.

2. Less Emphasis on Specialized Experience or Training

This is virtually a corollary of the first point. The Federal Service Entrance Examination and particularly its management intern option provide good examples of a calculated effort to select potential generalists in the field of public administration. By planned training and rotational assignments the new recruits are prepared for higher level responsibilities. The formal position classification system does not hamper this effort. In fact, by clearly delineating the various occupations to be found in the service, the classification plan helps point out the administrative fields such as budgeting, personnel, public relations, and program management into which potential generalists can be systematically rotated on their way up the ladder.

By executive development and training agreements, the Civil Service Commission encourages agencies to break down the walls between job specialties and allow employees to broaden their experience. For example, a scientist who shows an aptitude for administration can be moved into a personnel or budget job, despite his lack of formal qualifications, to prepare him for supervisory duties in his own field of science.[9]

The Army and particularly its Ordnance Corps have taken the leadership in showing how related specialized occupations can be combined into larger career fields to strengthen the career staffing concept for Army civilians and develop generalists in addition to specialists. For example, the narrow occupations of auditing, cost accounting, budgeting, management analysis, and progress

---

[8] Valid conclusions on career opportunities in the Federal Civil Service are difficult to reach because of the lack of a systematic data-collection plan which would show current rates of promotions and transfers by occupation, grade, and agency (preferably by educational attainment). The few sample surveys cited merely dipped into the vast unknown.

[9] For additional discussion on specialization, see Harold H. Leich, "Job Specialization in the Federal Service—Good or Bad?" 20 *Personnel Administration* 28–35 (March–April, 1957).

reporting can be combined into the broad career field of comptrollership, with freedom of movement among these specialties for competent trainees.[10]

3. Systematic Training for Advancement

Though some federal agencies have long trained their employees for career advancement, many could not use outside teaching institutions until July 1958 when the Government Employees Training Act clearly authorized and even directed agency heads to map out training programs in addition to encouraging employee self-development. However, few federal agencies now provide the systematic training for civilians that military officers have at many stages of their careers.

One recent development under the new Training Act is highly encouraging. The Civil Service Commission now publishes information on agency training programs in the Washington area that can be opened to employees of other federal agencies. To an increasing extent, the Commission is organizing its own courses open to selected employees of all agencies. This activity will become a part of the new Office of Career Development.

4. Flexibility of Assignment to Higher or Lower Posts

It is a principle of good personnel management to make the best possible fit between the qualifications of the employee and the requirements of his assignment. Normally we would not want to use a staff member in an assignment of *lower* rank or status than called for by his qualifications (his personal rank). To use extreme examples, an admiral does not command a landing craft, an ambassador does not stamp visas. Likewise, we usually would not want to place a staff member in an assignment of *higher* rank or status than called for by his qualifications.

Nevertheless, there are occasions when it makes sense to violate the "square peg-square hole" principle to some degree. In emergencies it is handy to be able to assign a person to a higher or lower billet than is usual for his rank or to move him laterally into a spot for which he does not have the expected qualifications.

In a military system this is easily done. But it can be done just as easily under the formal position classification plan of the Federal Civil Service. Administrators are authorized to "detail" employees to higher or lower grade jobs or laterally to jobs for which the employee is not formally qualified. Details may be

---

[10] Department of the Army, *Planning and Developing Civilian Career Programs* (December 10, 1959). See also Truman Benedict and LaRoy J. Bove, "The Career Cone: A Visual Planning Tool," 20 *Public Personnel Review* 138–144 (April, 1959).

made for six months without permission from the Civil Service Commission and can be extended beyond that time with Commission approval. Whether or not the term "detail" is used, other formal job classification plans have long provided this kind of flexibility.[11]

Some time limit on service at an inappropriate grade level would seem desirable in any personnel system. If the emergency assignment goes on indefinitely, the staff member is being under or over paid. The military system recognizes this and provides for "spot" promotions. Thus in wartime, a lieutenant who succeeded to command of a destroyer escort would be given a spot promotion to lieutenant commander for the duration of his command, even though his length of service would not entitle him to the permanent rank.

Detailing staff members to higher grade assignments is a good training device and gives a promising staff member a trial in a post of greater responsibility. If he makes good, the system will eventually catch up with him and he will receive a formal promotion to match his enhanced performance. On the other hand, if he proves unequal to the task, he can be returned to his appropriate level with minimum embarrassment.

Arguing strongly for this flexibility of assigning corps members to varied posts without loss of pay or status, the Second Hoover Commission's Senior Civil Service proposal called for personal rank. Yet two pages later the report recommended that corps members be given higher pay when they serve in higher ranking positions and be returned to lower rates of pay in lower ranking posts.[12]

A recent staff study of federal pay practices concluded that, while the personal contribution of the individual should be recognized in his compensation, a formal "rank-in-the-man" system should not be used at the higher levels as long as job-rank is used at lower levels. The staff report did propose two changes to attain some of the objectives of a "personal rank" system: (1) more attention should be paid to a position's long-range demands, those that can be expected throughout the entire cycle of the assignment, and (2) time limits on detail assignments should be sufficiently long to meet management needs.[13]

5. Freedom to Move Members to Any Task Anywhere

Supposedly, the personal rank system allows administrators to shuffle members anywhere on the world chess board, but under the position concept the staff

---

[11] *Position-Classification in the Public Service*, a report submitted to the Civil Service Assembly by the Committee on Position-Classification and Pay Plans in the Public Service, Ismar Baruch, Chairman (1941), pp. 132–133.

[12] *Op. cit.*, p. 40 and p. 42.

[13] Interdepartmental Committee on Civilian Compensation, "Report of Study, Civilian Pay Plans and Pay Benefits within the Executive Branch" (1958) as quoted in Department of Navy, *Manual for Position Classifiers* (May, 1959), p. 24.

member must first give his consent to a move. The Second Hoover Commission used this as another argument to support a personal rank system for the Senior Civil Service.

Actually this factor of obligation to move has nothing to do with either the rank concept or the position concept. In the U.S. Forest Service, which operates under a position classification plan, it is a tradition of the Service to accept assignment wherever headquarters requests. Civil Service investigators sign a written agreement when hired that they will serve wherever needed. There are many other organizations in the Federal Civil Service whose employees traditionally move when they are asked, just as military officers do.

As a matter of legal right, a federal administrator can ask any of his employees to move to an appropriate new assignment or a new location whether or not there is a written agreement. An employee who refuses to go can be discharged, although these things are usually settled by discussion.[14]

It is still true that military and foreign service personnel are shifted far more frequently than civilians in the rest of the service. The Congress has recognized the peripatetic nature of these careers and arranged government quarters, commissaries, and allowances for added expenses. More adequate arrangements along these lines will be needed if the Federal Civil Service, or parts of it, are ever to match the mobility of the personal rank services.

6. Systematic Screening for Promotion

Here is probably the area of greatest divergence between the personal rank systems and the Federal Civil Service as it operates today. Typical "rank-in-the-man" systems rely on central screening of all members of one rank for promotion to the next higher rank. In some cases "selection out" with liberal retirement benefits follows for those who are not selected for promotion. Under this "up or out" plan the entire "class" that entered together at the bottom some years before is considered as a unit for promotion to higher rank. Therefore the officer's immediate assignment prior to consideration for promotion is of relatively little importance; he is assured of consideration on his entire record wherever he may be serving.

In most parts of the Federal Civil Service, promotions are made to specific vacancies, and the special qualifications desirable for each vacancy are given considerable weight. Persons in the immediate office who have picked up directly-relevant experience naturally enjoy an advantage over their contemporaries in

---

[14] For a defense of the Hoover Commission recommendations against opponents of the right to reassign, see William Pincus, "The Opposition to the Senior Civil Service," 18 *Public Administration Review* 324 (Autumn, 1958).

other offices who lack the special experience but may have far superior all-around abilities.

This means, of course, that chance may play a large part in the relative progress of persons of equal ability. In one regional office there may be an unusual amount of turnover for several years, and anyone with moderate ability can be pushed along as fast as the regulations allow. In another regional office of the same agency turnover may be exceptionally low in the same years, and excellent people may stagnate. This tendency can be partly overcome by a good centralized promotion system; the new merit promotion program recently inaugurated throughout the service requires agencies to use broad areas of consideration.[15]

Another difference between the two systems is that in the military services, an officer who is merely adequate does not remain long to clutter up his rank. If he is not good enough to be promoted he does not stay. Presumably all in one rank form a homogeneous group of "comers" on their way up the ladder. In the Federal Civil Service, there is less stigma in being passed over. The person who is not fit for advancement may be retained at his present grade for half a generation. For the individual, that is certainly more humane than the military approach, and from the social viewpoint it may represent better utilization of abilities, but it does not lead to the high morale and keen rivalry that one finds in a military corps.

The Federal Civil Service career groups mentioned under Number 1, though usually providing centralized screening for promotions, have no "selection out" process.

* * * *

The Federal Civil Service, then, is moving toward many of the goals for which advocates urge a rank-in-the-man system. The common targets of the two personnel systems can be illustrated further by showing that each pays attention to the rank of both the job and the man.

PERSONAL RANK IN THE FEDERAL CIVIL SERVICE

Of course the very process of examining for a job opening in the Federal Civil Service is an effort to find a person who should rank with the job. Indeed, qualifications of candidates for the three top grades must be reviewed by the

---

[15] U.S. Civil Service Commission, Departmental Circular No. 927 (January 6, 1958) and supplements. In an activity as vast as the federal competitive service no precise geographical or organizational definition of "broad areas of consideration" is possible, but the intent is to make them broader than they ordinarily have been in the past.

Civil Service Commission as well as by the usual examining process. But in other ways, too, the job-oriented Federal Civil Service recognizes a rank in the man.

Status and perquisites often are based on GS rank. Perhaps more significant in bringing "our system closer to the rank-in-the-man concept than may be generally realized"—as the then chairman of the Civil Service Commission stated in 1956—is that the rank of the job often is adjusted upward as the capable incumbent attracts more responsibility—the man's rank, of course, rising with the job's.[16] Similarly, a poor incumbent can downgrade his job, and eventually the classification is adjusted downward.

It is true that the man and the job have not always meshed neatly in the Federal Civil Service. One reason for this may have been the separation until 1953 of the Commission's classification and examining activities. The "rank-of-the-man" or examining staff had little contact with the "rank-of-the-job" or classification staff. Some individuals tried to bridge the gap and drafts of standards were exchanged, but for the most part the two staffs had little impact on each other. Now, both examining and classification standards are produced by the same staff, the Standards Division in the Bureau of Programs and Standards.

To an increasing degree, new classification standards recognize that the phrase "qualification requirements" in the Classification Act is co-equal with the other parts of the trilogy: "duties, responsibilities, and qualification requirements." For example, new standards for psychologists add "level of professional performance" as a classification factor. The new attorney standards give weight to an individual's stature in his professional field as an element in evaluating his job. New standards for research scientists recognize superior qualifications as they are required and applied on the job. Even in the clerical ranks, standards for stenographer and typist now provide higher entrance grades for recruits who do well on the written test, on the assumption that they will perform better and be able to do more difficult work.

While there are still many situations where grades are controlled by manning tables and cannot be adjusted to the incumbent's qualifications, the new philosophy is coming to the fore, as shown in this recent statement by the Standards Division:

Scientists have long recommended recognition of a scientist's attainments and professional stature, through some sort of "rank in the man" procedure, in fixing grade levels for scientist positions. On the other hand, classifiers talk about "classifying the job, not the man." Although these points of view appear contradictory, in the case of research scientists the conflict is more apparent than real. Research is, by definition, a particularly unlimited activity, which involves stepping into the unknown; advancing

---

[16] Speech of Philip Young to the Society for Personnel Administration, May 16, 1956.

knowledge; discovering; creating; inventing. . . . In such circumstances, the job that is actually performed is the combined result of the work situation, or assignment, and the individual capabilities of the incumbent. The "man-in-job" concept which considers both the capabilities which the incumbent brings to the job, and the extent to which the job situation requires him to utilize these capabilities, is simply a means of recognizing and evaluating the position which actually results from this combination.[17]

THE POSITION CONCEPT IN THE MILITARY

At the same time, rank-in-the-man military systems make a definite effort to "put rank in the job," to insure that officers are placed in positions suitable to their rank. This is nothing new; the systems always have started juniors in lowly assignments and advanced them to posts of higher responsibilities as they demonstrated increased capacity and achieved higher rank.

Job analysis in the military has become all the more important in the space age. Millions of dollars have been well spent in studying military assignments to insure proper matching of officer and assignment. This activity is precisely what would be called job classification.

How systematic this process has become in the military is shown by the following description of what the Air Research and Development Command calls "Operation Square Peg":

The system will employ a procedure for the matching of job profiles (job specifications) against the personal profiles of research and development officers. . . . A mechanical processing procedure has been devised which will produce a tabulated listing of officers and their qualifications who possess the necessary codifiable mandatory and desirable qualifications for successful accomplishment of the job in question.[18]

Personal rank as an admiral or a general is not the whole story to a successful military officer. He is also deeply concerned about his current and future assignments and their prestige and opportunities. " 'What's my next command?' said the Colonel," as the old Army song has it.

It also is important to realize that military personnel systems provide for program staffing in appropriate situations. The National Guard, the reserve systems, and the direct commissioning of civilians in an emergency are examples.

---

17 "Classification of Research Scientists," *Classification News* (U.S. Civil Service Commission, November, 1959).
18 "Operation Square Peg," *Engineering and Scientific Manpower Newsletter* (No. 121, September 8, 1959).

CONCLUSION

This article has tried to demonstrate that "job-oriented" personnel systems pay substantial attention to the personal rank of their members, and that, conversely, "person-oriented" systems pay substantial attention to the level and requirements of the job.

From their beginnings, all viable personnel systems have paid attention both to the man and to his job. Some systems have occasionally emphasized one aspect at the expense of the other, but both have always been present.

Every personnel system should study both the man and the job to make the best possible match between the two, with sufficient flexibility to allow for emergency assignments and with broad training for future advancement.

The Federal Civil Service, though approaching "rank-in-the-man" ideas of the military, still falls short of all its advantages, particularly in lacking systematic training on the "staff college" principle, longer details to other jobs, job descriptions covering a longer work cycle, full reimbursement for the cost of a move, and "selection out."

For most of the service, the present mixture of career and program staffing may be a good solution. Certainly it would be unfortunate if our civil service system became a completely closed one in which interchange were no longer possible with private enterprise, universities, and state and local governments.

For the top group of career executives, this analysis suggests that only a few additional evolutionary changes may provide the kind of plan that the Second Hoover Commission envisaged.

32.

APPRAISAL ON THE JOB:
THREE TYPES OF APPRAISAL INTERVIEWS

NORMAN R. F. MAIER

One of the most common procedures in company executive-development programs is the appraisal of a man's performance, followed by an interview in con-

Reprinted from Norman R. F. Maier, *The Appraisal Interview* (New York: John Wiley & Sons, Inc., 1958), chap. 1. As adapted in *Personnel*, published by the American Management Association Inc., Vol. 54, No. 5 (March–April, 1958), pp. 27–40.

nection with the appraisal. This procedure may be set up in various ways but it is always adapted to the line organization and always requires the holding of interviews.

The skill of the interviewer is an important factor in the success of this plan and is a general managerial requisite, since appraisal interviews are conducted by supervisors at all levels. Unless skillfully conducted, however, such an interview may be an unpleasant experience for both parties and cause the interviewee to resist improving on the job. Fortunately, an interview that is satisfactory to the interviewer is likely to satisfy the interviewee as well and hence can be a constructive experience for both.

While it goes without saying that two interviewers may differ in skill, it is equally true that two *skilled* interviewers may practice quite different methods. It also follows that, while each method requires its own specific skills, more can be accomplished with the superior method even when skills are equal.

This differentiation between skill and method is important because the goal of the interview determines which method should be used to achieve it; and once we have clarified the goal in any activity, the problem of developing the necessary skills is greatly simplified. If, for example, in driving a golf ball, we are aiming at direction rather than distance, the skill we are concerned with is the orientation of the body while swinging rather than force of stroke.

Unlike our somewhat simplified example, however, appraisal interviews may have various and sometimes conflicting objectives. Among them we may note: (*a*) to let subordinates know where they stand; (*b*) to recognize their good work; (*c*) to point out how and where they can improve; (*d*) to develop them on their present job; (*e*) to develop and train them for higher jobs; (*f*) to let them know how they may progress in the company; (*g*) to serve as a record for assessing the department or unit as a whole, showing where each person fits into the larger picture; and (*h*) to warn some employees that they must do better. It is frequently supposed that several or all of these objectives may be achieved by a single interview, but this is not the case.

Conflicting Objectives.—The differences between these objectives, however slight, will affect the whole course of the interview. For example, "letting an employee know where he stands" suggests a fairly comprehensive report, while an interview for the purpose of recognizing an employee's good work can be much more selective in content.

When the interview serves as a warning, some companies require the employee to sign an appraisal form. This precludes his saying at a later time that he was not told his work was unsatisfactory. However, the requirement of a signature is inconsistent with goals other than warning.

A discrepancy between the goals of the interviewer and the interviewee may also cause difficulties. For example, in praising a very superior employee who has many virtues and few faults, the interviewer may make a minor criticism or pass over something as merely "satisfactory." However, the employee may regard this as unfavorable and feel crushed by any suggestion that he should improve.

On the other hand, a supervisor may treat a weak subordinate with kid gloves to avoid hurting his feelings. Thus he may call the employee's best point "quite satisfactory" although in reality it is only about average, and praise him highly for effort. The employee may emerge from the interview feeling relieved and and perhaps more secure than he should, considering his limited prospects.

This article will describe three types of appraisal interviews, each with a specific and slightly different objective. The differences are important in determining the skills required and, to a great extent, actually call for different skills from the interviewer's repertoire. A unique interaction characterizes each method, so that the three differ in kind rather than in degree. The three methods may be described as *Tell and Sell*, *Tell and Listen*, and *Problem Solving*.

THE TELL AND SELL METHOD

The initial aim of the *Tell and Sell* method is to communicate the employee's evaluation to him as accurately as possible. The fairness of the evaluation is assumed and the supervisor seeks (*a*) to let the employee know how he is doing; (*b*) to gain his acceptance of the evaluation; and finally (*c*) to get him to follow the plan outlined for his improvement. These three goals seem, at first glance, to be consistent with each other and in some circumstances, they undoubtedly are so.

If it is assumed that people desire to correct faults, that the superior's judgment is acceptable to the subordinate and that he is able to change in the direction specified, then the desired aims can be achieved. However, it is not unusual for subordinates to regard their supervisors' expectations as unreasonable, their criticisms unjustified, and the methods of work they suggest inefficient. It is also unrealistic to expect a person to improve merely because he wants to. He may strive to make wise decisions, be patient, get along with people, conduct conferences effectively, and stand up under strain, but such behavior may not be subject to his voluntary control.

While improvement in such things as getting to work on time, turning in honest expense accounts, and working hard is usually considered a matter of volition, here, too, more than a wish may be necessary. Frequently, the problem is one of adjustment rather than motivation. Emotional maladjustment requires therapy and improper attempts to make improvements may aggravate rather than correct the condition.

For purposes of this discussion it will be assumed that extreme cases are the exception and that the interviewer is going to deal with management people who are able to take criticism.

The Necessary Skills.—Considerable skills are necessary for success in the *Tell and Sell* type of interview. They include the ability to persuade the employee to change in the prescribed manner and this requires knowing how to use the incentives that motivate him and sometimes developing new ones. The salesman must know his customer and the selling of an evaluation makes the same demands on a supervisor.

The method becomes especially difficult if the interviewer encounters resistance. Since he usually sees himself in the role of doing something for the employee's good, any failure to appreciate this gesture places him on the defensive. Thus the situation may become strained or deteriorate into obvious hostility.

However, the employee usually senses his supervisor's increased aggression before it is too apparent, and consequently refrains from questioning the evaluation. The passive resistance and verbal agreement that follow are often taken as acceptance of the evaluation by the interviewer. When the employee retreats from discussion, the supervisor may feel more obliged to talk and may end up lecturing or preaching.

Defensive feelings, whether expressed or covered up, are a natural reaction of the employer to this type of interview. The supervisor is cast in the role of a judge, while the employee wants to make as good a showing as possible and tries to conceal any weaknesses. As the supervisor can never know all the circumstances and provocations, his criticism is apt to seem unjust.

Once the subordinate questions his superior's evaluation, a face-saving situation is created. Unless the interviewer is very patient or something happens to break the chain of events, the conflict will become more acute. Since the superior usually has some power at his disposal, the subordinate invariably learns to give in. Subordinates often develop a degree of insensitivity to criticism on these occasions. The general viewpoint in the organization may be, "everybody gets criticized during appraisal interviews, so you just take it with a grain of salt." Some interviewers attempt to comfort their subordinates by telling how they, too, are evaluated and criticized.

Although the *Tell and Sell* interview may be unpleasant for both parties, this does not prove that it lacks merit. Correction usually is unpleasant, and almost everyone can recall discarding faults because of criticism that once was painful. Certainly, faulty behavior can be inhibited or replaced by having someone point out a better way. The crucial issue is finding the most effective approach. Both motivation and training are essential to change.

When a man lacks the skill or knowledge to do his job in the way his superior desires, the problem is one of training or transfer. If an employee is worthy of development on his present job, the interviewer should clarify the job demands and indicate where and how the employee can acquire the desired knowledge or skills.

Motivation to Change.—The fact that people often want to do a job effectively may be sufficient motivation to adopt the correct methods and habits. The desire for the boss's approval may also provide motivation.

However, sometimes an employee has his own views about a job or does not wish to reveal his lack of ability to change. If he has "bad" habits or is negligent in certain respects, he may resist change because the undesirable behavior is attractive to him. In such instances, new motivation is necessary. One way is to make the old behavior unattractive by punishment and threats of discharge. This is similar to removing an undesirable growth by surgery. The *operative* approach is unpleasant for the employee because he must either give up the behavior he likes or suffer the consequences.

Another way is to make an alternate response attractive by rewarding it. This *substitution* method is usually more pleasant and effective than the operative, not only because punishment is unnecessary but also because an alternative is supplied. Thus a child's emotional disturbance is reduced if a broken toy is replaced by another, and a smoker will find it somewhat easier to give up cigarettes if he substitutes gum. However, something pleasant (a reward) must be added in order to make the choice attractive and voluntary.

Both methods require that an external motivating factor be added to one of the alternatives; a negative incentive (punishment) must be connected with the undesirable behavior or a positive incentive (reward) with the acceptable alternative. This form of motivation is *extrinsic* to the activity, in contrast with *intrinsic* motivation in which the activity itself is satisfying. When extrinsic motivation is used, the new behavior is not accepted for its own sake, but for other reasons.

Both the type of motivation used and the defensive attitudes aroused limit the effectiveness of the *Tell and Sell* method. Frequently the subordinate accepts the evaluation or says he does in order to get out of the interview situation. But the fact remains that a selling method permits only two courses of action: continue as before vs. change to the superior's plan. However, plans for improving a work situation and ways to deal with a behavior problem can seldom be reduced to two possibilities.

Advantages and Limitations.—A plan may be effective in one situation while it fails in another. The *Tell and Sell* method has its greatest potential with young and new employees, who are inexperienced and insecure and want the assurance of an authority figure. They are likely to respect the superior not only because of his position but also because of his greater knowledge and experience. Similar reactions usually occur in employees who are new on an assignment.

Individual differences also play a part in reactions to the *Tell and Sell* method. Persons who are easy-going, uncritical, somewhat unimaginative and ready to accept authoritarian leadership are most able to profit from it.

From the company's viewpoint the method is efficient, providing it works. Presenting an evaluation takes less time than discussing it and if the employee accepts the presentation, a fairly complete interview can be held in about 15 minutes. However, if the appraisal is resisted, considerable time may be required to achieve the potential gains of this method.

Although the *Tell and Sell* method may produce positive results under favorable conditions, it also may do more harm than good. When, for example, a subordinate thinks his appraisal is unfair, he may feel that his interests and the company's are no longer compatible. Loyalty depends on *mutual interests* and both the supervisor and the company may lose men's loyalties in the process of conducting appraisal interviews.

Again, if the interview is unpleasant, the day-to-day relationship between supervisor and subordinate may become strained and job satisfactions decreased for both.

However, the greatest risk occurs, particularly in appraising middle and top management, when the subordinate accepts the judgment of his superior and tries to please him instead of giving his best thinking to the job. Every language has a phrase for a "yes man" and no superior wants to develop one. Yet the *Tell and Sell* method is bound to encourage this type of subordinate for it assumes that the boss knows best—he is the father figure who dispenses rewards and punishments. Such an executive expects his men to want to please him and they soon learn what he expects of them, often competing with each other to gain his favors. Although the boss may ask his subordinates to make independent judgments and take initiative, the fact that he appraises and recommends motivates the weaker among them to find out what he wants and to do it his way. To forestall criticism, some even adopt the boss's manners and dress. Thus when this method works, it is likely to develop dependent, docile behavior, and when it fails, rebellious behavior may result. Needless to say, neither extreme is desirable.

Finally, what is the over-all effect on company philosophy and values? Organizations vary in the extent to which they are receptive to new methods and ideas. When evaluations are made from the top down, it is difficult for new ideas to enter, unless top personnel are recruited from outside the company. However, this may require overcoming resistance to changes down the line and is often impractical. Since the *Tell and Sell* type of interview makes no provision for upward communication, it tends to perpetuate existing values. Although changes may occur effectively when initiated from the top or when approved by the proper superiors, there is no means of stimulating new ideas. While both radicalism and conservatism with respect to change have unique values, each makes its contribution under different circumstances. Insofar as conservatism rather than change is desired, the *Tell and Sell* method is effective.

THE TELL AND LISTEN METHOD

The *Tell and Listen* method of conducting an appraisal interview is often viewed with skepticism because the role of the interviewer seems somewhat unnatural and ambiguous with respect to authority. The goal here is to communicate the evaluation to the employee and then let him respond to it. The interviewer covers his strengths and weaknesses during the first part of the interview, postponing points of disagreement until later. The second part is devoted to thoroughly exploring the subordinate's feelings about the evaluation. Thus the superior, while still in the role of a judge, listens to objections without attempting to refute them. In fact, he encourages the employee to disagree because the objective is not only to communicate the appraisal but also to drain off any negative feelings it arouses. The cathartic value of the verbal expression of frustrated feelings is assumed.

The initial reactions are similar to those of the *Tell and Sell* method since both begin with a presentation of the evaluation. However, the methods differ radically as regards the way disagreement and resistance are handled. Instead of the interviewer dominating the discussion, he sits back and becomes a nondirective counselor[1] during the second part of the interview.

Skills of This Approach.—The skills of this approach are (*a*) active *listening* —accepting and trying to understand the employee's attitudes and feelings; (*b*) making effective use of *pauses*—waiting patiently without embarrassment for the other person to talk; (*c*) *reflecting feelings*—responding to feelings to show understanding; and (*d*) *summarizing feelings*—to indicate progress, show understanding and emphasize certain points, as well as to end the interview. None of these skills implies that the interviewer either agrees or disagrees with the employee. Rather they suggest the possibility that the evaluation may be unjust and even incorrect, and that the employee should accept only ideas which may be helpful.

Since it is assumed at the outset that there are two sides to the appraisal, face-saving issues are not aggravated. As the superior doesn't expect the subordinate to agree, he feels no need to defend his evaluation. The unpleasant aspects of the interview are reduced for he has a method for dealing with the employee's defensive responses, and is better able to understand and respect his feelings. Consequently, he will be less inclined to avoid conducting appraisal interviews than the *Tell and Sell* interviewer, who may be over-anxious.

The motivating factors in the *Tell and Listen* interview are somewhat complex. Since fears of reprisals and of displeasing the superior are reduced, unadaptive defensive behavior fanned, in part, by these fears is less likely to occur. Thus the counter-motivation known as *resistance to change* is lessened by the counsel-

----

[1] C. R. Rogers, *Counseling and Psychotherapy* (Boston: Houghton Mifflin Company, Boston, 1942), p. 450.

ing process, but the tendency to change to avoid displeasing the boss is sacrificed. Which of these two opposing motivations is stronger will vary in individual instances.

There is also the positive motivation that comes from having a pleasant interview with the boss. Hostility is minimized and the subordinate feels accepted and important. These feelings are conducive to forming a constructive attitude toward growth. Thus a subordinate tends to want to please a supervisor he likes more than one he fears. When fear is dominant, a person, at best, shies away from wrongdoing, but does not extend himself to perform beyond the call of duty.

The motivations discussed so far are *extrinsic* in that they lie outside job activity and the work itself has not been made more interesting. However, some increase in job interest is possible. Intrinsic motivation would occur if the interview resulted in (*a*) solving some job problems; (*b*) clarifying certain misunderstandings between supervisor and subordinate; or (*c*) solving a personal problem. These gains are most probable in instances where the employee's job performances are deficient. The interview might also result in improvements in the work climate—another element of job interest.

If the superior listened and *learned* from the interview, additional gains would be possible. The superior might modify job assignments and expectations, alter his evaluation, perceive the subordinate's job differently, or discover his own negligence in training and assisting. However it takes an exceptional interviewer to learn from the interview. Since the appraisal is made before the interview, most interviewers feel committed to uphold it.

Benefits of the Method.—This method usually insures a good relationship between superior and subordinate during the interview. The employee is likely to leave with a positive attitude toward the supervisor, feeling that the interview has been worth while and that he is important to the company. The interview provides an opportunity for the superior to learn his subordinate's needs, although his impressions may be incorrect.

However, there is some risk that the interview may not achieve its first objective —letting the employee know where he stands. In addition, while the employee may gain new insights which may cause him to change, he is not likely to discover ways for improving job performance. Thus he may leave the interview with satisfaction but without a program for developing on his job.

The values promoted by the *Tell and Listen* interview are those of tolerance and respect for the individual. Thus the method tends to make supervisors employee- rather than production-minded, an attitude which generally stimulates higher morale.[2] However, while high morale and productivity frequently are

---

[2] D. Katz, N. Maccoby, and N. C. Morse, *Productivity, Supervision and Morale in an Office Situation* (Ann Arbor, Mich.: University of Michigan, Institute for Social Research, 1950), p. 84.

related, there may be variations in productivity among groups that have equally high morale.

The greatest value of this method comes from the fact that the interviewer may profit from the interview. Change initiated from below may occur when a subordinate is able to influence his superior's views on how the job may be improved in (*a*) supervision, (*b*) work methods, (*c*) job assignments and (*d*) job expectations. Frequently, superiors once performed the jobs of the men they now supervise, and very often expect their subordinates to act just as they did. Since people differ and times as well as jobs change, this expectation, while understandable, is usually impractical. In any event, a superior's expectations, at best, tend to restrict initiative and inhibit improvements. Although some of this loss may be recouped by using suggestion boxes, it is important not to stifle new ideas by an appraisal program that was designed to develop employees. A supervisor who listens and learns may encourage upward communication in deed as well as in word. The belief that constructive forces for change may spring from below can become an important part of organizational philosophy.

THE PROBLEM-SOLVING APPROACH

The *Problem-Solving* method of appraisal interview has grown out of the author's recent studies of executive development. Of the three methods presented here it deviates the most from common-sense views. It takes the interviewer out of the role of judge and makes him a helper. Although the interviewer may want to help his subordinate, in the other two types of interview this is difficult because the process of appraising is inconsistent with that of helping. It may appear that the purpose of the interview is lost if the appraisal is not directly communicated to the subordinate. However, one must also recognize that the development of the employee often is the primary reason for conducting an appraisal interview and that *this* objective may be lost in the process of communicating the evaluation.

As has been said, appraisal interviews may serve a variety of purposes of which development is one. Although the two other methods discussed communicate the appraisal to the subordinate, they do not assure his understanding and acceptance. The *Problem-Solving* approach has no provision for communicating the appraisal, and indeed it may be unessential for this purpose. If the appraisal is required for other reasons, it may be desirable to delay making it until after the interview.

The goal of employee development immediately establishes a *mutual interest* between the interviewer and his subordinate. Both would like the employee to improve on the job and agree that the boss could assist him. When the subordinate accepts this help-giving role of his supervisor he is more willing to describe his difficulties. However, when the boss passes judgment on his job performance, their interests conflict. On the one hand, the employee wants to impress his boss favorably and hide his weaknesses. The interviewer, on the other hand, wants to avoid being deceived and to discuss weaknesses. *Mutual interests* are present only so long as the employee's merits are being praised and end when the interviewer indicates that he is somewhat less than satisfied.

Since the objective is employee development, the interviewer cannot specify the area for improvement, because this would be making a judgment. He must limit his influence to stimulating thinking rather than supplying solutions, and be willing to consider all ideas on job improvement that the employee brings up. His function is to discover the subordinate's interests, respond to them, and help the employee examine himself and the job. He must forget his own viewpoint and try to see the job as the employee sees it. If the employee's ideas seem impractical, the interviewer should ask questions to learn more specifically what the employee has in mind. Often the ideas may seem difficult to accept because they are misunderstood or viewed from a different frame of reference. Communication may be faulty unless each person tries to understand the background, attitude, and experience of the other.

When the interviewer finds that a subordinate's thinking is naïve, he must be willing to assume that a problem-solving discussion is the best way to stimulate growth and sophistication. If an employee can grow in this manner, he need not know that he has had weaknesses and faults. The process may be compared to the training of children. Telling a child that he is gawky and uncoordinated does not help him to become graceful and skilled. As a matter of fact, he will probably improve more if left to himself, instead of being exposed to extensive fault finding. However, people are often so concerned with the faults they observe that they find it difficult to suppress comments and advice. Thus a supervisor's knowledge and experience will not help his subordinate unless he knows how to share them constructively.

Exploring Solutions.—Problem solving is characterized by the exploration of a variety of solutions. It is inhibited when a person feels threatened by an evaluation which directs attention to him rather than to the situation. When a person is placed in the spotlight he tries to hide his defects and to protect himself by defensive behavior. As long as he defends himself, he is not searching for new or better ways of performing. If an evaluation is very threatening it may arouse hostile and stubborn reactions which further delay problem solving.

The *Problem-Solving* approach uses non-directive skills similar to those of the *Tell and Listen* method—listening, accepting, and responding to feelings. The interviewer should be especially alert to expressions of concern at the start of the interview. Such a remark as "Well, this is the day we get overhauled, I suppose," should be met with a statement like, "I daresay you think these interviews are rough on people in some ways." However, the objective of the *Problem-*

Solving interview is to go beyond an interest in the subordinate's feelings to a discussion of the job. If the employee is not over-anxious, the interviewer can ask questions about the job at the beginning. While such questions are directive, they do not limit the views and feelings that can be expressed.

In some instances, the various job activities should be discussed and evaluated. Differences in perceptions of what the job is may account for some unfavorable points in the evaluation. Thus the interviewer might learn that the subordinate saw his job as "getting an assignment finished on time, regardless of the feelings of others" and that he had gained this mistaken impression from a previous reprimand. However, the differences should be passed over, serving merely to enlighten the interviewer about the need for better job descriptions, training, or communication. Once the job is analyzed in terms of the way it is done, some time can be spent discussing the ideal working conditions.

If mutual understanding of the job had been accomplished in previous interviews, the employee can be asked to review the year's progress and discuss his problems, and satisfactions. The idea is to make the interview an opportunity to get the boss's ear.

As has been said, the superior should consider all the ideas presented. By restating them in somewhat different words, the interviewer may test his understanding, and show his interest in considering the changes suggested. He need not agree or disagree with the ideas in order to understand and consider acting upon them.

When the employee expresses numerous ideas, it may be wise to jot them down. Making such a record is an act of accepting without taking a stand for or against. The ideas can be evaluated later on and the best ones selected. In this way none are called poor; some just fail to survive.

Skillful Questioning Is Needed.—Skillful questioning can stimulate a subordinate to evaluate his ideas and plans. The questions should not put him on the spot, but should indicate that the listener wants to get the complete story. The following may serve as examples of questions of this kind:

Can this plan of yours deal with an emergency situation, in case one should arise?
Would you have other people at your level participate in the plan?
What kinds of problems do you anticipate in a changing market?

Exploratory questions are effective in drawing a person out and making him think more clearly; they may also serve to direct analysis to areas that may have been overlooked.

The use of summaries and pauses, already touched upon in discussing the *Tell and Sell* method, is equally helpful in the *Problem-Solving* interview. Pauses, in fact, perform an additional function in the latter technique, since they allow the subordinate to explore and evaluate ideas without feeling the pressure of time. If a subordinate is free to analyze the job with the prospect of influencing improvements in it, he will be motivated to think constructively, in a mature and responsible way. The problem of gaining his acceptance of any changes is non-existent because he has suggested them.

The *Problem-Solving* approach motivates original thinking because it stimulates curiosity. Curiosity is a strong drive and as long as fear is not aroused, leads to exploratory behavior. For example, children will explore a free and secure environment but stop in the face of danger or threats of punishment. Problems offer opportunities to explore and their solutions lead to new experiences. Some *extrinsic* motivations such as gaining approval or avoiding failure may be present, but essentially the problem-solving activity has interest in itself. This *intrinsic* motivation is present in many things we like to do and is an important aspect of play. If it could be made a larger part of the job, then work would become more like play.

A re-examination of the job is bound to suggest some changes because certain aspects are usually more satisfactory than others.

CAUSE AND EFFECT RELATIONS IN THREE TYPES OF APPRAISAL INTERVIEWS

Method	Tell and Sell	Tell and Listen	Problem-Solving
Role of interviewer	Judge	Judge	Helper
Objective	To communicate evaluation To persuade employee to improve	To communicate evaluation To release defensive feelings	To stimulate growth and development in employee
Assumptions	Employee desires to correct weaknesses if he knows them Any person can improve if he so chooses A superior is qualified to evaluate a subordinate	People will change if defensive feelings are removed	Growth can occur without correcting faults Discussing job problems leads to improved performance
Reactions	Defensive behavior suppressed Attempts to cover hostility	Defensive behavior expressed Employee feels accepted	Problem-solving behavior
Skills	Salesmanship Patience	Listening and reflecting feelings Summarizing	Listening and reflecting feelings Reflecting ideas Using exploratory questions Summarizing

There are four different ways of improving job satisfaction: (*a*) the job itself may be reorganized or enlarged; (*b*) the subordinate's perception of the job may be changed; (*c*) the superior's understanding of a man's problems may be increased so that he will relate differently to his subordinate, supply assistance in the form that is needed, or improve communications; and (*d*) the opportunity may be created to solve problems of a group nature involving relationships between the various subordinates who report to the interviewer.

Since job satisfaction may be approached in various ways, some improvements should be possible for the employee. If none come under discussion, the interviewer may ask questions to stimulate exploration of the various areas. Once different possibilities are examined, a selection can be made in terms of practicality and interest. If the goal is to improve things in some way that is in line with the employee's wishes, then there is good assurance that a change will occur.

However, in order to achieve improvement in the direction desired by the subordinate, the superior must sacrifice his right to determine the change. It

CAUSE AND EFFECT RELATIONS IN
THREE TYPES OF APPRAISAL INTERVIEWS (*Cont.*)

Method	Tell and Sell	Tell and Listen	Problem-Solving
Attitude	People profit from criticism and appreciate help	One can respect the feelings of others if one understands them	Discussion develops new ideas and mutual interests
Motivation	Use of positive or negative incentives or both (Extrinsic in that motivation is added to the job itself)	Resistance to change reduced Positive incentive (Extrinsic and some intrinsic motivation)	Increased freedom Increased responsibility (Intrinsic motivation in that interest is inherent in the task)
Gains	Success most probable when employee respects interviewer	Develops favorable attitude to superior which increases probability of success	Almost assured of improvement in some respect
Risks	Loss of loyalty Inhibition of independent judgment Face-saving problems created	Need for change may not be developed	Employee may lack ideas Change may be other than what superior had in mind
Values	Perpetuates existing practices and values	Permits interviewer to change his views in the light of employee's responses Some upward communication	Both learn since experience and views are pooled Change is facilitated

may turn out that both will agree but in order to gain the change that the subordinate will accept, the interviewer must not attempt to impose his own views.

In the event that a subordinate does not express any ideas and fails to respond to the *Problem-Solving* approach, it may be assumed that this method has failed. However, the failure does not preclude the use of one of the other two methods.

Upward Communication.—The *Problem-Solving* approach affords both the participants a highly favorable opportunity for learning and communicating. Training is usually considered a one-way process in which the superior gives his knowledge to the subordinate. The *Problem-Solving* approach like the *Tell and Listen* method, stimulates upward communication. In addition, it creates a climate for high quality decisions and changes since it pools the thinking of two people who have supplementary experiences. Resistance to change is a common obstacle to progress but this approach removes sources of resistance and stimulates change.

The interviewer places *mutual interests* above personal interests, and respects the problem-solving ability of the subordinate. Exploring the job with an understanding superior stimulates new ideas and leads to increased job interest as well as a better use of the employee's talents.

The attitude of mutual respect cuts across barriers of rank, focusing attention on problems to be solved rather than on prerogatives, or status and personality clashes. It assumes that change is essential to an organization and that participation in change is necessary for individual growth.

This article has analyzed three methods of appraisal interviews and has shown that they produce different results. It has pointed out that the method is a function of the particular objective the interview is designed to serve; and has shown that interviewing skills must be related to the objective as well as the method. The manner in which skills and objectives vary with the interviewing method is shown in the accompanying chart.

The chart also emphasizes the psychological difference between the methods—in the attitudes they reveal and the motivations they develop. It is hoped that this analysis will assist interviewers in adopting the methods and skills that support their particular objectives.

As has been said, common sense is often misleading, and too many or opposing interviewing goals may make it impossible to achieve any of them.

33.

THEORY X AND THEORY Y

DOUGLAS MCGREGOR

UNDERLYING BELIEF SYSTEM: THEORY X

1. Most work is distasteful for most people
2. Most people prefer close and continuous direction
3. Most people can exercise little or no creativity in solving organizational problems
4. Motivation occurs mostly or only as a response to "bread-and-butter" issues —threat or punishment—and is strictly an individual matter

UNDERLYING BELIEF SYSTEM: THEORY Y

1. Most people can find work as natural as play, if conditions permit
2. Most people prefer and can provide self-control in achieving organizational objectives
3. Most people can exercise significant creativity in solving organizational problems
4. Motivation often occurs in response to ego and social rewards, particularly under conditions of full employment, and motivation is often dependent upon groups

---

The two belief systems derive from Douglas McGregor, *The Human Side of Enterprise* (New York: McGraw-Hill Book Co., 1960), esp. pp. 33–58.

34.

SHALL WE BARGAIN AWAY THE MERIT SYSTEM?

MURIEL M. MORSE

Even in a space age when events seem to kaleidoscope in many fields, we seldom have as good an opportunity as we have now in the field of collective bargaining to see a definite trend and pattern emerging. Many public administrators have been tranquilized by the Rooseveltian concept that collective bargaining as it exists in industry cannot be transplanted into public service; that the right to strike is opposed to the public interest; that a union shop is not compatible with a merit system. And so we have deluded ourselves into proposing a different definition for collective bargaining in government.

Collective bargaining in industry is described as requiring two adversaries of equal strength and authority bargaining in good faith, resulting in a written contract equally binding on both parties, and granting to employees the right to strike, other means of economic enforcement, and security of a union shop. On the other hand, public administrators in discussing this problem, and even in reporting in the literature (the recent PPA's publication "Management Relations with Organized Public Employees" is a good example) have generally tended to accept a definition of collective bargaining as a method whereby representatives of the union and the employer negotiate, perhaps informally, but without most of the economic sanctions cited above.

The events of the past few years make it abundantly clear that we cannot have collective bargaining under a definition of our own choosing. Unlike Humpty Dumpty, we cannot say "when I choose a word, it means exactly what I choose it to mean—no more no less."

CHANGING PICTURE OBSERVED

Tailor-made concepts of collective bargaining for the public service are unrealistic over the long run. They have occurred simply because we have been some 20 years behind the experience of industry in the use of this procedure. Events are changing that picture rapidly.

In an article in *Challenge*, November, 1961, Dr. Irving Bernstein, Professor of

---

Reprinted from *Public Personnel Review*, Vol. 24 (October, 1963), pp. 239–43.

Political Science, University of California at Los Angeles, points out that the American Federation of State, County, and Municipal Employees is the fastest growing union in the country next to the operating engineers. The drive to organize government employees has picked up speed since that time. Reasons cited for this growth include a narrowing of historic fringe benefits differentials between government and private industry, the growing variety in public employment, and the increased willingness of public agencies to experiment with collective bargaining. These experiments are bringing all of the weapons of the agreement into government.

In 1960, the Western Regional Director of the American Federation of State, County, and Municipal Employees described the scope and activities of union growth as follows. He said, "We have in our organization 302 local union agreements in 310 locals in 35 states and Canada. We have 209 bilateral contracts in 27 states and Canada . . . . We have 130 agreements granting the union exclusive bargaining rights as the bargaining unit. We have four union shop contracts in 59 agreements. We have maintenance of membership in 11 agreements. We have preferential shop agreements in two states. We have 103 agreements providing for arbitration."[1]

In appearing before the California Assembly Committee on Industrial Relations, a few years ago, Dr. Bernstein testified that, "the Metropolitan Transit Authority Act passed by the California Legislature in 1957, setting forth an experiment in collective bargaining, while not characterized by perfect smoothness, nevertheless was being carried forward successfully."[2] Part of that carrying forward was confirmation by the courts that, with the law silent, the strike was an integral part of this collective bargaining contract.

Also commented upon at that time were two interesting legal opinions of the State of Washington. The first was to the effect that a county may enter into a contract providing for a union shop. The Attorney General stated he could find nothing in the State Constitution, public policy, or statute law that would prohibit such a contract. His reasoning was that since the County Board of Commissioners enjoyed the right to select and hire employees, it was also free to require union membership as a condition of employment in the selection process. The same Attorney General also ruled that a school district might legally enter into a written collective bargaining agreement, because the power to employ embraced the authority to enter into contracts with employees either individually or collectively.

---

[1] Public Personnel Association, *Study of Collective Bargaining in the Public Service of the United States.* Prepared by San Francisco Bay Area Chapter. P. 6.
[2] *Ibid.*, p. 7.

MODIFIED CLOSED SHOP AGREED ON

The Philadelphia story is another example of "the weapons picture." While Eli Rock[3] may feel that collective bargaining in government does not necessarily involve formal negotiation or contract, and may consist of no more than discussion, conference, and negotiation, it does not work this way in Philadelphia. After a long history of negotiations with unions, and collective bargaining agreements on a year-to-year basis, Philadelphia finally embraced a form of its present contract in 1953. In 1959 employees were required to have union membership. A modified union shop with exclusive bargaining rights for a substantial segment of city employees was established. New employees in those classifications are now required to join the union within six months of appointment.

Philadelphia is not alone in this experiment. Exclusive bargaining rights are granted the union in 65 of their agreements with cities, the American Federation of State, County, and Municipal Employees reports. Indeed, the alternative to it, that is, multiple representation, or the job of bargaining with each recognized union or employee organization, is one on which many labor relations experts have commented in terms of loss of efficiency.

SETTLEMENT BY ARBITRATION GAINS

A third weapon, the settlement of disputes through arbitration, is progressing nicely in the public service. The 1961 San Francisco Bay Area Chapter report[4] on collective bargaining pointed out that the California Conciliation Service had intervened in 56 labor disputes in the public service fron 1947 to 1959. Incidentally, educational institutions and school districts were involved in the highest number of disputes served, and 21 labor unions and employee organizations were involved. Seven work stoppages occurred—five on the campuses of the University of California, and two others involving a city and a county in California.

We slid into arbitration in an interesting manner. The question of whether a public agency has the right to turn over to someone not responsible to the electorate certain decision-making has inhibited its use. There has been a tendency to view the use of arbitration as a good offices-type of approach in government where the arbitrator seeks a compromise and makes a recommendation to the final authority. But despite opinion that delegating authority in arbitration awards is not legal, at least 103 of the agreements reported by American

---

[3] Foster Roser, in "Management Relations with Organized Public Employees," edited by Kenneth O. Warner, pp. 105–106.
[4] PPA, San Francisco Bay Area Chapter, *op. cit.*, p. 7.

Federation of State, County, and Municipal Employees provide for it.[5] And where recommendations are universally upheld, *de facto* delegation has occurred.

ULTIMATE WEAPON—THE STRIKE

The ultimate weapon of the union is, of course, the strike. And here is where I think we have deluded ourselves perhaps most obviously. In an effort to get legislation approved which will permit collective bargaining in public agencies, proponents are all too willing to write in a no-strike clause. Strikes, although prohibited by law in the federal government and in many of the states, have occurred and are still occurring. This is true even when the so-called right to strike is prohibited either by law or by the terms of a collective bargaining agreement.

Sterling Spero, in *Government as an Employer*, points out that a no-strike policy for civil service unions is a policy of expediency rather than any recognition of the moral force of the claims of government as an employer.[6] H. Elliot Kaplan in *The Law of Civil Service* agrees that it does not answer the problem of preventing strikes by government employees merely to outlaw strikes. Leonard D. White philosophizes[7] that strikes should be prohibited only where such action could bring direct and serious danger to a community; namely, the consequence of the strike upon the public interest. To follow this thinking is to find oneself in an impossible tangle of definition.

Collective bargaining has made headway in police and fire services which use the no-strike pledge required by the American Federation. But if permission to strike is based on the nature of the employment rather than the violation of government's sovereign authority, it can cause hardships if carried out. For instance, a police force cannot function effectively without its communication facilities. Yet, the nature of the telephone operator's job is judged the same in public service as it is in a private public utility or corporation.

SUBSTITUTE COLLECTIVE BARGAINING?

The point of this commentary is simply that our concerns as public administrators should relate to the whole gamut of collective bargaining and the weapons which are used to enforce it. Industrial practices for making unions effective are present in the public service, and it is logical they should be. The changing

---

[5] PPA, San Francisco Bay Area Chapter, *op. cit.*, p. 6.
[6] Sterling Spero, *Government as an Employer* (Remsen Press, 1948), p. 219.
[7] Leonard D. White, "Strikes in the Public Service," *Public Personnel Review*, Vol. 10, No. 1, pp. 3–10.

face of management-employees relations in government proposes to substitute collective bargaining, and the means to enforce it, for the merit system. This is the fact we must face, and it brings some items of concern to most merit system administrators. I should like to list them.

(1) The right of an employee to join an organization of his choice and to be represented by that organization goes unchallenged. But in government there is a concept of an equal right, and that is a right not to join. Public jobs are distinguished from private employment in the concept of equal opportunity of all the citizens to compete for those jobs. The right of a county cited earlier to hire only workers who belong to a union flies in the face of this principle.

Furthermore, it is scarcely farseeing to say that while the closed shop might be a violation of the merit principle, the open shop is not. The very fact that someone must join a union in order to become the employee of a particular jurisdiction, limits recruitment. As a public service is entitled to the best without regard to race, creed, or color, it is equally entitled to the best without regard to any affiliation. The concept of equal opportunity for public jobs is certainly not compatible with the weapon of collective bargaining, namely, the union shop.

MEANS OF PROMOTION

(2) The right to compete for public jobs has been extended in most agencies to competitive promotion. The security found in the industrial union shop which provides for assignment by seniority, bidding for better jobs by seniority, and promotion by seniority, is quite opposed to many of the tools of the merit system. When we are talking on the one hand about better incentives for employee performance and better measurement of such performance, we might remind ourselves that seniority, not competition, is a corollary of collective bargaining.

(3) Another function of most merit system administrators is to provide information on wages and fringe benefits. If these are to be determined by collective bargaining, the prevailing wage theory goes out the window. A comment on the Philadelphia story is again in order here. Foster Roser reports that a major difficulty of collective bargaining in Philadelphia is that with no money, management can only negotiate on non-monetary terms, usually involving minor fringe benefits.[8] A similar difficulty has recently been reported in Cincinnati, Ohio.[9] Any personnel administrator faced with recruiting the best people he can for his jurisdiction would prefer being able to offer employees prevailing wages for comparable work. As a matter of fact, this system is more fair to all employees and

---

[8] Kenneth O. Warner, "Management Relations with Organized Public Employees," *Public Personnel Association*, 1963, p. 113.
[9] See annual report, Cincinnati, Ohio, 1962.

to the citizen than it would be to go, for salary, to the group which can bargain best.

(4) In representative government, it is generally conceded any individual employee has a right of petition, is entitled to speak for himself, and to use a counsel of his own choice in matters that affect his own welfare. If the efficiency of collective bargaining is achieved through exclusive recognition, or if representation can be accomplished only through a group, then there is a destruction of this concept. At a time when we are so concerned with retaining the benefits of an individualistic society as well as its responsibilities, it would seem that the right of representation of more than one group is equally fundamental to a merit system in representative government. It is so fundamental that it has been the great practical deterrent to collective bargaining legislation in California.

(5) Also fundamental is a means whereby elected officials are held accountable for their decisions. There is a growing tendency to degrade this concept of sovereignty by saying that elective officials delegate many of their acts, and the signing of a collective bargaining agreement is no different from any other delegation. I submit that there is a difference when public officials can abdicate their responsibilities in a matter usually involving over 80 per cent of the public's money in an operating budget, saying they are helpless to act because of commitments made in collective bargaining agreements.

(6) If we go back to our original definition of collective bargaining, requiring two adversaries of equal strength and authority to bargain in good faith, then the structure of management in public service presents a difficulty. In industry, levels generally are clear cut, and supervisory workers excluded from the union. The public service, on the other hand, is far from clear cut on this score. The fact is that all public employees work for one boss—the citizen. Membership which would provide a balance of power is difficult to achieve, since the citizen cannot be at the bargaining table.

(7) Another concern of public agencies is the extent of political activity of its employees. Dr. Bernstein, in his article in *California Management Review*, Spring 1962, urges more political activity on the part of labor unions, more education of membership for active political participation, supplying funds to candidates in behalf of issues which labor supports, and, where this is useful, to help in running campaigns.[10]

NONPARTISANSHIP IN DANGER

A tradition of the American scene at the local level has been the nonpartisan

---

[10] Irving Bernstein, "Labor's Power in American Society," *California Management Review*, Spring 1962, p. 10.

nature of government. I think most of us would agree that nonpartisanship has helped the merit system to flourish. If labor takes a greater part in the political picture, then we must surely expect partisan political activity on the part of merit system employees. This is inevitable if labor's part includes a large segment of state and local government employees represented by single bargaining agents with national affiliation.

Confirmation of this is found in a newsgram in the June 3, 1963 issue of *US News and World Report*—as follows:

> A new move in Washington is to be watched closely. It's a move to get employees of the vast Government establishment organized into unions.
>
> Checkoff of union dues has won White House approval. Unions of Government workers, assured of checkoff, will be able to grow in political strength. Postal workers long have had much political power.
>
> It's said that there is a law against political activity by Government workers. Actually, this law is largely a dead letter. What politicians are beginning to see is the chance to build a highly powerful political machine around the millions of people in Federal Government employment.

(8) Finally, the public personnel administrator's concern for the right of public employees to strike does not need to be labored. That it is inherent in the right to bargain is perhaps best expressed, apart from practice, by Dr. Arthur Bieriman, President of the AFL-CIO Teachers Union, in a statement made in San Francisco in 1959. He says; "It may be argued that the right to strike is implied in the right to bargain collectively. To this argument we make no reply. Whenever men organize to achieve a goal there is an implication that at great need they may act publicly and forcefully in defense of their rights as citizens and human beings. We feel that the right to strike is inherent, it is not a privilege. In extremity, whether legally or not, men strike."[11]

Here we have a clear-cut admission from a representative of a public employees' organization that strikes occur not as a matter of law, not as a matter of type of work, not even as a matter of recognition on the part of employees of the public interest (as indeed the teachers' strike in Gary, Indiana, during the last week of May 1963 confirmed), but rather as a right associated with collective bargaining.

CHOICE OF SYSTEMS NECESSARY

To sum up, the decision is not where to draw the line. The decision is about two kinds of personnel systems. Which are we going to have? They are different. They employ different principles, and they have different concerns. We can no longer believe that we can be half collective bargaining and half merit system.

---

[11] *San Francisco Examiner*, December 13, 1959.

This is well stated in an article in *Public Management*, May 1963 issue, by Douglas Weiford, City Manager, Eau Claire, Wisconsin. It points up clearly that the decision we really must make is whether the personnel administrator and the merit system are to survive.

If we believe in the merit system, more effective alternative machinery must be encouraged in government-employee relations. Drifting into collective bargaining is no answer. Unless we are to sow the seeds of our own destruction, we shall have to choose. Then it's up to us to devise a better climate than we have now for management-employee co-operation, and make statements of policy more explicit. They should include and spell out proper grievance procedures, the right of employees to be heard, regularly scheduled opportunities for consultations with representatives of employee groups, good channels of communication, and the ingredients of a sound personnel policy that allows employees to make recommendations for its improvement. They must and can be compatible with the basic principle of the merit system, responsive to the public interest, and flexible to meet today's personnel needs.

35.

HOW TO FEED BACK PERFORMANCE RESULTS TO TRAINEES

JAMES N. MOSÉL

Reduced to simplest terms, the process of personnel training consists of an "input" phase (the showing, telling, and explaining) and an "output" phase (the trainee's attempt to reproduce what is taught). The input is the instruction that goes into the trainee. The output is his response.

But there is still a third phase which is necessary if training is to be successful —the "feedback" phase. The trainee not only must attempt to make the responses which the trainer teaches, but he must also know how well he has succeeded in doing this. There must be a feedback from the output phase of the trainee's behavior into the input phase of the instruction. As training progresses the instruction must come more and more to incorporate information concerning the adequacy of the trainee's performance.

Reprinted by special permission from the February 1958 issue of the *Training Directors Journal.* Copyright 1958 by the American Society for Training and Development.

Feeding back to employees the results of their work embodies what psychologists call the "principle of knowledge of performance." This principle is one of the most thoroughly validated principles of learning. It is also one of the most neglected in industrial training. It may be stated as follows: *As knowledge of performance increases, learning increases both in rate and level.* A few studies will illustrate the kind of result we can expect.

In a government agency, calculating machine operators increased their performance by 60% as a result of seeing their output recorded in relation to the output of others.

In a Pittsburgh public utility, furnace stokers had no indication of how well they were doing. Gauges were installed to show the efficiency of the individual boilers and the data from these gauges were plotted to show individual improvement in the technique of firing the boilers. The result was an annual saving of $333,000 in coal.

In training operators to cut tungsten discs with a foot operated abrasive wheel, trainers developed a recording device which showed the learner his cutting patterns and thereby brought out the specific errors he was making in his cutting cycles. This technique was found to improve both the quality and quantity of work at various stages of training and also to decrease the use of abrasive wheels. After 11 weeks of training with this device, new employees reached the level of production of workers who had been on the job for 20 weeks.

In a wartime study, men were being trained to track aircraft with a tracking apparatus. Two groups of equal tracking ability, as determined by previous performance, were studied. One group was provided with knowledge of results in the form of a buzzer which the trainer sounded whenever a trainee was off the tracking point by more than two miles. The other group received no such information, and were given only the customary practice on the tracking apparatus. After only 68 minutes of practice, the group trained with the electric buzzer was found to be off target only 32% of the time while the group trained without the buzzer were off about 58% of the time.

Almost without exception, where knowledge of performance is given to one group of trainees and the same knowledge is withheld or reduced in the case of another group, the former group learns more rapidly and reaches a higher level of proficiency.

But the ways in which this principle works, and the conditions under which it works are many and complex. Consequently, it does little good merely to say, "Give your trainees knowledge of how well they are doing in training." As a matter of fact, as we shall see later, there are certain conditions under which giving knowledge of performance produces no effect. Rather, we need to know something about how to give the knowledge of performance, who should give the information, how much information and what kind should be given, and the conditions under which it should be given.

There is little to be gained by trying to develop gimmicks or packaged tech-niques for feeding back to employees the results of their performance. Instead, specific procedures must be designed to fit the individual training situation. The intention of this report is to present certain reasonably well validated principles from which the training official can tailor-make his own techniques.

HOW DOES IT WORK?

Feeding back knowledge of performance affects the trainee's learning in two ways. First, it gives the trainee information on what response he should learn. Research on human learning shows that very frequently the learner takes a long time to learn simply because he spends time in learning the wrong or irrelevant things which must then be unlearned.

To learn efficiently, he must be able to discriminate quickly those responses which he is to acquire. For instance, very often in supervisory training we tell the trainee that he must "create a non-threatening climate" in dealing with his subordinates. But "creating a non-threatening climate" represents a tremendous range of possible supervisor responses and the trainee is bound to be unsure, as to which ones are non-threatening. He needs an opportunity to react to situa-tions, make what he considers "non-threatening" responses, and then learn how well his behavior came close to the mark. Without feedback he may well under-stand and accept the principles of non-threatening behavior, but he will never learn actually to produce such behavior.

A second reason why knowledge of performance aids learning is that it affects motivation to keep learning. One of the basic requirements for motivation is that the trainee set goals for himself. But once goals are set, they will serve as incen-tives to performance only as long as the person experiences some sense of progress toward those goals.

One of the findings of research on human learning is that normal people tend to abandon a goal if they cannot move toward it. To do otherwise leads to frustration and tension. It is unnatural for a person to persist after a goal which he is unable to achieve. Consequently the sense of movement toward a goal is an absolute requisite for motivation to learn. Knowledge of performance enables the trainee to set effective goals and to experience the sense of movement toward them. There are some interesting experiments on learning in which people gave up their attempts at skill mastery even though they were making good progress, simply because they could not experience their progress. They felt all the frus-tration and loss of interest that ordinarily characterized a person who was failing to learn.

The experimental studies on this point suggest that *the incentive effect of knowl-edge of performance is likely to be more important in the later stages of practice than in the earlier.* In the earlier stages there is a certain initial enthusiasm which carries the trainee forward. Later, when the going is tougher, this initial drive must be replaced by a sense of progress which only knowledge of performance can give.

There is also a caution suggested by the same research. It seems that increasing knowledge of performance does not *always* increase motivation. There is probably little effect when the trainee is already performing at a high level of proficiency; and if he is doing poorly, increased knowledge of this fact may actually decrease his motivation. So we must go carefully in supplying knowledge of performance when the trainee's performance is at the extremes of the proficiency range.

WHAT INFORMATION TO GIVE?

Feeding back knowledge of performance will be effective only if we give the trainee information which will help him learn. Not all information about his performance does this. It goes without saying, of course, that the information we feed back must be relevant to the trainee's learning task. It must really be useful to him in achieving the training goals we impose on him.

But beyond this, *the information we give him must be unique or non-redundant.* By this I mean that it must be information which he does not already possess about his performance. The trainee always has some information of his own about his performance. In feedback we must add to this knowledge. The consequences of over-looking this point are nicely illustrated in a case of military training. In teaching aerial gunners to track aircraft, a special training device was used which made the view in the gunsight turn red when the trainee was on target. This device was found to improve the trainee's ability at fixing the target's range but not at tracking the target. The reason was that the trainees were receiving all the knowledge they needed about tracking just from looking into the gunsight. The red filter added no new information. In this case the knowledge of performance so ingeniously provided by the trainers failed to improve tracking skill because it was redundant.

In this connection we must realize that the trainee almost always has *some* knowledge of performance, whether we give it to him or not. If it is not provided for him, the trainee will attempt to develop his own. And in so doing, he is very likely to rely upon incorrect or irrelevant sources of information. Furthermore, research shows, if the trainee cannot discover such sources, he will *create* his own information. That is, he will set up his own standards about right and wrong performance, standards against which he can judge himself in some way. It is almost inevitable that in so doing he will adopt standards which do not correspond to those of the trainer. Under these conditions the trainee will indeed make progress toward his own self-developed standards, but his progress will not be the kind which the trainer intends.

Very frequently, what the training official perceives as a failure to learn is in reality learning of a different kind. The trainee learns all right, he just doesn't learn what we want him to learn. Thus we see that the trainee naturally seeks knowledge of performance, and that if it is not forthcoming, he will invent his own, which in turn usually leads to learning the wrong performance.

One of the commonest sources of such self-developed standards is other trainees. In the absence of external, trainer-provided standards, the training group will originate its own "myths" about what is a good performance and how to judge when you are producing it. These myths are psychologically very similar to rumors; they exist and flourish in the absence of adequate external information, and they are accepted by trainees because they want to accept them, because they have a need to know how well they are doing.

As to the content of feedback, it is extremely important that such information be positive as well as negative. That is, the information must tell him what to do, as well as what not to do. Negative information alone helps learning by telling the trainee what responses he should avoid, but this does not always make clear just what the correct response is. We see this principle violated in other areas of employee relations. Safety posters, for instance, which merely admonish the employee "to be careful" or to avoid accidents are usually worthless because they do not tell the employee what he needs to know in order to be careful or avoid accidents.

It is important, then, in critiquing a trainee's performance that the nature of the correct response be clearly communicated. This means that frequently the trainee must see a demonstration of the correct response, possibly from the trainer or from audio-visual aids. Ordinarily such displays are used only in the early stages of training for the purpose of giving an initial picture of what the correct performance looks like. This is a good practice. But often it is not realized that such devices should also be repeated later as a means for enabling the trainee to compare his performance with the correct one. *Such displays should be inserted as soon as possible after the employee's own performance in order that a comparison can be made.*

In general, then, whenever the trainee is not making the desired response, simply giving negative information will do very little toward installing the correct performance. Under these circumstances we must give positive information, and to do this we must include in our feedback a demonstration of the correct performance.

Furthermore, if feedback indicates only that the trainee is not making the correct performance, his motivation may decline. As we have already noted, people usually abandon goals when they do not experience progress toward them. To provide this experience of progress, the trainee must make some successful performances. And here again, demonstrations of the correct response are necessary—to be combined perhaps with guidance to insure the trainee's successful reproduction of what he has seen.

In cases where the trainee hits upon the correct performance and thus actually experiences the correct response, positive information to this effect should always be given. In this instance, the purpose of positive information is not so much to show the trainee what the correct performance is like, but to let him know that he has made it. In this way he learns the "feel" of doing it right so that in the future he is able to provide himself with sound knowledge of his own performance. Thus by teaching the trainee to recognize a correct performance in his own behavior, we prepare him to continue his self-teaching long after he has left the training situation. In this way he can train himself, and training official's efforts are supplemented by the trainee's own private efforts. But unless this happens, the trainee's performance is likely to deteriorate after leaving the training situation, simply because he cannot critique himself.

Finally, the information we supply the trainee should be specific. Experimental results in the field of learning give us a statement of this principle: *The more specific the knowledge of performance, the more rapid the improvement and the higher the level of performance.* Other things being equal, the more exactly the trainee knows how he has performed, the more he is able to make the appropriate improvements.

Research also shows, however, that there is an *optimum* specificity of information, and that knowledge of performance beyond this optimum will not improve performance or may even lead to its deterioration. This optimum represents the trainee's capacity to absorb and use the information we give him. When the knowledge we give exceeds this capacity, the trainee becomes confused. To protect himself against this confusion, he is likely to disregard the information we give him. The optimum amount of specificity of knowledge of performance is known to be related to the stage of training.

In the early stages of training, the trainee's ability to use feedback is limited so that a little information goes a long way. The trainee's progress is, in fact, dependent upon his ability to utilize the knowledge of performance we give him. *This means that effective training must not only provide the trainee with knowledge of his performance, but it must also teach him how to use it to improve his learning.* He must be shown how to relate the feedback to his own performance.

HOW TO GIVE KNOWLEDGE OF PERFORMANCE?

Once the content of the feedback information is determined, the question arises as to the most effective way of supplying the information. The time relations between the trainee's performance and provision of the feedback are an important factor. Again, experimental studies of learning have given us a generalization of this point: *The longer the delay in giving knowledge of performance, the less effect the information has.* This has been widely verified in a number of training investigations.

An illustration comes from the military problem of training men to receive telegraphic code. In the traditional method, a long series of code signals are presented by earphones and the trainee's reading of these was scored at the end of each training session. Thus, there was feedback but it was delayed until the end of the training period. A new method was developed, called the "code-voice" method, in which the presentation of each code-letter signal over the earphones was followed three seconds later by the name of the letter. This enabled the trainee to know immediately whether he had made a mistake. It was found that the voice-code method with its immediate knowledge of results was markedly superior to the conventional procedure.

Now we come to what is perhaps the most cardinal consideration in providing trainees with knowledge of performance; namely *that the information we feed back is always a carrier of social values and meanings for the trainee's concept of himself.* Our information is never completely impersonal and objective; it always constitutes "praise" or "reproof." It always contains implications for the trainee's ego and for the kind of mental picture which he has of himself. All of us hold a mental image of the kind of person we consider ourselves to be and of the kind we wish to become. Psychologists call this perception of ourselves the "self-concept."

Knowledge of performance always contains implications for the trainee's self-concept. If the information is consistent with this self-concept, or if it enhances it, the information will be accepted and used to improve performance. If the information we give is inconsistent with the self-concept, if it denies the kinds of things the trainee perceives himself to be, the information will be rejected or discounted. Stated in this way, we see that the question of how to give knowledge of performance is much broader than the simple question of which is more effective, praise or reproof. The real issue is whether the feedback affirms or denies the kind of person which the trainee wishes to be.

Psychologically, "praise" consists of giving a person experiences or evidence which indicate that he is the kind of person he wishes to become. Similarly, "reproof" consists of giving a person experiences which disaffirm that he is the kind of person he seeks to become.

Only when praise and reproof act in this way are they really praise and reproof; and only then do they have an effect on training. As popularly used by many trainers, however, "praise" means any kind of compliment, and reproof means any kind of criticism. But now we see that just any kind of compliment—or "praise," if you will—will not improve training. If the compliment merely affirms something which the trainee is *not* trying to be or become, it will not aid his learning. Furthermore, if it affirms something that he wishes not to become, it may even hinder learning. To tell a trainee, for instance, that his performance shows he has good mathematical ability will not motivate him to learn until he wishes to perceive himself as a capable mathematician. And to tell a person who likes to think of himself as a mathematician that he is a very capable garbage collector is not praise at all.

Our feedback will be effective only if it affirms to the trainee the kinds of things he is trying to assert himself. If this happens, the trainee will eagerly accept and use the information, because it "fits" into his customary way of viewing himself.

If, on the other hand, the feedback disaffirms or denies to the trainee the kinds of things he is attempting to assert about himself, the feedback becomes a form of psychological threat and will be resisted. The reason for the resistance is that we just naturally tend to defend ourselves against events which force us to experience ourselves in terms that we do not value. If the feedback gives this experience, we will defend ourselves by resisting the information.

There are several kinds of resistive reactions which trainees will make when faced with feedback which is threatening to their self-concept. One of the most common is *rigidity*—the trainee's behavior becomes fixed and unchanging. The result is that the trainee's incorrect responses become more deeply ingrained. Under these circumstances feedback will actually impede the process of training. On the other hand, research has shown that in the absence of threat, the person's behavior becomes more flexible and susceptible to change. The trainee becomes capable of accepting the feedback and using it to modify his performance in the desired direction.

We see then that feedback, indeed the entire training situation, must avoid arousing a threat to the trainee's self-concept. It must be permissive and accepting so that the trainee's behavior will remain open to change. Unfortunately, however, the training situation is often a threatening affair. Sometimes the very fact that an employee is sent to training threateningly suggests that he is in need of training because he is not such a "hot" employee.

Another resistive reaction to threatening feedback is for the trainee to accept the information but distort its meaning so that he escapes its threatening implications. The trainee is essentially protecting himself against the threatening information by misinterpreting its meaning. He may even interpret critical feedback as a sign that he is doing the right thing, rather than the wrong. He simply does not get the meaning to knowledge of performance which we wish to communicate. When this happens, knowledge of performance is of little value because the trainee resists making the necessary application.

Now, if the threatening information we give is so clear that the trainee finds it impossible to change its meaning, he can still resist simply by rejecting the information. He can do this in many ways. He may say it is inaccurate, unfair, or "asking too much." But in one way or another, he will discount or minimize it, and thus protect himself against its unwanted implications.

When we stop to think about it, we realize that whether our feedback re-enforces or denies the trainee's self-concept is to a large degree determined by the *manner* in which the knowledge is given to him, rather than by the actual content of the information. It is the "how" rather than the "what." And to employ the proper method requires that we know something about how trainees view themselves. We must see things from their view-point, in terms of what they are trying to accomplish in training, and understand a little about what kind of employees they consider themselves to be.

With these considerations in mind, we can now understand the experimental results which have been obtained in studies of human learning. In general, the evidence shows that praise tends to be slightly more effective than most reproof. More specifically, research suggests the following ranking in decreasing order of effectiveness:

1. Public praise.
2. Private praise.
3. Private reproof.
4. Public reproof.

However, reproof is sometimes helpful and sometimes detrimental. It appears that mild reproof can be rather effective in aiding learning. The reason being that such reproof is mild enough to avoid being threatening, and yet strong enough to motivate the trainee to keep improving. He tries to improve because improvement is seen as a feasible way to escape from the mild threat. Strong reproof, however, seems to be injurious to learning. It is threatening to the point that the trainee gives up; he ceases trying to improve because he cannot see how further effort will relieve him of the threat. In place of improvement, he adopts other reactions to escape the threat. Instead of learning what we want, he learns to protect himself against threat. He learns to do the things we have described above. This is especially likely if the training situation itself is threatening, for then the trainee learns that accepting and using our feedback is pointless (even though in itself it is non-threatening) because the total situation continues to be threatening.

Finally, it should be pointed out that the trainee's view of himself is different at different stages of training, and consequently, the implications of knowledge of performance for his view of himself will vary accordingly. In the early stages of training, the trainee may respond to a negative feedback by saying to himself, "I'm just a beginner, so it's natural for me to make mistakes." Later on when he is a more advanced learner, he may respond to the same information by saying, "Even old hands slip up occasionally." But note that in both instances the nature of the reaction is the same: the trainee is accepting the information by adjusting it so that it fits his view of himself.

36.

FEATURES AND PROBLEMS
OF THE FEDERAL SERVICE:
THE MANAGEMENT OF MERIT

FREDERICK C. MOSHER

Civil service employment involves many of the same activities and problems that face any large employer. But no other institution, private or public, approaches the federal service in terms of size (more than $2^1/_2$ million civilian employees), geographic spread (50 states and about 125 foreign countries, colonies, and dependencies) and occupational diversity (an extraordinary number of different occupations—representing just about every significant profession and calling known to man—are employed somewhere by the federal government). The government is in fact a loose aggregation of many different employers. But for some purposes and in some ways it operates as a single employer. The balance between agency operation and discretion on the one hand and central standardization, operation, and control on the other has long been the object of debate in the government. As will be shown below, the balance has swung dramatically in the last quarter-century away from the central office.

There are, nonetheless, strong centripetal and standardizing forces. The "board of directors" of the U.S. government is Congress, and some committees and some members of that body have long taken a rather unusual interest in the administration of federal personnel—unusual, that is, for a board of directors. Their inquiries sometimes lead to the passage of laws. Some of these laws apply only to specific categories of personnel—the Postal employees, the Foreign Service, manual workers, and so on—but the laws applicable to the general competitive civil service are usually sweeping and apply to hundreds of thousands of individuals in all sorts of occupations and programs. Some of them are fairly

Frederick C. Mosher, "Features and Problems of the Federal Service: The Management of Merit" in *The Federal Government Service*, Wallace S. Sayre, ed., © 1965. Reprinted by permission of Prentice-Hall Inc., Englewood Cliffs, New Jersey.

general in nature; many are specific and detailed; and some, though general in purport, are so phrased as to require highly specific procedures to make them effective. Most of the important phases of personnel administration are based upon laws of wide application—examinations, classification, pay efficiency ratings, veterans' preference, retirement, layoffs, and so on. Within or pursuant to the laws, the President has issued a variety of executive orders and the Civil Service Commission a large volume of more detailed instructions, all usually having application to a great proportion of employees in whatever agency they may work.

There are other more or less continuing forces in the direction of centralization and standardization of practice. One of these is the budget and appropriations process, which, among other things, forces each agency every year to bring together comprehensive information and plans about its operations and to defend them before their headquarters officials, the Bureau of the Budget, and the committees of Congress. Another is the President and the government-wide objectives and programs he supports. In recent years presidential impetus has been the dominant factor behind the drive for fair employment practices, greater employment of women, increased productivity of governmental manpower, and collective bargaining in the federal service. Personnel procedures are to some extent standardized by fiat from some of the central staff and service agencies (the Bureau of the Budget, the General Services Administration) as well as by rulings and judgments of the Comptroller General and the courts. Finally, nongovernmental organizations having interest in various aspects of public employment tend to exert a standardizing influence on employment policies—at least to the point of criticizing wide and unequal disparities in practice. Among those with great influence in this direction are the veterans' organizations, many labor unions, and professional associations.

Thus, the government continues to operate, in many ways, as *one* employer—one having enormous size, scope, and variety, but still only one. The ground rules are very nearly universal in application and in some fields, such as reductions-in-force, they are very specific (some would say distressingly so).

For the first half-century of its existence, the Civil Service Commission constituted the bedrock of centralized operations in the federal merit system. Viewed by itself and by many others as the mainstay and watchdog against partisan political practices in public employment, it both carried out many personnel operations itself and reviewed those operations which were performed in the executive agencies. In many respects, the most significant development in federal personnel administration since 1933 has been the decentralization of personnel powers from the Commission and the accompanying revolution in that agency's role and operations. Much of this development was the product of necessities of speed and scale rather than of design. Most of President Roosevelt's

New Deal emergency agencies were set up outside the civil service, at least partly because of the alleged cumbersomeness of civil service recruitment. In the late 1930s, the majority of these appointees were blanketed into the civil service system. In 1938, following the recommendations of the Brownlow Committee of 1937, the President directed all departments and agencies to set up personnel offices and thus equip themselves professionally to handle their own personnel work. Then, with the vast personnel requirements of World War II, personnel authority was delegated to the war agencies; the central system simply could not keep up with demands. After the war, efforts to re-centralize personnel matters resulted in widespread criticism, culminating in the report on personnel of the first Hoover Commission in 1949. Its central theme was decentralization of personnel administration. The great bulk of operating activities has moved from the Commission to the operating departments and agencies and from Washington to the field. Perhaps the most significant single event in this recent history was the passage of the Classification Act of 1949 which vested in the departments and agencies full authority and responsibility for evaluating and classifying jobs, according to standards promulgated by the Commission and subject to its periodic post-audit. In terms of work volume, the most striking decentralization has been in the fields of recruiting and examining, the traditional citadels of Commission activity. Of the 300,000 appointments to the competitive service in 1962, more than 85 per cent were recruited and examined by boards of examiners within the departments and agencies themselves.

Today the bulk of federal personnel work is performed by the operating agencies of the government, and a large proportion of it is done in their field establishments away from Washington. Personnel "programs" are, by and large, agency programs, not Civil Service Commission programs. And they comprehend, in addition to classification, recruitment, and examining, which have already been mentioned, the lion's share of training, placement, promotion, evaluation, labor relations, and other common personnel activities. Some of the principal debates on decentralization today relate not to the relative prerogatives of the Civil Service Commission and the rest of the executive branch, but, within individual departments and agencies, between their headquarters and regional offices and between the regional offices and the local installations.

In consequence of this transformation, the role and the complexion of the Civil Service Commission itself have been drastically revised. It is still in operation, but its largest operating activity—the conduct of security investigations for most of the government—did not exist thirty years ago. Today the security program accounts for almost half of the Commission's budget. Its other operating activities include some examining and the administration of the federal retirement system and of some other employee benefit programs, such as life insurance and health. It also continues to carry on some of its traditional functions—enforcing the basic laws of the civil service, the Hatch Acts, the Veterans' Preference Act, and others; hearing and deciding on employee appeals against agency decisions; issuing civil service regulations; and inspecting agency personnel management performance. But more than ever before, the Commission today is serving in a staff capacity as adviser, consultant, and planner at the levels of the President, of the departments in Washington, and of their installations in the field. It has been given, or has assumed, leadership in stimulating improvements in personnel programs in general, in eliminating discriminatory practices, in promoting efficiency, and in projecting a favorable "image" of the public employee and of public employment in the nation. And in recent years, these roles of leadership and of staff consultant have had growing importance.

Yet the Civil Service Commission[1] has many faces: its roles are confusing and in many senses contradictory. It is at once policeman, prosecutor, defender, and judge. It is an advocate before the Congress and an agent of the Congress; a security sleuth of, and a "union" for, employees; a rule-maker, an inspector, a disciplinarian, and a management consultant to other agencies; an adviser to and instrument of the President; an insurance agency; and a public relations office for the government in general. As indicated above, the Commission has considerably shifted its emphases in recent years. But many of the older functions, the older roles, remain. That it has been able to make this shift and still carry on its traditional responsibilities with as much grace and aplomb as it has is a considerable achievement of its leadership and its staff.

THE QUEST FOR QUALITY—PROBLEMS OF ENTRANCE

From their beginning, civil service systems have directed primary attention to recruitment and selection. At first, in fact, these were the only major functions of the Civil Service Commission. The extension of its activities into other areas of activity did not really begin until the time of World War I. It is thus no accident that when Americans think of civil service they think first of entrance examinations. This is the principal activity which provides the civil service system with direct contact with the general public. Examining and recruiting for the federal civil service has become an enormous, continuous business. In recent years, the government has announced an average of more than 20,000 examinations per year—about eighty every working day. It processes nearly two million applications and hires between two and three hundred thousand new employees annually.

---

[1] The term is used here generically to include the members of the Commission and its entire staff, headquarters, and field.

Open Competition

The basic procedure of civil service selection is about as old as the merit system itself. Its major steps are:

On the basis of requests for eligibles from agencies, examinations are planned and scheduled;
Examinations are publicy announced;
Candidates submit applications;
Applications are reviewed and candidates are notified as to their eligibility;
Examinations are given;
Examinations are graded and eligible registers are set up for those that pass in rank order of grade;
In response to an agency request, the top three names on the register are certified;
The agency selects and appoints one of the three.

Although there have been a number of variations in this procedure—including additional steps and shifting of sequence, particularly in recent years—the fundamental elements remain about as stated. The most important addition has been the requirement, for those who have passed the examination, of an investigation of security and suitability—by all odds the most laborious, time-consuming, and expensive step of all.

The crux of the process is the examination(s), and it is here that personnel administration in the public sphere has concentrated a large proportion of its energies and resources from the very beginning. The competitive procedure rests on the premise that the future performance of individuals in different kinds os work can be comparatively predicted with reasonable accuracy by tests of their qualifications and attributes given in advance. Starting from the simplest beginnings 80 years ago, testing has developed into an imposing applied science, comprehending measurements of: intelligence; different kinds of aptitudes, knowledge, and memory; performance of different kinds of tasks; attitudes; physical and athletic ability; character; and personality. The typical civil service examination comprises a battery of different kinds of tests, most of which are graded in quantitative terms; the various grades are then combined according to some formula of weighting to provide a composite examination score. It is of course presumed that all of the attributes measured, and the weights assigned to each, bear a valid relationship to the qualifications required for specific jobs.[2]

The procedure claims a number of advantages. First, it is *open*. Everyone can have a "crack" at a job, providing only that he meets the minimum qualifi-

---

[2] The subject of job testing and the problems associated therewith would warrant a volume —or a five-foot shelf. Let it suffice here to emphasize that civil service testing has advanced far beyond the paper and pencil examinations with which Americans commonly associate the civil service, and that in the development of testing technique, the federal government has been in the forefront.

cations which are themselves intended to be based upon what the job requires. Second, it is *competitive* in terms of the criteria of ability to perform the work of the job as such criteria are reflected in the examination itself. Third, it is *objective*. It systematically excludes political, personal, and other considerations. It separates the appointing agency as well as the examiners themselves from the individuals examined, making collusion or discrimination on the basis of factors other than merit difficult if not impossible. Fourth, it still permits the appointing agency a degree of *discretion* in its selection (one out of three), but only among candidates of proven qualifications. Finally, it is *efficient;* it takes advantage of the best available examining techniques, makes possible mechanized, mass examining, and avoids duplicating efforts among different appointing agencies.

Against these alleged advantages, critics of the civil service system make many counter-charges. One has been that the process is laborious, lumbering, and expensive, especially for a government of such vast size in an era of rapid change. Its slowness is such as to discourage the best qualified applicants and to detract from its effectiveness in meeting the changing needs of the using agencies. The very objectivity and impersonality claimed for it do not permit sufficient attention to human factors in employment such as personality, compatibility, dedication, and initiative. The employing agencies, not infrequently dissatisfied with the caliber of candidates from whom they may choose, complain that they are deprived of an essential ingredient to their responsibility for their programs—the determination of whom they may hire.

A related series of criticisms has gone to the heart of competitive examinations themselves. In a system of such vast size, there must be a great *distance* between the examiner and the hiring officer and consequently a tremendous difficulty in adapting the examination to the requirements of individual jobs. And persuading the hiring officer that the examination is so adapted is equally difficult. This is particularly true in those occupational fields of highly specialized skills and knowledges for which a central examining agency could hardly be equipped with qualified staff. Further, testing technicians recognize that even the best examinations are fallible—subject to a margin of error. There is doubt in some fields whether tests are reliable at all, and some have alleged that tests are negative indicators; that they measure the wrong kinds of things. Yet, the traditional competitive procedure requires that every passing candidate be ranked in accordance with his exact grade and that he be certified for possible appointment in accordance with his proper rank order. An 85 is superior to an 84.7 and below an 85.2.

The Civil Service Commission has, in recent years, shown flexibility in bypassing or overcoming many of these difficulties without doing too much violence to its underlying legal and idealistic principles of open competition, equal opportunity and objectivity. Foremost has been the decentralization already mentioned. Long ago, the Commission set up regional offices in major cities across the country, and a large part of this examining work has long been conducted at the regional level. The regional offices now account for about twice as many of new civil service appointments as the Washington headquarters. Second has been the delegation to boards of examiners, operating within the agencies and their field installations, of the bulk of day-to-day recruitment and selection. These steps have made possible quickening the response to personnel needs, bringing the selection process closer to where the work will be done and also closer to the labor market upon which it must depend. The examining operations of the Civil Service Commission headquarters have been reduced mainly to professional and administrative fields, for which it is desired to tap a nationwide employment market to produce eligibles in demand by a number of different federal agencies (such as the Federal Service Entrance Examinations, described below, and the management series).

The procedural restrictions involved in civil service examining have been relaxed for different categories of jobs. One device is the offering of continuously open examinations, particularly for semi-skilled and clerical jobs, such as typing and stenography. Under this system, it is possible for a candidate to apply, be examined, and appointed all on the same day. Another is the so-called *unassembled examination*, in which applicants are rated on the basis of their credentials in education, prior experience, evidences of achievement, and letters of recommendation. Such examinations are widely used for professional and specialized positions. The technique known as *selective certification* is frequently used to permit agencies to ask for candidates from general civil service registers who have particular specialties of education or experience to fit particular job needs.

The Shifting Significance of Competition

Despite these many steps to simplify and expedite entrance to the federal services on the basis of merit, the U.S. government is still hard pressed to recruit enough highly qualified personnel for many of its professional, scientific, and administrative posts. The civil service system has historically given great attention to the improvement of its techniques for selecting the best qualified among those who apply. But open competition among candidates can be futile if there are not any qualified applicants to begin with or if the best qualified potential candidates do not apply. There is evidence that in some fields this has been the case. In a few specialties, this is a reflection of a basic shortage in the society as a whole, a deficiency in the educational system. In others, it appears that the government has not been getting its share of the best available—they are drawn into other fields of employment. In these crucial areas, the competition among applying candidates is less significant than that between the government and other potential employers for the cream of the crop who are available.

Increasingly in recent years, the focus of federal efforts in recruitment has been to strengthen its competitive position in the labor market. This new approach to federal recruitment entails a near-reversal of two implicit and basic assumptions of the civil service which were grounded in the nineteenth century. The first of these was that the government was operating in an employers' labor market and that, in such a market, its position was a favorable one. Its fundamental procedures assumed that there were, and would continue to be, an ample number of qualified persons seeking federal employment—that is, unemployed or underemployed, or filling jobs considered less desirable than those in the government. A companion assumption, probably inherited from Andrew Jackson, was that government jobs (with certain exceptions) were basically simple, requiring no special knowledges and skills.[3] Armed with these two assumptions, the Civil Service Commission recruited passively by announcing examinations in small print in newspapers and on Post Office bulletin boards and by awaiting applications. Except in wartime, there appears to have been little positive effort to advertise opportunities and to seek qualified applicants before the Great Depression of the 1930s.

For the upper level jobs today, no assumptions could be more deceiving or more damaging. In many fields, these jobs are the most demanding, the most difficult, and the most important in their impact upon the society. Yet the assumptions have lingered long in civil service procedures, in the views of the Congress about the civil service, and, most important of all, in the minds of many influential individuals outside the government, including a significant share of scholars.

In recent years, a major focus of Civil Service Commission effort has been to combat these old assumptions. It has fostered continuing federal-university relations, "Career Days" on campuses, federal-industrial conferences, active public relations campaigns, articles and speeches on the excitement and the attractions of federal service.

Recruitment for Job or Career?

The open competitive system of selection provided by the Pendleton Act of 1883 has been referred to as "Americanizing a Foreign Invention"[4] (primarily a British one). The emphasis in this expression should be upon "Americanizing" because in some ways the American variations on the model were more important than the model itself. The British system contemplated the recruitment of its civil servants immediately upon the completion of their education and their retention in the service throughout their working lives. None were to come in

---

[3] There was apparently once much truth in this belief. It has been estimated that, at the close of the nineteenth century, only two per cent of the federal civil service were professionals. Most of these were probably lawyers and engineers.

[4] Paul P. Van Riper, *History of the United States Civil Service* (Evanston, Ill.: Row, Peterson and Company, 1958), p. 96.

except at the bottom; and the examinations were attuned to the educational system, not to the first job assignment. The Congress which passed the Pendleton Act rejected the concept of a closed career service with explicit intention. It removed from the bill a provision that would have permitted entrance only "at the lowest grade" and amended it to add an injunction that tests given for entrance be "practical in nature" and related to the duties to be performed.[5] These changes undoubtedly reflected a fear of a closed bureaucracy and a desire to maintain the democratic tradition in the public service. They have colored the nature and the administration of the civil service ever since. For while it is true that many thousands of civil servants have entered and stayed in the service for their entire careers, it is also true that the civil service does recruit new people at all levels, and always has.[6]

It is also true that the historic practice of the American system has been to frame examinations according to the requirements of the duties of specific jobs and not to measure the qualifications for progressive advancement in a life-long career. Critics and reformers—even including some of the Commissions themselves—have for a very long time urged the development of a career-oriented personnel system, including entrance examinations tailored for the purpose.[7] Examinations were administered for what amounted to career experience for some technical and professional specialists such as agriculturists, geologists, engineers, and foresters. Nonetheless, for the first half century of its existence, the Civil Service Commission did virtually nothing in the direction of attracting and examining college graduates for careers in the public service.

In the light of this background, the movement which began with the New Deal toward a career system for college educated people constitutes in some ways the most substantial achievement—and reversal of tradition—in recent personnel history. This development was, in part, a response to the growths in size of the federal government during the New Deal period, World War II, and the Korean War. It was more importantly a product of the obvious growth in importance and difficulty of federal undertakings. And in part, it has been a response to the intellectualization of the society and the governments which guide and service it. The push for a positive program of career recruitment, long advocated by civil service reformers, was strengthened during these years by the persistent and

---

[5] *Ibid.*, p. 100.

[6] In spite of this, some of the more professionalized bureaus of the government, such as the Forest Service, have developed closed career services in which lateral entry (i.e., direct appointment from outside above the bottom level) is virtually unknown. Paradoxically, in the U.S. Foreign Service, which was established in 1924 as a direct imitation of the closed British system, the majority of the top positions today are filled by persons who in fact entered laterally rather than in the orthodox manner.

[7] As long ago as 1905, the Commission in its *Twenty-Second Report* stated that "the great defect in the Federal Service today is the lack of opportunity for ambitious, well-educated young men" (p. 23).

repeated urging of a series of study groups, starting in 1935 with the Commission of Inquiry on Public Service Personnel. Its basic recommendations for a true career program were endorsed by and elaborated on by a variety of successors, notably the President's Committee on Administrative Management in 1937, and the First and Second Hoover Commissions in 1949 and 1955. All urged strengthening of recruitment and subsequent career opportunities for qualified, well-educated persons.

The response of the Civil Service Commission to these emerging needs and recommendations was sporadic, sometimes hesitant, but, over-all, remarkable. Behind the leadership of Commissioner Leonard D. White, an early appointee of President Franklin D. Roosevelt, the Commission offered its first examination designed for unspecialized college graduates in 1934—the Junior Civil Service Examiner examination. This test, which was offered again in 1936, provided a vehicle for the entry of a substantial number of able and well educated individuals into the federal service. In 1939, the effort was resumed with the offering of the first Junior Professional Assistant (JPA) examination, which aimed more specifically to draw college graduates who had majored in particular fields. Altogether, the first JPA included some 22 types of specialized options, including one for Junior Administrative Technicians, designed especially for persons who had specialized in administration or political science. The JPA was continued, though with changes in emphasis and options, through the war and until 1947. It was then succeeded by the Junior Management Assistant (JMA) program, which was the principal vehicle for general college recruitment from 1948 to 1954. The JMA was different from its predecessors in a number of ways. It drew the hiring agencies into the examining process to a much greater extent than before; it involved a much more extensive and presumably more thorough examining process; it was integrated with a systematic training and career development program to a much greater extent than its predecessors.

The JMA was probably a more effective device than any of the programs which preceded it for attracting and selecting young career professionals and potential career executives for the federal service. But it fell into hard times, for reasons not attributable to itself, during the late Truman Administration and the first years under President Eisenhower. The principal reason was the rapid decline in prestige and attractiveness of the federal service in general during the early 1950s, a decline resulting from security investigations, the hysteria attending Senator McCarthy's charges, the effects of veterans' preference (particularly its impact upon staff reductions), scandals in the public service, and "politics." Between 1951 and 1953, the number of applicants for the JMA dropped from 19,000 to about 8,000.

In 1954 the Civil Service Commission staff conducted a thorough investigation into its whole college recruiting program, and the following year launched upon a new one which was different from those that had gone before—the Federal

Service Entrance Examination (FSEE). This examination was designed as a vehicle for the recruitment and selection of college graduates and graduate students from a wide variety of fields of specialization—most of the major fields offered in colleges.[8] The FSEE test measured general intelligence and ability plus general information. It was supplemented by a test and program for Management Interns—a "blue ribbon" extension of the FSEE for the best qualified of applicants, leading to supervised intern programs in particular agencies. Applicants for Management Intern must pass the FSEE and then take more rigorous written and oral examinations. The select few who make the grade are appointed at higher levels and can anticipate rapid advancement to positions of high administrative responsibility.

After more than a decade of continuous experience, the FSEE and the Management Intern programs remain the basic general recruiting and selecting devices for federal college-level entrance. It may therefore be useful to discuss in somewhat greater depth their nature and content. The two tests represent the principal governmental response to the challenge of competition by other employers for young, educated persons aspiring to high-level professional and administrative positions. Although not restricted to upper division college students and graduates, the FSEE is clearly directed to them and they have constituted the bulk of those successful in the test. The test itself, a fairly brief short-answer exam of intelligence and general information, is sufficiently broad that college students and graduates can compete successfully regardless of their major field of study, and for most students it is now the principal means of entrance into the Federal service.[9] Through the device of selective certification, described above, a wide range of junior professional positions are filled from FSEE registers—park rangers, budget officers, tax accountants, geologists, mathematicians, air traffic control officers, to mention only a few.

The FSEE, which is one of the relatively few examinations which the Civil Service Commission itself still conducts, in many ways illustrates the degree to which civil service procedures and traditions can be adapted to the needs of the times. It is widely advertised on college campuses, and active recruiting is stimulated by visits of agency personnel representatives to the colleges and through faculty members. The examination itself is offered a number of different times each year, scheduled in relation to the rhythm of the academic year. Entrance grades and salaries are high enough to match the offerings of other employers in most (not quite all) fields. The results of these efforts have been impressive. In 1963, nearly 230,000 individuals applied for the FSEE; 140,000 took the examination; 58,000 passed; and over 8,000 were appointed to federal jobs.

---

[8] A number of other specialized examinations are still offered for majors in some fields, including the physical sciences, engineering, accounting, forestry and others.
[9] The FSEE replaced more than one hundred more specialized examinations.

The Management Intern examination is a much more rigorous and "exclusive" process. Those who pass it are assigned to tailored intern programs of training and practice in agencies and can expect rapid advancement, if they are successful, to positions of considerable managerial responsibility. The examination is offered less frequently than the FSEE but is given on the same days. Applicants must pass the FSEE and, in addition, more difficult tests of general abilities, knowledge of public affairs, and administrative problems. Those who pass the written tests later take an oral examination. The majority of those successful are graduate students. In contrast to the broad sweep of the FSEE, only 23,000 applied for the Management Intern part of the examination in 1963. Of these, about 2,500 passed the written examination, 700 reached the eligible register, and 300 were appointed to positions.

Together the FSEE and the Management Intern examinations approach the career idea at the entrance level and are far removed from the traditional philosophy of the civil service. But they are not yet a complete answer to the problem of professional and administrative personnel for the government. In spite of the impressive numbers of applicants, there is evidence that large numbers of the best potential applicants do not apply. It is increasingly clear that the top students normally proceed to at least one year of graduate training and that the "cream" of these are not attracted by the federal service. The majority of those appointed from FSEE registers have little background in social, political, and administrative fields, and one may question whether high academic ability in languages, music, or English literature is sufficient assurance in itself of adequacy in dealing with the governmental problems of today and tomorrow. Finally, it must be noted that most governmental agencies have not yet established systematic provision for the development and advancement to higher positions of their best qualified people. The planned career system ends soon after its beginning, and most of those in government, soon after their entrance, must fend for themselves.

37.

JUDICIAL REVIEW AND THE REMOVAL OF FEDERAL EMPLOYEES

Cornelius J. Murphy

During calendar year 1959, over forty-eight thousand federal civilian employees were either discharged from government service or separated for other administrative reasons. Because of the difficulty in obtaining judicial review of these actions, their legality will, in many cases, go unchallenged. It is the purpose of this article to reexamine the reasons why review is so limited and to suggest some means by which the end of justice can be better approximated.

The federal courts have been traditionally without power to review the removal of federal employees, except where there has been a violation of applicable statutes and regulations, or where there has been a manifest abuse of discretion. With this there can be little quarrel, such an approach to the problem reconciles the requirements of justice with the necessity that governmental operations be free of undue interference. The difficulty lies with the availability of a court to which an employee may turn for redress if his removal were procedurally defective or arbitrary.

It is repeatedly held that only the District Court for the District of Columbia has the power to order reinstatement of an illegally removed or separated federal civilian employee, reinstatement being achieved, theoretically at least, through the exercise of the power to issue original writs of mandamus.

In lieu of a petition for writ of mandamus, the adversely affected employee may sue, in the United States Court of Claims, for damages sustained as a result of the removal. This is, of course, a money judgment, and does not affect a reinstatement.

Both courts are located within the District of Columbia.

I. GEOGRAPHICAL DISTRIBUTION OF FEDERAL CIVILIAN EMPLOYEES

In pre-war America, the predominant geographic concentration of federal em-

Reprinted by permission of the Federal Bar Association from *Federal Bar Journal*, Winter, 1962, pp. 25–31.

ployees was in the metropolitan Washington, D.C. area. For example, in 1939, 126,000 people were employed there, more than the number employed in any of the States. Wartime America considerably changed this geographic distribution. Of the more than two million persons employed by the federal government in continental United States during calendar year 1960, only slightly more than 168,000 worked in metropolitan Washington, which was less than the number employed in California, where over 239,000 were employed, and New York with over 179,000, and Pennsylvania having in excess of 130,000 federal employees. More significantly, of 11,800 employees discharged during 1960, only 688 worked in the Washington area; of 19,000 separations for reduction in force, only 425 worked there.

Statistics such as these show the remoteness, for a substantial number of adversely affected employees, of the District Court for the District of Columbia and the Court of Claims. It is an obvious hardship for one living and working in California, or Texas, or even New York, for that matter, to go to the trouble and expense of prosecuting a suit in the District of Columbia. It is in the light of these statistics that the reasons precluding review in the District Courts located within the several states should be re-examined.

II. MANDAMUS

Ex parte Sawyer was the landmark case from which the courts evolved the rule that mandamus was the proper remedy for a federal employee either threatened with discharge or actually removed. In *Sawyer*, a municipal judge named Parsons in Lincoln, Nebraska, threatened with discharge by the Mayor and Councilmen of that City, obtained a restraining order from the Federal Circuit Court. Disregarding the order, the officials removed Parsons and made a new appointment. Contempt proceedings followed and the officials were imprisoned. They filed a petition for habeas corpus challenging the jurisdiction of the circuit court to issue the restraining order. In sustaining the petition, the Supreme Court, speaking through Mr. Justice Gray said:

. . . It is well settled that a court of equity has no jurisdiction over the appointment and removal of public officers, . . . The jurisdiction to determine the title to a public office belongs exclusively to the courts of law, and is exercised by *certiorari*, error or appeal, by *mandamus*, prohibition, quo warranto, . . . according to the circumstances of the case, and the mode of procedure established by the common law or by statute.

In view of the rule that only the District Court for the District of Columbia had jurisdiction to entertain original petitions in the nature of mandamus, jurisdiction to determine the legality of removal of federal employees has been confined to that court. A careful reading of the *Sawyer* opinion shows, however, that the court was concerned with equitable interference prior to removal, as distinguished from an equitable remedy of reinstatement following the discharge. This is clear from the dissent of Chief Justice Waite:

I am not prepared to decide that an officer of a municipal government cannot, under any circumstances, apply to a court of chancery to restrain the municipal authorities from proceeding to remove him from his office without the authority of law. There may be cases, in my opinion, when the tardy remedies of *quo warranto, certiorari,* and other like writs will be entirely inadequate. I can easily conceive of circumstances under which a removal, even for a short period, will be productive of irremediable mischief.

Some courts have not interfered, on the theory that only if a clear violation of the employee's statutory rights is alleged may the court intervene prior to a final administrative action, but the wisdom of such a practice is indeed dubious. A more pertinent inquiry should be: Following adverse administrative action and exhaustion of administrative remedies, can the district courts afford any relief if the action is shown to be wrongful? A strong argument can be made that the district courts, through their inherent power to issue mandatory injunctions, can afford relief by ordering, in an appropriate case, the reinstatement of a wrongfully affected employee. The equivalence of mandatory injunction and mandamus has long been established, and it has been held that a mandatory injunction may issue if mandamus is not available. In *Delaware and Hudson R. Corporation* v. *Williams*, the Court stated the rule: "Although in many instances a writ of mandamus will not issue, the courts are authorized to compel action through injunction when and if the facts warrant it." It is discouraging to see courts, faced with petitions by aggrieved federal employees, recognize the equivalence and then refuse to take jurisdiction.

III. THE ADMINISTRATIVE PROCEDURE ACT

Another argument favoring jurisdiction is that, in view of the abolition of the writ of mandamus by Rule 81(b) of the Federal Rules, the subsequent passage of the Administrative Procedure Act, making the form of judicial review include mandatory injunctions, was sufficient to confer jurisdiction to hear these suits upon all district courts. The theory that jurisdiction exists under the A.P.A. is supported by respectable authority but has found little support in the courts. Yet the act clearly provides that "any person suffering legal wrong because of any agency action . . . shall be entitled to judicial review thereof." Review is not limited to situations in which express provision is made therefor by statute but extends to . . . "every final agency action for which there is no other adequate remedy in any court . . ." Courts which deny that jurisdiction exists under the act seize upon the limitation that review is not available where the "agency action is by law committed to agency discretion." Yet, the Supreme Court has made it clear that it will not allow arbitrary actions affecting personal rights. In reviewing the legality of action by the Secretary of the Army in issuing a discharge certificate in form other than honorable, it expressly rejected the argument that the matter was not reviewable because committed to "agency discretion." If the Secretary of the Army exceeds his powers ". . . his action would not constitute exercises of his administrative discretion, and in such circumstances . . . judicial relief from this illegality would be available . . . ." The same reasoning should apply to personnel actions. This has been the theoretical position with respect to dismissal of federal employees, that in some cases arbitrary or ultra vires action is reviewable. The "discretion" reservation is particularly unfortunate because of its vagueness. It should properly apply, in cases of application of broad principles to particular cases, where the complexity of the problem involved requires the use of informed judgment or administrative expertise.

A reading of the act as a whole should lead to the same conclusion, as other questions of doubt should be resolved in favor of the existence of jurisdiction. For example, the statutory definition of "agency" lists several exclusions, none of which apply to personnel boards. It is true that standards for agency adjudications are specifically held to be inapplicable where there is involved "the selection or tenure of an officer of the United States." But that refers only to hearing requirements and does not in any way have reference to the availability of review of an administrative *decision*. The same is true with rule-making requirements which do not apply to personnel matters. It is, in fact, a more plausible interpretation of the act, that in view of its failure to exclude matters involving personnel from the definition of agency, that Congress intended to permit the review of these decisions. If such is the case, refusal to accept jurisdiction because of procedural anachronisms is not justifiable. Furthermore, in view of the substantial inequities involved under the present procedure, refusal to construe the Act as conferring jurisdiction seems unnecessarily conservative, since the act was intended to make review more available than it had been prior to its passage.

IV. DECLARATORY RELIEF

The development of the theory that district courts, other than that of the District of Columbia, are without jurisdiction to entertain original petitions in the nature of mandamus has led to the additional restriction that they are also without power to entertain petitions by federal employees for declaratory judgments as to the legality of the questioned administrative action. But the Declaratory Judgments Act specifically provides for such judgments regardless of availability of future relief. Furthermore, the Federal Rules encourage its use in appropriate circumstances if some useful purpose will be served thereby. It is important to note in this connection that it is possible, if the court finds that the employee's rights were violated, for courts in the District of Columbia at least, to issue a declaratory judgment to that effect, and retain jurisdiction until the employee is restored to his position. This is explained in *Borak* v. *Biddle.*

... It is enough for appellant's purposes, at least for the time being, that a declaratory judgment should be made by the district court establishing his right, prior to dismissal, to notice and the sort of hearing provided by the statute. But the district court should retain jurisdiction of the cause so that, if at the end of ninety days ... appellant (is not) restored to office, a writ may issue.

Sufficient "comity" probably exists between the governmental agencies and the various district courts so that any declaratory judgment of the courts with respect to employee's rights would be respected.

V. THE INDISPENSABLE PARTY

The case of *Blackmar* v. *Guerre* is considered authority for the proposition that a suit by a federal employee, seeking to review administrative action of a local official is not maintainable unless the superior officer or the agency entering final administrative appellate action is made a party defendant. In *Blackmar*, a Veterans Administration employee working in Louisiana was fired by a local official. He appealed the dismissal to a Regional Civil Service Board, which reversed and ordered reinstatement. The Veterans Administration then appealed to the Civil Service Commission in Washington which reversed the Regional Board and affirmed the original decision. The employee commenced suit in Federal District Court in Louisiana, naming Guerre, the local official who fired him and the Commission as defendants. He sought to set aside the original discharge and the Commission's action in reversing the Regional Board. He also prayed for a judgment declaring that he was entitled to an order from the Commission directing his reinstatement. Service on the Commission was attempted by serving the United States attorney and the regional director in Louisiana, and mailing copies of the complaint to the Commission in Washington. The action was dismissed as to the Commission for lack of jurisdiction over the person of the Commissioners. The Circuit Court affirmed. On certiorari to the U.S. Supreme Court, the affirmance was upheld. In the course of the opinion, the Court said of Guerre: "It is obvious that no relief can be granted against him." Despite severe criticism, *Blackmar* has been interpreted by the lower courts as requiring dismissal of an action where the superior officer of the department entering final agency action is not made a party, with little attention given to the importance of the distinction between the review of decisions made by a superior officer and those made by a subordinate.

VI. THE DOCTRINE OF PEDREIRO V. SHAUGHNESSY

Three years after *Blackmar*, the Supreme Court decided *Pedreiro* v. *Shaughnessy*. It concerned an attempt by an alien to have a deportation order declared void in a suit brought in the District Court for the Southern District of New York, against the Commissioner who had issued the order. The defendant District Commissioner had full power to issue the order. Prior to commencing suit, petitioner had exhausted his administrative remedies. A motion to dismiss on the grounds that the Attorney General was an indispensable party was granted. On appeal, the Second Circuit reversed. The Supreme Court affirmed. In the opinion, the following important language appears:

We also reject the government's contention that the Commissioner of Immigration and Naturalization is an indispensable party to an action for declaratory relief of this kind.   District directors are authorized by regulations to issue warrants of deportation, . . . The regulations purport to make these decisions of the district director final. It seems highly appropriate, therefore, that the district director charged with enforcement of a deportation order should represent the government's interest . . . Undoubtedly the government's defense can be adequately presented by the district director who is under the supervision of the commissioner . . . Our former cases have established a policy under which indispensability of parties is determined on practical considerations.

Professor Davis enthusiastically favors the view expressed in the above quote:

This ground for decision is both entirely new and entirely sound. It should become the foundation for future law. The beauty of the Pedreiro opinion is the emphasis on the practicalities of venue and geography and the complete absence of purported reliance upon such unworkable distinctions as those between action and inaction and between action of a subordinate and action of a superior through a subordinate.

Pedreiro has been well received in certain circumstances, but has been strictly interpreted in employee actions to require proof that the challenged official has the power to afford the relief requested. While in many situations reinstatement power actually exists, the employee's day in court should not turn on such distinctions. For it is well established that the Court can order a subordinate official to disobey his superior, although the subordinate normally is not empowered with authority to be disobedient. Further, such distinctions run against a basic tenet of our jurisprudence that the party who acts is the one who must account for the results. The courts also fail to see finality in action by the local official where the same is subject to administrative review. While there is some basis for this in veterans' appeals to the Civil Service Commission, there are other situations where the "appeal," so-called, does not include a formal hearing and results in a cursory confirmation of lower officials' decisions. Also overlooked is the Administrative Procedure Act's provision providing for review of agency action regardless of administrative appellate procedures. Finally, little consideration is given to the policy of the Federal Rules which makes joinder of parties defendant dependent on practical considerations.

VII. CONCLUSION

It would not take much equitable ingenuity to substitute mandatory injuction for mandamus, to enter declaratory judgments of rights to employment in the belief that sufficient comity exists between the judiciary and the executive to make them worthwhile, and to subject the indispensable party doctrine to practicability and convenience. The present judicial timidity in this area is perhaps grounded on the belief that to permit such suits in the federal courts would be an unwarranted intrusion on the doctrine of separateness and independent status of the executive branch. But there is no doubt that a cause of action exists within the area of procedure and good faith discretion, so that the issue is unreal. Perhaps the reluctance has its foundation in a belief that to permit suits in the districts where the action took place would unduly interfere with internal management of the government. Yet the results would be chaotic if the fifteen thousand employees discharged in 1959 all brought petitions in the District Court for the District of Columbia. It may well be that the proper solution would depend in part upon a venue statute as is the practice in some States. Whatever the result, the problem deserves more attention than it presently receives.

38.

APTITUDE TESTING FOR MACHINE OPERATORS

HUSAIN MUSTAFA

Use of semi-automatic machines to handle the tremendous number of repetitive operations that constitute mail-processing has created a need for a large number of keyboard operators. These operators must work at a constant prescribed rate of production for extended periods and sustain an accuracy rate of 99 per cent. Consequently, the mental and physical demands of a keyboard operator are unique. A high degree of mental alertness and concentration is necessary to make correct sorting decisions at rates up to one every second, reports the U.S.

Reprinted from *Public Personnel Review*, Vol. 27, No. 2 (April, 1966), pp. 102–05.

Post Office Department in *Criteria for Use of Multi-Position Letter Sorting Machines*, October 18, 1963. Incumbents must possess a high degree of manual and visual coordination and adequate finger dexterity. Moreover, they must sit in a relatively fixed position without being able to talk with each other while working.

Due to the difficult and exacting nature of the work, individuals lacking the required skills and aptitudes would not qualify as effective letter sorting operators. Therefore, measurement and identification of these skills and aptitudes should constitute the major part of the operator selection process. This discussion covers the progress achieved by the U.S. Post Office Department in developing scientific selection techniques and using established psychological and psychometric methods to identify and evaluate the skills and aptitudes needed for Letter Sorting Operator.

SHORTAGE OF OPERATORS

Sorters now in use incorporate the key-sort method. Under this system, mail is presented to the operator who reads the address and makes a mental memory association of this address with a numbered bin in the sorting machine. To sort the mail, the operator "keys" the proper bin number on a keyboard. This causes the mail eventually to be deposited in that bin.

The lack of aptitude necessary for "Letter Sorting Operator" among the majority of postal clerks was revealed following the installation of the first sorting machine in the Silver Spring, Maryland, Post Office, May, 1956. (Reported by Post Office Department, "Multi-Position Letter Sorting Machines," Memorandum from Bureau of Operations to Regional Directors of Operations, December 10, 1963.) Operator positions were put on bid and postal clerks were encouraged to take them. First, the clerk roster was exhausted, then the carrier group, and finally, substitute employees were approached. However, from the beginning it was found that turnover on the machine was great. Operators did not demonstrate, in actual operation, the ability to attain the prescribed speed or to sustain the required accuracy rate. A production study, conducted by the Post Office Department at the Washington City and Silver Spring, Md., post offices, employed the two variables of error rate and speed. Results showed no improvement after some training.

This, and similar experience in Washington, D. C., indicated that it is difficult to train an indiscriminately selected team of supervisors and operators to a point where acceptance and operation fall into a normal aptitude. Successful placement would depend upon prior identification and measurement of machine operator aptitude.

PRELIMINARY INVESTIGATIONS

Clearly, suitability for Letter Sorting Operator must be determined before actual placement in training. Such appraisals call for the use of established psychological and psychometric methods in the evaluation, measurement, and identification of the aptitudes and skills necessary for effective performance. In March, 1958, an experimental study was undertaken by the Department's Bureau of Personnel to test the following hypotheses:

1. That a paper and pencil test of memory and dexterity would yield scores related to criteria of the effectiveness of Letter Sorting Operators.
2. That a machine test measuring eye-hand coordination, dexterity of fingers, co-ordination of both hands, keenness of vision, memory, and accuracy yields scores related to criteria of the effectiveness of Letter Sorting Operators.
3. That these scores will correlate sufficiently with the criteria to be effective in the selection of potential Letter Sorting Machine Operators.
4. That criteria can be constructed that will reflect the effectiveness of Letter Sorting Operators with sufficient reliability and validity to be predicted within this test framework.

This study was conducted at the Washington City Post Office utilizing personnel assigned as operators on the Bell machine, and at Silver Spring, Maryland, Post Office where the experimental population consisted of Transorma Operators. Later, the study was extended to the Flint, Michigan, Post Office. The investigation's main objectives were to identify the effectiveness with which these operators performed their jobs and to eliminate those tests which did not measurably differentiate between effective operators and those identified as less effective. The criteria used in this study were:

1. Production records of each employee.
2. Performance records during the training period.
3. Records of recent scheme examination.
4. Supervisory evaluation of performance.

Sources of Data

Work samples in terms of pieces of mail worked and a count of errors for each operator were extracted from production records during the period of March 16–31, 1958. Production and performance records constituted the major source of data. All employees had proved satisfactory on the scheme examinations which are given on a pass or fail basis. Therefore, examination records have no value in securing criteria measures. Supervisory evaluations, because they coincided with production records, were also of limited value.

The experimental subjects included 177 Bell and Transorma trainees and operators in Washington, D. C., and Silver Spring, Maryland. In Washington, 90 girls from the substitute clerk-carrier group were tested for dexterity. Only 35 achieved 55 speed and two per cent accuracy. The rest either resigned or were reassigned. In Flint, Michigan, the examination was open to all distribution clerks who wished to take it. In this case, since all the subjects were already engaged in distribution, passing the examination was not made a condition for placement into the training. A group of 117 clerks participated in the training, but only 68 were found to be eligible. Forty clerks qualified to operate the keyboard at the rate of 50 a minute with a minimum of one per cent error. After six months of training, no one qualified to work at the rate of 55 and two per cent error. Finally, with further training, less than 5 per cent of the group achieved the higher production rate.

These experimental studies were highly useful in constructing objective criteria that reflect the effectiveness of Letter Sorting Machine Operators with sufficient reliability. In addition, they served to validate parts of the test battery employed and to eliminate those tests which did not distinguish between effective and ineffective operators. In effect, the need for two separate tests was established, for the realities of the situation called for a distinction between new employees and the regular clerks.

New employees must pass Civil Service Commission Examination (Aptitude Test) entitled "Distribution Clerk-Machines (Probational Exam. Spec. No. 2218 (1) Assembled)." Regular employees already on the rolls, and without other full-time assignments available to them, are given the CSC Examination, "Distribution Clerk-Machines," and basic training to the extent necessary to determine their ability to master machine distribution, regardless of whether they pass the CSC examination. Consequently, two registers of eligibles, the open competitive and the in-service, were established.

DISTRIBUTION CLERK EXAMINATION

The examination was developed over a two-year period beginning with installation of the Transorma machine in May, 1956. It was placed into effect as an in-service selection examination in Flint, Washington, Detroit, and Providence. Later, it was adopted as an open competitive examination, and the U.S. Civil Service Commission placed it into effect in December, 1959.

The examination consists of:

1. Written test;
2. Machine aptitude test;
3. Eye and physical examination.

The battery of tests includes a questionnaire about the person's history and interest.

The Aptitude Test

The aptitude test is administered individually and takes about 28 minutes to complete. There are four series of the examination on each roll of film; the one to be used should be designated before the examination. Time allowed is divided as follows:

Practice-keyboard (machine not in operation)	1 minute
Practice-numbers (machine in operation)	5 minutes
Test-numbers (machine in operation)	5 minutes
Memorizing scheme code	5 minutes
Practice-scheme code (machine in operation)	7 minutes
Test-scheme code (machine in operation)	5 minutes
Total time	28 minutes

The applicant is given the keyboard arrangement and is required to memorize it. The keyboard has five keys on each side. Only three on each side, outlined in red, are used for the test. The figures on the left keys are 20, 10, and 200; those on the right are 100, 1, and 2. When any one of these keys is pressed, it will register the digit for that key. When any two of the keys are pressed at the same time, the machine will register the combination of the two keys. For instance, when 200 is pressed at the same time as 100, the machine will register 300.

The participant is required to press the numbers on the keyboard corresponding to those appearing on the small screen in front of him. The numbers appear increasingly faster and the examiner records the total errors on an answer sheet. The actual test follows a prescribed period of practice on both numbers and scheme codes. Using the latter in operating the keyboard simulates what the operator is required to do when actually machine-sorting mail: reading the address, determining the separation to be made, and pressing the appropriate code-number keys.

A chart of the cities used in the test is placed 10 feet in front and slightly to the right of the machine. The chart shows five boxes in each of which the names of three cities appear. Each box has a number above it which is the code number for the cities in that box. In a five-minute period, the participant is required to memorize the code classification of the cities used. Following this, the machine is put into operation and he is required to press the numbers on the keyboard which correspond to the names of the cities appearing on the screen in front of him. During this practice period, he may refer to the chart of the cities whenever necessary. However, the chart is removed during the test. The number of errors committed during the test determines the rating attained.

The aptitude test requires individual testing of every candidate and is, therefore, slow and costly. During the 28-minute testing period, an examiner devotes full-time attention to timing the test and re-setting the machine at prescribed intervals to the proper rate of speed. Testing costs increased considerably since the test was adopted as an open competitive examination.

CONCLUSION

The construction and use of the aptitude test is based on the assumption that the ability to operate a sorting machine efficiently is either unquestionably present or unquestionably absent in a given individual's complex of aptitudes. Moreover, this ability to operate a machine can be measured and a positive relationship between the test scores and ranking of participants obtained. Basically, the test distinguishes between those who possess the desired measure of finger dexterity, memory, coordination of the eyes and hands, and of the two hands, and those who are of subnormal abilities. The test is, therefore, an important rejection factor.

Test scores were found to be related adequately to the effectiveness criteria of Letter Sorting Machine Operators. In Detroit, where a pass and fail group on the examination was placed into training, the fail group achieved the same level of production only after about 62 hours of additional training per individual. In Flint, Washington, and Silver Spring, production patterns indicated that the individuals who failed the examination and required longer training produced less than those who qualified on the examination and required less training.

These results indicate that there is a positive relationship between test scores and job success. Individuals selected specifically for machine operator positions would exhibit more acceptance of the changed operating procedures and training for future machine assignments. A stronger inference is difficult to draw at this time because the number of subjects studied is limited. Moreover, the performance of successful candidates actually selected for operator positions has not as yet been evaluated. For although the results obtained establish, at least initially, that the aptitude test has validity when used as a selection tool, its usefulness does not extend beyond that. The test is not useful as an indicator of motivation, interest, temperament, or work habits, all of which are important in determining job success.

Another conclusion can be tentatively drawn from the available data. A higher percentage of those seeking employment qualify by taking the test as compared to the in-service candidates. This may be explained, first, by the fact that the aptitude test, because it tests for motor skill, memory, and coordination, is correlated negatively with age; and that the incoming group is much younger, on the average, than the in-service group. At present, the median age of the clerks group is 42 as compared to college age for the other group. The second explanation lies in the fact that the distribution of the operators group by sex is changing. Men, at present, outnumber women in positions of operator. This distribution will prevail for some time. The percentage, however, is changing in favor of more women. Two factors are contributing to this change: increased emphasis on finger dexterity, and the adoption of the test as an open competitive examination.

It is important to note that the studies reported here were confined to a few of the largest post offices. National samples would probably modify present conclusions. Nevertheless, since economic considerations dictate that mechanization be limited to the largest post offices where the usefulness coefficient of mechanical equipment would be high, no substantial modification is expected.

39.

THE POLICE AND THE COMMUNITY: THE PROBLEM OF GRIEVANCE MECHANISMS

REPORT OF THE NATIONAL ADVISORY COMMISSION ON CIVIL DISORDERS

We have cited deep hostility between police and ghetto communities as a primary cause of the disorders surveyed by the Commission. In Newark, in Detroit, in Watts, in Harlem—in practically every city that has experienced racial disruption since the summer of 1964—abrasive relationships between police and Negroes and other minority groups have been a major source of grievance, tension and, ultimately, disorder.

In a fundamental sense, however, it is wrong to define the problem solely as hostility to police. In many ways the policeman only symbolizes much deeper problems.

The policeman in the ghetto is a symbol not only of law, but of the entire system of law enforcement and criminal justice.

As such, he becomes the tangible target for grievances against shortcomings throughout that system: against assembly-line justice in teeming lower courts; against wide disparities in sentences; against antiquated corrections facilities; against the basic inequities imposed by the system on the poor—to whom, for example, the option of bail means only jail.

Report of the National Advisory Commission on Civil Disorders, *The Police and the Community: The Problem of Grievance Mechanisms* (New York: Grosset and Dunlap, Inc., 1968), pp. 299–301, 310–12.

The policeman in the ghetto is a symbol of increasingly bitter social debate over law enforcement.

One side, disturbed and perplexed by sharp rises in crime and urban violence, exerts extreme pressure on police for tougher law enforcement. Another group, inflamed against police as agents of repression, tends toward defiance of what it regards as order maintained at the expense of justice.

The policeman in the ghetto is a symbol, finally, of a society from which many ghetto Negroes are increasingly alienated.

At the same time, police responsibilities in the ghetto have grown as other institutions of social control have lost much of their authority: the schools, because so many are segregated, old, and inferior; religion, which has become irrelevant to those who lost faith as they lost hope; career aspirations, which for many young Negroes are totally lacking; the family, because its bonds are so often snapped. It is the policeman who must fill this institutional vacuum, and is then resented for the presence this effort demands.

Alone, the policeman in the ghetto cannot solve these problems. His role is already one of the most difficult in our society. He must deal daily with a range of problems and people that test his patience, ingenuity, character, and courage in ways that few of us are ever tested. Without positive leadership, goals, operational guidance, and public support, the individual policeman can only feel victimized. Nor are these problems the responsibility only of police administrators; they are deep enough to tax the courage, intelligence, and leadership of mayors, city officials, and community leaders. As Dr. Kenneth B. Clark told the Commission:

This society knows . . . that if human beings are confined in ghetto compounds of our cities, and are subjected to criminally inferior education, pervasive economic and job discrimination, committed to houses unfit for human habitation, subjected to unspeakable conditions of municipal services, such as sanitation, that such human beings are not likely to be responsive to appeals to be lawful, to be respectful, to be concerned with property of others.

And yet, precisely because the policeman in the ghetto is a symbol—precisely because he symbolizes so much—it is of critical importance that the police and society take every possible step to allay grievances that flow from a sense of injustice and increased tension and turmoil.

In this work, the police bear a major responsibility for making needed changes. In the first instance, they have the prime responsibility for safeguarding the minimum goal of any civilized society—security of life and property. To do so, they are given society's maximum power—discretion in the use of force. Second, it is axiomatic that effective law enforcement requires the support of the community. Such support will not be present when a substantial segment of the community feels threatened by the police and regards the police as an occupying force.

At the same time, public officials also have a clear duty to help the police make any necessary changes to minimize so far as possible the risk of further disorders.

We see five basic problem areas:

The need for change in police operations in the ghetto to ensure proper individual conduct and to eliminate abrasive practices.

The need for more adequate police protection of ghetto residents to eliminate the present high sense of insecurity to person and property.

The need for effective mechanisms through which the citizen can have his grievances handled.

The need for policy guidelines to assist police in areas where police conduct can create tension.

The need to develop community support for law enforcement.

Our discussion of each of these problem areas is followed by specific recommendations which relate directly to more effective law enforcement and to the prevention and control of civil disorders. . . .

A third source of Negro hostility to police is the almost total lack of effective channels for redress of complaints against police conduct. In Milwaukee, Wisconsin, and Plainfield, New Jersey, for example, ghetto residents complained that police chiefs reject all complaints out of hand. In New Haven, a Negro citizens' group characterized a police review board as "worthless." In Detroit, the Michigan Civil Rights Commission found that, despite well-intentioned leadership, no real sanctions are imposed on offending officers. In Newark, the mayor referred complaints to the FBI, which had limited jurisdiction over them. In many of the cities surveyed by the Commission, Negro complaints focused on the continued presence in the ghetto of officers regarded as notorious for prejudice and brutality.

The 1967 Report of the Civil Rights Commission also states that a major issue in the Negro community is inadequate investigation of complaints against the police. It even reports threats of criminal actions designed to discourage complainants. A survey for the Crime Commission found substantial evidence that policemen in some cities have little fear of punishment for using unnecessary force because they appear to have a degree of immunity from their departments.

RECOMMENDATIONS

Objective evaluation, analysis, and innovation on this subject are vitally necessary. Yet attention has been largely, and unfortunately, diverted by protracted debate over the desirability of "civilian review boards." Research conducted by the Crime Commission and others shows that the benefits and liabilities of such boards have probably both been exaggerated.

In the context of civil disorder, appearances and reality are of almost equal importance in the handling of citizen complaints against the police. It is not enough that there are adequate machinery and procedures for handling complaints; it is also necessary that citizens believe these procedures are adequate. Some citizens will never trust an agency against which they have a grievance. Some irresponsible citizens will attempt to provoke distrust of every agency. Hence some police administrators have been tempted to throw up their hands and do nothing on the ground that whatever they do will be misunderstood. These sentiments may be understandable but the police should appreciate that Negro citizens also want to throw up their hands. For they believe that the "police stick together," that they will cover up for each other, that no officer ever receives more than token punishment for misconduct, and that even such expensive legal steps as false arrest or civil damage suits are foredoomed because "it is the officer's word against mine."

We believe that an internal review board—in which the police department itself receives and acts on complaints—regardless of its efficiency and fairness, can rarely generate the necessary community confidence, or protect the police against unfounded charges. We also believe, as did the Crime Commission, that police should not be the only municipal agency subject to outside scrutiny and review. Incompetence and mistreatment by any public servant should be equally subject to review by an independent agency.

The Crime Commission Police Task Force reviewed the various external grievance procedures attempted or suggested in this country and abroad. Without attempting to recommend a specific procedure, our Commission believes that police departments should be subject to external review.... Here, we highlight what we believe to be the basic elements of an effective system.

THE COMMISSION RECOMMENDS

Making a complaint should be easy. It should be possible to file a grievance without excessive formality. If forms are used, they should be easily available and their use explained in widely-distributed pamphlets. In large cities, it should not be necessary to go to a central headquarters office to file a complaint but it should also be possible to file a complaint at neighborhood locations. Police officers on the beat, community service aides, or other municipal employees in the community, should be empowered to receive complaints.

A specialized agency, with adequate funds and staff, should be created separate from other municipal agencies, to handle, investigate and to make recommendations on citizen complaints.

The procedure should have a built-in conciliation process to attempt to resolve complaints without the need for full investigation and processing.

The complaining party should be able to participate in the investigation and in any hearings, with right of representation by counsel, so that the complaint is fully investigated and findings made on the merits. He should be promptly and fully informed of the outcome. The results of the investigation should be made public.

Since many citizen complaints concern departmental policies rather than individual conduct, information concerning complaints of this sort should be forwarded to the departmental unit which formulates or reviews policy and procedures. Information concerning all complaints should be forwarded to appropriate training units so that any deficiencies correctable by training can be eliminated.

Although we advocate an external agency as a means of resolving grievances, we believe that the basic need is to adopt procedures which will gain the respect and confidence of the entire community. This need can, in the end, be met only by sustained direction through the line of command, thorough investigation of complaints, and prompt, visible disciplinary action where justified.

40.

DEPARTMENT-COMMISSION RELATIONS: SOME SWINGS OF THE PENDULUM

FELIX NIGRO

The central personnel agency is not the only part of the organizational framework for personnel administration. . . . As the operating departments grow large in size and come to employ increased numbers of employees, the need to establish such [departmental personnel] offices arises. Of course, proper recognition of the personnel function at the departmental level depends on more than just the question of size. We saw how late in point of time it was before the federal agencies created full-fledged personnel offices and how some of them in effect had to be coerced to do so by Executive Order 7916 issued in 1938.

In state and local governments, however, the smaller size of most of the administrative agencies means that the creation of personnel offices as such is usually not justifiable except for the largest departments. Nonetheless, even in these governments, there must be a competent staff which maintains contact with the central personnel agency—if the latter exists—and which in any event handles the personnel work of the department, no matter how few the employees. Wherever people work together, personnel administration emerges as an essential activity. Even the head of a small agency with only a dozen or more employees will normally need some help on personnel problems. Sometimes, it is a matter of salaries and working hours; other times simply of keeping basic records. In any case, personnel problems will arise, although obviously not in the same number or complexity as when the staff supervised totals hundreds or thousands.

When Reeves and David surveyed personnel administration in the federal government for the President's Committee on Administrative Management, they found that few departments had established strong personnel offices with trained technical staffs. Writing in 1936, they commented, "Twenty years ago the title 'personnel officer' was practically non-existent in the Federal service." Clerks had usually handled personnel matters, and "this condition continues to be typical even now among the older field services and may be found in many of the older establishments at Washington."[1]

Encouraged by such exceptions as the effectively functioning Office of Personnel in the Agriculture Department, Reeves and David strongly recommended that similarly adequate personnel offices be established in all the departments. They reasoned as follows: "The departments are self-contained operating agencies to a large degree, and must continue so in view of the limited extent to which it is physically possible for the Chief Executive to review their work. Direct responsibility for many of the most important phases of personnel work should therefore be lodged in the departments. From this it follows that major responsibility for the conduct of the entire personnel function must, to some extent, be divided between the central personnel agency and the departmental personnel offices."[2]

What should be the respective functions of the central personnel agency and the departmental personnel offices? Reeves and David warned against centralizing too much responsibility in the central agency, but, writing at a time when the federal departments were much smaller than they are today, they did envision that the commission would continue to be directly responsible for recruitment, classification, and transfer programs. The commission should, however, increasingly assume a role of positive leadership and initiative in improving personnel administration throughout the administrative branch and place less emphasis on routine operations as such.

The creation of the departmental personnel offices recommended by Reeves and David was required two years later by President Roosevelt in his Executive Order 7916. Slowly at first, but finally with a rush, the "modern" personnel office became standard equipment in the executive departments and agencies. Progressively, they were created also at bureau, field office, and sometimes even

---

[1] Floyd W. Reeves and Paul T. David, *Personnel Administration in the Federal Service*, President's Committee on Administrative Management (Washington, D.C.: U.S. Government Printing Office, 1937), p. 33.

[2] *Ibid.*, p. 43.

lower levels, depending upon the need. Indeed, by the time the first Hoover Commission appeared on the federal scene, a truly complicated organizational framework for conducting personnel administration had developed.

. . . much criticism had been heard during the war and immediately thereafter about the cumbersome nature of this machinery. The Task Force on Personnel placed part of the blame for this on a failure to establish the personnel function as an integral part of top management in the departments. Not only should the personnel officer report directly to the head of the agency or to a key assistant, such as the undersecretary, but he should be on a par with the budget director, management research officer, general counsel, and other key staff officers.[3] In other words, personnel management in general was not sufficiently strong at the operating levels of the government, although much progress had been made.

CENTRALIZATION VERSUS DECENTRALIZATION

An even more serious problem had arisen, however—the proper definition of the respective competences of the Civil Service Commission and the departmental and bureau personnel staffs. This is the issue of "centralization" or "decentralization," a vexatious problem which has become increasingly acute as total federal employment soared into the millions. Could the Civil Service Commission possibly continue to assume direct responsibility for such functions as recruitment and classification when this work force had grown so tremendously? Was this physically possible? Was it not too much for the commission?

. . . during the war, the commission itself saw the need to decentralize much of its detailed activities to the departments. Furthermore, in Executive Order 9830 issued in 1947, President Truman had clearly established that "personnel management is a primary responsibility of all who plan, direct, or supervise the work of Federal employees"—striking recognition of the key role of the operating agencies in personnel management.[4] But, even considering this latest step, had the decentralization policy gone far enough? The first Hoover Commission came to the conclusion *that it had not* and made sweeping proposals for the further delegation of authority to act in personnel matters to the departments.

This was not just a matter of pure theory—simply deciding what would be a new logical division of responsibilities. Rather, decentralization was urged as a matter of sheer necessity if the federal government was to be able to compete effectively with private industry in the labor market. Central recruitment by the

---

[3] *Task Force Report on Federal Personnel*, prepared for the Commission on Organization of the Executive Branch of the Government (Washington, D.C.: U.S. Government Printing Office, 1949), pp. 87–94.
[4] *Basic Acts, Rules, and Regulations Governing Employment in the Federal Competitive Civil Service* (Washington, D.C.: U.S. Civil Service Commission, February, 1955), pp. 14–16.

commission was much too slow and far too impersonal. By the time employment registers had been prepared, the best candidates had already accepted jobs with private firms. The commission was trying its best to reduce the delays, but it was attempting the impossible—to be the single employer for a federal service now so large it could no longer be served efficiently by centralized recruitment.

Said the task force, "If the Federal Goverment were a single, stabilized establishment with but a few simple tasks which anyone with ordinary intelligence could perform, the present system of procurement (of personnel) would perhaps be as adequate and economical as any which might be devised." However, the "government is the converse of singleness, stability, and simplicity in its employment needs today."[5] Centralized recruitment simply was not feasible "in a government which consists of thousands of activities with widely varying problems and requirements."[6] Recruitment and selection of new employees should be delegated to the maximum extent possible to the operating departments because "the objective of placing the right man, in the right job, at the right time can be most satisfactorily accomplished by allowing the operating activity to serve itself, as does a private employer, to the fullest extent."[7]

Specifically, the task force proposed that the major departments and agencies be given the authority to recruit and make final appointments to all high-level administrative, professional, and technical posts; to all positions peculiar to the agency; and to any other kinds of jobs which, in the opinion of the Civil Service Commission, could be more effectively filled by the agency. Each agency, however, would have to prepare a specific recruitment plan for review and approval by the commission which also would have the authority to inspect the operation in practice of these plans and to suspend the decentralization agreement if it were found that commission policies were not being observed.[8] These recommendations were approved by the first Hoover Commission, along with the related proposal of the task force that the authority to evaluate jobs for pay purposes also be delegated to the departments and agencies, under standards established and enforced by the commission.

In terms of a simple example, what was being proposed was that whenever a vacancy developed, the agency in which it occurred would decide the proper classification of the job, following published descriptions prepared by the commission of the different classes of positions. The agency would then fix the salary and also itself hire a qualified person to fill it, again respecting the commission's minimum standards governing decentralized recruitment and selection. This would make it possible to speed up hiring and the entrance on duty date of new

---

[5] *Task Force Report on Federal Personnel, op. cit.*, p. 20.

[6] *Ibid.*, p. 21.

[7] *Ibid.*

[8] *Ibid.*, pp. 21–22.

appointees, and at the same time allow the commission to exercise a role of leadership and guidance.

For a full understanding of these recommendations, it should be pointed out that besides a greater degree of decentralization, a *clear statement of the division of responsibilities between the commission and the departmental personnel offices was needed.* At times, operating officials had been baffled by the confused relationship between commission and agency personnel staffs and annoyed at the frequent disagreement of both over who was to provide a given personnel service. Personnel administration could not but suffer in the eyes of these line men when they saw the personnel experts themselves locked in combat. Although friction of this type is characteristic of any huge bureaucracy, it was felt by all concerned that a basis for smoother relationships could be found. . . .

REACTION TO DECENTRALIZATION PROPOSALS OF FIRST HOOVER COMMISSION

How did these proposals of the first Hoover Commission fare? As to classification of individual jobs, Congress acted in 1949 to decentralize this authority to the agencies, subject to post-audit by the commission.[9] A truly monumental step, this legislation reversed years of tight, centralized controls by the commission. For the first time since passage of the original Classification Act in 1923, Congress was willing to delegate to the departments the initial authority to decide a new appointee's salary. In this, the Congress had to balance its fear that salaries would not be controlled properly with the reality that to continue to require prior commission approval would sometimes mean as much as several weeks' delay before a new employee could enter on duty. The dictates of efficiency required a different approach: decentralization, under proper safeguards. As such decentralization has worked out in practice since 1949, it is generally considered a great improvement, although the Senate Subcommittee on Federal Manpower Policies, in a report printed in 1953, criticized the commission sharply for failure to publish adequate standards to guide the agencies in classifying the different types of jobs.[10] In its latest annual report, that for 1957, the commission, however, reports substantial progress in speeding the preparation of these standards.

The recommendations on personnel procurement were considered seriously by the Congress but not adopted. . . .

In June of 1949, bills to implement the decentralization and other personnel

---

[9] 63 U.S. Stat. 954, October 28, 1949.
[10] *Administration of the Classification Act of 1949 and the Compensation Process Established by the Act,* 83rd Cong., 1st Sess., Senate Document No. 34 (Washington, D.C.: U.S. Government Printing Office, 1953).

recommendations of the Hoover Commission were introduced in Congress.[11] A long period of hearings and debates followed, extending through the summer of 1951, but in the end no action was taken by the Congress to decentralize recruitment authority to the departments.

The then chairman of the Civil Service Commission, Harry B. Mitchell, told the Senate Committee on Post Office and Civil Service that if such decentralization were carried out on a sweeping basis, the commission would have very little to do. In fact, in his opinion there would be no excuse for its existence.

He pointed out that in many cases it had already delegated the preparation of examinations and of eligible lists to the departments under existing authority which had always been a part of the original Pendleton Act.[12] The latter states that "the Commission shall, at Washington, and one or more places in each State and Territory where examinations are to take place, designate and select a suitable number of persons, not less than three, in the official service of the United States, residing in said State or Territory, after consulting the head of the department or office in which such persons serve, to be members of boards of examiners. . . ."[13]

Some use of this power to decentralize recruitment had been made by the commission throughout its history, but not on any large scale until after World War II. In fact, when the first Hoover Commission made its studies, it estimated that 46 percent of all new appointments in the fiscal year 1949 would be made by boards of examiners, both in Washington and in the federal field services. (As Figure 40.1 shows, this had grown to 66 percent by fiscal year 1956.) When boards of examiners are used, the departments are responsible for giving examinations and preparing eligible lists, subject to inspection by the commission.

The Civil Service Commission, however, was willing to support legislation providing for gradual decentralization of recruiting authority to the departments. Under such a plan, the commission itself would decide when to decentralize such authority, and it would in any event be free at any time to do the recruiting job itself for any kinds of jobs it saw fit. Even this compromise proposal, however, was defeated, the reason being the strong opposition of the principal employee and veterans' organizations.[14]

---

[11] *Bills to Implement Recommendations of the Commission on Organization of the Executive Branch of the Government*, 81st Cong., 1st and 2nd sess. (Washington, D.C.: U.S. Government Printing Office, 1951), pp. 41–60.

[12] *Ibid.*, pp. 49–60 for testimony of Mr. Harry Mitchell.

[13] *Basic Acts, Rules, and Regulations Governing Employment in the Federal Competitive Civil Service, op. cit.*, pp. 4–5.

[14] See Harold H. Leich, "The Hoover Commission's Personnel Recommendations—A Progress Report," *American Political Science Review*, Vol. XLVII, No. 1 (March, 1953), pp. 100–25.

FIGURE 40.1. New Hires for Competitive Service, Fiscal Year 1956.

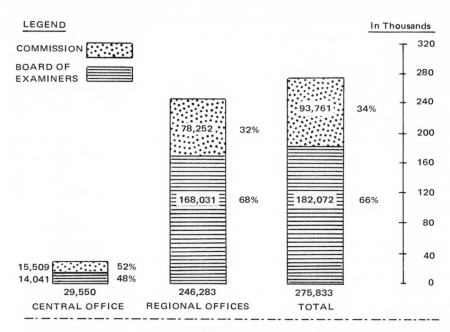

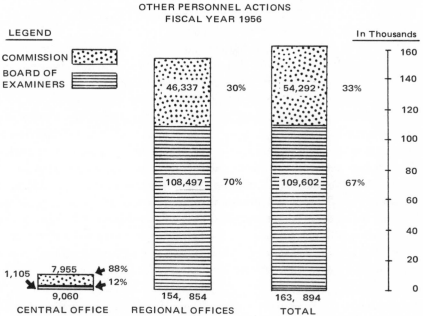

Source: *1956 Annual Report*, United States Civil Service Commission, p. 47.

OBJECTIONS OF EMPLOYEE AND VETERANS' GROUPS

What were the specific objections of the employee and veterans' groups? In general it can be said that they feared that decentralization would be carried too far and that the way would be opened again for the departments to make appointments on a political basis. This, again, was the "protectionist" school, anxious to preserve centralized controls by the commission and rejecting decentralization as a threat to the merit system. Charles I. Stengle, legislative representative of the American Federation of Government Employees, ably expressed this sentiment when he told the Senate committee that the "Civil Service Commission should be given a position of command in operating the civil service system and that it should share its prerogatives with none of the executive agencies of the Government." In the eyes of the organizations he represented, the proposed legislation would "weaken rather than strengthen the present civil service system by delegating to the agencies of the Government authority which should be retained in a single regulatory body, the Civil Service Commission."[15]

Luther Steward, president of the National Federation of Federal Employees, expressed the opinion that "the definition of merit would rest with operating officials." He continued: "I am not the one who is thoroughly cynical or is accustomed to thinking evil of my fellow man, but I cannot be blind to general and recurring tendencies, and I have heard not once but many times over the years high officials of Government with due solemnity indicate that in their opinion the basic factor in merit was the adherence to the dominant political party. . . . There seems to be still magic in the minds of some in the word 'decentralization.' Decentralization without definitely devolving the final decision in some central authority is merely the abdication of authority and an invitation to dissimilar systems and chaos."[16] Steward did not believe that the commission, once it decentralized as proposed, would be able to cope successfully with departmental evasions of the merit system. He was sure "the percentage of victories of agency heads would assume formidable proportions."[17]

Similarly, spokesmen for the principal veterans' organizations opposed the bill. Here the basic fear was that if recruiting were delegated to the departments, the latter would seek to evade the provisions of the Veterans' Preference Act of 1944. Under the latter, disabled veterans who pass an examination are automatically awarded ten additional points and all other veterans five points. Preference is also given veterans in reinstatements and layoffs, and the commission, of course, is required to observe these special arrangements for ex-servicemen.

---

[15] *Bills to Implement Recommendations of the Commission on Reorganization of the Executive Branch of the Government*, 82nd Cong., 1st sess. (Washington, D.C.: U.S. Government Printing Office, 1951), p. 34.

[16] *Ibid.*, p. 43.

[17] *Ibid.*, p. 45.

Although commission representatives repeatedly testified that it would continue to require compliance with this legislation, the various veterans' groups were not convinced. They suspected that once removed from tight commission scrutiny, the departments would seek loopholes and technicalities to get around veterans' preference. In general, their attitude could be summed up as follows: Why change the status quo and risk the possibility that some departments may use this added discretion to satisfy pressure from the operating official who wants a veteran passed up in order to have someone he knows appointed? Since complaints had been made by operating officials displeased with the veterans' preference requirements, these fears are understandable, but there was nothing in the proposed legislation that would have made it necessary for either the commission or the departments to yield to such pressures.

Perhaps the most interesting feature to be noted in these debates on the decentralization issue is that whereas the commission was willing to make additional delegations of authority to the departments, the employee and veterans' groups admonished and even rebuked it for such supineness. Here the commission was influenced by the "management" approach, so ably stated by Arthur Flemming when he told the Senate committee that "if we would put into effect a program which enables the Civil Service Commission to emphasize its responsibility for developing standards and permits the operating responsibility to rest with the departments and agencies, we would then make it possible for the commission to exercise really outstanding leadership."[18] The employees' and the veterans' organizations insisted that decentralization would weaken the traditional "protective" role of the commission. This was not without precedent, however, for in the previous history of civil service, at the state and local as well as federal levels, attempts to make procedures more flexible and to give appointing offices more leeway had met with strong resistance by the employees.

Does decentralization lead to abuses by appointing officials in the departments? In a careful study of a number of agencies included in the Sixth Civil Service Region, Gladys Kammerer does come to the inescapable conclusion that "decentralization of recruitment and examination to the departments makes possible an abuse of power and possible subversion of the merit principle nonexistent under the old federal system of centralization."[19] She found that an appointing authority determined to place a particular person in a position could do this more easily when recruitment was delegated to boards of examiners.

Although she was writing in 1952 and the Civil Service Commission has improved its inspection organization since then, sophisticated observers are not surprised at her conclusions. Whenever controls of any type are relaxed, some

---

[18] *Ibid.*, p. 15.
[19] Gladys M. Kammerer, "Revolution by Decentralization," *Public Personnel Review*, Vol. XIII, No. 3 (July, 1952), p. 141.

abuses will occur, but the real question is whether these disappointments are so great as to outweigh the many disadvantages of a tight centralization policy. Those imbued with the "efficiency" approach lean toward decentralization in federal personnel administration as a management necessity, in spite of the inherent threat to the "protective" function. This threat, they believe, can be brought under control. Even with so large a percentage of positions now being filled by boards of examiners, there has arisen no widespread evasion of the merit principle.

41.

IN SHORT: PERSONNEL ADMINISTRATION FOR LINE MANAGERS

PAUL PIGORS and CHARLES A. MYERS

Personnel administration is still a young profession—so young that even its name has not yet been generally agreed upon. Various other names such as "industrial relations" or "employee relations" are also used to designate the department in which men and women do personnel work. The quality of any profession depends on the aims and standards exemplified in the behavior of those who choose it as a career. Thus everyone who undertakes to represent a personnel-minded view—in his (or her) decisions and actions—helps to determine what personnel administration will become.

Unlike other professions, the character of personnel administration will be formed *not* primarily by those who specialize in it. *In any organization, personnel administration is what members of line management make it.* For this reason, a chief executive needs to be concerned with far more than personnel policies *as professed* in written statements. What he needs to know about personnel administration, and what every management representative should constantly ask himself, is this: In our daily behavior toward other employees, how consistently *are we implementing* valid principles for human relations?

The following questions and capsule conclusions represent the gist of a personnel-minded view. We believe that not only as a general philosophy, but also in practice, these ideas make sense for all those who, as management representatives, are responsible for personnel relations.

DEVELOPING A MANAGEMENT PATTERN

Managing involves coordinating resources to accomplish organizational objectives, but it is through the cooperative efforts of people that monetary and material resources are utilized most effectively. Every manager makes assumptions about the way people behave. These assumptions determine his pattern of management. Is this pattern closer to management by centralized direction and control, or to management by shared objectives and self-control? *Where* it is on the spectrum of management patterns and the *direction* in which it is moving will have tremendous significance for the ways in which people respond to managerial initiative in the organization. Certain environmental pressures, and the findings of recent behavioral science research, are leading more managers to move toward management by shared objectives and self-control. This way of managing matches the personnel point of view which has been presented in this book.

WHAT IS PERSONNEL ADMINISTRATION?

Personnel administration is a basic function of management. Unless it is effectively carried out by all members of line management, technical efficiency is inadequate to achieve organizational success. Personnel problems should not be thought of as something separate from technical problems. Both are parts of a single situation that needs to be understood and dealt with by line officials, *beginning with the chief executive.* Managing can become increasingly effective when it is carried out as a means of getting results *with* people, rather than *through* them (or in spite of them). This kind of managing depends on willing cooperation and on teamwork, as all organizational members work together toward shared objectives.

Naturally, in any organization the chief executive is captain of the "first team." However, he is also leader of the whole "squad." Therefore he is responsible for performance by all the teams. His policies (whether written or merely expressed in his behavior) set up conditions that determine the extent to which team spirit can be a natural response throughout the organization and the extent to which teamwork within small groups is likely to contribute to organizational aims which he shares. Unless the chief executive believes in personnel policies that reflect the principle of mutual responsibility, he is wasting most of the money spent to pay any specialist in personnel work.

RELATIONSHIP BETWEEN A CHIEF EXECUTIVE
AND A PERSONNEL ADMINISTRATOR

At best, a personnel administrator can help a chief executive to formulate a comprehensive system of personnel policies, to explain such policies to all management representatives, and to keep track of how useful such policies are when actually applied in specific instances. A personnel administrator succeeds to the extent that a personnel-minded view becomes the still, small voice which speaks to members of line management—and through them—even when he is not around. For example, how do line managers think about costs? In estimating the cost of a proposed program, do executives think of more than the dollars and cents directly involved? Do they also take account of the intangible losses and benefits which, although they cannot accurately be reckoned, will inevitably make themselves felt? A personnel administrator has reason for satisfaction when members of line management become so cost-minded that long-term benefits (and losses) in human values have a central place in their planning.

THE PERSONNEL ADMINISTRATOR'S ROLE
AS A STAFF MAN

Personnel-minded action, which expresses and evokes a spirit of cooperation, can greatly reduce the misunderstandings and friction that have often made relationships between line managers and staff specialists difficult and relatively unproductive. A personnel administrator can illustrate, in his own behavior, the role that goes with staff status. In doing so, he can make what may be his most important contribution.

A staff man properly works with people through ideas. In speaking for ideas, he does not give orders to line managers. He relies on the power of persuasion, not on the persuasion of power. To the extent that the ideas for which he speaks are valid, relevant, and timely, he can expect that members of line management will seek and take his advice. (If, however, a personnel administrator acts like an empire builder—promoting his ideas and blowing his own horn at every opportunity—then his function will naturally be resented by line managers, and he will have misrepresented the role of a staff man.)

A personnel administrator who succeeds, because his ideas carry weight, becomes influential to the extent that a personnel-minded view is consistently applied by line managers in their capacity as leaders of personnel. When members of line management effectively administer sound personnel policies, the personnel administrator probably will not get the credit. But he will have something better: the satisfaction of a job well done, because other people are doing their jobs better than might have been possible without his help. At best, he will witness a shift away from emphasis on the *authority of position* (according to which a person gets results primarily by giving orders) and toward emphasis on the *authority of the situation* (according to which employees of different status, and with a range of functions, work together, following the lead given by situational requirements). When this latter kind of authority is recognized, a line manager, as "a good leader," helps his associates to recognize and to meet situational demands. Having done so, all employees are entitled to take pride in organizational success and to say "we did this ourselves."

ORGANIZATION PLANNING AND MANAGEMENT DEVELOPMENT

The personnel responsibility of management, with staff help, begins with the development of managerial talent so that leadership in the organization can be continually replenished and improved. The structure of the organization, whether more decentralized or centralized, influences the way in which managers develop, as do other opportunities for self-development.

A formalized management development program may treat people as so many pawns on a chessboard, rather than as individuals who can grow in their managerial jobs as opportunities for self-development are provided. Management development is really getting somewhere, as a process which contributes to organizational strength, when the whole management group is engaged in an educational program in which (1) conference method is used frequently and informally, at and between all organizational levels, to solve problems; (2) coaching on the job is regarded as an important responsibility for every management representative; and (3) such coaching results in improved performance toward mutual objectives.

The personnel administrator can be seen by management as a source of help in advanced manpower planning for high-talent manpower needs. When he advises top executives in thinking about organization structure and management development he has moved into the front office as a member of the top-management team.

COMMUNICATING: A MANAGERIAL RESPONSIBILITY

Engineers have made tremendous achievements in mechanical communication and control systems, but experience shows that the premises and methods which work so well with wholly mechanical systems cannot successfully be applied without modification to communication between persons. When any human being tries to communicate with another, unilateral control by the sender becomes impossible. For one thing, every human receiver is always partly preoccupied with listening to messages on his inner circuit. The content and dynamics of these messages affect what filters through from outside.

Another circumstance that precludes a one-to-one correspondence between messages sent and messages received is that what is sent and received by human minds is always more than mere information. When a message reaches the mind of a human receiver he necessarily does something to it. The product of his interpretive activity is *meaning-for-him*, which is inevitably somewhat different from the sender's meaning. Other preconditioning factors (such as his personality and previous experience) make a difference in how he can interpret what he does receive. Many supervisors could testify that even simple, clear-cut orders can miscarry if they are blocked by feelings or purposes which convince an order-receiver that their meaning for him—as a person—is unacceptable.

Traditionally, managers have not bothered to take account of obstacles associated with the idea that feelings and purposes are integral elements in meaning as a whole. Some managers have apparently assumed that unilateral control can be exercised in person-to-person communication. They try to manage by sending inflexible directives (rules) down the line, imposing external controls, and counting on action reports up the line to keep informed. But recently, many managers have acted on the hypothesis that peak productivity depends on winning understanding and agreement from employees, who can then be expected to work with their supervisors toward long-range objectives of the organization as a whole.

MOTIVATION, INDIVIDUAL GOALS, AND TEAMWORK

Social scientists have shown that "man is a wanting animal." But what managers think an employee wants is not always what he needs most. Some seem to take it for granted that employees park their personalities with their cars. If that were so, rewards such as money and praise might be sufficient to motivate the "partial" men whose names are on the payroll. But that kind of indirect reward cannot release the strongest motive powers—the inner-directed drives by which man seeks to meet his deepest needs, such as the needs for belonging, responsibility, freedom to use initiative, and opportunity to grow by devoting his energies to something he believes in.

Recent research into human motivation has important implications for managers. Any executive could confirm, from his own experience, the general idea that work and work relationships can contribute to "true satisfaction in living" *if* high-level needs are met on the job. But often it has been assumed that high-level needs are important only to high-level employees. How many managers have considered following up the suggestion that the greatest hitherto-untapped resource for productivity might be released if the deepest and most enduring needs could be met, at every organizational level, as employees work together toward organizational goals?

Employees can find fulfillment in functioning as team members. And managers need teamwork. Why then is not teamwork always a positive force in organizations? Might there be more of it if managers tried to answer such questions as these: In our organization, where is effective teamwork operating? If any of it is motivated by aims that run counter to organizational objectives, how might this powerful counterforce be redirected so that it could benefit the organization as a whole?

A manager can do several things to promote teamwork: He can want it. He can believe in it. He can practice it. In such ways, he can create a climate where cooperative relationships develop. In trying to practice teamwork, a manager may take a leaf from the personnel administrator's book. *He can adopt a consultative approach*, conferring with his subordinates in a way that shows his wish to take account of their ideas and experience as organizational members, instead of degrading them to the level of "organization men."

An important managerial responsibility is to create and express—in words and action—a corporate personality. Personnel-minded managers can create a corporate character that invites every employee to express himself—in words and action—not merely as a superior and a subordinate, but also as a working partner. When a chief executive is receptive to new ideas, wherever they come from, he exemplifies an attitude which every organizational member needs to develop if he is to play his part in a situation which is constantly changing.

THE CHANGING WORK SITUATION

Does our present stage of technological advance represent a "critical turning point" in man's evolution? The answer to that question will gradually emerge as men and women work with each other and with new machines, in new ways. What must be done to develop the full potential of manpower supplemented and sustained by machine power? (Imaginative leadership will be needed to recognize and release potential capabilities, some of which have been "frozen" in employees, and some of which have not yet even been imagined—for machines.)

Automatic machines and automated processes have already eliminated many jobs which have traditionally been performed by human beings (including staff experts and line managers). Many other jobs have been, and will be, changed. Current trends and future developments will certainly bring even greater changes in the world of work—and of leisure. The extent to which such changes are beneficial will depend, in large measure, on how imaginatively and cooperatively employers, employees, and union officials can work together to find integrative solutions to their common problems.

Human monitors, communicators, and solvers of "ill-structured" problems are still needed today, even in "man-less" factories. The extent to which human beings make use of their unique advantages will doubtless play a large part in future decisions about whether it will pay to employ human beings in jobs whose technical functions could be performed by machines.

Man has capabilities which make him superior to present-day machines. For example, in listening and reading man can detect and respond to differences so slight that they baffle or elude machines. What is more, man is mobile, and at his best, he is both versatile and adaptable—able constantly to reprogram himself. Possibly man's greatest advantage is that, when he feels wholly enlisted in some goal, he can do the impossible.

However, in many organizations it seems clear that most employees are not exerting themselves to any marked extent. Too many of them are merely meeting minimum (externally imposed) requirements. If managers are seriously interested in creating a situation where employees would give—and could get—far more than they now do, it might be well to confer with first-level supervisors. They have often been referred to as "key men." Could they unlock that secret?

FUNCTIONS OF FIRST-LEVEL SUPERVISION

Certainly one of the first-level supervisor's key functions could be to help release the powerful inner drives that have been "frozen" in many employees. The supervisor's job has changed so much and so fast that few people—including supervisors themselves—seem to know precisely what that job is. Nowadays the first-level supervisor gets so much "help" from so many members of his organizational family that it is not clear what authority he retains or where the boundaries of his responsibility are. But studies of what is actually done by, to, and for supervisors have clarified some points. For instance, a first-level supervisor is still held responsible for getting out production (or overseeing service). In doing so, he spends most of his time on technical duties. He is rarely selected, prepared, or supported to function as a representative of management. Instead he is often the "man in the middle," hemmed in by standards and methods which he had no part in setting up, the target for a cross fire of unshared purposes and incompatible directives. The rise of unions and activities by staff specialists have greatly reduced the stature of the supervisor—who used to be an undisputed boss.

His job is still a big one. He gives out work assignments, issues orders and instructions, keeps track of production, schedules work (to some extent), exercises disciplinary authority, and handles complaints. Who helps him to develop and use the skills of personnel administration required by that many-sided job? Does he always receive from his immediate superior the kind of support that he is expected to give as a leader and teacher of subordinates? Can he learn from the example given by his organizational superiors how to elicit team spirit and help subordinates interact effectively in work teams? Does the organization structure make it possible for him to know the individuals who formulate organizational policy? Does anyone ever ask him for suggestions on how people at the work level might be helped to meet their personal goals while contributing to organizational objectives?

Any manager who asks such questions and follows through by getting facts might feel moved to reexamine some of the assumptions which have made the corporate personality what it has traditionally been. If some long-held but unrealistic assumptions could be changed, the first-level supervisor might become a new man. He certainly would be a new man if he were selected, prepared, and supported as a respected member of the management group. In that role, the supervisor's unique contribution could be enhanced by all those who work with him (in a staff or line capacity) as colleagues.

The first-level supervisor, like his superiors and subordinates, needs to belong and to grow on the job. If his position were such that he could meet these needs, he probably wouldn't feel the urge to join a union.

THE EMPLOYEE AND LABOR ORGANIZATIONS

Some managers have accepted the fact that their employees (principally blue-collar groups) want to join labor organizations to bargain collectively for terms and conditions of employment. Others either resent this or try to avoid unionization of their employees.

In many industries, however, unions are here to stay. The labor movement in the United States remains a powerful force to be dealt with. Can managers find a way to work with union officers toward shared objectives? Necessary preliminaries to a sound working relationship between a management and a union are mutual acceptance and mutual respect, assuming that employees have clearly indicated their desire to be represented by unions. Management can set the tone for such a relationship by accepting the idea that union demands and grievances can help managers to appraise their personnel decisions—thus making them better managers.

Not all union objectives are shared by management representatives, any more than all management aims are accepted by all employees or their union representatives. But managers embark on a self-defeating program if they fight a rearguard action, defending management prerogatives as their sole objective. The right to manage is safe just as soon, and just as long, as it is earned.

An effective personnel administrator or labor relations director can help management to develop workable relations with unions which represent part or all of a firm's employees. This staff help may extend to contract negotiations, and certainly to assistance and guidance in administering the contract, as shop law.

SITUATIONAL THINKING

Managers are responsible for diagnosing and caring for the health of the organizations they lead. One way to meet that responsibility is by making use of "situational thinking." This analytical tool is a personnel-oriented variant of the "systems" thinking called for, with increasing urgency, as automation comes of age.

Situational thinking is a methodical yet flexible way to explore a total work situation (in its larger contexts). It stresses the idea that every human being and each human relationship is constantly changing and should, therefore, always be regarded as being in process. This way of looking at any situation and of working in it can start at the level of enduring principles. For example, a personnel administrator can work with executives to think out and write down a comprehensive set of personnel policies. Policies need to be formulated, implemented, and kept up to date by persons who are in touch with current developments. If managerial thinking, as expressed in policies, is too rigid to keep up with the tide of human events and behavior, it will get further and further away from reality. Policies that remain unchanged in a changing situation will eventually fetch up high and dry—aground on the barren reef of outdated ideas.

Change is a constant factor in every situation where human beings play a part. A useful way to take account of change is to *set up a time frame for understanding*. Instead of thinking about a current situation as though it were an isolated fragment of time, one can look at it as a scene toward the middle of a three-act play. Current developments can be more fully understood in view of past happenings that helped to make them what they are. Wise decisions about what to do "here and now" take account of past experience and of foreseeable consequences.

Spatial relationships, such as the location and spacing of work stations, also need to be considered. In their effects on people, as well as on techniques, they can make a big difference in what a situation is—and in what it may become.

The technical factor is obviously of critical importance wherever people are at work. Recent technical innovations have been introduced at a rate that has "unmoored" many persons, and more technological changes are coming up, perhaps at an increasingly rapid rate.

Managers who try to keep up to date by becoming systems-minded may need reminding that the springs of human action cannot be operated mechanically. In fact, *human behavior* often demonstrates that the logics of technical systems cannot usefully be applied as a method to understand or control human nature. A more practical start toward understanding can be made by recognizing that *there is always some reason for behavior, no matter how unreasonable that behavior may look to someone else.*

APPLYING SITUATIONAL THINKING: AS CASE METHOD

Situational thinking can be useful in diagnosing and caring for organizational health only in so far as people use it to see and understand their ever-changing situation. For example, a timely and practical application of this method is when "hopeless" misunderstandings develop between organizational members. At such a time, perhaps the personnel administrator is called in because "human relations problems" are his specialty. If so, his best service may be to enlist a supervisor's interest and help. The personnel administrator can probably learn much of what he needs to know from the supervisor—who is, presumably, a man with information on facts of the case. But the supervisor may need a bit of coaching so that, next time, he will be able to apply a methodical system for proceeding from factual information through issue formulation to decisions that take account of facts and of valid principles, too.

When an outsider applies situational thinking to a "problem" case, he first tries to get inside the situation with his mind. He listens to incomplete and slanted statements by insiders and tries to appreciate the differences in ideas, purposes, and feelings that have produced tension and misunderstanding. After comparing these accounts with each other and checking objectively verifiable facts, the investigator has something that approximates the whole story. Now he is in a position to see what is at stake (at the level of long-term aims and principles) as well as what is at issue between persons who disagree with each other. The practical question then becomes: Can an impartial outsider help insiders to look with some degree of objectivity at the issue that has been dividing them? A personnel administrator or a personnel-minded manager knows better than to emerge from a period of solo case analysis with a full-fledged solution in his hands, exclaiming: "Boys, this is it!" Experience has taught him that the "boys" will find it easier to accept a solution which they have helped to work out.

However, even when a mutually acceptable short-term solution to a difficulty has been reached, no case-minded manager would regard his task as completed. The most fruitful part of situational analysis lies in learning from experience. How did the difficulty develop? What similar difficulties have been, and are being, experienced elsewhere in the organization? Was this difficulty handled as effectively as it could have been? Or did action on it begin so late that there was no time to think about prevention? If so, what might be done to prevent the recurrence of similar difficulties in future? What are the policy implications? Is there anything about this case which should be reported up the line to top management, because it highlights some flaw or gap in the system of personnel policies?

A management representative (line or staff) need not limit his use of situational thinking to analyzing other people's difficulties and trying to help others behave more reasonably. He can profitably apply situational thinking to get perspective on his own situation—particularly when he is emotionally involved. Without some such system for getting an outside angle on situations where he is an insider, no one can be sure that his decisions are (1) as securely founded on facts and (2) as well supported by reasons as they might be, that they are (3) not only planned as short-term solutions, but (4) also firmly grounded in valid principles, and therefore (5) may be expected to meet requirements of the case as a whole—and not merely one small part of a total situation.

INTERVIEWING

Management representatives, both staff and line, talk every day with other employees, formally or informally, in directed or nondirected interviews. Each such talk can be regarded as an experiment in human relations (because no one can predict precisely how it will turn out). It is also an opportunity to practice a wide range of skills needed in personnel administration. Everyone has these skills in some degree, but all of us need to develop more skill—especially as listeners, observers, and interpreters.

A nondirected interview (often held with employees who are having difficulties) makes greater demands on both participants than a *directed interview* (which is usually limited to getting factual information). Factors that favor success in interviewing include a setting which offers privacy and opportunity to relax, a sense of leisure, and security against outside interruptions. But even when the setting isn't ideal, an interviewer may be able to provide the essentials by the way he conducts the interview.

Here are a few simple rules for interviewing. Preparation can help both participants to make the most of such an opportunity to gain and share understanding. (It should be remembered that when anyone is notified that he is to be interviewed he, too, will be preparing himself—in some way.) After the interview starts, attentive, appreciative, and imaginative listening may be the interviewer's most useful contribution. Can he listen in a way that helps a troubled person to speak his mind? Will the interviewer be able to mirror that person's meaning in occasional comments that faithfully reflect feeling tone and help to clarify thinking? At best, such an interview culminates in greater self-awareness and self-confidence by the person who has been having difficulties and who now begins to see how to overcome them. Whether or not the interviewer thinks that an interview has been successful, he should (1) conclude it courteously, (2) follow through appropriately, and (3) review his notes to see what he might learn from this experience in human relations. If it seems not to have been fully satisfying to the interviewee, how might that undesirable consequence be avoided another time?

ASSESSING EMPLOYEE MORALE

If ability to understand is to become effective (in improved organizational health and stability, as a means to raise productivity), it must be matched by readiness to examine and analyze facts and then to take whatever action is indicated. A manager can never afford to indulge in wishful thinking. He needs to get facts and to follow their lead. If he has a personnel-minded view, it might be expressed in a soliloquy something like this: "How stable are the individuals and groups in our company? Our organization is certainly not just 'one big happy family.' What is it? Is it merely an aggregate of people held loosely and temporarily together by economic interest? Or is there a sense of united purpose and common membership? Is there perhaps more of this feeling in some sections of our company than in others? If so, what is accountable? And what might we do to help spread this attitude? Have we any effective work teams? If so, where? How were they built? How are they being maintained? Let's be sure to give credit where credit is due, and help where help is needed."

When a manager tries to diagnose organizational health, he should be able to rely on skilled assistance from the personnel administrator and other staff specialists. He is entitled to expect that the best current thinking will be made available to him by the specialists who advise him on (1) how to get reliable data on productive efficiency; (2) how to interpret current figures for tardiness, absence, and accidents; (3) whether it is worthwhile to conduct attitude surveys; if so, (4) how such surveys can best be carried out; and (5) how they might effectively be followed up, in action initiated by management.

For example, a personnel-minded view, whether presented by a personnel administrator or—better still—arising spontaneously in a manager's mind, might be stated in questions like these: Now that current statistics tell us the score, how is the game going, in all parts of the company and in every phase of the employment process? For instance, what *shows through* the data on attendance, labor turnover, transfers, and promotions? Is the current rate of personnel mobility strengthening the organization as a whole and building the morale of individuals? Or is it undermining teamwork? Who is leaving the company? Why? From which departments? What is labor turnover costing us in money and in human values? Could our transfer policies be more wisely formulated and more skillfully administered? Are employees satisfied with the possibilities and actualities of promotion?

Whatever the answers to such questions, it is to be hoped that the chief executive will not be wholly satisfied with them and that he will feel impelled to use them as leads to personnel-minded action. But whatever is done with the aim of increasing productivity, blaming people should be no part of the program. If any "unhealthy" condition is revealed, the realistic question to ask is *not* "Who is to blame?" but rather, "*What is accountable?*"

LEARNING FROM COMPLAINTS AND GRIEVANCES

Ideally, all management representatives should be seriously interested in uncovering and correcting what has been accountable for anything less than the highest attainable level of organizational health and productivity. Anyone who has such a view of his responsibility may be able to learn much that he needs to know by studying complaints and the procedure by which complaints (and grievances) are handled. For example, a chief executive should know: What kinds of complaints are being expressed? Where are they coming from? How does the complaint procedure work? Do some supervisors try to suppress "squawks" or to appease troublemakers? Or is every supervisor doing a good job in trying to learn about (and from) dissatisfactions and to remove all legitimate grounds for complaints? In a unionized concern, a manager should satisfy himself that the formal grievance procedure (1) is set up in such a way as to be fair (because it demonstrably meets requirements as an appeal procedure), (2) consists of adequate provisions, written out in clear-cut, simple language and known to all employees, and (3) can function fast. But no formal procedure can do all that needs to be done.

A key factor is the attitude of every supervisor. Can each supervisor take an objective and personnel-minded view of every complaint that reaches him? Can he regard it neither as a personal insult nor as just another headache, but as an opportunity to work for better understanding of, by, and with an employee? Now that a dissatisfaction has been brought into the open, perhaps it can be dealt with in a way that will remove what has been a hidden obstacle to high morale and good personnel (or labor) relations. Everyone who listens to complaints needs to develop skill in *listening for what speaks in each complainant.* Aside from the specific complaint that he makes, is he troubled by such negative feelings as resentment, jealousy, frustration, or insecurity? When a supervisor learns to get to the heart of a disguised complaint, he may find something that is unpleasant for him to contemplate, because it shows up something that needs to be corrected in his department, or perhaps even in a company policy. Such complaints can be eye-openers for management representatives. Everyone who wants to earn his right to manage must be prepared to open his eyes—to see what has been accountable—and to use his mind in figuring out what needs to be done.

When complaints become grievances, and especially when official grievances cannot be settled short of arbitration, a failure has occurred, but it need not be a sterile failure. How can such a breakdown be avoided next time? What does the arbitrator do that some management representative did not or could not do? A manager should wrestle with this question and should not let it go until he wins new insight.

Handling complaints is only one of many learning opportunities that occur during the employment relationship. At each stage in the employment process, from recruitment to retirement, there are special opportunities for gaining and sharing understanding and for making mutual accommodations. Each such opportunity can—and should—be treated as an integral part of a total process in which principles, policies, plans, procedures, and practices of personnel administration are all of a piece.

MAKING AND USING JOB DESCRIPTIONS

Making careful job (and position) descriptions and using them in a variety of ways can help to integrate personnel administration at every stage in the employment process.

In many companies, job descriptions are used primarily or wholly in connection with wage and salary administration, and often no position descriptions are written—the idea being that managers understand their jobs and relationships well enough without putting anything in writing. (Incidentally, research findings do not support that assumption.) But when careful descriptions are written for every job in the enterprise and fully and imaginatively used, many benefits accrue. For example, a complete set of position descriptions can serve as a mirror that gives an operational view of the organization chart. Does it reflect what top management wishes and expects to see? Or does some overlapping of duties show up?

In addition to all the standard uses for job and position descriptions, important benefits can be gained by using these word pictures as a means to bring misunderstandings into the open and talk them out. Even at high organizational levels there have been many misunderstandings about job requirements and report relationships. At lower organizational levels job descriptions, appropriately supplemented during progress appraisals, can be developed into what amount to position guides.

RECRUITMENT, SELECTION, AND PLACEMENT

Recruitment is the first stage of a relationship in which each stage should be planned and administered as part of an ongoing process which stimulates and frees the employee to develop and use his full potential as an organizational member and a teammate. To realize that aim, recruitment must be dignified. It must be effective in attracting a suitable number of qualified candidates for employment. *Placement* should be treated as a preliminary decision for routine workers and as part of a continuing experiment for promotional candidates. Discriminating *selection among* candidates, on the basis of company policies implemented by clearly defined procedures, can protect managers from the charge of improper discrimination *against* applicants. Members of the personnel department should set an example for other staff experts by the way in which they coordinate their activities with what is done by supervisors, to make a success of these initial hiring procedures.

INDUCTION, ORIENTATION, AND TRAINING

Sound procedures of induction, orientation, and training are essential to help employees with what they need to know, to feel, and to do. Because these stages in the employment process are important in connection with getting out production, they are the responsibility of line managers. Members of a personnel department can assist line managers by recommending induction and training procedures that incorporate up-to-date knowledge and fit the company situation.

PERFORMANCE APPRAISALS

Current performance on the job should be discussed with each employee in regular follow-up interviews. These talks should amount to joint appraisals in view of mutually agreed-upon performance standards. This practice is essential for mutual understanding and for maximum development by employees. When each employee knows how his immediate supervisor rates his performance in relation to his job description, he can adjust his expectations and behavior accordingly. Performance appraisal can also help managers to make sound decisions on promotion. When thorough, objective, joint appraisals of employee performance replace snap judgments by supervisors, all concerned—including union leaders—can find solid ground for agreement.

TRANSFERS AND SEPARATIONS

A personnel administrator may be of service to top management in formulating policies and procedures for transfers and separations. Established avenues of transfer should correspond to job families, set up according to job descriptions. These avenues should be made known to everyone concerned. Unless each employee can answer the question: "Where could I go from here?" he may be inclined to think that management's professed aims to develop and use employee ability are "just a lot of hooey."

DOWNGRADING AND LAYOFF

Decisions for downgrading and layoff are difficult for managers to make wisely and for unions to accept rationally. Only when personnel policies are demonstrably constructive and when efficient procedures are wisely administered can managers and union officials be sure that all employees are being treated fairly.

CONSTRUCTIVE DISCIPLINE

Disciplinary action also tests management's success in applying a personnel-minded view. A personnel administrator has not succeeded as a teacher if any supervisor fails to understand that daily discipline should be maintained within each work team, chiefly by self-discipline and by group controls. Such inner discipline should be encouraged by a constructive discipline policy and supplemented by a few simple rules that are promptly and consistently enforced.

When an employee has to be severely penalized, or even discharged, every management representative who has regularly dealt with him should look at the record and search his own memory for clues about what went wrong. Was this employee ever the right man in the right job? Was he the right kind of person to meet the standards for work and for conduct? Was he willing and able to carry his share of unassigned responsibilities for the organization as a whole? Was his follow-up adequate? Or did management fall down on the job at some stage after he was hired? A skillfully conducted exit interview may throw light on these points or management may never learn what was accountable for failure to get cooperation in this instance. Was it perhaps that the employee did not learn what was expected of him in time to adjust to requirements? If so, perhaps this failure can help some management representative to see that workers need to have advance notice, and adequate explanation, not only of their regular duties but also of changes in work routines, in work teams, and in rates of pay.

HANDLING JOB CHANGES

In a dynamic industrial economy, technological changes that affect employees and their job assignments are not only inevitable but also desirable. Such changes may be logical when considered from the viewpoint of cost and technical efficiency, but have line managers taken account of what these changes might mean humanly? Could a change be interpreted as a threat to current group relationships, to accepted work routines, or to a worker's skill? What has been done that could help employees to understand and accept necessary changes? Perhaps careful planning, consultation, and advance notice are already in effect. If so, what more could be done—or what might be better done—to reduce resistance to change? A manager who knows the score realizes that resistance (whether overt or covert) can prevent an organization from getting the full benefit of technical improvements.

Management decisions for production scheduling are technical in nature, but they have important human aspects, since production schedules are operated by people. By situational thinking, management representatives may be able to integrate technical and human requirements when they plan production schedules. Such planning is not easy. Often it has not even been attempted. It is simpler to limit one's self either to a purely technical view or to a person-centered approach. For instance, it is not hard to plan schedules solely with a view to meeting production demands. Nor is it difficult to adjust the schedule of one employee to fit his personal situation. But such special adjustments, if made for many people, produce chaotic work schedules, and if made for some people and not for others in the same situation, they do not meet policy requirements. Can a personnel administrator help top management to take a *situation-centered* view that starts with policy thinking, gives due weight to technical requirements, and takes account of human needs (and feelings) as affected by the timing of work schedules? In considering the human aspects of work schedules, a personnel-minded manager remembers that a company operates *not* in a vacuum but in a community. The location of a plant (geographically) and the timing of work shifts (on the clock and the calendar) are points of contact (and of possible friction) between a company and a community. Travel time, community customs, and work requirements (for example, in continuous-process industries) are matters that call for mutual accommodation, but special demands by a company on employees can be partly compensated for by extra payments.

* * * * *

THE CHALLENGE OF MODERN MANAGEMENT

In this second half of the twentieth century, managers face the challenge of establishing conditions under which people at work can meet high-level human needs, as they contribute their best efforts toward achieving organizational objectives in which they believe. This challenge is not new, but it becomes more evident and more urgent as the world-wide thrust toward independence makes people increasingly dissatisfied with any system of control which seems oppressive.

Management by rule (authoritarian management) was never good enough. Today it is transparently inadequate. Every person who gives himself to his work deserves what has been called "the basic wage"—an opportunity to realize his full potential for growth and service. But few people put enough of themselves into their job to earn that wage unless they can feel proud of the organization in which they work and can see that their contribution is important. Setting up conditions such that every employee could earn "the basic wage," if he felt like it, is a tall order, but a personnel-minded manager wants to fill it. Moreover, he knows that unless managers do meet this kind of challenge they are not earning the right to manage.

Any manager who does try to meet this challenge is tackling the kind of assignment in which he can never fully succeed, but he and those who help him (including staff specialists) may be sustained by the conviction that managing by shared objectives is worth working at. People can understand each other to a large extent. Personal goals can be harmonized with organizational objectives —if everyone concerned wants to do this and keeps on trying. And certainly people can work together effectively only in so far as they do understand each other and do work for the same objectives. Differences about short-term goals will often divide people, but anyone who has seen what flexibility, patience, and ingenuity can do, even in stress situations, knows that integrative solutions to human differences can often be found—especially when people start looking for them soon enough, and keep looking with imagination, perseverance, and good will.

Everyone with responsibility for performance by others is also obligated to keep searching for more productive ways to get results with other people—ways to reduce occasions for disagreement about organizational objectives and to multiply the means for settling differences. In recent years many bitter disagreements have been settled amicably after continuing conferences. In the years to come, perhaps conferring will increasingly replace conflict as a means to settle disputes.

To all who search for new and better ways of working with other people we would say: Do not give up. Keep on trying. Especially, keep on making experiments. Research in behavioral psychology has produced many new insights and new hypotheses, but this kind of research is too important to be left entirely to social scientists. The experimental approach and the questioning attitude that are prerequisites for fruitful research are open to all. Any manager might reexamine his assumptions about managing and being managed, in the light of actual experience—getting facts, comparing notes with colleagues, and developing hypotheses that can be tested today, and tomorrow.

If you are searching and researching for new ways to work productively with other people, we urge you to keep on believing that better ways can be found. Above all, keep on believing in people—including yourself. Put your trust in the spirit of mutual responsibility which—when strongly felt—can carry people through difficulties that would otherwise be insurmountable.

42.

A CRITICAL LOOK AT THE HATCH ACT

Henry Rose

Political activity by public employees was a matter of official concern in the federal government long before the Hatch Political Activities Act; in 1907 President Roosevelt ordered Civil Service Rule I amended to provide that persons "in the competitive classified service, while retaining the right to vote as they please and to express privately their opinions on all political subjects, shall take no active part in political management or in political campaigns." During the next thirty-three years the Civil Service Commission applied this general rule to particular cases, thereby building up a body of case law of over three thousand decisions. At irregular intervals during that period, the Commission published a pamphlet which contained a brief and concededly incomplete summary of the activities previously found to violate Rule I. The pamphlet was used by the Commission as a basis for rendering decisions in individual cases and for responding to requests for advice.

Rule I applied only to those federal employees who were in the "classified," also called "competitive," civil service, a category of employees who enjoy a measure of job protection. In 1939 there were 953,891 federal employees, of whom only sixty-nine per cent were in the "classified" civil service and thereby subject to Rule I. A principal legislative purpose of the 1939 installment of the

Reprinted from *Harvard Law Review*, January, 1962, pp. 510–16. Copyright © 1962 by The Harvard Law Review Association.

Hatch Act was to extend the proscription of rule I to most of the other thirty-one per cent; the 1940 installment had as its major purpose a further extension of coverage to state and local government employees who worked on federally financed programs. The 1940 amendments also included section 15, which states:

The provisions of this Act which prohibit persons to whom such provisions apply from taking any active part in political management or in political campaigns shall be deemed to prohibit the same activities on the part of such persons as the United States Civil Service Commission has heretofore determined are at the time this section takes effect prohibited on the part of employees in the classified civil service of the United States by the provisions of the civil-service rules prohibiting such employees from taking any active part in political management or in political campaigns.

To date, neither the Commission nor the courts have found it necessary to discuss in depth the construction of section 15. Two questions arise: (1) Exactly what is incorporated by that section, i.e., what is the referent? Does it give the force of statutory law to each of the thousands of individual prohibitions represented by the pre-1940 determinations of the Commission? Or does the section give statutory force to the Commission's summary of those determinations? Is the phrase "active part in political management or in political campaigns" meant to be coextensive with the pre-1940 determinations of the Civil Service Commission? That is, does section 15 refer to the prior determinations exclusively? Or does the section adopt by reference those prior determinations as a base, leaving the Commission to interpret the general prohibitory language to include activities not previously determined to be violative?

The latter question is answered with unusual clarity by the legislative history of section 15. The wording of section 15 in the amendatory bill which was the basis for most of the 1940 debate in the Senate was entirely different from the language finally enacted. The earlier section 15 read as follows:

The United States Civil Service Commission is hereby authorized and directed to promulgate, as soon as practicable, rules or regulations defining, for the purpose of this Act, the term "active part in political management or in political campaigns." After the promulgation of such rules or regulations, the term "active part in political management or in political campaigns," as used in this Act shall have the meaning ascribed to it by such rules or regulations. The Commission is authorized to amend such rules or regulations from time to time as it deems necessary.

The opposition in the Senate to such a broad delegation of authority to the Civil Service Commission was strong and persistent. After almost two weeks of debate on the entire bill, Senator Hatch proposed to substitute the present language of section 15. The change was obviously a substantial one and was intended to undercut this opposition. He introduced the proposal with the remark that "all the substitute does is to prescribe in the law itself that the present prohibitions . . . shall be the political activities prohibited by the Act; that it shall be limited to those interpretations . . . ." He then concluded that this would do away with the delegation-of-power question. At another point in the debate on the substitute section 15, he said:"[I]t seemed to me to be very wise not to give the Commission any more power to interpret further in the future." That he was successful in conveying his concept of the impact of section 15 was evidenced by the remarks of Senator Brown, who was opposed to the bill and to section 15 in particular, when he said: "We are asked to fix into hard and fast statute law every interpretation which has heretofore been made. . . . In other words, there could be no building up of a body of judicial interpretations which might hereafter change."

Although it is thus clear that Congress adopted by reference specific, existing prohibitions, not subject to change, there has been some confusion whether the statutory referent was the administrative determinations under Rule I or the Commission's summary of them in *Pamphlet 20*. The debates show that some senators apparently thought that the Civil Service Commission had a set of rules and regulations spelling out in detail the prohibited political activities until Senator Hatch informed his colleagues, during the last phase of the debate on section 15, that "there is but one rule of the Civil Service Commission . . . [which] is almost the exact language of the pending bill and the exact language of the law that was passed [the prior year]. . . . Under that rule, which has been in existence for more than 50 years, the Civil Service Commission has made certain definite findings that this thing is political activity within the meaning of the rule, or that something else is not . . . ." And it was at this point that the referent was seemingly made explicit, for Senator Brown asked Senator Hatch whether "section 15 relates to the interpretation of the rule . . .," to which the latter replied, "Yes. . . . [W]e are writing into the statute the interpretation of it."

Because the section 15 substitute was proposed by Senator Hatch and adopted by the Senate on the same day, without prior announcement that the particular proposal would be made, there was very little opportunity for members of the Senate to investigate and find out what was being incorporated by the section's reference. When Senator Brown protested that "before we make those interpretations in effect the statute law . . . we ought to have those interpretations . . . before us . . . ," the majority leader, Senator Barkley, expressed confidence that Senator Hatch had read "as many interpretations . . . as there have been cases before the Civil Service Commission upon which it had to pass," and argued that separate consideration of each Commission interpretation would unduly delay a vote on the bill. Shortly thereafter, the Senate approved the substituted section 15, but not before there was an accumulation of convincing evidence of a congressional purpose to adopt thereby the individual pre-Hatch Act Commission determinations, rather than the pamphlet summary.

It is possible of course that had Congress investigated in a responsible manner, it might still have voted as it did—but it is highly unlikely that it would have endorsed every one of the three thousand decisions. For example, would Congress knowingly have approved a proscription on writing an isolated letter to a newspaper on a political subject? Or would Congress have assented to the Commission's decision in *Archie B. Cole?* Mr. Cole was a rural mailcarrier who also happened to be a member of the Watch Tower Bible and Tract Society, better known as Jehovah's Witnesses. The evidence of Cole's "political activity" was

that he is a member of the faith or doctrine taught by the Watch Tower Bible and Tract Society, which is vigorously opposed to war ... that meetings of the Society have been held in the carrier's home ... that the literature published by the Society is devoted in a large part to vigorous criticism of our governments, statesmen, financiers, etc., as well as other governments, and the churches and clergy in general.

When Cole realized that he was in danger of losing his job (this was in the depression year of 1932), he promised to mend his ways and withdraw from such activities—but the Civil Service Commission sternly concluded "that Mr. Cole's participation in meetings, circulation of literature and other activities in connection with a society antagonistic to governmental policy is sufficient evidence of his unfitness for government employment to warrant his dismissal from the service" for political activity. Accordingly, the Commission recommended that he be removed, and the Post Office Department promptly dismissed him, though there was no evidence that his activities as a member of the Society interfered with performance of his duties.

Happily, no Hatch Act case has invoked the rule of the *Cole* case. It is even probable that during the past two decades the Commission has been as unaware of the *Cole* case as was the Congress in 1940, for no hint of the case appears in any Commission publication and the decision itself is buried in the raw file in a dusty storage cabinet. Thus, it appears that the Commission's blissful ignorance or disregard of the *Cole* rule has prevented the application of an outrageous and apparently unconstitutional rule.

By resorting to the hastily improvised incorporation-by-reference device in order to avoid either delegating the job or undertaking itself the onerous task of defining ambiguous key language, Congress unintentionally cast its net too far with the result that the statute proscribes conduct not within the legislative purpose, as in the *Cole* case. Conversely, some conduct of the general type Congress was seeking to halt fell outside of that carelessly cast net, as the following illustration shows. After a change of administration in Idaho, officials of the state's highway department allegedly discharged subordinate employees because their political allegiance was not to the party in power. Although a principal goal of the Hatch Act was to protect rank-and-file government employees from being pressured to engage in involuntary political activity, the Commission responded to the complainant that it was unable to do anything. It was helpless, in spite of the allegations of such flagrant political conduct by the Idaho officials, because such acts have

... never been considered to be contrary to and punishable under the particular provision of the rules specifically referred to by Congress in Section 15. ... Accordingly, on the basis of its precedent decisions which have in effect been written into the law by Section 15, the Commission must hold that the activities described in your complaint do not constitute "political management" within the meaning of the Hatch Act. On this basis the Commission can take no further action on your complaint.

The Commission has often recognized that it is bound by its pre-1940 administrative determinations. In *David B. Smith*, it stated: "It is established by determination of the Commission prior to enactment of Section 15 of the Hatch Act, that circulation of a political petition . . . comes within the prohibition . . . and that Section 15 precludes us from making any change in those determinations." In another case involving a finding that service on a political committee violated the act, the Commission remarked, "even if we were inclined to re-examine the question, it would be beyond our authority to do so. By Section 15 . . . Congress has adopted that rule. The Commission is as little able to change that, as it is to change any other enactment of Congress." And the Commission's Chief Hearing Examiner has concluded that

... if in Sections 9 and 12 of the Hatch Act Congress had simply prohibited those subject thereto from taking "any active part in political campaigns," there always would have remained an opportunity for logically reasoned conflicting arguments as to what falls within the scope of the prohibition. But Sec. 15 of the Hatch Act makes for inflexibility in interpretation, establishing what may be considered a mandatory principle of *stare decisis*.

The Commission's administration of the Hatch Act has not, however, adhered to its pre-1940 determinations as uniformly as the preceding quotation might suggest. It has implied at times that the summaries of decisions in *Pamphlet 20* and not the specific decisions themselves were given statutory force in section 15. In those cases where it feels called upon to cite authority for the proposition that certain conduct constitutes a violation of the Hatch Act, the Commission typically quotes from some portion of those summary pages in *Pamphlet 20*; sometimes a reference to section 15 is added, with the implication that the text of those few pages in the pamphlet have been given the force of statute. Individual pre-1940 cases are almost never cited; the Commission feels that *Pamphlet 20* "is an authoritative summary of its rulings (given the force of statutory law by section 15 of the Hatch Act) on what constitutes prohibited political activity."

In *Herbert S. Reed*, respondent was charged with executing "the affidavits of a 'qualified elector' to two nominating petitions" though he had not circulated them. In its decision the Commission announced that "an examination has been made of decisions rendered prior to July 20, 1940 (effective date of Hatch Act Section 15 . . .), which relate to political petitions. None is found in which a person was charged with executing a 'qualified elector's affidavit' and nothing more." If the Commission has no power to make additions to the list of prohibited activities, should not that be the end of the matter? Not in the view of the Commission, for it added, immediately after the above statement, "That still does not necessarily mean that Mr. Reed's role of affiant was not a violation." Because, the Commission went on,

It can not be expected that for every case there will be an exact factual prototype. Decisions must be made according to *authoritative* determinations by the Commission *in which the controlling principles are the same.* Summarizing in broad terms what the Commission's determinations have sought to effect, Form 1236 [*Pamphlet 20*] has said:

12. *In general.*—In brief it may be said that the law is designed to prevent those subject to it from assuming general political leadership or from becoming prominently identified with any political movement, party, or faction, or with the success or failure of any candidate for election to public office.

We, therefore, measure the instant case by that standard.

This kind of reasoning can be explained by two theories—both erroneous. It may proceed from the view that the Commission, although bound by section 15 to continue to hold violative those activities which were found to be prohibited prior to 1940, may add new activities to the prohibited list. Or the reasoning may be based on the view that when section 15 says the pre-1940 decisions are binding, it refers not to the individual decisions, but rather to the relatively few general principles culled from the Commission's analysis and synthesis of those thousands of decisions. By this theory the Commission applies to particular cases general principles which it has itself formulated. The latter theory appears to have been the one underlying the reasoning of the Commission in the *Reed* case. Note the anomalous result of such reasoning: Whereas Congress was unwilling to authorize the Commission further to interpret "active part in political management or political campaigns," the Commission arrogated to itself the power to interpret and apply the much broader and vaguer interdiction used in the *Reed* case. Either of these theories amounts to the rewriting of the act by the Commission. Congress debated at length a proposal to delegate to the Commission authority to define the specific activities to be prohibited under the act, and, in the face of opposition, that proposal was dramatically abandoned in the closing phase of the debate.

The *Reed* case is unusual in that the accompanying opinion makes an attempt to reconcile section 15 with the Commission's practice, so that the Commission's misreading of the act is demonstrable. More often, the cases reflect a lack of awareness of or an indifference to the congressional definition of "active part in political management or in political campaigns." In decision after decision, the Commission has ignored the statutory definition, i.e., section 15 and its referents. Of course it may be argued that an administrative agency does not require specific authorization to interpret and apply general prohibitory language in a statute which it enforces. Such power may be implied from the assignment of the enforcement function to the agency. However, it is clearly within the power of the Congress to limit the interpretative discretion of an agency.

The significance of the Commission's reliance upon *Pamphlet 20* depends on the accuracy of its summary of pre-1940 decisions. It is questionable whether a body of case law made up of thousands of decisions covering a wide variety of offenses can ever be accurately summarized in less than seven pages. Such a summary may be adequate for the general orientation of a new employee, but it is of doubtful value as a basic legal text. Furthermore, once such a summary was made after 1940, if accurate, it would require no modifications thereafter. However, over the years since 1940, modifications have been made in that summary. In addition, it is noteworthy that the portion of the pamphlet "devoted to a discussion of activities that, prior to enactment of section 15 of the Hatch Act . . . the Civil Service Commission had determined to be activities prohibited by the civil-service rules" contains material which clearly is not part of such "discussion." For example, it contains quotations from other statutory provisions and references to opinions of the United States Attorney General. Moreover, the text is liberally sprinkled with what employees "may" or "may not" do politically (although at other points, it states that the "Commission has held" various activities prohibited or permitted). At one point in the 1958 edition, employees are gratuitously warned that "it is regarded as contrary to the spirit of the law for a public servant to make a partisan display of any kind while on duty conducting the public business." Thus the "authoritative summary" does not warrant its characterization as such, and leaves the reader with insufficient guidance as to where authoritative summarizing leaves off and editorializing begins.

Although the Civil Service Commission generally uses the pamphlet as an authoritative listing of what specific political activity is prohibited, it has recognized on a few occasions that it is not safe to rely solely upon the pamphlet. It has cautioned that *Pamphlet 20*'s "general rules should be taken as of general and *prima facie* application, but not necessarily as without any possible exception." The Commission has not, however, enabled the bar or the regulated employees to determine what these exceptions might be or to contest a determination that none exists. There are no regular reports of the Commission's decisions. The pre-1940 decisions are not even available to the public. Copies of particular post-1940 decisions, under the Hatch Act, may be obtained from the Commission upon request. But since no adequate digest or topical index is available, it is unlikely that anyone would know which of the decisions, arranged by docket numbers— roughly a chronological order—should be requested. The expense of personally checking the approximately 350 formal decisions under the act would usually be prohibitive, especially since there is no bar specialized in Hatch Act proceedings and the average client has quite limited resources. The unavailability of administrative decisions is all the more regrettable in view of the small number of judicial decisions that have involved the act. The result is that *Pamphlet 20* is the principal source of guidance, not only to the regulated employees but also to both their lawyers and the Commission, in determining what is prohibited political activity.

Many of the decisions that are available may be less than enlightening; and since 1953 the Commission has followed a policy which largely relieves it even of the burden of preparing an opinion to support its decisions in Hatch Act cases involving federal employees. Since that date the Commission has explained with full opinion approximately one decision per year among its federal cases. The Commission disposes of the bulk of these cases by letters to the respondents or their attorneys with little or no explanation, a practice which flies in the face of good adjudicatory practice. Even in the cases where the Commission has issued opinions, they have been anonymous; it has not followed the practice, recommended recently by President Kennedy, of assigning to "individual agency members the responsibility of being individually responsible for the rationale underlying important agency decisions . . . ."

If the present regulatory scheme is to be continued, it is incumbent on the Government to make available in usable form all Commission determinations relating to political activity, whether made before or after passage of the Hatch Act. The persons subject to political-activity restrictions and their attorneys should have these available for whatever guidance they offer for predicting the legitimacy of future conduct. And if it is necessary for a democratic society to curtail the political liberties of some of its citizens, the necessity should be fully stated. Where political appointees administer restrictions on the political activities of millions of their fellow citizens, great effort should be made to avoid not only the possibility of partisan regulation, but also the appearance of it. Disclosure of decisions together with the Commission's reasoning would require it to give more attention to the consistency of its action with the law and would tend to dispel perhaps unwarranted suspicions. It would also provide Congress with a more adequate basis for review of national policy in this area of regulation.

The freezing of precedent decisions into doctrinaire rules to control decision of future cases is at odds with our adjudicatory tradition, is unsound, and is unworkable. The attempt of Congress to establish such a rigid precedent system by section 15 was doomed from the start—and the experience under the act lends additional support to Professor Llewellyn's observation that even where there is "deliberated determination to plant feet flat 'upon the ancient ways' movement and change still creep up on the blind side of the stagnators." It is time to acknowledge the failure of this attempt. The road to a fair balance of competing interests cannot be navigated with only a rear view mirror.

But providing administrative flexibility is not enough; it should be accompanied by fresh legislation based on a reappraisal of national policy regarding political behavior of public employees. Repeal of section 15 would legitimatize a measure of discretion in the Commission, but probably would not significantly affect the course of current decisions; after all, section 15 carried forward prior Commission policies. And it will be recalled that the adoption by reference was a substitute for undertaking or delegating the task of defining the activities to be proscribed. Thus, the removal of that prop should be coupled with a new look at the problem it was used to avoid. Ostensibly, the Hatch Act was primarily aimed at protecting public employees from pressures to engage in involuntary political activity. Yet the overwhelming majority of Hatch Act cases in recent years contain no suggestion of involuntary political activity. Indeed, it should be reconsidered whether the protection of public employees from involuntary political service requires the prohibition of any voluntary political activities. Consideration might also be given to whether the same restrictions should apply inflexibly to all covered employees, or whether the stringency of such restrictions should vary with the employee's governmental function, his contact with the general public, the degree of his job security, or other factors.

Even a much narrower inquiry by Congress could be useful, if it resulted in greater clarity as to the political-activity restrictions. A most unfortunate result of the present vagueness of the act is that because doubt as to the permissibility of a kind of political activity continues, an inestimable quantum of voluntary and desirable political participation goes undone, though it may be determined at a later date that such acts are permissible.

43.

THE TRIUMPH OF TECHNIQUES OVER PURPOSE

WALLACE S. SAYRE

I.

... The concepts and the methodology of contemporary public personnel administration are, of course, the product of the dominant objectives set by, and for, the students and the practitioners of the craft. It is possible to identify these goals in separate terms, even though they overlap and have always exerted powerful reciprocal influences upon each other. For the purpose of demonstrating the values of the Pigors-Myers text, it is useful to restate the main streams in the evolution of the premises and techniques which now characterize personnel administration in public agencies.

Reprinted from *Public Administration Review*, Vol. 8 (Spring, 1948), pp. 134–37.

The earliest of these, and still the source of the most distinctive public personnel practices, is the goal of eliminating party patronage from the management of the civil service. This definition of purpose has been the most enduring, the most widely understood and embraced, and consequently the most influential article of faith in the growth of the profession. From this premise the basic structure of civil service administration has been derived: central personnel control agencies, bipartisan commissions, quantitative techniques, the "rule of three," and the whole familiar arsenal of devices to neutralize and divert patronage pressures. On the whole, the means were once appropriate to the problem. But, as Gordon Clapp observed in this *Review* as early as 1941,[1] the merit system advocates having clearly won the day in most jurisdictions, the question now is what to do with the victory—which of these methods are today appropriate to the new priority objectives? And what are the new objectives?

A second, closely associated purpose was gradually made explicit in the development of the public personnel program. This goal is the guarantee of equal treatment to all applicants for public employment and among all public employees. This is clearly a positive ethic of great appeal in a democratic society, and it has won an increasing emphasis from public personnel specialists. The contribution of this goal to personnel methodology has been substantial. Its main effect has been to move personnel administration, in the words of Gordon Clapp, "into the cold objective atmosphere of tests, scores, weighted indices, and split-digit ranking" so completely that "these technical trappings have become the symbols of the merit system".

Still another stream of influence has contributed to the fulfillment of this tendency. The logic of scientific management, the paramount ideology of articulate business management between the two wars, has also exerted a powerful attraction for the personnel administrators. The impersonal goals of management logic made the precise, quantitative techniques of the efficiency engineer plausible and attractive methods for the "scientific" personnel manager. Job classification, factor analysis, numerical efficiency ratings, formal promotion charts, and all their procedural relatives acquired a new and impressive endorsement—the personnel system could now lay claim to the combined virtues of merit, equality in competition, and scientific management.

Finally, public personnel policies and methods have been measurably affected by the goal of a public career service. Stated in its most positive terms, this objective represents an effort to provide the conditions of work which will attract and hold a public service of optimum talents. In its negative aspects, the goal has been translated into an elaborate system of protectionism. In the area of methodology the negative connotations have slowly but surely won the dominant

---

[1] "The Rule of Three, It Puzzles Me," *Public Administration Review*, Vol. 1 (Spring, 1941), pp. 287–93.

position. The concept of status and the concept of rights earned by seniority, to use but two examples from a large network, have been molded from precedent to precedent into a personnel jurisprudence in which all but the most expert technicians lose their way.

In sum, the personnel administration produced by the confluence of these four streams of influence represents a triumph of techniques over purpose. This is not an unusual outcome in the field of administration. Nor does the conclusion mean that great historical accomplishments should not be recorded. What it does suggest is that both ends and means now urgently need fundamental re-examination.[2]

Private personnel administration has not escaped similar pressures. In particular, it has responded in its development to "scientific" management and to a modified version of careerism. The resulting complex of concepts and methods makes up a formidable system of quantitative techniques and formal rules in private personnel administration. Here, too, one may conclude that the ends have been made captive by the means.

Personnel administration, then, has tended to become characterized more by procedure, rule, and technique than by purpose or results. In the public field especially, quantitative devices have overshadowed qualitative. Standardization and uniformity have been enshrined as major virtues. Universal (and therefore arbitrary) methods have been preferred to experiment and variety. From the perspective of the clientele (the public, the managers, and the employees), these traits increasingly connote rigidity, bureaucracy, institutionalism;—and they are now beginning to evoke a reciprocal system of formal and informal techniques of evasion. Among personnel people there is an accompanying growth of frustration and a loss of satisfying participation in the real work of the organization.

Personnel administration, seen in this context, mirrors the dilemma of all orthodox administration. The traditional conceptual and methodological apparatus of administration has rested heavily upon the fallacy of an "administrative man" comparable to the synthetic, rational "economic man" of the classical economists. During the past fifteen years this fiction of the "administrative man" (which Elton Mayo so aptly called the "rabble hypothesis") has been steadily undermined not only by the painstaking inquiries of many students of human behavior but even more by the movement of great social forces. In the growth

---

[2] Those readers who find this judgment overdrawn are urged to examine anew *Better Government Personnel, Report of the Commission of Inquiry on Public Service Personnel* (New York: McGraw-Hill Book Co., 1935); the *Report of the President's Committee on Administrative Management* (Washington, D.C.: Government Printing Office, 1937), and the accompanying monograph by Floyd W. Reeves and Paul T. David, *Personnel Administration in the Federal Service* (Washington D.C.: Government Printing Office, 1937); the *Report of the President's Committee on Civil Service Improvement* (H. Doc. No. 118, 77th Cong. 1st sess.); and J. Donald Kingsley's *Representative Bureaucracy; An Interpretation of the British Civil Service* (Yellow Springs, Ohio: Antioch Press, 1944).

of personnel administration this rise of mature dissent may be traced, in large part at least, from its clearest beginnings in the reflections of John Dewey and Mary Follett upon the nature and structure of authority, in the efforts of Ordway Tead and Henry Metcalf to introduce more democratic precepts into the practice of personnel administration, and in the pioneering Hawthorne studies at Western Electric by Elton Mayo, F. J. Roethlisberger, and others. The efficiency engineer and the logician of management have slowly given way, at least at the level of administrative theory, to the psychologist, the sociologist, and other social scientists.

II.

Dissent from the "rabble hypothesis" of traditional personnel administration is the central virtue of the volume by Pigors and Myers. . . .

. . . The authors are not altogether successful in their attempt to transmute formal personnel procedures into useful human relations instruments.[3] This relative failure highlights one of the most difficult judgments which the human relations group must now make: to what extent can they accept and work within the present structure and methods of personnel administration? What are the hazards that any such acceptance will adulterate their concepts and inhibit further exploration and growth?

The answer, especially in public personnel administration, would seem to lie in a different perspective on the values and uses of quantitative techniques. It is not the techniques per se which have constructed the straightjacket that now imprisons so much of personnel administration. The basic techniques are, when properly used, of considerable value and of even greater potential promise. The real difficulty lies in the fact that (1) the techniques are usually inadequate for the full purpose they are relied upon to accomplish, yet accomplishment is gradually taken for granted; (2) the techniques are prematurely frozen into regulations and procedures for universal application in greatly varying administrative environments, thus stifling at birth the process of genuine research and technical development; and (3) the techniques gradually obscure the ends they were designed to serve. The contrast between this tendency of personnel specialists toward eager installation and canonization of rudimentary techniques and the stubborn experimentalism of the physical sciences is instructive. Even many of those who might be assumed to be the least susceptible to this tendency—the psychologists, with their strong experimental tradition—reveal their imprisonment with-

---

[3] As a textbook, *Personnel Administration* acquires immeasurable additional value from the case materials included. These provide real-life illustrations for most chapters. The cases are presented with satisfying completeness (190 pages are devoted to 19 cases), and each one is accompanied by a series of searching and provocative questions for discussion.

in the system by devoting their energies to the refinement of the installed methods of testing skills and personality "traits" rather than to the working out of new techniques and applications in the fields of attitudes, motivation, and group dynamics.

The immediate trends as well as some of the most deeply imbedded concepts of public personnel administration are opposed to the human relations points of view. Although this is not the whole problem, it is a revealing index of the crisis in civil service administration. At a time when the urgency, difficulty, and complexity of governmental performance are daily increasing, at a time when industrial personnel administration is moving toward a recognition of the values of experimental and thorough inquiry into human behavior, tempered in application by informality and flexibility in the human relations of organized effort, the public service becomes steadily more dependent upon a cold, impersonal, rigid quantification of human ability and worth in public employment. Nor is even this the full measure of the inadequacy. The methods relied upon lack the objectivity which is their sole claim to usefulness; they provide merely the appearance, not the substance, of the relevant measurement of ability and merit. The variables of personnel administration are too many and too subtle to be contained within a purely statistical frame of reference. In contrast, a prime virtue of the human relations group is its relative lack of conceit about the immutability of its concepts and techniques.

Some readers may wonder whether this review overlooks the "new trends" in federal personnel administration. These trends need to be more carefully examined than opportunity here affords. However, some tentative observations are in order. During the war years, many useful explorations were made in the direction of personnel policies and methods which would be appropriate and adequate for the great tasks of federal administration. Some of these experiments still endure, but the surrounding climate is not encouraging. With perhaps the sole exception of TVA among the federal agencies, there has been uniformly a net loss of opportunity for the development of agency personnel programs responsive to the special needs of agency assignments and climate. The prewar pattern of uniform rules, designed to impose an artificial appearance of order and objectivity upon the federal establishments, has been restored and strengthened, not relaxed. "Decentralization" has been the main theme of "progress" in the postwar federal personnel program. It is relevant to inquire: what is the substance of the program being decentralized? The ultimate values of the decentralization depend upon the quality of the program. The decentralization of work load under strict procedural instructions binding those who do the work is a dubious administrative economy; it certainly does not represent an important new trend in the development of an adequate philosophy and method of personnel administration.

44.

APPEAL ACTIVITIES IN THE FEDERAL GOVERNMENT

WILLIAM G. SCOTT

Most systems for the redress of grievances and complaints within the administrative framework of government are unilaterally established and maintained by the management of the agencies and civil service commissions. This is the case in the federal service as well as in state and municipal governments.[1]

The effect of rapid unionization of public employees on these systems is problematical. The administration of bilaterally negotiated grievance procedures, paralleling some of the governmental systems, seems to be one of the few functions in which government unions play a significant role at present. They cannot strike, nor can they participate in significant collective bargaining with the management of agencies since wage and fringe benefits are set by legislation.[2] They may, therefore, extend their efforts in the grievance area to provide an attraction for government employees.

However, this is speculative now. The chief avenues of redress for federal government employees still are the procedures set up by management. For certain important reasons, discussed here, these procedures are likely to remain paramount, although an aggrieved employee may get more effective presentation of his case by union representation.

We review certain appeal processes in the federal government in this section,

---

Reprinted with permission from William G. Scott, *The Management of Conflict* (Homewood, Ill.: Richard D. Irwin, Inc. and The Dorsey Press) pp. 30–35.

[1] For a study of appeal systems in local government see Melvin J. Segal, "Grievance Procedures for Public Employees," *Labor Law Journal*, December, 1958, pp. 921–24.

[2] This statement requires some modification since the promulgation of Executive Order 10988. This order titled Employee-Management Cooperation in the Federal Service issued January 17, 1962, allows for negotiation and union consultation on working conditions and personnel policy and practices. Congressional authority on wage levels and merit system principles is not interfered with. But even in these areas there are frequently wide gaps between maximum and minimum limits set by Congress in which negotiation can and does take place. Apparently there is room for negotiation even on the limits set by Congress. Section 5 (b) of the Order states, "When an employee organization has been formally recognized, the agency, through appropriate officials, shall consult with such organization from time to time in the formulation and implementation of personnel policies and practices, and matters affecting working conditions that are of concern to its members." This section might be construed to the effect that bargaining on wages and fringe benefit limits can be concluded with bureau chiefs and included in agency budgets *subject to congressional approval.*

duly noting that some local governments also have procedural activities of this nature. These latter systems are excluded from our discussion in the interest of space. Our inquiry is limited additionally by restricting the analysis to two major categories of federal appeal procedures—the appeal of adverse actions and the intra-agency grievance machinery. There are several other categories of appeal and grievance actions.[3] No particular purpose is served by going into them all.

APPEAL OF ADVERSE ACTION

Adverse actions are defined as removals, demotions, suspensions of more than 30 days, and reductions in rank.[4] Special channels of appeal are available to federal employees to seek redress from these serious, but limited, acts of agency administrators. The employee follows the route illustrated in Figure 44.1.

FIGURE 44.1. Employee Appeal of Adverse Actions

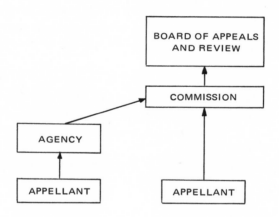

An employee seeking redress from adverse actions under this system may at his option initiate his appeal within the agency where he works or go first to

[3] Such as Performance Rating Appeals, Position Classification Appeals, and Discrimination Appeals. The reader is referred to an old but basic document for background information. It is *Appeals and Grievance Procedures in the Federal Government*, Subcommittee on Federal Manpower Policies, 83rd Cong., 1st sess., Doc. No. 33 (Washington, D.C.: U.S. Government Printing Office, 1953).

[4] A reduction in rank is an adverse action regardless of whether it is directed at an individual or is the result of reclassification of the position. In the latter instance, however, an appeal must be directed through the Position Classification Appeal procedure.

the Commission and forfeit his right to agency appeal. If he institutes his appeal action in the agency, then his next step for redress is to the Civil Service Commission, and finally to the Board of Appeals and Review of the Commission.

The agency system for appeal is a relatively new addition to the appeal network for adverse actions.[5] It was established by Executive Order 10987 in 1962 to ". . . provide a simple, orderly method through which an employee may seek prompt administrative reconsideration of a decision to take adverse action against him."[6] This system appears to be a reflection of the principle of getting appeals settled as close to their source as possible in the interests of decentralization at the agency level and of saving time.

The regulations provide one level of review in the agency by an administrative official higher than the one who made the adverse action. However, if the Commission approves, an agency may have more than one level of appeal ". . . when the delegation of authority or organizational arrangements . . . so require."[7]

The next step in appeal, outside the agency, is to the Civil Service Commission. The appeal is heard before a representative of the Commission and a decision is made by the Chief of the Appeals Examining Office or by a regional director of the Commission. The final step in the procedure, as noted before, is to the Board of Appeals and Review of the Commission.

The principle of non-suspension of administrative acts is present in this system as much as it is in . . . recourse in the church. That is, if an adverse action is sustained at the agency level against the appellant, the administrative act takes effect even though an appeal is carried to the Commission. In the case of removal the employee is dropped from the roles pending a reversal in the Commission at one or the other levels.

Civil service regulations require that an employee be given a 30-day notice of adverse action during which time, generally speaking, he remains on full duty status. If he wishes, he may prepare a case and answer charges within the agency or at the Commission depending on where he decides to initiate his appeal action. So for practical purposes the principle of non-suspension operates only after the 30-day notice period expires.

The source of this appeal process is traceable to the Lloyd-Lafollette Act of 1912. This Act was passed to cure some of the abuses of the spoils system which had not been eliminated by the Civil Service Act of 1883. The Lloyd-Lafollette Act did not include any provisions for the administration of appeals from adverse action by the Commission. It did establish, however, a statutory climate in which the Commission on its own authority, based upon civil service rules, created and set up the administrative machinery for the appeal programs.

---

[5] However, appeal of adverse actions directly to the Commission antedates this modification by nearly fifty years.

[6] Part 771—Remedies—*Federal Personnel Manual*, Subpart A, Definitions and Coverage.

[7] *Ibid.*, sec. 771.116.

The spirit of civil service reform was certainly grass-roots in character. Some have observed that the passage of the Lloyd-Lafollette Act was in no small part motivated by the assassination of President Garfield by a disappointed government job seeker. In any event it is interesting to see how reform was attempted by the civil service in keeping with the spirit of the law. One of the big problems was to hold efficient, trustworthy employees and drop the rest who were in government service thanks to the excesses of the spoils system. Of course this had to be done equitably with opportunity given to employees for redress. Thus the methods for appeal of adverse actions were part of the overall effort to accomplish the reform objective. It is important to note that under the regulations which evolved, *appeals could be based only on faulty administrative procedure in the processing of adverse actions.*

The basic law, which led to a change in the narrowly constituted appeal regulations, was the Veteran's Preference Act of 1944.

It provided a right to a hearing before the Commission as part of the adjudicative process, but its application was limited to veterans. Thus, a veteran could appeal to the Commission and get a decision on both procedural violations and the sufficiency of the agency reasons for taking adverse actions.[8]

Under this law the substantive and the procedural aspects of an adverse action were appealable by a veteran to the Commission. Non-veterans had to be content with appeals dealing just with procedural violations in the handling of actions against them.

The change in philosophy about what is appealable incorporated in the Veteran's Preference Act was extended to nearly everyone in the federal service by Executive Order 10988 in 1962. We have already seen how Executive Order 10987, issued the same day, required the development of regulations under which the *agencies* would introduce procedures for consideration of adverse actions.

GRIEVANCE PROCEDURES

In addition to the system for appeal of adverse actions, and the other procedures for specialized appeals referred to in the last section, there is a catch-all avenue for redress called the grievance procedure. This procedure has four distinguishing characteristics:

1. It is internal to the agency.
2. The Commission does not regulate it.

---

[8] Statement by Mr. L. L. Walton, Acting Appeals Examiner, United States Civil Service Commission, Chicago Regional Office. Mimeographed paper used for Civil Service Staff orientation to appeals activity.

FIGURE 44.2. Grievance Settlement in the Veterans' Administration

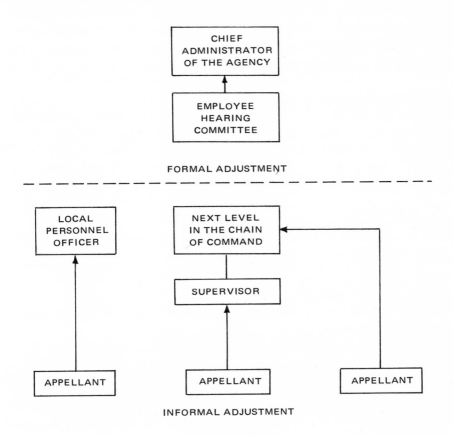

3. It is generated by administrative acts of agency officials.
4. It covers a wide number of problems that do not come within the scope of the specialized procedures.

These systems of appeal, which are procedurally different in each agency, are roughly analogous in spirit to the church's regulations for local handling of minor disputes. The Veterans' Administration approaches the grievance issue in the following way for its employees.

By "grievance" we mean a feeling of dissatisfaction with some aspect of your employment or with a management decision affecting you . . . .
It is the policy of the VA to identify, prevent, and make reasonable and proper effort to correct the causes of employee dissatisfaction "on the job." But when this

method fails, it is necessary that both employees and management have a final means of settling the issue. The VA grievance procedure provides this means.[9]

The method for adjustment of grievances proceeds along the lines shown in Figure 44.2. The policy provides that the aggrieved employee must first discuss his problem with his immediate supervisor. However, if the situation is such that he wants to avoid this step the opportunity for bypassing is available. Thus the employee may initiate his informal grievance action with a personnel representative or with the individual next above his supervisor in the chain of command. The employee's grievance can be carried into formal proceedings if an informal settlement is not reached. The appellant may request a hearing on his case by the Employee Hearing Committee. Appeal from the decision of the Committee is to the head administrator of the Veterans' Administration.

45.

THE PERSONNEL INTERVIEW

RICHARD STEPHEN UHRBROCK

THE INTERVIEWER'S RESPONSIBILITY

Men and women are rejected or hired mainly as the result of the impressions they make upon employment interviewers. What questions are asked during the interviews to form the groundwork for valid impressions? If you are an employer, do your interviewers have good judgment? How do you know? These are questions of vital concern to those responsible for personnel and public relations policies.

The average employment interviewer in American industrial concerns had approximately two years' high school education. He worked as a clerk in various departments and gradually shifted from record keeping to interviewing. If he had any coaching in employment methods, it usually was obtained from another clerk with similarly limited background. He may not have had friendly criticism of his interviewing procedures from a company official. He has not read books on how to interview. He does the best he can in terms of his understanding and training.

---

[9] VA Employee Letter 00-62-2, July 1, 1962, *The VA Grievance Procedure*, p. 1.

Reprinted with permission from *Personnel Psychology*, Vol. 1, No. 3 (Autumn, 1948), pp. 274–301.

Interviewing, according to Walter V. Bingham and Bruce V. Moore, authors of the widely read text *How to Interview* (1), is a conversation with a purpose. Therefore, some thought should be given to aims and methods (2, 3, 4). As a company representative, the interviewer has five main obligations:

1. To treat all applicants courteously;
2. To explore each applicant's background with sufficient thoroughness to decide whether immediate rejection or further investigation of potentialities is indicated;
3. To assist in the hiring of new people with characteristics like those of the best of the present group of employees;
4. To reject applicants whose services cannot be used in such a manner that they will not "lose face";
5. To maintain adequate records on his interviewing activities, so that the results and effects of his work can be evaluated periodically.

In general, the more applicants interviewed for each position to be filled, the more likely is the interviewer to select a good worker. In one company in 1941, the total number of applicants interviewed was 45,688. Of that number 2,190 persons were hired. In 1944, when wartime employment restrictions were in effect, there were 15,311 applicants. Of those, 2,807 were employed. Note that 30,377 *fewer* interviews were conducted in 1944 as compared with 1941. Six hundred seventeen *more* people were hired during 1944 than were hired in 1941. In other words, interviews were *down* 66.49 per cent; hires were *up* 28.22 per cent. The trend was slightly more favorable in 1945, 1946, and 1947. Table 45.1 shows

TABLE 45.1

INTERVIEW AND EMPLOYMENT TRENDS, 1941–1947

Year	Average Enrollment	Total Interviews	% Decrease Interviews from 1941	Total Hires	Number Interviews per Hire
1941	7,321	45,688	—	2,190	20.86
1942	7,011	33,111	27.53	2,441	13.56
1943	6,401	19,115	58.16	2,885	6.63
1944	6,430	15,311	66.49	2,807	5.45
1945	6,274	14,413	68.45	2,400	6.01
1946	6,650	16,499	63.89	1,734	9.51
1947	7,699	37,912	17.02	3,167	11.97

total interviews, total hires, and average yearly enrollments for the seven-year period, 1941–1947. Even so, who can say whether the employment interviewers selected the one best man out of each 21 applicants in 1941, or the ablest one out of each 5.45 applicants in 1944? The company necessarily relied upon the interviewers' judgments.

The employment interviewer is faced with a succession of psychological problems that run the gamut from establishing rapport with the applicant to rejecting the applicant while retaining his good will. These psychological problems are solved only by planning the steps in the interview, trying out the procedures, revising the method, and discussing the difficulties with others who have had similar experiences (5, 6).

The *Flow Chart of Selection Procedure* shows the steps leading from "reception of applicants" to "placement." In this schematic diagram, note that two interviews are scheduled in the employment office. The third and final interview is conducted by the foreman or department head in the operating department.

We will assume that the employment office is easily accessible to applicants; that a comfortable, clean reception and waiting room is provided; that the interviewer is an adequate representative of the company so far as tact and courtesy are concerned; and that interviews will be conducted in a private office, beyond the range of sight and hearing of other applicants who are waiting. What suggestions can be made that will help in planning the interview?

QUESTIONING THE APPLICANT FOR NON-TECHNICAL POSITIONS

The interviewer obtains facts through questioning and by stimulating the applicant to volunteer information. Therefore, each interviewer should prepare a list of questions that he can introduce into the conversation. Different lists of appropriate questions should be used in interviewing clerks, mechanics, unskilled workers, and college trained applicants. The phrasing and the order of the questions are important. Those which can be answered by giving a single fact, such as a date or the name of a former employer, halt the conversational flow of the interview. One experienced interviewer addresses the applicant by saying, "Good morning. What is your name?" After receiving the answer, he says, "Won't you be seated?" Usually he waits for the applicant to make the opening remark. The conversation is informal but moves along definitely planned lines. At first, direct questions are avoided. Instead of saying, "What is your line of work?" or, "What kind of work are you looking for?" he is apt to phrase the request somewhat in this manner, "Tell me what you have been doing on your last job." The facts about the most recent employment are explored first.

It is well to have the applicant account for all time in terms of schooling, vacations, work, or periods of unemployment. For example, one applicant for factory work failed to account for a period of three winter months. When questioned on this point he was naïve enough to admit that he had slowed down his work deliberately so that he would be discharged, and thus be eligible for

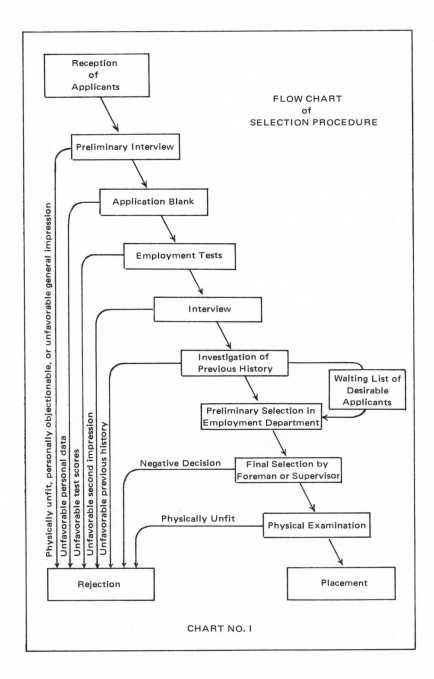

Reprinted from R. S. Uhrbrock, "Mental Alertness Tests as Aids in Selecting Employees," *Personnel* XII (May, 1936), p. 231.

unemployment insurance. To him it seemed like the best way to spend the winter. Needless to say, he was not hired.

The interviewer should be ready with an exploratory question when the applicant stops talking. He may inquire, "What were some of the more difficult things you had to do on your last job?" "Why do you want to change your job at this time?" "What are some of the important things you learned on that job?" "What type of work are you looking for now?" Each new question should dovetail with what went before. Previous length of service, earnings, marital status, and education can be discussed as details of former work are recited. The interviewer will find the *Dictionary of Occupational Titles* very useful in supplying background definitions, particularly when applicants use trade language in describing their jobs. It also will aid the interviewer in preparing questions designed to identify the novice who claims expert knowledge of a trade.

In a few minutes of skilled questioning, sufficient information can be obtained for the interviewer to make his first decision. Shall he reject the applicant? Or, shall he present an application blank with the suggestion that it be filled out, so that additional personal history data can be obtained? If the applicant appears desirable, there is no point in asking many questions that later would be recorded on the application blank. The interviewer should conserve his own time so that other applicants will not be kept waiting.

HOW SHOULD UNSUITABLE APPLICANTS BE REJECTED?

Each of the planned interviews indicated in the *Flow Chart of Selection Procedure* should have a series of terminal points where decisions should be made whether to reject the applicant or proceed further in the direction that may lead to the offer of a job. Terminal points are determined by job requirements and company policy. One interviewer will reject any applicant who makes derogatory statements about his former employers. Another will not waste time on the man who gives evasive or long-winded answers to direct questions. In pre-war days, in some companies where it was the practice to limit employment to single women, a terminal point was indicated when a female applicant stated that she was married.[1]

A few years ago an employment specialist used four preliminary questions in weeding out applicants when selecting a complete staff for a new hotel to be opened in New York City.

1. *"Where do you live?"* If the applicant said, "New York City" or "Manhat-

---

[1] Editorial Note: Such terminal points should, of course, be validated in terms of worker effectiveness or some other criterion of worker suitability.

tan" he had cleared the first hurdle. Those who lived in New Jersey or at distant points where transportation might be difficult or expensive were ruled out. For many applicants the interview was terminated as the result of their answer to a single question.

2. *"How long have you been out of work?"* If a man answered that he was still employed, but wanted to change jobs, he was ruled out. The employment man did not want to pirate labor. If the applicant said that he had been out of work more than a month, the interview was ended, on the assumption that any man who was any good would find a job in less than a month. If he named some period of unemployment of less than a month, he had cleared the second hurdle.

3. *"What hotel did you work in last?"* If the applicant had no hotel experience the interview was closed. If he named a New York City hotel he might or might not be considered further. The employment man had his own ideas about the value of experience in different well-known establishments. He preferred to hire men from certain hotels and would reject men who had worked at other places.

4. *"Who was your boss?"* The answer to this question was very important. The employment man, in this particular case, had a wide acquaintance among New York City hotelmen. Certain men have reputations as good trainers. He wanted to select men for the new hotel who had been exposed to good experience. Also, he wanted to be prepared to check references with men whose opinions he valued.

The procedure described above illustrates the concept of "terminal points" in the interviewing process. Even though it may appear abrupt and inconsiderate it gave some attention to each applicant. It was designed to identify, out of a mass of several thousand applicants, those who (a) had worked in well-known metropolitan hotels under men whose work standards were known and respected; (b) lived relatively near their work; (c) were not "floaters" since they had been employed recently. To be given further consideration, that might lead to employment, an applicant had to navigate successfully beyond these preliminary terminal points.

Closing the interview satisfactorily requires tact and careful planning. The questions used in an employment interview should progress from one possible terminal point to the next. It does not appear reasonable to assume that there is "one best way" to reject applicants. It probably is better to say frankly, "We have no suitable vacancies at this time and there is little prospect that we shall be able to employ you," than to hold out vague and indefinite hopes that "something may turn up and then we'll send for you if we need you."

When a vacancy exists, which the applicant is not qualified to fill, a different termination statement should be used. There is no point in precipitating an argument by telling a man flatly that he lacks essential qualifications for the job. Some interviewers state that several applicants are being considered and that a final decision will be made when all the facts are available. One man closes the interview by saying, "That is as far as we can go at this time. Thank you for letting us consider your qualifications." No promises are made to get in touch with the applicant at a later date.

THE INTERVIEW BY THE FOREMAN OR
DEPARTMENT HEAD

In normal times, from five to ten per cent of the applicants in the well-organized employment office will survive the preliminaries and be referred to the foreman or department head who placed a requisition for help.

The applicant presumably will have met certain definitely agreed upon pre-employment standards before being referred to the foreman. The foreman should be supplied with the application blank when the man is brought to him. A quick glance at it will give him the main facts about the man's age, education and experience. The interview with the foreman, conducted in the working environment, should *supplement* the information recorded on the application blank, or obtained from the applicant by the employment interviewer. In other words, the foreman should not ask the same questions previously answered in the employment office. In order to dovetail the two interviews successfully, there should be a previous understanding between the employment interviewer and the foreman as to what areas are to be covered by each. For example, the foreman is in a position to investigate the applicant's experience much more thoroughly than the employment interviewer ordinarily can do. The employment interviewer cannot be a specialist in all types of work. The foreman, who knows intimately the details of the work in his own department, can pursue details of the man's work history, so as to have an adequate basis for evaluating his skill, experience, and attitudes. At the same time he should stress the advantages in working for his company, as well as any disagreeable features that may be associated with the job.

Since this interview is conducted in the operating department, the foreman has an opportunity to observe the man's reactions to general working conditions such as noise, dust, fumes, humidity, lighting, temperature, cleanliness, and other factors that affect employees in the department. This interview ordinarily should not be conducted in an isolated section of the workroom. The applicant should be taken on a tour of the department. This type of peripatetic interviewing will reduce labor turnover by practically eliminating the "floater" who reports for work and says at the end of the first day, "If I'd known the work was like this, I wouldn't have taken the job."

In many companies the Employment Department could properly be called the Referral Department. It does the necessary weeding out and the paper-work, while foremen and department heads make the final decisions regarding employment. This is as it should be. The applicant should know that the foreman, and not the employment interviewer, had the authority to hire him. Then, if he is told to report for work, he knows that he has been selected by his foreman to be "on his team." Since the foreman makes the decision regarding hiring, he can offer the man a job, contingent upon passing a physical examination.

It is incumbent upon the foreman to terminate the interview in his department in a satisfactory manner. If the foreman wishes to see other men who may be referred by the Employment Department, he should explain the situation to the applicant and send him back to the employment interviewer.

It will help the employment interviewer in making future referrals if the foreman will discuss the applicants with him, so the interviewer will understand why some of the men who looked satisfactory to him were rejected by the foreman as a result of the interview in the department.

Few employers really know, except by hearsay, how applicants are being dismissed, or what their feelings may be toward the companies that decline to offer them employment. We need research data based upon verbatim reports of employment interviews and follow-up attitude studies to aid in answering the question, "How shall we reject applicants?"

INTERVIEWING COLLEGE TRAINED APPLICANTS

The problems involved in interviewing college seniors and graduates are not essentially different from those encountered in the average employment office. Many college students are totally inexperienced in job hunting. It is easy for interviewers to forget that some applicants are shy, embarrassed, and ill-at-ease when applying for their first jobs.

Many students fail to do themselves justice. An extreme example of this was told recently as the personal experience of a man who now is a professor of electrical engineering. He did not leave the home farm until he was twenty-one years old. He worked his way through the state university and was graduated at the head of his class. He never had applied for a job. The head of his department arranged an appointment for him with the representative of a company interested in employing technical men. The interview was to take place in the evening at the local hotel.

Because he wanted the job badly, the student carefully rehearsed all the things he would tell the company representative. He was nervous as he approached the hotel. He walked around the block several times and then entered the lobby.

It required considerable courage to approach the desk and ask for Mr. X. The clerk pointed out a man seated on a davenport in the lobby. The student walked to the davenport and sat down beside the man. Then he found that he was completely unable to address the stranger. Finally, he arose and returned to his dormitory. The next day he had no explanation to offer when he was asked why he had failed to keep the appointment.

There was nothing the interviewer could have done in this case. Many applicants, when applying for their first jobs, may be only slightly less shy. The interviewer's responsibility is very great after the first contact has been made.

One interviewer of technically trained college men looks for evidences of high scholarship, interest in manufacturing activities, physical energy, and integrated personality. He has found the following list of ten questions useful.

1. What was your major course, or field of concentration while in college?
2. How many men were in your graduating class?
3. Where did you stand in scholarship in that group?
4. Did you ever fail a school course?
5. Tell me, in detail, how you spent each summer since you were graduated from high school.
6. What college subjects have you *disliked* most? Why?
7. What illnesses or operations have you had?
8. What books (not assigned as part of your regular school work) have you read, during the past year, because of your interest in the author or the subject-matter?
9. What different careers have you considered seriously?
10. How do you spend your leisure time?

These questions usually are the landmarks of the interviews. Minor points are developed, depending upon the answers obtained. One applicant stated that he had "worked on a ship" during his summer vacation. The impression created by that reply was modified as a result of further questioning. When he was asked for details regarding his duties he replied that he had been engaged as escort for a ten-year-old boy who was sent from New York, on the Queen Mary, to join his parents at Southampton. His "work on a ship" had lasted less than five days! When the same general pattern (involving primary and secondary questions) is followed in talking with several men, a common basis is provided for comparing their merits.

Another interviewer has prepared a list of 63 questions for his own guidance. He said to himself, "What do I want to know about a man after I have finished interviewing him? What facts, or impressions, must I have in order to form a fair opinion about him?" The questions have not been memorized, and the list is not in sight during an interview. It serves as his guide when college graduates are rated and impressions are summarized after interviews are finished. The list is as follows:

I. *Appearance, facial expression, physique, carriage, and neatness*
   a. Is he well proportioned, without physical defects?
   b. Is he sensibly dressed?
   c. Is he clean? Note his hair-cut, linen, nails and shoes.

    d. Is his expression shy, diffident, surly, antagonistic, reserved, friendly?
    e. Does he know what to do with his hands?
    f. Does he have any objectionable mannerisms or peculiarities?
    g. Is his posture correct?

II. *Attitude toward the company interviewer*
    a. Is he at ease during the interview?
    b. Does he do half of the talking?
    c. Does he ask sensible questions?
    d. Does he give facts about himself?
    e. Does he answer questions definitely, or, does he "beat about the bush"?
    f. Does he know when the interview is over?

III. *Signs of intelligence*
    a. What did he say or do that indicated mental alertness?
    b. Is he logical in reaching conclusions?
    c. Does he use good judgment in presenting his ideas?
    d. Does he follow the conversation of the interviewer, or does he make "mental side-trips"?
    e. Is he "socially intelligent"?
    f. Would you judge that he would be intelligent in handling apparatus, and in dealing with mechanical situations?
    g. Did he graduate from college before the age of twenty-one?
    h. What quarter of his class was he in, scholastically, during his senior year?
    i. To what honorary scholastic societies has he been elected?

IV. *Does he have good health?*
    a. How recently has he had a physical examination?
    b. What conditions, at that time, needed correction?
    c. What corrections have been made?
    d. Has he been refused life insurance? If so, why?
    e. Is he overweight? Underweight?
    f. Does his hearing appear to be normal?
    g. Does he wear glasses?

V. *Is he keenly analytical?*
    a. What college courses demanding analytical ability has he taken?
    b. What special problems has he worked on that required careful analysis?
    c. Has he taken many "cinch" courses?
    d. What special reports, term papers, etc., has he prepared? To what extent do these deal with numbers and statistics?
    e. Did he seek specific and relevant information from the interviewer?

VI. *Character and integrity*
    a. Is he primarily concerned with immediate financial returns or promotional possibilities?
    b. Does he give the impression of having something to conceal?
    c. Would you be inclined to trust him in a matter involving your own reputation?
    d. Do his statements imply an unethical or anti-social attitude?

VII. *Is he well informed in his field of specialization?*
    a. What is his field of specialization?

   b. How long has he been interested in that field?

   c. What recognition has he received such as society membership, publications, etc.?

   d. Does he have plans for further work in his field of specialization?

   e. Does he have other related interests?

VIII. *Initiative and originality*

   a. Did he try to interview the interviewer?

   b. Did he ask any questions, or make any observation that distinguishes him from the ordinary run of applicants?

   c. Did he ever make tentative plans for a new mechanical device that he thought might be patentable?

   d. Did he ever undertake to sell any article? If so, with what degree of success?

IX. *English ability*

   a. Does he complete his sentences?

   b. Does he have any stock phrases that he repeats to an annoying degree?

   c. Is he unduly fond of long words, or foreign words?

   d. Is he slangy?

   e. Can he express an idea in several different ways?

   f. Is he sure of his grammar?

   g. Is he fluent?

   h. Does he stammer or stutter, or slur, or jumble his words?

   i. Was he a member of the debating team?

   j. Was he on the college paper?

X. *Is he decisive?*

   a. Was he interested in the details of the interview?

   b. Were his questions leading to a point where he could make an intelligent decision?

   c. Is he mature enough to make his own decisions, or will he be unduly governed by the advice of a parent or adviser?

   d. Will he be hasty in making decisions?

   e. Will he insist upon enough facts before deciding?

   f. Will he stand by a decision once made?

Who should do the most talking, the applicant or the interviewer? There is little factual data to support an opinion on this subject. Complete stenographic reports have been obtained on seven employment interviews. "Each interview was approximately twelve minutes in length. The number of words spoken by applicants ranged from 159 to 651. The interviewers spoke from 437 to 723 words. Applicants did one-quarter to one-half of the talking while interviewers did from one-half to three-quarters of the talking" (7). The best interviewer in the group talked 48 per cent of the time.

The pattern of the interview is more important than the actual number of words spoken. However, it probably is safe to suggest that the average interview could be improved by phrasing questions so that the applicant is encouraged to do at least half of the talking. Chapple's "Interaction Chronograph" (8) is the most promising research tool now available for the study of the pattern of the interview.[2]

Most employment interviewers (in common with the rest of us) believe that they are good judges of the abilities of other human beings. Their convictions regarding the characteristics of persons who will succeed on a given job seldom are verified in a systematic fashion. Few have tried the experiment of interviewing and ranking a number of applicants and then comparing their order-of-merit listing with the relative positions assigned these same men by other interviewers. Where this has been done by experienced and confident interviewers, exact agreement has been rare.

The interviewers' belief in their own infallibility usually is shaken when they compare notes. Each is curious about the questions the other men ask. Each wants to know what forms the basis for the final decisions as to the relative merits of the applicants. This can become the starting point for a short training course to improve the employment interview. Note the lack of agreement between seven interviewers who rated eleven applicants as indicated by the data in Table 45.2.

TABLE 45.2
ORDER OF MERIT RANKING

Applicants		Judges							Rank
Code	O.S.U. test score	I	II	III	IV	V	VI	VII	
Jn	224	3	8	4	3	1	5	5	3
Wy	219	10	9	9	7	6	11	9	10
De	208	9	7	5	4	8	8	4	8
Sn	207	8	10	10	9	7	7	8	9
Pt	205	1	2	1	1	5	1	2	1
Mc	195	6	1	2	2	4	10	1	2
Le	190	4	5	3	6	10	2	6	5
BW . . .	179	7	3	8	8	3	4	10	6.5
Bn	176	11	11	11	11	9	9	11	11
Dy	174	2	4	6	5	11	3	3	4
Ls	156	5	6	7	10	2	6	7	6.5

The applicants had been pre-selected at three different colleges by preliminary interviews and psychological tests. They were interviewed individually, during the course of one day, at Manufacturing Headquarters, by a Vice President, General Superintendent, three Division Superintendents, a Factory Superinten-

---

[2] If the Interaction Chronograph is viewed as a promising research tool, *Personnel Psychology* would agree. As a completed product of research, ready for use, *Personnel Psychology* views the *Interaction Chronograph* with considerable skepticism. Its protagonists have made rather sweeping claims for the device but have not published sufficient data permitting an impartial evaluation by unbiased technicians. The evidence is not yet at hand on the basis of which we may either accept, qualify, or reject the claims made for the machine.—Ed.

dent, and the Director of Industrial Relations. "Mc" was assigned first place by two executives and tenth place by another. "Dy" was rated 2 and 11 by two different judges.

RECORDING OPINIONS CONCERNING APPLICANTS

Our memories regarding the details of interviews are notoriously poor. Each applicant for positions of importance should be rated at the conclusion of the interview. This rating may consist of a few notes that could be used in the future when referring to the man. Or, a rating scale containing a fairly comprehensive list of statements may be prepared so that all applicants will be evaluated against the same background. If a five-step form of rating scale is used it would contain items similar to the following:

How does his appearance impress you? Consider his facial expression, physique, carriage.

Creates poor effect.	Makes somewhat unfavorable impression.	Appearance satisfactory.	General effect is fairly good.	Creates a definitely favorable impression.

Interviewers may wish to rate applicants on such characteristics as judgment, common sense, leadership, initiative, technical proficiency, command of English, and other qualities that are thought desirable. *It must be remembered, however, that a rating is not a measure of a trait. It is only the record of an opinion.*

A check list containing fifty statements was used by 20 interviewers to rate 140 college graduates who were applying for positions. No judge rated more than 15 persons. The figures which appear before the statements in Table 45.3 indi-

TABLE 45.3

FREQUENCY OF USE OF FIFTY DESCRIPTIVE STATEMENTS WHEN 140 COLLEGE GRADUATES WERE RATED BY TWENTY JUDGES

Frequency	Statement
45	Is dressed neatly.
38	Would probably cooperate well.
32	Presents an alert, lively, responsive appearance.
27	Appears to have sufficient health and stamina for this job.
27	Has strong desire to adapt himself to meet any set of conditions.
26	Is self-confident, yet conservative, in his opinion of his own abilities.
26	Talks about what he knows better than does average man.
25	Shows a good choice of words and phrasing in his conversation.
24	Has himself under adequate control.
24	In the long run could not stand the competition.

TABLE 45.3   (*Cont.*)

Frequency	Statement
23	Is a steady, solid individual—dependable yet not brilliant.
22	Possesses considerable initiative.
20	Knows what he wants to do about as well as the average.
18	Has no leadership qualities.
18	Would be good on specific assignments.
18	Is a fluent talker.
18	Is a careful and systematic thinker.
17	Has an analytical mind.
17	Has a somewhat retiring nature.
17	Has not had much actual working experience.
15	Knows what he wants and is determined to get it.
15	Probably could rise no higher than rank of supervisor.
14	Has a noticeable lack of objective.
14	Respects seriousness of situation, but has well developed sense of humor.
13	Has not formed definite goals as yet, but will as he matures.
12	Is slow to express own ideas during interview.
11	A good prospect for research, but not for executive development.
11	Would have difficulty in finding common ground with workmen.
11	Gives impression of possessing ability to handle people.
9	Is a "rough diamond."
9	Sets a definite goal for himself and works toward this end.
8	Is a little slow to catch on.
7	Has an excellent "public contact" personality.
6	Prefers to be a follower rather than a leader.
6	Gives impression of being opportunist.
6	Rough edges haven't worn off as yet.
5	Is very opinionated.
5	Is not highly adaptable socially.
5	Must be carefully handled to bring out his best.
5	Is hesitant to talk about himself and his objectives.
4	Is not sufficiently trained in his own field.
4	Suggests instability of emotional control.
3	Expects too rapid advancement.
2	Is unlikely to apply himself.
2	Appears to be somewhat antisocial.
2	Has reached his upper level of development.
1	Apparently has never learned ordinary manners.
1	Talks disrespectfully of former employers.
1	Compares favorably with the best men we have hired.
1	Is outstanding in all respects.

cate the number of times each descriptive phrase was noted as a characteristic of an applicant. The following directions appeared at the head of the check list of fifty statements.

Place a check-mark (√) in front of the statements which describe this man most accurately.

Check not less than *five* and not more than *ten* of the statements.

Check only such statements as you yourself might use in describing this man.

Do not check statements which are typical of someone either *better* or *worse* than the man you are rating. For example, "Is a good routine worker," should not be checked if the man you are rating is capable of independent thought and action in matters of importance. The statement, "Is a good routine worker," even though it may be true, does not give a correct impression of such a man's abilities in this respect.

These statistics have little value in themselves. They indicate that within the group of 140 college graduates interviewed, each of the fifty descriptive statements was found serviceable by one or more judges in recording his impressions. Favorable statements were checked more frequently than uncomplimentary ones. The selection of items included in the check lists, the liberality of the judges and the distribution of personal characteristics within the group of college graduates interviewed, undoubtedly operated to skew the distribution of ratings. The lists of rating statements are presented only to illustrate a form that may prove serviceable to other employment interviewers.

Whatever method of recording is used, an employment interviewer should make a definite decision regarding his disposition of each case. He should indicate over his signature whether he (a) recommends the man for employment, (b) would not offer employment, (c) would offer employment with reservations.

It is very helpful when reviewing the qualifications of technical men if interviewers will supplement the check-list rating scales with a sentence or two indicating their estimates of each applicant's strong and weak points. After several interviewers have talked with a man, their comments can be assembled as follows:

"Probably has good ability to apply theory."

"Technical knowledge and ability apparently very good."

"Good mind—capable and intelligent. Reads widely but unsystematically. Makes a good first impression. Good, clean-cut appearance. Possesses a good academic background, and sufficient intelligence to acquire a working knowledge of almost any problem. Is polite and well-mannered with some store of 'social grace'."

"May prove to be below average in speed when wholly responsible for his own work."

"Looks like an able research man."

By keeping ratings made at the time of employment, follow-up studies can be made on the men hired, who succeed or fail on the job. The interview, as a selection procedure, then can be evaluated. Also, the expertness of individual interviewers can be determined, roughly, in terms of the work histories of the men they rate high and recommend for employment.

THE PANEL INTERVIEW

The panel interview, during which two or more persons question the candidate, has much to recommend it when several positions are to be filled. This type of interviewing has been practiced in finding jobs for unemployed men; in interviewing college seniors; by civil service examining boards; and in sizing up executives before inviting them to change jobs.

A form of panel interviewing was practiced in 1921 by Urbain J. Ledoux, who auctioned off unemployed men on Boston Common, in Boston, Massachusetts. The men were stripped to the waist and Ledoux described their work histories and abilities. The crowd, containing a few employers, asked questions. Either Ledoux or the unemployed workman supplied the answers. Then the bidding started. Out of 150 men who offered themselves for employment, two found jobs that gave them a week's board and lodging and $2.00 pocket money (9).

One large company, employing technically trained college graduates, has used a modification of this technique. The employment men from several of its plants visited a university on the same day. Seniors interested in being considered for jobs came before the group and were interviewed individually. The senior was questioned, first by one man and then another. Each interviewer attempted to get answers to questions that he considered important. He had an opportunity to listen to all the other questions and answers. For example, the plant personnel man who put his faith in the single question, "What are the principles of free wheeling?" had an opportunity to note the type of questions the others used.

After the joint interview was concluded, the qualifications of the applicant were discussed. A student did not need a majority vote to be employed. Each interviewer had his own quota to meet. He had the benefit of the opinions of his colleagues. He could hire a man for his plant even though all of the other interviewers had rejected him. Each employment man took the full responsibility for his own selection. There was no bidding on a salary basis. Each college man hired was started at the same salary, set by the central personnel office of the company.

The best example of "group" interviewing that has been conducted in recent years was provided by the United States Civil Service Commission. The Commission wished to provide an eligibility register for directors and assistant directors of personnel for major departments, agencies, and establishments of the Federal government. Applications were filed by 6,616 candidates. Experience ratings were assigned by a Board of Examiners. A total of 689 persons reported for a five-hour written examination; 547 passed the test. The 160 candidates who stood highest on the list, on the basis of experience ratings and written test results, were interviewed by a board of three members who made a circuit of 30 different cities. The interviews were recorded. Each interview was approximately one hour in length. The members of the interviewing board noted their impressions on rating scales. The candidate's final place on the eligibility list was determined by (a) rating on experience and training; (b) written examination results; (c) character investigation; (d) evidence of accomplishment adduced in the oral interview.

Eligible registers were prepared, listing the names of 84 men and 11 women. Thirteen months after the examinations, eleven men and two women had been appointed to positions paying between $3,800 and $6,500 per annum (10).

The panel interviews that were conducted by the three members of the Board of Oral Examinations in connection with the selection of directors and assistant directors of personnel were unique in a number of respects. The points of view underlying the procedures have been described by Ordway and O'Brien (11).

In the first place the scope of the oral examination was limited to a consideration of evidences of ability that could not be demonstrated on written or performance tests. Subjective characteristics such as appearance, manner, neatness, dignity and other *"factors of personality"* were minimized. In the oral examination, *"factors of performance"* were sought as evidence of personal fitness for the work of director of personnel.

In defining this concept Ordway and O'Brien have written (12):

"What each candidate has actually done (performance) can be evidenced factually and we submit that where *possession of a required capacity* related to performance of the duties of the particular position *has actually been demonstrated in the past*, the demonstration imports possession of subordinate elements of personality requisite to the accomplishment. For example, if one of the requisite factors of performance for a particular job is capacity to obtain cooperation from others, the fact that an applicant has faced difficult situations in which he has needed to overcome opposition and has successfully obtained cooperation (supported by details as to time, place, and circumstances) is evidence of the capacity. The question of degree—evaluation— is another matter. We are dealing with evidence now. Whatever the elements of neatness, facial expression, or posture which might have hindered or aided in the result, the action speaks for itself. Whether or not observable 'Appearance' substantially aided or hindered his capacity in this respect is less important than the fact determined that he has demonstrated, in some degree, the required capacity."

It might be argued that written questions could be phrased that would stimulate candidates to supply the essential facts about their past performances. That position misses the point entirely. Each separate fact, as it is brought out in the oral examination can be explored and investigated by the board of examiners (through the use of supplementary questions) until it is stripped of all non-essentials. No formal, written examination procedure can introduce appropriate additional questions to reveal the experience of each individual candidate.

The legalistic approach of Ordway and O'Brien has made a contribution to the philosophy of personnel administration as well as to its technique. They applied the rules of evidence to the oral interview. Their thesis is explained as follows (13, 14):

"The details of past action constitute the best evidence. Examiners should seek to place upon the record the circumstances surrounding each relevant incident of experience offered, as a setting for the probative facts: *what the candidate did under the circumstances.*

"What did he do which shows initiative, or perseverance? What did he do to obtain cooperation, and what happened? What factors did he weigh before making some decision, and what decision did he make? How long did he vacillate, and what was the effect of the decision made? Facts, facts, facts are what we are seeking. What did he do in preparing a plan? What did he consider? What did he do in seeking to carry through a program once planned, or to adapt the program to changing conditions? What obstacles did he meet? What did he do under the circumstances?

"The candidate's statements, as direct evidence, are thus placed upon the record. The examiner is now free to follow up the statements offered and to enlarge upon relevant detail of time, place, and circumstance. Cross-examination is permissible. This does not mean that the candidate is to be heckled as an adverse witness, but by leading the candidate on into detailed descriptions of the situations presented, with time, place, and names connected, it is possible for a good examiner to disclose mis-statements or exaggeration as is done in court. Having adduced the detail of place and circumstance and names of others familiar with each incident, further verifica-tion, if needed, can be made by field investigation. By this process factual and verifiable evidence can be adduced; and the evidence so adduced can be recorded by mechanical devices or by stenographic or stenotype reporting of the questions and answers. This record contains the facts or demonstration of possession or lack of demonstration of possession of the requisite factors and is a reviewable basis for the application of the rating standards."

The interviewing methods described by Ordway and O'Brien probably are most effective when used by men with legal training. However, the underlying prin-ciples are simple and straightforward and may be applied, either by one inter-viewer or by a group. The irrelevant is excluded so far as possible. The search is for evidence that will support the interviewer's opinion as to the applicant's ability, even if that opinion is challenged in a court of law. That is the ideal toward which all employment interviewers should move.

NEW-TYPE SELECTION BOARDS IN INDUSTRY

The reports on the success of the group methods being developed by the National Institute of Industrial Psychology, London, for the selection of management train-ees, will be followed with interest. In a country where over 92 per cent of the firms in production industries have fewer than 250 employees, it frequently is necessary to recruit management trainees from sources outside the company. In addition to possessing ability and interest, the man must have characteristics that will insure his acceptability by his new associates if he should be employed. The staff psychologist from the National Institute of Industrial Psychology assists in interviewing, testing, and evaluating the credentials of the men who are recommended for consideration. As a result of this preliminary winnowing process, a "candidate group," (preferably eight in number) is selected to be observed, in action, by the "employer group," which usually is limited to three members. The candidates and employers have dinner together. The occasion is entirely informal and social (15):

> "After dinner, all adjourn to a suitable room where the candidates sit round a table while the members of the board occupy chairs suitably placed in the corners. The psychologist then introduces a subject for discussion, generally something which links up with the candidates' interests, such as the opportunities in business for ex-officers. After starting the ball rolling he, too, retires to a corner and listens. It is essential that the members of the board should not take part in the discussion, for it is clearly impossible for them to observe objectively if they get involved in the situation."

The candidates discuss the topic among themselves for about an hour. The members of the employer group observe from their corners, but do not participate. Questions are answered, during an open session, which follows the discussion.

A second meeting is held the following morning. A specially designed problem, such as might be encountered in business, is presented for consideration. The candidates are asked to discuss the issue and arrive at a solution. Again, the employer members act as observers. Later, with the aid of the psychologist, the members of the employer group review the significant points concerning each candidate. The procedure was used twenty times in 1946. "So far there has been no case where the board has failed to agree on the candidate to whom the post should be offered." (16).

EVALUATION OF ACCOMPLISHMENT

The major portion of the time of interviewers is devoted to persons who are soliciting work. The bulk of these applicants has just entered the labor market, or are unemployed workers with varying lengths of service. It is not unusual to interview thirty such applicants to find one who meets the needs of a particular employer.

The problem is quite different when the interviewer sets out to engage a man already employed to fill a responsible position. In the first place, he has to develop a procedure for discovering such men. Some employment interviewers are adept at locating likely prospects among younger executives who attend professional meetings. In conversation they describe their difficulties in finding a man to fill a particular position in their organization. If the man is interested he will indicate that he would like further details.

One or more interviews may be held in which different executives participate.

Gradually the man's history is pieced together. The executives who are considering him wish to be satisfied on points such as the following:

1. What are the details of his most active year?
2. Was he able to overcome antagonism and opposition to programs for which he was responsible?
3. How frequently has he found it necessary to retreat from positions or stands he has taken on different issues?
4. How extensive are his personal contacts with groups of persons with various interests and viewpoints?
5. Has he ever failed in a case where personal adjustment was attempted?
6. How successful has he been in convincing a man, or group, that one procedure should be substituted for another?
7. Is he able to handle disciplinary cases successfully?
8. Has he passed the peak so far as his personal achievement is concerned?
9. Has he used good judgment in handling his personal finances?
10. Does his home life provide an adequate degree of happiness and stability?

When the man is not an avowed candidate for a position, informal employment interviews may not progress beyond a preliminary, exploratory stage. In fact, where the first conversations are handled with subtlety, he may not even know their real import. The apparently casual talks and interviews may terminate at any time without definite mention of the possibility of an offer of employment.

Men who are alert can read the signs when an employer shows an interest in them. Although those holding responsible positions wait for invitations to join other firms, they may stimulate interest in themselves by volunteering information that will weigh in their favor. Also they may discuss different aspects of the situation with friends who are in a position to refer to their qualifications and accomplishments.

When conducted with finesse, employment interviews of this type (after they have progressed beyond the initial phase) are works of art. The executives on one side are asking the question, "Do we want to invite this man to join our firm?" The prospect is saying to himself, "What do they have to offer? Would I be interested? What do I need to do to get them to put their cards on the table?" Win, lose, or draw, such interviews will test the ingenuity of anyone who survives the preliminaries.

ATTITUDE INTERVIEWING

Good industrial relations presuppose a knowledge of changing currents of opinion within the employed group. The importance of interviewing employees to ascertain their attitudes is becoming recognized. The procedure has been described by Putnam (17), Mayo (18), Whitehead (19), Roethlisberger (20), Roethlisberger and Dickson (21), Raphael (22, 23) and others. The training of interviewers in this phase of personnel work is very much neglected. Men like to talk about their jobs—especially the elements that irritate them. When the same "irritation point" is referred to time and time again during an employee attitude survey, management is provided with a danger signal that indicates where attention is needed. The workman who made the following statement intended to be helpful (24):

"Well, the main trouble with that Wage-Incentive as I see it is that it's too complicated for the ordinary working man to understand. Practically nobody that's working on Wage-Incentive has any idea how to figure the bonus he's supposed to make. I think it ought to be fixed up so that if you have two girls and a man working side by side here on a certain job, they can *look* at the production they're getting out and make a pretty fair guess as to what bonus they're making. Some time ago some of the departments complained about that to the Superintendent and they sent a man over to explain it. Well, he came into one department that I know of and called every man aside and said, 'Now, here, I want to explain your Wage-Incentive Plan to you.' Well, now this fellow that they sent over was a very competent man, I think. I have no reason to believe that he didn't know his job fine. He explained it in a way that *he* understood, but I'd be willing to bet that not a single one of the fellows that he talked to had any more idea about it when he finished than when he started. It's just too complicated, that's all. It ought to be made simpler."

A statistical table that indicates that ten per cent of the employees are dissatisfied is a lifeless item, But a series of short paragraphs that recite, in worker language, what was said, gets attention. After reading such an attitude report one superintendent asked, "Who said that about this Company? What's his name?" When he was reminded that it had been decided that no one would be hurt as a result of the interviewing program and that all names were withheld to preserve the confidential nature of the information, he readily agreed, and said, "We must do something about that situation. We can't have employees feeling and talking like that."

EMPLOYEE COUNSELLING

Employee counselling is part of the supervisory job. Most of this is done on a very informal basis. Occasionally, it is necessary to conduct a "warning" interview to deal with such factors as poor performance, improper attitude, laziness, and infraction of company rules (25). Such an interview is conducted in private. In some companies a copy of the warning is given to the employee and a duplicate is filed in the personnel office. If it should be necessary to terminate an employee after he has had a warning interview, he cannot claim that he did not know that his work was unsatisfactory.

Employee counselling dealing with "problem" cases requires considerable psychological insight. Thomas and Muchmore have stated (26):

"The facts are simple in themselves, but a knowledge of them may well mean the difference between success and failure in the interview. They include: the fact that true motives are usually hidden and that what we see at first are only symptoms; the fact that there is always resistance to be nullified, but that a lessening of it usually occurs after the interview is felt to be ended; the fact that the solution may come through changed attitudes as well as changed conditions; and the fact that a human being values his sense of security and self-respect, and desires recognition. Finally, the interviewer should remember never to judge a case from the viewpoint of morality, and to reserve decision until all the details are known."

THE "EXIT" INTERVIEW

"Exit" interviews or conferences probably are just as important as "entrance" interviews (27, 28, 29, 30, 31, 32). They provide the personnel department with reasons why employees are seeking work elsewhere. Opportunities are afforded for creating good-will toward the company. In one group of 4,600 employees, quitting over an eleven month period, 195, or 4.2 per cent, decided to remain on the job as the consequence of the exit interview (33).

RECOMMENDATIONS

When we discuss methods of improving the personnel interview, we immediately think of the employment interview because of its numerical importance. Probably greater progress can be made if we attack the problem in reverse order.

It is recommended that interviewers be trained first in conducting exit conferences; secondly, in making employee attitude surveys, using conversational methods, and finally, by participating in the actual hiring of new employees. A series of stenographic, phonographic or dictated reports should be provided for analysis and criticism (34, 35). As these reports are discussed with personnel and operating heads, improved phrasing of questions will be agreed upon. Coaching of the novice by an experienced interviewer should aid in developing judgment in interpreting the facts revealed by skilled questioning. An excellent list of "selected readings for the interviewer" has been published by the American Management Association (36).

The selection of employees, or the report on their attitudes, will be no better than the "social wisdom" of the interviewers. The problem, therefore, is to train men and women in the techniques of good interviewing, and to sample their work by means of reports, observations, and objective data, so as to provide convincing evidence that they are serving effectively in a field where, "Art is long, life short; judgment difficult, opportunity transient."

REFERENCES

1. Bingham, Walter Van Dyke, and Moore, Bruce Victor, *How to Interview*. Harper & Bros., New York, 1941.
2. Arthur, Guy B., "Interviewing Techniques,"*Management Review*, 1945,Vol. 34, pp. 169–171.
3. Purcell, Dale B., "Hiring Interviews," *Personnel Journal*, 1944, Vol. 22, pp. 263–267.
4. McMurry, Robert N., "The Knack of Interviewing Applicants," *Industrial Relations*, 1945, Vol. 2, pp. 8–9, 26.
5. Fear, Richard A., and Jordan, Byron, *Employee Evaluation Manual for Interviews. The Psychological Corporation*, 1943, p. 39.
6. *Manual of Employment Interviewing*. American Management Association, Research Report No. 9, 1946, p. 75.
7. Uhrbrock, Richard S., "Analysis of Employment Interviews," *Personnel Journal*, 1933, Vol. 12, pp. 98–101.
8. Chapple, Eliot D., "A Method for Evaluating Supervisory Personnel," *Harvard Business Review*, 1946, Vol. 24, pp. 197–214.
9. *New York Times*, September 9, 1921, 1 : 5; September 10, 1921, 1 : 5; November 8, 1927, 29 : 4; April 10, 1941, 25 : 8. See *New York Times Index* 1921–1941.
10. Correspondence with James C. O'Brien, Chairman, Board of Oral Examiners, United States Civil Service Commission, Washington, dated February 26, 1940 and March 21, 1940.
11. Ordway, Samuel H., Jr., and O'Brien, James C., *An Approach to More Objective Tests*. Society for Personnel Administration, Washington, D.C. Pamphlet No. 2, June, 1939, p. 31.
12. Ibid., pp. 11–12.
13. Ibid., p. 17.
14. Ibid., pp. 19–20.
15. Fraser, John Munro, "New-Type Selection Boards in Industry," *Occupational Psychology*, 1947, Vol. 21, pp. 170–178.
16. Ibid., p. 177.
17. Putnam, M. L., "Improving Employee Relations," *Personnel Journal*, 1930, Vol. 8, pp. 314–325.
18. Mayo, Elton, *The Human Problems of an Industrial Civilization*. Macmillan Co., New York, 1933. Chapter IV, "Development of the Western Electric Inquiry. The Interview Program," pp. 77–98.
19. Whitehead, T. N., *The Industrial Worker*, Vol. 1. Harvard University Press, Cambridge, 1938, pp. 136–151.
20. Roethlisberger, F. J., *Management and Morale*. Harvard University Press, Cambridge, 1941, pp. 16–18, 40–43, 81–84, 88–108.
21. ——, F. J., and Dickson, William J., *Management and the Worker*. Harvard University Press, Cambridge, 1939, pp. 226–229.
22. Raphael, Winifred, "A Technique for Surveying Employees' Opinions and Attitudes," *Occupational Psychology*, 1944, Vol. 18, pp. 165–173.
23. ——, "A Study of Some Stresses and Strains Within the Working Group," *Occupational Psychology*, 1947, Vol. 21, pp. 92–101.
24. Uhrbrock, Richard S., *A Psychologist Looks at Wage Incentive Methods*. Institute of Management Series, No. 15, American Management Association, 1935, pp. 8–9.
25. Michaels, E. G., "The Warning Interview," *Personnel*, 1944, Vol. 20, pp. 105–106.
26. Thomas, R. L., and Muchmore, John H., "Getting Results in 'Problem' Interviews," *Personnel*, 1944, Vol. 21, pp. 31–37.
27. "Mechanics of the Exit Interview," *Personnel*, 1944, Vol. 20, pp. 231–239.
28. McMurry, Robert N., "Exit Interviews Keep Workers on the Job," *Commerce*, 1943, Vol. 40, pp. 23, 42–43.
29. Onarheim, J. I., "Exit Interviews Help Us Check Personnel Policies," *Factory Management and Maintenance*, 1944, Vol. 102, pp. 121–122.

30. Palmer, Dwight L., Purpus, Eugene R., and Stockford, LeBaron O., "Why People Quit," *Industrial Relations*, 1944, Vol. 2, pp. 8–10, 36–37.
31. Patric, John, and Taylor, Frank J., "Once Through the Gate, He's Gone," *Nation's Business*, 1942, Vol. 30, pp. 24–26.
32. Drake, Charles A., "The Exit Interview as a Tool of Management," *Personnel*, 1942, Vol. 18, pp. 346–350.
33. *The Exit Interview.* Policyholders' Service Bureau Group Insurance Division, Metropolitan Life Insurance Company, 1942, p. 18.
34. Covner, Bernard J., "Studies in Phonographic Recordings of Verbal Material. IV. Written Reports of Interviews." *Journal of Applied Psychology*, 1944, Vol. 28, pp. 89–98.
35. *Psychology Bulletin*, 1942, Vol. 39, p. 794.
36. *Manual of Employment Interviewing*, American Management Association, New York, 1946, pp. 74–75.

46.

DEPARTMENT-COMMISSION RELATIONS: THE PRESIDENT'S FORMAL POSITION

U.S. CIVIL SERVICE COMMISSION

As the central personnel agency of the Federal Government, the Commission has a leadership function in personnel areas, including the one of evaluating how personnel management is contributing to the mission accomplishments of agencies. In the larger sense, the Commission is concerned not with personnel programs *per se*, but with personnel programs as they have a positive or negative effect on the basic job the manager has to do. Its program of providing leadership and assistance to agencies in carrying out the personnel job in Government is carried out through:

1. Setting up standards and guides for agency personnel activities.
2. Inspecting personnel activities to see that they meet the standards and conform to requirements of law.
3. Developing better personnel management methods.
4. Advising agencies in personnel matters.

Reprinted from U.S. Civil Service Commission, *The Role of the Civil Service Commission in Federal Employment* (Washington, D.C.: U.S. Government Printing Office, 1963), pp. 28–30.

AGENCIES TAKE PERSONNEL ACTIONS; COMMISSION CHECKS COMPLIANCE WITH RULES AND STANDARDS

Where once the Commission passed on agency personnel actions in advance on an individual basis, now agencies do hiring, firing, position classifying, and other personnel transactions on their own responsibility, in accordance with standards set by the Commission.

Decentralization has removed many bottlenecks in Federal personnel matters. Employees may be hired and moved from one job to another with much less delay. To insure that agencies fulfill their responsibilities, Commission inspectors check their actions to see that the standards have been observed. The Commission is responsible for seeing that personnel actions decided on by the agencies do not violate the Civil Service Act and other laws or the policies and procedures established for the operation of the merit system.

COMMISSION'S INSPECTIONS ARE AN AID TO MANAGEMENT

Simultaneously with checking merit-system compliance, the Commission's inspections provide aid to agency management in developing better personnel management methods.

At the installation and bureau level, inspectors help the manager solve his personnel problems through actions he can take locally, and report problems not solvable locally to higher levels of agency management for action. Their service to the highest levels of the agency includes presenting an objective review of how delegated personnel authority is being exercised. They develop information for the President and other high officials in the Administration on how their policy interests are being met.

Specific areas with which civil service inspectors concern themselves include manpower utilization, employee-management relations, and equal employment opportunity (with special emphasis on minority groups, senior citizens, women, and the physically handicapped).

FEDERAL PERSONNEL MANAGEMENT DEPENDS ON AGENCY-COMMISSION COOPERATION

The management of Federal personnel matters is a kind of partnership in which the agencies and the Commission share responsibility for the well-being and development of the Federal personnel system.

The Commission has an extensive program for preparing qualification and classification standards, with substantial cooperation from the departments and agencies.

The Commission's Interagency Advisory Group, composed of top personnel officials of Federal agencies, was established to provide an opportunity for departments and agencies to discuss and work out solutions to mutual personnel problems and to encourage the initiation of proposals and ideas on personnel policies and practices. The Executive Director of the Commission acts as chairman of the group, which meets monthly or more often. Project committees are formed from time to time to study and report on specific issues or proposals that require research or development. Regional offices have established similar groups to consider local problems.

Federal Executive Boards, established by the Chairman of the Civil Service Commission at the request of the President, composed of heads of field installations, are in operation in 12 cities with substantial concentrations of Federal employees. The Boards provide for cooperation and coordination across agency lines in programs and activities of common interest with the objective of improving the effectiveness and economy of Government field operations.

In addition to inspections and interagency advisory group contacts, there is daily contact between the Commission's staff and agency personnel offices which actually take personnel actions. The best of standards, regulations, and instructions cannot cover all situations or answer all questions; so the Commission's staff in the central and regional offices gives advice and assistance to agency personnel officials on general problems as well as individual cases.

The Commission, the agencies, and the Federal personnel system benefit from these relationships.

47.

DETERMINING THE CLASSIFICATION OF A POSITION: ANALYZING POSITIONS

U.S. CIVIL SERVICE COMMISSION

Analysis goes on throughout the classification process. It involves a critical examination of a position and the interpretation of its work and requirements in terms of classification criteria. It is, in effect, a process of breaking down a position into meaningful, identifiable elements, relating those elements to one another and determining the importance of each and of all together. The elements of positions may exist in an infinite variety of combinations. The aim of the process of analysis is to identify and arrange them, to the extent necessary, in terms of the criteria—as spelled out in applicable classification standards, or in the absence of standards, in other guides—with which the classifier determines the series and grades of positions.

An essential and often final step in the analytical process is perhaps the reverse of that process itself. Equally as important as breaking down the position into its basic parts in order to compare them with available classification criteria is the process of bringing together the parts of a position—a synthesis—in a logical and meaningful pattern in order to see the position as a whole. Only in this way can the ultimate purpose of a position, its place in the organization, and its true worth be clearly recognized—and its worth may be more or less than is apparent by merely adding the value of each of its parts.

IDENTIFYING CLASSIFICATION FACTORS

A most important step in the analytical process is identifying the factors that are significant for determining a position's grade and series. These factors provide an essential frame of reference for arranging the information about the tasks, responsibilities, or other elements of a position in a form suitable for its evaluation.

The Commission's classification standards are the primary guides for this step. Specific factors used in the standard vary to suit the occupation and type of work concerned.

Reprinted from U.S. Civil Service Commission, *Classification Principles and Policies*, Personnel Management Series No. 16 (Washington, D.C.: U.S. Government Printing Office, 1963), pp. 29–34.

Where published standards are available for a given type of position, factors used in the standards are necessarily of first consideration. But in any particular position other factors may be significant beyond those treated in the standards which apply to the bulk of positions in an occupation. Factors discussed in a given standard are not intended to exclude consideration of other factors when present in a position; in a given case it is essential that the presence of any factors beyond those expressly covered in the standards be recognized and its effect determined. Where published standards or similar guides are not available, the classifier must depend on his knowledge of standards for other series, his occupational knowledge, and his awareness of characteristics of positions generally which contribute to their classification value.

DUTIES TO BE CONSIDERED

In most positions, certain duties are performed from time to time that do not affect the position's classification. Eliminating these duties from consideration at the start facilitates analysis.

Major vs. Minor Duties.—In analyzing positions major duties must be identified and distinguished from other, minor duties which are not significant for classification purposes and can be disposed of without extensive analysis. In the preliminary analytical process major duties should be grouped or otherwise related to each other to insure a full understanding of the sequence of events and purposes of actions.

Distinguishing between major and minor duties is usually not difficult. Major duties typically are those which are the reason for the position's existence and govern its qualification requirements. Typically, they occupy most of the time of the incumbent. Minor duties generally occupy a small portion of time, are not the primary duties for which the position was established, and are not significant in determining qualification requirements.

Regular vs. One-Time-Only and Temporary Duties.—Regular recurring duties are the foundations of most positions. They may be performed in a continuous, uninterrupted manner or they may be performed at recurring intervals. In some circumstances it is difficult to distinguish between duties that recur over a relatively long cycle and those that are really only one-time duties and not significant in evaluating a position.

Within reason, the time period of cyclic duties is not important; there is no magic cut-off point beyond which a duty cannot be considered as recurring. The important factors are that the duty recurs on a reasonably anticipated schedule and the position concerned is involved with the entire cyclic process.

One-time-only or temporary duties generally are clearly such. Their value to a position is that of diversity or training—they generally do not affect the series or grade. When such duties extend over a long period of time, however, they cannot be ignored. In some circumstances they may be the basis for the grade of the position as long as they are performed, with their termination calling for a new description and reevaluation of a position. Thus unusual, emergency, or one-time-only assignments may be required of any employee generally without effect on his grade. Their possible effects on his grade should be carefully considered, however, if such conditions as the following exist:

If the unusual duty lasts over a long period of time, e.g., several months.

If the unusual duty occurs repeatedly and if it is reasonable to assume that it will continue occurring even though not on a precisely predictable pattern.

If one person is singled out of a group to receive all the unusual and emergency assignments because of an ability to solve novel problems.

Projected Duties.—*As a general rule, a position is classified on the basis of the duties being performed. In some cases, however, projected duties are advanced as the basis for a proposed grade.* In determining whether projected duties are to be given any weight in classifying a position, the best rule is for each case to be decided on its own merits.

Generally, there seems to be no justification for a hard and fast rule prohibiting the evalution of duties before they are performed. In effect, we do this everytime we classify a vacancy and recruit an employee—we assume he will soon perform the duties that are assigned to him when he enters on duty.

In some instances it is difficult to evaluate duties that have not been and are not being performed. If it is necessary to base the grade of a position on these duties for recruiting or other sound reasons, the position can be reviewed later, after the work concerned is being performed.

RESPONSIBILITIES

All positions have both duties and responsibilities, although the emphasis on each from a classification standpoint varies greatly from position to position. Generally, more emphasis is placed on duties in positions in the lower grades, and on responsibilities in positions in the higher grades.

In some positions the assigned responsibility—as for a given project or a given program—is the essence of the position, and the specific methods used and tasks performed are largely within the discretion of the incumbents, generally without effect on the position's classification. Even in this type of situation, however, the intensity of the program, the way in which it is carried out, and the results achieved may vary to such an extent as to affect materially the basic concept of the position and its classification worth. The classifier must concern himself with these matters and consider the impact that the incumbent has on the job.

QUALIFICATION REQUIREMENTS

As a third grade-determining factor, the Classification Act lists *qualification requirements*. In essence, required qualifications involve the skills and knowledges necessary for satisfactory job performance. One critical consideration regarding qualifications is the necessary distinction between *simple possession* of certain qualifications on the one hand and, on the other, the *necessity* for *possession* of certain qualifications that are required for successful performance of duties and competent assumption of responsibilities of the position.

IMPACT OF THE MAN ON THE JOB

It is a basic tenet of position classification that it is the position which is classified, not the particular individual who is performing the work of the position. Yet consistent with this basic tenet is the concept that an incumbent of a position may have an important impact on the position he holds, sometimes to the point where the position is so changed that its classification must also be changed. In other words, the qualifications and ability of the individual can have a material effect on the *kind* or the *level* of work of the job as he performs it.

Impact on Grade Level of Work.—The opportunity for an incumbent's special talents or capacity to be reflected in the responsibilities assumed varies, of course, with the occupation. *On the one extreme, a highly routinized, carefully structured job—one, for example, dependent on some mechanical or flow process—is not likely to leave much room for "impact of the man."* In such instances, differences between individuals are reflected in the usual performance distinctions in volume and accuracy of the work product—for which within-grade pay increases, special recognitions, awards, or promotional opportunities may be used to reflect management's acknowledgement of their value. *On the other extreme, the influence of personal differences in capacity on the work assignment is most likely to be significant in professional, managerial, analytic, or secretarial positions.* Between the two extremes, there is a broad gray area; in this area, the opportunity for an employee to have an impact on the dimensions of his job cannot be prejudged and must be evaluated on an individual basis.

Classification standards typically recognize the differences with which different people perform what is superficially the same job by the description of grade levels in terms of all important classification factors, rather than by pegging particular duties to a specific grade. Duties, in and of themselves, provide only part of the basis for determining grade level. Even in the oldest standards on the books the same types of duties will be found described over a number of grade levels which reflect different combinations of values of such factors as: the nature of supervision and guidelines controlling the work; the preselection of assignments on the basis of level of difficulty; the need for originality, imagination, and inventiveness; the kinds and importance of authorities delegated; and public contact considerations.

In some of the more recent standards dealing with specific occupational areas where the man-job relationship is particularly evident and important and may be reflected in relatively intangible ways, the published standard has provided specific guidelines for weighing and evaluating the effect of the individual on his job. (*See particularly the material on this subject in the classification standards for attorneys and for research scientists.*) Where a published standard provides specific methods and guidelines for considering the impact of the man on his job, these methods should be followed with full appreciation of their underlying purpose; that is, not to evaluate the man alone, but rather to provide for full consideration of the total dimensions of the position as it has been affected by the incumbent.

The absence of specific reference to this relationship in a standard does not justify a conclusion that the impact of the individual should not be considered in the evaluation of positions in the occupation in question. Each position should be carefully considered in terms of its total duties, responsibilities, and qualification requirements. The use of standards in evaluating a position must consist of a measurement of this total job against the standards, with full weight given to the degree to which the individual in the job has changed it in any direction. Exceptional ability might have resulted in the attraction to the job, for example, of especially difficult work assignments, of unusual freedom from supervision, or of special delegation of authority to act for the agency. Unusual weakness in the ability of the incumbent might have resulted in limitations being placed on the job in terms of closer supervision, for example, or especially easy work assignments, or less-than-normal delegations of authority. *A final grade-level decision* must take into account the full effect of all these considerations.

It should be clearly understood that the mere fact that an individual in a position stands out from other individuals in comparable, or what otherwise may have been assumed to be identical, positions should not by itself be interpreted as grounds for a higher grade for the incumbent. A careful review must be made of the positions with which comparison is being made to determine whether they are really being fully and adequately performed. In other words, the job which is thought to reflect the impact of the highly competent incumbent must be evaluated a*gainst a general standard*, not merely against other comparable jobs around it. One of the earmarks of such a job is that it is one in which a change in incumbency would require a reevaluation of the job and frequently the filling of it at a lower grade.

In sum, the impact of the man on the job is reflected in the classification when and because it actually makes the job materially different than it otherwise would have been. This difference may require a change in classification of the job to a higher or lower grade or to a different series.

Reflection of Impact in Job Descriptions.—In establishing true impact-of-man-on-job, it is essential that the employee's duties are management-recognized and endorsed, and are performed in a climate that permits continuing contributions of real significance. Duties and responsibilities must be specifically stated. Thus recognition of the impact of a man on his job should be manifest from statements in the job description or other records which identify the higher level duties or responsibilities and give examples which clearly show the way in which the employee's performance has changed his job materially. This change can occur in positions of like organizational rank or like job content, as well as in positions which are unique to one employee. In the former instance, of course, a penetrating analysis must be made of the significance of the employee's job contributions, keeping in mind particularly the fact that all positions of like duty content must be compared against a standard, not merely against each other.

48.

HOW FEDERAL JOBS ARE FILLED: COMMISSION-AGENCY ROLES

U.S. CIVIL SERVICE COMMISSION

In its 80-year history, the Civil Service Commission has assumed many responsibilities in Federal personnel management, but one of its primary objectives is still to recruit the best qualified workers for the executive branch.

COMMISSION OVERSEES COMPETITIVE RECRUITING AND EXAMINING—BUT AGENCIES DO THE ACTUAL HIRING

The Commission's recruitment activity often is confused with the actual hiring of Federal workers. The Commission directs recruitment and examination programs, but the agencies do the actual hiring.

The Constitution empowers the Congress to vest appointing power for subordinate officers of the Government in the President, in the heads of departments,

Reprinted from U.S. Civil Service Commission, *The Role of the Civil Service Commission in Federal Employment* (Washington, D.C.: U.S. Government Printing Office, 1963), pp. 5–9.

and in the courts. Generally speaking, the Congress has conferred appointing authority for employees in the executive branch on the heads of agencies. Heads of agencies may redelegate this authority to the heads of various subordinate units, and these appointing officers have the final say as to who shall be appointed to Federal jobs under them. No independent body such as the Commission may direct them to employ any specific individual.

The appointing officer's area of choice is limited, however. The Civil Service Act of 1883, the Veterans' Preference Act, and other laws lay down the primary conditions for a merit system which requires appointing officers to select employees from among persons who have been found qualified for the work.

The merit system is designed to provide (1) the best-qualified available personnel for the Government service, (2) equal opportunity for all interested citizens to be considered for Federal jobs on the basis of their qualifications and suitability for the work to be done, without discrimination as to race, creed, color, national origin, sex, or politics, and (3) continuity of service through periodic changes in political administration.

The Civil Service Commission is the major instrumentality for maintaining the merit system. The Civil Service Act directs the Commission to recommend to the President rules to govern hiring in the Federal service. When approved by the President, these rules become binding on the Commission as well as on other Federal agencies.

AGENCIES DECIDE ON METHOD OF FILLING VACANCIES

Agencies have the prerogative of determining the *method* of filling vacancies in the Federal service. They may promote, transfer, or reassign present employees who are qualified; reinstate qualified former employees; or appoint someone from outside the Government. A large proportion of Federal jobs are filled by promoting, transferring, or reassigning employees from other jobs.

Competitive examinations, open to all qualified citizens, are used generally to bring new workers into the career service. Applicants are rated under practical and uniformly applied qualification standards, and qualified veterans are given the added points to which they are entitled by law. Eligibles are arranged in order of their ratings except that certain disabled veterans are placed at the top of lists for some kinds of jobs as required by law. Lists of eligibles may be subdivided on the basis of residence. When a vacancy occurs, and the appointing officer decides to make an original appointment, names on the top of the appropriate list are referred to the employing agency for consideration. The employing agency is required to make a selection on the basis of merit and without discrimination because of race, creed, color, national origin, sex, or politics.

AGENCIES DECIDE WHEN TO FILL JOBS; COMMISSION DOES NOT SET NUMBER OF EMPLOYEES AGENCIES MAY EMPLOY

Examinations for all kinds of jobs are not open at all times. There must be jobs to fill before an examination is scheduled and applications are accepted. Agencies —not the Commission—decide how many employees to hire and when to fill jobs, subject to appropriations made by the Congress and controls exercised by management in the executive branch.

When an agency has or expects to have vacancies and there is no existing list of eligibles for the jobs, the Commission may be asked to schedule an examination. When an examination is scheduled, an examination "announcement" is issued. It lists the title, duties, pay, location, and agency which has the jobs to be filled; the requirements of experience and training; the basis for evaluating the candidates; instructions as to how persons may apply; and the time limit for submission of applications. The announcements are widely distributed and the examinations adequately publicized to give qualified and interested citizens an opportunity to compete for the positions.

Those who submit applications within the time limit are then examined as prescribed in the announcement. A written test may be given—this is called an assembled examination because a group of applicants take a test in a central place at the same time. But for many jobs there is no written test. Applicants are rated on the basis of the experience and training they describe on their application forms. This is called an unassembled examination. Other examining techniques may be included—knowledges, skills, and personal characteristics may be measured through confidential inquiry to competent persons who know the applicants' work records, and the applicants may be examined in interviews in which their personal characteristics are observed.

COMMISSION SENDS NAMES OF ELIGIBLES TO AGENCY, AND APPOINTING OFFICER MAKES CHOICE FROM AMONG TOP THREE ELIGIBLES

When an agency wants to fill a job by an original appointment, the appointing officer requests the names of people who are eligible for the job. Names from the top of the appropriate register are referred to the appointing officer for consideration. He may then select 1 of the highest 3 who say they are available. He may not pass over these three persons to select a lower ranking eligible and he may not pass over a veteran on the list to select a lower ranking nonveteran without giving reasons for this action to the Civil Service Commission. The Commission then passes on the sufficiency of these reasons. If the Commission finds these reasons to be insufficient, the nonveteran or the lower ranking eligible may not be appointed.

BOARDS OF EXAMINERS HOLD EXAMINATIONS, RATE TESTS, AND MAINTAIN LISTS OF ELIGIBLES UNDER COMMISSION SUPERVISION

Much of the actual work of announcing examinations, rating candidates, and maintaining lists of eligibles is done by boards of civil service examiners in the agencies. These boards are made up of agency personnel, nominated by the agencies and subject to Commission approval. The Commission trains board members, directs and supervises their operations, and inspects their work to make sure that they adhere to Commission standards.

Boards of examiners are established so that examinations will best meet the needs of individual agencies, and candidates for employment will be available as soon as they are needed. About 900 boards now examine and refer candidates for about three-fourths of the vacancies filled through competitive examination. The Commission conducts examinations for positions which are common to a number of agencies or for which it has been impracticable to set up boards of examiners.

CAREER-CONDITIONAL APPOINTMENT SYSTEM ASSURES STABILITY, FLEXIBILITY OF UNITED STATES PERSONNEL SYSTEM

The career-conditional appointment system, which has been in effect since 1955, is designed to give the Federal personnel system the flexibility needed during expansions and contractions of the work force resulting from limited emergencies and to assure stability of the career service.

The system recognizes that not all those who accept Government employment intend to spend all of their working lives in public service and that the Governmend may not have continuing jobs for all those who may be employed at a given time, such as during an emergency. A conditional period of service enables employees to demonstrate their interest in careers in Federal service and establishes the ability of the Government to provide reasonable assurance of continuing career opportunities.

Career-conditional appointments are given to persons who pass open competitive examinations and are selected for continuing positions in regular order from civil-service lists of eligibles. Career-conditional employees automatically acquire full career standing after a conditional period of 3 years.

Career-conditional employees who meet qualification requirements may be reassigned, promoted, transferred, or reinstated to other positions in the competitive service without again taking an open competitive examination. In reductions in force, however, they rank below employees with full career standing. Thus, career-conditional employees enjoy most of the benefits of competitive status, but not the tenure rights reserved for those with full career standing.

AGENCIES AUTHORIZED TO MAKE NONCAREER
APPOINTMENTS UNDER CERTAIN CONDITIONS

The system takes into account the fact that there are always some jobs in the competitive service which cannot or should not be filled on a competitive or continuous basis.

When it is necessary to fill strictly temporary jobs, agencies are authorized to make temporary limited appointments for not to exceed 1 year. If appropriate lists of eligibles exist, they must be used, as a general rule. However, agencies may make temporary appointments of qualified persons without regard to lists when the appointment is at grade GS-7 or below and does not involve more than 700 hours of service. Agencies may also make 1-month appointments to meet special needs without regard to usual competitive requirements.

In other cases, there are times when an agency needs to fill continuing positions and the Commission does not have available a list of eligibles appropriate for filling the jobs. Then agencies may obtain permission from the Commission to make temporary appointments pending the establishment of a register. Persons given such appointments are subject to displacement when an adequate list of eligibles is established. In making these appointments, agencies must make certain that appointees at least meet minimum qualifications for the jobs. They also must give preference to veterans. Hiring of this kind is subject to close inspection by the Commission.

Still another type of noncareer appointment is the term appointment. Term appointments are used only for work that is of a project nature that will be completed within 4 years, at the end of which the employees' services will not be required. These appointments are made from lists of eligibles but, because the work is for a limited amount of time, they do not confer career status. They do, however, carry with them removal protection after 1 year of service.

AGENCIES CAN PROMOTE, TRANSFER, OR
REASSIGN QUALIFIED WORKERS
WITHOUT PRIOR COMMISSION APPROVAL

Career or career-conditional employees may be moved to other positions at the same or higher grades in their own or different agencies without again competing with persons outside the Federal service.

For such shifting within the Federal service, the Commission prescribes standards to assure that the candidate is qualified to do the job for which he is being considered. The standards specify the experience, training, and other qualifications persons must have to qualify for the jobs. Agencies have been given authority to determine whether individual employees meet these standards, and they can promote, transfer, or reassign their employees without prior approval of the Commission. The Commission inspects agency operations to make certain that the standards are observed. If violations of the standards are found, the Commission may revoke the agency's authority to act and require that the agency obtain specific prior approval of the Commission before taking such actions.

Career and career-conditional employees may also transfer without loss of career rights to Federal agencies with merit systems of their own, with whom the Commission has interchange agreements. They are the Atomic Energy Commission, the Tennessee Valley Authority (white-collar positions only), and the Canal Zone Government (positions under the Canal Zone Merit System).

49.

SALARIES BY GENERAL SCHEDULE (GS) LEVELS, WITH WITHIN-GRADE STEP INCREASES

U.S. Civil Service Commission

PAY RATES OF THE GENERAL SCHEDULE AS PROVIDED BY SECTION 5332
OF TITLE 5, UNITED STATES CODE, AS AMENDED BY FEDERAL SALARY ACT OF 1967

General Schedule—Basic per Annum Rates

Grade	1	2	3	4	5	6	7	8	9	10	Amount of within-grade increase
GS-1	$3,776	$3,902	$4,028	$4,154	$4,280	$4,406	$4,532	$4,658	$4,784	$4,910	$126
GS-2	4,108	4,245	4,382	4,519	4,656	4,793	4,930	5,067	5,204	5,341	137
GS-3	4,466	4,615	4,764	4,913	5,062	5,211	5,360	5,509	5,658	5,807	149
GS-4	4,995	5,161	5,327	5,493	5,659	5,825	5,991	6,157	6,323	6,489	166
GS-5	5,565	5,751	5,937	6,123	6,309	6,495	6,681	6,867	7,053	7,239	186
GS-6	6,137	6,342	6,547	6,752	6,957	7,162	7,367	7,572	7,777	7,982	205
GS-7	6,734	6,959	7,184	7,409	7,634	7,859	8,084	8,309	8,534	8,759	225
GS-8	7,384	7,630	7,876	8,122	8,368	8,614	8,860	9,106	9,352	9,598	246
GS-9	8,054	8,323	8,592	8,861	9,130	9,399	9,668	9,937	10,206	10,475	269
GS-10	8,821	9,115	9,409	9,703	9,997	10,291	10,585	10,879	11,173	11,467	294
GS-11	9,657	9,979	10,301	10,623	10,945	11,267	11,589	11,911	12,233	12,555	322
GS-12	11,461	11,843	12,225	12,607	12,989	13,371	13,753	14,135	14,517	14,899	382
GS-13	13,507	13,957	14,407	14,857	15,307	15,757	16,207	16,657	17,107	17,557	450
GS-14	15,841	16,369	16,897	17,425	17,953	18,481	19,009	19,537	20,065	20,593	528
GS-15	18,404	19,017	19,630	20,243	20,856	21,469	22,082	22,695	23,308	23,921	613
GS-16	20,982	21,681	22,380	23,079	23,778	24,477	25,176	25,875	26,574		699
GS-17	23,788	24,581	25,374	26,167	26,960						793
GS-18	27,055										

* Effective on the first day of the first pay period on or after October 1, 1967. Retroactive generally October 8, 1967.

CSC Form 2968-A October 1967.

This schedule was effective through July, 1968, at which time approximately a 4.5 percent increase went into effect.

50.

STRUCTURE OF THE FEDERAL POSITION CLASSIFICATION PLAN

U.S. CIVIL SERVICE COMMISSION

The Federal position classification plan originated with the Classification Act of 1923. That act was amended several times and was replaced by the Classification Act of 1949. The 1949 Act also has been amended and otherwise interpreted and supplemented, but it remains the principal legal authority for classifying positions within the Federal Government.[1]

The primary objectives of the Federal classification plan are:

1. Pay shall be based on the principle of equal pay for substantially equal work;
2. Differences in pay shall be in proportion to substantial differences in *difficulty, responsibility, and qualification requirements* of the work performed and *to the contributions of employees to efficiency and economy;* and
3. The position classification plan should facilitate all phases of personnel administration.

The Classification Act includes a pay plan and a classification plan. The Pay plan consists mainly of the General Schedule of salary rates for 18 GS grades and rules for use of the rates. The classification plan provides general definitions of 18 grades into which all positions under its coverage are to be placed and specifies the authority of the Civil Service Commission and the agencies as well as general classification procedures. It does not, however, prescribe the occupational groupings for positions or evaluation methods; the development of these features of the plan are responsibilities of the Civil Service Commission.

The structure of the Federal classification plan beyond the 18-grade statutory framework involves several groupings of positions, a related coding system, and certain mechanical devices. Together, they provide a framework for the classification of positions.[2]

Reprinted from U.S. Civil Service Commission, *Classification Principles and Policies*, Personnel Management Series No. 16 (Washington, D.C.: U.S. Government Printing Office, 1963), pp. 13–17, 19–21.

[1] For a summary of the development of position classification, see part I of *Basic Training Course in Position Classification*, Personnel Methods Series, No. 11.

[2] For an outline of the Federal position classification plan showing a division of the General Schedule into occupational groups and series and for series definitions, see the *Handbook of Occupational Groups and Series of Classes Established under the Federal Position Classification Plan.*

DEFINITIONS AND GROUPING OF
POSITIONS UNDER THE PLAN

Position

"Position" means the work, consisting of the duties and responsibilities, assignable to an employee.

Class of Positions

A "class" or "class of positions" includes all positions which are sufficiently similar, as to (1) kind or subject-matter of work, (2) level of difficulty and responsibility, and (3) qualification requirements of the work, to warrant similar treatment in personnel and pay administration. For example, grade 3 clerk-typist positions constitute a class.

Series of Classes

A "series" or "series of classes" is an occupational or type-of-work grouping that consists of all positions in a particular kind of work. Positions within a series are similar with respect to subject-matter of the work and exist at all grade levels appropriate for the kind of work. A series may be thought of as including the normal steps in the line of promotion for a particular kind of work, for example, the Medical Biology Technician or the Structural Engineer series.

Grade

A "grade" is a level of work *or a zone of difficulty, responsibility, and qualification requirements.* A grade includes all positions under the Classification Act whose difficulty, responsibility, and qualification requirements are sufficiently similar to warrant one range of rates of basic compensation. A grade does not identify kind or subject-matter of work.

Occupational Group

An "occupational group" embraces generally several series of classes in associated or related occupations, professions, or activities.

Under the Federal classification plan a position is the basic organizational unit through which management directives are carried out.

Work is accomplished through positions; therefore, their control is an essential part of management. Since there are about one million Federal positions that fall under the Classification Act, in a wide variety of professional administrative, technical, and clerical occupations, the difficulty, if not impossibility, of managing this number of positions individually is obvious. *Thus, bringing together similar positions into classes reduces the number of discrete units that must be controlled and facilitates selection, training, setting pay, and other personnel and administrative transactions.* The very essence of classification, then, is placing positions in their appropriate class; that is, determining the level of the kind of work that the job involves.

CODE AND TITLE STRUCTURE

For precise identification and administrative convenience code symbols have been assigned to the occupational structure. In effect, the code identifies the class of positions to which a particular position has been assigned. The three-part code has a symbol for the schedule, series, and grade:

(1) The Symbol for the General Schedule is GS.
(2) The series symbol is expressed numerically. (Each occupational group has been assigned a number of an even hundred. The various series within that group are assigned numbers within that hundred. Thus, the symbol for the "Biological Sciences" group is 400 and the symbol for the "Medical Biology Technician" series within that group is 404).
(3) The final symbol of the code structure is the General Schedule number of the grade. For example, the code for all General Schedule grade 5 Medical Biology Technician positions (a class of positions) is GS-404-5.

TITLING PRACTICES

The Classification Act provides that the official class titles shall be used for personnel, budget, and fiscal purposes, but this requirement shall not prevent the use of organizational or other titles for internal administration, public convenience, law enforcement, or similar purposes. Thus an agency in its discretion could authorize a GS-14 Supervisory Chemist, for example, to use a title in correspondence or professional articles such as Senior Research Associate.

Published standards specify titles to be used for positions in classes covered by the standards. There are, in addition, certain general prescriptions concerning the use of titles which are set forth in the *Introductory Material to Position Classification Standards*, Section III, "Titling Practices." These include a statement of the principles to be followed in titling supervisory positions and the principles to be followed in using parenthetical words "Typing" and "Stenography" after certain class titles. These prescriptions are considered to be part of the standards, and are published in the Introduction because they have general applicability.

Authority for establishing additional class titles for occupations covered by printed standards is centralized in the Standards Division, Bureau of Programs and Standards, United States Civil Service Commission. It is recognized that the classes and specializations covered by published standards may be subject to change as functions or qualification requirements change. To meet this situation, the Civil Service Commission, upon receipt of adequate and complete supporting information in writing, will consider altering the class structure to allow for the proper identification of new specializations or needed combinations.

Recommendations for such changes may be submitted either by agencies or by operating offices of the Commission. Proposed new classes and titles covering specializations not provided for in published standards must have the prior approval of the Civil Service Commission before they are established and used for the classification of positions. When such classes or titles are established, official notification is given to all agencies by means of an addition to the standards defining the new classes and giving the official class titles.

When standards prescribing titles have not been published for an occupation, agencies are free to use suitable titles of their own choosing. Since consistency in title construction is highly desirable, even in the absence of published standards, the *Introductory Material to Position Classification Standards* includes a statement of suggested principles for the construction of class titles for positions in series not covered by published classification standards.

Keeping the Classification Structure Current

Because occupations themselves are dynamic and changing and because new occupations emerge from time to time, it is necessary for the Government's occupational structure to be flexible in order to keep pace with changes.

The Commission has a number of means for keeping abreast of occupational changes and is continuously revising the occupational structure, as well as its standards, to keep up with changes. For example, when the activities of the Soil Conservation Service called for a large number of employees with a unique combination of knowledges in the agricultural sciences, the Commission responded to the need by defining and developing standards for a new occupation —the Soil Conservationist Series. In response to the almost overnight advent and development of the digital computer, the Commission defined and developed standards for a group of new digital computer occupations. The development of these standards to facilitate personnel activities in the computer field has contributed to the Government's progress in automatic data processing.

Similarly, in response to the development of nuclear energy, two new series— Nuclear Engineering and Health Physics—were recognized and defined. The Commission is also in close touch with unfolding aero-space activities and occupations. The astronomy series has been redefined as the Astronomy and Space

Science Series; an Aero-space Engineering Series has been defined in lieu of the former Aeronautical Engineering Series, and the Commission is making further studies of this field to determine the need for other changes in its occupational structure.

The Commission solicits suggestions from agencies, utilizes information obtained by its operating activities, and receives information from interested employee groups concerning occupational changes and needs for revision in the occupational structure or the standards. In addition, the Commission conducts periodic studies of each occupation and makes appropriate revisions in the occupational structure and standards to reflect changes in technology and changes in the content or concept of occupations.

POSITION CLASSIFICATION STANDARDS— PURPOSE AND NATURE OF STANDARDS

Title IV of the Classification Act of 1949, as amended, provides that the Civil Service Commission shall define the various classes of positions that exist in the service in terms of duties, responsibilities, and qualification requirements; establish the official class titles; and set forth the grades in which such classes have been placed by the Commission.

In fulfilling its responsibilities under the Classification Act, the Commission strives to make its standards practical and useful aids to good management, aids that are responsive to the changing and dynamic nature of occupations in our modern society.

The role of standards in assuring a sound Federal classification system becomes increasingly significant as agencies decentralize more personnel authority and as occupations grow more complex. With the greater delegation of personnel (including classification) authority, classification standards are now applied by personnel and operating officials at practically all organizational levels of agencies. At the same time, *because of the growing complexity of today's occupations, standards can no longer be catalogs of specific duties and responsibilities. If new standards are to remain usable over a reasonable period of time, they must be written in terms of those elements of difficulty, responsibility, and qualification requirements that capture the essential character of the field of work.*

Classification standards place a great responsibility upon the user (agency personnel specialist and operating official alike) for care, understanding, judgment, and insight in their application. It is vital that they be applied with full understanding of their importance and their intent, and with a full sense of the responsibility which goes with their use.

The Classification Act requires that departments and agencies classify positions in conformance with, or consistent with, standards published by the Commission. The official class titles in published standards must be used for personnel, budget, and fiscal purposes although departments may use organizational or other titles for internal administration, public convenience, law enforcement, or similar purposes. To comply with this requirement, each office with authority for classifying positions must have the published standards available for reference. Each office need not maintain a complete set of standards, but it must have those which apply to its positions. Published standards should be made available for review by employees and officials of the departments.

Position classification standards may be defined as a set of documents published by the Civil Service Commission which provide information for distinguishing the duties, responsibilities, and qualification requirements of positions in one class from those of positions in other classes, and which thus provide the criteria for placing each position in its proper class. These standards distinguish both as to level of difficulty and responsibility and as to kind of work.

Classification standards are prepared at the same time, and on the basis of the same occupational analysis, as *qualification* standards for determining whether candidates meet the requirements of the job. Within the Civil Service Commission the responsibility for developing both types of standards lies in one office. Because of this total study of an occupation in depth, classification and qualification standards can be inter-related to better serve the needs of program officials. Classification standards provide guides for placing the job in the right series and grade level, and qualification standards provide guides for filling the job with a person qualified for that series and grade. This process of matching the man and the job is the heart of good personnel management.

USES OF POSITION-CLASSIFICATION STANDARDS

Position-classification standards have, of course, a definite function to serve in classifying positions to their appropriate series and grades. In this respect they:

(1) Aid in an understanding of why *certain kinds of positions are classified to particular classes,* by showing the work factors with respect to kind and level of work which cause positions to fall in one class rather than another.
(2) Help to secure *uniformity and coordination in classifying positions,* by providing an established standard for common reference and use in the classification of positions in different organizations, locations, or agencies.
(3) Help to *expedite the process of classifying positions to schedule, series, and grades,* by furnishing a convenient ready reference for comparing the work factors of a particular position with those of another position and with those stated in the standards.

Their use, however, goes beyond the procedures of position classification. For example:

(4) *Position classification standards facilitate and clarify recruiting and placement*

processes, because their qualifications statements are guides in recruiting, testing, and selecting employees.

(5) *Position classification standards aid administrators and supervisors in general management, because they make available, in concise written form, information used by administrators in organizing or reorganizing, in delegating authority and responsibility, or in changing flow of work;* and by supervisors in checking on the assignments of duties and responsibilities to members of their staffs. They serve as a basis for common understanding of personnel matters and as a means of simplifying a multiplicity of job details. They assist management in utilizing personnel, so as to avoid dilution of scarce skills, for example; and in grouping duties into jobs so as to facilitate recruiting, promoting, and reassigning personnel. In the field of career development, they provide clues to career patterns, and in conjunction with organizational charts, to career ladders, and they may aid in the development of training programs. They provide a means for promotions and transfers and a basis for more orderly reduction-in-force procedures.

(6) *Such standards material is also used by employees, not only in satisfying themselves about the classification of their positions, but also in finding out the characteristics of other classes open for possible promotion or transfer.*

(7) Position classification standards are *aids for performance rating purposes in the development of performance standards.* Supervisors and administrators will find them helpful in determining performance requirements of various types of positions. Employees will find them of value in reaching a better understanding of the ratings.

DEVELOPMENT OF STANDARDS

The great majority of position classification standards are prepared by the Commission itself. In some instances, when a type of position exists only or primarily in one agency, [the agency] concerned may develop the standard under the guidance and direction of the Commission.

The development of classification standards is a very extensive and complex activity. It requires not only a thorough knowledge of general and personnel administration, and of the principles of classification; it also requires extensive occupational study, a realistic understanding of the nature and characteristics of the occupation being studied, and a thorough understanding of the duties and responsibilities which make up positions in the occupation. Further, it calls for an appreciation of the career aspects of the work situation and environment surrounding the occupation.

51.

THE EXTENT OF THE PROTECTED/COMPETITIVE SERVICE: SOME DISTINCTIONS AND DATA

U.S. CIVIL SERVICE COMMISSION

A. THE PROTECTED/COMPETITIVE SERVICE: SOME DISTINCTIONS

Congress founded the competitive civil service in response to public protests against the evils of the "spoils system" which developed early in the Nation's history.

Merit and fitness for a job were the primary considerations of the first Presidents in making Federal appointments, but gradually these factors were subordinated to the question of party loyalty. By 1829, the full-scale spoils system had arrived, bringing to vogue the cry: "To the victor belong the spoils!" Incoming administrations made mass removals of Government workers and awarded the jobs to supporters of the victorious party.

While the structure and responsibilities of the Federal Government expanded and grew complex, appointments were made with little regard to the skills and experience the jobs required. Despite evidences of inefficiency and corruption fostered by the spoils system, the growing evil was tolerated for many years. It was only after President Garfield was assassinated by a disappointed jobseeker that public indignation mounted and Congress enacted the Civil Service Act of 1883.

This law created the Civil Service Commission "to regulate and improve the civil service of the United States." It established the merit system, providing for competitive examinations and the making of appointments to the competitive service from among those graded highest in the examinations.

Competitive Service Now Covers 85 Percent of Federal Jobs

From its meager beginning, the competitive service has grown to embrace 85

Reprinted from U.S. Civil Service Commission, *The Role of the Civil Service Commission in Federal Employment* (Washington, D.C.: U.S. Government Printing Office, June 1963), pp. 2–4.

percent of all jobs in the Federal Government and 91 percent of those in the United States. Unless an executive-branch job is specifically excepted by law or by action of the Civil Service Commission, it is in the competitive service and subject to civil-service rules. With the extension of the competitive service to about 10,000 positions in Alaska in 1955, and about 20,000 positions in foreign countries in 1956, the competitive service is now operated on a worldwide basis.

"Excepted" Jobs Total 355,100 But Few Are "Patronage" Positions

The 14 percent of Federal positions that are excepted from civil-service requirements number 355,100. Of them, 158,000 are excepted by statute and the remainder by action of the Civil Service Commission. Some people believe that all of these are patronage positions; actually, relatively few are true patronage jobs.

Examples of positions excepted by statute are doctors, dentists, and nurses in the Department of Medicine and Surgery of the Veterans Administration, and all positions in the Tennessee Valley Authority, the Atomic Energy Commission, the Foreign Service of the Department of State, and the Federal Bureau of Investigation of the Department of Justice.

Positions excepted by action of the Civil Service Commission are placed in 1 of 3 schedules—A, B, or C—after a study of all pertinent facts (such as the duties, pay, and location of the positions) has been made by the Commission.

Schedule A Defined

Schedule A is for positions for which it is not practicable to hold any examinations, except as noted below. Examples are: Chaplains, professional and technical experts for temporary consultation purposes, narcotics agents for undercover work, certain part-time positions at isolated localities, and many positions in foreign countries. There are 155,000 positions in this schedule.

Schedule B Defined

Schedule B is for positions for which competitive examinations are impracticable but for which *noncompetitive* examinations are given. Examples are positions assigned exclusively to Navy or Air Force Communications Intelligence activities. There are about 21,000 jobs in this schedule.

Schedule C Defined

Schedule C is for positions whose occupants serve in a policy-determining capacity to the politically appointed heads of agencies or in a confidential capacity to them and their key officials. It was established to more clearly define the career service by setting apart from it positions properly in the political area. It contains key positions which should be filled by the administration in power with persons who will fully support its political aims and policies.

No examination is required for appointment to Schedule C jobs except as noted below. Departments and agencies have authority to assign duties to any position. They may recommend to the Commission that a position be placed in Schedule C if they feel the duties assigned are either policy determining or require the incumbent to serve in a confidential relationship to a key official. The Commission considers the duties of the position—if they are actually policy determining in nature or if they establish a confidential relationship to a key official, it places the position in Schedule C; if not, it rejects the recommendation. Each job is considered on an individual basis. Thus, the true career service is set apart from the effects of political change, and a new administration is enabled to carry out its program more effectively. There are about 1,400 jobs in Schedule C.

Determining Qualifications for Appointment to Positions in Schedules A, B, and C

Agencies have authority to establish qualification standards and to determine the qualifications of persons selected for Schedule A and C positions *except* for those positions in GS-16, 17, and 18. The Commission is required by law to approve the qualifications of persons proposed for positions in these grades before appointment.

Persons proposed for positions in Schedule B must have their qualifications approved by the Commission, regardless of the grade of the position.

B. THE PROTECTED/COMPETITIVE SERVICE: SOME DATA ON COVERAGE

There is no easy characterization of the "federal employee." The material below only begins the job of giving order and form to the complexities of those employed in public work. The *Annual Report 1966* of the U.S. Civil Service Commission provides some initial sense of that complexity:[1]

On June 30, 1966, Federal civilian employment totaled 2,759,019.

Of this total there were 2,595,770 full-time employees, 105,717 scheduled part-time workers, and 57,532 intermittent employees. In June part-time and intermittent workers served approximately 54 percent of the time they would have worked if on a full-time schedule.

---

[1] U.S. Civil Service Commission, *Annual Report 1966*, p. 25.

Pay rates of Federal employees are set in many ways. The largest group includes employees subject to the Classification Act. On June 30, 1966, this group included 1,188,586 or 46 percent of the total 2,595,770 full-time employees. Second in size was the wage-board group which included 686,328 full-time employees or 26 percent. Wage-board rates are set in accordance with prevailing rates in the localities where they work. Full-time postal employees whose rates are set by Title 39 of the United States Code, numbered 569,715 or 22 percent of total full-time employment. All other pay systems combined included 151,141 employees or 6 percent.

Of total employment, 1,991,261 were serving under career or excepted appointment which contain no conditional or time limitations.

52,512 U.S. citizens were stationed in foreign countries or U.S. territories. In addition there were 113,958 foreign nationals working for Federal agencies overseas.

Approximately 56,000 were hired as extra summer employees in furtherance of the President's Youth Opportunity Campaign.

76 percent of the total Federal employment were men.

In December 1965, 1,312,345 or 51 percent of the total Federal work force had veteran preference. About 17 percent of these employees were disabled veterans. About 96 percent of the number with preference were men. Approximately 1 percent of the veteran work force were widows of veterans and wives or mothers of disabled veterans entitled to preference.

Trends in total federal employment and coverage of the protected/competitive service permit more simple summary. Both trends have risen sharply, only to level off in recent years. The data below, for selected years only, show the peaks and plateaus for total employment and percentage of employees under the protected service.[2]

Selected Year Ending June 30	*Total Number of Employees*	*Number in Protected Service*	*Per Cent under Protected Service*
1884	131,208	13,780	10.5
1891	166,000	33,873	20.4
1895	189,000	54,222	28.7
1899	208,000	93,144	44.8
1904	290,858	154,093	53.0
1909	376,794	234,940	63.9
1914	482,721	292,460	60.6
1919	842,214	592,961	70.4
1924	521,641	415,593	79.7
1929	559,579	445,957	79.7
1934	673,095	450,592	66.9
1939	920,310	. . .	. . .
1944	3,312,256	622,832	67.7
1949	2,090,732	. . .	. . .
1954	2,346,718	1,750,823	83.7
1959	2,382,807	1,991,261	84.9
1963	2,527,960	2,042,034	85.7
1966	2,759,019	2,164,163	85.6

[2] Commission on Organization of the Executive Branch of the Government, *Report on Personnel and Civil Service* (Washington, D.C.: U.S. Government Printing Office, 1955), pp. 97–98, and U.S. Civil Service Commission, *Annual Reports, 1955–66.*

52.

SPOILS AS DYSFUNCTIONAL AND FUNCTIONAL

PAUL P. VAN RIPER

THE SPOILS OF WAR

In all probability, the American Civil War has the distinction of being the most extensive modern conflict won with the aid of a public service built up primarily by means of the spoils system. In fact, there is good reason for maintaining that the war could not have been won by the North without a highly partisan exploitation of the patronage. The value of the spoils system must therefore be judged in terms of ends as well as means.

Under Abraham Lincoln the spoils system reached new heights. The most complete sweep of the offices thus far was made. For instance, 1,457 out of a total of 1,639 presidential officers were replaced.[1] Subordinate employees suffered in proportion. In all fairness, it must be admitted that Lincoln had more factions to conciliate than his predecessors. The Republican party was a conglomerate of disunities, a civil war was in the offing, and loyalty, political and national, was paramount.

From 1861 to 1865 the policy of Washington, selection according to relative capacity and fitness, was almost entirely forgotten. Until the opening of hostilities Lincoln's appointive policies were devoted essentially to maintenance of the Union. After the beginning of the conflict the problem became one of maintaining Northern unity. Normally taking a direct hand only in the filling of the most important offices, Lincoln left the bulk of the nominations for presidential as well as for subordinate offices to his political friends and advisors. The military forces as well as the civilian establishment were exploited freely, and political generals were notoriously numerous. With more offices at his disposal than any president up to that time, and faced with the urgency of the imminent disintegration of the Union, Lincoln appears to have used—or permitted the use of—the appointing powers at his command as deliberately as they could have been used for practical, and usually partisan, political purposes. The only thread of consistency in the executive appointing policy during the years from 1861 to 1865

From pp. 43–56, *History of the United States Civil Service*, by Paul P. Van Riper. Copyright © 1958 by Harper & Row, Publishers, Incorporated. Reprinted by permission of the publishers.
[1] Carl R. Fish, *The Civil Service and the Patronage* (New York: Longmans, Green and Co., 1905), p. 170.

seems to have been the practical one of preservation of the Union via preservation of the Republican party.

That the Union was preserved lends considerable merit to the judgment that the process was not ineffectual. As Fish has pointed out, "If Lincoln had made appointments for merit only, the war might have been shortened; on the other hand, he might not have preserved a united North to carry on the war."[2] Lincoln was, however, far from insensitive to the problems posed by the methods of appointment used by his administration. On one occasion, contemplating the throng of office-seekers and Congressmen in his outer office, he was moved to observe that the spoils system might in the course of time become far more dangerous to the Republic than the rebellion itself.[3] When pressed to sweep the offices anew after his reelection in 1865, the President flatly refused. For the first time since 1829 the principle of rotation in office received a forthright setback. The decline of the spoils system may well be dated from this decision by President Lincoln.

THE "SYSTEM" OF SPOILS

Thus far we have considered the political rise of the spoils system and its meaning in terms of broad theoretical and practical ends. But what were the mechanics of patronage politics? What was sought and received? How was the patronage managed? What was the meaning of the spoils system as an administrative device?

From an administrative point of view, the spoils sytem was primarily designed to man, finance, and control the political machines of the new democracy. However, the spoils system performed another important managerial function for which it has seldom been given due credit. It also provided a much-needed channel for the recruitment of personnel for the rapidly expanding national government. While with respect to either of these functions we cannot precisely plot the spoils system with straight lines and boxes in the manner of modern organization charts, it is, nevertheless, entitled to be called a "system." By the eighteen fifties its general form, structure, and methods of operation were plainly observable and well understood.

The Sinews of Politics.—In understanding the spoils system we must first remember that before the Civil War politics and administration were inextricably intermixed in the American public service at all levels. There were few politically

---

[2] *Ibid.*, p. 172.

[3] Frederick Bancroft (ed.), *Speeches, Correspondence and Political Papers of Carl Schurz* (6 vols.; New York: G. P. Putnam's Sons, 1913), Vol. II, pp. 155–56; Vol. III, p. 295. This story seems to have been a favorite with Schurz, for he repeated it many times. For a detailed analysis of the patronage politics of the Lincoln administration, see Harry J. Carman and Reinhard H. Luthin, *Lincoln and the Patronage* (New York: Columbia University Press, 1943).

neutral, professional managers in the modern sense of the term. From the first days of the Constitution there had always been a certain mutuality of political interest among politicians, administrators, and employees. This the Jacksonians had sought, with signal success, to turn to patently partisan ends. While Federalist and Jeffersonian Republican executives had often required only the proper political opinion, the Jacksonians and those who came into power after them usually required—indeed, took for granted—positive partisanship. The civil servant received not only a livelihood and an opportunity to serve but often also an opportunity for personal gain. He might even expect to rise into a position of political power and prominence, with potentially immense pecuniary and psychological rewards. That politics was often a touchstone to success in private enterprise via land grants, franchises, and government contracts only heightened interest in public office. In return, however, public servants were expected to contribute their votes and a portion, often substantial, of their time, energy, and income to the political party to which they were indebted for their employment. All this was not a matter of contract, though such might be implied. Rather, it was usually a recognition of a sort of partnership, often entered into with considerable enthusiasm by all concerned. Loyalty to one's political party was as appropriate, and just about as frequently assumed, as loyalty to the nation, a church, or an individual state. Most frequently the penalty for both administrative and political failure was removal. In addition, however, one might be cut off from any access to other types of political favors, both those directly at the command of the party, such as nominations, and those available only through governmental channels, such as contracts. On the whole the motivations and methods of private enterprise were those of the spoils system.

From an organizational point of view, the President was at the top of the system, acting both as party chief and chief executive. Underneath were the members of the Cabinet, the most important of whom, from a party organization point of view, were the Postmaster General and the Secretary of the Treasury. Their key position stemmed not only from their duties but also from the fact that the agencies under their control were by far the largest in the civil establishment and the closest to the grass roots of the nation. At first the Treasury predominated in influence as a result both of its early close relationship to Congress and of the Four Years Law of 1820, which especially affected Treasury employees. The rise of the Post Office to partisan prominence came with Jackson. The terms of postmasters were limited to four years for the first time in 1836, and, in addition, senatorial confirmation was then first required for postmasters receiving over $1,000 a year. Then, too, the Post Office had by this time become by far the largest of the executive departments. For more than a century the Post Office continued to be at the center of the administrative workings of the spoils

OFFICE-SEEKERS AT WASHINGTON DURING THE INAUGURATION

These Gentlemen who are ready, like good Patriots, to serve their Country, are all ORIGINAL LINCOLN MEN. 'Tis true, they voted for PIERCE and BUCHANAN; but this was a deep game to insure the Election of LINCOLN in 1860.

From HARPER'S WEEKLY, March 16, 1861.

system, an arrangement which Congress and party leaders are still loath to disturb.[4]

Especially were employees in the field office outside Washington, then as now comprising about 90 per cent of the federal civil service, impelled to contribute their energies to the rapidly consolidating political party system. District attorneys, postmasters, collectors of customs, and a host of other officials were frequently representatives of both the public service and the party. More often than not the greater portion of their efforts was devoted to partisan rather than administrative purposes.

Energy, however, was not all that was required. Financial contributions, historically known as "political assessments," were also expected. The practice of assessment of office-holders for political purposes was well developed by 1840. Even Lincoln is reported to have written to remonstrate with an office-holder who refused to pay up.[5] Demands were usually whatever the traffic would bear, and by 1860 assessments were wrested from office-holders almost in the name of civic duty. Especially prevalent in the states but still far from unknown in federal circles, this practice continued on into the twentieth century. "Two per cent clubs" are still to be found among state employees, and candidates for public office are still expected to contribute substantially toward party campaign expenses.

Considering the traditionally close relationship of the press to politics, it is not surprising that from 1830 to 1860 many editors were appointed to office. The awarding of printing contracts to friendly printers and publishers was an old political custom which the creation of the Government Printing Office in 1860 helped to counteract.[6] But the appointment of large numbers of newspapermen to positions of administrative responsibility in the federal government dates primarily to the time of President Jackson. Two of the General's principal advisers, Amos Kendall and Isaac Hill, were editors of note, and Kendall was appointed Postmaster General in 1835. The editors of the *Cincinnati Advertiser*, the *Ohio People's Press*, and the *New York Courier and Enquirer* were among those receiving awards for their orthodoxy after the election of 1828. Over fifty representatives of the press were so honored by Jackson and nearly the same number by

---

[4] Dorothy G. Fowler, *The Cabinet Politician* (New York: Columbia University Press, 1943), contains one of the best analyses of the "system" in the spoils system, with special reference to the key position of the Post Office in the control of federal patronage. See also Fish, as cited in footnote 1, ch. viii, "Machinery of the Spoils Systems," pp. 173–85.

[5] Fish, as cited in footnote 1, p. 180. For a brief history of political assessments during the middle of the nineteenth century see Frederick W. Whitridge, "Political Assessments," *Cyclopedia of Political Science*, John J. Lalor (ed.), Vol. I (1882), pp. 152–55. For the earlier developments of this and related practices discussed in this section, see Leonard D. White, *The Jacksonians* (New York: The Macmillan Co., 1954), pp. 325–46 and elsewhere.

[6] See especially White, as cited in footnote 5, pp. 284–99, on this then serious problem.

Lincoln.[7]   The fact that for many years postmasters possessed the personal
privilege of "franking," frequently worth a substantial sum, explains in part why
some seemingly negligible rewards for party orthodoxy proved so attractive.   The
press has always been close to partisan politics, but in the period before 1865
the relationship was perhaps more blatantly on a *quid pro quo* basis than in any
other period of our history.   Appointments of newspapermen to office contributed in no little measure to the affinity.   Fortunately for a democratic society
concerned with the freedom of the press, this practice has gradually declined,
partly as a result of the increasing circulation and financial stability of newspapers
since the Civil War.   However, the relationship of the parties and the press,
especially with respect to printing contracts, is often still quite close in state and
local governments.

Finally, we come to a species of political middlemen who served as patronage
brokers.   In return for partisan support, segments of the patronage were frequently delivered up by the President and cabinet members to governors, other state
officials, national and local party committeemen, and political bosses.   However,
for constitutional as well as practical reasons, the bulk of the most attractive
patronage posts gravitated into the hands of the legislative members of the party
in power.   The Senate has always possessed the legal power of confirmation of
appointments.   As the Constitution fails to draw a clear line between offices which
are subject to confirmation and those which are not, it quickly became accepted
practice for the Senate to draw its own liberal rules.   The practice of confirmation
was gradually applied to a wide variety of the middle and upper level offices and
even to some of the lesser ones, such as the smaller postmasterships.   From the
beginning President Washington consulted closely with many members of the
House of Representatives as well as the Senate on appointment matters before
nominations, and all presidents have followed this example.   But within three
months of the beginning of the first session of Congress, the Senate had pressed
even further.   At this point Benjamin Fishbourn, a well-qualified nominee for
the post of naval officer for the port of Savannah, was rejected by the Senate as
a whole because the two senators from Georgia desired to press their own candidate in opposition to the declared choice of the President.   Here the Senate was
clearly endeavoring to extend its authority to the actual nomination process and
to substitute its judgment for that of the President, something clearly not contemplated by the Constitution.   By the time of the Jacksonians this sort of practice, in which the whole Senate bows to the personal desires of a majority party
senator from the home state of a nominee, was by no means unusual.   Eventually
dubbed "Senatorial Courtesy," the procedure has continued on into mid-twen-

---

[7] Erik M. Eriksson, "The Federal Civil Service under President Jackson," *Mississippi Valley
Historical Review*, XIII (March, 1927), pp. 525–32; and Carman and Luthin, as cited in
footnote 3, pp. 118–29.

tieth century. Thus, one way or another, much of the nominally presidential and cabinet patronage fell to senators of the party in power; and some of it, such as postmasterships, gradually came to be considered the perquisite of representatives.

Even legislators themselves often sought office during this period. For the higher offices, especially those comprising the Cabinet, this has always been considered proper; but pressure by senators and representatives for even the lower administrative offices was pronounced in the period before the Civil War. The information is most complete for Jackson's administration, though the tendency antedated his term. One list shows fifteen ex-senators and twenty-six ex-representatives as recipients of presidential appointments between 1829 and 1834.[8] Nor did all of these appointments represent "lame ducks." Long continuation of this practice for other than top positions might have undermined the cherished American principle of separation of powers. However, as legislative salaries and alternative occupational opportunities in private enterprise improved, the practice declined, except with respect to senators and congressmen who have been retired to private life by defeat at the polls.

Underlying all this was the meaning of the patronage to the President in terms of political control and direction of the government. In a political system rent by federalism and the separation of powers, some means had to be found to bridge at least some of the gaps in this dual division of authority. Otherwise nothing might be accomplished. It is not too much to say that one of the few major forces which lay at the command of a nineteenth century president who wished to think and act in terms of national rather than local interests was the power of the patronage. From 1829 on, public offices became recognized pawns in this as well as other political bargaining processes.

Such was the anatomy of the spoils system as a support for partisan politics. As political parties assumed a more modern form, characterized by national conventions, central committees, and large scale requirements for funds, the civil service became more and more intricately tied in with the party organization at all levels. By 1860 the two were almost inextricably entangled. That the administrative efficiency of the civil service should to some extent suffer was to be expected, though the decline was considerably less precipitous than is commonly supposed. The Jacksonian genius lay in politics rather than administration. Spoils politics was played according to the fluid rules of personal and political loyalty and expediency, a fascinating sort of game which the politicians and most of the public thoroughly understood, supported, and appeared to enjoy.

The Spoils System as a Recruiting Device.—Probably Washington has been the only president in our history to know personally a large proportion of the federal public servants. Between 1792 and 1861 the federal civil service increased

---

[8] Eriksson, as cited in footnote 7, p. 333.

fiftyfold—from roughly 1,000 employees to 50,000 or more. During the same period the population increased only eight times. The prediction of James Madison in 1788, that "the numbers of individuals employed under the Constitution of the United States will be much smaller than the number employed under the particular states," proved hopelessly wrong.[9] The growth of the country was demanding constant expansion of the public service, regardless of the Jeffersonian conception—accepted by many of the Jacksonians as well—of government as a necessary evil.

Finding interested and qualified applicants and making appointments soon became more than a one-man job, if it had ever been that. Even Washington had found it continually necessary to consult his friends on personnel matters. As the years went by, it became increasingly urgent for the President to obtain help and counsel, not just because it was politic to do so, but because in the United States no effective system had yet been devised to nominate large numbers of competent men for public office. The Constitution provided no answer, and the senatorial proposal of the eighteen thirties, for devolution of the selection of personnel almost entirely upon individual members of Congress to the exclusion of the President, would have been, if anything, a step backward.

In a real sense, the development of the "courtesy" system, senatorial and otherwise, was an answer to internal executive as well as external partisan problems. That it was not the only answer is clear from both the experience of the Federalists and the Jeffersonian Republicans, and from the later lessons of modern civil service reform. But, for the time being, the system sufficed.

Even so, the chief executive's appointment and removal burden often reached intolerable proportions. The diary of President Polk reveals especially well the anguish and torture to which American chief executives have often been subjected under the spoils system. The deaths of Presidents Harrison and Taylor have been related in part to the unrelenting pressure brought by seekers of public office. Even Lincoln said that he felt like "a man so busy in letting rooms in one end of his house that he cannot stop to put out the fire that is burning the other."[10] It is no wonder that much of the initiative for reform of the spoils system was later to come from the White House.

JACKSONIAN PERSONNEL ADMINISTRATION

Though the spoils system was triumphant by 1865, continuity with the past was never completely lost. One of the important contributions of Leonard D. White's analysis of the Jacksonian bureaucracy has been to point out a certain persistence

---

[9] *The Federalist* (Modern Library ed.; New York: Random House, [1937]), p. 301.
[10] Ward Hill Lamon, *Recollections of Abraham Lincoln* (Chicago: A. C. McClurg and Co., 1895), p. 212.

of the Federalist and Jeffersonian Republican tradition of tenure in office through-out the period immediately prior to the Civil War.[11] We have already noted that Jackson dismissed no more federal officers than did Jefferson. Despite the rising tide of spoils, there constantly remained a stratum of the civil service which helped to maintain continuity and competence in administration. Even the most partisan of executives could comprehend the need to maintain a basic level of administrative efficiency by retaining a few key officials. Hence the comptrollers, auditors, and chief clerks of the departmental service in Washington frequently kept their positions through several administrations. So did a portion of the minor clerks, a number of the small group of scientific and technical personnel, and the officer corps of the army and navy. In the field agencies politics reigned, though not always to the exclusion of integrity and competence. In a sense the federal service was manned and managed through two personnel systems, though at this time that governed by the principle of spoils was by far the most dominant. Ever since the time of Jackson the proper relationship between these two systems has been a matter of considerable concern and argument.

The Chief Clerks.—The details of personnel administration were largely under the jurisdiction of the chief clerks in each of the major establishments both in Washington and in the field. They maintained the employment rolls and records, exercised general supervision of employee activities, assigned work, oriented new employees, and maintained other relevant records. Training was unknown in a modern sense; promotions were relatively few, efficiency ratings in an embryonic state, and retirement policies nonexistent. There was, of course, no more legal protection against removals in the public service than in business. The government labor policy toward both blue collar workers and unions resembled that of the private administrative world. There was as yet no concept of the government as a model employer. The major difference between public and private employment lay in the hours of work. While the government offices in Washington were open from eight to ten hours a day in the eighteen thirties, for example, most clerical employees actually were on duty only six hours a day,[12] as compared to the ten to twelve hour day then common in the commercial world. Short hours, coupled with the frequent fees and other income supplements of public office, may partially account for the great interest displayed throughout the nineteenth century in all levels of public employment.

Examinations.—Only in a few aspects did the public service of the pre-Civil War era presage that of the twentieth century. Following several congressional discussions of governmental efficiency in the later eighteen forties and early fifties, the Senate on March 7, 1851, requested the cabinet officers to submit their

---

[11] As cited in footnote 5, pp. 347–62. Fish also supports this view.
[12] White, as cited in footnote 5, p. 400.

recommendations on the examination, promotion, classification, and pay of clerks in the federal establishment. The entire cabinet, except for Daniel Webster of the State Department, recommended the use of a simple, qualifying test, then described as a "pass-examination," for the initial appointment of clerks. However, in light of the constitutional appointment prerogatives of the executive, there was hesitation to make examinations compulsory. Nevertheless, in 1853 Congress made pass-examinations a requirement for entrance into a large proportion of the clerical offices in Washington. Since the testing procedure was at the mercy of department heads, its administration lacked uniformity. Pass-examinations were taken seriously mainly in connection with the appointment of fiscal employees, though the statute requiring them remained in effect until the Pendleton Act of 1883 established the present Civil Service Commission.

Where the idea of examinations for entrance into the public service originated is hard to say now. Certainly formal examinations were no part of business personnel practices at this time; and the British experience with civil service examinations, then barely under way, had as yet made no impact in America. Entrance examinations for the military academies dated from 1818 and 1819, and examinations for army surgeons were given as early as 1814. Also, before 1853 the Treasury had for a while conducted examinations for entrance into some of its accounting positions. These examinations seem to have stemmed from the practical necessities of Treasury administration, which, more than in many departments, made knowledge of certain elementary commercial techniques essential. In a report by the Secretary of the Treasury in 1854 we find the modest requirements then current:

This course of examination has required that the applicant shall—1st, be able to write an ordinary business letter, in a fair and legible hand; 2d, that he shall show himself to be acquainted with the first four rules of arithmetic, and capable of ordinary celerity in the use of them, and 3d, that he shall evince some knowledge of the generally received principles of accounting.[13]

The pre-Civil War applicants for Treasury posts were evidently not overtaxed. In all likelihood, however, these requirements were comparable to those—applied more informally, no doubt—of the typical commercial houses of the day.[14]

Shortly after the approval of pass-examinations for clerical employees, Congress provided for similar examinations for a limited number of consular "pupils." But this first attempt at deliberate development of a career foreign service died a quick death a year after its initiation. It was revived in an emasculated form in 1864. Senator John P. Hale of New Hampshire, in a typical contemporary objection to this form of recruitment, is reported as saying, "I am opposed to

---

[13] U.S. Treasury Department, *Report of the Secretary of the Treasury on the State of the Finances for the Year Ending June 30, 1854*, 33d Cong., 2d sess., House Exec. Doc. 3 (Washington, D.C.: A. O. P. Nicholson, 1854), p. 98.
[14] Unfortunately there is no history of private personnel practices in this country.

it, not because I think our consuls are educated too highly as a general fact, but I dislike this way of doing it. If we begin here where is it to stop? We shall have then to appoint pupils as ambassadors, and when you begin that, there is no ending!" General John A. Quitman, a representative from Mississippi, put it even more bluntly, saying in effect, "that consuls were diplomats and that the best diplomacy was the diplomacy of the backwoods, the honest diplomacy of republican freemen." The controversy, in the opinion of Henry Adams, reflected a continuation of long-standing legislative-executive antagonism. Congress seemed to be afraid its patronage would be cut and the President's increased.[15]

Salary Scales.—A far more lasting contribution to public personnel administration was initiated by the "classification" law of 1853. For some years departmental clerks had been complaining about the insufficiency and inequality of pay in relation to duties and responsibilities, but little had been done about it. The pay for departmental employees was still based on legislation dating from 1818.[16] Intervening enactments, which, in the continuing congressional attempt to control the executive, were becoming more and more detailed, had left the problem of regularization of pay and duties pretty much up in the air. The result was a hodge-podge of administrative and legislative regulation. A cabinet report in 1852 had recommended that some system of classes for clerical employees be devised and that pass-examinations then be required for applicants to these positions. Congress finally agreed that something should be done. By an act of March 3, 1853, it directed the heads of all the departments except the Department of State, which was included two years later, to group their Washington clerical employees under four classes, keeping in mind their actual duties. In 1854, the classes and their pay scale were as follows: Class I at $1,250, Class II at $1,400, Class III at $1,600, and Class IV at $1,800. Chief Clerks of Bureaus and Chief Clerks of Departments were to receive $2,000 and $2,200 respectively. These salaries represented, however, no great improvement over those of 1818. On the average, the increases meant perhaps a raise of $200 or so at the bottom and $100 or less at the top of the clerical grades.

Department heads were given a great deal of leeway in the required adjustment and were supposed to organize their employment force so that there was equal pay for equal work. But there was no central agency to see that this was done. Moreover, the new legislation provided systematic pay scales for less than a tenth of the federal positions. The more important officials, the employees in the field services outside Washington, and the sub-clerical and blue collar workers were excluded. In present-day terms, the laws were really nothing but salary stan-

---

[15] Hale and Quitman are quoted in Henry Brooks Adams, "Civil Service Reform," *North American Review*, Vol. CIX (October, 1896), pp. 462–63 and elsewhere.
[16] Salaries were temporarily increased in the eighteen thirties by a bonus system. The bonus system was also employed from 1864 to 1867.

dardization acts, providing only incidentally for a minimal duties-classification. Certainly they are most unimpressive to the modern classification expert. But they seem to have been the best that anyone then either could invent or considered desirable to invent. Moreover, it is important to note that the laws of 1853, 1854, and 1855[17] remained major bases for the classification and pay of the federal government's clerical employees for nearly seventy years. No major change occurred until the Classification Act of 1923 radically revised the legal and administrative bases for the description and pay of government jobs. Compensation and classification remained for the most part a matter of day-by-day legislative whim, typically applied to individual positions or small groups of positions, until the resulting unwieldy edifice threatened to collapse during World War I.[18]

In general, we can say that before the Civil War no one devised a practical program for administrative reform of the civil service. If anyone deserves credit for prophetic insight in this period, it is not Clay, Calhoun, or Webster but Senator Robert M. T. Hunter of Virginia. It was largely at the inspiration of this southerner that the pass-examination statutes of the eighteen fifties were enacted. Unfortunately, Hunter joined the Confederacy as its first Secretary of State and was thereafter lost to the federal scene.[19]

Whether the difficulty lay in the paucity of ideas or in the unfavorable political climate is difficult to determine. Undoubtedly the fact that modern standards of private business management were still in an embryonic stage had much to do with the failure to develop more systematic procedures in the public service. Certainly, almost the entire weight of contemporary political theory and practice militated against any attempt at more modern methods. A civil war and recurrent political and economic crises would be necessary to convince the average voter and the average legislator of any need for reform. There is little evidence to contradict the view that most people were quite satisfied with the organization, if not the immediate personnel, of the federal bureaucracy of pre-Civil War days.

A RADICAL INSTITUTION

In conclusion, let us briefly review the spoils system as a dynamic social institution. With the rise of the new democracy of the Jacksonian era, the public service established by the Founding Fathers became a major focal point of

---

[17] The State Department and Census Office were included at this time.

[18] The major study of the development of classification and pay standards in the American public service is Ismar Baruch, *History of Position-Classification and Salary Standardization in the Federal Service, 1789–1941* (2d ed., P.C.D. Manual No. A-2; Washington, D.C.: U.S. Civil Service Commission, 1941). See also White, *op. cit.*, pp. 376–93.

[19] See Leonard D. White, "Centennial Anniversary," *Public Personnel Review*, Vol. XIV (January, 1953), p. 3, for the story of Hunter's endeavors.

attack by the political leaders of the newly-enfranchised electorate of the nineteenth century. To the voters of 1829 the holdover bureaucracy with its roots in the discredited Federalist regime seemed the final bastion of aristocracy—hardly an object of pity in a democratic revolution.

The selection of Andrew Jackson as President personalized the power and aspirations of the new electorate. It also placed at his mercy the administrative service of the federal government. Jackson sought to adapt these services to the newly vitalized ideals of equality of opportunity, social mobility, individual freedom, and popular government. Equality was reflected in attempts to limit the tenure of office and to pass the offices around. Any suggestion that a man of average intelligence was not fit for any and all public offices was indignantly rejected as a denial of the power and wisdom of "the people." The validity of class and institutional barriers to the free rise of individual talent was vehemently attacked. Above all, the new democracy felt, if it did not always logically perceive, that exploitation of the patronage by and for the grass roots was vital to the control of a government which for so long had represented position and property.

The development of the spoils system into so pervasive an institution was undoubtedly intensified by the various constitutional, sectional, and administrative problems of the period. Spoils politics was related to the democratic ideals of an expanding nation as well as to the political and economic framework within which these ideals functioned. After 1829 the federal offices, like state and local offices before them, were used openly and explicitly as fuel for partisan purposes. In the eyes of the common man of Jacksonian persuasion, unquestionably the spoils system represented a "reform" which tightened the bond between the people and their government.

In the days of its youth the spoils system was a *radical institution* which, to the fastidious and apprehensive, did not appeal any more than the tumultous democracy it represented. Even President Jackson and many of the more responsible exponents of "reform" in 1829 would have been astonished at the "pillaging" which later developed. Still, those who would reform all things too often forget that the American federal service was politically recast to keep it responsive to the will of the people.

For many years events were such that no other system seemed possible or desirable. But, as all social institutions may carry within themselves the impetus for their own destruction, so with the spoils system. Some of the very forces behind the development of this democratic device began, even before the Civil War, to lay the groundwork for its eventual decline, if not for its complete downfall.

53.

THE TAPROOTS OF AMERICAN
PUBLIC PERSONNEL ADMINISTRATION

PAUL P. VAN RIPER

What about American public personnel management as a total conception? That is, can we describe public personnel administration in the United States as a coherent system, having some inner unity, an internal consistency, a basic logic, a form and design all its own, capable of general analysis, description and implementation?

I believe it can be so described, and this I wish to try and do, not in a final way, but perhaps in a way which may have some general utility by providing an overview of our American public service. At least let me make an attempt to see the forest of American public personnel management rather than the trees.

Expressed in another way, let me try and make some order out of chaos. For what is to follow is in direct contradiction to a frequently expressed view which says that American public personnel management is chaotic, a hodgepodge of policies and procedures, combining the worst of all worlds. We have, I think, a tendency to be hypercritical of what we have for two reasons: (1) we have not thought through what we have and why we have it; and (2), the grass in other personnel systems seems so much greener, mainly because we've never really been close enough to other systems to perceive their own many problems.

Let me offer a warning now, that what is to follow contains a distinct point of view as well as a framework of historical analysis. With respect to both I will, of necessity, somewhat overstate and oversimplify. But my analysis is based on considerable research,[1] and I believe it to be essentially correct. My point of view is quite another matter. All I can say is that it *is* my point of view, and I hope it may be useful to those who are charged with the task of formulating American public personnel policy in the critical years to come.

BASIC CHARACTERISTICS

Let us begin by briefly examining the fundamental characteristics of our public

Reprinted by permission from the March–April, vol. 25, 1962, *Personnel Administration*, pp. 12–16, 32. Copyright 1962, Society for Personnel Administration, Suites 485–487, National Press Building, 14th and F Streets, N.W., Washington, D.C. 20004.
[1] See Paul P. Van Riper, *History of the United States Civil Service* (Evanston, Ill.: Row, Peterson and Co., 1958).

personnel system as it has developed in the last 75 years since the Pendleton Act of 1883.[2]

The Pendleton Act itself cast in permanent form at least five conceptions. First, it provided for the apportionment of offices in Washington, D. C., among the states in proportion to their population. This was to guarantee a representative group of permanent civil servants in the capital, as well as to encourage opportunity for all for employment at the center of the government. Noting, for example, the lack of Southern representation in the apportioned service of the early nineteen hundreds, President Theodore Roosevelt stimulated a major drive to redress the balance. He was successful. While this clause is of relatively little significance now, it served a fundamental purpose during the first decades of the Act of 1883.

More important was the introduction of the idea of competitive examinations. These were to be nation-wide in coverage, open to all on a truly competitive basis, limited to no particular universities, no social class, and no special political point of view. Competitive examinations were by no means a new idea in 1883, but this conception of their openness and availability to all was and still is distinctive in comparison to the rest of the world.

Next was the specific requirement that the examinations be practical and as little tied in with formal educational requirements as possible. The American public service today is, in terms of formal educational requirements, as little "degree bound" as any public service in the world. We are concerned more with actual qualifications in fact, and less with pieces of paper.

Fourth, the Pendleton Act set no age limits for entrance. Indeed, Congress specifically amended the original draft of the statute by removing a provision allowing initial entrance into the service *only* "at the lowest grade." An American citizen—and even aliens in some cases—may enter whenever and wherever they are able to do so.

Finally, the result of this last provision combined with the open, practical examination system has been the concept of lateral entry—movement in and out of the service, between government and private enterprise—so noticeable under both Roosevelts and Wilson, during the Korean War, and often since, including recent months.

What does all this mean?

Except for the idea of examinations, these provisions were unique in the world of the 19th century. Together, they formed an equally unique prescription for a public service designed to recognize talent wherever it lay, in any geographical area, at any age, and regardless of formal degrees, diplomas or social status.

In passing the Pendleton Act, I do not give Congress credit for having any

---

[2] Actually one might go back to 1871 and the first Civil Service Commission under President Grant. The Pendleton Act and much subsequent public personnel policy and practice derived from this earlier experience.

explicit civil service theory, nor do I credit the civil service reformers too much, for they would have introduced the British system intact, with all its age, degree, university, and perhaps even class limits. In the U. S. we do not operate theoretically; we operate pragmatically. Almost without being aware of it Congress created in 1883 a civil service system uniquely fitted to a classless society[3] in which the individual's capabilities mattered, rather than where he was from or his formal educational or other status.

Basically, the central theme of the Pendleton Act was absurdly simple, but, in its simplicity, also revolutionary. Whenever the common man could pass a test for a job, he could come into the government, often to high place. There were few other barriers. This was a new and radically different approach to developing a national civil service from any put into law before this.

MORE RECENT DEVELOPMENTS

In support of this new approach to public personnel management a number of additional actions have been taken since 1883.

We have refused to allow only for promotion from within. Though not specifically provided for in the Pendleton Act, access by all qualified persons, whether in the government or not at any specified time, to all types of positions was clearly implied by no age limits for entrance as well as by open, competitive examinations. Nor have we ever tied promotion to many formal requirements.

We have developed a classification system which permits and encourages movement in and out. Work has been divided into segments capable of using interchangeable parts, so to speak.

Contrary to England and elsewhere in Europe, we have not segregated the scientific and professional man off to the side. If he can do the work, he, too, may aspire to a top post in general management.

We have gone far to eliminate discrimination, not only on the grounds of politics and religion (as provided since 1883) but also because of race, sex, and national origin.

We have not bound our top political management, or our career management, so tightly that there is no discretion in the recognition of talent—especially not in comparison to foreign systems.

We have refused to countenance the closed shop in public employment. For a firm—and still final—statement and stand on this issue we are again indebted to Theodore Roosevelt.

We have refused to accept seniority as the sole basis of promotion.

---

[3] Classless in the sense of European classes and European sensitivity to the permanence of class position and boundaries.

We have strengthened, by a statute of 1956, the rules against requiring formal education to qualify for other than certain scientific and professional work.

And we have refused to close the door to lateral entry at all levels and all ages.

All in all, what we have developed is a civil service system which is one of the best attuned in the world today to the requirements of a mobile society, which would recognize talent wherever it is and from whatever social or economic strata of American life. We have developed what I have elsewhere chosen to term an "opportunity" type of career system,[4] as opposed to the closed career systems typical of the rest of the Western world—and most of the Eastern.

Our system *is* a "system," a coherent one, which is in its main parts internally consistent. They are all aimed at the same end, the free entry of talent into the government and its relatively free movement therein.

INTO THE FUTURE

Looking into the future, is such a system still relevant? I strongly hold that it is, for a number of reasons.

Above all, we must utilize all of our available talent to the utmost. The why's and wherefore's of this are patently obvious.

If talent can rise regardless of prior economic and social status, it is channeled constructively to constructive social purposes, and not into frustration, agitation, and often fruitless conflict and unrest.

Our opportunity system of public employment is the only approach to governmental administration which gives management a real opportunity to manage and to select and recognize talent wherever it can find it.

This is the only approach which is consonant with the basic social concept, recognized since 1776, of equality of opportunity.

Indeed, this is the only approach consonant with democracy itself and with individual freedom, for freedom is not such without opportunity to rise through one's own efforts as far as one can.

What I am proposing is simply this: that the measure of all proposals to further refine and refurbish our civil service system at all levels shall be *one basic and essentially simple criterion: do any such proposals not only permit but encourage our government, whatever the governing party, to utilize quickly such administrative and technical talent as may be available throughout our great nation?*

To put the matter another way, in the form of a series of questions:

1. Are we capable of reducing not only the traditional barriers of politics, race, sex, religion and national origin, but also what I will call the newer barriers of formal degrees and diplomas, seniority, versions of the closed shop, economic status, promo-

---

4 Van Riper, *op. cit.*, pp. 553–58.

tion solely from within, and overly managed development programs which may prematurely limit and discourage as well as assist upward movement?

2. Are we capable of developing administrators who are willing to recognize talent wherever it is and give it a chance along with a suitable reward in terms of money, status, and power to act?

3. Will we permit our administrators to manage and to continue to select subordinate managers with as few limits as possible in terms of seniority, degrees, status, position-classification requirements, promotion and transfer regulations, appeals and the like?

4. Are we willing—and here we've not done all we could—to take the consequences of the recognition of talent? That is, in the name of the future of our country —which depends on an able, efficient civil service, are we willing to permit, with a minimum of interference and without tying up everything in the courts, the weeding out of the service of those who are not just corrupt and grossly inefficient, but also those who are marginal or even average? This is the other side of the coin of equality of opportunity, and it is equally crucial.

5. Finally, are those of you actively engaged in personnel and general administration helping positively not only to bring in and recognize those of skill and ability, but are you also helping in a positive way to weed out—call it "selection out" if you like a softer term—those who are in the way of those who are better? Yours is a double-barrelled task and it must be dealt with as such!

We claim to be democratic and we ascribe (sic) to the concept of equality of opportunity. Moreover, we are fortunate in that the bulk of our people are ambitious, eager to learn, eager for something useful and important to do, socially and geographically mobile, uncommitted to the limited ideals of any single social class, and openminded and pragmatic rather than ideologically limited in their concepts of action.

The basic framework of our public personnel system has recognized and has been built on the foundations of this kind of mobile social system. And our personnel systems, both public and private, have thus far in turn reinforced this social system by providing upward channels of mobility for those with vision, talent, and drive. Contrary to some popular opinions, all present evidence points to the conclusion that it is as easy in the United States as it ever was for men and women of ability to move from low socio-economic status to high position in one lifetime.[5] It is absolutely crucial that, in every aspect of American life, this characteristic social tendency not only continue but in every way be reinforced— and reinforced, above all, in public life.

CONCLUSION

To sum up, I do not argue that our personnel system is now perfect. My criticisms are implicit in the above criteria. But I maintain that its basic conception

---

[5] See, for example, W. Lloyd Warner and James C. Abegglen, *Occupational Mobility in American Business and Industry* (Minneapolis: University of Minnesota Press, 1955), pp. 35–36.

is both coherent and sound. The problem is to realize it fully.

This suggests, in turn, that the public personnel—indeed, much of the general administrative—task today is double-barrelled: (1) to devise and support procedures which bring in to the public service and reward talent wherever it may be found, and (2) to devise and support procedures which weed out or hold to their maximum role those of lesser ability.

Public administrators must be ruthless in both, for this is the price of excellence, and we can have no less in our public service. But pay and procedures are not enough, and it is one of the mistakes of the past decade to often assume that they are. They are important; but after all, it was in the thirties, when public personnel administration was a procedural chaos and pay was anything but munificent, that there occurred one of the most impressive free flows of talent into the service that has ever been seen.

That is, the final task is more subtle. What I have proposed with respect to public personnel management means nothing if we do not at the same time emphasize the long-run meaning and importance of the administration of public affairs. If we are to attract men and women of great ability and energy into the public service, we must somehow bring home to them and the public at large the exciting ultimate and overriding values of taking an active part in directing the affairs of a nation which is engaged in the greatest competitive struggle for national survival and national purpose the world has ever known.

54.

VETERANS' PREFERENCE: POLICIES AT POTENTIAL CROSS-PURPOSES

PAUL P. VAN RIPER

. . . Out of the First World War came the first full scale, enforced veteran preference regulations.[1] This time the veretans did not make the mistake of Civil War veterans who waited until memories were dim. They organized quickly and secured the swift enactment of several sweeping preferential provisions by

From pp. 269–271, and 423–424, *History of the United States Civil Service*, by Paul P. Van Riper. Copyright © 1958 by Harper & Row, Publishers, Incorporated. Reprinted by permission of the publishers.
[1] The principal reference work on veteran preference is USCSC, *History of Veteran Preference in Federal Employment* (Washington, D.C.: U.S. Government Printing Office, 1955).

Congress. The first was contained in a section of the census act of March 3, 1919, which granted preference in the Washington departments only. The second was a part of the deficiency act of July 11, 1919, and provided for preference generally throughout the classified service. Not only were honorably discharged veterans themselves included but also their widows and the wives of those too disabled to obtain government employment. Finally, by congressional act and executive order, age limits were waived; veterans were permitted to go to the top of the registers for which they received passing marks; their passing mark was made five points lower than that for nonveterans; many physical requirements were waived; and reinstatement privileges were liberalized. The Civil Service Commission analyzed the situation in its report for 1919 and concluded that, while the preference laws might not then react to the detriment of the service, they might in the future when there were fewer veterans and only the more inefficient were searching for employment.[2]

From March, 1919, to November, 1920, the Commission received 80,000 claims for preference. Of these 75,000 were allowed, and 60,000 claimants succeeded in passing the examinations. A total of 15,750 of these were appointed. About 1,500 veterans were reinstated in the same period.[3] The result was that for the year 1920 veterans comprised 13.6 per cent of the total number appointed. This figure rose to 28.91 per cent the following year and to the highest figure that it ever reached before World War II, 34.12 per cent, in 1923. During only one year from 1921 to 1940 were veterans less than 20 per cent of the total number of appointees.[4]

At its second national convention the American Legion indicated that it had established satisfactory liaison with the Civil Service Commission and that veterans were actually receiving the preference to which they were legally entitled.[5] Of course, from time to time there developed questions of interpretation and policy as to the relative preference of various classes of appointees as well as the total amount and form of the preference. President Harding made a major adjustment in these factors in 1923 when he distinguished between nondisabled and disabled veterans and established our present form of 5 and 10-point preference for nondisabled and disabled veterans, respectively. Both types of veterans lost their privilege of going to the top of the registers, but retained their below-normal passing marks of 65 and 60. After complaints that disabled veterans were not receiving adequate appointments, President Coolidge again placed dis-

---

[2] USCSC, *Thirty-sixth Report* (Washington, D.C.: U.S. Government Printing Office, 1919), pp. xvi–xix.
[3] USCSC, *Thirty-seventh Report* (Washington, D.C.: U.S. Government Printing Office, 1920), pp. xiv–xvi.
[4] USCSC, *Fifty-seventh Report* (Washington, D.C.: U.S. Government Printing Office, 1940), p. 134.
[5] USCSC, *Thirty-seventh Report* (Washington, D.C.: U.S. Government Printing Office, 1920), p. xiv.

abled veterans, along with the wives of those too disabled to obtain employment and the widows of all kinds of veterans, at the top of the registers. At the same time all veterans were accorded preference over nonveterans of equal efficiency in case of reductions-in-force. During the twenties and thirties no other special preference was granted veterans with respect to removals.[6]

By 1934 veterans occupied approximately one-fourth of the total positions in the federal civil service. This was a large proportion of the service to come from a group which then composed less than 10 per cent of the total adult population.[7] A few studies have been made of the effects of veteran preference upon the nature of the government service, but most of these indicate no more than that a number of types of positions have been largely occupied by veterans.[8] The results in terms of morale and efficiency have not been measured. It is questionable if they could be, and with the influx of veterans from World War II it is unlikely that the full effects of the preference resulting from the First World War will ever be determined.

From a chronological standpoint, veteran preference has antedated the merit system in most governmental jurisdictions. However, a full application of veteran preference is possible only under a centralized personnel system, and the two have developed hand in hand. The principal impetus for the preference system seems to have arisen from a combination of humanitarianism and recognition of the importance of veteran voting power. In 1920 preference aided the civilian relocation of veterans by providing an additional source of employment for ex-military personnel. At the same time it also provoked additional administrative friction and dislocation in a government service already suffering from an increasing turnover in personnel. As preference came more into prominence, merit probably tended to retreat, for the two have seldom been synonymous. However, there is very little evidence from which to draw satisfactory conclusions for the period between the two World Wars. . . .[9]

. . . In accord with the intent of the Veterans' Preference Act of 1944, a special effort was made to attract qualified veterans into the service, as well as to see that veterans' rights were protected. A special Veterans Service Section was formed within the Commission. An extensive program, involving the cooperation

---

[6] For other details, such as credit for military experience, reinstatement, apportionment, etc., see USCSC, *History of Veteran Preference in Federal Employment, op. cit.,* pp. 6–14.

[7] This estimate is by the Chief Examiner of the Civil Service Commission, April 12, 1934, as quoted in Commission of Inquiry on Public Service Personnel, *Problems of the American Public Service* (New York: McGraw-Hill Book Co., 1935), p. 277.

[8] See, for example, the statistics on veterans contained in the Commission's *Forty-eighth Report* (Washington, D.C.: U.S. Government Printing Office, 1931, pp. 10–11, and 96.

[9] For a comparative study of veteran preference here and abroad, see Albert G. Huegli, "A Study of Veterans' Preference in the Civil Service" (unpublished Ph.D. dissertation, Department of Political Science, Northwestern University, 1944). See also John P. McCarthy, "Veterans' Preference in Public Employment" (unpublished Master's thesis, Department of Political Science, University of Chicago, 1947).

of regional veterans federal employment representatives, the Federal Personnel Council, and the officials of veterans organizations was also undertaken. As a result of both the great number of returning veterans and the Commission's special efforts to place them, there was an increase in the percentage of the civil service with veteran status from 31 to 47 per cent between June 30, 1946, and June 30, 1949.[10] What the full effects of veteran preference have been or will be is a highly arguable question, capable of generating considerable heat in Washington and elsewhere. The fact that the veteran population is relatively young and represents a full-scale cross-section of potential employees with somewhat more than average health and ability means that the service should not suffer for some time to come. Moreover, preference does not apply to promotions. Still, it is clear that preference fosters procedural red tape and that it may hamper the employment or retention of the most qualified persons.

From the point of view of recruitment and placement, the greatest criticism has been levied against the so-called "absolute" 10 point preference, granted primarily to disabled veterans and resulting in their placement at the top of a register even though their passing score may only be 60. Legislation in 1953 modified these preference provisions by permitting the 5 and 10 point preference bonus to be added to a veteran's score only if he first made a passing grade of 70. In addition, persons receiving the 10 point preference bonus were no longer entitled to be placed at the top of the register unless they had been certified as having at least a 10 per cent disability. These amendments to the veteran preference legislation somewhat reduced the criticism against veteran preference, but did not fully resolve the problem. This was especially true for appointing officers who still frequently found the tops of appointment registers clogged with disabled veterans and other 10 point preference recipients, with the result that it was difficult to reach for appointment many of those really best qualified. There are various ways to circumvent this difficulty, but they are often time-consuming or politically dangerous, with the result that administrators are reluctant to use them. The matter of 10 point absolute preference has been a constant source of irritation contributing neither to the efficiency nor morale of the service, however beneficial to those receiving the preference. Several attempts were made during the Truman administration, particularly after the report of the First Hoover Commission, to modify the preference provisions, but none was successful. . . .

---

[10] USCSC, *Sixty-sixth Report*, 1949, p. 13. By 1949 some 57 per cent of the men and 10 per cent of the women in the service were entitled to preference. *Ibid.*, p. 42. The employment of veterans then leveled off and the proportion of veterans in the civil service remained at approximately 50 per cent during the period from 1949 to 1958. For a more complete analysis of veteran preference in the federal service, see USCSC, *History of Veteran Preference in Federal Employment* (Washington, D.C.: U.S. Government Printing Office, 1955). For a critic's view of preference at this time, see Samuel H. Ordway, Jr., "The Veteran in the Civil Service," *The Annals*, Vol. CCXXXVIII (March, 1945), p. 133.

55.

STATE AND LOCAL MANPOWER:
A CHALLENGE TO CREATIVE FEDERALISM

David B. Walker

THE INTERPRETERS

"Creative federalism"—like federalism itself—means many things to many people. To conservative critics, "It could," in the words of one recent Wall Street *Journal* editorial, "only make the federal government more the senior partner in anything and everything, than it already is" and it becomes thus "an ingenious concept, . . . but too ready a cover for governmental giantism." According to the Free Society Association, a conservative group headed by Senator Goldwater's campaign manager Denison Kitchel, creative federalism "simply decentralizes a few administrative activities—just for convenience' sake and . . . all vital decisions are made at the top, in Washington, where the power rests." Thus the Appalachia, National Teachers' Corps, Demonstration Cities, and rural renewal programs—to mention only a few—are attacked by these conservatives on grounds that none of them "disperse power along with their generous handouts." "The real difficulty with all these developments, insofar as the federal system is concerned," as Robert Taft, Jr. put it in a recent article, "is that State and local responsibility and concern evaporate when financial support and control move elsewhere."

Unlike these conservatives, cynical observers fail to find much direction or substance in "creative federalism." Some view it as a slogan used only for political purposes and without any precise meaning. Other skeptics see it as a device for putting the Johnson brand on divergent and frequently inconsistent proposals, programs, and procedures involving Federal-State-local relations. The President's failure thus far to provide an in-depth explanation of the concept, and the Administration's tendency to tag nearly all new domestic programs with this label, lend some support to these contentions.

More sympathetic interpreters of the President's efforts, however, see in "creative federalism" a new and meaningful approach to resolving the Nation's economic and social problems. One Presidential adviser recently explained it this way:

Reprinted from remarks made at the Public Personnel Association, 38th Eastern Regional Conference, San Juan, Puerto Rico, June 7, 1966. Some editorial omissions have been made.

We have more national programs because new problems are recognized as national problems. But we realize these problems have different aspects in each region or state or town, and there must be flexibility. The President cannot be governor of 50 states and mayor of 2,000 communities. Creative federalism is essentially a search for ways to get that flexibility in federally financed programs.

. . . . .

CREATIVE FEDERALISM: A MEANINGFUL GOAL?

What, then, is "creative federalism"? Are the conservative critics correct in their assessment? Are the cynics? Or are the proponents?

. . . . .

Careful analysis of these Presidential pronouncements, and of the Administration's programs and practice, will—I believe—show that "creative federalism" is a meaningful goal, not a simplistic slogan.

First, creative federalism emphasizes that there should be greater cooperation and more effective and flexible administration in joint-action pregrams—between all levels of government, and between government and private organizations and individuals. At the same time, it recognizes that competition and problems of program coordination inevitably arise as the pluralism of American life is enriched with the development of new centers of power and influence.

Second, creative federalism does not make the national government, as conservative critics contend, the senior member in a partnership to improve the economic and social welfare of all people; instead, it relies on joint Federal-State-local efforts, joint planning, and joint financing to achieve this high purpose, rather than on direct Federal action; and this is best symbolized by the extraordinary expansion of grants-in-aid during the past $2^1/_2$ years.

Third, creative federalism is not a Machiavellian maneuver to make the States and their localities financially dependent on the national government, as critics like Roscoe Drummond allege; the tax cut early in the Johnson Administration did much to strengthen the fiscal position of these jurisdictions, and the doubling of Federal grant funds from 1961 to fiscal year 1967 merely constituted a national response to the staggering fiscal burden under which these other levels labor.

Fourth, creative federalism is not a devious device to strengthen the power position of the Federal bureaucracy. Federal personnel, after all, increased by 200,000 since 1961, but declined by more than 100,000 between 1946 and 1966, while State and local employment increased by 4.7 million during this 20-year period. Moreover, those who know anything of the national legislative process and of how grant programs are enacted are acutely aware of Congress' constant concern with protecting State and local interests. Further, those who know anything of the administration of Federal grant programs know that governors and other State administrators, county executives, mayors, and interest groups are neither voiceless nor powerless when confronting Federal administrators.

Finally, as Senator Edmund S. Muskie declared in a major Senate address on this topic March, 1966:

Creative federalism is not concerned with the dialogue of States' rights and local rights versus centralized Federal power. This debate belongs to the past. Instead, it accepts the expanding role of State and local governments to take on greater political and administrative responsibilities as the Nation grows. At the same time, it relies on a strengthened Federal role to provide new ideas, incentives, and resources to the States and localities to meet common goals.

Greater cooperation, greater financial assistance, more effective administration of joint-action programs, and a greater recognition of the States and local governments as positive partners in our federal union—these are some of the integral features of "creative federalism," and these are concrete concerns of this Administration.

THE MISSING DIMENSION

One of the most critical dimensions of contemporary intergovernmental relations—manpower—has yet to become a major focal point of "creative federalism." The President briefly touched on it in his May 11 address at Princeton University when he endorsed a national program to assist "State and local gevernments seeking to develop more effective career services for their employees." But this was the first Administration recognition that the personnel problems of these jurisdictions constitute a challenge to "creative Federalism" and to the Great Society.

Thanks largely to the fact that Congress is not oblivious to critical intergovernmental issues, we already have such a national program. On May 25th, Senator Edmund S. Muskie, chairman of the Senate Subcommittee on Intergovernmental Relations, introduced the proposed Intergovernmental Personnel Act of 1966. This measure grew out of an increasing awareness on the part of the Senator and his Subcommittee:

That good management practices alone will not improve intergovernmental relations;
That additional Federal financial assistance alone will not resolve the difficulties of State and local governments;
That greater flexibility and uniformity in the administration of grant programs alone will not lessen the tension between the levels of government; and
That a greater decentralization of decision-making alone will not reduce the pressures on Washington.

In its survey "The Federal System as Seen by Federal Aid Officials," the Subcommittee on Intergovernmental Relations found that interlevel personnel problems were one of the weakest links in the chain of intergovernmental collaboration. The 109 middle-management administrators of Federal grants participating in this study indicated a basic awareness that the success of their programs depended in large measure on the talents of their State and local administrative counterparts. With the increase in the number and scope of Federal aids, they recognized that implementation of joint-action programs has become a major responsibility of State and local governments, and they conceded that the rapid expansion of this administrative partnership necessitates a reexamination of intergovernmental personnel relationships.

In general, these Federal aid administrators were skeptical of, indeed largely hostile to, existing State and local personnel practices. A substantial majority expressed concern over low salaries, the inadequacy of in-service training programs, and the lack of across-the-board merit systems. More than three-quarters considered the inability to transfer retirement benefits and the loss of seniority rights as significant deterrents to job mobility. And, in a rare display of innovative enthusiasm, a majority agreed that the operation of their programs would benefit with the establishment of a federally-supported in-service training program.

The responses of these Federal executives were largely conditioned by their desire to extend their own standards of specialized competence to their administrative counterparts at the other levels, and to thwart any injection of partisan politics into their functional relationships. These concerns underscore the accuracy of Professor Charles Adrian's assessment that in our cooperative federal system, conflict does not stem from the relations between the levels of government as such, but in two other ways. First, "friction results whenever the administrative personnel of a particular level for a particular function is not fully professionalized." Second, there is friction between the bureaucracy and the legislature at all levels, and this rises out of "the difference in values, interests, constituencies of the two decision-making groups." In effect, the Federal middle-management aid officials participating in the Subcommittee's survey were seeking in their own way to reduce tension in both areas.

While the particular purpose of these administrators may be questioned—and the Subcommittee staff was conscious of their special bias—the survey's findings deserve the close attention of all who are seriously interested in creating a genuinely creative federalism. The report dramatized what may be obvious to you, but not so obvious to many public officials at all levels and to the public-at-large:

That, on a day-to-day basis, intergovernmental relations today are chiefly administrative relations;

That the administration of joint-action programs is always a mutual and, ideally, a professional undertaking;

That the failure of State and local governments to upgrade the caliber of their public service has generated one of the basic tensions in contemporary Federal-State-local relations; and

That a manpower crisis presently exists at these levels, and the Federal Government, the States, and their localities must join in confronting it, if the goals of the Great Society are to be achieved.

THE DYNAMIC METABOLISM OF STATE AND LOCAL GOVERNMENTS

As a follow-up on these survey findings, Senator Muskie instructed the Subcommittee staff to determine the dimensions of the manpower crisis and what steps might be taken to alleviate it. Our research revealed that the roots of the crisis stemmed from the paramount fact that States and localities—not Washington—have shouldered most of the burden of meeting the mounting public demand for more and better governmental services—during the past two decades. This dramatic performance can be chronicled in terms of money and in terms of manpower.

First, the facts of fiscal federalism reveal there has been a shift in the balance of governmental finances over the past two decades:

Of total revenues raised by all levels of government in 1946, State and local governments accounted for only 23 percent; by 1965, their share was 43 percent.

Of total governmental expenditures in 1946, State and local governments accounted for only 15 percent; in 1964, this had increased to 42 percent.

State and local governments accounted for only 5 percent of the total public debt in 1946; today their share has increased to 23 percent.

State and local governments, then, have been and are under great pressure to increase outlays for public services, and this will continue for the foreseeable future. They have made extraordinary efforts in the past two decades to meet their rising needs—to the extent that last year, their expenditures constituted 68 percent of all spending for civil government. And five years from now, their expenditures are expected to reach the $120 billion mark—or $10 billion more than the projected Federal budget for all purposes—including defense and foreign policy commitments.

Second, developments in the manpower area have paralleled those relating to money. State and local employment has now reached the 8 million mark, an increase of 130 percent over the 1946 figure. Analysis of the evolving employment pattern for State and local governments reveals some striking shifts from that of a generation ago. From 1954 to 1964, special districts, school districts, townships, and States—and in that order—enjoyed higher employment rates than the 4.3 percent average annual increase that characterized overall State and local hiring during this decade. In terms of functional categories, State and local employment in police protection increased by 30 percent from 1957 to 1965, and in public health and hospitals by 41 percent. The number of full-time public employees in education soared by 60 percent, and those in public welfare by 62 percent. Finally, of the total manpower involved with civil governmental functions, the State and local sector now accounts for over 80 percent. In short, the State and local public service has experienced a remarkable transformation during the past two decades—in terms of size, hiring units, occupational composition, and added responsibilities.

The reasons for this massive growth are known to most of us. The population boom, the demand for expanded services generated by it, the physical and social problems stemming from urbanization and suburbanization, and the unwillingness of an increasing number of American citizens to settle for the level and quality of services provided a generation ago—these are the more obvious causes for this employment explosion. But others should be noted. The rejuvenation of the States and of the smaller, non-metropolitan local governments figure in this development. The disproportionate growth in the size of those age groups requiring extensive public services—the young and the old—is another factor that must be considered. And the stimulating effect of expanded Federal grant-in-aid programs and activity cannot be ignored.

Much of the recent Federal aid legislation merely provides the funds necessary to attain certain general goals, but leaves the job of implementation to the States, the counties, and the cities. These jurisdictions then have had to "staff up" to accomplish the objectives of this legislation. And with project grants, Federal departments merely play the role of disbursing agencies that underwrite plans and projects that are initiated, developed, and ultimately administered by States and localities.

Most of this largely unheralded revolution in State and local employment, then, can be explained in terms of dynamic demographic and social developments that have affected all levels. But, as I have noted, Federal action, directly or indirectly, has also been a contributing factor. So we have reached the point now where States employ more than 2 million workers with a monthly payroll of $850 million, and where local governments employ nearly 6 million workers with a monthly payroll of $2.5 billion. We have also reached the point where we can take little comfort in these figures.

THE GROWING MANPOWER GAP

The foregoing clearly demolishes the myth that the States and localities are withering under the glare of a Federal sun. But it does not clearly indicate that manpower is one of the most critical intergovernmental issues confronting us.

The galloping growth rates, after all, tend to conceal the many troublesome topics that have combined to create a crisis situation.

Recent reports, however, indicate that there already exists a shortage of well-trained and highly-qualified personnel—especially in the administrative, professional, and technical categories—at all levels. As you so well know, many well-trained and well-qualified employees of State and local government were hired during the Depression years and are now approaching retirement age. More than one-third of all municipal executives, for example, fall into this category and are slated for retirement in this decade. And a recent survey of New York City revealed that one out of every five budgeted positions of a professional, managerial, or technical nature (but excluding education) was vacant, and that many others were filled with people not fully qualified. Equally significant, more or less similar conditions exist in many other cities.

When the long-range implications of prospective State and local manpower needs are considered, this gap yawns even wider. As the President pointed out in his recent Princeton University speech:

By 1970, our State governments must grow by more than 600,000 to keep pace with the times. Employment for State and local government will exceed 10 million persons. Each year over the next decade, our Nation will need 200,000 new public school teachers to keep up with the growing population.

Other somber statistics can also be cited. Witness these facts:

Approximately half the Nation's municipal health directors will be eligible for retirement within the next ten years;

Two hundred vacancies for traffic engineers will occur annually in the years ahead, but only approximately 50 new graduates will be available each year in this specialized field;

Two vacancies will exist for every graduate of a university course in city or regional management; and

By 1980, local governments alone will have to recruit approximately 300,000 additional administrative and professional employees to maintain their current program objectives.

These forecasts of manpower shortages have implications extending far beyond the individual programs, communities, and States that are affected. They indicate that we cannot be sanguine about that 8 million employment figure. They reveal that State and local governments generally—and not just a few of these jurisdictions—are having serious difficulty now in attracting and holding professional, managerial, and technical personnel, and that these jurisdictions will face even greater difficulties in the years ahead. Finally, they underscore the accuracy of Stephen K. Bailey's assessment—in a *Reporter* magazine article—of the real threat to Great Society programs:

Probably no series of legislative enactments in U.S. history has created more conflicts and administrative problems than those recently passed under Lyndon Johnson's leadership. They have three things in common: their implementation cuts across existing departmental and agency lines within the Federal Government; they demand heroic responses from State and local governments if they are to succeed; they require a combination of technical and administrative skills that are critically scarce in the society at large. Despite the demands of the war in Vietnam, the critical shortage is not money but people to carry out the programs and effective administrative machinery. Neither Medicare nor aid to education nor the poverty program has either of these at the moment.

THE REASONS FOR A FULL-FLEDGED FEDERAL RESPONSE

These estimates of State and local personnel shortages, then, clearly indicate that manpower is as critical to improved intergovernmental relations and to "creative federalism" as any other single issue. At the Federal level, the personnel problem has received almost continuous attention since President Kennedy's appointment of the Randall Commission in 1961. At the State and local levels, however, it is only beginning to be recognized as a topic worthy of national concern.

During the past quarter of a century, Federal involvement in the intergovernmental personnel field has been largely restricted to three areas: political neutrality, merit requirement in certain aid programs, and training for personnel involved with specific grants-in-aid. The control respecting neutrality in politics has brought to life significant problems in achieving compliance, and about the pertinence and scope of the statutes themselves. Merit requirements, on the other hand, as Professor Harry W. Reynolds has pointed out, "have strengthened fledgling professionalism in State personnel systems, but encountered impediments insofar as rectifying shortcomings in many traditional wellsprings of patronage." And, while training assistance has been increasing in recent years (some estimates put the annual figure at $2.5 billion in Federal funds), it is still geared largely to certain categories of specialized personnel, and to needs as seen by Federal aid administrators.

The findings of the Senate Subcommittee on Intergovernmental Relations indicate to me that today this Federal response is inadequate. As I see it, we must mount a broad-gauged attack on the many forces that face us on the manpower front. Piecemeal resistance no longer will suffice. The threat is just that critical.

Economy and efficiency dictate this kind of Federal concern, for the wisest use of the grant-in-aid dollar depends in part on the caliber of State and local administrators. Improved public administration makes it necessary, for the success of all State and local programs and most Federal grants depends on the competence of these officials. Improved intergovernmental cooperation requires it, for administrative conflict develops when administrators at the State and local levels are not fully professional. The manpower requirements of State and local governments—both present and prospective—clearly dictate it, since the Federal Government needs an effective public service at these levels as much as do these jurisdictions themselves. Finally, the ultimate fate of most of the Great Society programs directly depends on the career competence of thousands of State and local employees.

A NATIONAL INTERGOVERNMENTAL PERSONNEL PROGRAM

At Princeton, the President called for a national program of assistance to "State and local governments seeking to develop more effective career services for their employees." On May 15th, Senator Edmund S. Muskie introduced the proposed Intergovernmental Personnel Act of 1966 (S. 3408). I believe this measure constitutes a realistic response to many of the critical challenges that confront us in this vital area. I also believe that it constitutes a national program that will implement the President's stated goal.

The main purpose of this legislation is to encourage State and local governments to improve the quality of their own public service. It does this by focusing on three prime problems in the personnel area: merit requirements, personnel administration, and in-service training programs.

First, this legislation authorizes the President to extend merit system requirements to more grant-in aid programs. At present, only nine grants contain such requirements. And only 28 States and only our larger cities have broad-gauge merit systems in operation today. But, as one expert has explained it:

A merit system provides a quest for and a flow into public career jobs, through open competition, of the highest available competence for current performance and potential for growth to meet the future needs of dynamic government. It is responsive to the democratic mandate, and excludes from the career service jobs of political leadership to determine political change.

To most of us, merit, like motherhood, is above debate. But this provision of the bill has already generated considerable debate. After all, for 22 States the merit principle applies primarily to those departments administering Federal grants subject to this requirement and, in only a few other instances, to one or more additional executive departments. Moreover, in smaller non-metropolitan jurisdictions and in many counties, merit is truly a principle and rarely a practice.

Yet the record shows that the impact of the Federal legislation requiring merit standards has been a primary factor in sustaining the principle in these jurisdictions. Moreover, the administration of these regulations has been carried out with a minimum of discomfort and political controversy.

For these reasons, I believe that requirements establishing "a system of public employment, operating under public rules, and based, among other factors, on competitive examinations, equal pay for equal work, tenure contingent on successful performance, promotion on evaluated capacity and service" should be extended to more grant-in-aid programs.

Title I of the proposed legislation provides for this by giving the President the authority to apply them to such additional grant programs as he sees fit. The language of this provision recognizes the difficulties of extending the merit system to all grant-in-aid programs. It recognizes the troubles inherent in attempting to apply it to many of the recently enacted programs. Yet, it encourages action in those grant programs which involve sizeable Federal funds and are continuing, rather than experimental, endeavors.

The proposed measure also strengthens the merit system in yet another way by providing that the grants authorized for improving State personnel administration in Title II may be used to strengthen or extend the career civil service. In short, nearly all personnel experts, most of the larger cities, the majority of the States, and the Federal Government recognize the relationship between recruiting and retaining capable public servants and the presence of a meaningful merit system. These provisions of the Intergovernmental Personnel Act are rooted in this relationship.

· · · · ·

Second, the proposed legislation recognizes that State and local resources in personnel administration have not kept pace with the growth of the programs they administer. With few exceptions, State and local personnel agencies have not been equipped or given additional support for new workloads. For example, 27 States in 1961, according to one Public Personnel Association report, had no employees engaged in full-time training activities in their central personnel offices. Today, only 10 States have as many as 25 professional, administrative, and technical employees in their civil service or merit system agencies to cope with their continuing responsibilities—let alone to undertake expanded efforts. Again, a fiscal fact tells the story: the combined budgets for these agencies amounted to a mere .06 percent of total State expenditures for fiscal 1964.

The Muskie measure comes to grips with the personnel management problem. Title II authorizes a program of grants to enable States to strengthen their personnel administration, to provide State personnel services to smaller local jurisdictions, and to stimulate projects for the improvement of personnel administration in our larger cities. Qualifying States would develop programs of personnel improvement which might cover such timely topics as planning for a State's future manpower needs, extension of the State merit system, improved recruitment and examination programs, or even demonstration projects in electronic data processing and motivational research. In 1963, the New England civil service directors recommended:

Federal personnel policy should include more assistance to State civil service agencies in establishing new classifications, administering examinations and certifications relating to new programs supported by Federal funds. Policies should be refurbished in concept to emphasize "assistance to States" as the true operational symbol.

This provision of the bill implements this proposal.

Grants are also authorized under the title to improve the personnel administration of smaller units of local government. There is a pressing need here for pioneering State assistance to our non-metropolitan local jurisdictions. Generally, such units are not in a position to establish modern personnel systems, and they have comparatively greater difficulty in recruiting competent professional personnel. Funds are provided, then, for development State plans that might involve broader coverage of local employees under a merit system, State technical personnel services to these units of government, cooperative research and demonstration projects between these levels, or cooperative interlevel efforts with regard to loans, transfers, or promotion of personnel.

The last part of this title authorizes a separate program of Federal assistance for personnel improvement in our larger cities. Project grants are authorized for metropolitan personnel management that might cover a wide variety of purposes, including long-range personnel planning, the upgrading of personnel agencies, the improvement of one or more of the traditional personnel functions, or initiation of pilot projects geared to meeting special urban needs—such as the identification of new types of auxiliary jobs that will be required to meet shortages in many professional and technical fields—and exploration of the possibilities for job training and employment of the disadvantaged.

This title of S. 3408 would be administered by the Division of State Merit Systems of the Department of Health, Education, and Welfare, in that this unit has had more practical experience with State personnel systems than any other in the Federal Government. The concurrence of the Department of Housing and Urban Development, however, would be required before HEW could approve projects for metropolitan jurisdictions.

In addition to these grants for strengthening personnel administration, the proposed legislation provides another means for improving intergovernmental collaboration in this field. Title V of the Act authorizes the Civil Service Commission to join on a shared-cost basis with States or units of general local government, or both, in cooperative recruitment and examinations. A current draft report on "Modernizing Local Government"—prepared by the Council for Economic Development—urges that Federal registers be made available for the use of State and local governments, and that these governments cooperate whenever it appears to be advantageous. This title implements this recommendation.

In these ways, the Muskie bill squarely confronts many of the more difficult personnel management questions to which all levels of government must today provide answers. The amounts authorized are modest, and cooperative arrangements are permissive. Nevertheless, the funds will be seed money well spent, and the devices for cooperation will facilitate a concerted attack on a critical common problem.

. . . . .

Third, closely linked to the merit system and personnel management problems is the need for more and better training opportunities. The traditional functions of State and local government have been revolutionized by new technology and the changing character of American society. Skilled and professional personnel are needed in State and local governments today where ten years ago neither the skill nor the profession existed. And, as I pointed out earlier, even the most conservative projections of future personnel needs suggest an intensification in the demand for better trained and more specialized personnel.

Yet today only California, New York, Michigan, and a few other States have training programs for State top management. Less than a third of the States, according to one survey by the International City Managers Association, regularly sponsor post-entry training for local government officials. And, according to another ICMA study, no city today has anything approaching a model training program. Where training exists, it is largely geared to improving the routine skills of office workers, policemen, and firemen. Yet, the critical problem is the need to retain and develop more and better professional, administrative, and technical talent.

The proposed legislation attacks this problem in four ways. First, it authorizes Federal departments and agencies conducting training programs for their own employees to open them up to State and local personnel in counterpart agencies. Second, it authorizes Federal departments and agencies administering grant-in-aid programs to initiate training programs for counterpart State and local personnel in short-supply categories. Third, it gives prior Congressional consent to interstate compacts or other agreements for cooperative efforts relating to the administration of State and local personnel training. Fourth, it establishes a grant-in-aid program for in-service training of State and local employees.

This last provision, of course, is the most significant of the four. Under it, the States could be given the whole responsibility for developing plans for the training of their own employees and the initial responsibility for joining with local governments in developing such programs for local personnel. Plans would include provisions for continuing assessment of training needs, for equitable standards relating to the selection and assignment of training candidates, and for efficient utilization of such personnel, including continued service for a reasonable period of time. A State plan also would include guidelines covering the selection of universities or other non-governmental facilities when such institutions are to be used for training purposes.

The title authorizes general units of local government, either jointly or separately, to submit training plans if, within a year from the effective date of the Act, a State fails to submit a plan which includes significant provisions covering local training activities. Further, it would be administered by the Civil Service commission, but the concurrence of the Secretary of Housing and Urban Development again is required for approval of training projects for our Nation's cities.

It is important to note that Title IV of S. 3408 is residual. Personnel receiving training under other Federal statutes are specifically excluded from its coverage. But, more importantly, it meets the training needs of the States and localities, as these jurisdictions see them. It concentrates on the critical professional, administrative, and technical sector. It replaces the piecemeal method that has to date characterized the Federal approach to in-service training.

CONCLUSION

Improved merit systems, improved State and local personnel management, and improved in-service training programs—these are the three basic concerns of the proposed Intergovernmental Personnel Act of 1966. These must become national concerns, if the States and their localities are to be vigorous members in the great partnership that was established in 1789.

More than a half-century ago, Brooks Adams wrote, with the foresight so characteristic of all the Adamses:

There can be no doubt that the modern environment is changing faster than any environment ever previously changed; therefore, the social centre of gravity constantly tends to shift more rapidly; and therefore, modern civilization has unprecedented need of the administrative or generalizing mind. But, as the mass and momentum of modern society is prodigious, it will require a correspondingly prodigious energy to carry it safely from an unstable to a stable equilibrium.

Our environment is certainly changing more rapidly than it did in the days of Brooks Adams and Woodrow Wilson. Our modern civilization certainly has as great a need for the masterful administrative mind as it did then. And our federal system today presents a greater and more creative challenge to successful public administration than it did in that earlier era.

Author Index

Abegglen, James C., 536
Acheson, Dean, 194, 195, 196
Acton, Lord, 195
Adams, Brooks, 553
Adams, Henry Brooks, 529
Adrian, Charles, 544
Albouze, Achille R., 35, 48, 85–93
Allport, G. W., 331
Altshuler, Alan, 118
Anshen, M., 159
Appleby, Paul, 117, 118
Argyris, Chris, 92, 165, 199, 209, 221, 231
Arthur, Guy B., 492
Atkins, Stuart, 222

Bach, G. L., 159
Bailey, Stephen K., 547–48
Bancroft, Frederick, 520
Baritz, Loren, 232
Barnes, Louis B., 230
Baruch, Ismar, 361, 530
Baum, Bernard H., 16, 34, 49, 103–12
Beckhard, Richard, 229
Benedict, Truman, 360
Benne, Kenneth D., 226, 231
Bennis, Warren G., 62, 64, 199, 206, 208, 209, 212, 226, 229, 231
Bernstein, Irving, 381, 382, 386
Bernstein, Marver, 95, 96, 134
Bieriman, Arthur, 387
Bingham, Walter Van Dyke, 471, 492
Bion, W. R., 231
Blake, Robert R., 213, 283

Blood, J. W., 277
Blumberg, Arthur, 229, 230
Bolster, Mel H., 57
Bosworth, Karl A., 224
Bove, LaRoy J., 360
Bradford, Leland P., 226, 231
Bright, James R., 158, 161, 169, 170
Brogan, Raymond F., 255–56
Brown, David S., 208
Bruner, Jerome S., 53, 57
Burke, Kenneth, 118

Canter, R. R., 165
Cantril, H., 331
Carlin, Jerome, 119
Carman, Harry J., 520, 524
Chapple, Eliot D., 492
Clapp, Gordon, 13, 461
Clark, Kenneth B., 422
Cleveland, Grover, 317
Cohen, Michael, 7, 17, 24, 30, 69, 70, 76, 80, 112–37
Cole, Archie B., 455
Cooke, J. E., 169
Coolidge, Calvin, 538
Cornog, Geoffrey Y., xiii
Corson, John J., 71, 148–55
Couch, Virgil L., 85
Covner, Bernard J., 493
Crossman, E. R. F. W., 158, 159, 169
Crowder, Norman A., 175

Dalton, Melville, 216
David, Paul, 357, 426, 462

Davis, Louis E., 23, 64, 155–73
Dawson, Raymond, 127
Dechert, Robert, 97
Dewey, John, 463
Dickson, William J., 490, 492
Dolmatch, Theodore B., 58, 173–82
Downs, Anthony, 115, 124
Drake, Charles A., 493
Drucker, Peter F., 151, 156, 157, 158, 159, 277
Drummond, Roscoe, 542

Eisenhower, Dwight D., 5, 127, 132, 343, 344, 406
Elkins, W. A., 329
Eriksson, Erik M., 524, 525
Etzioni, Amitai, 69, 115
Everett, R. Permin, 49, 183–92

Farley, James, 320
Fear, Richard A., 492
Fellner, William, 132
Fenno, Richard F., 136
Finer, Herman, 112, 113, 120, 122
Finley, Robert E., 173
Fish, Carl R., 519, 520, 523, 527
Fishbourn, Benjamin, 524
Flemming, Arthur, 433
Follett, Mary, 463
Folsom, Marion, 132
Ford, Pamela, 78
Foulke, William Dudley, 4, 192–93
Fowler, Dorothy G., 523
Franklin, Benjamin, 196
Fraser, John Munro, 492
Friedrich, Carl J., 112, 113, 119, 120

Galanter, Eugene, 180
Galitz, W. O., 165
Garfield, James A., 468
Gellhorn, Walter, 80, 81, 122
Ghiselli, E. E., 215
Gibb, Jack R., 226, 231
Gibson, Frank, xiii
Gladstone, Richard M., 70, 72, 267–77
Glaser, Robert, 180
Goldwater, Barry, 12, 16, 194–98, 541
Golembiewski, Robert T., xiii, 19, 58, 59, 65, 66, 198–232
Gomersall, Earl R., 43, 58, 232–49
Goode, Cecil E., 90, 92

Goss, Mary E., 119
Grandpré, Donn R., 249–56
Grant, Ulysses S., 532
Gray, Justice, 410
Grazia, Alfred de, 124
Greiner, Larry E., 230
Griffiths, William E., 23

Haire, Mason, 92, 215
Hale, John P., 528–529
Hall, Clyde C., 358
Halloran, Daniel F., 64, 65, 256–61
Halset, Walter G., 16, 24, 71, 72, 261–66
Harding, Harold F., 45
Harding, Warren G., 538
Harris, Joseph P., 115, 135
Harrison, Benjamin, 526
Heisel, W. D., 70, 72, 267–77
Herbst, P. G., 212
Herzberg, Frederick, 50, 282
Hill, Isaac, 523
Hilsman, Roger, 127
Hoos, Ida R., 23, 64
Hoover, J. Edgar, 153
Hoslett, S. D., 331
Huegli, Albert G., 539
Huitt, Ralph K., 132
Hunter, M. T., 530
Huntington, Samuel, 71
Hurja, Emil, 320
Huse, Edgar F., 54, 276–87

Jackson, Andrew, 21, 23, 404, 521, 523, 524, 525, 527, 531
Jefferson, Thomas, 527
Jensen, Ollie A., 13, 287–295
Johnson, Lyndon B., 8, 78, 126, 127, 295–03, 310, 315, 547
Jones, Roger W., 5, 38, 54, 304–25
Jordan, Byron, 492

Kallen, Arthur D., 131
Kammerer, Gladys, 433
Kaplan, H. Elliot, 384
Karl, Barry Dean, 224
Katz, D., 373
Kaufman, Herbert, 7, 8, 43, 325–46
Kay, E., 277
Kendall, Amos, 523
Kennedy, John F., 126, 127, 311, 459, 548
Kingsley, J. Donald, 462

Kitchel, Denison, 541
Klaw, S., 232
Knudson, Harry R., Jr., 49, 65, 346–55
Kofmehl, Kenneth, 130
Kuriloff, Arthur H., 222

Lalor, John J., 523
Lamon, Ward Hill, 526
Lawrence, Paul R., 200, 201
Leavitt, H. J., 157, 162
Ledoux, Urbain J., 485
Lehman, W. P., 358
Leich, Harold H., 56, 65, 355–66, 430
Lesieur, F. G., 164
Levine, Robert A., 22
Levinson, Daniel J., 71
Levinson, Harry, 15, 283–84
Lewin, K., 331
Likert, R., 92
Lincoln, Abraham, 519, 520, 523, 524, 526
Lindblom, Charles E., 123
Lockwood, Howard C., 289
Long, Norton, 7, 8
Lorsch, Jay W., 200, 201
Lumsdaine, A. A., 180
Luthin, Reinhard H., 520, 524
Lysaught, Jerome P., 180

Maccoby, N., 373
Macy, John, 34
Madison, James, 526
Maier, Norman R. F., 55, 366–79
Mandell, Milton M., 358
Mann, Dean E., 6, 39
Mannes, Marya, 152
March, James G., 228, 231
Marrow, Alfred, 231
Marting, Elizabeth, 173
Maslow, A., 282
Mayo, Elton, 238, 462, 463, 489, 492
McCarthy, John P., 539
McCleery, William, 155
McGregor, Douglas, 50, 92, 199, 247, 277, 283, 285, 380
McKinney, A. C., 165
McMurry, Robert N., 50, 51, 492
McQuie, Robert, 251–54
Metcalf, Henry, 463
Michaels, E. G., 492
Miller, Warren E., 130
Millett, J. D., 92

Mitchell, Harry B., 430
Moore, Bruce Victor, 471, 492
Morse, Muriel M., 16, 72, 381–88
Morse, N. C., 373
Mosel, James N., 58, 388–97
Mosher, Frederick C., 12, 21, 319, 397–408
Mouton, Jane, 213, 283
Muchmore, John H., 491, 492
Murphy, Cornelius J., 79, 409–15
Muskie, Edmund S., 543, 549, 550, 551
Mustafa, Husain, 41, 415–21
Myers, Charles A., 29, 30, 31, 34, 35, 48, 434–52, 460, 463
Myers, M. Scott, 43, 58, 232–49, 282

Neustadt, Richard E., 115, 125, 129
Nigro, Felix, 34, 425–34
Normanbrook, Lord, 70

O'Brien, James C., 486, 487, 492
Odiorne, George, 231–32
Onarheim, J. I., 492
Ordway, Samuel H., Jr., 486, 487, 492, 540

Palmer, Dwight L., 493
Parnes, Sidney J., 45
Patric, John, 493
Paul, R. Shale, 71, 148–55
Pennock, J. Roland, 112
Perkins, James A., 154–155
Pigors, Paul, 29, 30, 31, 34, 35, 48, 434–52, 460, 463
Pinchot, Gifford, 328
Pincus, William, 362
Pipe, G. Russell, 132
Polk, James K., 526
Pollock, James K., 342
Pollock, Ross, 357
Porter, Lyman W., 215
Powell, Norman John, 355
Purcell, Dale B., 492
Purpus, Eugene R., 493
Putnam, M. L., 489, 492

Quitman, John A., 529

Raphael, Winifred, 490, 492
Reed, Herbert S., 456, 457
Reeves, Floyd W., 426, 462
Reynolds, Harry W., 548

Rock, Eli, 383
Rockwell, Willard F., 95, 96
Roethlisberger, F. J., 91, 238, 463, 489, 492
Rogers, Carl R., 45, 372
Roosevelt, Franklin D., 340, 398, 406, 426, 452
Roosevelt, Theodore, 319, 533, 534
Rose, Henry, 6, 77, 452–60
Roser, Foster, 383, 385
Rourke, Francis E., 113

Sayles, Leonard, 152, 153, 165
Sayre, Wallace S., 12–13, 20, 93, 319, 335, 397, 460–64
Schein, Edgar H., 209, 226, 229, 231
Schinagl, Mary S., 55
Schurz, Carl, 520
Scott, Andrew, 127
Scott, William G., 72, 465–70
Segal, Melvin J., 465
Selznick, Philip, 117
Shepard, Herbert A., 228, 231
Sherif, M., 331
Sherwin, Chalmers, 149–50
Simon, H. A., 159, 325, 334
Skinner, B. F., 174, 175
Slater, Philip E., 212, 226
Smith, Bruce L. R., 22
Smith, David B., 456
Smithburg, D. W., 334
Somers, Herman M., 126
Spero, Sterling, 384
Sprague, Robert, 95, 96
Stahl, O. Glenn, 41–42, 90–91, 355
Stanley, David T., 42
Stengle, Charles I., 432
Steward, Luther, 432
Stock, Dorothy, 231
Stockford, LeBaron O., 493

Tacheron, Donald G., 130
Taft, Robert Jr., 541

Taylor, Frank J., 493
Taylor, Zachary, 526
Tead, Ordway, 463
Telford, Fred, 47
Thelen, Herbert A., 231
Thomas, R. L., 491, 492
Thompson, Victor A., 119, 334
Tocqueville, Alexis de, 197
Truman, Harry S., 427

Udall, Morris K., 130
Uhrbrock, Richard Stephen, 41, 470–91, 492
Uris, Auren, 233

Van Riper, Paul P., 4–5, 11, 14, 20, 31, 57, 78, 344, 404, 519–40

Walker, David B., 8, 541–53
Walker, Charles R., 158, 161
Walton, L. L., 468
Warner, Kenneth O., 383, 385
Warner, W. Lloyd, 536
Washington, George, 317, 524, 525, 526
Webster, Daniel, 528, 530
Weiford, Douglas, 388
Weitzel, Frank H., 24
Werling, R., 163, 165, 171
Wernimont, P. F., 165
White, Leonard D., 142, 384, 406, 523, 526, 527, 530
Whitehead, T. N., 489, 492
Whitridge, Frederick W., 523
Wikstrom, Walter S., 37–38
Wilcox, Herbert G., 215
Wildavsky, Aaron, 124
Williams, Wade J., 49, 183–92
Wilson, Woodrow, 318, 533, 553
Winn, Alexander, 211

Young, Philip, 364

Subject Index

Acculturation, organizational, 325–34, 106–12
  in Civil Service Commission, 106–12
  in Forest Service, 325–34
Administrative Procedure Act, 411–12
Administrative responsibility, 69–81, 112–18, 148–55, 261–66, 325–46
  agency controls over, 72, 114–16, 325–34
  and discretion, 112–14
  and interest groups, 116–18
  and New Politics, 335–46
  and professionalization, 261–66
  and unionization, 72
  by sharing power, 79–81
  external controls over, 75–79
  perceptions of at top levels, 148–55
  personal control relevant to, 69–72
  (*See also* NEW POLITICS; OMBUDSMAN; PROFESSIONALIZATION; and UNIONIZATION.)
Agencies, federal, 34–35, 103–12, 425–34, 502–6
  relations with Civil Service Commission, 34–35, 103–12, 425–34
  roles in personnel actions, 502–6
Agriculture, U.S. Department of, 335–46, 357
American Management Association, 231
Appeal procedures at federal level, 466–70
  for adverse actions, 466–68

  for grievance procedures, 468–70
Appraisal, 367–77
  objectives of, 367–68
  three types of interviews for, 368–79
    problem-solving, 374–77
    "tell and sell," 368–71
    "tell and listen," 372–74
    (*See also* COUNSELLING; and INTERVIEWING.)
Assignment, flexibility of, 360
Automation, 23, 64–65, 155–73
  and job design, 23, 161–72
  and position classification, 64–65
  theories regarding, 156–60
  types of, 160

Brookings Institution, 305, 314
Budgeting, xiii, 124–25
  and incrementalism, 124–25
Bureau of the Budget, 128, 34
Bureaucracy, 20–21, 62–64, 201–3
  effects of, 20–21, 62–64
  properties of, 201–3

California State Personnel Officers' Council, 85
Career conditional appointment, 504–5
Career development, 55–57, 146–55, 304–9
  and manpower planning, 304–8
  and mobility, 308–9

and perceptions of administrative
    responsibility, 148–55
at executive level, 146–48
Career Executive Board, 135
Career orientation, 38–39, 249–51,
    304–8, 404–8
and manpower planning, 304–8
lack of in public systems, 249–51,
    404–8
Certification, 41–42
Chicago Tribune 196
Civil Service Commission, U.S., 30–
    34, 103–12, 125–40, 425–34, 454–
    60, 493–506
and federal hiring, 501–6
and Hatch Act, 454–60
and interest groups, 432–34
organization of, 32–33, 127–32,
    137–40
relations with agencies, 34–35, 103–
    12, 425–34
relations with Congress, 30–31,
    125–28, 130–37, 493–95
relations with President, 33–34,
    126–31, 137–40
roles of, 493–95
    (*See also* DECENTRALIZATION.)
Civil War, 5
Civilian review boards, 423–25
Civil service movement, 317–25, 335–
    46
and New Politics, 335–46
and Spoils Politics, 317–25
underlying values of, 320–24
Classes in federal classification system,
    508–9
Classification, 103–12, 155–73, 183–
    92, 496–514
    (*See also* POSITION ANALYSIS; and
    POSITION CLASSIFICATION.)
Classification Act of 1923, 508
Classification Act of 1949, 507–12
Climates in organization, 217–32,
    284–85
changes in, 217–32
to enhance personal growth, 284–85
Closed vs. open shop, 383–84
Collective bargaining, 381–88
definition in industry, 381
issues in public administration,
    381–87
versus merit system, 387–88

Committee for Economic Develop-
    ment, 40, 145
Committees, congressional, 30–31,
    125–37
relations with U.S. Civil Service Com-
    mission, 30–31, 125–28, 130–37
Competitive service, 515–18, 532–37
exceptions from, 516–17
extent of, 515–16, 517–18
taproots of, 532–37
    (*See also* MERIT SYSTEM.)
Conflict of interest, 21–22, 94–103
and effects on recruitment, 97–103
restrictions against, 94–95, 98–100
    (*See also* LEGISLATIVE OVERSIGHT
    OF ADMINISTRATION.)
Conformity, voluntary, 334–35
Confrontation design, 228–29
    (*See also* LABORATORY APPROACH.)
Congress, 30–31, 125–37, 192–93
and relations with U.S. Civil Service
    Commission, 30–31, 125–28,
    130–37
and "spoils," 192–93
Cornell University, 154
Counselling, 366–79
three types of, 366–79
    (*See also* APPRAISAL; and INTER-
    VIEWING.)
Creative federalism, 541–53
description of, 541–43
relevance of personnel administra-
    tion for, 543–53
Creativity, 45–46

Decentralization, 106–12, 425–34,
    501–6
and Hoover Commission, 429–31
in federal hiring, 501–6
objections to by employees and vet-
    erans, 432–34
of personnel functions in federal
    agencies, 106–12, 425–29
    (*See also* ORGANIZATION OF PER-
    SONNEL ACTIVITIES.)
Defense, Department of, 95–96, 141
Departmental personnel officer, 34–
    35, 86–93, 106–12
functions of, 86–87
objectives of, 89–93
perceived role of, 87–89
reactions and attitudes of, 106–12
Duties, classification of, 497–501

Emotions and attitudes, 217–49
anxiety and performance, 232–49
as they affect competence and creativity, 235–36
training relevant to, 217–32
Employment, trends at federal level, 518
Examiners, boards of, 504
"Excepted" positions, 5, 147, 516–17
Schedule A, 516
Schedule B, 516
Schedule C, 5, 147, 516–17
Executive Assignment System, 309
Executives, public, 39, 97–98, 145–55, 516–17
career, 146–55
number of, 145–46
perceptions of administrative responsibility by, 148–55
top presidential appointees, 145–46, 516–17
Exit interview, 491

Federal Aviation Administration, 307
Federal Executive Boards, 495
Federal Housing Administration, 94
Federalism, 8, 314–15
and intergovernmental personnel matters, 314–15
Federal Service Entrance Examination, 407–8
Feedback, 381–97
definition of, 388
significance of in training, 389–90
underlying dynamics of, 390–91
useful properties of, 391–97
(*See also* TRAINING.)
Forest Service, U.S., 150, 325–34
identification with, 325–34
transfer and promotion in, 326–30

General Accounting Office, 131
General Schedule (GS) Levels, 507
Generalist, personnel, 347–54
advantages of, 349–50
compared to specialization in personnel function, 347–48
disadvantages of, 350–51
illustrative experience with, 351–54
Government Employees Training Act of 1958, 132, 304, 309
Grade structure, 48

Grades, in federal classification system, 508–9
Grievance procedures, 386, 421–25, 445–47, 468–70
and collective bargaining, 386
and personnel administration, 445–47
at federal level, 468–70
for police and community, 421–25

Hatch Act, 6, 452–60
interpretations of by U.S. Civil Service Commission, 454–60
legislative intent of, 453–54
provisions of, 452–53
Hoover Commission, 137–40, 250

Identification with agency, 326–34
and internalization of values and perceptions, 333–34
as affected by transfer and promotion, 326–30
effect of symbols on, 330–33
Incrementalism, 124–25
Inspections, personnel, 103–6, 494–95
federal policies concerning, 494–95
implementation of policies, 103–6
Interagency Advisory Group, U.S. Civil Service Commission, 495
Interest groups, 116–18, 432–34, 468, 537–40
Intergovernmental Personnel Act of 1966, 543–45, 553
Intergovernmental relations, 542–49
and "creative federalism," 542–45
personnel needs at state and local levels, 545–49
Intergovernmental Relations, Senate Subcommittee on, 548
Interior, U.S. Department of, 357
Internal Revenue Service, 141
Internalization, as a vehicle for organizational acculturation, 333–34
International City Managers Association, 552
Interviewing, 366–79, 470–91
and counselling, 490–91
and exit interview, 491
approaches to, 477–85
by panels, 485–87
by selection boards, 487–88
flow chart for, 472–77
responsibilities involved in, 470–72

terminal points in, 474–76
three types for appraisal, 366–79
(*See also* APPRAISAL.)

Jacksonian age in personnel administration, 526–30
Job design, 23, 161–72, 201–16
impact of automation on, 23, 161–72
patterns for organizing work and, 201–16
(*See also* AUTOMATION; and ORGANIZING, PATTERNS FOR.)
Job enlargement, 161–72, 232–34
and anxiety reduction, 232–34
and automation, 161–72
(*See also* JOB DESIGN; ORGANIZING, PATTERNS FOR; and POSITION CLASSIFICATION.)
Judicial review and removal of federal employees, 409–15
Junior Management Assistant Program, 406–7
Justice Department, 141

Kellogg Foundation, 92

Laboratory Approach, 217–31
and T-Groups, 217–18
basic questions about, 228–31
bibliography about, 231–32
in Organization Development, 227–28
properties of, 218–24
underlying values of, 224–27
(*See also* ORGANIZATION DEVELOPMENT; and T-GROUPS.)
"Lateral entry," 140
Leadership, 146–47, 219, 340–41, 519–31
at policy level, 340–41
at presidential level, 146–47, 519–31
in a T-Group, 219
Legislative oversight of administration, 30–31, 76–79, 95–101, 125–37
by committee action, 30–31, 95–97, 125–28, 130–37
by law, 76–79, 97–101
(*See also* COMMITTEES, CONGRESSIONAL, and CONFLICT OF INTEREST.)

Limited government, 194–98
relation to administration, 195, 197–98
tenets of, 194–97
Line administrators, 183–92, 337–40
and personnel dilemmas, 337–40
and position classification, 183–92
Loyalty, 16–25, 140–45, 381–88
and administrative responsibility, 17
and conflict of interest, 21–22
and professionalization, 140–45
and sub-unit identifications, 16–17
and technological change, 21–25
and unionization, 16, 381–88
multiple forces acting upon, 22–25
(*See also* ADMINISTRATIVE RESPONSIBILITY; PROFESSIONALIZATION; and UNIONIZATION.)

Management Development, 278–87
climate for growth in, 284–85
important relations in, 278–84
results of one approach to, 285–87
Manpower planning, 304–16, 541–53
and career development, 304–8
at federal level, 304–16
at state and local levels, 541–53
Merit, 13–14
Merit system, 317–25, 381–88, 397–405
and "New Politics," 335–46
and unionization, 381–88
characteristics of, 397–400
maturity of, 317–21
new developments affecting, 322–25
underlying values of, 400–5
(*See also* MERIT SYSTEM; "NEW POLITICS;" and UNIONIZATION.)
Middle managers, 39–40, 140–45
recruitment and training of, 140–45
Minorities, 228–94
and selection as public employees, 288–94
Mobility of federal employees, 308–9
Motives, 50–51, 199, 282–83
types of, 282–83
underlying theories of, 50–51, 199

National Guard, 365
National Intergovernmental Personnel Program, 549–53
National Park Service, 357
National Teachers' Corps, 541

National Training Laboratories, 231
"New Politics," 5–8, 335–46, 543–53
and federalism, 8
and policy leadership, 340–41
basic trends of, 341–44
implications for traditional merit system, 345–46
personnel dilemmas posed by, 337–40, 543–53
(*See also* MERIT SYSTEM; PRESIDENT; and SPOILS POLITICS.)
New York Port Authority, 217

Occupational group, 509–10
Ohio State University, 92
Ombudsman, 75, 80–81
(*See also* ADMINISTRATIVE RESPONSIBILITY.)
"Operation Square Peg," 365
Organization Development (OD), 200–32
as a new personnel function, 205–16
contra bureaucracy, 200–3
one approach to, 217–32
(*See also* LABORATORY APPROACH; and ORGANIZATION OF PERSONNEL ACTIVITIES.)
Organization of personnel activities, 29–35, 48–49, 103–12, 183–92, 200–16
and decentralization, 106–12
as staff, 29–30, 48–49
at departmental level, 34–35, 86–93, 103–12
in federal government, 30–35
in relation to line management, 183–92
new emphases in, 200–5, 207–16
(*See also* DECENTRALIZATION; and ORGANIZING, PATTERNS FOR.)
Organizing, patterns for, 46–51, 62–65, 155–73, 198–216
and automation, 155–73
traditional approaches, 46–48, 62–63, 201–3
underlying theories, 59–51, 198–200
unorthodox approaches, 62–65, 203–16
Orienting the employee, 42–43, 232–49, 325–34
an unconventional approach to, 232–49

conventional approach to, 42–43
in Forest Service, 325–34

Pay and fringe benefits, 309–11, 507
and General Schedule, 507
central emphases in, 309–11
Peace Corps, 217
Pendleton Act of 1883, 4, 532–34
Performance appraisal, 54–55, 276–77
useful properties of, 276–77
Personnel, 346
Personnel administration, 183–92, 337–40, 435–50, 460–64
characterizations of, 435–37, 460–64
functions of, 437–50
role of "line" in, 183–92, 337–40, 436–50
Personnel administration, broad conditioning environments of, 2–25, 64–65, 317–26, 460–64
political, 2–8, 256–57
social, 10–17, 317–26
technological, 18–25, 64–65
Policy vs. implementation, 113–14
Policy-making process, 123–40
and unions, 128–29
impact of form of organization on, 137–40
in personnel administration, 123–37
Political appointments, 6, 145–46, 519–31
Political parties, 145–46, 192–93, 317–25, 335–46, 519–31
and personnel matters, 340–41
and spoils politics, 192–93, 317–25, 335–46, 519–31
relation of President to, 145–46
(*See also* MERIT SYSTEM; and SPOILS POLITICS.)
Polling techniques, 330–31
Position analysis, 46–48, 155–73, 365–66, 496–501, 508–14
concept of position in military, 365–66
effects of automation on, 155–73
factors in, 496–501, 508–14
overview of, 46–48
Position classification, 23, 46–48, 64–65, 103–12, 157–73, 184–91, 251–61, 355–57, 496–501, 508–14
and GS grades, 507

and Modified Classification Review, 184–91
concerns about, 251–54, 256–61
effects of automation on, 23, 64–65, 155–73, 261
factors considered in, 496–501
in practice, 103–12
overview of, 46–48
role of "line" in, 83–92
standards for, 512–14
structure underlying federal plan of, 508–14
systems for, 355–57
training for, 188–89
(*See also* POSITION ANALYSIS; RANK-IN-JOB; and RANK-IN-MAN.)
Post Office and Civil Service Committees, 130–35
Post Office, U.S., 135
Praise, functions and dysfunctions of, 395–97
President, 33–34, 126–46, 137–47, 519–31
and appointments of supergrade career executives, 146–47
and early personnel administration, 519–31
political appointees of, 145–46
relations with Civil Service Commission, 33–34, 126–31, 137–40
(*See also* MERIT SYSTEM; POLITICAL PARTIES; and SPOILS POLITICS.)
Professionalization, 16–25, 140–45, 261–66
and impact on loyalty, 16, 261–66
and technological change, 22–25
at middle levels, 140–45
Programmed instruction, 173–82
managerial perspectives on, 175–79
major approaches to, 174–75
(*See also* TRAINING.)

"Rabble hypothesis," 463
RAND Corporation, 22
Randall Commission, 548
Rank-in-job, 256–61, 363–64, 409–11
advantages of, 363–64
contra personal rank, 257–61
in American personnel administration, 256–57
including impact of man, 409–11

(*See also* POSITION CLASSIFICATION; and RANK-IN-MAN.)
Rank-in-man, 256–61, 356–63
advantages of, 356–63
contra American approach, 256–57
in foreign countries, 257–61
(*See also* POSITION CLASSIFICATION; and RANK-IN-JOB.)
Raytheon Company, 351–54
Realpolitik, 116
Recruiting, 37–41, 97–98, 140–46, 232–49, 287–95
and interviewing, 40–41
and manpower planning, 37–38
and orientation, 42–43, 232–49
and testing, 41
at career levels, 39–40, 140–45
at executive levels, 39, 97–98
at political levels, 39, 95–97, 145–46
cultural biases in, 287–95
"Rule of three," 41–42

Schedule C, 5, 147, 516–17
Scientific management, 201–3, 460–64
and bureaucracy, 201–3
impact on personnel administration, 460–64
Selection of employees, 288–94
and "fairness," 288
and testing, 288–89
reducing bias in, 291–94
"Senatorial courtesy," 524–25
Sensitivity training, 217–32
(*See also* LABORATORY APPROACH; and T-GROUPS.)
Situational thinking, 442–44
Specialization, 46–48, 62–63, 201–16, 347–48
and patterns for organizing, 46–48, 62–63, 201–16
disadvantages of in personnel function, 347–48
Spoils politics, 4–5, 192–93, 256–57, 317–25, 519–31
developments beyond, 317–25, 335–46
effects on position classification, 256–57, 527–31
in Congress, 192–93
mixed consequences of, 519–31

(*See also* MERIT SYSTEM; and NEW
POLITICS.)
Standards in federal position classifica-
tion, 512–14
State, U.S. Department of, 217, 306

Technological change, 16–25, 64–65,
155–73
and automation, 23, 64–65, 155–73
and position classification, 23, 64–
65
and professionalization, 16, 22–25
and unionization, 16
Tennessee Valley Authority, 464
Testing, 41, 287–95, 401–8, 415–21,
460–64
and neglect of purpose, 460–64
cultural biases in, 287–95
for aptitudes, 415–21
overview of at federal level, 401–8
Texas Instruments, 232–49
T-Groups, 217–31
basic questions about, 228–31
purposes of, 219–24
types of, 217–18
underlying values of, 224–27
(*See also* LABORATORY APPROACH.)
Theory X vs. Theory Y, 50–51, 199,
380
(*See also* ORGANIZING, PATTERNS
OF.)
Training, 54–58, 140–45, 173–82,
217–49, 276–87, 325–34, 389–97
and emotions, 217–31, 232–49
and feedback, 58, 389–97
and management development,
276–87
and programmed instruction, 173–
82
at middle levels, 140–45
by reducing anxiety, 232–49

for organization change, 57–58
in Forest Service, 325–34
overview of, 54
using T-Groups, 217–31
(*See also* FEEDBACK; RANK-IN-JOB;
and RANK-IN-MAN.)
Transfers, personnel, 326–30
Transitional appointments, 295–96

Unionization, 311–12, 378–88, 432–
34
and closed shops, 383–84
and decentralization, 432–34
and loyalty, 16
and strikes, 378
criticisms of, 381–88
development of at federal level,
311–12
(*See also* ADMINISTRATIVE RESPON-
SIBILITY; and COLLECTIVE BAR-
GAINING.)

Values, 224–27, 297–303, 261–75
and ethics of federal employees,
297–303
and off-the-job conduct, 267–75
conflicts in public service concerning, 261–66
in Organization Development, 227–
28
in T-Groups, 224–27
Veterans, 432–34, 468, 537–40
and Preference Act of 1944, 468,
539–40
impact on public personnel administration, 432–34
preference for, 468, 537–40
Veterans' Administration, 468–70

Wayland Laboratory, 351–54
Work Planning and Review, 277–86

BOOK MANUFACTURE

People in Public Service: A Reader in Public Personnel Administration composition was by Henkes-Holland. Offset printing and binding was by Kingsport Press, Inc. The paper is Perkins & Squier Company's Glatfelter Old Forge Wove. Internal and cover design was by John Goetz. The type in this book is Times Roman.